A COUNSELOR'S GUIDE

TO

CAREER ASSESSMENT

INSTRUMENTS

FIFTH EDITION

NCDA opposes discrimination against any individual based on age, culture, disability, ethnicity, race, religion/spirituality, creed, gender, gender identity and expression, sexual orientation, marital/partnership status, language preference, socioeconomic status, any other characteristics not specifically relevant to job performance.

(January 2008)

A COUNSELOR'S GUIDE

TO

CAREER ASSESSMENT

INSTRUMENTS

FIFTH EDITION

EDITED BY:
Edwin A. Whitfield
Rich W. Feller
Chris Wood

National Career Development Association
In Cooperation with the Association for Assessment
in Counseling and Education

Printed in the United States of America

Library of Congress
Cataloging in Publication Division
101 Independence Avenue, S.E.
Washington, DC 20540-4320

Library of Congress
CIP 20540-4320
9140 East Hampton Drive
Capitol Heights, MD 20743

Library of Congress Cataloging-in-Publication Data
A counselor's guide to career assessment instruments. -- 5th ed. / edited by
Edwin A. Whitfield, Rich W. Feller, Chris Wood.
  p. cm.

ISBN 978-1-885333-24-7
1. Occupational aptitude tests--Evaluation. 2. Vocational
interests--Testing--Evaluation. I. Whitfield, Edwin A. II. Feller, Rich.
III. Wood, Chris (Christopher Todd) IV. National Career Development
Association (U.S.) V. Association for Assessment in Counseling and Education
(U.S.)
 HF5381.7.C68 2008
 153.9'4--dc22

                              2008034244

TABLE OF CONTENTS

ABOUT THE EDITORS

Edwin A. Whitfield recently retired from the Ohio Department of Education where he served as an Associate Director. His responsibilities included providing leadership and coordination for school guidance and counseling programs, Safe and Drug Free Schools, GED testing and career and academic assessment initiatives in the state of Ohio. Prior to that he served as a coordinator of guidance and counseling in California, and as a teacher and counselor in Iowa and Ohio. He received his B.A. from Loras College, his M.Ed. from Ohio University, and the Ph.D. from the University of Iowa. Dr. Whitfield has served as NCDA president and as president of NCDA state divisions in California and Ohio. He served as editor of the Career Development Quarterly for six years, as coordinator of NCDA publications, and as chairperson of the American Counseling Association's Council of Journal Editors. He has received the NCDA Merit Award twice. Dr. Whitfield has published works addressing career development, assessment, evaluation, and guidance program planning and implementation.

Rich W. Feller is Professor of Counseling and Career Development and University Distinguished Teaching Scholar at Colorado State University where he teaches courses in career development, counseling and performance and change. A Nationally Certified Counselor (NCC), Nationally Certified Career Counselor (NCCC), and NCDA Fellow he has served on the NCDA, CACREP and ACTE Guidance Board of Directors, and editorial boards for the *Career Development Quarterly,* the *Journal of Career Development* and the *Career Planning and Adult Development Journal.* Author of over 75 publications including *Career Transitions in Turbulent Times* (with Garry Walz), *Knowledge Nomads and the Nervously Employed* (with Judy Whichard), the CDM's *Tour of Your Tomorrow* video series and the Ability Explorer's Making the *Most of Your Abilities* video program (both with Joe Vasos). He has served as Visiting Scholar at the University of Canberra in Australia, the University of North Carolina at Greensboro, and as Fellow at the Japan Institute for Social and Economic Affairs.

Chris Wood is a counselor educator at Seattle University. He has been a faculty member at The Ohio State University and the University of Arizona. A Nationally Certified Counselor (NCC) and Nationally Certified School Counselor (NCSC). Dr. Wood is on the editorial board for the *Professional School Counseling* journal and has published articles in *Professional School Counseling, Journal of College Counseling, Counselor Education & Supervision, The Elementary School Journal* as well as numerous book chapters. He has previous experience as a high school counselor, a guidance department chair, a counselor/group leader at a residential youth facility for troubled teens, and a career counselor at an alternative school serving grades 7-12. He was a career assessment coordinator and research assistant on a $1.3 million dollar Community Employment Education Center grant from the Office of Adult and Vocational Education and a Faculty Research Associate on a grant from the National Research Center for Career and Technical Education.

FOREWORD

The four previous editions of this outstanding resource have been widely used by counselors, career development professionals, assessment specialists, and counselor educators for decades. Work on the four previous editions of the *Guide,* dating back to 1979, represent multiple years of professional dedication and commitment by previous co-editors Jerome T. Kapes, Marjorie M. Mastie, and Edwin A. Whitfield. The legacy provided by these editors continues with the publication of this fifth edition, under the excellent leadership of Edwin A. Whitfield, Rich W. Feller, and Chris Wood.

None of the work on this and previous editions of the *Counselor's Guide to Career Assessment Instruments* would have been possible over the past 30 years without the collegial and professional commitment of time and expertise by assessment and career development professionals who have served as advisory committee members, chapter authors, and reviewers of hundreds of assessment instruments. In addition, test publishers have supported our efforts through providing materials and resources for the reviewers and information to accompany each review in the *Guide.* We are truly indebted to all of these professionals for their outstanding contributions to the improvement and growth of the career assessment field.

The editors have made several changes in this edition to enhance the *Guide's* overall value and contribution to the field, including new material in Chapters 2 and 7, as well as revisions to each of the other chapters. The Additional Instruments chapter has been revised by eliminating out-of-date instruments and adding new instruments. In addition, the editors have made a concerted effort to include reviews of a significantly increased number of assessments that are useful in adult career decision making.

This fifth edition of *A Counselor's Guide to Career Assessment Instruments* is an example of a very productive and collaborative effort between the National Career Development Association (NCDA) and the Association for Assessment in Counseling and Education (AACE), both of which are divisions of the American Counseling Association (ACA).

We hope that you will use this resource to enhance your work with clients of all ages!

Donna Gibson
President, 2007-2008
Association for Assessment
  in Counseling and Education

Darrell Luzzo
President, 2007-2008
National Career Development Association

ACKNOWLEDGEMENTS

This is the fifth edition of *A Counselor's Guide to Career Assessment Instruments*, and the first without the editorship, dedication, leadership and commitment of Dr. Jerome T. Kapes. Jerry Kapes, who passed away since the last edition of the *Guide* was published, was the primary reason that *Counselor's Guide* came into existence and still exists today, 30 years after an initial meeting of NCDA and AACE members who met in the late 1970s to discuss the need for such a resource. He, along with Marjorie Mastie chaired that meeting and coordinated the first edition of the *Guide*. Because of his belief in its value and his continuing commitment, it has remained over the intervening quarter century as a quality resource for career development and assessment professionals. We owe him a debt of gratitude.

Since its inception, the *Guide* has benefited from an array of talent and professional commitments that have produced over 300 career assessment reviews. Hundreds of career development and assessment professionals have volunteered their time and expertise to develop and produce these reviews and content chapters making it a resource produced by and for the profession. Also, the five editions of the *Guide* have been enhanced and improved through the work of various committee members and individuals who advised the editors on test selections, available resources and research related to career assessment.

In addition, over the years, hundreds of test publishers have provided complementary copies of instruments and manuals to the reviewers of their instruments featured in each edition of the *Guide*. The formatted information preceding each review also is provided by the publishers. When the opportunity arises we encourage you to thank them for their support of our profession.

Each edition of the *Guide* has benefited from the support of the Buros Institute at the University of Nebraska-Lincoln, producer and publisher of the Mental Measurement Yearbooks (MMY), a revered and respected standard in the field of assessment, and multiple other publications and guides addressing assessment quality and use. Buros has graciously allowed the editors of the *Guide* to approach MMY reviewers and to allow them to adapt their work previously published in recent editions of the MMY to fit the format for the *Guide*.

The fifth edition of the *Guide* is the first edition that Deneen Pennington, Executive Director of NCDA, and her staff have been involved in the development and publishing of the Guide. Their efforts in turning our work into a finished product are appreciated; especially Mary Ann Powell, who coordinated our efforts with NCDA headquarters and book design and printing contractors, and provided a polished final product.

The timeline for completion of each edition of the *Guide*, once work is started, usually requires about three years from initial contact to finished product. Such a span of time can require adjustments that affect family commitments and priorities. Recognizing this, we extend our thanks to our families. In addition, appreciation from:

- Ed Whitfield...to his wife Marjorie for her support for this work, times five.
- Rich Feller...to his parents Martha and Edward Feller for support over a lifetime.
- Chris Wood...to his wife Angie for her patience and understanding.

Rich Feller and Chris Wood offer tremendous gratitude to senior editor Ed Whitfield for his vision, leadership, and perseverance in the publication of this work. His incredible respect for the history and importance of *A Counselor's Guide to Career Assessment Instruments* is a testimony to his commitment to this 30 year project, career development, and NCDA. Few in our profession have added as deep a contribution to the assessment literature as has Ed Whitfield.

CHAPTER 1

A Counselor's Guide:
Introduction to the Fifth Edition

Edwin A. Whitfield
Associate Director (Retired)
Office of Supportive Learning Environments
Office of Assessment
Ohio Department of Education

Rich W. Feller
Professor
Counseling and Career Development
School of Education
Colorado State University

Chris Wood
Department of Counseling and School Psychology
College of Education
Seattle University

Background

The first edition of *A Counselor's Guide* was published in 1982, and subsequent editions published in 1988, 1994 and 2001. Given the rapid changes that continue to occur in career assessment instruments and in the professions that use them, it appears that this approximate time is the maximum time between revisions if this work is to remain current. The time needed to plan and produce the *Guide* is approximately three years, with decisions about which topics and instruments to include made relatively early in the process, while other content such as the additional instruments chapter and appendices continue to evolve, even until press time.

The first edition of the *Guide* contained 259 pages. As can be seen, the number of pages has grown appreciably over the quarter of a century since that first edition. The Additional Career Assessment Instruments chapter includes instruments that are not reviewed in this fifth edition but are available from various publishers listed in Appendix B. Also, a User's Matrix is provided that lists and categorizes all instruments included in this edition. Several of the chapters and most of the reviews have different authors from any of the previous editions. Overall, there are 71 separate instruments included in 55 reviews using a standard format that includes Description, Use in Counseling, Technical Considerations, Computer-Based Version (if applicable), Overall Critique, and References.

To correspond with NCDA or the editors concerning this Guide, please visit our website at www.ncda.org for NCDA Headquarters contact information or phone toll-free (866) 367-6232.

The reviews include instruments that were not reviewed in the fourth edition as well as new reviews of instruments reviewed in previous editions. Typically, when an instrument from the previous edition warrants a new review, it is assigned to a different reviewer for the current edition of the *Guide*. When contacted to send technical manuals and other descriptive information to the new reviewers, some test publishers asked that the previous review in the fourth edition of the *Guide* be reprinted, due to the absence of any changes to or additional research on the instrument since the last edition of the *Guide*.

Since the fourth edition will no longer be available upon the publication of this fifth edition, and the instruments in question remain available and popular, the absence of these instruments in this fifth edition would deprive readers of these most recent reviews, and possibly create confusion by their absence. Consequently, four reprints of instrument reviewed in the fourth edition are included in this fifth edition. Appropriate caveats are placed at the start of each of these reprints alerting readers to these decisions.

Reviews and Reviewers

The decisions as to which instruments to include for review were based on a review of the literature, publisher web sites, professional associations' journals and newsletters and input from career development professionals. The principles underlying the decisions to select instruments for review include the following:

- Major instruments identified by the sources listed above
- Previously reviewed instruments that have undergone extensive revision or update
- New instruments that appear to have promise of extensive use
- Instruments, not otherwise included, that could be used by employers to facilitate career development of employees and adults in career transition
- Instruments with proven utility for persons with disabilities or disadvantages
- Buros Institute publications
- NCDA's annual review of career assessment developments in the *Career Development Quarterly*

Given the continuing expansion of computer-based versions of career assessment instruments, it was decided to again include, if applicable, a section in each review to cover these versions. Also, Chapter 5 discusses the rapidly evolving developments in computer-assisted career assessment and on-line adaptations.

As was the case for previous editions, permission was obtained from the respective publishers for use of reviewers who had previously published reviews in their publications and journals. Typically, these reviewers made extensive revisions in their previously published manuscripts both to update the information and to accommodate the *Counselor's Guide* format. Other members of AACE and NCDA, or professionals who publish in the journals of these associations, were recruited to write reviews for new or revised instruments. Lastly, other reviewers with unique expertise and experience with a particular instrument also were used. As before, all reviews published in *A Counselor's Guide* were subjected to an external evaluation by the editors. However, the opinions expressed by the reviewers are their own. All test publishers were offered the opportunity to examine their instrument(s) reviews for accuracy. Final decisions on content rested with the editors and the reviewers.

Context Information for Users

Before deciding to employ psychometric instruments for career assessment, the user needs prerequisite contextual information. This includes knowledge of the instruments available for the particular intended use, access to sources of good information about the available instruments, and awareness of the various legal, ethical, and social considerations that have an impact on the career assessment process. A brief discussion of each of these context considerations follows.

Instrument Availability and Use

Trustworthy information about which career assessment instruments are most used for career counseling and related purposes is difficult to obtain. The primary reason for this difficulty is that most users are familiar with only a few of the many available instruments. When users are asked to rate or rank the usefulness or applicability of a large number of instruments, they tend to place the ones they use at the top and then rank others by name recognition only somewhere below these choices. Several surveys conducted in the past have included instruments that are no longer available, yet they still received relatively large numbers of nominations for use, presumably because their names were familiar. In previous editions of *A Counselor's Guide,* the editors have reported such surveys conducted by others (Engen, Lamb & Prediger, 1982; Zytowski & Warman, 1982), Kapes & Mastie, (1988), Watkins, Campbell and Nieberding (1994) and Kapes & Whitfield, (2001). Given the dated and somewhat unreliable nature of this information, especially at the lower end of the rankings, these rankings were not included in the previous edition and are not included here.

Some instruments are appropriate for more than one population and are reviewed in the most appropriate section (chapter) of the *Guide.* For example, Ashland Interest Assessment (AIA) is reviewed in Chapter 12 (Special Populations) also is appropriate for Chapter 9 (Interest and Work Values) while Self Directed Search (SDS) and Harrington-O'Shea Career Decision-Making System (CDM-R), although appropriate for the Special Populations (Chapter 12), are reviewed in Chapter 9 (Interest and Work Values). Various uses of instruments by various populations are discussed at length in Chapter 7. Other instruments such as Armed Services Vocational Aptitude Battery (ASVAB), Career Occupational Preference System (COPS), CareerScope, Career Planning Survey (CPS), Kuder Career Planning System and Occupational Aptitude Survey and Interest Schedule (OASIS), are found in Chapter 8 (Aptitude/Achievement and Comprehensive or Combined Measures) but contain separate multiple instruments (achievement, aptitude, interest and/or values built into a career assessment system). In many cases, separate publisher-provided information for each instrument precedes the review of the full system. Readers are encouraged to check the Index for reference to specific instruments.

Sources of Information about Available Instruments

When the first edition of *A Counselor's Guide* was published in 1982, the only comprehensive source of information about career assessment instruments available was the Buros Institute's publication, Tests in Print II and its companion set of reviews, the *Eighth Mental Measurements Yearbook* (MMY. Since that time, the Buros Institute has published Tests in Print III, IV, V, VI and VII (1983, 1994, 1999, 2002, 2006), and the *Ninth, Tenth, Eleventh, Twelfth Thirteenth, Fourteenth, Fifteenth, Sixteenth, and Seventeenth Mental Measurements Yearbooks* (1985, 1989, 1992, 1995, 1998, 2001, 2003, 2005, 2007). Also, the Institute has established an online database through Bibliographic Retrieval Service (BRS) that makes reviews for subsequent yearbooks available as they are received.

The professional journals continue to publish reviews. Those likely to contain reviews or articles about the use of career assessment instruments are the Journal of Counseling and Development, the Career Development Quarterly, the Journal of Career Assessment, and the Measurement and Evaluation in Counseling and Development Journal. Also, the Association for Assessment in Counseling and Education (AACE) publishes test reviews in its organization newsletter, NewsNotes, many of which deal with career assessment instruments.

Those desiring additional information about the sources described here as well as other sources of information about testing and career assessment are encouraged to consult Appendix A, which contains an annotated bibliography of available sources.

Legal, Ethical, and Social Considerations

Today's users of career assessment instruments need to consider many more external factors than by those who pioneered the field. Very few laws existed 60 years ago when the post-World War II expansion of the use of tests in career counseling began. Since that time, both state and federal laws have been enacted that either govern, promote, or sometimes even require their use. Federal legislation that has promoted the use of tests for career counseling programs can be traced back to 1958 when the National Defense Education Act was passed with its emphasis on counseling and guidance in the public schools. This law was followed by The Elementary and Secondary Education Act of 1965 and its later amendments that continued to promote school guidance and counseling activities, including testing and assessment.

A second stream of federal legislation that at first promoted vocational or career guidance and eventually required the use of tests in the public schools began with the Vocational Education Act of 1963 and was expanded by its subsequent amendments in 1968 and 1976. The 1984 Carl D. Perkins Vocational Education Act included in section 204 (c) a specific requirement for handicapped and disadvantaged students that stated:

Each student who enrolls in a vocational education program and to whom subsection (b) applies shall receive (1) assessment of interests, abilities, and special needs of such student with respect to completing successfully the vocational education program . . .

The 1990s produced several pieces of federal vocational education legislation with implications for career assessment as part of guidance and counseling services. In 1990, the Carl D. Perkins Vocational and Applied Technology Education Act replaced the earlier Perkins act; eight years later it was superseded by the Carl D. Perkins Vocational and Technical Education Act of 2006. Although these acts have not explicitly required the use of career assessment instruments, they included extensive provisions for career guidance and counseling services. Both Perkins acts have also required performance standards that have increased the use of applied achievement assessments.

This increased attention to student achievement assessment was stimulated by the first SCANS report (Secretary's Commission on Achieving Necessary Skills, 1991). In the middle of the 1990s, Congress also enacted the School to Work Opportunities Act of 1994, which was intended to provide all students with salable skills upon leaving high school. The major focus of the act was to integrate school- and work-based learning using connecting activities that include many career guidance services.

Parallel to federal vocational education legislation, which has focused on public schools and community college/postsecondary institutions, were the several acts directed at adults in the labor force who were unemployed or underemployed and who were economically disadvantaged. These include the Manpower Development Training Act of 1962, Comprehensive Employment Training Act of 1973, Job Training Partnership Act of 1982 and the recent Workforce Investment Act of 1998. Many of the programs developed by the states to implement these acts included various career counseling and assessment services.

Operating alongside federal vocational education legislation have been The Education of All Handicapped Children Act of 1975 and its subsequent amendments including the Individuals with Disabilities Education Improvement Act of 2004" and its subsequent amendments. These laws have required the use of tests and other assessment devices as input to constructing Individualized Education Plans (IEPs) for individuals with disabilities through age 21 in the public schools. In addition, they require transition planning beginning at age 14 to enable students to participate "... in advanced placement courses or a vocational education program" [Sec. 614 (d) (1) (A) (vii)]. Since students with disabilities in the public secondary schools are served in vocational education programs, tests targeted to this group have expanded greatly in quantity, if not in quality, over the past two decades.

Emerging over somewhat the same period as vocational education and handicapped/disability legislation, the Career Education movement also contributed to the use of tests in career guidance and counseling. Beginning in 1971, this movement was promoted by separate legislation in 1974, 1976, and 1977. The major impact this movement had on career assessment was the development and use of instruments in the schools, including at the elementary and middle school level.

Although the above-described legislation promoted the use of assessment as part of the career guidance and counseling function of schools and agencies, other laws were passed that regulated its use. In 1979, the Department of Health, Education, and Welfare's

Office of Civil Rights issued federal Vocational Education Programs Guidelines for Eliminating Discrimination and Denial of Services on the Basis of Race, Color, National Origin, Sex, and Handicap. These guidelines, based on three previous civil rights laws (Civil Rights Act of 1964, Title IX of the Education Amendments of 1972, and section 504 of the Rehabilitation Act of 1973), prohibit the use of tests in ways that would limit a person's options to pursue training in vocational education programs. The 1974 Family Educational Rights and Privacy Act (The Buckley Amendment) and the National Institute of Education's 1978 Guidelines for Assessment of Sex Bias and Sex Fairness in Career Interest Inventories also govern or influence the use of tests.

Professional associations have provided guidance for the use of tests in career counseling as well as in other areas. The *Standards for Educational and Psychological Testing* (American Educational Research Association, American Psychological Association, & National Council on Measurement in Education, 1999) published by the American Psychological Association (APA) on behalf of a joint committee of APA, the American Educational Research Association (AERA), and the National Council for Measurement in Education (NCME), govern the development and use of all career assessment instruments. The National Board for Certified Counselors (NBCC) also produced a code of ethics that included a section on measurement and evaluation.

In 1980, the American Personnel and Guidance Association (now the American Counseling Association, ACA) published its policy statement, *Responsibilities of Users of Standardized Tests* (RUST). This document, which contains much information relevant to the use of career assessment instruments, was revised in 2003 (ACA, 2003). A similar publication, *Code of Fair Testing Practices in Education* (Joint Committee on Testing Practices, 2004), was developed by a Joint Committee on Testing Practices (JCTP), which involved six professional associations including ACA and AACE. This committee has also published *Rights and Responsibilities of Test Takers: Guidelines and Responsibilities* (JCTP, 1999). These last three documents are included in their entirety in Appendix C. An abbreviated checklist, based on the standards and guidelines described above, is included in Chapter 6.

Using the Guide

To choose wisely from the array of assessment instruments in this fifth edition, it is helpful to reflect on the purpose of career assessment and its role in enhancing career and human development.

The choice and use of career assessments can be based on three basic beliefs. First, career development is an integral and inseparable part of learning and human development; second, career guidance and career development programs should be a part of the total instructional program in schools, colleges, and training divisions of business and industry; and third, all assessment enhances learning as well as personal and career development.

It is also important to note certain principles that apply to all assessment:

- Assessment is something that is done with and by learners, not something that is done to them. It is much more than taking a test, regardless of purpose. Assessment is a process, a part of instruction, not an event. It is a process for gathering information and using results to inform decisions.

- All assessments must complement and supplement each other. Assessment of achievement, aptitudes, interests, values, career development, and personality traits are a part of learning and development.

- All assessment should promote self-assessment, the involvement of the learner, and his/her ownership of the process and the results.

- Two major purposes of assessment are to improve and to prove: to improve individuals' learning and development and the programs provided for them, and to prove the effectiveness of such programs.

- Assessment is inseparable from instruction, learning and development.

Although all assessments of learners contribute to their overall growth and development, career assessment provides additional information for the enhancement of career development and career success. Career assessment instruments provide one form and format of assessment. When combined with other assessment modes, experiences, professional assistance, and other influences, these instruments assist learners/clients in forming and seeking answers to questions such as *What can I do?* (aptitude), *What can I be?* (aptitude/achievement), *What should I be?* (interest/personality/values), *What do I want to be?* (interest), and *How can I be what I want to be?* (career development/career maturity/career planning).

In Appendix C, Testing Standards and Codes, *The Responsibilities of Users of Standardized Tests* standard describes four specific areas related to the purpose of testing: Description, Accountability, Prediction, and Program Evaluation. In a similar vein, Herr (1994) described four main uses of career assessments:

1. **Prediction:** What is the probability of a learner's success in an educational program, occupation, or career?

2. **Discrimination:** How similar is a learner to those who are successful in a given program or occupation.

3. **Monitoring:** What is the status of a learner's career maturity, decision-making skills, or planning skills?

4. **Evaluation:** How effective are career interventions or program activities? What is the success of a program in terms of learner improvement or achieving the intended results of the program?

The first three of Herr's uses of assessment results seek to improve the choices and career success of individuals; the last purpose adds the dimension of program accountability by using assessment data in aggregate.

Mau (2007), in reviewing studies addressing career program interventions, noted that the U. S. Department of Education has recently revised the National Career Development Guidelines in order to bring them into alignment with the goals of the No Child Left Behind Act of 2001 (2001). These revised guidelines now address three domains; Personal Social Development, Educational Achievement, and Lifelong Learning and Career Management. [See America's Career Resource Network (ACRN) entry in Appendix A.] Also, in an earlier review of 40 studies, Mau, Sudarijanto, and Wine (2006) found career interventions are most effective with career management outcomes and least effective with educational achievement outcomes.

Wall (2007) suggests both broad and narrow evaluation questions in planning and implementing a career development program evaluation. Her downloadable guide http://www.home.earthlink.net/~sagesolutions discusses sources of data including commercial assessment instruments.

Mastie (1994) also described four uses of assessment in career counseling and discussed the appropriateness of each. She labeled these uses of career assessments as Compass, Credential, Process, and Empowerment.

Career assessment as **Compass** is the process of amassing information about an individual (interests, aptitudes, values, skills, etc.) in order to improve the accuracy of a decision. In light of the limitations of available assessment instruments, Mastie cautioned of the dangers of using such information to find a right career path.

Career assessment as **Credential** is seen as limiting access and opportunity for those tested. She cautioned that if assessment is used to qualify learners for intended training opportunities and career paths, counselors must be aware of these hurdles and incorporate them into ongoing career development programs and provide intervention for counselees to prepare for them. In Chapter 7, Podmostko and colleagues examine this use of assessments in more detail.

Career assessment as **Process** is based on the view of career development as an ongoing process, a series of choices. Thus, any particular career decision is merely a single instance in a lifetime of career choice points. Career assessment can assist learners to approach career choice points as times to reevaluate opportunities; to reassess their skills, interests, and values; to seek assistance if needed; and to use the information to create career plans and initiate action. The emphasis is more on *choosing wisely* than on making a *wise choice.*

Career assessment as **Empowerment** is based on the premise that career planning is the work of the client, and not the work of the counselor. Career assessments are seen as questions for the learner, not answers. Using assessment results helps learners take control of, inform, and enrich their own explorations of possible choices. Sauser, in his instrument review in Chapter 10 of this *Guide,* emphasizes this use of assessment instruments when he states, "The real value of the instrument … is dependent on the degree to which the job seeker engages in this experience and the counselor provides insight and guidance."

Clearly, choosing assessment instruments is neither a simple nor an isolated decision. Career assessment is both process and product. It is a vital ingredient in the process of planning and choosing and an important source of information about how learners/clients are progressing in their career development. It provides information on self-knowledge, career knowledge, and career planning skills, all of which are necessary for the learner/client to enhance his/her career development and career success. It complements other assessments and instructional processes and draws from these to enhance career development. At the same time it allows for the benchmarking of learner progress singularly and in aggregate to enhance intervention techniques and allow us to assess and improve program effectiveness. Career assessment, used properly, can provide form and focus to career development and to a career development program. Inappropriate, misused, or unconnected to other program efforts, it offers little and has the potential to interfere with career development and career success.

This fifth edition of *A Counselor's Guide to Career Assessment Instruments*, while providing a plethora of career instruments from which to choose, also provides advice on choosing appropriate assessment strategies and using the assessment results to best serve the learner. Chapters 2 through 7 lead the reader through discussions of recent trends and concerns in the use of career assessment and the competencies needed to choose and use assessment wisely. Edwin Herr (Chapter 2) views career assessment as one form of (as well as an adjunct to) career intervention that must be kept constantly relevant to changing contextual factors within which workers and potential workers must negotiate their career development, career identity, and employability. He includes within contextual factors the changing nature of work, the development or adaptation of career assessment cross-nationally, the merging of technology and career assessment, accountability, empirically supported treatments as well as evidence-based practice.

Valerie Schwiebert follows in Chapter 3 with a review of factors that must be considered in selecting career instruments. While assuming some basic understanding, the chapter provides an excellent overview of the many factors and actors in the selection process. Schwiebert discusses such factors as the intended purpose, technical and statistical information, and other practical issues.

In Chapter 4, Norman Gysbers and Richard Lapan look at societal changes, the challenges they represent for assessment, as well as the potential for career assessments to help shape sound policy and guide program implementation and evaluation. They envision three roles for assessment: personal advocacy, program evaluation, and formulation of public policy. They conclude with an example of a policy brief to consider.

James Sampson, Darrin Carr, Jill Lumsden, Cassandra Smission, and Casey Dozier (Chapter 5) explore the benefits, limitations and potential of computer applications in career assessment. Their discussion of necessary competence and experience for persons who use computer-assisted assessment focuses on the various roles of the computer, the counselor, and the client/individual in career assessment. Like Herr (2003), who warned of the threat of multiple career practitioners with varying qualifications who use career assessments, Sampson and colleagues caution that "irrespective of background, certification, or licensure, practitioners should only deliver career services within the limits of their training and experience." Other topics include the types of career assessment, current trends, problems related to computer technology, and assessment standards.

Thomas Krieshok and Michael Black (Chapter 6) provide an informal self-evaluation method for career development professionals to assess their own testing and counseling competencies, responsibilities, and practices in career assessment. They cover the basic concepts of counseling skills, assessment skills, administration procedures, score interpretation and reporting procedures, and technical considerations.

Mary Podmostko, Joe Timmons, and Christine Bremer (Chapter 7) address the four domains of assessment strategies (educational, vocational, psychological, and medical) in career planning and development that can reduce or eliminate barriers created by disability. Their chapter focuses primarily on supporting clients in the vocational domain, specifically, vocational interest assessment and vocational aptitude and skills assessment. Like Herr in Chapter 2, they emphasize that career assessments are one form of career interventions, and a part of the total intervention strategy.

A total of 71 instruments in 55 test reviews comprise the heart of this fifth edition. These are divided into five categories to facilitate location and selection of appropriate instruments: Chapter 8 — Aptitude/Achievement and Comprehensive or Combined Measures, Chapter 9 — Interest and Work Values Instruments, Chapter 10 — Career Development/Maturity Measures, Chapter 11 — Personality Assessments, and Chapter 12 — Instruments for Special Populations.

Each review begins with publisher-provided descriptive information in a standardized format, followed by a brief critical review of the instrument's strengths and limitations. Users will find in these entries the answers to daily application questions, such as:

> For what ages is this test appropriate? Who publishes it? What is the date of this inventory? Is there a new edition? Can it be given within one of our class periods? Can it be hand-scored? How expensive would it be for me to test an entire group? What kinds of scores would we get from this instrument?

Beyond these factual answers, users will find here the kind of practical information that they need for evaluating instruments:

> Are there reasons to believe this instrument may not be appropriate for the use I have in mind? Does this test really measure what we want to measure? What other instruments of this type are there for me to consider? Is there an entire category of measures we have overlooked?

In the final chapter (13), Chris Wood, Edwin Whitfield, Brenda Gerhardt, and Sibyl Cato, provide an overview of additional career assessment instruments that are available to the practitioner. When such are available, readers are referred to more complete reviews. The *Guide* concludes with the appendices provided to facilitate the use of this, as well as other, career assessment resources:

- Rich Feller and Jackie Peila-Shuster provide an annotated bibliography (Appendix A) that contains a manageable number of current references in testing and career assessment.
- Publishers' full addresses, phone numbers, e-mail addresses, and/or web pages when available are provided in Appendix B to simplify requests for specimen sets or other assistance and to facilitate ordering.
- Appendix C provides the complete text of professional association position statements on the responsibilities of test users, code of fair testing practices, the rights and responsibilities of test takers, and standards for multicultural assessment.

- The user's matrix updated by Edwin Whitfield and Sibyl Cato (Appendix D) lists all instruments included in the guide and should help the reader to find instruments appropriate for selected purposes.

Once the reader has an overall picture of what is available here, thoughtful consideration should be given to perspective. Fairness and balance in the treatment of reviewed instruments drove all deliberations by the editors, reviewers, and authors. We have made this reference as dependable, honest, and accurate as it was in our power to achieve. Nevertheless, limitations of length, technical documentation, and the occasional divided professional opinion suggest that serious readers will need to undertake additional investigation using the technical manuals and the sources referenced. This guide can neither teach a measurement course nor make a selection decision for a busy practitioner. The user must assume his or her responsibility to achieve full professional competency through ongoing professional development programs and through a great deal of experience with the instruments described here. With this perspective in mind, we are pleased to offer this tool to assist in clarifying and managing the complex body of knowledge about career assessment.

References

American Counseling Association. (2003). *Responsibilities of users of standardized tests.* Alexandria, VA: Author.

American Educational Research Association, American Psychological Association, & National Council on Measurement in Education. (1999). *Standards for educational and psychological testing.* Washington, DC: American Psychological Association.

Department of HEW, Office of Civil Rights. Vocational education programs guidelines for eliminating discrimination and denial of services on the basis of race, color, national origin, sex, and handicap. Washington, DC: 44 Fed. Reg. 6 (March 21, 1979).

Engen, H. B., Lamb, R.R., & Prediger, D. T. (1982). Are secondary schools still using standardized tests? *Personnel and Guidance Journal,* 60, 287–290.

Herr, E. L., (1994). The counselor's role in career assessment. In J. T. Kapes, M. M. Mastie, & E. A. Whitfield (Eds.), *A counselor's guide to career assessment instruments* (3rd ed.) Alexandria, VA: National Career Development Association.13-22.

Herr, E. L. (2003). The future of career counseling as an instrument of public policy. *The Career Development Quarterly,* 52(1), 8–17.

Joint Committee on Testing Practices. (1999). *Rights and responsibilities of test takers: Guidelines and responsibilities.* Washington, DC: American Psychological Association.

Joint Committee on Testing Practices. (2004). *Code of fair testing practices in education.* Washington, DC: American Psychological Association.

Kapes, J. T., & Mastie, M. M. (1982). *A counselor's guide to vocational guidance instruments.* Falls Church, VA: National Vocational Guidance Association.

Kapes, J. T., & Mastie, M. M. (1988). *A counselor's guide to career assessment instruments* (2nd ed.) Alexandria, VA: National Career Development Association.

Kapes, J. T., Mastie, M. M., & Whitfield, E. A. (1994). *A counselor's guide to career assessment instruments* (3rd ed.) Alexandria, VA: National Career Development Association.

Kapes, J. T., Parrish, L. H., & Funderburg, D. L. (1993). Vocational assessment for students with special needs: A survey of Texas public schools. *Occupational Education Forum, 21(2),* 31–44.

Kapes, J. T., & Whitfield, E. A. (2001). *A counselor's guide to career assessment instruments* (4th ed.). Columbus, OH: National Career Development Association.

Mastie, M. M. (1994). Using assessment instruments in career counseling: Career assessment as compass, credential, process and empowerment. In J. T. Kapes, M. M. Mastie, and E. A. Whitfield (Eds.). (1994). *A counselor's guide to career assessment instruments* (3rd ed.) Alexandria, VA: National Career Development Association. 31-40.

Mau, W. C. (2007) Impacts of school-based career interventions on NCDG outcomes. *Career Convergence,* Broken Arrow, OK. National Career Development Association. Retrieved April 1, 2007 from source.

Mau, W. C, Sudarijanto, R., & Wine, T. (2006, July). *Effectiveness of Career Interventions in college/university settings.* Paper presented at the annual meeting of National Career Development Association, Chicago, IL.

No Child Left Behind Act of 2001. (2001). 107 U.S.C. § 1424 (2002). Secretary's Commission on Achieving Necessary Skills. (1991). *What work requires of schools: A SCANS report for America 2000.* Washington, DC: SCANS, U.S. Department of Labor. (ERIC Document Reproduction Service No. ED332054)

Wall, J. E. (2007) Is your program working? Resources for evaluating your career program. *Career Convergence.* Broken Arrow, OK National Career Development Association. Retrieved October 1, 2007 from source.

Watkins, C. E., Jr., Campbell, V. L., & Nieberding, R. (1994). The practice of vocational assessment by counseling psychologists. The Counseling Psychologist, 22(1), 115–128.

Zytowski, D. G., & Warman, R. E. (1982). The changing use of tests in counseling. *Measurement and Evaluation in Guidance, 15(2),* 147–152.

CHAPTER 2

CAREER ASSESSMENT: PERSPECTIVES ON TRENDS AND ISSUES

Edwin L. Herr
The Pennsylvania State University

Background

Since the earliest years of the twentieth century, career assessment, like other forms of career intervention, have been seen by policy makers, theorists, and counselors as important instruments to achieve social, economic, and political goals, both at national and individual levels. In this sense, career assessment is often perceived to be an important sociopolitical instrument by which to achieve outcomes of significance to national aspirations. In oversimplified terms, goals to which career assessment is expected to contribute include such examples as (1) the prevention of long-term unemployment, the development of an effective workforce, and the matching of workers and employers; (2) the adjustment by potential or active workers to rapidly changing requirements for employment or for retention; (3) intervention programs for persons considered marginally employable because of poor academic or technical skills, functional disabilities, interpersonal or other social problems, or discrimination; and (4) the provision of assistance to those who have become unemployed or underemployed as a result of industrial reorganization, outsourcing, or international economic competition.

These national goals and related ones have been reflected in a continuing stream of public policies and legislation in the United States and other nations affecting the form, substance, and purposes of career assessment, career counseling, career education, and other career interventions. Such policies and legislation have been direct responses to changing conditions in the society at large at particular historical periods as issues of recession, national defense, civil rights, war, technological affects on work processes or worker functions, skill shortages, or the consequences of the global economy dominate. Embedded in each of these historical periods are assumptions about what types of assistance individuals need in order to develop the knowledge, skills, and attitudes that will facilitate their transition through various stages of career development: choosing the particular types of work they wish to do, preparing for that work, being inducted into the work force, and adjusting to its requirements and changing conditions.

These goals, purposes, policies, and legislative actions related to work and to workers are an important backdrop against which career assessment and career interventions in general are developed, refined, and implemented. Because of their responsiveness to change and to individual needs to choose, adopt, and function within shifting conditions of change, career interventions must be kept constantly relevant to the contextual factors within which workers and potential workers must negotiate their career development, their career identity, and their employability. This is true not only in the United States but increasingly throughout the world as nations come to terms with the reality that the major asset of any nation is not its wealth or its raw material and natural resources: its major assets are the literacy, the numeracy, the communications ability, the computer skills, the teachability, and the flexibility of its work force as it is able to learn about and to implement new work processes and changes in the organization of work.

Nations tend to share many of the same goals for career interventions regardless of their specific cultural traditions. Among them are helping persons to distribute their abilities across the nation's occupational structure and to have equal opportunities for access to educational and occupational opportunities. These are fundamental stimuli to the broadening of the techniques employed in career assessment and in other types of career interventions, to increased comprehensiveness of the persons and the settings served, and to the range of individual needs and societal purposes to be addressed. The result is that while still uneven in availability in many nations, career assessment, career counseling, career guidance, career education, and other career interventions have become worldwide phenomena.

These observations are not to suggest that the use of career assessments or other career interventions is the same from nation to nation. They are not. As I will discuss in the next section on trends, there is an increase throughout the world in indigenous approaches to the delivery of career interventions that are compatible with the resources, cultural traditions, and policies of individual nations. In this sense, the theories and practices of career assessment do not exist in a vacuum; they are affected by economic, political, and social events that spawn new needs and goals for career assessment. In a continuous progression, visionaries, theorists, researchers, and practitioners emerge who can help to convert ideas related to career assessment into action.

Some Perspectives on Career Assessment

Career assessment originated in the United States, primarily as an adjunct to career counseling. Thus, in many cases, the contents of career counseling were seen as the scores and their interpretations that result from career assessment. Many professionals in the United States and in other countries continue to view career assessment as a part of the career counseling process, not as a separate intervention, even though the use of career assessments in self-directed, counselor-free, and computer-mediated career guidance systems have demonstrated their unique contributions as interventions in their own right.

A further way to view career assessment is as a bridge from career development theory to practice, a method of operationalizing theoretical constructs by incorporating them into career interventions and, in particular, into tests and other measurements. This has been true in Holland's theoretical constructs as these are embedded in the Vocational Preference Inventory, My Vocational Situation, and the Self-Directed Search; in the use of his theoretical framework (RIASEC) as the organizing and interpretive structure for the most recent iterations of the Strong Interest Inventory and for some of the informational and self-assessment components of the DISCOVER computer-mediated career guidance system; and the use of Holland's three letter coding system of major personality types as a way of organizing U.S. government educational and occupational information through such sources as the Dictionary of Holland Codes (Holland, 1997).

In a similar fashion, Super, from the beginning of his theory development, used assessment instruments to operationalize and to evaluate his theoretical constructs (Super, 1990; 1994). Like Holland, he made his theoretical constructs accessible to researchers and to practitioners by using assessment to bridge theory and practice. Examples of the instruments that evolved from his theoretical propositions include the Career Development Inventory, the Adult Career Concerns Inventory, the Work Values Inventory, the Values Inventory, and the Salience Inventory. These instruments describe or measure such constructs as one's level of career maturity or career planfulness, knowledge and attitudes about career choice, intrinsic and extrinsic life-career values, and the relative importance to the client of major life roles beyond those of occupation or career. These instruments, then, are useful in defining goals for career counseling as well as for explicating and assessing particular types of content of importance to the decision making of individual clients. Super also developed models of career counseling, particularly the C-DAC Model (Osborne, Brown, Niles, & Miner, 1997), in which career assessment and career counseling are intimately interactive as interventions.

Other theorists also use assessments to translate theory into practice. Among them is Krumboltz, who has developed several important theoretical concepts and innovative assessment devices that have emerged from his work in behaviorism, social learning, and cognitive behavioral theory. One example of such assessment that has linked his theoretical work to interventions is the Career Beliefs Inventory (Krumboltz, 1994), a counseling tool that can identify presuppositions and irrational beliefs that may block people from achieving their career goals.

The Changing Context for Career Assessment

These preliminary comments suggest the richness and the dynamic character of the history of career assessment. Obviously, the development of new career assessments and the refinements of older instruments is ongoing as new contextual and measurement challenges are addressed. Indeed, there are several trends emerging that will continue to spawn new types and uses of career assessments and adaptations of the old. In many cases, these trends include specific issues that require new career assessments or modified theoretical perspectives. While it is not possible to be exhaustive in this brief chapter about such matters, there are several categories of trends and issues that exemplify the emerging pressures for new career assessments, new practices, and new theoretical perspectives. They include the changing nature of work; the development or adaptation of career assessment cross-nationally; the wedding of technology and career assessment; and accountability, empirically supported treatments and evidence-based practice. Each of these trends and issues will be discussed in the following sections.

The Changing Nature of Work

The ways in which work is done and organized are rapidly changing. There are multiple factors influencing that change and affecting the types of career assessments that will be required in the future. Among the most significant factors are those spawned by the global economy. These include the pervasive use of advanced technology in the workplace and a global labor surplus, including a large number of highly educated and skilled workers, seeking opportunities in whatever nation offers employment opportunities and economic security. As the migration of workers across national boundaries continues to take place and the ways in which work is organized and implemented are changing rapidly, there are needs for new definitions of workplace skills, personal attributes, personal flexibility, and career assessments of these competencies and behaviors.

In preparation for and adjustment to the workplaces now in transition, there is currently increased interest in assessing "soft skills" such as the ability to work in teams, to work in diverse cultural environments, to participate in decision making in the workplace, to be resilient in workplaces that are in a constant state of change, to be teachable and adaptable as new products and processes are created and implemented in shorter intervals of time, and to think in new ways about career planning that focuses on short time horizons (e.g., five years) rather than decades. Within such contexts, however one views work or career development in the twenty-first century, it will no longer be linear, or easily separated into sequential life stages of growth, exploration, advancement, maintenance, and decline. Very few individuals will remain in one job, one firm, one occupation throughout their working life; they are likely to be in career transition many times during their working life, susceptible to organizational changes occasioned by mergers and consolidations of workplaces leading to the shedding of redundant workers and the use of technology to stimulate productivity and reduce the costs of retaining workers who are not central to the particular goals of a given workplace. As workforces are reduced in size to only those workers who have the technical and managerial skills absolutely essential to the mission of the workplace, the workers terminated will, in many places, become members of the contingent, part-time workforce, be self-employed, or be employed by outsourcing firms.

Knowledge Workers

In the United States, and in a growing number of other countries, educational requirements for many forms of work are rising as the work place is becoming more fully automated, applying more computer-driven lathes, robots, data analysis, diagnoses, design processes, often supported by the Internet, telecommunications, and global supply chains of products and services. These changes have increased the need for knowledge workers, persons who know how as well as why they are implementing specific work processes. Now more than 60% of the U.S. workforce, knowledge workers must be able to adapt to rapid changes in work processes and problems, troubleshoot, solve problems, and apply new knowledge. As Peter Drucker (Beatty, 1998) has contended, knowledge has replaced experience as the principal requisite for employment in most of the emerging occupations in the world. Because of the needs to link science and technology more fully to produce new products and services, more workplaces have become "learning organizations" (Senge, 1996) where assessing ideas and creativity are major elements in the continuous improvement of the content and processes being used (Florida, 2004). There are also work places where jobs as clearly defined, fixed sets of tasks, the principal way of organizing work, are giving way to new terms like boundaryless careers and multitasking. Some observers have argued that "jobs" as a way of organizing work are social artifacts that have outlived their usefulness. Increasingly, employers are expecting workers to get work done that needs to be done regardless of the artificial boundaries that separate specific sets of tasks (Bridges, 1994). In such contexts, it is likely that career assessments in the future will emphasize individual initiative, creativity, problem solving, and the ability to multitask and to take risks.

Lifelong Learning

Embedded in the identification and preparation for and the continuous adjustment to work of knowledge workers, in workplaces where continuous learning is essential, lifelong learning becomes a major part of one's ability to function effectively in the "new" workplace. For more and more workers, learning skills and achievements are major elements of individual career development. In a society of change, intense competition, creativity, and knowledge work, mastery of basic academic skills becomes a prerequisite for employability, for lifelong learning, and as foundation skills for technical and occupational processes.

The World Bank (2003) suggests that the status quo for workers in a global economy is to be engaged in continuous learning and to feel constantly on edge, off balance, as workers are expected to be prepared to adjust and adapt to the ongoing transformation in the organization of work, a constant theme in the lives of workers engaged in a global economy. In response to such conditions, career assessments are likely to include more attention to individual ability to cope with ambiguity, with stress, and with resilience.

Some Implications from the Changing Nature of Work for Career Assessment

There is much more to be said about the changing nature of work, the global economy, and the changing nature of skills that workers will need to possess to function within a work world in transition. Available perspectives suggest that the worker of the future must be his or her own career manager, keeping employability skills honed and attractive to employers, and engaging in continuous learning and attention to trends that will affect his or her inventory of employable skills. Implicit in such perspectives is the view that although constancy and stability (homeostasis) have frequently been cited in the psychological literature as desirable traits for individual growth and development, career planning and choices in the future are likely to be more spontaneous, more values oriented, and more influenced by environmental and organizational flux, unpredictability, and turbulence.

The question relative to career assessment is: do our current instruments measure personal flexibility, commitment to continuous learning, comfort with cultural diversity, ability to work in teams, willingness to engage in multitasking, self-initiative, the ability to be creative, and the motivation to be responsible for one's own career development? These are among the major competencies seen as essential to functioning well in a global economy. At the least, it would seem useful to inventory our current career assessment instruments to determine to what degree there exist scales or subscales that measure such individual traits and abilities. If these measures do not exist, it will be necessary to construct them.

The Development or Adaptation of Career Assessment Cross-Nationally

Although one can identify career assessments that include measures of particular competencies or abilities important in a changing world of work or, barring such availability, constructing new assessments, it is also possible to adapt career assessments constructed in other nations. To an increasing degree, as career assessment and other career interventions have become worldwide phenomena, they have become increasingly indigenous to their own nations' characteristics and to the career concerns of importance in that nation. Until recently, the adaptation of career assessment instruments have primarily focused on measurement instruments constructed in the United States or Western Europe and translated into the language of a nation interested in validating the instrument's suitability for use in that nation. While the principal adaptation of career assessments still tends to be from the United States or Western Europe to other nations, that trend may be less pronounced in the future. As the utility and comprehensiveness of career interventions, including career assessment, from nations around the world becomes increasingly accessible, provides culturally sensitive content, and procedures of relevance and high quality, the adaptation of indigenous instruments that measure skills, altitudes, or behaviors of interest to another nation will proceed rapidly. This process will likely accelerate since "many of the world's largest testing companies are making their tests available through the Internet" (Oakland, 2004).

The importance of adapting accurately and validating thoroughly career assessments from another country is a growing issue. At the least, it requires a knowledge of the methodological processes that led to the instrument, its purposes, its psychometric properties in the country of origin, and the external and internal conditions that gave rise to the assessment instrument. To oversimplify the matter, then, its uses in a new culture, in a nation hoping to adapt the assessment, must be validated, its language standardized across cultures, its reliability measured, and local or national norms developed. In professional terms, it is necessary for any adaptation of a test or assessment to adhere to copyright provisions, obtain the consent of the test's author and publisher, and observe the ethical standards that apply to test adaptation as provided by counseling or psychological associations located in some 80 countries around the world as well as the International Test Commission (Bartram, 2001).

Rossier (2004) compared the cross-cultural equivalence of several personality inventories frequently used in career counseling (e.g., 16PF, NEO-P1, Internal-External Locus of Control Scale). His very strong point is that when counselors use a translated instrument particular attention must be paid to its cultural validity or cultural replicability. Neglecting to do so can result in erroneous conclusions about the meaning of the scale scores. In addition to linguistic, conceptual, and scale equivalence, there also needs to be culture-specific normative equivalence if the scale is to be used in career counseling.

Duarte (2004) has made the important point that adaptation of career assessment instruments from one nation to another is not simply a linguistic exercise. Rather, those who "translate" instruments from one language to another are obliged to do complete literature reviews related to the development of the instrument as well as to the meanings of the constructs assessed by the instrument. In the case of indigenous instruments being adapted from other nations to the United States, this will require U.S. researchers to become familiar with the published work in European, Asian, and other national journals and with the languages in which they are published (e.g., French, Japanese, Spanish, German).

To the degree that such a trend intensifies, there will likely be a greater sensitivity in the United States to excellent research occurring in other nations and bring researchers to greater cooperation transnationally as they fashion instruments that are truly international in their concepts and content or adapt career assessments that are found to have high validity and reliability in many nations beyond their originating nation.

Technology and Career Assessment

One of the trends that will facilitate the cross-national development, adaptation, and use of career assessments is the pervasive use of computers and the Internet for research, statistical analyses, management of data banks, and other tasks associated with the construction of career assessment instruments. As computers and available software continue to become more user friendly and comprehensive in their content and less expensive to purchase and use, these tools and the access to the Internet they provide will create conditions by which new measurement instruments will be made available.

In the past decade as the Internet achieved significant growth in websites that provided career advice, career information, job placement, and career assessments (Harris-Bowlsbey, 2003), research studies indicated that the career assessment instruments in these websites varied from poorly constructed, locally used instruments to highly professional, standardized instruments with strong psychometric properties. Many of the latter were developed during the 1970s and 1980s when computer-based career guidance systems (e.g., DISCOVER, SIGI Plus) were being developed and used in state career information delivery systems, schools, colleges, employment counseling agencies, and some workplaces. In many of these systems, career assessments were prominent parts of the content as they helped users clarify the status of their interests, values, abilities, and career goals and the databases they should explore. As computer-assisted career guidance systems and the Internet became increasingly common in their use over the past several decades, the importance of career assessment as a complement to career counseling and other career interventions has been demonstrated empirically and in relation to the roles of career counselors.

Indeed, when one thinks of interventions on computer-assisted career guidance systems or on the Internet, one can think of the career assessment itself as an intervention, the career assessment and the other elements of a computer-based system or website as an intervention, or the career assessment, other elements of a program or website, and a counselor as a career intervention. The results obtained tend to become more positive as these increments of interventions are added together in combination with the group or individual intervention of counselors (Herr, Cramer, & Niles, 2004).

Whiston, Brecheisen, and Stephens (2003) found in their research that counselor-free interventions were not as effective as were inventions that involved a counselor. In addition, they found that individuals who used a computer-assisted career guidance system that was supplemented by a counselor's individual counseling attained better outcomes than persons who used a computer system not supplemented by counseling. As computer-assisted career guidance systems and Internet websites have rapidly grown in number and use, ethnical standards for the use of these interventions have been created by the

National Board for Certified Counselors, National Career Development Association, Association of Computer-Based Systems for Career Information, and other groups. Even so, there are still ethical problems occurring in the use of these interventions, probably more so on the Internet than in the more mature computer-assisted career guidance systems.

Thus, what has been said by a number of observers is that the Internet provides a huge array of websites which essentially offer a "smorgasbord of disjointed" information that is available to the public free of charge and without consumer protection (Harris-Bowlsbey, 2003). At the same time, however, the Internet provides enormous possibilities for high-quality occupational information, video portrayals of work environments and occupations, online access to the best in professional literature, publications, summaries of research findings, cybercounseling, e-mail, chat rooms, text messaging, online discussion, e-learning, video conferencing, telephone help lines with replies online (Offer, 2005), and career assessments. What is at issue, to an increasing degree, is a research base that analyzes material on the Internet to identify those items which meet quality standards and those career interventions, including career assessments, that are determined to be best practices, empirically supported, and evidence-based.

Evidence-Based Assessments, Empirically Supported Treatments, and Accountability

As one uses terms like "best practices," "empirically supported treatments," and "evidence-based" implicit, if not explicit, is the role played by assessments in achieving such outcomes. To an increasing degree, the whole range of interventions and the results they achieve individually and collectively are being questioned by legislators, policy makers, and institutional administrators. They are asking: "What are we receiving for our investment of resources in career services?" "How do we know what interventions or combinations of them are the most effective?" Do career services or interventions add value to the education of adolescents or college students, or to the purpose and productivity of adult workers?" "How do we know?" "Why do we need counselors if counselor-free interventions are effective?" In one sense, the question is: can we create a matrix that identifies individual career presenting problems — stress, anxiety, indecision, indecisiveness, overcommitment to work, undercommitment to work, etc. — and the interventions and theories that have been found to affect these career concerns in positive and effective ways, for different subpopulations, under varying conditions. These questions ask how does intervention A compare with the effects of intervention B or C or D vis-a-vis a particular presenting problem? What are the comparative costs of intervention A, B, C, or D in achieving the goals sought? How do we assure that the values achieved exceed the costs of the interventions? These are questions of accountability, of cost-benefit ratios, and of evidence-based or empirically supported practices.

There are now hundreds of career assessment instruments available, many of which have been studied at length in terms of their validity, reliability, and other psychometric properties. One issue is which of these instruments most likely measures most directly and comprehensively the outcomes of most concern (career maturity, career adaptability, information seeking, developmental status on necessary career tasks, personal flexibility) in comparing the impact of different interventions on the outcomes chosen. A second issue is the need to reinvigorate career outcome research that assesses both single and comparative effects on the major career outcomes that are inherent in the most influential career theories in the field. Whiston, Brecheisen, and Stephens (2003) reported that there has been a decrease in career outcome research over the past 15 years, even though there have been new techniques, including the Internet, and new career outcomes to be assessed. A third issue has to do with the consistency of the instruments used to assess the effects of career interventions on career outcomes. If different instruments are used to assess the same outcomes, unless it is clear that their contents are highly correlated, it becomes difficult to know what the obtained results mean. A further issue is that unless career outcome research grows in its coverage and immediacy across a large spectrum of career interventions, used singly and in combination, editors, practitioners, and researchers may conclude that approaches to career counseling, career education, career guidance, and other career interventions are not empirically supported or evidence-based practices.

While one can argue persuasively that, "in the broadest or aggregate sense," there is no longer a major question about the ability of career counseling and other career interventions to improve or change career behavior (e.g., Brown & Ryan Krane, 2000; Campbell, Connel, Boyle, & Bhaerman, 1983; Oliver & Spokane, 1988; Rounds & Tinsley, 1984; Whiston, 2003; Whiston, Brecheisen, & Stephens, 2003; Whiston, Sexton, & Lasoff, 1998), the large array of research studies available have not really addressed accountability, empirically supported treatments, or evidence-based practice questions systematically. Meta-analyses and other research techniques have permitted researchers to summarize large numbers of studies and to determine the collective effect of research studies of a particular process on different forms of behavior. But, in general, these studies have not compared the effects of intervention A to that of intervention B in relation to particular career-presenting problems. Nor have these studies essentially contrasted the utility of theory A versus theory B for understanding and intervening in specific career concerns. Increasingly, researchers and theorists are contending, as has Whiston (2003), that "there is not an established method or model for conducting career counseling that is consistently used in the field and evaluated by researchers. Hence, career counseling professionals do not have a clear understanding of precisely *what* is effective, nor has the field made great strides in comparing different approaches with different populations" (p. 40).

Unlike some other mental health emphases (e.g., psychotherapy), career counseling protocols or treatment manuals have not typically been developed to assure that practices being evaluated are standardized so that they can be examined relative to their efficacy in promoting particular types of behavior, reframing irrational thoughts, facilitating counselee decision making, or obtaining other desired outcomes. Without such standardization of practices, it is difficult to compare the implementation of theory A versus theory B. Nor can one deconstruct various approaches to career intervention into their components to assess which ingredients of that practice are essential and necessary or acceptable but not necessary (Wampold, 2001) as compared with other approaches. While such research approaches may not occur in the foreseeable future, pursuit of such goals would better enable the field to articulate differences among its major theoretical and intervention processes; describe the importance of its contributions to societal goals to policy makers, legislators, and administrators; improve the training of practitioners; and address cost-benefit ratios of career interventions.

Cost-Benefit Analyses

One of the most important ways to examine accountability in the provision of career services for the future is cost-benefit analyses. Cost-benefit analyses tend to complete the circle from the creation, implementation, and evaluation of career assessments or other career interventions to their likely costs and benefits. A century ago, early career interventions, including career assessments, were largely philosophical and conceptual, not really theoretical and rarely empirical. Assessment instruments were created by early pioneers of career counseling to serve such practical purposes as identifying interests and aptitudes. However, during the course of the twentieth century, a science of assessment, measurement, and evaluation has evolved, largely, but not exclusively, as a complement to career counseling. The counseling profession at large has become increasingly accomplished in generating and presenting research evidence of the efficacy of career counseling and other career interventions for many purposes. Within such a context, career assessments have been used as measures by which to determine the efficacy of career interventions in facilitating such outcomes or viability of particular theoretical propositions.

More recently, career assessments have been studied as stand-alone or counselor-free career interventions in their own right, as portals by which counselees can identify and gain access to selected modules in computer-assisted career guidance systems, or as accountability monitors in such federal legislation as No Child Left Behind. At the same time that career assessments have been used as measures of dependent variables in research designs studying the effect sizes of different career interventions or as important adjunctive measures supporting career counseling and providing content for counselor-counselee dialogue, career assessment devices have also been studied in terms of their validity, reliability, and utility for different purposes. In general, career assessments have validated that career counseling and related career interventions are effective for many purposes and that, as these purposes change and expand, measurement methodologies and career assessments continue to be created.

To return to the issues of cost-benefit analyses: in spite of a clear set of philosophical assumptions about the value of career interventions and an enlarging research base that validates the importance of career interventions, it is fair to suggest that researchers and theorists in counseling, with the possible exception of those engaged in rehabilitation or in drug and alcohol research, have not systematically taken the next step of translating the available research findings into cost-benefit analyses. Even though one can make the oversimplified observation that every positive or negative correlation between a particular career intervention and a desired outcome carries with it economic costs and economic benefits, most theorists and researchers in career counseling and related career interventions have not focused on these issues. There has not been systematic examination of the costs of providing counseling or assessment to various populations for specific purposes compared to the economic and social benefits derived from such services. Nor have analyses accrued that have focused on the added value to an institution — school, university, employer, government, or society at large — of providing career services or to the individual who participates in career services.

Given limited economic resources available for counseling and competing human services, and rising demands for such resources, a strategic issue for the future will be the need to train counselors, theorists, and researchers in the mentality and methodology of cost-benefit analyses. Assessment strategies will be critical as they produce relevant measures of the added value of career interventions and the productivity of counselors in different settings. Such approaches will likely be effective tools in advocating to legislators and administrators policies that incorporate career counseling, career assessment, measurement, and evaluation as important assets in addressing major social and individual career goals.

Summary

This chapter has demonstrated that career assessment, both as a stand-alone career intervention and as an adjunct to career counseling and other career interventions, has sunk its roots deep into U.S. policy, theory, and practice as well as that of other nations. Clearly, the purposes for which career assessment is expected to be a useful process have expanded and taken on new content, formats, and venues. Career assessments are now frequently available on the Internet as part of the growing presence of online career counseling and access to job information. Rather than adapting assessments developed in the U.S., nations around the globe are increasingly creating career assessment instruments with content and procedures that are indigenous to their goals for career services for those choosing, preparing for, making the transition to, and adjusting to work.

As important as current career assessments are, the organization and substance of work itself is changing rapidly and qualitatively as are the expectations of workers. Workers need to become their own career managers or investors of their time, talent, and effort systematically in the choices available to them. Since such career choices and career transitions will likely occur more often, workers will need to be personally flexible, able to cope with change, and engaged in continuous learning. The need to assess these types of competencies will broaden the content of career assessments yet to be developed.

As the use of career assessments is worldwide, it is likely that major trends will include the development or adaptation of career assessments cross-nationally and the increased use of technologies (e.g., the Internet) to administer and interpret career assessments as counselor-free interventions or as the source of much of the content analyzed and discussed in the growing increase of online career counseling. Each of these trends will increasingly rely on the creation of new career assessments that address the changing nature of work and its reflection in career theory as well as providing measures of major dependent variables for purposes of accountability, empirically supported treatments, and evidence-based practices.

References

Bartram, D. (2001). The development of international guidelines on test use: The international test commission project. *International Journal of Testing*, 1(1), 33–54.

Beatty, J. (1998). *The world according to Peter Drucker*. New York: The Free Press.

Bridges, W. (1994, September). The end of the job. *Fortune*, 130, 62–74.

Brown, S. D., & Ryan Krane, N. E. (2000). Four (or five) sessions and a cloud of dust: Old assumptions and new observations about career counseling. In S. D. Brown & R. W. Lent (Eds.). *Handbook of counseling psychology* (3rd ed, pp. 740–766). New York: Wiley.

Campbell, R. E., Connel, J. B., Boyle, K. K., & Bhaerman, R. (1983). *Enhancing career development. Recommendations for action*. Columbus, OH: The National Center for Research in Vocational Education, The Ohio State University.

Duarte, M. E. (2004, June). *Assessment and cultural riches: Adaptation of psychological instruments and the global research village*. Paper presented at the symposium on International Perspectives on Career Development, San Francisco, CA.

Florida, R. (2004). *The rise of the creative class. And how it is transforming work, leisure, community and everyday life*. New York: Basic Books.

Harris-Bowlsbey, J. (2003). A rich past and a future vision. *Career Development Quarterly*, 52(1), 19–25.

Herr, E. L. (2003, October). *The measurement of career guidance outcomes*. Invited paper presented the international conference *Career guidance and public policy: Bridging the gap*. The Organization for Economic Cooperation and Development and the World Bank. Toronto, Canada.

Herr, E. L., Cramer, S. H., & Niles, S. G. (2004). *Career guidance and counseling through the life span: Systematic approaches*, Boston, MA: Allyn and Bacon.

Holland, J. L. (1997). *Making vocational choices: A theory of vocational personalities and work environments* (3rd ed.). Odessa, FL: Psychological Assessment Responses.

Krumboltz, J. D. (1994). The career beliefs inventory. *Journal of Counseling and Development*, 72, 424–428.

Oakland, T. (2004). Use of Educational and Psychological Tests Internationally. *Applied Psychology: An International Review*, 53(2), 157–172.

Obsorne, W. L., Brown, S., Niles, S. G., & Miner, C. (1997). *Career development assessment and counseling: Donald Super's C-DAC Model*. Alexandria, VA: American Counseling Association.

Offer, M. (2005, Summer). E-guidance: Can we deliver guidance by email and what issues does that raise? Recent research and evaluation in HE. *Career Research and Development, The NICEC Journal*, 12, 32–33.

Oliver, L. W., & Spokane, A. R. (1988). Career intervention outcome: What contributes to client gain? *Journal of Counseling Psychology*, 35, 447–462.

Rossier, J. (2004). *An analysis of the cross-cultural equivalence of some frequently used personality inventories*. Paper presented at the Symposium on International Perspectives on Career Development, San Francisco, CA, June, 2004.

Rounds, J. B., Jr., & Tinsley, H. E. A. (1984). Diagnosis and treatment of vocational problems, In S. Brown & R. Lent (Eds.), *Handbook of counseling psychology* (pp.137–177). New York: Wiley.

Senge, P. M. (1996). Leading learning organizations: The bold, the powerful, and the invisible. In F. Hesselbein, M. Goldsmith, and R. Beckhard, *The leader of the future, new visions, strategies and practices for the next era* (pp.41–58). San Francisco, CA: Jossey-Bass.

Super, D. E. (1990). A life-span, life-space approach to career development. In D. Brown & L. Brook (Eds.). *Career choice and development: Applying contemporary theories to practice* (pp.197–261). San Francisco, CA: Jossey-Bass.

Super, D. E. (1994). A life span, life space perspective on convergence. In M. L. Savickas & R. W. Lent (Eds.) *Convergence in career development theories: Implications for science and practice* (pp.63–74). Palo Alto, CA: CPP Books.

The World Bank (2003). *Lifelong learning in the global knowledge economy, challenges for developing countries*. Washington D. C.: Author.

Wampold, B. E. (2001). *The great psychotherapy debate: Models, methods, and findings*. Mahwah, NJ: Lawrence Erlbaum Associates.

Whiston, S. C. (2002). Application of the principles. *The Counseling Psychologist*, 30, 218–237.

Whiston, S. C. (2003). Career counseling: 90 years and yet still healthy and vital. *Career Development Quarterly*, 52(1), 35–42.

Whiston, S. C., Brecheisen, B. K., & Stephens, J. (2003). Does treatment modality affect career counseling effectiveness? *Journal of Vocational Behavior*, 62. 390–410.

Whiston, S. C., Sexton, T. L., & Lasoff, D. L. (1998). Career intervention outcome: A replication and extension. *Journal of Counseling Psychology*, 45, 150–165.

CHAPTER 3

SELECTING A CAREER ASSESSMENT INSTRUMENT[1]

Valerie L. Schwiebert
Professor of Counseling
Western Carolina University

Purpose

This chapter reviews the steps involved in selecting a career instrument for use with a particular client or group of clients. Assuming readers are enrolled in or have had a course or courses in assessment and are qualified professional counselors, this chapter is intended to facilitate the process of selecting a career instrument(s) for use with a client or a group of clients. When selecting an assessment instrument it is important to consider the specific instrument to use, the information the counselor has available, and the information the instrument will hopefully provide. Selecting any instrument based on how it will help the counselor and serve the client to be more informed or to make better decisions is essential. To meet these needs, it is necessary for counselors to have information on the test itself, the purpose of the test, qualifications needed by test users, and information on the practical and technical qualities of the instrument before making a final selection.

The purpose of any assessment is first to gather data to facilitate decision making by the counselee or client. Many of these decisions may be related to career development plans and choices involving educational and occupational plans, as well as other vocational and personal attributes and assets that can be added to the totality of the information needed to choose wisely. It is important to note that counselors may be choosing from tests in several categories outside the typical "career or vocational" categories, such as interest, values, aptitude, intelligence, achievement, and personality tests. Using these types of tests, a counselor may help the client explore hidden interests and aptitudes, assess intelligence level to ascertain if the client's educational goals are consistent with the client's intellectual functioning, and much more. However, before selecting any instrument to assess this information, it is necessary to specifically determine what information is desired, how it may best be obtained, and why that information would be useful.

In selecting an instrument, the counselor must first consult the test manual to see if his/her intended purpose of using the test is congruent with the test developers stated purpose. There are descriptions of tests throughout this *Counselor's Guide* that include statements of purpose. For other instruments, consult the test manual for the statement of purpose. *The Responsibilities of Users of Standardized Tests* (3rd edition) (Association for Assessment in Counseling [AAC], 2003) clearly states, "Responsible use of tests requires

---

[1] Note: This chapter is an updating of a previous chapter by William A. Mehrens, which appeared in the fourth edition of this book.

that the specific purpose for testing be identified. In addition, the test that is selected should align with the purpose, while considering the characteristics of the test and the test taker. (p. 3)" It goes on to state that tests should not be administered without a purpose or need for information, and describes in detail four specific areas related to the purpose of testing: description, accountability, prediction, and program evaluation (AAC, 2003).

Who Should Be Involved in Instrument Selection

An assessment may be intended for an individual or a larger group (e.g. a client or all eighth-grade students). If the assessment is intended for a specific individual, it is important that the counselor work with the client in this process. If the assessment is to be given to a large group to assess the career interest areas in a large urban high school, it may not be appropriate to involve the students in the process of selecting the test. While a client would not select a specific test, he or she should be involved in the discussions of what types of information may be available from different types of instruments, and how that information may be of benefit to the client. Involving the client in the process of instrument selection may increase the motivation, cooperation, and empowerment of the client in the test taking process. It also may assist the counselor in helping clients to accept the results and interpretations of their test results (Hood and Johnson, 2006).

If the assessment is to be administered to a large group of individuals, it may not be realistic to involve each of them in the selection process. However, the selection process still should be a cooperative venture among professionals and the community. These individuals can contribute by helping to determine the need for the assessment, the purposes of the assessment, and in the general stages of instrument selection. In this way, assessment becomes a community effort and may lead to more enthusiastic test use and administration than if the program is dictated by a single person. The final test selection should be overseen by professional staff with the appropriate training to select such assessment instruments.

Sources of Information about Specific Instruments

After the purpose of the assessment has been appropriately determined and the appropriate individuals consulted in the assessment process, the counselor must locate and select the assessment that will provide the needed information. There are multiple sources of information regarding assessments. A counselor may begin by talking with colleagues, consulting test publishers, using textbooks and guides such as this publication, and by using test review compilations such as Buros *Mental Measurements Yearbooks* as well as Appendix A of this book.

After the counselor has identified an assessment or assessments that match the specified purpose, an examination kit from the test publisher may be requested (sometimes at no cost). After reading the manual and any accompanying technical materials to assess the suitability of the test for the specified purpose, it is also important for the counselor to take the test. This provides the counselor with invaluable information regarding the test items, clarity of directions, results, etc. and familiarity with the test itself.

Technical Information Regarding Instruments

While examining the information regarding the prospective assessments, it is important to carefully examine the major technical characteristics of the test. These include, but are not limited to, the adequacy of the norms, the reliability and validity of the instrument, the types of scores provided, and the instrument's appropriateness for various clients or groups (e.g., various cultural or ethnic groups).

Norms

The use of norm referencing and/or criterion referencing adds meaning to test score(s). It has been argued that at times the validity of the inference of interest is not enhanced through norm referencing. However, for most of the inferences the counselor is interested in making (e.g., interest in a particular career choice or aptitude for becoming an airplane pilot) it is important to add meaning to a score by comparing it to the scores of others or to a standard or norm. If norm referencing is used, it is imperative that the norm group is clearly defined (usually in the test manual) and that it be both representative and relevant to the client(s) being tested. It is also important for the counselor to consider if the year(s) in which the norms were gathered might have an impact on the test's usefulness. That is, if the norms are not recent, are they still relevant for the test taker of today?

A norm group is typically a sample of individuals from a larger population. If the counselor is making an inference regarding how an individual compares to the population, it is important that the sample be representative of that population. One consideration is the size of the sample. It should be large enough so that it provides reasonably stable values. A value is stable in a sampling sense if another sample would have produced a similar value. However, a large sample alone is not enough. If the sample is not representative of either the population the test is measuring or the client(s) to test, the test is not appropriate.

It is also important for the counselor to examine the sampling procedure. Most readers are not sampling statisticians and cannot be expected to delve into the sampling process extensively. In general, however, a counselor should look to see whether the publisher considered relevant variables in the sampling procedure, such as age, gender, socioeconomic status, ethnicity, size of community, and geographic location. The manual or technical manual should explain in at least a general fashion how the relevant variables were considered in the sampling design and how the sample proportions compare with the population values. It is also important to examine how many individuals responded to the normative sample testing.

The relevance of the norm group depends upon the degree to which the population sampled is comparable to the group with which users of the instrument wish to be compared. For example, if an individual client (a high school senior) is interested in making a decision about which college to attend and wishes to consider his or her academic ability using the SAT in making the choice, norm groups are useful. Knowing his or her ability compared with a representative sample of high school seniors or even the set of all high school seniors in the nation who took the particular test would be informative. However, it would be even more useful to know how the SAT score compared to individuals attending the colleges under consideration. Hood and Johnson (2006) reported, for example, that a SAT Verbal score of 540 would place an individual at the 3rd percentile at a particular Ivy League university (almost assuring they would never get in without an exceptional circumstance) and at the 99th percentile at a particular state college (almost assuring they would get in without an exceptional circumstance). In conclusion, because counselors often work with diverse clients, they need access to differing norm groups. Therefore, many test publishers furnish a variety of norms. The most important point in instrument selection is that the relevant norms for the particular client(s) are available to the counselor.

Reliability

Reliability means consistency of scores. Technically, reliability is a characteristic of the scores, not the instruments. The scores are reliable if they are consistent, that is, if they do not fluctuate due to random errors. There are several types of reliability, including test-retest, split half, internal consistency, parallel forms, and inter-rater reliability. A discussion of each of these types of reliability is outside the scope of this chapter. However, which estimate is of interest depends upon the purpose of the assessment. Typically, if the counselor uses a total score in interpretation, and wishes to know if the score represents a homogenous characteristic, internal consistency reliability information is useful. If the counselor is considering a timed test, then internal consistency reliability is not an appropriate measure of consistency. If the purpose of assessment is to encourage career exploration and enhance current self-understanding, evidence regarding the long-term stability (or instability) of the scores may be unimportant. If the counselor is using an interest inventory to assist a client in making a decision about a career, the counselor also should be interested in evidence regarding the stability of the scores. If the counselor is interested in assessing change across some time span and wishes to use two different forms of the assessment, then the counselor would need information regarding the equivalence of the forms.

At times, it is not the reliability of the scores, but rather the reliability of a decision made from the scores that is important. For example, some career instruments unlike other instruments are not used for "pass/fail" decisions. For those decisions where one is interested in a dichotomous classification of individuals, the reliability of the set of scores is not nearly as important as the reliability of the classification. In those cases, the test publisher should provide some evidence of the decision reliability.

Validity

The Responsibilities of Users of Standardized Tests (RUST) (AAC, 2003) states that "validity is the accumulation of evidence to support a specific interpretation of the test results. Since validity is a characteristic of test results, a test may have validities of varying degree, for different purposes. (p. 2)" Further, the RUST statement requires the counselor to be conversant and competent in aspects of testing including validity. Evidence of validity may be found in the manual or technical manual of the assessment. In judging validity, the counselor must have in mind just what specific inferences are intended to be drawn from the scores and must look for evidence to support such inferences. There are five types of validity: face validity, criterion-related validity (predictive and concurrent), content validity, and construct validity. Though there is not space to define each type of validity here, it should be noted that face validity refers only to the concept of "does the test look like it measures what it is claiming to measure?" Therefore, face validity is not evidence to support the interpretation of test scores entailed by the proposed use of tests. It is only useful in possibly increasing client motivation and interest.

Types of Scores and Interpretative Materials

Test publishers frequently provide a variety of score types (e.g., percentiles, T-scores, stanines, IQ scores, etc.). However, in communicating norm-referenced scores to clients, it is typically preferable to use a type of score that is easily understood. The percentile or percentile rank is typically the score easiest for clients to understand. Caution should be used, however, when explaining percentile scores because many individuals may interpret them as percentages or percent correct.

In most situations, counselors are using assessment instruments to assist clients in making decisions about their own lives. Because the decision is the client's, it is important that he or she not only understand the score, but also its technical quality and the implications of that score for the decision to be made. One way to communicate the reliability of the test score is to use a band interpretation (this is usually one standard error of measurement above and below the score). In this way, the client has a more realistic picture of the meaning of the score and its bearing on the decision at hand.

Finally, clients may understand the particular score and the meaning of the band interpretation and still not have a good understanding of how the information is useful to them. Other things being equal, the counselor should choose an instrument that has available good interpretative materials that can be shared with the clients. However, the responsibility of interpreting a score always lies with the counselor to share this information with the client in her/his career planning and career development. It cannot be delegated to some computerized interpretation or test publisher's handout.

Appropriateness for Various Groups

At times, a counselor may be interested in obtaining information from an instrument about a particular client (or group of clients) who is a member of a particular group (e.g., non-English speaking individuals, persons with physical disabilities, an ethnic group). Attention should be paid to the appropriateness of an instrument for that group. The instrument may be inappropriate because the items are offensive or biased, or because the total scores are not valid for making the particular inference of interest for that particular group.

Major test publishers are quite alert to the importance of these issues and have been taking steps over the last few years to maximize the value of the instrument for a variety of groups. For example, test publishers typically have sensitivity reviews of the items, they do statistical analyses to detect items that function differently for different groups, and they obtain separate validity evidence for various groups. Also, as mentioned above, normative samples are obtained from various groups that makes test results more applicable to a wider audience. However, it is important to note that no test publisher can ever possibly gather evidence on the appropriateness of the instrument for all possible groups, and some test publishers do not gather sufficient data for any groups. It is incumbent upon those counselors selecting and administering instruments to determine whether data exist relating to the appropriateness of the instrument for the particular group that represents their clients. If these data do not exist, the counselor must not use the assessment or may choose to gather his or her own normative data for that particular population. This should only be undertaken if the counselor has sufficient training to undertake this task.

Practical Issues in Instrument Selection

The most important practical issue in instrument selection is to select (and use) only those instruments that the counselor is qualified to administer and/or interpret. This is echoed in the American Counseling Association's Code of Ethics (2005) and the RUST statement (AAC, 2003). For example, counselors generally are not trained to give individual intelligence tests and, hence, such an instrument should not be selected. The exception to this would be if a counselor were to have taken specialized training to qualify him or her to administer such tests. Test usage requirements depend on the complexity of the test. Test publishers often distinguish between tests with no restrictions (Level A), Level B tests (purchaser must have a four-year college degree and must have completed a college course in tests and measurements), and Level C tests (purchaser must have completed an advanced degree in an appropriate profession, belong to an appropriate professional organization, or be licensed or certified in an appropriate profession).

Other practical issues include the time it takes to administer and score an instrument, the costs involved, and the availability of a test publisher's administration and interpretation of the instrument. It is important to weigh if the information the assessment instrument will provide may be obtained though alternate means that are equally as valid and reliable, and cost less, require less time, etc.

One final note on practical issues is for all counselors to be aware of the ongoing legislative efforts to limit the assessment practices of counselors. Counselors should stay aware of current state and national regulations related to their practice of assessment. In addition, counselors should be aware of legal and ethical issues related to appropriate use of tests with populations whose culture or native language may unfairly bias test results against them.

Test Evaluation Outline

The review format and publisher-provided information used in this *Counselor's Guide* for each of the reviews in chapters 8 through 12 can serve as an evaluation for those instruments as well as other instruments listed in chapter 13. Also, the following outline by Mehrens, Lehmann, Eberly, and Denny (1991) may prove useful in organizing test evaluation information. It provides a systematic outline of the information necessary for the reviewer/counselor to ultimately accept or reject the assessment instrument based upon data gathered from several sources.

- Purpose for testing
- Group that will be tested (for example, age or grade)
- Name of test
- Author(s)

- Publisher
- Copyright dates of all materials (manuals, reviews, scoring keys, test booklets, answer sheets)
- Purpose and recommended use as stated in the manual
- Grade/age levels for which the instrument was constructed
- Forms: Are equivalent forms available? Is there evidence of equivalence of forms?
- Format: comment on legibility, attractiveness, convenience, and durability
- Cost
- Content of test and types of items used
- Administrative and timing requirements
- Scoring processes available (e.g., machine scoring vs. hand scoring)
- Types of derived scores available
- Types and quality of norms
- Adequacy of reliability evidence presented in the manual
- Validity evidence
- General quality of administrative, interpretive, and technical manuals
- Comments about the instrument by outside reviewers

References

American Counseling Association. (2005). *Code of ethics and standards of practice.* Alexandria, VA: Author.

Association for Assessment in Counseling. (2003). *The responsibilities of users of standardized tests* (3rd ed.). Alexandria, VA: American Counseling Association.

Hood, A .B., & Johnson, R. W. (2006). *Assessment in counseling* (4th ed.). Alexandria, VA: American Counseling Association.

Mehrens, W. A., Lehmann, I. J., Eberly, C. G., & Denny, G. S. (1991). *Instructor's manual to accompany Measurement and Evaluation in Education and Psychology.* Fort Worth, TX: Holt, Rinehart, and Winston, Inc.

CHAPTER 4

USING ASSESSMENTS FOR PERSONAL, PROGRAM, AND POLICY ADVOCACY

Norman C. Gysbers
Professor with Distinction
Educational, School, and Counseling Psychology Department
University of Missouri–Columbia

Richard T. Lapan
Professor and Chair
Student Development and Pupil Personnel Services
University of Massachusetts at Amherst

Introduction

In this the first decade of the twenty-first century, Friedman (2005) declared that the "world is flat." Why is the world flat? According to Friedman, the world is flat because of ten forces at work: the falling of the Berlin wall, the introduction of Netscape, work-flow software, open-sourcing, outsourcing, offshoring, supply-chaining, insourcing, informing and, finally, by something he called the steroids – digital processing.

As the power of these forces continue to unfold, they are causing substantial and long lasting changes in the occupational, industrial, and social structures of the United States, changes that are having dramatic impact on the workplace. Workplaces are becoming more global, characterized by technological change moving at near light speed. "More and more workers and the organizations in which they work are developing global identities" (Feller & Whichard, 2005, p. 23).

Societal structures and social and personal values also continue to change and become more diverse. People are on the move too, from rural to urban areas and back again and from one region of the country to another in search of economic, social, psychological, and physical security. Our population is getting older and is becoming increasingly more diverse (Shrestha, 2006).

All of these changes are creating substantial challenges for children, adolescents, and adults. A rapidly changing work world and labor force in a global economy; violence in the home, school, and community; divorce; teenage suicide; substance abuse; and sexual experimentation are just a few examples. These challenges are not abstract aberrations. These challenges are real, and they are having and will continue to have substantial impact on the personal/social, career, and academic development of children, adolescents, and adults in the twenty-first century (Gysbers & Henderson, 2006).

Given societal changes such as these and the challenges they represent, what roles can assessment play in assisting children, adolescents, and adults to respond directly and positively to them? We envision three roles. First, there is a personal advocacy role in which assessments can assist individuals to become personally empowered. Through the use of aptitude, achievement, interest, values, and personality and career development measures, valuable information can be provided as "tools of discovery," assisting them to explore, consider options, and make informed personal, academic, and career decisions. Second, there is a program advocacy role in which assessment instruments can be used to measure the effectiveness of guidance and counseling programs and their activities and services. In turn, such data can be used to advocate for and to expand, extend, and adjust these services and activities to the benefit of individuals of all ages and circumstances. Third, there is a policy advocacy role in which assessment data from personal advocacy and program effectiveness can be used to help formulate policy to guide and direct guidance and counseling programs at the national, state, and local levels. This chapter focuses on each of these roles, beginning with personal advocacy, followed by program advocacy, and ending with policy advocacy.

Personal Advocacy

Now, more than ever before, given the challenges of the twenty-first century, it is imperative that individuals of all ages and circumstances feel empowered by having purpose for and direction in their lives. Assessments, used as "tools of discovery," can improve the chances that all individuals will be able to create more satisfying career options, effectively respond to life's possibilities and challenges, take advantage of life's anticipated and unanticipated events (Goodman, Schlossberg, & Anderson, 2006), and find greater satisfaction in their life roles (Gysbers, Heppner, & Johnston, 2003). Used as "tools of discovery," assessments can empower individuals by providing them with vocabulary to describe themselves in various ways and, then, they can use their new vocabulary to explore and gain insight into their personal, educational, and career options. The goal is to empower individuals with the knowledge and skills to become active and involved advocates for themselves.

What must individuals know and be able to do to become self-advocates? Lapan (2004) recommended that individuals must be able to:

(a) interact with a sense of purpose and direction; (b) orient themselves to valued opportunities and choices; (c) act in agentic and empowered ways; (d) exhibit a mature commitment to a self-defined direction; (e) be hopeful, motivated, and optimistic about the present and the future; (f) persevere and overcome obstacles, as well as turn unexpected events into positive opportunities; (g) be creative and curious; and (h) balance an ability to be entrepreneurial with the need to care for others and the environment. (p. 25)

What is required for individuals to acquire the knowledge and skills to become self-advocates? Lapan (2004, p. 25) identified six primary constructs that promote self-advocacy development. They are:

- positive expectations, including self-efficacy beliefs and attributions
- identity development through interrelated processes of career exploration and goal formation

- an enhanced understanding of oneself, the world of work, and how best to fit or match this self-understanding to occupational possibilities
- the pursuit of one's intrinsic interests and preferences
- the ability to achieve academically and become a self-regulated, lifelong learner
- a range of complex social skills and work-readiness behaviors to be used in one's everyday interactions with others

These constructs form the basis for guidance and counseling programs and services for individuals of all ages and circumstances because they are the knowledge and skill base that promotes positive development leading to self-empowerment. Assessments play a key role, because, as "tools of discovery," they expand and extend individuals' understanding of themselves, others, and their worlds. Assessments can open doors allowing individuals to see, explore, and consider new possibilities personally, educationally, and occupationally.

Assessments facilitate self-advocacy for individuals because they offer vantage points that highlight critical aspects of experiences. These are perspectives that may be missed without the use of such assessments. As "tools of discovery," assessments provide a medium though which critical issues can be identified, explored, and eventually reintegrated. They can empower individuals to make informed choices.

In advocating for individuals, assessments can be used to measure the extent to which development of these six constructs is occurring and to identify barriers to such growth. For example, recently a high school senior participated in a school-to-work evaluation study. She is a very strong student, ranking in the upper 10% of her class, and possesses a clear sense of efficacy about her ability to master a wide range of academic subjects. Unfortunately, her father died the previous year. In talking about her future plans, it was clear that she had a good sense of her talents and self-confidence. However, as she talked her concerns about finances surfaced. She very articulately spoke of the financial challenges currently being faced by her mother. From her perspective, finances for her future educational and career plans would now not be available. Finances had become a perceived barrier that she would not be able to overcome (Luzzo & Jenkins-Smith, 1998). Without an assessment procedure that took a "wide lens" in addressing the range of critical career constructs necessary for developing a more adaptive orientation to the world of work (Savickas, 1999), these negative attributions would not have surfaced. Because of this assessment process, this young woman became an active and involved advocate for herself, for her goals and her aspirations.

Program Advocacy

Today, the issue of program accountability is in the forefront of professional dialogue. Is this focus on accountability new or has our profession always been concerned about assessing the effects of our work? The answer is no, it is not new, it has been of concern since the work of counselors began in the early 1900s (Gysbers, 2004). As a result of the continued focus on accountability, counselors are increasingly being asked to assess the results of their work with children, adolescents, and adults. Assessments are one of the major tools counselors and other career development professionals use to evaluate the outcomes of their work.

The role of counselors as advocates for effective programs based on evaluation data has significant consequences for both the assessments used and assessment users (Gysbers & Henderson, 2006). For example, assessments used in program evaluation may face skeptical audiences. Policy makers and those who try to influence legislation, especially those who demand results-based program accountability, will ask critical questions of the evaluation results. Counselors will not be able to answer these questions adequately unless the assessments used address program content standards and meet rigorous psychometric standards. Counselors choosing tests to evaluate program outcomes may need to ask different questions about the psychometric adequacy of the tests than might typically be asked when working with individuals. A test-retest reliability question might focus on whether or not there is enough reliable variance in the range of possible test scores to show change over time. Some scales may be more vulnerable to ceiling effects that would create a restricted range of test scores, thus reducing variability and ultimately co-variability or possible mean changes over time. Finding significant differences may elicit a "so what" reaction from those who control the budget. Counselors will need to answer this validity question by arguing that the significant effect size changes measured by instruments robustly predict outcomes of concern to policy makers. Normative samples must include the perspectives of the diverse population living in the United States. Test makers will need to justify construct validity by demonstrating that their tests are not confounded by unmeasured background variables.

Some counselors may experience some anxiety in expanding their role to include program advocacy through evaluation. This reaction could be due to a number of factors. For example, graduate training for many counselors is likely not to have included a course teaching students how to evaluate program interventions. Counselors may have been required to take introductory statistics courses, but such coursework likely did not instruct them in practical program evaluation strategies. From our experience, counselors-in-training at the graduate level may experience a significant amount of anxiety in subject matter related to mathematics. Most counselors would identify with Holland's Social theme (i.e., wanting to promote individual growth and development by helping others) and not with the Investigative theme (i.e., analyzing and questioning) (Holland, 1997). These feelings and self-definitions may interact to make program evaluation appear much more daunting than is warranted.

To counteract the fear of evaluation, Missouri counselor educators, the Missouri Department of Elementary and Secondary Education, and the Missouri School Counselor Association set out to empower school counselors to conduct results evaluation of their work without fear of data. The concept used is a train-the-trainer model called Program Results-Based Evaluation (PRBE). School counselors in Missouri are being trained to use and analyze local data to improve their work with students and their parents as well as to share results-based evaluation evidence with administrators, boards of education, teachers, the community, and with each other. The data they collect and analyze are used to improve the programming and services they provide as well as to provide data to advocate for the importance of their work with students and their parents (Gysbers, Lapan, & Stanley, 2006).

Policy Advocacy

A policy is "any plan or course of action adopted by a government, political party, business organization, or the like, designed to influence and determine decisions, actions, and other matters" (Morris, 1969, p. 104). Currently, there is no one national, state, or local policy that guides and directs guidance and counseling programs across the age span. Policies emanate from various sources. Federal and state agencies, professional associations, and many other groups shape and influence policy content and direction. As a result, there is a diffuse set of policies in operation that influence and determine decisions and actions regarding the nature, structure, and content of guidance and counseling programs and the activities and services they provide.

Given our system of regulatory entities at the local, state, and national levels and the many and various groups vying for attention and influence, it is highly unlikely that there ever will be one overall policy at any level that will guide and direct guidance and counseling programs. This, however, should not stop us from using our professional expertise to influence and shape policy at all levels. Unfortunately, our profession has attended to this important area only sporadically. Our professional associations, working alone or in concert, have worked hard to develop and influence legislation at state and national levels. In fact, the American Counseling Association has created an Office of Public Policy and Legislation, and the American School Counselor Association has established an Office of Research. Various documents emphasizing preferred roles and functions of professional personnel including school counselors, career counselors, vocational rehabilitation counselors, and mental health counselors have been disseminated, as have professional association position statements on topics of national, state, and local importance.

Although efforts such as these by professional organizations and others have had some impact on shaping and influencing national, state, and local policy formulation and legislation, much more needs to be done. We propose that a concerted effort be made to gather and organize student client assessment and program legislation at all levels. We further propose that policy briefs be developed for local, state, and national decision makers and policy analysts that make the connection between the effects of guidance and counseling programs on individuals of all ages and circumstances and the needed policies and legislation that will promote and sustain such programs.

To accomplish these proposals will require that we "build a constantly evolving knowledge base about what works and what is promising" (Schorr, Sylvester, & Dunkle, 1999, p. 27). Unfortunately, much that we do as professionals still is fragmented and disconnected across the age span, as are the assessment data that we collect. Also, current "public policy often tends to segment problems artificially by age group or subject matter" (Research and Policy Committee of the Committee for Economic Development, as cited in Herr & Gysbers, 2000). In addition to building a knowledge base (in part derived from assessment data), there is a need to connect and coordinate policies on career services based on such data across all levels of government. As Herr & Gysbers (2000) recommended:

There is the need for coordination and integration of career services across settings and government levels. Public policy at the federal level must connect with public policy at state and local levels and vice versa. Similarly, as voids in public policy are identified and life-cycle approaches are considered, counselors must be made available and their services must be coordinated. In any locale, counselors in schools, employment services, rehabilitation agencies and other settings must take each other into account, and public policy must support the systematic integration of the skills each of these counselors have, rather than divide and isolate these professionals. In this regard, employers and workplaces need to be seen as part of a continuum of career guidance and counseling programs and services, not separate from and unrelated to such provisions. (p. 274)

Formulating and adopting coordinated policies for guidance and counseling programs and services across all levels of government (based in part on assessment data) require substantial and sustained work, but it is work that we must undertake. To begin, we can use currently available assessment data to develop "policy briefs" to be used with decision makers and legislators. A format for a two-page "policy brief" might look something like the following:

- Statement of Need. The career, personal/social, and academic development needs of a particular group or groups are described briefly.

- A Response. The work of professional counselors that responds to the needs is outlined. Assessment data and research studies that demonstrate the effectiveness of this work are highlighted.

- The Keys. The necessary organization, structure, resources, and staffing to carry out the effective guidance and counseling work are discussed briefly.

- Problem. Any problems in developing and implementing effective guidance and counseling programs are presented.

- Recommendations. Recommendations for policy formulation and legislation, if required, are presented.

Empowering the children, adolescents, and adults of our country to face the challenges of today and tomorrow requires the strongest overall system of guidance and counseling programs and services that our nation can provide. We believe this will occur only if policies that guide and direct guidance and counseling programs and services for individuals of all ages and circumstances are based in part on sound assessment data. Thus we urge professionals to take assessment data beyond their offices in school buildings, public or private agencies, and colleges and universities into the world of policy makers at all levels. Only then will we realize that one of the important but often neglected uses of assessment data is policy advocacy.

Summing Up: A Call to Action

In these challenging and turbulent times assessments can play key roles in personal, program, and policy advocacy. As we have seen, they can facilitate individuals' positive growth and development by providing them with critical information that can empower them to make informed decisions about potential life-work choices. They also can assist career practitioners to be accountable, to evaluate their work with their clientele to ensure they are providing them with the best possible programs and services. Finally, they can inform policy makers at all levels as they seek to create sound policies to guide the development and implementation of sound guidance and counseling programs and services. Given these important roles, it is time to use assessments and assessment data to the fullest for personal, program, and policy advocacy.

References

American School Counselor Association (2004). *Ethical standards for school counselors.* Alexandria, VA: Author.

Feller, R. W., & Whichard, J. (2005). *Knowledge nomads and the nervously employed: Workplace change and courageous career choices.* Austin, TX: Pro-Ed.

Friedman, T. L. (2005). *The world is flat: A brief history of the twenty-first century.* New York, NY: Farrar, Straus, and Geroux.

Goodman, J., Schlossberg, N. K., & Anderson, M. L. (2006). *Counseling adults in transition: Linking practice with theory* (3rd ed.). New York, NY: Springer Publishing Company.

Gysbers, N. C. (2004). Comprehensive guidance and counseling programs: The evolution of accountability. *Professional School Counselor, 8,* 1–14.

Gysbers, N. C., & Henderson, P. (2006). *Developing and managing your school guidance and counseling program* (4th ed.). Alexandria, VA: American Counseling Association.

Gysbers, N. C., Heppner, M. J., & Johnston, J. A. (2003). *Career counseling: Process, issues, and techniques* (2nd ed.). Boston, MA: Allyn & Bacon.

Gysbers, N. C., Lapan, R. T., & Stanley, B. (2006). No fear results evaluation: The Missouri story. *ASCA School Counselor, 43,* 35–37.

Herr, E. L., & Gysbers, N. C. (2000). Career development services and related policy issues: The U.S. experience. In B. Hiebert & L. Bezanson (Eds.) *Making waves: Career development and public policy.* Proceedings from the international symposium, May 2-4, 1999. Ottawa, Canada: Canadian Career Development Foundation.

Holland, J. L. (1997). *Making vocational choices: A theory of vocational personalities and work environments* (3rd ed.). Odessa, FL: Psychological Assessment Resources.

Lapan, R. T. (2004). *Career development across the K–16 years: Bridging the present to satisfying and successful futures.* Alexandria, VA: American Counseling Association.

Luzzo, D. A., & Jenkins-Smith, A. (1998). *Development and initial validation of the Assessment of Attributions for Career Decision-Making.* Journal of Vocational Behavior, 52, 224–245.

Morris, W. (Ed.). (1969). *The American dictionary of the English language.* Boston: Houghton Mifflin Company.

National Career Development Association (2003). *National Career Development Association code of ethics.* Tulsa, OK: Author.

Savickas, M. L. (1999). The transitions from school-to-work: A developmental perspective. *The Career Development Quarterly*, 47, 326–336.

Schorr, L., Sylvester, K., & Dunkle, M. (1999). *Strategies to achieve a common purpose: Tools for turning good ideas into good policies.* Washington DC: Institute for Educational Leadership.

Shrestha, L. B. (2006). *The changing demographic profile of the United States.* Washington DC: Congressional Research Service, The Library of Congress.

CHAPTER 5

COMPUTER-ASSISTED CAREER ASSESSMENT: STATE OF THE ART

James P. Sampson, Jr.
Professor, Department of Educational Psychology and Learning Systems
College of Education
Co-director, Center for the Study of Technology in Counseling and Career Development
The Career Center

Darrin L. Carr
Coordinator of Information
The Career Center

Jill A. Lumsden
Coordinator of Career Development Services
The Career Center

Cassandra Smisson
Career Advisor
The Career Center

Casey Dozier
Career Advisor
The Career Center

Florida State University

Background

Computer applications in career assessment have become an established feature of the delivery of career services. Similar to other computer applications, computer-assisted career assessment presents a mixture of benefits and limitations, with much of the potential of the technology yet unrealized. Personal computers were a crucial step in the evolution of assessment, enabling important improvements in the administration, scoring, profiling, and interpretation (Sampson, 2000a). Although most computer-assisted assessments were simply computer versions of established paper-and-pencil measures, innovation in computer-based test interpretation resulted in important contributions to the field. With the advent of the Internet, dramatic changes occurred. Access to assessments increased substantially, while the quality of assessments appears to have decreased markedly. But, the nature and amount of counseling support to help individuals use assessments is less apparent.

The purpose of this chapter is to help counselors to be aware of and to make effective use of available computer-assisted career assessments. It also is intended to help counselors and test developers in collaborating to improve the design and use of computer-assisted career assessments. The chapter is both critical of current computer-assisted career assessment and hopeful for the future. This chapter begins with persons using computer-assisted career assessment and continues with types of assessment. Roles, benefits, limitations, trends, and future innovations in computer-assisted career assessment are then discussed.

Persons Using Computer-Assisted Career Assessment

Computer-assisted career assessment is used by a wide variety of persons with assistance provided by counselors for clients who seek help. Persons seeking career assistance are categorized in this chapter as clients or individuals. *Clients* use career assessment within the context of a counseling relationship with a career counselor. *Individuals* use self-help assessments available on the Internet. For the sake of simplicity, both clients and individuals will be referred to as "persons," except when the content applies to only a client or individual. Furthermore, in this chapter, *computer-assisted career assessment* (singular) is a broad term used to designate the use of technology to gather and report information in the appraisal process. The plural (i.e., *assessments*) is used when referring to specific instances of such technology.

A variety of practitioners provide services to persons seeking help with career choices. (A career choice can be an occupational choice, an educational choice, a training choice, or an employment choice.) In addition to counselors, practitioners can include career development facilitators, psychologists, vocational rehabilitation specialists, teachers/faculty/academic advisors, librarians and media specialists, human resource specialists, social workers, practitioners-in-training, and student peer counselors (Sampson, Reardon, Peterson, & Lenz, 2004). Irrespective of background, certification, or licensure, practitioners should only deliver career services "within the limits of their training and experience." Specific practitioner competencies are needed for ethical use of computer-assisted career assessment. These competencies include (a) an understanding of the construct being measured; (b) an understanding of assessment constructs, item selection, and scale construction, standardization, reliability, validity, and utility; (c) an understanding of the test interpretation, including scale interpretations and recommended interventions based on scale scores; and (d) an understanding of any available computer-based test interpretation, including evidence of interpretive validity (Sampson, Shy, & Purgar, 2003). These competencies apply to counselors as well as any practitioners using the computer-assisted assessments included in this book. Being certified or licensed is no guarantee that practitioners have obtained the competencies needed to make effective use of computer-assisted career assessment. Moreland, Eyde, Robertson, Primoff, and Most (1995) found that in order to determine who is qualified to administer assessments, screening professionals based solely on their credentials or professional degree is not the most effective way of determining eligibility. They recommended a competency-based approach, instead of a more general credential or degree, to help ensure that practitioners can use assessments effectively in delivering services. In addition to degrees which provide important fundamentals in communication skills, counseling theory, and appraisal, specific competency in assessment (e.g., test selection, administration, scoring, profiling, and interpretation) is required.

Types of Computer-Assisted Career Assessment

There are two types of career assessment: self-assessment and practitioner-assisted assessment. *Self-assessment* is designed to be used by individuals without help from a practitioner to select, administer, score, profile, and interpret the assessment. *Practitioner-assisted assessment* is designed for use by clients within the context of a helping relationship with a qualified practitioner (Sampson et al., 2004). Counselors should not limit their focus to only clients using practitioner-assisted career assessment. Clients may have already used self-assessments on the Internet, and this experience may influence their expectations for practitioner-assisted assessment. As a result, counselors need to be generally aware of the self-assessment resources that are available on the Internet.

Optimizing Roles in Computer-Assisted Career Assessment

The ultimate effectiveness of computer-assisted career assessment is dependent upon making the optimum use of the capabilities of the computer, the counselor, and the client or individual receiving assistance in making a career choice.

Role of the Computer in Career Assessment

Computer technology can be used to enhance the effectiveness of career assessment. In particular, computers and counselors can be assigned tasks that best suit their capabilities. Computers are not an effective or appropriate replacement for the counselor in delivering career counseling. Computers are best suited to perform computational and repetitive tasks, such as administering items, scoring tests, and constructing interpretive reports from predetermined algorithms. Practitioners are best suited for cognitive, affective, and problem-solving tasks, such as helping clients integrate assessment results from multiple sources into their existing knowledge about themselves and formulating a plan for action to meet their needs. Another way that computer technology can enhance the career assessment process is by improving the quality of test instruments and procedures through the development of previously unavailable techniques. For example, computer technology has resulted in the development of adaptive devices that allow persons with disabilities to complete assessments independently (Sampson, 2000a). In self-help situations, the computer can be programmed to suggest that the individual seek counseling when potential problems are identified by the individual or the computer system (Offer & Sampson, 1999).

Role of the Counselor in Career Assessment

The role of the counselor is to ensure, to the best of his or her ability, that clients are given access to, or referred to, assessments that are valid and reliable for the purposes to which they are being used (American Educational Research Association, American Psychological Association, & National Council on Measurement in Education, 1999). During the counseling process, counselors must ensure that (a) clients are given access to, or referred to, assessments that are appropriate for their needs; (b) clients are properly oriented to the nature of assessments and the use of the results; (c) clients are offered tentative interpretations and hypotheses based upon assessment results; (d) higher order problem solving skills are modeled for clients; and (e) clients have the opportunity to give the counselor feedback on the assessment process. Furthermore, to meet ethical obligations counselors must ensure that (a) assessments do not have any systematic bias with regard to gender, race, ethnicity, age, sexual orientation, or disability; (b) adequate steps are taken to maintain confidentiality of any client assessment records that are transmitted or stored on a computer; and (c) lack of financial resources does not pose an unreasonable barrier for individuals to gain access to computer-assisted career assessments. Finally, counselors should conduct regular evaluations to determine the effectiveness of the computer application in service delivery and that its implementation results in a full realization of its potential benefits (Campbell, 2000; Mastie, 1994; Reile & Harris-Bowlsbey, 2000; Sampson, 1998; Sampson, Peterson, & Reardon, 1989; Sampson & Pyle, 1983; Walz, 1984; Watts, 1986). Other practitioners (such as career development facilitators) should also assume a role in career assessment appropriate for their training, supervised experience, and credentials (Sampson, Reardon, Peterson, & Lenz, 2004).

Role of the Client and the Individual in Career Assessment

As stated previously, career assessments can be used by either "clients" involved in a counseling relationship or by "individuals" using self-help resources without counselor assistance. The role of both clients and individuals includes (a) seeking professional counseling assistance if prompted to do so by self-help career assessments; (b) following the directions provided by the counselor or the software to keep test use congruent with the standardization procedures that contribute to assessment reliability and validity; (c) responding to test items in an honest and complete manner; (d) confirming and expanding upon interpretations offered by the counselor based upon assessment data (Mastie, 1994); (e) evaluating whether the goals of assessment were accomplished (Campbell, 2000); (f) following through with the application of assessment results in developing a plan of action to meet their needs; and (g) being a self-advocate for good assessment by reporting fraudulent assessment practices associated with software and practitioners to appropriate regulating entities, such as states' attorney offices, licensure boards, certification boards, and professional associations' ethics committees.

Current Trends in Computer-Assisted Career Assessment

The vast majority of personal computers are connected to the Internet. While some assessments are still available only on personal computers, the trend is clearly to deliver assessments from remote computer servers, with personal computers serving only as an access point for obtaining access to the software. Also, larger assessment vendors appear to be implementing integrated, web-enabled delivery platforms through which they can deliver a variety of instruments from their portfolio of holdings using a common interface. Such platforms then allow for the centralized maintenance of client assessment records as well as easy purchase of additional test administrations. Many Internet-based career assessments remain available at no cost, with the cost-recovery for development and delivery supported by advertising or supported by public sector organizations or the government as a public good. (Internet-based career assessment can be categorized as one type of computer-assisted career assessment.) Figure 1 shows the relationships among access options, quality, and cost recovery for development and delivery of career assessment, with the most common kinds of assessments shaded in gray.

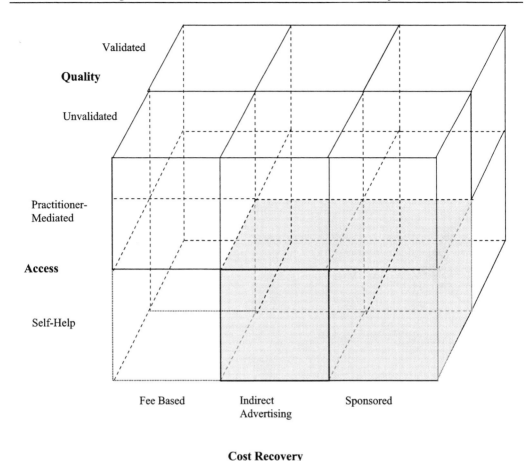

Figure 1. Organizational Schema for Internet-Based Career Assessments

Many counselors and career development professionals have encountered clients who request to take a "career test" that will magically answer their questions. Fortunately the counselor is there to disabuse the client of the magic and place the assessment results in a learning context (Krumboltz & Jackson, 1993). But, a quick search for the text string "career test" on the popular World Wide Web search engine Google resulted in more than 1,000,000 hits. While the search engine, to its credit, suggested more accurate terms like "career assessment" and "career aptitude test," it can at most recommend options.

A cursory review of the variety of websites returned by this search suggests that it could be difficult for the typical individual to choose among competing sites with different agendas. Often sites appear to pass individuals to another website for a referral fee. Others offer a "career test" which appears to be a loss-leader to encourage the purchase of additional products and services (e.g., a book or online degree). Disturbingly, a website published by one assessment aficionado offers a career assessment on the same screen as a "personality disorder" test based on the DSM-IV which has no professional restrictions.

Savvy individuals, however, would find among this milieu of websites well-established career assessments with evidence of strong psychometric properties. Unfortunately, these websites did not appear to consistently provide test development information that already existed in print form. This information would be important for counselors and consumers to make informed decisions about the selection and use of these assessments. The few sites that appeared to provide this information did so in terminology requiring a level of technical sophistication unlikely to be possessed by the average individual or even some practitioners. It is important for those developing career assessments for the Internet to accurately describe the reliability, validity, standardization, and potential biases of their assessments in terms understandable to the general public. This is a challenging, yet not impossible, task for the counseling profession which prides itself on its ability to communicate.

Computer-assisted career assessment is widely available as one function of career information delivery systems (CIDS). The three components of a CIDS are (a) assessment of varying combinations of values, interests, skills, and employment preferences; (b) the capability to use assessment data to identify potentially appropriate occupational or education options; and (c) occupational and educational information delivery. These three components are integrated so that the information from one component is used in completing another component. Examples of integration include using assessment results to search for occupations, or looking up educational programs for an occupation being researched. Three types of assessments that are used in CIDS are (a) standardized tests administered online, (b) standardized tests administered offline and then input into the CIDS, and (c) sorting of self-assessment variables. CIDS are available in almost all states and include occupational and educational information specific to each state. While many of these systems are used in both self-help and practitioner-assisted modes, most schools, colleges, and agencies where the systems are available provide varying types of career services to help clients make effective use of the CIDS. Many CIDS are now available via the Internet. The design and use of these systems, including the assessments, is guided by voluntary standards established by the Association of Computer-Based Systems for Career Information (ACSCI, 2005). Information on voluntary compliance of specific CIDS with ACSCI standards can be found at http://www.acsci.org/standards.asp.

Benefits of Computer-Assisted Career Assessment

Computer technology has contributed to the reliability and validity of career assessment, improved client integration of assessment data in counseling, and enhanced staff efficiency and cost-effectiveness of career assessment (Sampson, 2000a). This section begins with a discussion of improvements in the elements of assessment and continues with improvements in test interpretation and access to career assessment.

Improvements in the Elements of Assessment

In the area of test administration, clients can input answers via keyboard with fewer errors in comparison with paper-and-pencil tests. Test scoring can be completed by the computer in a quick and consistent format. The computer also can generate test score profiles customized for the client and the counselor, as well as narrative interpretive reports.

Clients can be provided with multimedia-based generalized test interpretations that review basic concepts and general test results before they receive a specific test interpretation from a counselor. With the exception of generalized test interpretations, the elements above are available with computer-assisted career assessment.

Improvements in Test Interpretation

Computer-based test interpretation (CBTI) "uses information technology to integrate theory, practitioner judgment, and empirical evidence, as one source of data, to help practitioners and test takers better understand the meaning of test scores for the purpose of gaining insight and making decisions" (Sampson, Shy, & Purgar, 2003, p. 89). Although there are differing schemas for the classification of CBTI (Fowler, 1987; Lanyon, 1987; Roid & Gorsuch, 1984), there is a clear consensus about the role of CBTI in service delivery. CBTI should be used in a consulting role, integrating a variety of data in creating an assessment (McMinn, Ellens, & Soref, 1999; Sampson, 2000b). It should not be used to replace the practitioner (Garb, 2000; Zachary & Pope, 1984) or as a stand alone psychological report (Butcher, 1995). When individuals use CBTI in a self-help situation, one of its roles is to indicate to them the circumstances when counseling assistance may be needed (Sampson et al., 2003).

In comparison with traditional test interpretation, potential benefits of CBTI include (a) the capability to process a greater number of complex variables (Snyder, 2000); (b) access to an expanded knowledge base as a result of the research data and practitioner judgment available (Sampson, 2000b); (c) the capability to organize and systematically access the extensive and rapidly growing databases related to popular measures (Krug, 1987); (d) being less affected by subjectivity (Butcher, 1995) and interpreter bias (Butcher, 1987; Garb, 2000; Nurius, 1990; Snyder, 2000); (e) increased consistency and reliability of interpretations (Butcher, 1987, 1995; Snyder, 2000); (f) rapid access to interpretative reports during preliminary stages of service delivery (Butcher, 1995; Snyder, 2000); and (g) rapid updating of interpretations as new research data become available (Krug, 1987). The use of CBTI in career assessment is less common than narrative interpretive reports.

Improvements in Access to Career Assessment

Improved access to Internet-based career assessment adds the potential benefit of improving access to career assessment and counseling for persons with disabilities, for persons living in remote locations, or for persons who have traditionally been reluctant to seek career services (Robinson, Meyer, Prince, McLean, & Law, 2000; Sampson, 2000b; Sampson & Lumsden, 2000). The use of visual images may improve the effectiveness of career assessment for various multicultural groups (Sampson, 1990). Also, Internet-based career assessment has the capability for immediate updating of software, opportunity for immediate feedback, and reduction in scoring and interpretation variability due to these events occurring at a centralized location.

Limitations of Computer-Assisted Career Assessment

The benefits of using computer-assisted career assessment may be compromised by a variety of issues related to questionable quality of computer-assisted assessment, problems in the design of interpretive reports, lack of screening before using assessments, inappropriate access to career assessment, inadequate funding for the development of assessments, problems related to computer technology, ethical issues, and confusion regarding the appropriate application of assessment standards.

Questionable Quality of Computer-Assisted Assessment

The quality of career assessments available on the Internet varies in terms of validity and reliability (Robinson et al., 2000). "Ethically and scientifically sound material coexists on the Internet with shoddy work that has not been evaluated at any level" (Clark, Horan, Tompkins-Bjorkman, Kovalski, & Hackett, 2000, p. 87). The Internet provides a point of access for many who may not otherwise use career assessments, but it also poses a problem when there is so little regulation about the credibility of the information being released (Barak, 2003).

Oliver and Zack (1999) completed a comprehensive review of career assessments available on the Internet. Using common search methods, such as search engines and gateway sites, Oliver and Zack identified 24 Internet sites that offered no-cost career assessments. Each site was then subjectively rated using a descriptive form covering ease of use, informative interpretation, fit of the assessment into a career planning schema, and the application of guidelines and standards. The results showed that few career assessment sites provided evidence of the psychometric quality of the assessments available. The fact that no fee was charged to individuals who accessed the career assessments reviewed does not absolve developers from the responsibility of documenting the quality of their assessments.

Three distinct quality issues are associated with computer-assisted career assessment. First, new career assessments are being delivered exclusively by computers that provide little or no evidence of quality. A likely assumption is that a "caveat emptor" (or "buyer beware") environment exists on the Internet similar to the magazine publishing environment that has regularly printed unvalidated psychological self-assessments in the guise of "quizzes" or "checklists." Individuals using the Internet may be unable to differentiate valid and invalid software, especially given the general positive perceptions among the public concerning the inherent accuracy of computer-based resources. Prince, Chartrand, and Silver (2000) provide an example of how psychometric evidence can be presented on the quality of new career assessments developed for the Internet. In developing their Internet-based career assessment system, they chose or created instruments that had evidence of validity for self-help use.

Second, test manuals and assessment websites often fail to provide evidence of the equivalency of the results obtained from traditional paper-and-pencil assessments that are subsequently available in computer-based versions. Enough evidence of score differences in administration modes for the same instrument exists to necessitate studies to establish the equivalence of paper-and-pencil and computer-based versions (Sampson, 2000b). Oliver and Chartrand (2000) stated, "no matter how well standardized, widely used, and highly regarded the instrument is, researchers and counselors cannot automatically assume that the measure will perform on a website as it does in the usual environment for test administration" (p. 98–99). The most recent *Standards for Educational and Psychological Testing* (American Educational Research Association, American Psychological Association, & National Council on Measurement in Education, 1999) require that developers provide evidence of the equivalence of various test administration modes (standards, 4.10, 6.11, and 13.8), as demonstrated by Prince et al. (2000).

Third, establishing the validity of a computer-based test interpretation is as important as establishing the validity of the instrument. Even in cases where well-established instruments provide substantial evidence of the validity of the measure, little evidence is often provided on the validity of the computer-based test interpretation. It may be that a "halo effect" exists where counselors and clients assume that a "good" test must have a "good" interpretation. The *Standards for Educational and Psychological Testing* (American Educational Research Association, American Psychological Association, & National Council on Measurement in Education, 1999) requires that developers describe the basis of any interpretation (standard 5.11) and evidence supporting the interpretation given (standard 6.12).

Problems in the Design of Interpretive Reports

The provision of valid and useful narrative reports is crucial to the effectiveness of computer-assisted career assessment. Oliver and Zack (1999) found that the complexity of narrative interpretative reports varied for each assessment instrument. From the sites included in the Oliver and Zack study, we can identify three levels of interpretive reports. The simplest level of interpretation was characterized by *categorization* (e.g., labels such as "highly promotable") and screening suggestions (e.g., "You would benefit from reading our book."). A second more complex level of interpretation was *narration*, where the instrument generated a possible categorization with an additional narrative explaining the meaning of the categorization. The third level of interpretation provided *integration*, offering categorization, a narrative context, and referral to/guidance on additional information resources and services based upon specific user results. These three levels of interpretive complexity reside on a continuum that is analogous to the functions performed by a counselor. It appears that the majority of Oliver and Zack sites resided on the lower end of this continuum. Furthermore, Oliver and Zack found interpretation to be "inadequate in many cases" (p. 330). Thus even those assessments using the most complex interpretation scheme may need to be approached with caution by clients, individuals, and counselors.

The design and use of computer-based test interpretation has several potential limitations. Potential problems of CBTI include (a) a lack of appropriate qualifications of test developers, which may lead to poor quality interpretations (Moreland, 1985); (b) the potential for inclusion of biased expert judgment in interpretations (Garb, 2000); (c) the perception of test users that test interpretations are more accurate when more nonspecific statements are used (Snyder, 2000); (d) the danger of CBTI lending itself to unrealistic credibility and assumptions of validity (Wetzler, 1990); (e) the possibility that overworked or inadequately trained counselors may become overly dependent on CBTI (Sampson & Bloom, 2001); and (f) the possibility that differences among CBTI reports exist for the same test generated from different software programs (Eyde & Kowal, 1987). An additional concern is the lack of validity evidence for CBTI. The validity of a CBTI is distinct from the validity of the test (Butcher, 1987; Snyder, 2000), and it is possible to have an invalid interpretation of a valid test. Therefore, the validity of the test and the CBTI must be established independently (Sampson et al., 2003).

Given the Oliver and Zack data, it is not surprising that there is little evidence for Internet-based assessments that provide multimedia-based generalized test interpretation, despite the capability of the Internet to deliver this type of resource. Instead there appear to be many text-based interpretations that provide simple categorizations or narrations without reference to specific user needs. An example of multimedia-based generalized test interpretation would be a video presentation explaining the theoretical constructs that undergird an instrument (e.g., the Holland hexagon or the five factor model of personality) and where the person generally relates to these constructs. These types of generalized multimedia interpretations have several advantages. The first is alleviating the counselor from routine communication of basic information. These routine duties often become tedious for the busy counselors, and this tedium can be perceived by the client as boredom with the client's case. A second reason is that different clients have different learning styles. Providing the same interpretive information in different ways (e.g., text, audio, and pictorial) allows the client to select a learning mode that best meets his or her needs. Furthermore, presenting generalized interpretive information in a multimedia format can be beneficial to those clients with cognitive or sensory disabilities as more than one channel of communication is used. The potential outcome of multimedia-based generalized interpretation is that clients may come to the counselor better prepared to participate in a discussion about their assessment results, thus maximizing client-counselor time.

Lack of Screening Before Using Assessments

The Joint Committee on Testing Practices (American Educational Research Association, American Psychological Association, & National Council on Measurement in Education, 1999) states that test users should, "select tests through a process that includes persons with appropriate knowledge, skills, and training." The problem with online assessments is that even when guidelines are clearly stated, people often disregard them and take assessments without the adequate vocabulary level necessary for the assessment, which can then jeopardize the validity of the assessment (Barak, 2003).

Inappropriate Access to Career Assessment

The global nature of the Internet is simultaneously a strength and a weakness. Individuals from all over the world can use career assessments, regardless of ethnicity, culture, or language. This can become a problem, however, when individuals take tests that are intended to measure traits in a specific country, language, or culture that is not their own (Barak, 2003). This can cause difficulties because the norms used to interpret the results may not be applicable to them or because cultural differences may have a significant impact on test results (Anastasi and Urbina, 1997). There also is concern that computer and Internet access are not readily available to all individuals or groups due to economic, social, or cultural reasons. This lack of equal opportunity, which is correlated with socioeconomic status, is a problem because assessment cannot be offered equally to all those who need it (Barak, 2003; Sampson, 2000a).

Inadequate Funding for the Development of Assessments

Although the cost of delivering career assessments on the Internet is relatively low, the cost of developing valid assessments and interpretive reports remains high irrespective of the delivery method. In the past, the costs associated with developing tests and interpretive reports were recovered through royalties paid to publishers by organizations delivering services or by clients receiving counseling. Oliver and Chartrand (2000) noted that numerous assessments are available at no charge on the Internet. It may be increasingly difficult to meet professional standards if adequate funding is not available for research and development (Harris-Bowlsbey, Riley-Dikely, & Sampson, 2002). Stable public and private sources of funding for developing Internet-based computer applications are needed to avoid a reduction in the quality of assessments available.

Problems Related to Computer Technology

An additional problem of computer-assisted assessment includes the validity-related issue of construct irrelevant variance, or the measurement of examinee characteristics that are irrelevant to the construct being measured, which may include computer proficiency, computer platform and interface effects, speediness, and test anxiety (Huff & Sireci, 2001).

Ethical Issues

Numerous ethical issues have been raised related to computer-assisted assessment. In addition to the quality issues raised above, the confidentiality of assessment data transmitted and stored on personal computers and computer networks can be compromised if appropriate security measures are not consistently followed. Individuals who need counseling along with using self-help computer software may be unaware of the potential value of counseling or they may be unable to locate an appropriate professional. Counselors may misuse or become dependent on computer-based test interpretation software as a result of being inadequately trained or overworked. Inadequate awareness of important location-specific circumstances may cause a counselor in a remote location to misinterpret client data or fail to recognize relevant issues. Clients with limited financial resources may have difficulty gaining access to computer resources, especially Internet-based resources. Also, gaining access to the Internet from a residence that is shared with other persons may not allow the auditory and visual privacy necessary for test administration and related counseling. It is also uncertain how state counselor licensure laws will apply to a counselor delivering career assessment and related counseling services across state and national boundaries. (Allen, Sampson, & Herlihy, 1988; Bartram, 1997; Bloom, 2000; Offer & Watts, 1997; Peterson, Murray, & Chan, 1998; Reile & Harris-Bowlsbey, 2000; Robinson et al., 2000; Robson & Robson, 1998; Sampson, 1998; Sampson, Kolodinsky, & Greeno, 1997; Sampson & Lumsden, 2000; Wilson, Jencius, & Duncan, 1997). Standards for Internet-based assessment are included in ethical statements of the Association of Computer-Based Systems for Career Information (2005), National Board for Certified Counselors and the Center for Credentialing and Education (2001), and the National Career Development Association (1997).

Confusion Regarding the Appropriate Application of Assessment Standards

The Joint Committee on Testing Practices (American Educational Research Association, American Psychological Association, & National Council on Measurement in Education, 1999) established the Standards for Educational and Psychological Testing, which are the most often used standards in assessment. However, there may be confusion as to which assessments these standards apply. Although there appears to be general agreement that personal-computer–based assessments from test publishers should abide by the standards, there is less agreement about Internet-based tests. One problem has to do with terminology. On the Internet, the terms test, instrument, scale, measure, questionnaire, and checklist appear to be used interchangeably. One position is that the standards apply only to assessments developed by members of the professional associations who approved the standards. Another position is that if individual items build to a scale, or if individuals rate themselves on a particular construct that leads to the development of insight, then assessment is taking place, and the standards apply irrespective of the professional association membership of the authors.

In the first position, the focus is on the nature of the assessment developer, whereas in the second position the focus is on the outcome of using the assessment. In the second position, if it works like a scale, or a self-assessment of constructs, then it is assessment. In other words, "If it walks like a duck and quacks like a duck, then it's a duck." We endorse this second position that focuses on the nature of assessment outcomes rather than the nature of the assessment developer. The problem, however, is that some assessments on the Internet have been developed by individuals who are either ignorant of the Joint Committee standards or who are aware of standards but choose to ignore them to save time and reduce costs. This may also be due to a lack of awareness of the potential harm that unvalidated assessments may cause to unsuspecting users. In court cases, judges are increasingly using testing standards to establish an appropriate "standard of care" for assessment practice. As a result, providers and users of assessments need to become more aware of, and consistently apply, appropriate standards to ensure quality in computer-assisted career assessments.

Future Innovations in Computer-Assisted Career Assessment

Several future innovations have the potential of improving the quality and effectiveness of computer-assisted career assessment. These innovations include expansion of the communication aspect of computer-assisted career assessment, voice input, use of multimedia technology, and improved reviews.

Expansion of the Communication Aspect of Computer-Assisted Career Assessment

Internet-based career assessments belong to the broad category of information and communications technology (which is abbreviated internationally as ICT) (Offer, Sampson, & Watts, 2001). The communication aspect of ICT has not been developed in career assessment. Synchronous communication via voice conferencing or videoconferencing would allow clients the opportunity to discuss assessment results in a group, as well as facilitating interaction between counselors and clients. Asynchronous communication through a group Listserv or e-mail would also facilitate discussion about assessment results among clients and counselors. Integrating distance counseling into career services would make it easier to serve clients who have barriers to accessing career services, such as disabled clients or clients who live in geographically isolated areas (Sampson & Bloom, 2001). Telephone help lines have been shown to be effective in providing information and support to individuals who are making career choices (Watts & Dent, 2002). This type of distance support can be used to improve the effectiveness of career assessment for persons who might not otherwise receive the help they need.

Voice Input

Voice input in response to test items has been anticipated for some time. While gradual progress has occurred in voice recognition software, a highly reliable system that would be required for assessment purposes is not yet cost-effective. As voice recognition software improves over time, voice recognition will clearly become a reality. While the availability of this technology will be generally useful to many persons, the benefits will be substantial for persons with disabilities who have difficulty in responding to paper-and-pencil or standard keyboard assessments.

Use of Multimedia Technology

The availability of assessments that take advantage of multimedia technology to administer test items and present interactive interpretations remains elusive. The majority of current computer applications in career assessment are either computer versions of existing paper-and-pencil tests or simple assessments with limited interpretation of the results. Problems do exist in the use of videos, such as the validity of item presentation for various multicultural groups and the cost of video production. However, these challenges need to be weighed against the potential to create multimedia stimuli that more closely reflect reality as well as increasing the potential for persons to learn from interactive interpretations that combine text, sound, pictures, graphics, and video.

Improved Reviews of Computer-Assisted Career Assessment

The Internet provides numerous opportunities to design more effective self-assessments and counselor-assisted assessments in the delivery of career services. In order to innovate successfully, an in-depth and rigorous review of the current state of computer-assisted career assessment is necessary. Problems which might confront such a review include (a) how to select which assessments are described from the countless options available, (b) the rapid nature of change on the Internet, and (c) the timely compilation and distribution of information to practitioners and consumers given this rapid change. One option would be to adopt a comprehensive review model similar to that used by this book, *A Counselor's Guide to Career Assessment Instruments*. In this guide, reviews are written by practitioners for practitioners, researchers, and other parties interested in career assessment. Their work could be expanded and used by the larger professional audience afforded by the Internet. The review model used by the Buros Center for Testing could be similarly adopted.

Clients and individuals also need information on the use and quality of computer-assisted career assessment. Information from *A Counselor's Guide* could also be presented in layman's terms. To be effective, such "Consumer Reports" reviews would need to be featured prominently in any Internet search engine when terms such as "career tests" or "career assessment" are used. The information gathered from this effort could be provided to both practitioners and test publishers for a fee to recover costs, while consumers could access the information for free. However, obtaining adequate funding and identifying qualified practitioners to write the reviews is a formidable challenge.

Conclusion

Computer-assisted career assessment has undergone a substantial change in the evolution from personal computers to the Internet. The number of assessments now available has increased dramatically. The quality of assessments has always been a concern since the first tests were developed in the early 1900s. Evidence of the quality of Internet-based assessments is scarce at best. The chance that individuals will use the results from invalid assessments to make important decisions is a reality. Also, the distance counseling that could be used as an adjunct to self-help assessments is rarely available. It is ironic that the Internet may provide clients and individuals with improved access to inferior assessments (Sampson, 1999). Counselors need to be proactive in using Internet web sites to help individuals identify quality assessments and understand the role of assessment making important decisions.

The Internet in particular offers unique opportunities to improve test selection, orientation, administration, scoring, and interpretation. Career assessment is clearly in a transition phase from being paper-and-penci-based to being computer-based. This transition will occur gradually as the costs of developing Internet-based assessment resources decline, as test developers gain more experience in developing computer-based assessments that take better advantage of computer capabilities, and as a greater proportion of our population gains easier access to computers that can deliver assessment resources and services.

Our success in developing and delivering cost-effective computer-assisted career assessments will depend on keeping the best of past psychometric rigor and counseling integration, while exploring future uses of multimedia and distance counseling to deliver quality assessments that provide clients with useful data as well as provide new opportunities for promoting interaction among counselors and clients. To achieve the potential of computer-assisted career assessment, the limitations identified in this chapter need to be carefully addressed. The Internet offers enormous potential to improve face-to-face and distance career assessment and counseling as well as the quality of self-help career assessments. The opportunity to innovate and improve access to quality assessments is unprecedented.

References

Allen, V. B., Sampson, J. P., Jr., & Herlihy, B. (1988). Details of the new 1988 AACD Ethical Standards. *Journal of Counseling and Development*, 67, 157–158.

American Educational Research Association, American Psychological Association, & National Council on Measurement in Education. (1999). *Standards for educational and psychological testing.* Washington, DC: American Educational Research Association.

Anastasi, A., & Urbina, S. (1997). *Psychological testing* (7th ed.). Upper Saddle River, NJ: Prentice Hall.

Association of Computer-Based Systems for Career Information. (2005). *Handbook of standards for the operation of computer-based career information systems.* Retrieved January 9, 2007, from http://www.acsci.org/standards.asp

Barak, A. (2003). Ethical and professional issues in career assessment on the Internet. *Journal of Career Assessment, 11,* 3–21.

Bartram, D. (1997). Distance assessment: Psychological assessment through the Internet. *Selection and Development Review, 13,* 15–19.

Bloom, J. W. (2000). Technology and web counseling. In H. Hackney (Ed.), *Practice issues for the beginning counselor.* Needham Heights, MA: Allyn and Bacon.

Butcher, J. N. (1987). The use of computers in psychological assessment: An overview of practices and issues. In J. N. Butcher (Ed.), *Computerized psychological assessment: A practitioner's guide* (pp. 3–14). New York: Basic Books.

Butcher, J. N. (1995). How to use computer-based reports. In J. N. Butcher (Ed.), *Clinical personality assessment: Practical approaches* (pp. 79–94). New York: Oxford University Press.

Campbell, V. L. (2000). A framework for using tests in counseling. In C. E. Watkins, Jr. & V. L. Campbell (Eds.), *Testing and assessment in counseling practice* (2nd ed.). Mahwah, NJ: Lawrence Erlbaum Associates.

Clark, G., Horan, J. J., Tompkins-Bjorkman, A., Kovalski, T., & Hackett, G. (2000). Interactive career counseling on the Internet. *Journal of Career Assessment, 8,* 85–93.

Eyde, L. D., & Kowal, D. M. (1987). Computerised test interpretation services: Ethical and professional concerns regarding U.S. producers and users. *Applied Psychology: An International Review, 36*(3/4), 401–417.

Fowler, R. D. (1987). Developing a computer-based test interpretation system. In J. N. Butcher (Ed.), *Computerized psychological assessment: A practitioner's guide* (pp. 50–63). New York: Basic Books.

Garb, H. N. (2000). Computers will become increasingly important for psychological assessment: Not that there's anything wrong with that. *Psychological Assessment, 12,* 31–39.

Harris-Bowlsbey, J., Riley-Dikel, M., & Sampson, J. P., Jr. (Eds.). (2002). *The Internet: A tool for career planning* (2nd ed.) (pp. 1–9). Tulsa, OK: National Career Development Association.

Huff, K. L., & Sireci, S. G. (2001) Validity issues in computer-based testing. *Educational Measurement: Issues and Practice, 20*(3), 16–25.

Krug, S. E. (1987). Microtrends: An orientation to computerized assessment. In J. N. Butcher (Ed.), *Computerized psychological assessment: A practitioner's guide* (pp. 15–25). New York: Basic Books.

Krumboltz, J. D., & Jackson, M. A. (1993). Career assessment as a learning tool. *Journal of Career Assessment, 1*, 393–409.

Lanyon, R. I. (1987). The validity of computer-based personality assessment products: Recommendations for the future. *Computers in Human Behavior, 3*, 225–238.

Mastie, M. M. (1994). Using assessment instruments in career counseling: Career assessment as compass, credential, process, and empowerment. In J. T. Kapes, M. M. Mastie, & E. A. Whitfield (Eds.), *A counselor's guide to career assessment instruments* (3rd ed.). Alexandria, VA: National Career Development Association.

McMinn, M. R., Ellens, B. M., & Soref, E. (1999). Ethical perspectives and practice behaviors involving computer based test interpretation. *Assessment, 6*, 71–77.

Moreland, K. L. (1985). Validation of computer-based test interpretations: Problems and prospects. *Journal of Consulting and Clinical Psychology, 53*(6), 816–825.

Moreland, K. L., Eyde, L. D., Robertson, G. J., Primoff, E. S., & Most, R. B. (1995). Assessment of test user qualifications: A research-based measurement procedure. *American Psychologist, 50*, 14–23.

National Board for Certified Counselors and the Center for Credentialing and Education. (2001). *The practice of Internet counseling.* Retrieved January 9, 2007, from http://www.nbcc.org/webethics2

National Career Development Association. (1997). *NCDA guidelines for the use of the Internet for provision of career information and planning services.* Retrieved January 9, 2007, from http://www.ncda.org

Nurius, P. S. (1990). A review of automated assessment. *Computers in Human Services, 6*, 265–281.

Offer, M., & Sampson, J. P., Jr. (1999). Quality in the content and use of information and communications technology in guidance. *British Journal of Guidance and Counselling, 27*, 501–516.

Offer, M., Sampson, J. P., Jr., & Watts, A. G. (2001). *Career services technology and the future.* Manchester, United Kingdom: Higher Education Careers Services Unit and the National Institute for Careers Education and Counselling.

Offer, M., & Watts, A. G. (1997). *The Internet and careers work.* Cambridge, United Kingdom: National Institute for Careers Education and Counselling.

Oliver, L. W. & Chartrand, J. M. (2000). Strategies for career assessment research on the Internet. *Journal of Career Assessment, 8*, 95–103.

Oliver, L. W. & Zack, J. S. (1999). Career assessment on the Internet: An exploratory study. *Journal of Career Assessment, 7*, 323–356.

Peterson, D., Murray, G., & Chan, F. (1998). Ethics and technology. In R. R. Cottone & V. M. Tarvydas (Eds.), *Ethical and professional issues in counseling* (pp. 196–235). Upper Saddle River, NJ: Merrill.

Prince, J. P., Chartrand, J. M., & Silver, D. G. (2000). Constructing a quality career assessment site. *Journal of Career Assessment, 8*, 55–67.

Reile, D. M., & Harris-Bowlsbey, J. (2000). Using the Internet in career planning and assessment. *Journal of Career Assessment*, 8, 69–84.

Robinson, N. K., Meyer, D., Prince, J. P., McLean, C., & Law, R. (2000). Mining the Internet for career information: A model approach for college students. *Journal of Career Assessment*, 8, 37–54.

Robson, D., & Robson, M. (1998). Intimacy and computer communication. *British Journal of Guidance & Counselling*, 26, 33–41.

Roid, G. H., & Gorsuch, R. L. (1984). Development and clinical use of test-interpretive programs on microcomputers. In M. D. Schwartz (Ed.), *Using computers in clinical practice: Psychotherapy and mental health applications* (pp. 141–149). New York: Haworth.

Sampson, J.P., Jr. (1990). Computer-assisted testing and the goals of counseling psychology. *The Counseling Psychologist*, 18, 227-239.

Sampson, J. P., Jr. (1998). The Internet as a potential force for social change. In C. C. Lee & G. R. Walz (Eds.). *Social action: A mandate for counselors* (pp. 213–225). Greensboro, NC: University of North Carolina at Greensboro, ERIC Clearinghouse on Counseling and Student Services.

Sampson, J. P., Jr. (1999). Effective design and use of Internet-based career resources and services. *IAEVG (International Association for Educational and Vocation Guidance) Bulletin*, 63, 4–12.

Sampson, J. P., Jr. (2000a). Computer applications. In C. E. Watkins, Jr. & V. L. Campbell (Eds.), *Testing and assessment in counseling practice* (2nd ed) (pp. 517–544). Hillsdale, NJ: Lawrence Erlbaum Associates, Inc.

Sampson, J. P., Jr. (2000b). Using the Internet to enhance testing in counseling. *Journal of Counseling and Development*, 78, 348–356.

Sampson, J. P., Jr., & Bloom, J. W. (2001). The potential for success and failure of computer applications in counseling and guidance. In D. C. Locke, J. Myers, & E. L. Herr (Eds.), *The handbook of counseling* (pp. 613–627). Thousand Oaks, CA: Sage.

Sampson, J. P., Jr., Kolodinsky, R. W., & Greeno, B. P. (1997). Counseling on the information highway: Future possibilities and potential problems. *Journal of Counseling and Development*, 75, 203–212.

Sampson, J. P., Jr., & Lumsden, J. A. (2000). Ethical issues in the design and use of Internet-based career assessment. *Journal of Career Assessment*, 8, 21–35.

Sampson, J. P., Jr., Peterson, G. W., & Reardon, R. C. (1989). Counselor intervention strategies for computer-assisted career guidance: An information processing approach. *Journal of Career Development*, 16, 139–154.

Sampson, J. P., Jr., & Pyle, K. R. (1983). Ethical issues involved with the use of computer-assisted counseling, testing and guidance systems. *Personnel and Guidance Journal*, 61(5), 283–287.

Sampson, J. P., Jr., Reardon, R. C., Peterson, G. W., & Lenz, J. G. (2004). *Career counseling and services: A cognitive information processing approach.* Pacific Grove, CA: Brooks/Cole.

Sampson Jr., J. P., & Shy, J. D., & Purgar, M. P. (2003). Computer-based test interpretation in career assessment: Ethical and professional issues. *Journal of Career Assessment,* 11, 22–39.

Snyder, D. K. (2000). Computer-assisted judgment: Defining strengths and liabilities. *Psychological Assessment,* 12, 52–60.

Walz, G. R. (1984). Role of the counselor with computers. *Journal of Counseling and Development,* 63, 135–138.

Watts, A. G. (1986). The role of the computer in careers guidance. *International Journal for the Advancement of Counselling,* 9, 145–158.

Watts, A. G., & Dent, G. (2002). Let your fingers do the walking: The use of telephone helplines in career information and guidance. *British Journal of Guidance and Counselling,* 30(1), 17–35.

Wetzler, S. (1990). Computerized psychological assessment. In D. Baskin (Ed.), *Computer applications in psychiatry and psychology* (pp. 43–56). New York: Brunner/Mazel.

Wilson, F. R., Jencius, M., & Duncan, D. (1997). *Introduction to the Internet: Opportunities and dilemmas.* Denver, CO: Love Publishing Co.

Zachary, R. A., & Pope, K. S. (1984). Legal and ethical issues in the clinical use of computerized testing. In M. D. Schwartz (Ed.), *Using computers in clinical practice: Psychotherapy and mental health applications* (pp. 151–164). New York: Haworth.

Note: The senior author may be reached at the University Center, Suite A4100, Florida State University, Tallahassee, Florida 32306-2490, (850) 644-2490, jsampson@admin.fsu.edu, http://www.career.fsu.edu/techcenter/

CHAPTER 6

ASSESSMENT AND COUNSELING COMPETENCIES AND RESPONSIBILITIES: A CHECKLIST FOR COUNSELORS[1]

Thomas S. Krieshok
Department of Psychology and Research in Education
University of Kansas

Michael D. Black
Staff Psychologist
Veterans Affairs Eastern Kansas Health Care System
Leavenworth, Kansas

Introduction

This checklist provides a practical means for counselors to evaluate their testing and counseling competencies and practices. It is intended to cover the basics and should not be viewed as a comprehensive statement of all responsibilities and competencies involved in assessment. Since each item is considered to be important, there is no pass-fail score.

As used here, the terms, "test" or "assessment" subsume the various types of instruments covered by this *Counselor's Guide* — single tests, test batteries, inventories, card sorts, and various self-report scales. The term "client" is meant to include anyone to whom assessment instruments are administered (e.g., a sixth grader, college senior, or adult). Items in the Interpretation section of the checklist refer to the use of tests in individual counseling. Relevance of items to the use of tests with groups and in consultation with other professionals or parents should be evident. Some checklist items address computer-based assessment. Counselors interested in computer applications should consult the *Standards for Educational and Psychological Testing* (American Educational Research Association, American Psychological Association, and National Council on Measurement in Education, 1999) and Chapter 5 of this *Counselor's Guide*.

Much of the content of this revised checklist was adapted from resources cited at the end of this chapter. *Standards for Educational and Psychological Testing* (American Educational Research Association, American Psychological Association, and National Council on Measurement in Education, 1999), *Test Interpretation and Diversity* (Sandoval, Frisby, Geisinger, & Associates, 1999), *Standards for Multicultural Assessment* (Association for Assessment in Counseling, 2003) and *ACA Code of Ethics and Standards of Practice* (American Counseling Association, 2005) were major resources for this chapter.

---

[1] This chapter is a revised version of a previous chapter by Nancy J. Garfield and Thomas S. Krieshok in the fourth edition of this book.

Counselors wishing to improve their assessment skills in general will find Appendix A (Sources of Information about Testing and Career Assessment) to be helpful. Although a number of test selection and interpretation responsibilities are cited in this checklist, Chapter 3, (Selecting a Career Assessment Instrument), Chapter 4 (Using Assessments for Personal, Program, and Policy Advocacy), and Chapter 5 (Computer-Assisted Career Assessment: State of the Art) provide more extensive suggestions.

COUNSELING SKILLS

Basic counseling skills are critical to providing effective career counseling. The section below provides a review of these skills.

Use the following key in responding to the statements:

3 = I am able to apply the concept.

2 = I have some knowledge, but little experience in applying the concept.

1 = I have little or no knowledge of this concept.

Enter the appropriate number in the blank at the left of each statement.

_____ 1. Build rapport with the client.

_____ 2. Be sensitive to diversity, including socioeconomic status, culture, gender, age, and differing abilities.

_____ 3. Consider developmental differences (e.g., be certain the instrument is age appropriate).

_____ 4. Attend to the client throughout the counseling process, noting verbal and nonverbal cues, soliciting feedback, and responding to his or her needs as the process unfolds.

_____ 5. Be knowledgeable of career theories.

_____ 6. Be able to integrate career development and personal issues in counseling.

_____ 7. Be knowledgeable of a repertoire of assessment instruments, both quantitative and qualitative (e.g., genogram, timeline).

_____ 8. Be knowledgeable of self-help materials and outside resources for further reading.

_____ 9. Help client balance strengths and opportunities for improvement.

_____ 10. Give feedback in language the client will understand.

_____ 11. Relate results of assessments to the real world of work.

_____ 12. Be able to integrate results from different measures into a coherent interpretation for the client.

_____ 13. Write reports that provide integrated, concrete, and useful recommendations for the client.

_____ 14. Practice within legal, ethical, and professional guidelines, attending to matters such as confidentiality and counselor competence with instruments used.

_____ 15. Provide feedback in a manner that does not convey that the instruments say a client may not choose an educational or career path.

_____ 16. Take the initiative to stay current in the fields of career and personal counseling.

_____ 17. Be aware of the research on decision making from other branches of psychology (e.g., social psychology, cognitive psychology, neuroscience).

ASSESSMENT SKILLS

Concepts important to the use of tests are listed below. Persons with final responsibility for evaluating and selecting assessment instruments will require knowledge beyond these basic concepts.

Use the following key in responding to the statements:

3 = I am able to apply the concept and explain it to others.

2 = I have some knowledge, but little experience in applying the concept.

1 = I have little or no knowledge of this concept.

Enter the appropriate number in the blank at the left of each statement.

STATISTICS USED IN TESTING AND TEST MANUALS

_____ a. Measures of central tendency (mean, median, mode)

_____ b. Measures of variability (range, variance, standard deviation)

_____ c. Distributions (frequency, normal)

_____ d. Scales of measurement (nominal, ordinal, interval, ratio)

_____ e. Correlation coefficients (Pearson product-moment, point biserial)

TYPES OF INSTRUMENTS

_____ a. Measures of maximum performance

_____ b. Measures of typical performance

_____ c. Similarities and differences among measures of intelligence, aptitude, ability, and achievement

_____ d. Similarities and differences among self-reports, self-ratings, inventories, and tests

SCORE REPORTING PROCEDURES

____ a. Percentile ranks

____ b. Standard scores (including stanines)

____ c. Grade placement (equivalent) scores

____ d. Score profiles and profile analysis

____ e. Group similarity indices ("Your scores are similar to the scores of people who ...")

____ f. Expectancy (experience) tables

____ g. Estimates of probability of success and/or level of success; standard error of estimate

STANDARDIZATION AND NORMS

____ a. Standardized administration and scoring

____ b. Limitations of raw scores

____ c. Types of norms (e.g., local, national, gender, grade); their applications and limitations

____ d. Norm-based vs. criterion-referenced interpretation

RELIABILITY

____ a. Meaning of test reliability

____ b. Sources of measurement error

____ c. Types of test reliability (test-retest, parallel forms, internal consistency — including split-half, inter-rater)

____ d. Standard error of measurement and error bands

VALIDITY

____ a. Meaning of test validity

____ b. Implications of test use for validation procedures

____ c. Types of test validity (content, criterion-related, construct)

____ d. Factors affecting test validity (e.g., the "criterion problem")

____ e. Differential validity of test batteries for diverse criteria

____ f. Potential sources of bias affecting validity

RESPONSIBILITIES/COMPETENCIES

Test user responsibilities and competencies are listed in the next three sections.
Use the following key in responding to the statements:

3 = I do this routinely — as a regular practice.

2 = I have done this on occasion.

1 = I do not do this — but should give it consideration.

NA = Not applicable to the assessment instruments I am using.

Enter the appropriate number in the blank at the left of each statement.

PREPARING FOR TEST USE

_____ 1. Avoid unnecessary testing by determining whether existing information can meet the needs of your clients and institution.

_____ 2. Review advertisements for tests, promotional brochures, catalog descriptions.

_____ 3. Read professional reviews of the test — for example, in the *Journal of Counseling and Development, the Mental Measurement Yearbooks.* (See Appendix A for more information.)

_____ 4. Obtain and review up-to-date copies of the administration, interpretation, and technical manuals for any test you are considering.

_____ 5. If not qualified to evaluate the instrument, obtain help from a qualified supervisor or consultant.

_____ 6. Determine whether the test's reading level is appropriate for your client.

_____ 7. Determine if the language in which the test is written is appropriate for the client you will be assessing.

_____ 8. Verify that the test items, norms, and score-reporting procedures minimize bias due to gender race, sexual orientation, ethnic and cultural background, disability, or age. Bias can occur if an instrument does not retain its psychometric properties across different groups.

_____ 9. Assure that if there are special administration circumstances (e.g., large print tests, which take longer to read; English as the second language; a client needs more time due to individual needs) you will still be able to use the results with confidence.

_____ 10. Determine if test-takers are fluent in English, or establish that the instrument reliability and validity will not be compromised by language difficulties.

_____ 11. Be aware of the complexity of culture, understanding that a client may belong to several different cultures simultaneously.

_____ 12. Make necessary modifications to the administration or interpretation of the instruments for clients whose differing abilities will affect their test taking. Modifications may involve instrument presentation, response format, timing, time setting, etc.

_____ 13. Be aware that modifications to the administration or interpretation of instruments may alter their validity.

_____ 14. Know whether you possess the qualifications (e.g., specific training and/or experience) required for use of a given assessment instrument. Apply the same criteria to anyone with delegated responsibility for assessing clients.

_____ 15. Determine whether research shows that the instrument measures what you are seeking to measure.

_____ 16. Evaluate the basis for any cutoff scores or decision rules advocated for interpretation.

_____ 17. Avoid an instrument that requires the comparison of a client's raw scores unless research shows that equal raw scores for each of the test's scales (e.g., interest type) indicate equal amounts of the characteristic being measured.

_____ 18. Determine that computer-administered instruments meet the same standards (have been normed and determined to be reliable and valid for this mode of administration) as paper-and-pencil instruments.

_____ 19. Examine the basis for occupational attribute descriptions (e.g., relevant abilities, work activities) used to link client characteristics (e.g., abilities, interests) to occupations. Determine whether the descriptions and links are justified.

_____ 20. Before final adoption of an instrument, evaluate usability by administering and interpreting it to a small number of clients. (See subsequent checklist items.) If possible, arrange to take the instrument yourself.

ADMINISTRATION AND SCORING

_____ 1. Acquire the training necessary to administer the instrument. Study the directions for administration and know whether additional materials (e.g., timer, scratch paper) are needed.

_____ 2. Provide appropriate training for test administrators and proctors.

_____ 3. Ensure that reasons for testing are understood and accepted by clients, such as why the instrument is being given, what it can and cannot do, who will receive the test results, how they will be used.

_____ 4. Maintain the security of assessment materials before, during, and after administration.

_____ 5. Provide a testing room and psychological climate that will allow each client to achieve optimal performance.

_____ 6. Plan for special circumstances affecting the administration of an assessment instrument (e.g., late arrivals, persons with disabilities, left handers).

_____ 7. Ensure that test administration directions are followed explicitly and completely.

_____ 8. Determine, in advance, appropriate answers to questions about guessing, skipping questions, and using time efficiently.

_____ 9. Note unusual behavior by any person(s) being tested. If the test results are not invalidated, consider whether a report of the unusual behavior should accompany the scores.

_____ 10. Periodically rescore a sample of "self-scored tests" to verify scoring accuracy. Routinely rescore the tests of clients who, in your judgment, may have difficulty with self-scoring.

_____ 11. Develop a system for dating, recording, maintaining the confidentiality of, and scoring test results.

_____ 12. If the instrument is computer administered, ascertain the client's computer literacy. For those unfamiliar with computers, provide training about how to take a computer-administered instrument.

INTERPRETATION

_____ 1. Provide test interpretations based on documented bridges between scores and their real-world implications. Be sure your interpretations, including those provided on the score report and/or a computer terminal, are warranted by research conducted on the instrument.

_____ 2. Initially, and periodically thereafter, discuss your interpretations with a qualified colleague.

_____ 3. Review, with the client, the purpose and nature of the assessment — why it was given (e.g., its relevance to client goals); what the test can and cannot do; who will receive the results.

_____ 4. Obtain the consent of the client before using assessment results for purposes other than those described prior to the testing.

_____ 5. Consider whether a client's reading level, primary language, race, sexual orientation, ethnic and cultural background, disability, computer literacy, or age may have influenced the test results. Take such information into account in any report of results.

_____ 6. Encourage clients to discuss how they felt about the testing experience in general (e.g., did they see potential personal benefit?), their performance, and any problems encountered (e.g., nervousness, fatigue, language difficulty, and distractions).

_____ 7. Provide a simple explanation of measurement error and its implications, especially for score differences and profiles.

_____ 8. Help the client to think of assessment interpretations as hypotheses to be checked against past experience, compared with other information, tested via mutually planned activities, and periodically reviewed and modified.

_____ 9. Be aware of the research on the limits of individual rationality and biased self-reporting. Do not assume that the client has the degree of personal awareness, or awareness of the world of work, that he or she needs to make an optimal choice.

_____ 10. Apply good counseling techniques to test interpretation by attending to the client first and the results second (e.g., by listening attentively and encouraging feedback and discussion); allowing sufficient time for the client to assimilate information and ask questions; checking the client's understanding from time to time; and correcting any misconceptions.

_____ 11. Help the client begin (or continue) the career planning process by cooperatively identifying career options, steps for exploring the options, and criteria for evaluating the options.

_____ 12. Monitor and encourage career-planning activities through informal contacts, scheduled progress reports, or follow-through counseling sessions.

_____ 13. In general, observe the Golden Rule of Assessment: "Administer and interpret unto others as you would have them do unto you."

REFERENCES

American Counseling Association. (2005). *ACA code of ethics and standards of practice.* Alexandria, VA: Author.

American Educational Research Association, American Psychological Association, and National Council on Measurement in Education. (1999). *Standards for educational and psychological testing* (2nd ed.). Washington, DC: Author.

Association for Assessment in Counseling. (2003). *Standards for multicultural assessment.* Author.

Sandoval, J., Frisby, C.L., Geisinger, K.F. & Associates. (1999). *Test interpretation and diversity: Achieving equity in assessment.* Washington, DC: American Psychological Association.

CHAPTER 7

ASSESSING YOUTH AND ADULTS WITH EDUCATION AND CAREER DEVELOPMENT CHALLENGES

Mary Podmostko
National Collaborative on
Workforce and Disability for Youth,
Institute for Educational Leadership
Washington, DC

Joe Timmons
Institute on Community Integration
University of Minnesota

Christine D. Bremer
Institute on Community Integration
University of Minnesota

Introduction

This chapter, adapted from material in the National Collaborative on Workforce and Disability for Youth (NCWD/Youth) publication, *Career Planning Begins with Assessment* (Timmons, Podmostko, Bremer, Lavin, & Wills, 2005), addresses assessment strategies in career planning and development that can reduce or eliminate barriers to successful outcomes created by disability. The value-neutral term "focus client" will be used to discuss individuals who may need extra or modified assessment strategies and services. Understanding individual needs and developing an empathetic approach to supporting these individuals are critical to reaching desired outcomes.

Each focus client brings a unique set of characteristics and goals that will affect the career assessment process, including a number of risk factors. By understanding the issues addressed in this chapter and ensuring that appropriate strategies are used, career counselors and other career development professionals can help individuals cope with and manage their risk factors and improve the quality of assessment services. These services provide a foundation for improving the lives of focus clients by helping them develop meaningful individualized career plans.

The primary issue affecting the career development of focus clients is usually their limited experience in career exploration and work-based activities. Both practically and culturally, these limitations hinder accurate assessment and may prevent identification of skills, aptitudes, and interests that might appear after exposure and opportunity. Youth and adults who have had a wide range of positive experiences in school, community and work, and who have had opportunities for leadership, generally have a better understanding of career development and can make more reasoned choices in many assessment activities. Therefore, assessment activities administered within a wide range of experiential settings and flexible or extended time frames are optimal.

A key issue for many focus clients is that often their career planning process has not reflected the values of choice and self-determination. Many individuals with disabilities have been relegated to passive roles in their own career planning process, which resulted in

- very few options being recommended or offered,
- options that reflected the low expectations of advisors,
- options that featured perceived needs for protection and support, and
- options driven primarily by community availability rather than an individual's choices. (Timmons, Podmostko, Bremer, Lavin, & Wills, 2005)

As a result, many focus clients have been guided into jobs and careers that are neither motivating nor satisfying, and that have not allowed them to use the skills, knowledge, and abilities that they have to contribute to the workplace. A large part of the planning effort lies in assisting the focus client identify her or his assets and sharing this information with families, other career development professionals working with the focus client, and potential employers. Effective assessment, both formal and informal, is the foundation on which the career planning process rests.

Four Domains of Assessment

Career assessments address the range of interests, skills, knowledge, and expertise that are needed for success in work and life, such as those identified by the Partnership for 21st Century Skills (n.d.):

- Core subjects and twenty-first century themes, such as English, reading, languages, mathematics, science, civics, financial and economic literacy, and health literacy
- Learning and thinking skills, such as creativity, innovation, critical thinking, problem solving, communication, and collaboration
- Information and Communications Technology (ICT) skills
- Life skills, such as adaptability, initiative, self-direction, social and cross-cultural skills, productivity, accountability, and leadership

Thorough career assessment for individuals with disabilities encompasses the skills described above and covers four major domains (educational, vocational, psychological, and medical) and the use of career assessment instruments in the overall career assessment strategies selected by the career professionals and their clients. These domains overlap, and assessment in one domain will often lead to useful information or understanding in another. Assessments in the educational and vocational domains are designed to measure achievement, aptitudes, skill levels, interests, physical and functional capacities, and cognition. These data are then used to help form educational, training, and/or employment plans specific to the individual's situation.

In psychological and medical domains, assessment for focus clients is typically conducted to identify or diagnose mental or physical problems that may impede an individual's academic progress, vocational growth, or career development; to develop treatment or therapy plans to alleviate these problems; and to identify appropriate accommodations for school, home, and workplace. These types of assessments are conducted by licensed physicians, other medical personnel, and psychologists.

In the four domains, testing and performance assessments are subdivided into seven areas commonly used in career development: academic performance or achievement; cognitive abilities; behavioral, social, and emotional considerations; vocational interests; job aptitudes and skills; occupation specific certification; and physical and functional capacities. Cognitive abilities may fall under the educational or psychological domain. Physical and functional capacities may fall under the vocational or medical domain.

This chapter focuses primarily on supporting focus clients in the vocational domain, specifically (a) formal and informal vocational interest surveys that match a focus client's interests, goals, and values to potential career options, and (b) vocational aptitudes and skills assessments that measure a focus client's ability or potential to learn or perform skills required in certain careers. (A third type of vocational assessments, occupation-specific certification tests, is usually administered by licensure boards, businesses, and workforce preparation programs to measure the ability to perform specific work compared to industry standards.)

Vocational assessments range from informal interest surveys that may be used to help the focus client start thinking about careers to comprehensive vocational evaluations conducted by trained and certified evaluators resulting in in-depth vocational profiles and recommendations. These assessments often need little or no modification for use with focus clients. Note that no assessment outcome stands alone and that assessment data from all four domains, as well as information from observations, interviews, and record reviews, may be needed to assist the focus client in developing complete and well-documented plans. Care should be taken to avoid duplicating assessment activities unnecessarily, and career decisions should never be made on the basis of a single assessment.

Potential Risk Factors and Disclosure

It is not the career development professional's responsibility to diagnose disabilities. Because of the variety and high incidence of disabilities (approximately 20% of the population), access to specialists (e.g., special educators, vocational rehabilitation counselors, health care professionals) who can evaluate potential focus clients and assist with individual assessment issues is needed, as is awareness of the risk factors of focus clients that can affect the selection and administration of career assessment strategies and instruments. These factors, which may be hidden or apparent, include:

- diagnosed disabilities, (e.g., visual, hearing, orthopedic, and neurological impairments; learning disabilities, Attention Deficit/Hyperactivity Disorder, mental health or emotional problems, cognitive or intellectual disabilities)
- undiagnosed or unidentified disabilities
- chronic illnesses or conditions (e.g., asthma, diabetes, rheumatoid arthritis, cystic fibrosis, spina bifida, colitis, seizure disorders, cerebral palsy, cancer, HIV/AIDS, anemia, lupus)
- alcohol and chemical use, both legal and illegal

Some focus clients have readily apparent disabilities or conditions (usually sensory or physical disabilities such as visual impairments, hearing loss, or orthopedic or neurological impairments). Others have somewhat less obvious but still recognizable cognitive disabilities (such as developmental disabilities or autism). The majority of these individuals have had concrete interventions in school to alleviate the effects of the disability. Families often develop a good understanding of the dynamics of the client's disability, and chances are good that educational and vocational transition plans include documentation of accommodations and supports needed for academic and career development.

Other focus clients have hidden or nonapparent disabilities or illness. Hidden disabilities include learning disabilities, Attention Deficit Hyperactivity Disorder (AD/HD), Attention Deficit Disorder (ADD), mental health or emotional problems (such as depression, anxiety disorders, or conduct disorders), and traumatic brain injuries (TBI). Because of the nature of hidden disabilities, identification and the provision of needed interventions and supports are more difficult. Families, as well as professionals, often have inadequate understanding of the nature of hidden disabilities. Most importantly, clients with hidden disabilities are less likely than others to disclose their disability to avoid being stigmatized or labeled. This means that clients with these disabilities may enroll and enter educational, training, and career development programs without communicating their disability or their needs for accommodations and special assistance.

Undiagnosed or unidentified disabilities may be suggested by evidence found in a focus client's records of low literacy levels, inconsistent academic performance, limited vocabulary, behavior, assessment results, or interview responses. A screening process may be needed to determine whether further diagnostic assessment by a trained specialist should be provided. However, clients have the right to refuse screenings and diagnostic assessments.

Beyond disability status, additional risk factors often come into play and also require consideration in career counseling settings. For example, many focus clients come from challenging family circumstances, have not completed high school, have been in foster care, are involved in the juvenile or adult justice system, or have a primary language other than English.

Focus clients may have previously received services or are currently receiving them via special education, vocational rehabilitation, or workforce development systems. They may have participated in career assessments and/or have an Individualized Education Program or Individualized Plan for Employment that include employment and postsecondary education goals. In some cases, available medical or psychological records may be helpful. However, these documents are protected by privacy rules and may not be available to the career planning professional.

Some clients will choose to not disclose their specific diagnosis or prognosis, or that they have previously qualified for or received disability-related accommodations or services. In many cases, adults avoid disclosure because they wish to avoid being stigmatized or labeled as having a disability. Nondisclosure is an established right under the Americans with Disabilities Act (ADA). For the focus client, whether or not to disclose a disability or illness to prospective employers or others is an important decision that may have both short- and long-term ramifications. To help individuals understand the complex issues involved, NCWD/Youth has published *The 411 on Disclosure*, a workbook to help individuals make informed decisions about disclosure and show how these decisions can impact their education, employment, and social lives.

Working with focus clients who have received or are receiving services from a number of agencies and programs may become confusing as they transfer from one program or service provider to another at various times. Each time a youth or adult begins working in a new program or with a new career development professional, the need for assessment should be revisited since the purpose and form of assessment may vary by program and changing client goals. Also, it is important to remember throughout the interview and on-going transition process that many focus clients have had limited or negative experiences with tests and testing which may impact their responsiveness to assessment opportunities.

Person-Centered Planning

For focus clients, assessment should support a consistent process for goal setting that includes "person-centered planning" in which the career planning process is driven by an individual's needs and desires. In career assessment, person-centered planning focuses on a person's assets (interests, aptitudes, knowledge, and skills) and not on his or her perceived deficits. Career development professionals who use person-centered planning seek to involve the people who are active in the life of an individual, such as family members, educators, employers, friends, and service providers. Person-centered career planning will include multiple options, self-advocacy, bridging of academic and career needs, access to critical information, and professional assistance.

Whatever the age of the focus client, family members have important roles in supporting and preparing him or her for the world of work. Although there is a natural tendency for focus clients to seek independence and to rely less and less on parents and other family members for support, all participants in the process should understand that career planning is a process requiring flexibility and negotiation, in which each focus client and family member may have a role to play.

Streamlining the Assessment Process

Often, the assessment process can be completed in less time and at lower cost by making use of the focus client's existing records, provided permission to view and use these records has been obtained. To be useful, records containing background information, prior interviews and observations, histories, and testing must be up-to-date. Whether or not prior assessment results are considered current can often be determined from publishers' materials. If a focus client's situation has recently changed (because of schooling, training, onset of a disability, therapy, treatment, etc.), new assessments may be needed. Records should be reviewed with an eye to assessing their value in supporting a focus client's future academic or career planning needs. If outdated or lacking validity, records may inappropriately limit an individual's options.

Older individuals with disabilities who have established academic credentials or clear vocational goals may not need extensive testing to measure achievement or uncover vocational interests. Others may have complicated situations requiring an extended process of supported planning and implementation. In more complex cases, it is good practice to have written plans with objectives and timelines that formalize the activities, make all participants aware of the process, and hold everyone accountable. Deciding which formal tests should be administered and in what order is part of this process. Plans can be amended and updated depending on testing outcomes, and the focus client's input should be considered as much as possible.

Assessment Activities

Prior to beginning formal or informal testing or performance reviews, career counselors can gather a lot of information by observation and interviews. The initial interview establishes rapport with the individual and his or her family and helps them develop a realistic understanding of what a career counselor has to offer. Personal information about health or disability issues may be part of the interview process and must be handled with tact and sensitivity. The Americans with Disabilities Act provides guidance and language in this regard. Privacy and confidentiality must be maintained, and securing information from other agencies, when appropriate, must be done ethically and legally, using signed consent forms when needed.

Helping focus clients make informed choices and achieve desired outcomes requires a structured, well-defined assessment process. The following principles should guide the assessment process:

- Self-determination based on informed choices should be an overriding goal of assessment.
- Assessment is a dynamic intervention process.
- Assessment facilitates self-discovery of talents, goals, strengths, and needs.
- The purposes and goals of assessment should be clear.
- Assessment should be integrated into a larger plan of person-centered planning and individualized services.
- Assessment should consider environmental factors affecting the individual.
- Formal assessment instruments should be carefully chosen with attention to their documented reliability and validity.
- Formal assessments should be administered and interpreted by qualified personnel.
- Assessment reports should be written in easily understandable language.
- Assessment activities should be experienced as positive and should empower the focus client to communicate their goals to family members and others, and to make decisions about next steps.

Assessment instruments are used to help determine a person's specific abilities, strengths, and challenges. The results of assessments should not be used merely to categorize an individual with a disability but rather as tools to develop strategies to help him or her reach desired goals. Assessments also help identify areas to probe in order to understand an individual's potential strengths and functional abilities in educational or community settings.

Providing Accommodations

Accommodations are changes made in a classroom, work site, or assessment procedure that help people with disabilities learn, work, obtain an accurate assessment, or receive services. Accommodations are intended to do more than just comply with federal regulations and maximize the effectiveness of assessments; they are designed to alleviate the effects of a disability, not to lower expectations for performance in school or work. Common accommodations include allowing a focus client with a learning disability extra time to complete an assignment or a test, providing amplification equipment for a student with a hearing impairment in a classroom, or providing a special computer keyboard for someone with dexterity problems.

Provisions of the Americans with Disabilities Act and other federal laws provide for the use of appropriate testing accommodations for clients with disabilities for the purpose of increasing access and participation to public education and employment. Accommodations are of particular concern when using criterion-referenced or norm-referenced instruments. The goal of providing accommodations is to change the way that a test is taken without changing the validity of the test results.

Sometimes a question arises about the reliability or validity of certain tests when accommodations are used. In such cases, the test publisher should be contacted for clarification. At no point should an individual be penalized or denied services because of unreliable or invalid test results. If a particular assessment cannot be conducted in a way that assures validity, other methods of assessment should be used. Testing accommodations are categorized into four classes (Thurlow, House, Boys, Scott, & Ysseldyke, 2000):

- *Presentation format:* changes in how tests are presented, including accommodations like providing Braille versions of the tests or orally reading the directions to students
- *Response format:* changes in the manner in which students give their responses, including accommodations such as having a student point to a response or use a computer for responding
- *Setting of the test:* home, or in small groups
- *Timing of the test:* including extending the time allowed or providing more breaks during testing

Specific accommodations may affect the validity or fairness of individual tests. Familiarity with local practice is needed since states, local agencies, and school districts have their own guidelines, and inconsistencies are widespread.

Career assessment of focus clients may lead to practical ideas for job accommodations in training programs and workplaces. Effective assessment can examine potential needs for accommodations that will enable an individual to perform the essential functions of a chosen job. On-site and off-site accommodations that might improve the job placement success of focus clients include modifications to a job, restructuring of tasks, use of job coaches to assist with training, or use of American Sign Language interpreters. The Job

Accommodation Network (JAN) is a free consulting service that provides information about workplace accommodations, the ADA, and the employability of people with disabilities. JAN has information for employers and people with disabilities, including a Searchable On-line Accommodation Resource (SOAR) on their website (http://janweb.icdi.wvu.edu/).

Situational Work Assessments

Situational work assessments are contextualized assessments that focus on performance of tasks in realistic settings. Focus clients often benefit from the assessment of occupational skills. Work behaviors can be examined in situational work assessments and may include capacities and competencies for performing essential job duties of specific competitive employment positions. For example, the measurement of a youth's keyboarding proficiency may be predictive of his or her ability to succeed in a job requiring a minimum speed for data entry or word processing. Allowing youth to try essential job functions of different jobs will help them decide if they really enjoy the work and if they have the stamina to meet work requirements.

While the outcomes of occupational skills assessment are not entirely predictive of future success in a competitive job situation, they often can lead to job skills training, apprenticeships, or internships that help focus clients increase their competency and productivity. They can also lead to the development of creative, individualized job placement plans such as customized employment or "job carving (a restructuring of job duties or tasks so that an individual with more significant disabilities can perform job functions of high interest). Typically, job carving is provided for people who, for a variety of reasons, cannot perform the entire job or the whole range of skills required.

In special education programs and community rehabilitation organizations, situational work assessments are also often used to study the "soft skills" needed in employment. They include an assessment of basic work behaviors and skills through practical hands-on work experiences.

Youth with identified behavioral disorders or learning disabilities can benefit greatly from situational work assessments. Many young people who struggle in the classroom for one reason or another nonetheless flourish in work settings where hands-on activities better fit their learning styles.

A Word about Work Environments. Ecological or environmental assessments examine the workplace context, which may contribute significantly to the success of an individual at work. These may include, but are not limited to, availability of close supervision; style of supervision (e.g., casual vs. autocratic); physical building structures and layout of the learning or working environment; flow of product or service processes; effects of formal and informal rules; social interaction demands of others (e.g., coworkers, classmates); sensory stimuli such as noise, motion, temperature, air quality, etc.; work schedules and time requirements; opportunities for independence and decision making; performance expectations of authorities; and opportunities for self-correction. Temperaments (preference for working with data, people, or things; preference for indoor vs. outdoor work; working with people or alone) play a large role in ecological assessments, as the fit of temperament to context can be of great importance in determining the success of an individual in a job.

Assessment results can be used to build a case for finding fitting employment opportunities for the focus client. Too often, individuals are not hired because prospective employers cannot see how their needs will be met if they hire an individual with a disability, a chronic illness, or other perceived barriers. Assessment results can provide a communications tool for discussing with employers the actual capabilities of individuals with disabilities. Functional skills are critical to successful employment and include transportation, communication, interpersonal skills, self-care, self-direction, and work tolerance. Most people develop these skills over months or years and can discuss or demonstrate them in the course of a job interview. Focus clients with disabilities, chronic illness, or other barriers who have developed an understanding of their strengths and their limitations can address the concerns of employers, coworkers, and customers by explaining their compensatory strategies, including any needed accommodations or assistive technology. Because employers look for employees with two sets of skills — the functional skills that all workers need and the specific work skills needed to do a specific job — it is important that job seekers understand what these skills are and how to develop them if they are lacking.

Functional limitations refer to an activity or behavior that an individual cannot perform or performs with difficulty. These may also result from behaviors that the individual has difficulty performing with sufficient frequency, adequate intensity, in the appropriate manner, or under socially expected conditions. Functional limitations may also result from behaviors that occur too frequently, too intensely, last too long, or occur when and where they should not normally occur. Disability specialists in educational and vocational rehabilitation settings can assist with strategies to overcome work-related functional limitations.

Independent Living Skills Assessments

This category of testing does not fit specifically in any domain but can be an important piece of the assessment puzzle. By late adolescence, many youth are making plans for living on their own. Skills needed for independent living are taken for granted by many youth, but youth with disabilities or chronic illnesses may have physical or intellectual limitations that prevent them from engaging in adult activities without support or assistance. Additionally, independent living skills are closely related to the functional work skills discussed above. Assessment and instruction in these activities of daily living (ADLs) are common in schools and rehabilitation programs serving students with more significant disabilities. These are important to consider when planning for transition. ADL assessment areas include:

- transportation and mobility
- personal care (clothing, grooming, nutrition, medical)
- recreation and leisure
- home maintenance
- communication skills

Specially trained teachers, instructors, and therapists can assess individuals in these and other areas. Often service providers have specialty areas (vision loss, deafness, mental retardation, etc.) and will work with individuals in the community, in schools, or in residential settings. In some cases, extensive longer term training is required and is done in the rehabilitation centers found in many communities. This training is sometimes called prevocational because it may need to be completed prior to individual participation in vocational activities.

Systemic Challenges

Focus clients who seek assistance from publicly funded organizations often find that they must navigate a complex maze of laws, regulations, and policies in order to access assessment services. Additional constraints include funding, lack of information on available assessment resources and expertise, privacy protections, and reporting and evaluation requirements.

In addition to providing potential funding sources for career assessments and planning, federal legislation encourages collaborative cross-agency cooperation (both statewide and in local communities) to address systemic problems. Resource mapping, a type of environmental scanning, is a useful means for agencies and service providers to identify, record, and disseminate related resources and services that comprise a delivery system. By detailing current capacities, needs, and expertise, an organization or group of organizations can begin to make strategic decisions to efficiently broaden their collective assessment capacity and create an equitable and effective division of labor.

Resource mapping also allows states and communities to form partnerships and identify service gaps and service overlaps — information that is essential to aligning the assessment services and strategic planning of multiple agencies and organizations. The resource mapping process may also reveal that some agencies or organizations have expertise in particular areas of need. For example, partners may wish to draw on the expertise of the state department of education in developing assessment accommodation guidelines that will ensure consistency across agencies.

Outcomes of the resource mapping process may include (a) a list of assessment resources and available expertise; (b) a common policy and release form for authorizing the receipt and sharing of confidential data or assessment information from focus clients, schools, family members, and partner agencies; and/or (c) a division of labor for local assessment services such as academic assessments provided by the public school system and/or community college, disability and functional evaluations provided by the vocational rehabilitation office, and vocational assessments provided by the local One-Stop Career Center (funded by the Workforce Investment Act). Resource mapping and strategic planning processes are also useful in developing assessment services and aligning on-the-job supports for employers in the community.

Summary

There are a number of assessment strategies in career assessment and planning that can reduce or eliminate barriers to successful outcomes, including (a) thorough career assessment encompassing the four domains of assessment; (b) access to specialists who can evaluate potential focus clients and assist with individual assessment issues as needed; (c) ameliorating the risk factors of focus clients that can affect the selection and administration of career assessment strategies and instruments; (d) accommodations, situational assessments, and life skills assessments; (e) understanding various government and community support systems, including those providing medical, mental health, financial, and independent living services; and (f) eliminating systemic challenges to effective career assessment through partnerships and resource mapping.

References

Partnership for 21st Century Skills. (n.d.). *21st Century skills outcomes.* Retrieved July 24, 2007 from http://www.21stcenturyskills.org/index.php?option=com_content&task=view&id=254&Itemid=120

Thurlow, M., House, A., Boys, C., Scott, D., & Ysseldyke, J. (2000). *State participation and accommodations policies for students with disabilities: 1999 update.* Retrieved July 16, 2007, from http://www.education.umn.edu/NCEO/OnlinePubs/Synthesis33.html

Timmons, J., Podmostko, M., Bremer, C., Lavin, D. & Wills, J. (2005). *Career planning begins with assessment: A guide for professionals serving youth with educational & career development challenges* (rev. ed.). Retrieved July 24, 2007, from http://www.ncwd-youth.info/resources_&_Publications/assessment.html

CHAPTER 8

APTITUDE/ACHIEVEMENT AND COMPREHENSIVE OR COMBINED MEASURES

- Ability Explorer (Second Edition) (AE)
- Adult Basic Learning Examination (Second Edition) (ABLE)
- Armed Services Vocational Aptitude Battery (ASVAB)
  Career Exploration Program (CEP)
- Career Planning Survey (CPS)
- CareerScope: Career Assessment and Reporting System (Version 8.0)
- COPSystem Career Guidance Program (COPS) (CAPS) (COPES)
- Differential Aptitude Tests (Fifth Edition) (DAT) and Career
  Interest Inventory (CII)
- Employability Competency System Appraisal Test (ECS Appraisal)
- EXPLORE and PLAN
- Highlands Ability Battery (tHAB)
- Kuder Career Planning System (KSA) (KCS) (SWVI-r)
- Motivational Appraisal of Personal Potential (MAPP)
- O*NET Ability Profiler (AP)
- Occupational Aptitude Survey and Interest Schedule (Third Edition)
  (OASIS-3)
- System for Assessment and Group Evaluation (SAGE 2001)
- Tests of Adult Basic Education (TABE 9 & 10)
- Wonderlic Basic Skills Test (WBST)
- WorkKeys Assessments
- World of Work Inventory (WOWI)

Ability Explorer, Second Edition (AE)

Joan C. Harrington and Thomas F. Harrington

JIST Publishing, Inc.
8902 Otis Avenue
Indianapolis, IN 46216
www.jist.com

Target Population: Middle school to adult

Statement of the Purpose of the Instrument: The Ability Explorer helps individuals discover their best abilities and then connects their top abilities to related courses, activities, and careers.

Titles of Subtests, Scales, Scores Provided: Self-rating scores for 14 abilities: Artistic, Clerical, Interpersonal, Language, Leadership, Manual, Musical/Dramatic, Numerical/Mathematical, Organizational, Persuasive, Scientific, Social, Spatial, Technical/Mechanical. The top two ranking abilities are then connected to related activities, courses, and careers.

Forms and Levels Available, with Dates of Publication/Revision of Each: Ability Explorer, Second Edition assessment; Ability Explorer Administrator's Guide. Ability Explorer Professional Resources CD-ROM. No special qualifications required. All in 2006.

Date of Most Recent Edition of Test Manual, User's Guide, etc.: 2006

Languages in Which Available: English only.

Time: Actual Test Time: 30–45 minutes
Total Administration Time: 30–45 minutes (can be self-administered)

Norm Group(s) on Which Scores Are Based: Norm Groups: middle/high school students and postsecondary students and adults are available in the Professional Resources CD-ROM.

Manner in Which Results Are Reported for Individuals: Scores for each ability are reported in a range from 0 to 60 and then converted into High, Medium, and Low percentile ability ratings. Self-scoring and self-interpreting. A video, "Getting the Most from the Ability Explorer," is available.

> **Types of Scores:** 14 raw scale scores for each of the abilities can be converted to the percentile and T-score norms developed for the assessment.

> **Report Format/Content:** Basic Service: Assessment is self-scoring and self-interpreting.

Report Format/Content for Group Summaries: Not available.

Scoring

> **Machine Scoring Service:** Not available.
> **Hand Scoring:**
> *Scored by:* Counselee.

Time required for scoring: 5–10 minutes. Included in administration time.

Local Machine Scoring: Not available.

Computer Software Options Available: Not available.

Cost of Materials: Due to possible price changes since publication date be sure to check with publisher web site.

Specimen Set: A free sample is available from the publisher.

Technical Manual: Ability Explorer Professional Resources CD-ROM, Second Edition includes illustrative cases, follow-up activities for grades 6–12, and detailed normative and technical information, $29.95.

Counselee Materials: Each package contains 25 sixteen-page self-scoring and self-interpreting booklets and an administrator's guide. 1–9 packages, $39.95; 10+ packages, $35.95.

Additional Comments of Interest to Users: The video program, "Making the Most of Your Abilities", offers the viewer a "connection" between abilities, their development, and career fulfillment. The DVD uses heartfelt interviews with real life job occupants and shows how these individuals developed their abilities and took advantage of opportunities that helped them land their current job and created the foundation for future success in work and lifelong learning. It prepares viewers to consider the connections between their abilities, careers, and satisfaction. It also teaches viewers how to interpret their scores from the *Ability Explorer* assessment.

Published Reviews of the Instrument in the Last 15 Years:

Borman, C. (2001). Review of the Ability Explorer. In J. T. Kapes & E. A. Whitfield (Eds.) *A counselor's guide to career assessment instruments* (4th ed., pp. 74–81). Columbus, OH: National Career Development Association.

Hoffman, A. (1997). Ability Explorer: A review and critique. Paper presented at the Annual Meeting of the Southwest Educational Research Association, Austin, TX.

Mau, Wei-Cheng. (2001). Test review: Ability Explorer (AE). NewsNotes. Association for Assessment in Counseling.

Reviewed by:

Wei-Cheng J. Mau
Professor
Department of Counseling
Educational and School Psychology
Wichita State University

Description

The *Ability Explorer (AE)*, a self-report inventory, assesses 14 work-related abilities congruent with skill areas identified by the U.S. Department of Labor. The *AE* is a 2006 revision of a previously published instrument (Harrington & Harrington, 1996) designed to "provide middle school/junior high, high school, and postsecondary students, as well as adults with information about their abilities as they directly relate to the world of work and to educational and career planning" (Harrington & Harrington, 2006, p. 3).

The *Ability Explorer*, Second Edition, now published by JIST, is available in English and is self-scored. The machine and Internet editions of the earlier *Ability Explorer* as well as the Spanish version have been dropped. Some improvement and enhancement have been made to the new edition. The *Ability Explorer* has integrated O*NET into its materials. Through O*NET titles and the *Occupational Outlook Handbook (OOH)*, the career areas displayed by the *Ability Explorer* represent those occupations where over 50% of U.S. workers will be employed in 2012.

The *Ability Explorer*, written at a grade 8 or lower level, provides assessment for two age levels (adolescent and adult). A unique design of this assessment is that it links assessed abilities with various activities, courses, and occupations. The assessment is divided into three parts: (1) the self-rating of abilities, (2) the self-rating of past performance on activities, and (3) the self-reporting of school course performance. The administration time and scoring for the assessment booklet is estimated to be 35 to 45 minutes.

In Part One, a total of 140 items were selected to represent the 14 ability scales (10 hypothetical statements per scale). Of the 140 items, 112 items are based on past performance on various activities and 28 items on course work. The 14 work-related abilities include language, numerical/mathematical, clerical, mechanical/technical, spatial, manual, scientific, interpersonal, leadership, musical/dramatic, organizational, persuasive, social, and artistic. A color-coded, brief description is provided for each of the 14 abilities. The questions in the ability inventory are answered on a six-point Likert scale ranging from very good to very poor. Hand scoring involves summing responses for each column and transferring the summed scores to a summary sheet. Only raw scores are provided. Users must refer their raw scores to a table in order to understand how they compare to other people's scores in terms of "high," "medium," or "low."

Part Two of the Ability Explorer surveys an individual's involvement in activities related to the 14 ability areas. The individual is then asked to identify activities he/she did best in and activities to try or do better in. In Part Three, the individual is asked to circle the grades he/she earned for the courses related to the 14 ability areas. Again in this part, the individual is given a chance to identify courses he/she did best in and courses he/she wants to take in the future. Finally, the individual is asked to examine two highest rated abilities in relation to the performance of the abilities, activities, and course grades.

The assessment design is based on the assumption that ability can be improved. This inventory provides feedback not only in terms of the individual's highest rated abilities but also ability areas that can be improved through courses. Users are shown ways to improve a desired ability area and to evaluate the current status of their ability development relative to planned career goals. Technical, administration, and counselor manuals are also available.

Use in Counseling

The *Ability Explorer* can be used in conjunction with an interest inventory to compare and contrast results. The information obtained from the AE can become an integral part of the career portfolio. "Just as the individual should use a career portfolio to record what is best about him or her, so the Ability Explorer profile report is a record of what the person considers his or her strongest abilities" (2006, p.28).

Counselors could use *AE* to help their clients develop a functional based resume, at least in part, on abilities. The individual's highest rated abilities can be highlighted in the resume, perhaps as a section heading in the body of the resume.

The *Ability Explorer* could be used as a tool when practicing for job or informational interviews. "The counselor or teacher can extend this further by allowing the individual to reflect upon his or her *Ability Explorer* results during a counseling session. This encourages the student or adult client to articulate his or her best strengths, a skill that can certainly make for successful interviews. The individual's peers and/or parents or guardians could also be encouraged to participate in 'interviews' focused on his or her *Ability Explorer* results" (2006, p.29).

The publisher also provides a resource CD that contains an administrator's guide, administrator's record, illustrative cases, and follow-up activities that are very useful for test users.

Technical Consideration

The inventory items were developed through writing initial statements and reviewed by experts, field tests, and an item analysis procedure. All statements in all three parts of the *Ability Explorer,* as well as the directions, were reviewed by a panel of minority experts.

The second edition used the standardization groups established in the previous edition. The norm group for the *Ability Explorer* contains 4,837 cases, including 3,532 middle/junior high and high school students and 1,305 college students and adults. The normative sample is representative of the U.S. population, although the African American group is overrepresented. The *AE* uses a single, large norm group. It does not break down information by grade level, sex, or race, although data show that there are differences among groups. The authors argued that "The focus of the *Ability Explorer* is on what abilities are needed to perform an occupation, not the abilities for males performing an occupation or females performing the same occupation. The source of the questions on the instrument was job analysts' findings. These job analysts looked at the abilities and skills needed to do a job, as opposed to whether a male or female, Black or Hispanic, etc. used the same abilities to do the same job" (2006, p.32–33). Although separate norms for each grade level are provided in the professional manual, a single norm table is used for interpretation in the test booklet.

AE has good internal consistency reliability estimated for ability scales. The median coefficient for abilities is .88, with a range of .83 to .91. No gender difference for the

[Editors' Note: In 2008, after this review was completed, the test publisher added the "Making the Most of Your Abilities" DVD program (Feller & Vasos, 2008) as a resource available to users.]

coefficients was noted. The median Standard Error of Measure (SEM) is 3.48. The internal consistency reliability of the activity scale is lower than the ability scale. The median coefficient for activities is .70, with a range of .64 to .77. On four scales—Clerical, Interpersonal, Language, and Social—the alpha reliabilities estimated for male students are higher than for female students. The relatively lower reliabilities estimated for female students are also reflected in larger SEM scores. It is important to take into consideration the SEM scores when interpreting the activity scales for female students.

AE appears to be a fairly stable measure for college students. The test-retest reliability, based on 73 college students over a two-week period, averaged .84 for skill scales and .75 for activity scales. The authors did not provide estimates of score stability based on middle/high school students. One should not automatically infer that *AE* can be stably measured for middle or high school students.

Validity

Intercorrelations among ability subscales were used to provide partial evidence of construct validity. In general, most of the scales are moderately correlated, which show that the scales are distinct yet measure a similar construct.

Evidence of criterion-related validity was shown by the correlations with measures of career-related aptitude tests. However, the provided evidence tends to be low. For example, the correlations with the Differential Aptitude Test (DAT) are low to moderate, ranging from .08 (clerical) to .46 (numerical). Correlations with the G score of the General Aptitude Test Battery (GATB) also tend to be low, ranging from .01 (manual) to .33 (numerical/mathematical). Correlation with SAT aptitude test language is .27 and with the numerical/mathematical scale is .25.

Another criterion-related validity evidence was based on comparisons of 14 ability scale profiles of eight college majors against the skills required on the job based on the U.S. Department of Labor job analysts' data reported in the *Guide for Occupational Exploration (GOE)*. Results indicated that there was a 73% match between students' self-rated abilities and job analysts' data reported in the *GOE* (Harrington & Harrington, 2001).

The authors also reported validity evidence inferred from Harrington and O'Shea's (2000) study, which compared ability profiles of the Career Decision-Making System (CDM) based on five college majors and four employed worker samples. Findings showed that 67% matched. The CDM and the *AE* each have 14 ability scales, and 12 of the abilities have similar names. Another study by Harrington and Schafer (1996) examined the concurrent validity inferred from a comparison of the CDM self-reported abilities and the GATB Occupational Aptitude Pattern Structure (OAP) abilities. The authors concluded that the self-reported work abilities of employees are generally consistent with the *GOE*.

Overall Critique

The second edition of *AE* has made some improvement over the previous version in that it attempts to align the assessment with national standards and career development guidelines and to link its design with the *O*NET* system and the *No Child Left Behind* national trend. The authors have followed a rigorous test item development procedure to ensure a high quality of content validity. Supplemental materials, such as the administrator's record, administrator's guide, and professional manual, are features of the new edition. These supporting documents provide a better guidance for users in the administration and interpretation of the assessment results. Nevertheless, there are several weaknesses that deserve some attention for further improvement.

A common problem shared by many self-assessment tests is rating bias. Raters tend to either overestimate or underestimate their abilities, depending on the difficulty of the tasks or subject matter, as pointed out by many researchers (e.g., Kruger, 1999; Myers, 1998). The categories of the rating scale, "above average" and "below average," are not clearly defined. The accuracy of self-assessment also may have been compromised by the unclear definition of the rating categories used in *AE*.

Another weakness is limited information on validity, especially in the area of predictive validity and construct validity. The authors did a nice job of providing content validity, and the evidence appears to be fairly adequate. Although some initial evidence of construct validity has been substantiated by the literature and theoretical/logical reasoning, more direct evidence for validity is needed (Mau, 2001). Most of the criterion-related evidence of validity was drawn from college students or adults. The validity of *AE* for middle/high school students remains questionable. Some of the validity data are questionable, especially comparing results to traditional aptitude tests (Borman, 2001). The authors have toned down the value of predictive validity of the instrument and stressed the importance of the guidance purpose. The authors believe that "an individual's wide range of potential talents needs to be identified and explored before a prediction of success or failure is made" (Harrington & Harrington, 1996, p. 8). Perhaps, users of *AE* should place more emphasis on using the assessment results for personal awareness and self-efficacy intervention rather than for prediction of occupational obtainment or job satisfaction.

References

Borman, C. (2001). *Ability Explorer* review. In J. Kapes & E. A.Whitfield (Eds.), *A counselor's guide to career assessment instruments* (4th ed., pp. 74 – 81). Columbus, OH: National Career Development Association.

Feller, R., & Vasos, J. (2008). *Making the most of your abilities*. [DVD] St. Paul, MN: JIST Publishing.

Harrington, J., & Harrington, T. (1996). *Ability Explorer.* Itasca, IL: Riverside Publishing.

Harrington, T., & Harrington, J. (2001). A new generation of self-report methodology and validity evidence of the ability explorer. *Journal of Career Development*, 9, (1), 41–48.

Harrington, J., & Harrington, T. (2006). *Professional manual, Ability Explorer,* 2nd ed. Indianapolis, IN: JIST Publishing.

Harrington, T., & O'Shea, A. (2000). The *Harrington-O'Shea career decision-making system revised.* Circle Pines, MN: American Guidance Service.

Harrington, T., & Schafer, W. (1996). A comparison of self-reported abilities and occupational ability patterns across occupations. *Measurement and Evaluation in Counseling and Development*, 28, (4) 180-190.

Kruger, J. (1999, August). Lake Wobegon be gone! The "below-average effect" and the egocentric nature of comparative ability. *Journal of Personality and Social Psychology*, 77(2), 221–232.

Mau, W. (2001). Test review: Ability explorer (AE). *Association for Assessment in Counseling NewsNotes*. Retrieved January 20, 2003 from http://aac.ncat.edu/newsnotes/y01fall1.html.

Myers, D. (1998). *Social psychology*. New York: McGraw-Hill.

Adult Basic Learning Examination (ABLE)

Bjorn Karlsen and Eric F. Gardner

The Psychological Corporation
19500 Bulverde Road
San Antonio, Texas 78259
1-800-872-1726
http://harcourtassessment.com

Target Population: Adults.

Statement of the Purpose of the Instrument: ABLE is a battery of tests designed to measure the achievement levels of adults who have had varying amounts of formal schooling.

Titles of Subtests, Scales, Scores Provided: (1) Vocabulary, (2) Reading Comprehension, (3) Spelling, (4) Language, Total Language (3 & 4), (5) Number Operations, (6) Problem Solving, Total Mathematics (5 & 6).

Forms and Levels Available, with Dates of Publication/Revision of Each: Forms E, F, Level 1, Level 2, Level 3, ©1986.

Date of Most Recent Edition of Test Manual, User's Guide, etc.: 1986.

Languages in Which Available: English, Spanish edition of Level 2, Form E.

Time: Actual Test Time: Untimed.
Total Administration Time: Approximately 3 hours.

Manner in Which Results Are Reported for Individuals: Profile/Score form.
Types of Scores: Raw scores, percentile ranks, stanines, grade equivalents.

Report Format/Content for Group Summaries:
Basic Service: Group record is completed by counselor. The same scores as on individual reports can be accommodated.
Options: Item-Response Summary Report.

Scoring
Machine Scoring Service: Not available.
Hand Scoring:
Scored by: Clerk; Counselor.
Time required for scoring: 10 minutes.

Computer Software Options Available: Not available.

Cost of Materials: Due to possible price changes since publication date be sure to check with the publisher website.

Specimen Set: ABLE-Examination Kit, $50.00 (10/16/2007)

Counselee Materials: ABLE Screening Battery Test Booklets, pkg of 25, $85.00; ABLE Hand-Scorable or Reusable Test Booklets, pkg of 25, range from $125.00 to $130.00; ABLE Hand-Scorable Test Sheets, pkg of 50, $62.00; ABLE SelectABLE (Form C) includes Group Record and SelectABLE Handbook, $100.00 (10/16/2007)

Published Reviews of the Instrument in the Last 15 Years:
None cited.

Reviewed by:

Kurt F. Geisinger
Meierhenry Distinguished University Professor
Director, Buros Center for Testing
University of Nebraska – Lincoln

Description

The Adult Basic Learning Examination (ABLE) is a battery of tests designed to measure basic levels of educational achievement or functional academic skills and abilities among adults. It was developed originally as an instrument (1) for adults rather than children and (2) able to be administered to adults who may have quite varied levels of formal education. The current edition, the second, was published in 1986. Three levels of the test are available: Level 1 (1 – 4 years of education), Level 2 (5 – 8 years of education), and Level 3 (at least 8 years of education). An untimed screening test composed of items measuring verbal and numerical concepts takes from 15 minutes to an hour to complete, and may be used in determining which level to administer to a client. All three levels include five subtests: Vocabulary, Reading Comprehension, Spelling, Number Operations, and Problem Solving. Each level has material that increases in difficulty. Items on the Level 1 Vocabulary, Spelling, and Problem Solving subtests (as well as the first five questions on the Number Operations subtest) are dictated (rather than given in writing). Level 2 contains the same five subtests at a more advanced level as well as a Language subtest that covers grammar, capitalization, and punctuation. On the levels 2 and 3 tests, no items are dictated. All answers are made on answer sheets. The manuals for administering the tests are very explicit with regard to the required procedures. Subtests may be administered separately or together. Each level of the examination takes approximately 2 hours, 40 minutes to administer, but none of the tests are timed.

The publisher's website indicates that a Spanish form of the instrument is available, although no information was presented to this reviewer regarding this form, its development, or the psychometric basis for using it.

Uses in Counseling

This measure could be used in career counseling setting with individuals who have limited academic history (the target user market) but who are considering educational and vocational options. The measure is not as vocationally-oriented as some of its competitors, such as the Test of Adult Basic Education (TABE) (Geisinger, 1998). ABLE is appropriate for use with adults in a variety of contexts, including adult education programs. Level 3 would most appropriate within GED programs, and Levels 2 and 3 are likely appropriate in various technological education programs. ABLE could be used to help adults decide whether to pursue a GED.

The norms of the measure are adequate enough to permit a counselor to assess the academic skills of a student who is pondering assorted vocational possibilities. The measure is reasonably non-threatening and could be used, for example, with adults who have been out of the workforce but are considering rejoining. It also could be used in a variety of institutional education programs as well (such as in prisons) to help individuals decide their possible options once released.

A Handbook of Instructional Techniques and Materials (Karlsen & Gardner, 1986a) is available for teachers of classes of adult learners and is enhanced by a Reading Supplement (Karlsen & Gardner, 1986b). Both can be used in helping instructors to design instruction for the appropriate level and are available from the test publisher.

Technical Considerations

Norms. The norm sample was used to derive norms in terms of percentile ranks, stanines, and normal curve equivalents. The norming population for Levels 1 and 2 included adults in GED programs and adults in prison education programs whereas, at Level 3, it was comprised of adults in vocational/technical high school programs (Fitzpatrick, 1992). All populations were described in terms of their age, race, and geographical breakdowns. Grade equivalents are also available through analyses that linked scores on the ABLE with those of the Stanford Achievement Test series.

Reliability. The internal consistency reliability of the measures was evaluated using the standard Kuder-Richardson formulations, equivalent to coefficient alpha when items are scored as correct and incorrect as they are in ABLE. Subtest values range from the high .70s through the low .90s—in my opinion, these values are probably acceptable for the low stakes purposes for which it is used. One previous reviewer characterized these coefficients as approaching acceptable reliability (Williams, 1992). Some indication of temporal stability also would be useful.

Validity. Correlations between one of the experimental forms of the ABLE and a form of the Stanford Achievement Tests were respectable. The contents of the two tests do not overlap highly, however, and one concern might be that to some extent the measure assesses general developed mental ability (or intelligence) rather than educational attainments per se. This correlation is found, of course, in most or all tests of academic achievement. Also, the test is supported primarily by arguments of content validity. While the materials provided to me did not permit me to assess the content validity evidence, one can differentiate two aspects of content validation. It is clear that the items well represent the domains for which they were written, although one might assert, as has Fitzpatrick (1992), that the Level One Vocabulary subtest is really a test of "auditory comprehension." The authors of the test, Bjorn Karlsen and Eric Gardner, are both exceedingly well experienced in test construction. However, one might question the choice of some of the scales. Perhaps tests of spelling and vocabulary are not the best way to assess a person's verbal ability, especially with examinees who have been out of the educational process for some time or who have had little formal education. Moreover, vocabulary is a strong component/correlate of intelligence and may represent a sense that the test is measuring general developed mental ability as well as educational development. On the other hand, such scales may be less threatening for individuals lacking significant formal education than tests of critical reading or business writing.

Some evidence of fairness and appropriateness for use with ethnic minorities and individuals with disabilities would greatly enhance the value of the measure to counselors.

Overall Critique

The ABLE series is one of the better tests for use towards its intended purpose. A key component of score interpretation is based upon the last grade completed by individuals in the norming reference population (Fitzpatrick, 1992). The measure should probably be used in conjunction with a measure of interests, so that a counselor can assess not only one's educational attainments but also the nature of his or her interests. It should also be used with an interview, so that the counselor can determine just how much the individual has been using his or her academic skills. It is possible that a person who once succeeded adequately in school some time ago has let these skills lie fallow; perhaps in such circumstances, a brief refresher could enhance them substantially. Monsaas (2007) observed that validity evidence for the Tests of Adult Basic Education (TABE) scores matched General Educational Development (GED) Test performance better than the ABLE, making an argument for the TABE, a competitor battery.

The measurement of language use has moved beyond assessments of spelling and vocabulary, even though they are economical techniques for assessing verbal ability quickly. One problem is that vocabulary is so highly related to intelligence. Nevertheless, this measure has a satisfactory purpose, one that it meets at least adequately and perhaps substantially better than other less well constructed measures. Some mention of its use with language minorities and those with disabilities is needed, and neither such statements were provided. The measure appears professional, is attractive, and well made.

References

Fitzpatrick, A. R. (1992). Review of the Adult Basic Learning Examination, Second Edition. In J. J. Kramer & J. Close Conoley (Eds.), *The eleventh mental measurements yearbook* (pp. 19 – 21), Lincoln, NE: Buros Institute of Mental Measurements, The University of Nebraska.

Geisinger, K. F. (1998). Review of the Tests of Adult Basic Education Work-Related Foundation Skills. In J. C. Impara & B. S. Plake (Eds.), *The thirteenth mental measurements yearbook* (pp. 1086-1088), Lincoln, NE: Buros Institute of Mental Measurements, The University of Nebraska.

Karlsen, B. & Gardner, E. F. (1986a). *Handbook of instructional techniques and materials.* San Antonio, TX: Harcourt.

Karlsen, B. & Gardner, E. F. (1986b). *Reading supplement.* San Antonio, TX: Harcourt.

Monsaas, J. (2007). Review Tests of Adult Basic Education, Forms 9 & 10. In K. F. Geisinger, R. A. Spies, J. F. Carlson, & B. S. Plake (Eds.), *The seventeenth mental measurements yearbook,* Lincoln, NE: Buros Institute of Mental Measurements, The University of Nebraska.

Williams, R. T. (1992). Review of the Adult Basic Learning Examination, Second Edition. In J. J. Kramer & J. Close Conoley (Eds.), *The eleventh mental measurements yearbook* (pp. 21-23), Lincoln, NE: Buros Institute of Mental Measurements, The University of Nebraska.

Armed Services Vocational Aptitude Battery (ASVAB) Career Exploration Program (CEP)
U.S. Department of Defense
Personnel Testing Division

U.S. Department of Defense
Defense Manpower Data Center Monterey Bay
400 Gigling Road
Seaside, CA 93955
www.asvabprogram.com

Target Population: High school sophomores, juniors, seniors, and postsecondary students

Statement of the Purpose of the Instrument: The Armed Services Vocational Aptitude Battery Career Exploration Program (ASVAB CEP) is a comprehensive career exploration and planning program that includes a multiple-aptitude test battery, an interest inventory based on Holland's theory, and various career planning tools designed to help students learn about themselves and the world of work and gain confidence in making career decisions.

Titles of Subtests, Scales, Scores Provided: The ASVAB has eight subtests (General Science, Arithmetic Reasoning, Word Knowledge, Paragraph Comprehension, Mathematics Knowledge, Electronics Information, Mechanical Comprehension, and Auto and Shop Information) and three Career Exploration Score composites (Verbal Skills, Math Skills, and Science and Technical Skills). Military Entrance Scores (AFQT) are provided for students interested in the military. The Find Your Interests (FYI) inventory yields six RIASEC scores: Realistic, Investigative, Artistic, Social, Enterprising, and Conventional.

Forms and Levels Available with Dates of Publication/Revision of Each: ASVAB Forms 23/24, 2002; FYI, 2005

Date of Most Recent Edition of Test Manual, User's Guide, etc.:
Technical chapters are posted on the Program's web site as they are developed.
ASVAB Career Exploration Program Counselor Manual, 2005
ASVAB Career Exploration Program Overview Guide, 2005
Exploring Careers: The ASVAB Career Exploration Guide, 2008
Educator and counselor brochure, 2007
Student and parent brochure, 2007
Conducting ASVAB Interpretations: A Training DVD, 2006
ASVAB Career Exploration Program Discover Your Future 2-minute DVD for students, 2006
Military Careers, 2008

Languages in Which Available: English only.

Time: Total Administration Time ASVAB 3.5 hours, FYI 15 minutes

Norm Group(s) on Which Scores Are Based: ASVAB norms are based on the Profile of American Youth (PAY97) project by the U. S. Department of Defense and the U.S. Department of Labor. Two nationally representative samples were obtained. The norms for 10th, 11th, and 12th grade students are based on 4,700 youth who expected to be enrolled in grades 10, 11, and 12 as of the fall of 1997. The norms for post-secondary students are based on approximately 6,000 American youth age 18 – 23 as of June 1997.

FYI norms are based on the results of a national sample of 1,958 high school students from 19 high schools. The schools were randomly selected, and the resulting sample was weighted to be nationally representative.

Manner in Which Results Are Reported for Individuals:

Types of Scores: Students are provided with norm-based standard scores and percentile scores for the eight ASVAB subtests and three Exploration Score composites. Standard scores are provided based upon norms for the same grade, combined sex group. The same grade standard scores are also presented graphically with error bands to pictorially show strengths and weaknesses. Norm-based percentile scores are provided as follows: same grade/same sex, same grade/opposite sex, and same grade/combined sex.

The paper-and-pencil version of the FYI is self-scored. Students determine their top three RIASEC codes based on gender combined norms. An additional scoring step allows students to determine gender-based results.

Report Format/Content:

Basic Service: Two copies of the ASVAB Summary Results (ASR) are provided, one for the student and one for the counselor. The ASR reports scores, provides definitions of each scale and composite, and provides a brief summary of the meaning of the scores.

All participants receive a posttest interpretation from trained CEP personnel. During the interpretation, the ASVAB scores are explained; students have an opportunity to ask questions; students take and self-score the Find Your Interests (FYI) inventory; students learn about the role of work-related values , the OCCU-Find, and how to explore careers via the CEP website, www.asvabprogram.com. On the ASR, participants are provided with an access code to the website that will allow them access to take the FYI online and use an expanded OCCU-Find with links to the Occupational Outlook Handbook, O*NET, and www.careersinthemilitary.com. The students have access to this website for up to 2 years.

Options: Schools can elect to have students complete the interpretation session in a computer lab using their access codes from the ASR. This allows students to take the FYI electronically in approximately eight minutes. Students are presented with both combined group and gender specific RIASEC codes. The online OCCU-Find facilitates career exploration, providing students with immediate information on occupations of interest.

Report Format/Content for Group Summaries:

Basic Service: Counselors are provided with a copy of each student's ASVAB Summary Results sheet as well as a group summary.

Scoring:

Machine Scoring Service: There are no costs either to participating schools or students.

The maximum time required for scoring and returning is two weeks.

Hand Scoring: Hand scoring of the ASVAB is not available. Students can take the FYI inventory and self-score it or take it online and have it scored electronically.

Local Machine Scoring: Local machine scoring is not available.

Computer Options Available: Students can use both the FYI inventory and OCCU-Find online.

Ways in Which Computer/Online Version Differs: Students are provided with up to two years access to their personal page. They can retake the FYI up to two times and explore occupations electronically. Their personal page saves the results of the FYI.

Students are provided with three Career Exploration Composites: Verbal Skills, Math Skills, and Science and Technical Skills. A competency-based linkage was developed between the knowledge, skills, and abilities (KSAs) in O*NET occupations and the eight ASVAB subtests. In the online version, students can sort occupations based upon their top RIASEC codes and by Skill Importance Ratings.

Cost of Materials: All materials are provided free of charge.

Specimen Set: Sample CEP materials are available free of charge. The ASVAB is a secure test.

Counselee Materials: All materials are provided free of charge.

Published Reviews of the Instrument in the Last 15 Years:

Rogers, J. E. (2001). Armed Services Vocational Aptitude Batter Career Exploration Program (ASVAB). In J. T. Kapes, & E. A. Whitfield (Eds.), *A counselor's guide to career assessment instruments,* (4th ed., 95 – 101. Columbus, Ohio: National Career Development Association.

Reviewed by:

John Patrick
Associate Professor

Christopher W. Blosel
Christi L. Gross
Graduate Students

School Counseling Program
Counselor Education Department
California University of Pennsylvania

Description

The Armed Services Vocational Aptitude Battery Career Exploration Program (ASVAB CEP) is a comprehensive print and web-based career exploration and planning program that has been developed and maintained by the U.S. Department of Defense and is comprised of the ASVAB, which is a multiple aptitude test battery and an interest inventory, as well as other structured career-related activities designed to assist high school (Grades 10 – 12) and postsecondary students in exploring the world of work and making career decisions. The purpose of the ASVAB CEP is "to give students the opportunity to explore a variety of careers using knowledge they have gained about their interests and skills through assessment components and structured activities" (U.S. Department of Defense, 2005a, p. 1). Additionally, the ASVAB CEP is used by the United States military services to identify students who may qualify for entry into the military and the assignment of qualified individuals to specific military occupational training programs (U.S. Department of Defense, 1999). The results of the ASVAB CEP may facilitate students to evaluate their aptitudes and interests, explore occupations congruent with their interests and skills, and discern potential careers.

The ASVAB CEP has undergone extensive revisions since 2001 and is now comprised of the following components: (1) The ASVAB, a general multiple aptitude test battery; (2) The Find Your Interest (FYI) occupational interest inventory; (3) ASVAB Summary Results, a score report provided to students that describes their standard and percentile scores on individual ASVAB tests, Career Exploration Score composites, and military entrance score; (4) *Exploring Careers: The ASVAB Career Exploration Guide* designed to assist students in understanding and using their ASVAB scores with the OCCU-Find, a list of almost 500 occupations grouped by the six John Holland RIASEC interest areas; (5) www.asvabprogram.com, the program website that contains the online FYI and OCCU-Find and has links to the Occupational Outlook Handbook, O*NET Online, and www.careersinthemilitary.com; (6) *Military Careers,* a publication that offers a broad overview of career opportunities in the military; (7) www.careersinthemilitary. com, a website that provides extensive information on approximately 140 military occupations; (8) *My Educational and Career Plans,* an activity for students to assist them in making future educational and career plans; (9) *Coursework Planner,* a worksheet to help students plan remaining high school courses based on tentative career choices; and

(10) A *Program Benefits Video* that discusses why students should participate in the ASVAB Career Exploration Program (U.S. Department of Defense, 2005a). Additional career planning tools included with the ASVAB CEP are the *My Educational and Career Plans Summary Sheet,* which encourages students to explore occupations based on their interests, personal experiences, work values, and post–high school goals; *Coursework Planner,* an activity intended to assist students determine what high school courses they should take based on the requirements of occupations they are interested in; and Idea Sheets, activities that aid teachers and counselors integrate the ASVAB CEP into the classroom. The three primary components of the program that will be reviewed here include the ASVAB, FYI, and the OCCU-Find feature found on the program website (www.asvabprogram.com).

The ASVAB itself is recognized as one of the most widely used multiple aptitude test batteries in the world. The test (Forms 23 and 24) consists of 200 items, requires three hours to complete, and generally is administered as a paper and pencil test. A computerized version of the test battery (CAT-ASVAB) is now available for use in Military Entrance Processing Stations and is not available for distribution to schools over concern for test security (Sands, Waters, and McBride, 1997). The eight subtests are (1) *General Science* (GS/25 items), measuring knowledge of life science, earth science, and space science; (2) *Arithmetic Reasoning* (AR/30 items), measuring the ability to solve basic arithmetic word problems; (3) *Word Knowledge* (WK/35 items), measuring the ability to understand the meaning of words through synonyms; (4) *Paragraph Comprehension* (PC/15 items), measuring ability to obtain information through written material; (5) *Mathematics Knowledge* (MK/25 items), measuring knowledge of mathematical concepts and applications; (6) *Electronics Information* (EI/20 items), measuring knowledge of electrical current, circuits, devices, and electronic systems; (7) *Auto and Shop Information* (AS/25 items), measuring knowledge of automotive maintenance and repair, and wood and metal shop practices; and (8) *Mechanical Comprehension* (MC/25 items), measuring knowledge of the principles of mechanical devices, structural support, and properties of materials. The eight subtests are power tests that allow generous time limits to complete the test battery. In addition to the eight subtest scores, three *Career Exploration* composite scores are yielded. *Verbal Skills* is a general measure of vocabulary and reading skills covered in the WK and PC tests. *Math Skills* is a general measure of mathematical ability covered in the MK and AR test results. Similarly, *Science and Technical Skills* is a general measure of science and technical skills covered in the GS, EI, and MC subtests. A fourth composite score, the *Military Entrance Score* is derived from the AR, MK, PC, and WK subtests and is the score used in determining military career fields in which an individual may qualify. ASVAB results are reported both to students and counselors on the *ASVAB Summary Results* sheet. This report shows grade-specific, gender-specific, and combined standard scores and score bands for all eight subtests and the three Career Exploration Scores. It also provides students with percentile-based interpretations of those scores (U.S. Department of Defense, 2005a).

Find Your Interests (FYI) is an interest inventory based on John Holland's theory of career choice and can be taken on-line at www.asvabprogram.com or as a paper-and-pencil self-scoring version. The FYI assesses an individual's correspondence to each of the six RIASEC (Realistic, Investigative, Artistic, Social, Enterprising, and Conventional) types. The FYI consists of 90 items, usually requires about 15 minutes to complete, and employs a three-point scale of *Like* ("I would like to do this activity"), *Indifferent* ("I don't care one way or the other"), and *Dislike* ("I would not like to do this activity") with each item. In scoring the FYI, a *Like* receives a score of 2, an *Indifferent* is scored as a 1, and *Dislike* is assigned a 0. Raw scores range from 0 to 30, with higher scores reflecting higher interest in that domain (U.S. Department of Defense, 2005a).

The OCCU-Find feature found on the program website organizes close to 500 occupations by RIASEC interest codes so that individuals can rapidly discover occupations that match their own interests. Individuals are provided with occupational information derived from the Occupational Information Network (O*NET) database for each occupation selected. Links to the Occupational Outlook Handbook and www.careersinthemilitary.com also are given.

Use in Counseling

As the core component of the ASVAB CEP, the ASVAB continues to be used as the admissions and placement test for entering the Armed Services. However, its use has been expanded so that it can also be used as a career exploration and planning assessment tool for counseling students in the 10th grade and higher about military as well as civilian job and training opportunities (Erford, 2007). More specifically, the ASVAB CEP can be employed by counselors to aid high school and postsecondary students in learning more about themselves through interest and aptitude skills assessment (ASVAB and FYI) and explore occupations by engaging in specific structured career planning activities such as the OCCU-Find, *My Educational and Career Plans, and Coursework Planner.* A key feature of the ASVAB CEP is the ability to assist students in identifying high school courses that can increase their skills and readiness for future employment and postsecondary education. Additionally, school counselors may find the ASVAB CEP helpful when initiating career exploration and planning programs consistent with provisions of the "No Child Left Behind" Act.

The materials that comprise the ASVAB CEP are of exceptional professional quality. The test booklets, manuals, and other ASVAB publications are well-designed, easy to read, and attractive to the user (Rogers, 2001). *The ASVAB Career Exploration Program Counselor Manual* (U.S. Department of Defense, 2005a) provides school counselors with comprehensive information on program components, ASVAB and FYI test content, reliability, validity, and norms, as well as sections on ASVAB and FYI test administration and interpretation. *The ASVAB Career Exploration Program Overview Guide* (U.S. Department of Defense, 2005b) provides an overview of the ASVAB CEP and provides answers to the most frequently asked questions about the program. A practice test comprised of sample ASVAB test questions from each subtest is included in the program guide. Another publication, the *ASVAB Exploring Careers: The ASVAB Career Exploration Guide* (U.S. Department of Defense, 2008) assists students through the interpretation of their ASVAB and FYI scores and how to use the OCCU-Find to interpret their test results. Finally, the *ASVAB Technical Manual for the ASVAB 18/19 Career Exploration Program* (U.S. Department of Defense, 1999) provides comprehensive information on the validity, reliability, and normative data on various components of the ASVAB CEP. This manual is outdated and is in the process of being revised. The revision will be posted on the www.asvabprogram.com website upon release.

Students are provided with their ASVAB test results on the *ASVAB Summary Results Sheet*. This report shows grade-specific standard scores and score bands for all eight tests as well as the three Career Exploration Scores. Students also receive a Military Entrance Score that determines if they have met entrance requirements for military service (U.S. Department of Defense, 2005a). Counselors also receive a copy of the summary results for each student tested.

The ASVAB is administered by the U. S. Department of Defense or U.S. Office of Personnel Management employees so as to ensure test security. Test administration times and dates are usually arranged by making contact with a military recruiter or an Education Services Specialist at a local Military Entrance Processing Station. Schools are responsible for scheduling ASVAB test sessions, making necessary arrangements for proctors, and providing facilities for test administration (U.S. Department of Defense, 2005a).

It should be noted that ASVAB testing is exempt from the provisions of the Family Educational Rights and Privacy Act of 1974 and does not require a signed parental release statement (U.S. Department of Defense, 2005a). Participation by students remains voluntary. Also, school officials must inform the military prior to testing which of the eight options they select to provide ASVAB test results to military recruiters. Only options 7 and 8 forbid the release of ASVAB test results to military recruiters. This is perhaps the component of the ASVAB CEP that draws the most criticism and remains an impediment to wider civilian use of the ASVAB CEP. If schools make the decision to release test information to military personnel, then the testing data provided can be used by military recruiters to make contact with students in the 11th grade and higher. This may warrant unsolicited contact by military recruiters for some students.

Technical Considerations

The ASVAB is one of the most highly developed and researched aptitude test batteries of its kind (Jensen, 1988; Rogers, 2001). ASVAB Forms 23/24 were equated with ASVAB Form 8(a), thus ensuring that percentile scores on all test forms can be interpreted in the same way. Anchor norms for the current forms were derived from aptitude test data collected as part of the Profile of American Youth (PAY97) project. This large-scale research project was sponsored by the U.S. Department of Defense in cooperation with the U.S. Department of Labor to update current national norms for the ASVAB. The norming samples for the current forms of the ASVAB were drawn to be representative nationally of two groups of American youth. The first norming sample was comprised of approximately 6000 American youth age 18 to 23 as of June 1, 1997, with oversampling of Hispanic and Non-Hispanic Black youth. Norms for students in postsecondary schools (two-year colleges) were obtained from these data. The second norming sample was comprised of approximately 4700 youth who were matriculated in grades 10, 11, and 12 as of fall 1997. The norming samples were drawn based on a stratified clustered random sampling design and are considered generally representative of the U.S population for grades 10, 11, and 12 and postsecondary students (Sims & Hiatt, 2004).

Reliability estimates for the ASVAB are based on item response theory. The reliability estimates across grades for the ASVAB composite scores range from .88 to .91 while estimates for the eight individual tests range from .69 to .88. Since the ASVAB is primarily used by the military for the effective classification of recruits, numerous criterion-related studies have been conducted that indicate the ASVAB is a valid predictor of success in military training and entry-level job performance (Welsh, Kucinkas, & Curran, 1990). However, there have been only a few studies that have examined the criterion-related validity of the ASVAB in predicting success in civilian occupations (Holmgren & Dalldorf, 1993; Hunter, Crosson, & Freedman 1985). Holmgren and Dalldorf (1993) found significant correlations between ASVAB composite and individual test scores and measures of success with eight of eleven popular civilian occupations. Hunter (1983) noted that the General Aptitude Test Battery (GATB), a multiple aptitude test battery used by the U.S. Employment Service, is psychometrically equivalent to the ASVAB. Since the GATB has long been recognized in the literature as a predictor of job performance in the civilian sector, Hunter concluded that the ASVAB also predicts performance in civilian occupations. Since psychometrically equivalent tests share similar validity coefficients with external data, Hunter et al. (1985) determined that the ASVAB was a valid predictor of military and civilian job performance. Given the paucity of research as to the efficacy of using the ASVAB to predict civilian job performance, counselors should exercise some caution in using the ASVAB for this purpose. Additional studies are needed in order to make a conclusive determination if the ASVAB can be used alone as a predictor of success in civilian occupations. However, use of the ASVAB in conjunction with the FYI and other components of the ASVAB CEP are superior to use of the ASVAB alone in facilitating career exploration and planning of civilian occupations because it also incorporates interests and work values into the career exploration program. The ASVAB is considered to have sufficient content and construct validity by Welsh et al. (1990).

The other testing instrument included in the ASVAB CEP is the FYI. The FYI is based on John Holland's theory of career choice and assesses an individual's resemblance to each of the six RIASEC types. More than 1000 items were initially written and administered to more than 5,000 high school students in 48 randomly selected schools. The best performing 120 items were selected for further review in a second large scale study (N = 1,958) that was roughly equal in the number of males and females, exhibited ethnic diversity, and was weighted to be nationally representative, so as to identify the best 90 items that would comprise the final version of the FYI. The ASVAB Career Exploration Program Counselor Manual (U.S. Department of Defense, 2005a) indicates that the internal consistency of the six RIASEC scales as assessed by coefficient alpha ranged from .92 to .94. The manual also makes reference to additional evidence that was obtained from 259 students who took the FYI on two occasions over a two to two and one-half week period. Test-retest correlations ranged from .89 (Enterprising) to

.93 (Artistic) indicating stability of scores over time. Initial reliability studies of the FYI indicate that the inventory is reliable (U.S. Department of Defense, 2005a).

The U.S. Department of Defense (2005a) also reports that initial validity information for the FYI was obtained from two types of analysis: (1) FYI item and scale interval relationships, and (2) relationships between FYI scales and the various scales in the 1994 version of the Strong Interest Inventory. The results of these analyses indicate that the FYI has substantial evidence for the construct validity of the FYI at the item level. Multidimensional scaling techniques were used to assess the degree to which the FYI scales fit the RIASEC hexagonal pattern hypothesized by John Holland. This analysis indicated that the FYI had an excellent goodness of fit and exhibited the same type of hexagonal shape as other RIASEC based interest inventories. Other data presented in the ASVAB CEP counselor manual suggests that the FYI has content and criterion validity also.

Gender and diversity concerns have been raised with previous editions of the ASVAB and FYI. The test authors have taken considerable time and effort to update current national norms for the ASVAB so that individual scores are compared to a nationally representative sample of youth at their particular grade level (Sims & Hiatt, 2004). Complete information on the sex and racial/ethnic composition of the reference sample will be provided in the next revised technical manual for the ASVAB CEP. A primary issue with the ASVAB is how the test scores are used in predicting future educational and career outcomes. U. S. Department of Defense research personnel and civilian review panels have investigated the ASVAB thoroughly and have concluded that the test is as free of bias as possible (U.S. Department of Defense, 2005a). Wise, Welsh, Grafton, Foley, Earles, Sawin, and Divgi (1992) have concluded after the most recent wide-scale investigation of the ASVAB that the test is a sensitive predictor of training and performance for all applicant groups. According to the ASVAB CEP Counselor Manual (U.S. Department of Defense, 2005a) a variety of statistical decision rules and statistical analyses were employed to help select items for the FYI that minimized gender differences and did not favor one applicant group from another.

Overall Critique

As the ASVAB CEP continues to evolve, the ease of use of this career exploration and planning program, as well as its relevance to the field of counseling, continues to grow. We agree with Rogers (2001) that the materials comprising the ASVAB CEP are of excellent quality, and include visually appealing test booklets, a logical approach to design and layout, and text that are readable for the test taker. The ASVAB CEP has also been enhanced with the recent revisions to the ASVAB and FYI that appear to have reduced gender and diversity bias to the extent possible. Both the ASVAB and FYI represent the state of the art in test construction. The ASVAB functions exceptionally well as the admissions and placement examination for the armed services, but its predictive validity when applied to civilian occupations is questionable. This can be attributed to the paucity of research examining how predictive the ASVAB is to job performance among civilian occupations. It is hoped that this can be addressed in the near future with further research.

The ASVAB Career Exploration Program also provides an exceptionally professional comprehensive website (www.asvabprogram.com) well designed for use by both students and counselors. Along with general program information, the site includes assessments that students can use to identify strengths, work values, and vocational interests, as well as structured activities to explore nearly 500 occupations. The website also offers the OCCU-Find to assist students with researching the educational and skill requirements, projected outlook, and expected salary range for specific occupations. Additionally, the site provides helpful information for interested educators, counselors, and parents. The website is easily navigable and very informative, and serves to enhance the overall ease of use and relevance of the ASVAB CEP. The ASVAB CEP is a good choice for aptitude and interest assessment as well as for career exploration and planning by its intended audience.

References

Erford, B. T. (2007). *Assessment for counselors.* New York: Lahaska Press.

Holmgren, R. L., & Dalldorf, M.R. (1993 October). *A validation of the ASVAB against supervisors' ratings in the General Aptitude Test Battery (GATB).* Washington, DC: United States Employment Service.

Hunter, J. E. (1983). *The prediction of success in the military: A preliminary report.* Rockville, MD: Research Applications.

Hunter, J. E., Crosson, J. S., & Friedman, D. H. (1985). *The validity of the Armed Services Vocational Aptitude Battery (ASVAB) for civilian and military job performance.* Washington, DC: Office of the Assistant Secretary of Defense (Force Management and Personnel).

Jensen, A. R., (1988). Review of the Armed Services Vocational Aptitude Battery. In J.T, Kapes & M. M. Mastie (Eds.) *A counselor's guide to career assessment instruments* (2nd ed., pp. 59 – 62). Alexandria, VA: National Career Development Association.

Rogers, J. E. (2001). Review of Armed Services Vocational Aptitude Battery (ASVAB) Career Exploration Program. In J. T. Kapes & E. A. Whitfield (Eds.), *A counselor's guide to career assessment instruments* (4th ed., pp. 93 – 101). Columbus, OH: National Career Development Association.

Sands, W. A., Waters, B. K., & McBride, J. R. (Eds.) (1997). *Adaptive testing: Inquiry to operation.* Washington, DC: American Psychological Association.

Sims, W. H. & Hiatt, C. M. (2004). *Description of student testing program norms.* Alexandria, VA: The CNA Corporation.

U.S. Department of Defense, (2005a). *ASVAB career exploration program counselor manual* (DD Form 1304-SCM). Seaside, CA: Defense Manpower Data Center.

U.S. Department of Defense, (2005b). *ASVAB career exploration program overview guide* (DD Form 1304-5OV). Seaside, CA: Defense Manpower Data Center.

U.S. Department of Defense, (2008). *ASVAB exploring careers: The ASVAB career exploration guide* (DD Form 1304-5WB). Seaside, CA: Defense Manpower Data Center.

U.S. Department of Defense, (1999). *Technical manual for the ASVAB 18/19 career exploration program.* Seaside, CA: Defense Manpower Data Center.

Welsh, J. R., Kucinkas, S. K., & Curran, L. T. (1990). *Armed Services Vocational Aptitude Battery (ASVAB): Integrative review of validity studies* (AFHRL-TR-90-22). Brooks Air Force Base, TX: Air Force Human Resources Laboratory.

Wise, L., Welsh, J., Grafton, F., Foley, P., Earles, J., Sawin, L., & Divgi, D.R. (1992). *Sensitivity and fairness of the Armed Services Vocational Aptitude Battery (ASVAB) technical composites* (DMDC Technical Report 92-002). Monterey, CA: Defense Manpower Data Center.

CAREER PLANNING SURVEY
ACT, Inc.

ACT
500 ACT Drive
P.O. Box 168
Iowa City, IA 52243-0168
www.act.org

Target Population: Grades 8 – 10

Statement of the Purpose of the Instrument: The Career Planning Survey is a comprehensive guidance-oriented career assessment system designed to help students in grades 8 through 10 identify and explore personally relevant occupations and high school courses.

To provide students with a general sense of direction for career exploration, the Career Planning Survey uses the World-of-Work Map (WWM). The WWM provides both a visual overview of the work world as well as specific career areas for exploration.

Titles of Subtests, Scales, Scores Provided: The assessment components consist of an interest inventory (the ACT Interest Inventory; UNIACT), an inventory of ability self-estimates (the Inventory of Work-Relevant Abilities; IWRA), and two optional academic ability tests (Reading Skills and Numerical Skills).

UNIACT and IWRA

- *Scales:* Administration & Sales; Business Operations; Technical; Science & Technology; Arts; Social Service
- *Scores Provided:* stanines, score ranks, and WWM regions

ABILITY TESTS

- *Scales:* Reading Skills; Numerical Skills
  Scores Provided: Ability "label" based on percentile scores (labels are upper 10%, upper 25%, middle 50%, lower 25%, and lower 10%).
- *Scale:* Reading + Numerical Composite
  Scores Provided: standard (T) score and percentile score band.

Forms and Levels Available, with Dates of Publication/Revision of Each: Single form, first published in 1997. There have been periodic updates of accompanying materials (student guidebook, etc.)

Date of Most Recent Edition of Test Manual, User's Guide, etc. Student Guidebook: 2007 Assessment Booklet: 2001; Counselor's Manual: 2001; Technical Manual: 2001

Languages in Which Available: English only.

Time:

The Career Planning Survey can be completed with or without optional Ability Tests.

Actual Test Time Without Optional Tests: 23 minutes

Actual Test Time of Optional Tests: 30 minutes

Total Administration Time Without Optional Tests: 44 minutes

Total Administration Time with Optional Tests: 90 minutes

Norm Group(s) on Which Scores Are Based: For UNIACT, nationally representative samples of 13,400 8th, 10th and 12th graders. For IWRA and the ability tests, nationally representative samples of 16,300 8th and 10th graders.

Manner in Which Results Are Reported for Individuals:

Types of Scores: For UNIACT and IWRA: Stanines, score ranks, and WWM regions. For Ability Tests: Ability "label" based on percentile scores (labels are upper 10%, upper 25%, middle 50%, lower 25%, and lower 10%). For Reading + Numerical Composite: standard (T) score and percentile score band.

Report Format/Content:

BASIC SERVICE: Two copies of the Student Score Report, including color highlighting of the student's World-of-Work Map regions based on assessment results.

OPTIONS: Score Report Labels and additional copies of the Student Score Reports.

Report Format/Content for Group Summaries:

Basic Service: None.

Options: The following are available for single schools or multiple schools in combination: Group Summary Reports, data CD-ROM, data diskette. Student List Reports are available for single schools.

Scoring:

Machine Scoring Service:

COST OF BASIC SERVICE PER COUNSELEE:

Student Assessment Sets (answer sheet, a student guidebook, and two copies of the Student Report) include prepaid scoring:

Student Assessment Set Option A (with Ability Tests): $4.45

Student Assessment Set Option B (without Ability Tests): $3.80

Volume discounts available.

Cost of Options:

Score Report Labels (2 copies): $0.31 per student

Student List Reports: $0.16 per student

Summary Report (single school): $31.00

Summary Report (multiple schools): $42.00

Data Diskette (single school): $31.00

Data Diskette (multiple schools): $42.00

CD-ROM (single school): $31.00

CD-ROM (multiple schools): $42.00

Time required for scoring and returning (maximum): 2 weeks

Hand Scoring: Not available.

Local Machine Scoring: Not available.

Computer Software Options Available: Not available

Cost of Materials: Due to possible price changes since publication date, be sure to check with publisher web site

Specimen Set: $13.50

Counselee Materials: (Itemize and indicate what is reusable)

Student Assessment Sets include answer sheet (scored by ACT), a student guidebook, prepaid scoring, and two copies of the Student Report.

Student Assessment Set Option A (with Ability Tests): $4.45
Student Assessment Set Option B (without Ability Tests): $3.80

Reusable Test Booklets: $0.80.

Additional Comments of Interest to Users: New in 2007, students can do career exploration on the web at the Career Planning Survey website. Up-to-date information is available on hundreds of occupations, all organized to work seamlessly with the Career Planning Survey Student Report and guidebook.

Published Reviews of the Instrument in the Last 15 Years

Lowe, S. A. (2003). Review of the Career Planning Survey. In B.S. Plake, J.C. Impara, & R.A. Spies, (Eds.), *The fifteenth mental measurements yearbook.* Lincoln, NE: Buros Institute of Mental Measurements.

Reardon, R. C., & Vernick, S. H. (2001). Career Planning Survey. In J.T. Kapes, & E.A. Whitfield, (Eds.), *A counselor's guide to career assessment instruments* (4th ed., pp. 110 – 115). Columbus, OH: National Career Development Association.

Reviewed by:

Margaret M. Nauta
Associate Professor
Department of Psychology
Illinois State University

Description

The Career Planning Survey (CPS) (ACT, 2001a) is a multi-faceted assessment package that is intended to facilitate early high school (grades 8 – 10) students' exploration of educational and occupational fields. It comprises three instruments: The Unisex Edition of the ACT Interest Inventory (UNIACT) (Swaney, 1995), the Inventory of Work-Relevant Abilities (IWRA) (ACT, 2001a), and an optional set of academic ability tests. The CPS instruments have been available through other ACT packages for several years. The current versions of the UNIACT and IWRA were each most recently updated in 1989, and the ability tests were updated in 1997. The CPS, first introduced in

1998, replaced two earlier ACT programs, the Career Planning Program and the Career Survey.

The three CPS instruments are administered together via a 16-page booklet with a separate answer sheet that is sent to the publisher for computer scoring. The CPS can be administered in about 45 minutes when only the UNIACT and IWRA portions are used and in 90 minutes if the optional ability tests are used.

The UNIACT assesses interests with respect to each of six Career Clusters (Administration & Sales, Business Operations, Technical, Science & Technology, Arts, Social Service) that parallel Holland's (1997) six RIASEC types. The items emphasize activities (e.g., conduct a meeting) that are familiar to high school students. Students rate their interest for each of the 90 items using a three-choice response format (dislike, indifferent, like).

The IWRA assesses self-estimates of 15 abilities. Some of the ability areas assessed by the IWRA (e.g., manual dexterity) can be assessed objectively, but many (e.g., helping others) are not included in standard objective ability batteries. Like the UNIACT items, the IWRA items comprise activities that are familiar to students. For instance, when asked to rate their "meeting people" abilities, students are provided with example activities including talking with people, getting along with others, and making a good impression. For each item, students use a five-point scale to rate their ability as high [top 10%], above average [upper 25%], average [middle 50%], below average [lower 25%], or low [bottom 10%] when compared to others their age. The IWRA abilities are grouped into six Career Clusters that mirror those on the UNIACT.

The final CPS component, the Reading and Numerical Skills ability tests, is optional. These ability areas were chosen because they are important in all occupations (ACT, 2001a). The 32-item Reading Skills test assesses reading comprehension and the ability to make inferences and draw conclusions. The 24-item Numerical Skills test primarily assesses basic arithmetic operations (e.g., addition, division), with a smaller number of items assessing more complex skills requiring the understanding of ratios and averages. Unlike the UNIACT and IWRA, the ability tests are administered under timed conditions.

After the publisher scores students' responses, a two-page CPS Report is provided along with a 24-page *Career Planning Guide* (ACT, 2007) designed to facilitate students' exploration of occupations and fields of study. The CPS Report links students' UNIACT and IWRA scores to each other and to occupational options using a graphic tool called the World-of-Work Map (WWM), an empirically based extension of Holland's (1997) hexagon that organizes occupations into 12 regions based on similarity of basic work tasks (working with data, ideas, things, people). The CPS Report shows the three map regions that correspond most closely to the student's interests and the three that correspond to the student's highest ability self-estimates. On the back of the report, students' UNIACT and IWRA results appear as ranks and stanine scores. The Reading and Numerical Skills test results are norm based and reported in the form of labels (e.g., Upper 10%, Lower 25%, etc.) comparing the student's performance to that of a same-grade norm sample. An ability test composite score is also reported along with a percentile rank band based on a comparison to the national norm group. A variety of group summary reports are available for counselors, teachers, or school administrators.

Use in Counseling

The CPS is intended for use with students who are in the early stages of career planning. The goal is to help students consider and seek information about occupations that are consistent with their interests and self-rated abilities so that they can begin to formulate career goals and choose appropriate high school classes. Although the CPS could be used in individual counseling, it was designed for group administration and interpretations, making it appealing for use in classrooms.

The *Counselor's Manual* (ACT, 2001b) indicates that the ability tests may help school professionals identify students who need remedial training. Another possible use is as a tool for encouraging students to examine the accuracy of two of their ability self-estimates. If there are wide discrepancies between students' ability self-estimates and their ability test scores, counseling could be used to explore reasons for the discrepancy and, if necessary, challenge students to appraise their skills realistically.

Technical Considerations

As described in the *Technical Manual* (ACT, 2001a), the CPS norms are based on large, nationwide samples of 8th-, 10th-, and 12th-graders. The UNIACT and 12th-grade IWRA norming data were derived from more than 13,000 students between 1992-1994. The IWRA 8th- and 10th-grade norms and the ability test norming data were collected in 1997 from more than 16,000 students. The 9th-grade ability test norms were established by interpolation. The norm samples were generally representative of the U.S. population for gender and race (ACT, 2001a).

The *Technical Manual* provides detailed information about the UNIACT and IWRA scores' reliability and validity; much less attention is devoted to the ability tests' validity. A portion of the psychometric research is based on earlier versions of the instruments. Because there is considerable overlap between the earlier and current versions, extending the earlier findings to the current instruments is reasonable, but test users should use some caution when making assumptions about the generalizability of these findings to student groups who are administered the current versions of the CPS instruments.

UNIACT scores' internal consistency estimates ranged from .85 to .92 among the norm sample (ACT, 2001a). Test-retest coefficients obtained from a smaller sample of students over an average five-month time period ranged from .68 to .82. Convergent and discriminant validity are supported by Career Cluster scale score intercorrelations that are consistent with Holland's (1997) hexagonal structure of interests. Factor analyses have supported the structural validity of the UNIACT scales, and the scale scores correlate in expected ways with scores on other interest inventories. Finally, the UNIACT scores' criterion-related validity is supported by expected interests among individuals in various criterion groups (e.g., predominant Scientific interests among biology majors).

Internal consistency is not estimated for the IWRA because it was not designed to have item homogeneity. The Technical Manual does report 1 – 2 week test-retest reliability coefficients ranging from .69 to .78 for the IWRA Career Cluster scores based on a sample of approximately 1,000 students. The IWRA's construct validity has been supported by factor analyses that revealed a good fit between the IWRA's factor structure and the data/ideas, things/people dimensions that are used to place the abilities on the WWM. The Career Cluster factor structure has also been supported. Finally, the IWRA's criterion-related validity is supported by expected Career Cluster ability self-estimate scores among particular criterion groups (e.g., predominant Scientific ability self-estimates among students who aspire to science careers).

Internal consistency estimates for the ability tests, based on the norm samples, ranged from .80 to .88. Data regarding the ability tests' validity are not reported in the CPS *Technical Manual.* The development of the ability tests did involve extensive input from high school teachers and other content experts, suggesting that the tests have good content validity.

The CPS Technical Manual reports information and data suggesting that the CPS instruments have similar structures across race and gender groups.

Computer-Based and/or Online Versions(s)

The CPS is only available as a paper-and-pencil inventory, but once students receive their CPS Score Reports, they may visit ACT's CPS website (http://www.act.org/cps). The website, which was implemented in 2007, contains an interactive WWM, like that on the CPS Report, that allows students to find up-to-date information about hundreds of occupations.

Overall Critique

The CPS has been developed and revised based on sound theory and empirical findings and with input from content experts. The coordinated assessment of interests and ability self-estimates allows students to identify occupations for further exploration based on constructs that are theoretically central to career decision making. The CPS instruments are brief and can be split over multiple administrations (ACT, 2001c), which makes them convenient for use within the usual school schedule.

The items comprising the CPS are developmentally appropriate, allowing students to answer them in an informed way. This makes the CPS preferable to instruments that assess interests and ability self-estimates based on occupational titles, which may be difficult for students to rate because of their limited experiences (ACT, 2001a). The manner in which scores are reported is also developmentally appropriate. Stanine scores and ranks encourage students to think about their relative interests and ability self-estimates without over-interpreting small differences.

A key strength of the CPS, as noted in earlier reviews (Loew, 2003; Reardon & Vernick, 2001), is its high-quality ancillary materials. The *Technical Manual* (ACT, 2001a) is clearly written and thorough. The *Counselor's Manual* (ACT, 2001b) and *Directions for Administration* guide (ACT, 2001c) allow new users to administer and interpret the instruments responsibly. The CPS *Career Planning Guide* (ACT, 2007) and website promote the meaningful use of CPS scores by linking them to curriculum choices and occupational information.

As noted in a review of an earlier CPS version (Loew, 2003), the optional ability tests probably have fairly limited practical value. More detailed achievement estimates are available from other instruments. Moreover, little attention to the ability tests is given in Counselor's Manual, and the ability scores are not integrated into the student's Career Planning Guide; thus, students may not benefit from the ability test information unless a counselor works individually with them to examine the relationships between the ability test scores and IWRA and UNIACT scores.

Users should keep in mind that there will be at least a two-week delay between the administration and interpretation of CPS scores because answer sheets must be sent for computer scoring. If it is desirable for scores to be immediately available, an online program, such as DISCOVER (ACT, 1995), which includes the UNIACT and IWRA, may be preferable.

References

ACT (1995). DISCOVER for colleges and adults: Professional manual. Hunt Valley, MD: Author.

ACT (2001a). *Career Planning Survey: Technical manual.* Iowa City, IA: Author.

ACT (2001b). *Career Planning Survey: Counselor's manual.* Iowa City, IA: Author.

ACT (2001c). *Career Planning Survey: Directions for administration.* Iowa City, IA: Author.

ACT (2007). *Career Planning Survey: Career planning guide.* Iowa City, IA: Author.

Holland, J. L. (1997). *Making vocational choices* (3rd ed.). Odessa, FL: Psychological Assessment Resources, Inc.

Loew, S. A. (2003). Review of the Career Planning Survey. In B. S. Plake, J. C., Impara, & R. A. Spies (Eds.), *The fifteenth mental measurements yearbook* [Electronic version]. Retrieved April 11, 2007 from EBSCOHost Mental Measurements Yearbook database, http://web.ebscohost.com/

Reardon, R. C., & Vernick, S. H. (2001). Career Planning Survey (CPS). In J. T. Kapes & E. A. Whitfield (Eds.), *A counselor's guide to career assessment instruments* (4th ed., pp. 110 – 115). Columbus, OH: National Career Development Association.

Swaney, K. B. (1995). *Technical manual: Revised Unisex edition of the ACT Interest Inventory (UNIACT).* Iowa City, IA: ACT, Inc.

CAREERSCOPE® CAREER ASSESSMENT & REPORTING SYSTEM (CAREERSCOPE®)

Vocational Research Institute

Vocational Research Institute

1528 Walnut Street, Suite 1502
Philadelphia, PA 19102
info@vri.org
www.vri.org

Target Population: Adolescents and adults reading at or above the 4th grade level and able to use a computer.

Statement of the Purpose of the Instrument: Establish career interest and aptitude score profiles and occupational clusters in which the consumer can experience work activity satisfaction and probable success in occupational training.

Titles of Subtests, Scales, Scores Provided:

CareerScope Interest Inventory

CareerScope Aptitude Battery: General Learning Ability, Verbal Aptitude, Numerical Aptitude, Spatial Aptitudes, Form Perception, Clerical Perception.

Forms and Levels Available, with Dates of Publication/Revision of Each: CareerScope version 8.0, copyright 2007.

Date of Most Recent Edition of Test Manual, User's Guide: CareerScope User Guide version 8.0, copyright 2007.

Languages in Which Available: English and Spanish.

Time:

Actual Test Time: Interest Inventory: Untimed (typically 15 minutes); Aptitude Battery—25 minutes.

Total Administration Time: 45 – 60 minutes.

Norm Group(s) on Which Scores Are Based: Please review VRI Research Briefs (referenced) for details. Interest Inventory: 18 years of age or older (separate norms also reported by gender). Aptitudes: 9th grade v. 10th grade v. adult.

Manner in Which Results Are Reported for Individuals:

Types of Scores:

INTEREST INVENTORY—Scale percentile ranks as compared to total age appropriate norm group and as graphically displayed and statistically analyzed as standardized idiographic 12-scale profile. APTITUDE BATTERY—Reported as standardized scores (mean = 100, sd = 20), as numerical percentile ranks and as a composite profile histogram display.

Report Format/Content:

BASIC SERVICE: The consumer's Assessment Profile includes interest and aptitude score tables and graphic displays, with supporting narrative text, and career cluster recommendations (with descriptions of general work activities). The Counselor Report presents raw scores, corresponding percentile and standardized scores and viable career clusters in a concise tabular format. The Summary Report provides a one-page graphical overview of Interest Results, Aptitude Results, and Work Group Recommendations.

OPTIONS: Assessment Profile career recommendations can be founded upon the synthesis of interest and aptitude results; career recommendations can be presented in formats consistent with GOE/DOT, O*NET, or U.S. Department of Education's Career Cluster/Pathway system; illustrative high-growth/high – replacement-rate occupations can be included/excluded.

Report Format/Content for Group Summaries:

Basic Service: The Career Scope Management System supports local configurations and generation of group summary reports that identify examinees with specific score or recommendation outcomes.

Scoring:

Machine Scoring Service: Not available.

CareerScope assessment software is self-scoring. The license owner generates reports on a local/network printer.

Hand Scoring: Not available.

Local Machine Scoring: Not available.

Computer Software Options Available:

CareerScope with Audio includes a voice that slowly reads the Login, Orientation, Instructions, and Practice Items, as well as the Interest Inventory Items. (Additional cost)

CareerScope English w/Spanish presents the Interest Inventory, Numerical Reasoning, and Word Meanings items in Spanish. (Additional cost)

For evaluees with reading difficulties, Numerical Reasoning and Word Meanings can be administered as *untimed assessments,* providing as much time as needed to finish the two tasks that emphasize reading comprehension. (No additional cost)

Cost of Materials: Due to possible price changes since publication date, be sure to check with the publisher website.

Specimen Set: Two pricing plans are available, the Licensed Plan and the Metered Plan.

Licensed Plan: A single-user license of CareerScope costs $3,000. This license entitles the user to administer the assessment to an unlimited number of evaluees *on a single computer.* Multiple workstation and site licenses are also available; volume purchase discounts start with the second license.

Metered Plan: The CareerScope Metered Plan is a "pay by the administration" plan that allows users to use CareerScope on an unlimited number of computers at a single address. The initial software license costs $500 (one-time cost), plus the cost of administrations (ranging from $5 to $14 per administration, depending on quantity purchased).

Two additional-cost options are available. The *Audio* option includes a friendly voice that slowly reads the Login, Orientation, Instructions, and Practice Items, as well as the Interest Inventory Items. This option costs $495 for a single workstation or $1295 for use on unlimited workstations at a single site. The *English w/Spanish* option presents the Interest Inventory, Numerical Reasoning and Word Meanings items in Spanish. This option costs $795 for a single workstation or $1995 for use on unlimited workstations at a single site.

A five-administration evaluation copy of CareerScope is available at no cost (as a "specimen set") to those qualified, interested professionals looking to evaluate CareerScope in order to make a purchase decision. The request must come in writing, on official letterhead, and be approved by VRI's local representative.

Counselee Materials: All assessment questions are administered on the computer workstation, and evaluee responses are automatically stored on the computer. Therefore, no consumable test forms or answer sheets are necessary. The only additional materials required are scratch paper and pencil, which should be provided to each evaluee for completion of tasks involving numerical operations.

Additional Comments of Interest to Users: CareerScope operates on Windows networks and workstations. Program updates/upgrades, with enhanced feature sets and/or revised scoring algorithms, are typically scheduled for annual release.

Published Reviews of the Instrument in the Last 15 Years:

Brown, C. D. (2001). Review of CareerScope® Career Assessment and Reporting System. In J. T. Kapes & E. A. Whitfield (Ed.), *A Counselor's Guide to Career Assessment Instruments*, (4th ed.). Columbus, OH: National Career Development Association.

Lustig, D., Brown, C., & Lott, A. (1998). Reliability of the CareerScope Career Assessment and Reporting System. *Vocational Evaluation and Work Adjustment Journal*, 31, 19 – 21.

Lustig, D., Brown, C., & Lott, A. & Larkin, V. (1998). Concurrent validity of the CareerScope Career Assessment and Reporting System. *Vocational Evaluation and Work Adjustment Journal*, 31, 28 – 31.

Reviewed by:

Mary Boylan
Rehabilitation Psychologist
National Learning Network,
Cork, Ireland

Description

The CareerScope: Career Assessment and Reporting System was first implemented by the Vocational Research Institute (VRI) in 1997. The Vocational Research Institute conducted annual revisions with Version 8 released in 2007. The goal of CareerScope is to assist individuals and/or counselors to focus on matching appropriate career interests with career aptitudes. CareerScope is comprised of the CareerScope Interest Inventory and the CareerScope Aptitude Battery. Twelve interest areas are structured around the U.S. Department of Labor categories: Artistic, Business Detail, Scientific, Selling, Plants/Animals, Accommodating, Protective, Humanitarian, Mechanical, Lead/Influence, Industrial, and Physical Performing. Similarly the aptitudes are correlated with those identified by the Department of Labor in their General Aptitude Test Battery (GATB) (Vocational Research Institute, 2007) and include: General Learning Ability, Verbal Aptitude, Numerical Aptitude, Spatial Aptitude, Form Perception, and Clerical Perception.

The CareerScope is a self-administered assessment that takes approximately one hour. Completing the CareerScope Interest Inventory requires 15 minutes on average. It is a series of statements about tasks from various occupations. Participants are asked to respond to the statements as quickly possible indicating their like for, dislike of, or lack of knowledge about the task. The CareerScope Aptitude Battery consists of seven separate tasks in the following areas: object identification, abstract shape matching, clerical matching, pattern visualization, computation, numerical reasoning, and word meanings. Each task is timed and takes from one to seven minutes. Between each task, a 90 second break is available.

CareerScope includes three reports: 1) the Assessment Profile, 2) the Counselor Report, and 3) the Summary Report.

1) The Assessment Profile is made up of three parts. The first part presents the evaluee's Interest Results in both tabular form and graphic display, including the VRI-developed Individual Profile Analysis. Part two of the Assessment Profile graphically reports and displays the evaluee's Aptitude Results as standard scores and as percentile scores. Part three of the Assessment Profile provides Recommendations based upon the overlap of the evaluee's high interest and high ability areas. These recommendations can be presented in three formats: GOE/DOT, O*NET, or U.S. Department of Education's Career Cluster/Pathway system.

2) The three-page Counselor Report provides the counselor with a quick overview of pertinent assessment information in tabular format.

3) The one-page Summary Report is a graphical overview of assessment information, and is available in two formats: GOE/DOT and U.S. Department of Education's Career Cluster/Pathway system.

Use in Counseling

Career counseling has a major role to play in high-school and postsecondary educational settings as well as in industry. It can provide a focus relatively early in the process of career exploration. CareerScope can significantly assist counselors in creating accurate profiles of students and their interests and aptitudes, and thus be better able to direct them to relevant courses, colleges, and career options. Because CareerScope is computer based, self-administered, and can be networked (i.e. conducted at various stations in a computer laboratory setting), it also can assist counselors in doing career exploration with groups of students as well as with students individually. Similarly, CareerScope can assist college counselors in helping students to explore relevant or appropriate first jobs, as indicated by their aptitudes and interests scores. It is important that the counselor help individuals in understanding and using the pertinent information from their reports. Counselors should be very familiar with the instrument, its purpose and the information it provides.

CareerScope also can be used by career counselors in private practice or those hired by organizations.. It can assist people to think about options. It is common for individuals to change careers and jobs regularly. Many individuals seek career counselors to assist with such transitions. The purpose of this particular counseling relationship is to pursue career goals and clarification. The CareerScope can be a valuable tool for individuals to assess interests and aptitudes in preparation for a career change. Similarly, the CareerScope has potential utility when exploring job or career opportunity within a company or organization. It is this variety of recommendation formats that sets CareerScope apart and makes it useful in a variety of settings (such as education, workforce development, and vocational rehabilitation) and in developing resources such as career development portfolios, Individualized Educational Plans (IEP), transition plans, employee training plans, and employment retention plans.

Other CareerScope options include: Audio (a voice slowly reading login, orientation, instructions, practice items and Interest Inventory item), English with Spanish (includes the Interest Inventory, Numerical Reasoning and Word meanings in Spanish), and untimed assessments (providing enough time as needed to finish the reading comprehension tasks). These accommodations allow CareerScope to be used with individuals with special needs.

Technical Considerations

CareerScope is normed on both adolescents and adults. The adolescent norm is based on a national sample with an average age of 16.6 years and mean educational level of 10.4 (Brown, 2001). The adult norm is also based on a national sample with an average age of 28.1 years and mean educational level of 11.9 years (Brown, 2001).

The concurrent validity of CareerScope's aptitude battery was examined in 1998 by utilizing 115 employees of the Philadelphia Jewish Employment and Vocational Service (JEVS) (Vocational Research Institute, 2006a). Participants ranged in age from 18 to 65 years and 74% were female with 79% Caucasian. All participants were administered the CareerScope and the General Aptitude Test Battery (GATB) developed by the Department of Labor (Vocational Research Institute, 2007). Correlations were computed between the scores of the CareerScope aptitude tests and the GATB tests. The correlations were found to be at least moderate ranging from a high of .80 to a low of .52 (Vocational Research Institute, 2006a).

The retest reliability of CareerScope's aptitude battery was examined in 1998 (Vocational Research Institute, 2006b). The participants were 307 Louisiana seventh through twelfth graders, of which 57% were females and 75% were Caucasian. The ages ranged from 12 to 18, with an average of 14.6. Students completed two administrations of the CareerScope with a gap of 25 – 40 days between administrations. Results indicated that the aptitude battery is a reliable measure for secondary students with reliability measures ranging from .80 to .70 (Vocational Research Institute, 2006b).

The same sample was used to examine the retest reliability of the CareerScope Interest Inventory Scales (Vocational Research Institute, 2006c). With retest reliabilities ranging from .73 to .87, it was suggested the interest inventory tests were reliable measures for secondary school students (Vocational Research Institute, 2006c).

The internal consistency of the CareerScope Interest Inventory Scales was examined with the 115 employees of the Philadelphia JEVS. The coefficient alpha was computed for each of the twelve scales and ranged from .81 to .91. These findings suggested good internal consistency among the scales (Vocational Research Institute, 2006d).

Computer-Based Version

CareerScope 8.0 requires a computer to have Microsoft Windows 2000 or above. It also requires approximately 300 MB of free hard-drive space with 256 MB of available physical memory (Vocational Research Institute, 2007). CareerScope can be installed on one computer or can be installed as part of a shared network (Vocational Research Institute, 2007).

This version of CareerScope provides an introduction to the program, including its history, uses, and requirements. It provides an interactive session with the mouse for people who may not be familiar with a computer. The interest inventory and aptitude battery are very well explained, and adequate practice is provided before a participant is asked to complete any task. The instructions are clearly stated or presented and easy to follow. The graphics and use of color contribute to the ease with which this product can be used. The three reports generated at the end of the assessment can be saved as PDF, Word, or Rich Text Files.

Overall Critique

A major strength of the CareerScope is that it combines individuals" interests with their aptitudes in one assessment period and produces one report. Individuals can infer from this information their career path possibilities. An individual can also be assisted by a counselor in accessing and understanding the appropriate information and options. Prior to CareerScope, individuals completed interest inventories and aptitude tests separately. They may have completed one or other or both. The interpretation of the results of these inventories and tests was solely in the hands of the counselor.

The reading ability needed for the CareerScope is at the fourth-grade level. The requisite computer skills are not difficult and can be easily acquired. Thus the assessment is accessible to a large number of people. Despite the required reading ability for the test, the reports generated by CareerScope are quite detailed, and how they relate to career groups could be a little difficult. To understand without some assistance. CareerScope is a computer-based assessment thus it cannot accurately test for an individual's dexterity or motor skills.

The CareerScope is based on the U.S. Department of Labor's categorization of careers and it is important that clients and counselees are familiar with them. It would be interesting to investigate how accurately CareerScope identifies interests and aptitudes in other industrialized countries. More research is needed on the use of the CareerScope within the US as most of the was conducted on two very small specific samples totaling 422 individuals.

References

Brown, C. D. (2001). Review of CareerScope Career Assessment and Reporting System. In J. T. Kapes and E. A. Whitfield (Eds.) *A counselor's guide to career assessment instruments.* (4th ed). Columbus, OH: National Career Development Association.

Vocational Research Institute. (2007) CareerScope: Career Assessment and Reporting Software. Start Up Guide. Philadelphia, PA: Author

Vocational Research Institute. (2006a). *Concurrent validity of the CareerScope aptitude battery* (Research Brief # 1). Philadelphia, PA: Vocational Research Institute.

Vocational Research Institute. (2006b). *Retest reliability of the CareerScope aptitude battery* (Research Brief # 2). Philadelphia, PA: Vocational Research Institute.

Vocational Research Institute. (2006c). *Retest reliability of the CareerScope interest inventory* (Research Brief # 3). Philadelphia, PA: Vocational Research Institute.

Vocational Research Institute. (2006d). *Internal consistency of the CareerScope interest inventory scales* (Research Brief # 4). Philadelphia, PA: Vocational Research Institute.

COPSystem Career Guidance Program

Career Occupational Preference System Interest Inventory (COPS)

Career Ability Placement Survey (CAPS)

Career Orientation Placement and Evaluation Survey (COPES)

R. R. Knapp, L. Knapp, and L. Knapp-Lee

EdITS/Educational and Industrial Testing Service
PO Box 7234
San Diego, CA 92167
Phone: 800-416-1666
Fax: 619-226-1666
customerservice@edits.net
www.edits.net

Target Population: Junior high, high school, and adult (4th grade and up).

Statement of the Purpose of the Instrument: The COPSystem instruments are designed to provide individuals with coordination measures of interest, abilities, and work values in terms of eight major career clusters. Scores on any one, two, or three of the assessments provide a starting point for career exploration.

Titles of Subtests, Scales, Scores Provided: All three assessment keyed to 14 COPSystem Career Clusters: Science Professional, Science Skilled, Technology Professional, Technology Skilled, Consumer Economics, Outdoor, Business Professional, Business Skilled, Clerical, Communication, Arts Professional, Arts Skilled, Service Professional, and Service Skilled. CAPS subtests include: Mechanical Reasoning, Spatial Relations, Verbal Reasoning, Numerical Ability, Language Usage, Word Knowledge, Perceptual Speed and Accuracy, and Manual Speed and Dexterity. The COPES scales are: Investigative vs. Accepting, Practical vs. Carefree, Independence vs. Conformity, Leadership vs. Supportive, Orderliness vs. Flexibility, Recognition vs. Privacy, Aesthetic vs. Realistic, and Social vs. Reserved.

Forms and Levels Available, with Dates of Publication/Revision of Each: COPS (1995), COPS Professional level (COPS-P, 2002), COPS Form R (COPS-R,1992), COPS Intermediate Inventory (COPS-II, 2003), COPS Picture Inventory (COPS-PIC, 1993), Spanish COPS (SPOC, 1995), Spanish CAPS (1976), Career Ability Placement Survey (CAPS, 1976), and Career Orientation Placement and Evaluation Survey (COPES, 1995). COPS, COPS-R, CAPS, and COPES all renormed in 2004.

Date of Most Recent Edition of Test Manual, User's Guide, etc.: COPS Technical Manual (1990, 2007, in press), CAPS Technical Manual (1992), COPES Manual (1995)

Languages in Which Available: English, Spanish non reading, Some translations of directions for the COPS-PIC, CAPS, and COPES in: Spanish, Hmong, Russian, Croatian, Laotian, and Vietnamese.

Time:

Actual Test Time: COPS: 20 – 30 minutes; CAPS: 40 minutes; COPES 20 minutes

Total Administration Time: 2 hours: COPS: 25 – 35 minutes; CAPS 50 minutes; COPES: 25 – 35 minutes.

Norm Group(s) on Which Scores Are Based: Junior high, high school, and community college/college norms.

Manner in Which Results Are Reported for Individuals:

Types of Scores: Raw scores, Percentiles, Stanines, Verbal Labels.

Report Format/Content:

BASIC SERVICE: COPSystem scores keyed to 14 COPSystem Clusters as described in the interpretive booklet. The interpretive booklet provides information about each cluster, including a definition of each career cluster, related courses of study, sample occupations, related college majors, necessary skills and abilities, activities for experience, career planning worksheet, educational planning worksheet, and local job interview sheet.

OPTIONS: self scoring, machine scoring through EdITS, or local onsite machine scoring (Machine scoring provides individual printouts).

Report Format/Content for Group Summaries:

Basic Service: Summary of Interest shows the percent of times one of the 14 career clusters was chosen by examinees as one of their top three areas of interest; Needs Assessment Summary provides a summary of student responses to a career planning questionnaire; Examinees by Interest Area is a listing of students interested in one of three top Career Clusters. Basic List Report is a condensed summary of student responses to the COPS, CAPS, and COPES. Record Labels have same information as basic list on self-adhesive levels.

Options: Data may be summarized by any grouping and is available electronically for the machine scoring version.

Scoring:

Machine Scoring Service:

COST OF BASIC SERVICE PER COUNSELEE: Depends on the quantity; this price includes the cost of the booklets and scoring service combined and ranges from $6.16 to $6.81 for all three instruments. $1.80 per assessment.

COST OF OPTIONS: File Copy, $0.40 for all three assessments ($0.40 per assessment). Basic List Report, $0.40 per examinee. Summary of Interests, $0.20 per examinee, Needs Assessment Summary, $0.20 per examinee. Examinees by Interest Area, $0.20 per examinee.

Time required for scoring and returning: 10 business days.

Hand Scoring:

SCORED BY: Counselee; Clerk; Counselor

TIME REQUIRED FOR SCORING: approximately 15 – 20 minutes per test

Local Machine Scoring:

PROVISIONS/CONDITIONS/EQUIPMENT REQUIRED: Windows PC, laser printer, and an Optical Mark Read Scanner with pencil dual-read-head capacity.

Computer Software Options Available: Available late 2008

OTHER: Software for scoring only, not administration.

Ways in Which Computer/Online Version Differs:

CAPS test #8 will be different.

Cost of Materials: Due to possible price changes since publication date, be sure to check with the publisher website.

Specimen Set: $44.50

Counselee Materials: All materials are consumable. Each assessment may be used as a stand-alone instrument. Prices vary according to quantities. Self-Scoring of all three assessments combined ranges from $4.24 to $5.82. Contact publisher for prices of individual assessments.

Additional Comments of Interest to Users: Online version should be available late 2008. New technical manuals in process. Specific information regarding new norms, reliability, and validity available on website and in newsletters.

Published Reviews of the Instrument in the Last 15 Years:

Wickwire, P. N., & Faldet, B. (1994). Review of the Career Occupational Preference System Interest Inventory (COPS). In J. T. Kapes, M. M. Mastie, & E. A. Whitfield (Eds.), *A Counselor's guide to career assessment instruments* (3rd ed., pp. 158 – 161). Alexandria, VA: National Career Development Association.

Wickwire, P. N. (2001). COPSystem (COPS, CAPS, and COPES). In J. T. Kapes & E. A. Whitfield (Eds.), *A Counselor's guide to career assessment instruments* (4th ed., pp. 210-217) Columbus, OH: National Career Development Association.

Reviewed by:

Emily E. Bullock
Michael B. Madson
Department of Psychology
University of Southern Mississippi

Description

The Career Occupational Preference System (COPSystem; Knapp, Knapp, & Knapp-Lee, 1990) includes three coordinated instruments that are designed to assess career interest, abilities, and values. The purpose of these instruments is to increase self-awareness in junior high students, high school students, college students, and adults pursuing the career decision-making process.

The three instruments within the COPSystem are the Career Occupational Preference Interest Inventory (COPS), Career Ability Placement Survey (CAPS), and the Career Orientation Placement and Evaluation Survey (COPES). The development and revision of these instruments has a strong theoretical and research basis. Original versions of these instruments appeared between 1975 and 1995 and the latest normative data were gathered between January 2000 and June 2002.

The Career Occupational Preference Interest Inventory (COPS) is a measure of job activity preference in relation to 14 clusters of related occupations. It takes 20 – 30 minutes to respond to the 168-item inventory. The items are composed of activities associated with specific work environments such as "care for patients in a hospital" and "arrange flower displays." Test takers respond to items using the response choices of "like very much", "like moderately", "dislike moderately", or "dislike very much" (Knapp, Knapp, & Knapp-Lee, 1990).

Results are presented in percentiles that represent a comparison of the examinee's scores to the normative sample. The results provide the test taker information relative to the strength of his or her interests in relation to 14 Occupational Career Clusters. The Professional and Skilled distinctions reflect differences in level of training and responsibility for occupations within that cluster. The 14 Career Clusters are listed below (Knapp, Knapp, & Knapp-Lee, 1990):

Science Professional	Business Skilled
Science Skilled	Clerical
Technology Professional	Communication
Technology Skilled	Arts Professional
Consumer Economics	Arts Skilled
Outdoor	Service Professionall
Business Professional	Service Skilled

The Career Ability Placement Survey (CAPS) is a battery of eight ability tests grouped into the categories listed below. Each test is administered by cassette or CD-recorded instructions and has a five-minute time limit. The total administration of the CAPS takes about 50 minutes. Each item on the CAPS requires the test taker to complete a task relevant to the ability category. For example, in Word Knowledge the test taker must choose the best one-word definition for the term "synchronize" (Knapp, Knapp, & Knapp-Lee, 1992).

The CAPS can be used and interpreted as a stand-alone measure of vocationally oriented ability by interpreting the resulting percentile and stanine scores relative to the eight ability tests. As recommended, it can also be used and interpreted within the COPSystem by interpreting the resulting percentile scores relative to the 14 Career Clusters. The reported scores represent a comparison between the examinee's scores and the normative sample. Through extensive factor analytic research, the eight CAPS abilities have been keyed to the 14 Career Clusters to help examinees identify within which career clusters his or her abilities best match (Knapp, Knapp, & Knapp-Lee, 1992):

Mechanical Reasoning	Language Usage
Spatial Relations	Word Knowledge
Verbal Reasoning	Perceptual Speed and Accuracy
Numerical Ability	Manual Speed and Dexterity

The Career Orientation Placement and Evaluation Survey (COPES) is a measure of vocational values. There is a self-scoring form (128 item) and machine scoring form (160 item) of the COPES and each takes 30 – 50 minutes to complete. Each item allows the test taker to choose one of two statements that best reflect his or her values by completing the sentence, "I value activities or jobs in which I ...." To complete the sentence test takers can, for example, mark either "team up with others "or "work on my own." The items were written with consideration of the 14 Career Clusters and numerous previous factor analytic studies of values (Knapp & Knapp-Lee, 1996).

Results are reported in percentile scores that represent a comparison between the examinee's scores and the normative sample. Interpretation of COPES results begins by identifying the three most salient or highest percentile values for the examinee. The COPES results can then be used in the interpretation of the full COPSystem. Extensive research aided in determining which COPES values fit best with the occupations represented in each of the 14 COPS Career Clusters. The work values measured by the COPES are composed of eight work values dichotomies as listed below (Knapp & Knapp-Lee, 1996):

Investigative vs. Accepting	Orderliness vs. Flexibility
Practical vs. Carefree	Recognition vs. Privacy
Independence vs. Conformity	Aesthetic vs. Realistic
Leadership vs. Supportive	Social vs. Reserved

Currently, the COPSystem is only available in paper-and-pencil versions. The test taker can score all three COPSystem inventories by hand, and self-scoring is recommended (Knapp, Knapp, & Knapp-Lee, 1990). Machine scoring that provides a summary of the entire battery's results is available through EdITS. Computer scoring software for the paper/pencil version is currently available and an online version of the assessments is scheduled for release in late 2008. Time to score and interpret the instruments within the COPSystem will vary depending on clinician choice of how to use it (e.g., self-scoring, in groups) and what support tools to incorporate.

Use In Counseling

The COPSystem is a set of coordinated career assessment instruments composed of separate measures of interest, ability, and values for use with junior high students, high school students, college students, and adults. It appears the COPS Interest Inventory serves as the anchor instrument within the system. The results of the COPS Interest Inventory communicate the level of a test taker's interest in 14 Career Clusters, which are composed of occupations with similar job activities. Knapp, Knapp, & Knapp-Lee (1992) state that the results of the ability and values measures are best used when interpreted in light of the 14 Career Clusters as an integrated COPSystem battery. The eight scales of the CAPS (ability) and the eight scales of the COPES (values) have been keyed to the 14 Career Clusters through extensive factor analytic research.

Support materials

A variety of supportive materials can be ordered to supplement the interpretation or use of the COPSystem results. Support materials for purchase from the publisher's website (http://edits.net/copsystem.html) include *Visuals, Career Brief Kits, Career Clusters Booklets Kit, Comprehensive Career Guidebook and Leader's Guide,* and *Career Clusters Charts.* The Visuals are a set of overhead transparencies also available in PowerPoint format to aid in the explanation of the combined use and interpretation of the three instruments. *Career Brief Kits* are composed of 485 color-coded cards that explain one occupation in detail and provides a key to various occupational classification systems such as O*NET and the DOT. The *Career Cluster Booklets Kit* is composed of booklets that detail information on each career cluster. The *Guidebook* provides in-depth interpretative information. *Career Cluster Charts* serve as wall- or pocket-size visuals of how the Career Clusters and associated occupations are organized (COPSystem, n.d.).

Uses

The COPSystem Technical Manual outlines several ways and environments in which it is appropriate to use the coordinated inventories. Environments such as schools, businesses, and private practice counseling settings are all suggested. In the school system, the COPSystem can be used for career planning, self-awareness, or early career awareness programming. Relevant norm groups make the COPSystem appropriate for use at the junior high, high school, and college levels. The use of the COPSystem may be lead by a school counselor or individual teachers through a group or individual interpretation format. In business and industrial settings, the COPSystem may serve as a tool for personal development, increased self-awareness, and selection and placement (Knapp, Knapp, & Knapp-Lee, 1990). Knapp and Knapp-Lee (1996) cite the COPES as being especially useful in counseling settings when the therapist is working with an adult in career transition.

Alternate versions

The COPS Interest Inventory has multiple versions to meet the needs of the test administrator and potential examinees. The standard version of the COPS is for use with junior high students, high school students, college students, or adults. The COPS-P is specifically designed for college students and adults. The COPS-R is for use with those in the 6th grade through high school. The COPS II was designed for use with those in 4th grade through high school and with special education populations. Any of the versions of the COPS can be ordered for use with the COPES and CAPS. There are Spanish versions of the COPS and CAPS with norms composed of Spanish-speaking students from the U.S. combined with a Spanish-speaking sample from Mexico (COPSystem, n.d.).

Technical Considerations

Updated normative data were collected for the COPSystem in five geographic regions between January 2000 and June 2002. The data consisted of a sample of 18,991 7th through 12th grade students and an additional sample of 1,898 college students. Because there is a significant difference in the manner in which males and females respond to the COPS items, gender based norms are provided. The collected normative sample appears to adequately represent each gender (EdITS, 2006).

COPS Interest Inventory Reliability and Validity

Reliability coefficients ranging from .86 to .92 are reported for the scales of the COPS Interest Inventory (EdiTS, 2006). Based on the 1974 version of the instrument, a one-year interval test-retest procedure yielded coefficients ranging from .62 to .80 for all scales of the interest inventory (Knapp, Knapp, & Knapp-Lee, 1990).

Numerous studies supporting the validity of the COPS Interest Inventory are reported. In a study including the Kuder scales and the COPS Interest Inventory, correlations between similar scales ranged from .21 to .49. Eighty-nine percent of those sampled in this study chose at least one of same top three interest areas on both instruments. Correlations between similar scales of the COPS Interest Inventory and the Vocational Preference Inventory ranged from .5 and .7. Concurrent validity was indicated in a study reporting that 71% of the sample declared college majors that aligned with interests measured on the COPS Interest Inventory. In support of predictive validity, a study demonstrated that 64% of the sample was in a job or college major that aligned with their COPS interests areas one to seven years after being assessed (EdITS, 2006, Knapp, Knapp, & Knapp-Lee, 1985).

CAPS Reliability and Validity

The development of the CAPS focused on creating a reliable measurement of cognitive ability that would fit into the typical time allotted for cognitive assessment within a career battery. This task was pursued with the understanding that a shorter instrument would result in lower reliability. In a sample of 90 high school students, test-retest reliability coefficients ranging from .70 to .95 after a two-week interval. Alternate form reliability was measured during the test development process and ranged from .70 to .89 for all CAPS scales. Numerous studies citing the intercorrelations among CAPS scales, other measures of ability, and career choice support the criterion and construct validity of the CAPS (Knapp, Knapp, & Knapp-Lee, 1992).

COPES Reliability and Validity

Internal consistency reliability coefficients ranged from .70 to .83 for the COPES scales. Concurrent validity evidence is based on moderate correlations among the 1977 version of the COPES scales and similar scales on other values inventories. A predictive validity study involving a 1 – 4 year follow-up with 9th through 12th graders concluded that 89% of those that responded to the follow-up survey were currently pursuing a career congruent with their original COPES results (Knapp & Knapp-Lee, 1996). In addition, Knapp and Knapp-Lee (1996) cite the theoretical factor structure of the items that was confirmed through factor analytic research as evidence for the construct validity of the instrument.

Overall Critique

The COPSystem is a uniquely coordinated career development assessment battery composed of a measure of interest, values, and skills. The foundation for the development of each of the instruments is based in well-established theory, 30 years of sound research, and confirmed factor analysis. The psychometric properties of each instrument appear adequate for making decisions about individuals. Reports of the psychometric properties of the instruments was confusing at times due to the use of different versions of the instruments for the establishment of reliability and validity. Further, caution needs to be exercised in relation to the new norms and psychometrics as the results were provided by the publishers and not peer reviewed.

There are a variety of versions and supportive materials that allow for tailoring the COPSystem to a variety of client populations. Yet, the presentation of inventory materials, manuals, and support materials can be confusing to one unfamiliar with the system. A manual or web page that provides an overall explanation of the system, its possible uses, support materials, and various versions would be helpful in understanding how the COPSystem could be integrated into potential test administrators' environments.

Overall, the COPSystem is an impressive and intriguing set of coordinated instruments. As stated in a previous review (Wickwire, 2002), the COPSystem is suggested for consideration by counselors in primary schools, secondary schools, colleges, business, and private practice settings.

References

EdITS (2006, Spring). Brief summary of the reliability and validity of the COPSystem assessments. *Career Research and Test Development*, 1.

COPSystem: Career measurement package. (n.d.). Retrieved December 18, 2006, from http://edits.net/copsystem.html.

Knapp, L., & Knapp-Lee, L. (1996). *Manual: COPES: Career Orientation Placement & Evaluation Survey*, 1995 ed. San Diego, CA: EdITS.

Knapp, L., Knapp, R. R., & Knapp-Lee, L. (1992). Career Ability Placement Survey (CAPS): *CAPS technical manual*. San Diego, CA: EdITS.

Knapp, R.R, Knapp, L., & Knapp-Lee, L (1985). Occupational interest measurement and subsequent career decisions: A predictive follow-up study of the COPSystem Interest Inventory. *Journal of Counseling Psychology*, 32, 348-354.

Knapp, R. R., Knapp, L., & Knapp-Lee, L. (1990). *COPSystem technical manual*. San Diego, CA: EdITS.

Wickwire, P. N. (2001). COPSystem (COPS, CAPS, and COPES). In J. T. Kapes, & E. A. Whitfield (Eds.), *A counselor's guide to career assessment instruments* (4th ed., pp. 210 – 217). Columbus, OH: National Career Development Association.

Differential Aptitude Tests (DAT) & Career Interest Inventory (CII)

G.K. Bennett, H.G. Seashore, and A.G. Wesman (DAT only)

Harcourt Assessment
19500 Bulverde Road
San Antonio, Texas 78259
1-800-872-1726
http://harcourtassessment.com/

Target Population: 8th, 9th, and 10th grade high school students, (level 1) grades 7 – 12 and adults.

Statement of the Purpose of the Instrument: The DAT is a battery of eight tests designed to measure students' ability to learn or to succeed in a number of different areas. The DAT is designed to be used alone or in conjunction with the *Career Interest Inventory,* a career guidance instrument designed to provide information about students' educational goals, interest in a variety of school subjects and activities, and interest in fields of work. When the DAT is used in conjunction with the *Career Interest Inventory,* a complete profile of students' interests and aptitudes can be developed.

Titles of Subtests, Scales, Scores Provided: DAT: Verbal Reasoning, Numerical Reasoning, Abstract Reasoning, Perceptual Speed and Accuracy, Mechanical Reasoning, Space Relations, Spelling, and Language usage; additional score: Scholastic Aptitude (VR + NR), *Career Interest Inventory* Occupational Groups: Social Science, Clerical Services, Health Services, Agriculture, Customer Services, Fine Arts, Mathematics and Science, Building Trades, Educational Services, Legal Services, Transportation, Sales, Management, Benchwork, and Machine Operation.

Forms and Levels Available, with Dates of Publication/Revision of Each: Two levels of the DAT and *Career Interest Inventory* are available. Level 1 is designed to be used with students in grades 7 – 9, Level 2 is designed to be used with students in Grades 10 – 12. Both levels of the DAT can be used with adults. However, it is recommended that only the Level 2 of the *Career Interest Inventory* be used with adults.

The publication date of both the DAT and CII is 1990.

Only one of the two forms of the DAT is currently available, Form C. Only one form of the *Career Interest Inventory* is available. A Partial Battery is also available for both Levels 1 and 2 of the DAT. It consists of two tests, Verbal Reasoning and Numerical Reasoning. *The Partial Battery* may also be used with or without either level of the *Career Interest Inventory.*

Date of Most Recent Edition of Test Manual, User's Guide, etc.: Technical manual 1992.

Languages in Which Available: English and Spanish language edition with norms for students in Mexico only; available only from IEGE in Mexico DF, Mexico.

Time:

Actual Test Time: 2.5 hours for complete DAT battery; 1.5 hours for partial DAT battery; 30 minutes for the CII (untimed).

Total Administration Time: Approx. 196 minutes for complete DAT battery; CII is 30 minutes (untimed).

Norm Group(s) on Which Scores Are Based: DAT norms for each grade 7 – 12, males, females, and combined gender; DAT norms for four groups of adults. See norms booklets.

Manner in Which Results Are Reported for Individuals:

Types of Scores: raw scores, percentile ranks, stanines, national percentile bands for DAT; raw scores for CII.

Report Format/Content:

BASIC SERVICE: DAT/CII: Individual Report; CII only; Individual Report.

Report Format/Content for Group Summaries:

Basic Service: Group summary available upon request.

Options: DAT/CII list report by Teacher/Counselor or school, Student Profile, Counselor's Report (by teacher/counselor or school/district), Occupational Interest Report (by school), Career Planning Summary (by teacher/counselor, school, or district).

Scoring:

Machine Scoring Service: Prices valid through October 16, 2007.

COST OF BASIC SERVICE PER COUNSELEE: Individual report, $2.25; DAT Partial Battery/Career Interest Inventory, $4.50; additional copies of reports $0.50 each.

TIME REQUIRED FOR SCORING AND RETURNING: 21 calendar days

Hand Scoring:

SCORED BY: Counselee (CII only); Counselor (DAT)

TIME REQUIRED FOR SCORING: Approximately 10 minutes.

Local Machine Scoring:

Provisions/conditions/equipment required: NCS SENTRY Scanners.

Computer Software Options Available: DAT/CII Scoring Assistant helps produce computer reports for results from hand-scored instruments.

Ways in Which Computer Version Differs: Reports are formatted differently from those obtained from TPC scoring services. Less interpretive text is provided. User sites can add special text to CII report, as an option.

Cost of Materials: Due to possible price changes since publication date, be sure to check the publisher's website.

Specimen Set: DAT with CII is $50; CII only is $26; prices valid through 10/16/07. DAT Technical Manual, $50.50; DAT with CII Counselor's Manual, $78.00.

Counselee Materials: DAT Partial Battery Examination Kit, $50; CII Hand-Scorable Booklets, Level 1, $83; CII Hand-Scorable Booklets, Level 2, $88; DAT Test Booklets, Level 1 & Level 2, $180 each; DAT Test Booklets Form C, Level 1 & Level 2, $80 each.

Additional Comments of Interest to Users: The new edition of the Career Interest Inventory will be linked to the U.S. Department of Labor's O*Net.

Published Reviews of Instrument in the Last 15 Years:

Hattrup, K. (1995). Review of the Differential Aptitude Tests, Fifth Edition. In J. C. Conoley and J.C. Impara (Eds.), *The twelfth mental measurements yearbook.* Lincoln: Buros Institute, University of Nebraska – Lincoln.

Schmitt, N. (1995). Review of the Differential Aptitude Tests, Fifth Edition. In J. C. Conoley and J.C. Impara (Eds.), *The twelfth mental measurements yearbook.* Lincoln: Buros Institute, University of Nebraska – Lincoln.

Wang, L. (1995). Review of the Differential Aptitude Tests (DAT). *Measurement and Evaluation in Counseling and Development, 28,* 168-170.

Wilson, V. L. & Stone, E. (1994). Review of the Differential Aptitude Tests. Fifth Edition with Career Interest Inventory. In J. T. Kapes, M. M. Mastie, & E. A. Whitfield (Eds.), *A counselor's guide to career assessment instruments* (3rd ed.). Alexandria, VA: National Career Development Association.

Reviewed by:

Karl N. Kelley
Chair, Science Division
Department of Psychology
North Central College
Naperville, IL

Description

In the 1940's, George K. Bennett, Harold G. Seashore, and Alexander G. Wesman (Bennett, Wesman, 1947; Bennett, Seashore, & Wesman, 1948; Seashore, 1950) argued that individual aptitudes predict career and academic success. They defined an aptitude as the capacity of an individual to learn. Thus, aptitude assesses an individual's ability to learn specific skills and acquire knowledge. Rather than advocating a single aptitude to learn (similar to the "g" intelligence), these researches viewed aptitudes as a collection of different factors. The challenge became to identify and assess the key aptitudes in predicting career and academic performance.

First published in 1947, the Differential Aptitude Test (DAT) was designed to empirically demonstrate the relationship between aptitudes and performance. The four revisions of this test (the most current being in 1990) have continually refined these measures and expanded the normative basis for the test.

Currently, the DAT consists of eight specific tests (Verbal Reasoning, Numerical Reasoning, Abstract Reasoning, Perceptual Speed & Accuracy, Mechanical Reasoning, Space Relations, Spelling, and Language Usage) that can be conceptually organized around three global aptitude dimensions (Cognitive, Perceptual, and Clerical/Language). Each specific test is linked to courses of study and career fields. For example, high scores on the Verbal Reasoning scale is correlated with success in general academics classes and occupations including business, law, education, journalism, and the sciences. The global aptitude dimensions are linked to skills that are more general.

Cognitive — Contains tests of Verbal Reasoning and Numerical Ability. These tests measure the ability to learn from books and manuals, self-instruction, or trainers/teachers.

Perceptual — Contains tests of Abstract Reasoning, Mechanical Reasoning, and Space Relations. Assesses aptitudes in understanding things, rather than people or words.

Clerical /Language — Contains tests of Spelling, Language Usage, and Clerical Speed/Accuracy. Tests skills necessary to perform various types.

The test consists of 510 items and takes 2 hours and 36 minutes to complete. All items are presented in a multiple-choice format and responses are recorded on machine scorable optical scan forms. Sample items for each test are provided in Table 1.

Table 1.

Scale	Sample
Verbal Reasoning	Analogies ___ is to pencil as ink is to ___ 40 items, 25 minutes
Numerical Reasoning	What number should replace R in the equation $7R + R = 88$ 40 items, 30 minutes
Abstract Reasoning	Participants are presented with a series of figures and to select the next logical figure in the series. 40 items, 20 minutes
Perceptual Speed & Accuracy	Participants are given 5 letter/number combinations with one item underlined. They are to find the underlined combination on the answer sheet. two 100 items sections, 3 minutes each
Mechanical Reasoning	Participants are asked to draw logical physical conclusions from drawings 60 items, 25 minutes

Space Relations	Participants are presented with a pattern where some sections are shaded and are asked to select the appropriate three-dimensional figure represented the assembled figure. 50 items, 25 minutes
Spelling	Identify the misspelled word in a set of four terms 40 items, 10 minutes
Language Use	Identify grammatical errors in sentences. 40 items, 15 minutes

Use in Counseling

This test is designed to assist high school students (and to a lesser degree young adults) in selecting appropriate courses and exploring career paths. Counselors can administered this test in group or individual sessions. The tests can be returned to the publisher for machine scoring or can be scored by the counselor or student.

When machine scored by the publisher (Harcourt Assessment), several report options are available. All of these standardized reports are clear and generally helpful. Reports include raw score, percentile, and stanine information. With some training, students and parents should be able to understand their scores. However, individual sessions with students may be beneficial since there are multiple scales to interpret and students particularly in the earlier grades may become confused. To assist in this interpretation process, the publisher also provides 10 supplemental publications for understanding and using scores. Some of these publications directly address student and parent concerns whereas others are focused the questions for professional counselors. All of these materials are well written and easy to read. They do not get bogged down in technical considerations. Technical manuals are available for those who are interested in the test psychometrics. In addition to the interpretative materials, practice tests are available to students so that they can become familiar with the types of test items and requirements for the various subtests.

It is important to note that the interpretative materials stress that although these tests can provide useful information, they should be interpreted with caution. The test results provide clues and the first steps in the career development process. Counselors are encouraged to seek converging evidence with other information including actual academic performance, results from others tests, and the student's interests (the test manual suggests a benefit of coupling the results of the DAT with the Career Interest Inventory (CII)).

Although there are many potential benefits to using this test, it is a lengthy assessment (testing time is over 2 hours and 30 minutes). When instructions and break times are included, the total testing time can approach 3 hours.

Technical Considerations

As noted above, this test has been in print since 1947 and is currently in its fifth revision (1990). The most recent Technical Manual (published in 1992) contains a wealth of information about the development of the test and appropriate psychometrics.

The basic structure of the test has remained stable over time, measuring the same basic aptitudes. The current version has made several substantial revisions in the content of the items. The first major change was to divide the test into two levels—a basic level for grades 7 to 9 and a more advanced version for grades 10 to 12. All of the items (with the exception of the Perceptual Speed and Accuracy (PSA) tests) are new in this version. More than 4000 new items were developed and refined into the final 310 items (not including the 200 items from the PSA sections).

Test developers carefully screened items for readability and bias. They defined readability as adhering to the guidelines established by Taylor's (1989) research on core vocabulary. Bias was addressed by establishing a nine-member panel of subject matter experts (SME) who reviewed each item for potential gender and racial stereotypes or the existence of demeaning or offensive terms.

The normative base for this test included 84,000 students who participated in the National Item Tryout Program in 1988. These students were from more than 150 school districts varying in socioeconomic status, enrollment, and region. The Technical Manual lists all of participating school districts and provides basic demographic information. Norm tables provide descriptive information including stanine and percentile ranks for females, males, and combined sex. Same sex interpretation is suggested for mechanical reasoning, space relations, and perceptual speed and accuracy scales. The developers recommend using combined-sex norms for all other scales.

The test developers assessed internal reliability using Kuder-Richardson 20 (KR-20) analyses. All scales yield high internal consistency (coefficients ranging from .82 to .95). These statistics are not computed for the Perceptual Speed & Accuracy Tests, which is appropriate.

In addition, the standard error of measurement (SEM) is computed for each scale for each grade tested (including separate analyses for males, females, and combined sex). These SEMs range from 2.6 to 5.5 for individual scales.

This test makes the theoretical argument that there are multiple discrete aptitudes. In order to establish the validity of this claim, intercorrelations among the scales are presented. The only two scales showing consistently high correlation are the verbal reasoning and numerical reasoning scales (with correlations around .70). These correlations do not vary substantially between sexes or across grade levels. Other scales are moderately interrelated.

Construct validity is supported by a multi trait matrix which includes a collection of correlations with other tests of aptitude and achievement. In general, specific scales on this test demonstrate logically consistent correlations tests such as the Otis-Lennon School Ability Test, the American College Testing Program Battery, and the Armed Services Vocational Aptitude Battery.

The criteria validity of the test is established by correlating test scores with student

GPAs. As could be expected, the combination of verbal and numerical reasoning (VR + NR) yields the highest correlations with GPAs (correlations range from .36 to .84 with a median correlation of .66). Other scales do not yield correlations as high or as consistent as the VR and NR scales.

Overall Critique

The Differential Aptitude Test has been in use since 1947 and has been a popular test among high school career counselors. This test brings many strengths to the table, including a comprehensive set of tests covering conceptual, perceptual, and clerical/language skills. Broad-based normative data provide a sound reference point for interpreting scores. In addition, the test publisher provides clear and helpful interpretation materials. The technical manual provides support for the internal reliability of the test and evidence for construct validity. Content validity is strong with particular attention being paid to avoiding unfair item bias and offensive content. The readability and the face validity of the test are also strengths.

The DAT has been around for a long time but it has not inspired much recent research, and there are many important unanswered questions remaining. One of the major drawbacks in using this test in career development is the lack of predictive validity studies in areas beyond GPA. Additional research needs to be conducted to establish this important area. Counselors need to be very cautious in making recommendations without this information. In addition, more research should be conducted to more firmly establish the construct validity of the test and test-retest reliability.

Another caution in using this test is the length. The full test required over two and a half hours of testing time, and younger students could lose interest and motivation. More research needs to be conducted in this area. Future revision of this test should also link results to U.S. Department of Labor's O*Net resources.

Although there are some important cautions in using this test, it does provide a sound starting point for helping students consider their academic lives while helping them plan for a career. It should be noted, that this test is a starting point and is not giving specific directions. At this point, there are no plans to update or revise this test.

The Career Interest Inventory (CII)

Description

The Career Interest Inventory (CII) is an easy to use self-report test for helping students explore a variety of academic and career choices. The results of this test are linked to the Differential Aptitude tests scores to allow students to understand the convergence (or divergence) of their interests and aptitudes.

The test presents participants with a set of tasks/jobs (such as draw pictures for books; work in a hotel; raise dogs to sell) and has them rate each one on a 5-point scale from liking the activity very much to disliking the activity a great deal. There are two levels of this test corresponding to the DAT levels (level 1 is designed for students in grades 7 to 9 and level 2 for students in grades 10 to 12).

The responses to the job/activity statements are organized into 15 career fields described in the U.S. Department of Labor's (1991 Dictionary of Occupational Titles (DOT).

Agriculture—working with plants and/or animals (Farmer, Forest Ranger, Gardener, Horse Trainer)

Health Services—provide a variety of services to the sick, injured or disabled (Nurse, Doctor, Physical Therapist, Veterinarian)

Management—help establish goals, direct operations, and control activities within an organization (Accountant, Banker, Manager)

Clerical Services—prepare/store records and data plus operate office machines (Bookkeeper, Cashier, Clerk, Secretary, Typist)

Customer Services—guard or clean buildings, prepare/serve food, cut/style hair, etc. (Cook, Flight Attendant, Police Officer)

Sales—buying/selling products or services (Fund Raiser, Real Estate Agent, Insurance Agent),

Fine Arts—use special skills in creative arts/entertainment (Artist, Editor, Journalist, Musician, Photographer, Singer, Writer)

Mathematics and Science—do research, observe things, and do experiments (Chemist, Computer, Scientist, Engineer)

Educational Services—help people learn (College Professor, Librarian, Museum Worker, Teacher)

Social Science—concerned about the social needs of people (Counselor, Historian, Social Worker, Psychologist)

Legal Services—advise people about legal matters (Attorney, Judge, Paralegal)

Benchwork—use hand tools to make and/or repair small products (Jewelry Repair, Locksmith, Video Repair)

Building Trades—skilled work (Bricklayer, Carpenter, Plumber, Painter, Roofer, Welder)

Machine Operation—use/operate machines working with metal, paper or wood (Band Saw Operator, Furnace Operator, Press Operator)

Transportation—operate vehicles like trucks, buses, tractors (Ambulance Driver, Service Station Attendant, Truck Driver)

Use in Counseling

The Career Interest Inventory provides another tool in helping students understand their academic and career directions. It is very different from the DAT in that this test focuses on the student's interests rather then aptitudes. The results of the test are more focused on specific jobs as opposed to general tasks. The materials provided with this test are clear and organized. Students, parents, and counselors should not have any difficulty interpreting the testing results. When taken in conjunction with the DAT and machine scored, results link the tests scores together.

The Counselor's Manual for Interpreting the Career Interest Inventory provides detailed about the theoretical and practical aspects of this test. It is well organized and easy to understand. One of the helpful features of this manual is it covers how to interpret scores for special needs populations.

Feedback to the student includes the raw score for each occupational group and a consistency index. This index provides information about scoring patterns (a score of 3 could indicate a balanced number of high and low interest scores or a collection of neutral scores). The consistency index allows a more detailed interpretation of the raw score.

Technical Considerations

The two forms of the test are designed to take about 30 minutes (Level 1 consists of 152 statements and Level 2 has 170 statements).

The normative sample for this test included approximately 100,000 participants representing a reasonable cross-section of the population in terms of geographic region, socioeconomic status, urban classification, and ethnicity. Items were linked logically (as opposed to empirically) to the 15 DOT career fields. Items were retained for this test if the exhibited good item-scale correlations. After the initial item scaling, internal consistency reliability coefficients (alphas) were computed and ranged from .82 to .94 for Level 1 and from .87 to .94 for Level 2.

Construct validity was established through by linking items to the DOT scales and correlations with matched scales from the Ohio Vocational Interest Survey Second Edition (OVIS II). Correlations were generally strong.

Overall Critique

The Career Interest Inventory is an easy to use and understand test for assisting students with career development plans. Reports and summary information from the publisher are clear and helpful. This test will be most valuable when used in conjunction with the Differential Aptitude Tests, and the publisher does a very good job of linking the results of these two tests.

The major drawback of this test is the connection with the Dictionary of Occupational Titles, which is no longer in print. The DOT has been replaced by O*NET, the Occupational Information Network. Rather than using the 15 DOT career fields, students and counselors would benefit by linking test results to the O*NET 2006 SOC (Standard Occupation Classification) Taxonomy. Although the O*NET 2006 SOC Taxonomy is more complex than the DOT classification (having 23 major occupation groups as opposed to 15), it is more accurate and comprehensive in representing the job market today.[1]

---

[1] Editors Note: Harcourt Assessment has informed the editors that the new edition of the CII will be linked to the O*NET taxonomy.

References

Bennett, G. K. & Wesman, A. G. (1947). Industrial test norms for a southern plant population. *Journal of Applied Psychology,* 31, 241-246.

Bennett, G. K. Seashore, H. G. & Wesman, A. G. (1948). *Validation of the Differential Aptitude Tests.* San Antonio, TX, US: Psychological Corporation.

Seashore, Harold G. (1950). Understanding the individual through measurement. *American Council on Education Studies,* 14, 41-51.

Taylor, S. E. (1989). *EDL core vocabularies in reading, mathematics, science, and social studies.* Columbia, SC: Educational Development Laboratories.

U.S. Department of Labor (1991). *Dictionary of occupational titles* (4th ed.). Washington, DC: U.S. Government Printing Office.

Employability Competency System Appraisal Test (ECS Appraisal)

CASAS – Comprehensive Adult Student Assessment Systems

CASAS – Comprehensive Adult Student Assessment Systems

5151 Murphy Canyon Road, Suite 220
San Diego, CA 92123
800-255-1036
www.casas.org

Target Population: Youth from age 16 and adults.

Statement of the Purpose of the Instrument: The ECS Appraisal test is a paper and pencil instrument developed to assess students' basic skills in reading and math within an employability context. The test items expand through four instructional levels, or CASAS Skill Levels A through D (Beginning Literacy through Adult Secondary Education). Corresponding grade level equivalents are approximately 4th through 9th grade on Form 120 and 4th through 12th grade on Form 130. Counselors can use ECS Appraisal test score results to determine appropriate placement of students into academic instructional programs, including those aligned with career and technical education cluster areas required to meet the Carl D. Perkins Career and Technical Education Improvement Act of 2006. Students and counselors also can use ECS appraisal test scores to help determine if student basic skill levels in reading and math generally meet those required for selected occupations of interest, such as described in O*NET occupational descriptions. O*NET is the nation's primary source of occupational information and is based on new data from the U.S. Department of Labor and other job information sources.

Titles of Subtests, Scales, Scores Provided: Form 120, Reading Test, 20 test items, Scale Scores 197 – 228; Form 120, Math Test, 20 test items, Scale Scores 197 – 228; Form 130, Reading Test, 25 test items, Scale Scores 200 – 245; Form 130, Math Test, 25 test items, Scale Scores 200 – 245. Both forms include two additional and optional test items in critical thinking and 12 skills for preemployment and work maturity (purchased separately). Students can take the additional items after the reading and math tests or at another time. Test booklets include self scoring answer sheets.

Forms and Levels Available, with Dates of Publication/Revision of Each: Form 120 includes Reading Test and Math Test, recommended for CASAS Skill Levels A and B, published 1991. Form 130 includes Reading Test and Math Test, recommended for CASAS Skill Levels B and above, published 1994, 1996, and 1998.

Date of Most Recent Edition of Test Manual, User's Guide, etc.: ECS Appraisal Test Administration Manual published 2002.

Languages in Which Available: English only.

Time:

Actual Test Time: Suggested total administration time is 40 minutes for Form 120 and 50 minutes for Form 130. However, a definite time is not required and extra time for testing accommodations does not affect standardized administration of the instrument.

Norm Group(s) on Which Scores Are Based: The ECS Appraisal Test is a criterion-referenced test. Test items were drawn from the CASAS item bank of more than 6,000 calibrated items field-tested with youth and adults in high school completion, job training, adult basic education, English as a Second language, and correctional programs.

Manner in Which Results Are Reported for Individuals:

Types of Scores: Scores are reported on a common numerical scale that is divided into five instructional skill levels A – E (Beginning Literacy/Pre-Beginning, Beginning Basic Skills and Intermediate Basic Skills, Advanced Basic Skills, Adult Secondary, and Advanced Adult Secondary).

Report Format/Content:

BASIC SERVICE: Self-Scoring Answer Sheets report test information and results.

OPTIONS: Agencies can contract with CASAS for group scoring options.

Report Format/Content for Group Summaries: Not available.

Scoring:

Machine Scoring Service: Not available.

Hand Scoring:
SCORED BY: Counselee; Clerk; Counselor
TIME REQUIRED FOR SCORING: One minute per form.

Local Machine Scoring:
Provisions/conditions/equipment required: Counselors can use CASAS TOPSpro software if adult basic education program in district uses CASAS and has already purchased the software program. The TOPSpro standalone license costs $1,395.00; a LAN (local area network) license at one site costs $1,695.00. Hardware requirements include a PC running Windows XP or later, 512 MB RAM, 5 GB of available harddisk space, and a monitor with 1024 X 768 resolution. A Scantron Scanmark in the 2000, or 8000 series, or NCS Opscan 3, 4, 5, 6, or 7 is needed in order to scan answer sheets.

Computer Software Options Available: Standard administration online.

Other: Computer-based (CBT): The ECS Appraisal, Form 130, is available in computer-based administration.

Ways in Which Computer Version Differs: The ECS Appraisal can be administered within CASAS eTests, which runs on Windows based computers as a standalone or on a LAN. Minimum system requirements are Windows 2000 or higher, and a monitor with 1024 x 768 resolution. The application is available with 50, 100, 500, or 1,000 administrations, or multiples of these numbers. No other hardware is needed besides the computer.

Cost of Materials: Due to possible price changes since publication date, be sure to check the publisher's website.

Specimen Set: The ECS Appraisal Manual is a specimen set and includes test administration directions and samples of both Forms 120 and Forms 130 with corresponding answer sheets.

Counselee Materials:

REUSABLE MATERIALS:

ECS Appraisal Test Administration Manual, Forms 120 and 130, $66.00 (unless specimen)

Test Booklets, Form 120 – Reading & Math, Set of 25, $70.00

Test Booklets, Form 130 – Reading & Math, Set of 25, $70.00

Test Booklets, Form 130 in Large Print – Reading & Math, one test booklet, $30.00

Critical Thinking for Employability, 15 questions/hypothetical situations per test booklet, $15.00

CONSUMABLE MATERIALS:

Self-Scoring Answer Sheets, Form 120, Set of 25, $33.00

Self-Scoring Answer Sheets, Form 130, Set of 25, $33.00

Critical Thinking Items A & B optional use with Form 130, tablet of 100, $20.00

Large-Print Answer Sheets, Form 130, tablet of 25, $15.00

ECS Checklists (career awareness, preparing a resume, cover letter, filling out an application, interviewing, work maturity, job experience/training, assessment summary) –complete set (tablets of 100 pages per checklist), $125.00.

Computer-Based Form 130 Appraisal Administrations start at 50 administrations for $85.00 up to 1000 administrations for $750.00.

Reviewed by:

William D. Schafer
Affiliated Professor (Emeritus)
University of Maryland

Description

CASAS was designed as part of a system that includes curriculum development, instruction, and assessment for adult basic education programs. According to the second edition of the Test Administration Manual (2003), CASAS "meets Workforce Investment Act (WIA) requirements" (p. 1).

The domain of the CASAS was designed to be related to the SCANS competencies of the U.S. Department of Labor, among others. An Instructional Materials Quick Search was referenced in the Administration Manual, but was not provided for this review.

There are two primary series of assessments in CASAS: Life Skills and Employability, both testing reading and math skills. Listening comprehension tests are available for English as a second language (ESL) students. Four levels of difficulty range from beginning literacy to high school. Certification tests are available for reading in the life skills series and reading and math in the employability series.

Three other series are available. These are Life and Work, Workforce Learning Systems, and Citizenship. Other assessments include certain academic subjects and Spanish literacy.

Tasks may be multiple choice, written response, or performance based. For the first two, the assessments may be delivered using paper or computer. The assessments are not timed, but each takes about an hour to complete.

The materials provided by the publisher and therefore the focus of this review is on the Employability series of assessments. Pretests and posttest forms are available at each of the four levels in reading and math and at the first three levels (not including high school) in listening. These tests are entirely multiple choice.

The Test Administration Manual recommends which form a student should take. In general, the recommended forms yield most accuracy at the level of scoring expected of the student. The reading, math, and listening tests are vertically linked, separately, but the scale derives from an earlier edition of the tests in which reading and math were scaled together. Users may convert raw scores to scale scores on each form using tables in the Manual.

Use in Counseling

CASAS has been developed to allow assessment of students' current skill levels as well as progress after instruction. Uses suggested in the Administration Manual include placement into instructional programs, establishing a baseline, diagnosis of learning needs, monitoring to establish progress, and certification of skill level. Training is a requirement for using the system.

Technical Considerations

Item Bank Development and Maintenance

A Technical Manual (CASAS, 2004) describes the background of the assessment system, item bank development, psychometric properties of the item banks, and technical characteristics of the Life Skills Series and Employability Competency system, separately.

Development of the CASAS item banks was initially guided by a survey of the competencies that were represented across several California agencies and national projects. The competencies are reviewed every year by a nationally representative group and currently number about 300, divided among eight content areas: basic communication, consumer economics, community resources, health, employment, government and law, learning to learn, and independent living; the full list of competencies are listed in the Technical Manual. The competencies are tested in functional contexts such as workplace communications.

The initial pool of about 1,000 items was written to this domain, piloted, and field tested. New items are added to the pool on a continual basis, and there are over 6,000 calibrated items at present.

Scaling

The items on the reading and math tests were initially scaled and scores reported together. After about 1985, the tests were separated and are now scaled and reported independently.

CASAS uses the one-parameter logistic (Rasch) model to relate item response probabilities to person abilities. At the initial calibration, items were divided among 10 forms with embedded linking items (items common among forms and used to place the item parameters on a single scale). Items on the forms spanned the range from beginning through advanced levels of achievement.

New items are calibrated using field tests with embedded live items. They are evaluated with small samples before field testing and after field testing are re-evaluated for location, discrimination, differential item functioning, and fit to the Rasch model. Field testing uses sample sizes of at least 300, but the Technical Manual does not provide information about how these examinees are selected.

Validity and Reliability

Match between items and the skill or competency it is intended to assess is supported in the Technical Manual through a description of the process by which it is evaluated, including item writers' judgments and experts' evaluations. However, the ways by which these individuals were selected and data about the consistency of their judgments were not presented.

The currency of the domain of the CASAS has been evaluated in four state-level studies: Iowa in 1995, Indiana in 1996, Connecticut in 1997, and California in 1999. In each case, respondents were supportive of the domain as covering the needed skills and competencies needed in their contexts.

Principal components analyses (exploratory factor analyses) of the matrices of inter item tetrachoric correlations were generated for each form in order to evaluate unidimensionality. The Technical Manual presented the first two eigenvalues and the scree plots of all the eigenvalues. The data are supportive of unidimensionality of the reading and math tests separately and seem to justify the decision to scale and report them separately.

Confirmatory factor analyses were generated for both one- and two-factor models. Better fit was found for the two-factor solutions.

A study of parameter invariance was conducted in 2002. In this study, examinee responses to two forms, each containing both reading and math subtests, were selected from banked data for two samples aged 16 to 22: (1) youths who were incarcerated and (2) youths in the California Conservation Corps and adult education programs. For each form, reading and math were calibrated separately for each population (eight calibrations), and the item parameter estimates correlated with the banked parameters. (The Technical Manual calls these item difficulties, which normally are percents correct; it is assumed here that they are Rasch parameters.) The eight correlations ranged from .76 to .89, which is supportive of invariance. Interestingly, the four correlations between the two youth samples ranged from .97 to .98, which suggests that stability may be higher when other population characteristics and/or time of data collection and/or linking error are controlled.

Differential item functioning was evaluated using the Mantel-Haenszel delta-difference procedure for gender and ethnicity (Dorans & Holland, 1993), although the classification rules described in the reference incorporate statistical significance and those described in the Technical Manual do not. Items that showed statistical DIF were reviewed by committees and were used only if needed. Tables of numbers of items on forms showing different degrees of DIF, however, show (a) several examples in which the numbers of items in DIF categories do not sum to the total number of items on the form, and (b) forms in which the number of items in the greatest DIF category exceeded 10%, and (c) as noted by Parke (2005), lack of indication of the numbers of items where statistical DIF favored the focal or the reference groups.

CASAS scores have been related to scores on several external measures. Results in the Technical Manual are expressed as expectancy tables for score ranges or as CASAS means and standard deviations for students scoring in ranges on the external instrument. Where correlations were reported, they were generally supportive of a reasonably strong relationship between the CASAS and the external measure (e.g., .71 between CASAS Reading and ACT WorkKeys Reading for Information; .70 between CASAS Math and ACT Work Keys Mathematics).

Alpha coefficients for the various reading test forms for reading in the Employment Competency System range from .88 to .95; for the math test forms, they range from .86 to .96, all based on data from 1996 through 2000. In addition, tables show the scale scores that correspond to the raw scores on each of the forms along with the conditional standard errors. Unfortunately, the conditional standard errors are given in scale score units whereas the means and standard deviations in the tables of descriptive statistics are given in raw score units. Since interpretation is always in terms of scale scores, it would be better to report all results in the scale score metric.

Overall Critique

The CASAS tests have been carefully developed from a well-documented content domain that is reviewed regularly by a nationally representative committee. The items have been thoroughly tested using both classical and item-response-theory methods and the scaling is consistent with modern practice. They can be recommended as reliable and valid for interpretations consistent with their stated purposes.

Earlier reviews have noted some areas of concern. These are that few items assess higher order cognition (Flowerday, 2005), lack of test-retest or split-half reliability (Flowerday, 2005), lack of documentation of appropriateness of use with Native American and Asian American examinees (Flowerday, 2005), sparse information on relating CASAS to a curriculum and instruction program (Flowerday, 2005; Parke, 2005), and lack of completeness in describing studies in the Technical Manual (Parke, 2005). The one additional deficiency I noticed is the lack of representative norms. Attention to these needs would enhance an already attractive series of assessments.

References

Comprehensive Adult Student Assessment System (2003). *Test administration manual* (2nd ed.). San Diego, CA: author.

Comprehensive Adult Student Assessment System (2004). *Technical manual* (3rd ed.). San Diego, CA: author.

Dorans, N. J. & Holland, P. W. (1993). DIF detection and description: Mantel-Haenszel and standardization. In Holland, P. W. & Wainer, H. *Differential item functioning.* Hillsdale, N. J.: Lawrence Erlbaum Associates.

Flowerday, T. (2005). [Review of the Comprehensive Adult Student Assessment System (CASAS)]. In R. A. Spies & B. S. Plake (Eds.), *The sixteenth mental measurements yearbook* (pp. 256 – 258), Lincoln, NE: Buros Institute of Mental Measurements.

Parke, C. S. (2005). [Review of the Comprehensive Adult Student Assessment System (CASAS)]. In R. A. Spies & B. S. Plake (Eds.), *The sixteenth mental measurements yearbook* (pp. 258 – 261), Lincoln, NE: Buros Institute of Mental Measurements.

EXPLORE
ACT, Inc.

ACT
500 ACT Drive
P.O. Box 168
Iowa City, Iowa 52243-0168
www.act.org

Target Population: Grades 8 and 9

Statement of the Purpose of the Instrument: The EXPLORE® program is designed to help 8th and 9th graders explore a broad range of options for their future. EXPLORE prepares students not only for their high school coursework, but for their post–high school choices as well. It marks an important beginning for a student's future academic and career success. EXPLORE can serve as an independent program or as the entry point into ACT's Educational Planning and Assessment System (EPAS). Both 8th- and 9th-grade norms are available for EXPLORE.

Titles of Subtests, Scales, Scores Provided: The EXPLORE Program includes the following components:

Four Multiple-choice tests of academic achievement:
- English (providing a total test score and two subscores: Usage/Mechanics and Rhetorical Skills)
- Mathematics (providing a total test score)
- Reading (providing a total test score)
- Science (providing a total test score)
- A Composite score (average of four test scores)

UNIACT Interest Inventory (an interest inventory score is provided)
Needs Assessment
Plans and Background Information

Forms and Levels Available, with Dates of Publication/Revision of Each: Form 02B was put into operational use in the fall of 2004. A new form is available every one to three years.

Date of Most Recent Edition of Test Manual, User's Guide, etc.:
Technical Manual (2001) (Updated manual available in 2007)
Administrator's Handbook (2006 – 2007)
It's Your Future, Using Your EXPLORE Results, 2006 – 2007
ACT's National Curriculum Survey 2005 – 2006
Technical Manual: Revised Unisex Edition of the ACT Interest Inventory (UNIACT), 1995.

Languages in Which Available: Multiple choice academic achievement tests are available in English only. Preparing/planning guide and interpretive guide available in Spanish also.

Time:
Actual Test Time is 120 minutes (30 minutes per academic test)

Total Administration Time is 135 minutes for test component plus 50 minutes for non test components including the Interest Inventory, Needs Assessment, Plans and Background Information.

Norm Group(s) on Which Scores Are Based: Norms are reported as "percents at or below" (cumulative percents) on EXPLORE® reports. They indicate the percent of examinees in the fall 2005 norming study who received the same scale score or a lower scale score. For example, if a student has a percent at or below 75, it means that 75% of the examinees in the norm group received the same score, or a lower score, than the student.

• Norms are provided for the following three groups:

• Fall Grade 8—Eighth-grade students who test August through January will receive fall 8th-grade norms.

• Spring Grade 8—Eighth graders testing February through July will receive spring 8th-grade norms.

• Grade 9—Ninth-grade students will receive 9th-grade norms regardless of their test date.

Manner in Which Results Are Reported for Individuals:

Types of Scores: World-of-Work Map career areas and regions for UNIACT. Scale Score (1 – 25) for each academic achievement test. Scale Score (1-12) for each subscore reported for the English Test. Composite score, which is the average of the four achievement test scores. Estimated PLAN composite score range. Percents at or above for each scale score reported for the achievement tests based on the national representative norms.

Report Format/Content:

BASIC SERVICE: Results and follow-up materials are shipped to the school three weeks after test materials are received at ACT's scoring center. Routine score reports include two copies of the Student Report including color highlighting of UNIACT results on World-of-Work map graphic and career areas. College Readiness Standards, statements of skills, and knowledge that the student are likely to know and be able to do based on the student's scores are provided on the back of the student report.

Report Format/Content for Group Summaries: Results and follow-up materials are shipped to the school three weeks after test materials are received at ACT's scoring center.

Basic Service: Standard Reporting

• student roster (includes self-reported career plans, self-reported educational plans for high school and beyond, scale scores, and both national and local percentiles)

• profile summary report

• early intervention roster (helps identify students needing extra attention)

• presentation packet

Options:

Additional Supplemental Reports

• alternative student roster and score labels

• College Readiness Standards Information Services

• customized summary report

• district summary report and presentation packet

• CD-ROM/disk service

• EXPLORE to PLAN linkage report

Scoring:

Machine Scoring Service:

COST OF BASIC SERVICE PER COUNSELEE: $5.10 per answer sheet, $2.00 per test book

COST OF OPTIONS:

Pregridding service, $0.26 plus $50 set up fee

Data CD, $33 for school/$44 for multischool district

Local Norms, $85/school norms; $175 district norms

College Readiness Standards Reports, $94

District Profile Summary Report, $94

EXPLORE-PLAN Linkage Report, $175

Hand Scoring: Not available.

Local Machine Scoring: Not available.

Computer Software Options Available: Not available.

Cost of Materials: Due to possible price changes since publication date, be sure to check with publisher website

Specimen Set: $7.60

Counselee Materials: Included in cost of scoring

Using Your EXPLORE Results — Interpretive Guide for students (reusable)

Student Score Report (not reusable)

www.explorestudent.com — Interpretive web site for students and parents

Additional Comments of Interest to Users: ACT offers Braille test books, audiocassettes, CD's, reader's scripts, large-print test booklets, and large-print worksheets for EXPLORE.

Published Reviews of the Instrument in the Last 15 Years: None cited

PLAN

ACT, Inc.

ACT
500 ACT Drive
P.O. Box 168
Iowa City, Iowa 52243-0168
www.act.org

Target Population: Grade 10

Statement of the Purpose of the Instrument: The PLAN® program helps 10th graders build a solid foundation for future academic and career success and provides information needed to address school districts' high-priority issues. It is a comprehensive guidance resource that helps students measure their current academic development, explore career/training options, and make plans for the remaining years of high school and post graduation years.

PLAN can help all students—those who are college-bound as well as those who are likely to enter the workforce directly after high school.

As a "pre-ACT" test, PLAN is a powerful predictor of success on the ACT. At the same time, many schools recognize the importance of PLAN testing for all students, as it focuses attention on both career preparation and improving academic achievement.

Typically, PLAN is administered in the fall of the sophomore year.

Titles of Subtests, Scales, Scores Provided: The PLAN Program includes the following components:

Four Multiple-choice tests of academic achievement:

- English (providing a total test score and two subscores: Usage/Mechanics and Rhetorical Skills)
- Mathematics (providing a total test score and two subscores: Pre-Algebra/Algebra and Geometry)
- Reading (providing a total test score)
- Science (providing a total test score)
- A Composite score (average of the four total test scores)

UNIACT Interest Inventory (an interest inventory score is provided)
Needs Assessment
High School Course/Grade Information
Plans and Background Information

Forms and Levels Available, with Dates of Publication/Revision of Each: A new form is provided every year and released to the students after administration.

Date of Most Recent Edition of Test Manual, User's Guide, etc.:
Technical Manual (1999) (Updated manual available in 2007)

Administrator's Handbook (2007 – 2008)

Using Your PLAN Results (2007 – 2008)

ACT's National Curriculum Survey (2005 – 2006)

Technical Manual: Revised Unisex Edition of the ACT Interest Inventory (UNIACT), 1995.

Languages in Which Available: Multiple choice academic achievement tests are available in English only. Preparing/planning guide and interpretive guide available in Spanish also.

Time:

Actual Test Time is 115 minutes.

Total Administration Time is 135 minutes for test component plus 60 – 75 minutes for non test components including the Interest Inventory, Needs Assessment, High School Course/Grade Information, Plans, and Background Information.

Norm Group(s) on Which Scores Are Based: Norms are reported as "percents at or below" (cumulative percents) on PLAN® reports. They indicate the percent of examinees in the fall 2005 norming study who received the same scale score or a lower scale score. For example, if a student has a percent at or below 75, it means that 75% of the examinees in the norm group received the same score, or a lower score, than the student.

Norms are provided for the following groups:

• Fall Grade 10—Tenth-grade students who test August through January will receive fall 10th-grade norms.

• Spring Grade 10—Tenth graders testing February through July will receive spring 10th-grade norms.

Manner in Which Results Are Reported for Individuals:

Types of Scores: World-of-Work Map career areas and regions for UNIACT. Scale Score (1 – 32) for each academic achievement test. Scale Score (1 – 16) for each subscore reported for the English and Mathematics Test. Composite score, which is the average of the four achievement test scores. Estimated ACT composite score range. Percents at or above for each scale score reported for the achievement tests based on the national representative norms.

Report Format/Content: Student report includes Test Scores, course plans compared to core, college readiness indicators, profile for success regarding their career area preference, career information based on their Interest Inventory results, their item response information for each question, and narrative statements for suggestions on improving their skills based on their scores.

BASIC SERVICE: Results and follow-up materials are shipped to the school three weeks after test materials are received at ACT's scoring center. Routine score reports include two copies of the Student Report.

Report Format/Content for Group Summaries: Results and follow-up materials are shipped to the school three weeks after test materials are received at ACT's scoring center.

Basic Service: Standard Reporting
- High School List Report (includes self-reported career plans, self-reported educational plans for high school and beyond, scale scores, and national percentiles)
- Score labels
- Profile Summary Report
- Early Intervention Roster (helps identify students needing extra attention)
- Presentation Packet

Options:

Additional Supplemental Reports
- Local School and District Norms Reporting
- College Readiness Standards Information Services
- Customized Profile Summary Reports
- Low N-count Student Profile Summary Report
- Item Response Summary Report
- District Profile Summary Report and Presentation Packet
- Research Data File (CD-ROM/disk service)
- College Readiness Standards Information Services
- EXPLORE to PLAN Linkage Report
- PLAN to ACT Linkage Report

Scoring:

Machine Scoring Service:

Cost of basic service per counselee: $9.20

Cost of options:

Pregridding service, $0.26 plus $50 set up fee

Data CD, $33 for school/$44 for multischool district

Local Norms, $85/school norms; $175 district norms

College Readiness Standards Reports, $94

District Profile Summary Report, $94

EXPLORE-PLAN Linkage Report, $17

PLAN-ACT Linkage Report, $175

Item Response Summary Report, $94

Hand Scoring: Not available

Local Machine Scoring: Not available

Computer Software Options Available: Not available

Cost of Materials: Due to possible price changes since publication date, be sure to check with publisher website

Specimen Set: none.

Counselee Materials: Included in cost of scoring

Using Your PLAN Results – Interpretive Guide for students (reusable)

Student Score Report (not reusable)

www.planstudent.com – Interpretive web site for students and parents

Additional Comments of Interest to Users: ACT offers Braille test books, audiocassettes, CD's, reader's scripts, large-print test booklets and large-print worksheets for PLAN.

Published Reviews of the Instrument in the Last 15 Years: None cited

Reviewed by:

Brian J. Taber
Assistant Professor

Howard H. Splete
Professor Emeritus
Department of Counseling

Oakland University
Oakland, MI

Description

EXPLORE and PLAN are the first and second of the three sequential assessments in ACT's Educational Planning and Assessment System (EPAS). The third is the ACT test. All of these assessments are group administered, paper and pencil achievement tests designed to measure acquired published curriculum-based knowledge and skills. The intended overarching goal of the EPAS program is to assess academic development of students and gauge their readiness for college (ACT, 2006a). Accordingly, each of the assessments in the EPAS program is taken sequentially, with EXPLORE administered in the 8th or 9th grade, PLAN in the 10th or 11th grade, and the ACT in the 11th or 12th grade. Within the EPAS framework, EXPLORE provides a baseline assessment of academic achievement, PLAN a review of academic performance, and the ACT assesses academic readiness for college. This longitudinal approach to assessment facilitates the identification of academic strengths and weaknesses at differing points in a student's education. The results from the EPAS assessments inform students, counselors, educators, and parents regarding academic performance in four different scholastic areas for the purposes of educational and career planning.

Both EXPLORE and PLAN contain four timed multiple-choice tests covering English, Mathematics, Reading, and Science Reasoning. The guiding principle in the development of these tests is that the item content should reflect the knowledge and skills necessary for further education. To accomplish this, item content for each of the tests was derived from three sources. First, the test developers gathered information on the objectives of instruction for each grade level for all states that had published them. Second, test developers reviewed the contents of state-approved text books for each grade level. Third, they consulted with educators to acquire information on the knowledge and skills necessary for successful academic performance in high school and postsecondary education. The results of these efforts culminated in the creation of each of the following tests.

The English Test has 40 items in EXPLORE and 50 items in PLAN. This test assesses a student's knowledge of standard written English in regards to punctuation, grammar, usage, and sentence structure, and also rhetorical skills in relation to strategy, organization, and style. The test contains four prose sections, each followed by multiple-choice test items. In addition to the composite score for the English Test, subscores are reported for Usage/Mechanics and Rhetorical Skills in both EXPLORE and PLAN.

The Mathematics Test has 30 items in EXPLORE and 40 items in PLAN. This test assesses a student's quantitative reasoning in four content areas. In EXPLORE, the math content areas are Pre-Algebra, Elementary Algebra, Geometry, and Statistics/Probability. In PLAN, the math content areas are Pre-Algebra, Elementary Algebra, Coordinate Geometry, and Plane Geometry. Items on the Mathematics Test cover knowledge, skills, direct application, and understanding and integrating concepts. The use of calculators for EXPLORE and PLAN is permitted. In PLAN, subscores are reported for Algebra and Geometry as well as a Mathematics composite score. In EXPLORE, there are no subscores.

The Reading Test has 30 items in EXPLORE and 25 items in PLAN. This test assesses a student's reading comprehension in terms of being able to refer to what is explicitly stated and the ability to derive conclusions, comparisons, and generalizations. The test is comprised of three prose sections on topics in the social sciences, fiction, and the humanities, each followed by a set of multiple-choice questions.

The Science Reasoning Test has 28 items in EXPLORE and 30 items in PLAN. This test assesses scientific reasoning skills in the context of different scientific disciplines. In EXPLORE, the science reasoning content domains are life sciences, Earth/space sciences, and physical sciences. In PLAN, the science reasoning content domains are biology, Earth/space sciences, chemistry, and physics. Scientific information is conveyed in different formats: data representation (e.g., graphs and tables), research summaries, or conflicting view points. Multiple-choice items assess such things as the student's ability to critically examine the information provided and conclusions drawn from it, as well as the ability to make generalizations from the information given to draw conclusions and make predictions.

In addition to the academic achievement tests in EXPLORE and PLAN, students provide noncognitive information that are purported to help in the educational and career planning process. The noncognitive assessments includes such things as self-reported academic needs, scholastic plans, and the UNIACT — a vocational interest inventory in which the student responds "like," "dislike," or "indifferent" to 72 work-relevant activities. Additionally, a school or school district can add up to 12 additional noncognitive supplemental items of their choosing. For example, supplemental items may cover topics such as hours spent studying, interest in adding additional types of courses in the curriculum, or student opinions about the school environment.

Uses in Counseling

Score reports for EXPLORE and PLAN provide scale scores for the English, Mathematics, Reading, and Science Reasoning tests. Additionally, percentile scores are reported for each student in reference to a national norm group by grade as well as their performance relative to others in their school, the district, and the state in which they reside. PLAN also provides norm-referenced scores for 10th graders planning to attend a 2-year or 4-year college. Both EXPLORE and PLAN score reports show estimated composite score ranges for the next test in the sequence of the EPAS program. The score reports provide feedback on college readiness based on the results of the four tests in terms of whether their scores are below, at, or above bench mark scores for college admissions. Suggestions are offered on the back of the score reports on how students can improve their academic skills in each of the four areas covered by the tests.

In addition to the achievement test results, information is provided for the noncognitive assessments regarding their self-reported academic needs and vocational interests. Students are provided with feedback in regard to how their high school course plans compare to the recommended courses necessary for admission into college as well as to their self-reported academic needs. This is important information for students who are considering college and need guidance on course selection and academic preparation. On the PLAN score report, a range of ACT assessment composite scores of college sophomores in majors related to the student's career area preference is provided. UNIACT results are reported using the World-of-Work Map which highlights the regions and job families that coincide with students' interests.

In order to help the students better understand and make use of their results for educational as well as career purposes, booklets are provided for both EXPLORE and PLAN. The informational booklets explain what the results on the score report mean as well as information about the World of Work Map and tips on conducting career exploration. Additionally, a course planner is located at the back of each booklet for the student to plan what courses to take in successive years in high school. Apart from the print material, there are EXPLORE and PLAN websites with informational links for students, counselors, and parents. While no specific guidelines for use in counseling are offered from the test publisher, score reports and ancillary materials present an ample amount of user friendly information that can be considered in educational and career planning.

A useful feature of EXPLORE and PLAN is that they are conceptually and statistically linked permitting academic skill assessment at different stages of educational and career development. This provides a source of information in identifying academic strengths and weaknesses over time. Another advantage is that in the context of the EPAS program EXPLORE and PLAN are linked to the ACT assessment, which helps prepare students for college admissions testing. Further, it is purported that taking EXPLORE and PLAN assessment encourages completion of more challenging course work and increases students' readiness for college (ACT, 2006b).

Technical Considerations

The most recent norming of EXPLORE and PLAN took place in the fall of 2005, and information regarding these groups is provided in supplements to the technical manuals (ACT, 2007a, ACT, 2007b). EXPLORE was normed on 3,001 8th graders and 3,960 9th graders. PLAN was normed on 4,356 10th graders and 2,556 11th graders. As part of the sampling strategy, schools were stratified by size, and weights were applied to schools in order to approximate regional and national representation. Despite efforts to attain national representation, no data from either EXPLORE or PLAN are provided. Therefore, it can not be determined whether these norms are in fact related to the demographic makeup of students and school characteristics nationally.

The EXPLORE and PLAN Technical Manuals (ACT, 1999, 2001) give thorough and detailed information regarding the creation of the tests. In developing these tests, ACT uses information from state instructional objectives, approved text books, and national survey data from educators from various educational settings to ensure that EXPLORE and PLAN tests cover essential material in each of the four content areas. Accordingly, the item content of EXPLORE and PLAN generally conforms to expectations of the academic skills that should be acquired at each grade level being tested. Items are reviewed for content and fairness and undergo item tryouts and subsequent analyses before being incorporated into the tests.

Internal consistency reliability estimates for the EXPLORE and PLAN scale scores range from upper .70s to high .80s. The standard error of measure ranges from 1 to approximately 2 points for each of the four test scores. The reliability and standard error of measurement estimates indicate an acceptable level of test score consistency given the nature and purpose of these tests.

Validity evidence for EXPLORE and PLAN is somewhat limited. For EXPLORE, the technical manual reports observed correlations between EXPLORE and PLAN for a sample of 90,125 students who have taken both tests. These correlations ranged from .63 on the Science Reasoning tests to .77 on the English tests. The observed correlation between the EXPLORE and PLAN composite scores was .85. This indicates that a student's score on EXPLORE has moderate to high correlation to their scores on PLAN. These results indicate that in general, test performance does not change much from the baseline assessment of EXPLORE to the midpoint assessment of PLAN within the EPAS system.

Validity evidence for PLAN also is somewhat limited. The technical manual reports data on the relationship of self-reported grades, courses completed, and the intention to complete future courses, and performance on the PLAN tests. The sample was drawn from 83 schools in a southeastern state in 1990. Examination of the correlations among the variables indicates that these relations are low to moderate. Based on a sample of 6,500 students from 1993, the PLAN technical manual reports correlations between PLAN scores and whether students have completed related course work or intend to take college prep course work related to the PLAN. Results indicated modest relations between PLAN scores and completed course work ranging from .35 for Science Reasoning to .47 for Mathematics. Correlations for PLAN test scores and plans to take future course work ranged from .27 from the Usage/Mechanics English subscores to .32 for Mathematics.

Other than some psychometric information for the UNIACT, the technical manuals for EXPLORE and PLAN do not provide any research information on the other noncognitive variables in EXPLORE and PLAN. Readers are referred to the *UNIACT Technical Manual* (Swaney, 1995) for more detailed information regarding the psychometric properties of the UNIACT. Internal consistency estimates of reliability as well as tests of temporal stability of the UNIACT are quite good. Additionally, a number of studies have substantiated the construct, convergent, discriminant, and criterion validity evidence for the UNIACT.

Overall Critique

The EXPLORE and PLAN assessments are painstakingly developed achievement tests. A great deal of attention is paid to ensuring content validity and item integrity. The tests focus primarily on higher order cognitive abilities rather than rote memory. The accompanying score reports and additional materials are thoughtfully and professionally prepared. The ancillary booklets and websites are user friendly and provide solid information on how students can make the most of their score results. However, the technical manuals for EXPLORE and PLAN should be updated with the more recent norms and any subsequent validity information to support its purported use.[1]

As with any singular assessment tool, counselors using results from EXPLORE and PLAN should do so in conjunction with self-reported academic needs, grades, and other teacher assessments in order to create an overall picture of a student's strengths and weaknesses to formulate useful educational and career plans.

EXPLORE and PLAN seem useful in educational and career planning for those who intend to pursue postsecondary education. Given the increased complexity of many occupations, the percentage of students who will need to consider some sort of postsecondary training beyond high school will continue to increase. Therefore, by linking academic achievement and occupational interests via UNIACT results, students can be helped to see the relationship between achievement in different scholastic areas and occupations. Indeed, EXPLORE and PLAN are useful assessment tools in helping high schools student to see the relationship among academics, occupational exploration activities, interests, and planning for continued learning and development.

[1] Editor's Note: Updated manuals due for publication in 2007.

References

ACT, Inc. (1999). *PLAN technical manual.* Iowa City, IA: Author.

ACT, Inc. (2001). *EXPLORE technical manual.* Iowa City, IA: Author.

ACT, Inc. (2006a). *College readiness standards.* Iowa City, IA: Author.

ACT, Inc. (2006b). *EPAS: A system that works.* Iowa City, IA: Author.

ACT, Inc. (2007a). *Norming section of the EXPLORE technical manual.* Iowa City, IA: Author.

ACT, Inc. (2007b). *Norming section of the PLAN technical manual.* Iowa City, IA: Author.

Swaney, K. B. (1995). *Technical manual: Revised unisex edition of the ACT Interest Inventory (UNIACT).* Iowa City, IA: ACT, Inc.

The Highlands Ability Battery (tHAB)

Robert McDonald
Paper & Pencil Version and CD Version

Lazar Emanuel
CD Version and Online Version

The Highlands Company
1328 Boston Post Road
Larchmont, NY 10538
www.highlandsco.com
www.highlandslifeandcareercenter.com
CD version: www.highlandscd.com
Online version: www.abilitybattery.com

Target Population: All ages 15 and above with universal application to male and female.

Statement of the Purpose of the Instrument: To compare the user's scores on each of 19 work samples with the scores of all users who have completed the Battery in the same format (CD or online). Also, to conduct feedback with clients either individually or in groups (e.g., corporate groups, student groups.) Each work sample measures a different innate ability by requiring the client to respond on his or her keyboard to visual and aural stimuli. In this way, we measure whether the client is a specialist or a generalist, and whether he or she is an introvert or an extrovert. We also measure the client's orientation to time management, as well as to the abilities we describe as classification, concept organization, idea productivity, spatial relations (abstract and structural), verbal memory, tonal memory, image memory, kinesthetic memory, number memory, pitch discrimination, observation, visual speed, visual accuracy, and vocabulary. We adjust results to compensate for ranges in typing speed. Instructions are given both on screen and orally.

Titles of Subtests, Scales, Scores Provided: The Battery consists of 19 work samples or subtests. They are: Generalist/Specialist scale, Extrovert/Introvert Scale, Time Frame Orientation, Classification (Inductive Reasoning), Concept Organization (Analytical Reasoning), Time Frame (Foresight), Idea Productivity (Ideaphoria), Spatial Relations Visualization (Structural), Spatial Relations Theory (Abstract), Design Memory, Verbal Memory (Associative Memory), Observation, Tonal Memory (Auditory Memory), Pitch Discrimination, Rhythm Memory, Number Memory, Visual Speed, Visual Accuracy, Vocabulary Level.

All the subtests are scored in the range of 5 – 99. The individual receives a separate score for each subtest, measured on the following scale: Low 5 – 34; Mid-range 35 – 64; High 65 – 99.

Forms and Levels Available, with Dates of Publication/Revision of Each: Screen shots of each screen of each work sample are supplied. The CD version was first published in the year 2000 and has not been revised. It is available on a CD-ROM disc. The online version was published in April 2004 and was revised in August 2006.

Date of Most Recent Edition of Test Manual, User's Guide, etc.: The most recent edition of the Test Manual was published in 2006. Instructions for registration and technical support are supplied to each user. Directions for completing the subtests are contained within the CD itself and within the online version.

Languages in Which Available: English only.

Time:

Actual Test Time: Approximately three hours in all.

Total Administration Time: The Battery is scored during the assessment process. A report is available to the client immediately upon completion of the assessment. The report contains 32 pages of text and graphics.

The Company employs a full-time technician who is available at all hours to answer any questions relating to the CD version and the online version.

Norm Group(s) on Which Scores Are Based: Norms were based originally on all clients who completed the paper and pencil version of the Battery. The norms were tested and confirmed by Dr. C. L. Holland in 1994. In 2002, the Chauncey Group, an ETS subsidiary, examined 4,307 CD reports. The Chauncey Group computed sample sizes, means, standard deviations, and complete norms tables for each of the 23 CD-based scores for four groups of examinees ages 15 – 21, 22 – 30, 31 – 39, 40 and older. Each norms table provided the percentile rank and the raw score for that age group at that percentile rank. Tables were provided that included the comparison of these data among each other and, where available, to the norms assigned by Highlands in the CD-based Highlands Ability Battery. In its report, the Chauncey Group concluded:

Overall, the data from the CD-based Highlands Ability Battery shows that each test score in the battery correlates sufficiently so as to provide indirect evidence that the tests in the Highlands Ability Battery are sufficiently reliable for their use in the test battery for feedback purposes, since the feedback report provides a combination of the scores for personal growth purposes.

Also, examination of the frequency distributions among the four age groups shows consistent similarities for scores at the different percentiles regardless of age group. Those differences in scores by age group that did exist were consistent across the different age groups.

Since completion of the Chauncey Group report, the company has been drawing data in an online databank based upon the test results of each client. We now have a separate set of data for (1) a 500-client sampling of paper and pencil results; (2) all CD results to date; (3) all online results to date; and (4) all results of a group in the construction industry which we refer to as the X Group. Norms based on the CD results (a total of 2,036 at this date) are computed by age and sex and are compared with the paper and pencil results to assure reasonable conformity. Since the introduction of the online version, a separate set of data has been maintained for it (a total of 6,800 entries to date). These are also distributed by sex and age. The age range is 15 – 21, 22 – 30, 31 – 39, 40 – 55, and 56+. Data are also maintained by sex. Each subdivision of age and sex is separately normed.

Manner in Which Results Are Reported for Individuals:

Types of Scores: A score expressed in percentile ranking is issued for each work sample.

Report Format/Content:

BASIC SERVICE: A 32-page report is issued to each client. The report contains a bar chart showing the client's score on each work sample. The results and their significance are explained in narrative form, as well as graphically. A sample report is attached.

After the report is issued and analyzed by a user and an Affiliate of the Company, we conduct an individual feedback conference lasting two hours. During the conference, the results are explained to the client. In some situations, as with corporate teams or a class of students, feedback can be accomplished effectively in group feedback sessions lasting 4 to 8 hours.

OPTIONS: The Battery is used in many corporate and student settings for training in individual development, team building, and leadership.

Report Format/Content for Group Summaries:

BASIC SERVICE: For each type of group, we have designed both a facilitator's manual and a participant manual. Manuals are available in Personal Development, Team Building, and Leadership.

Before each program, we prepare and issue a Group Profile showing the distribution of scores among the participants. This enables the affiliate/facilitator to focus on the strengths and challenges of the group as a whole, as well as of the individual participants.

OPTIONS: We have conducted programs utilizing the Battery in mentoring and in in-house training of HR and other corporate personnel. The training enables these employees to administer and interpret the Battery for other employees of the company.

Scoring:

Machine Scoring Service: All scores are computed and stored electronically in a common data base housed on the Company's own server. Scores are collected and scored immediately.

Scoring is done online as a work sample is completed.

COST OF BASIC SERVICE PER COUNSELEE: The Battery and the two-hour individual feedback are treated as one integrated service. The cost for both in direct sales by the Company to the individual user is $450. The Company pays one or another of its Affiliates for conducting the individual feedback. When they deal with their own clients, Affiliates of the Company are permitted to establish their own prices for the Battery and feedback.

The Company sells access to the Battery to its Affiliates, who then fix the charge for the Battery and feedback themselves. The cost to each Affiliate for a key permitting registration online is $90; the cost for a single CD disc is $80. The CD price, but not the online price, is subject to volume discounts.

COST OF OPTIONS: When group programs are substituted for individual feedback, the cost varies depending on the size of the group, the nature of the program, and the length of the program.

Hand Scoring: Not available.

Local Machine Scoring: Not available.

Computer Software Options Available: Computerized adaptive administration; because each work sample is scored by applying its own unique formula, software was designed, implemented, and copyright by the company.

Ways in Which Computer/Online Version Differs:

The CD and online versions make unnecessary:

• Travel by the client to an office or classroom

• Hand scoring and the resulting possibility of error

• Interpretation of results by a fallible human being

• Translation of results onto paper—a source of potential error.

Further, the CD and online versions permit:

• Immediate registration and completion

• Instantaneous receipt of scores and report

• Sophisticated instructions, both on-screen and in audio

• Graphics in color and with movement

• Common treatment for all, instead of varying treatment by individual instructors

• Translation of individual results into data by sex and age for all clients

Cost of Materials: Due to possible price changes since publication date be sure to check with publisher web site.

Specimen Set: No additional cost for individual clients. Clients in a group feedback are charged $50 each for the Participant's Manual.

Counselee Materials: Various manuals and instruction sheets.

Additional Comments of Interest to Users: We are contemplating an online version in the Spanish language. We regularly design and produce new group feedback programs. We are now in the process of completing a program in Leadership. All programs relate human abilities to the functions and roles of the school or the workplace.

Published Reviews of the Instrument in the Last 15 Years: None cited.

Reviewed by:

Manivong Ratts
Assistant Professor
Department of Counseling and School Psychology
College of Education
Seattle University

Description

The Highlands Ability Battery (tHAB) is based on the initial work of Johnson O'Connor, a research scientist devoted to studying innate abilities. O'Connor (1928) theorized that people are born with certain natural abilities that develop from infancy and can be measured upon maturation, usually at the age of 14. tHAB was developed primarily for use in career counseling with high school and college students and for working adults in career transition. Initially offered as a paper and pencil test in 1992 by its publisher, The Highlands Company, a CD version was developed in 2000, an online format followed in 2004 (Tavantzis, 2007). The paper and pencil version can be administered in individual or group formats. Both tHAB CD and online versions may be taken in one sitting or in intervals.

tHAB consist of a series of 19 worksamples. Each worksample measures a particular ability and is categorized under one of the following sections: (1) *Personal Style Assessment* (Generalist-Specialist, Introvert-Extrovert Scale, and Time Frame Orientation), (2) *Driving Abilities* (Classification, Concept Organization, Idea Productivity, Spatial Relations Theory, and Spatial Relations Visualization), (3) *Specialized Abilities* (Design Memory, Observation, Verbal Memory, Tonal Memory, Rhythm Memory, Pitch Discrimination, Number Memory, and Visual Speed and Accuracy) and (4) *Vocabulary* (Vocabulary).

Each worksample is timed to determine the ease with which an individual is able to complete a particular task. The paper and pencil and CD versions take approximately 3 hours to complete, while the online version can be completed in 2 hours and 30 minutes. Both tHAB CD and online versions include written and voice-recorded instructions. All three versions of the Battery provide examples of how to complete each worksample and offer test takers practice worksamples.

Results of both tHAB CD and online versions are available immediately in electronic format upon completing the Battery. The report includes a detailed 30-page summary of each worksample compiled in a personal profile and bar chart to illustrate ability patterns and how certain abilities cluster. A copy of the results also is automatically transmitted via the Internet to a trained and certified Highlands affiliate. Certified Highlands affiliates are individuals who have participated in *The Highlands Company Affiliate Training Program*. This training qualifies people to interpret tHAB results and offer consultation for test takers. Trained and certified affiliates are available live or via phone for two-hour individual or group interpretation of results. Live interpretations can also be recorded on a CD-ROM and mailed to test takers. Certified Highlands affiliates are either employed through the Highlands Company or one of the 175+

trained and certified consultants from around the world (e.g., United States, United Kingdom, Singapore, and Canada).

Individual reports vary depending on whether the test taker is a student or an adult. A new report issued in 2007 relates natural abilities to the functions of leadership. Certified affiliates who consult with students are likely to explore college choices, college curriculum, college majors, and college selection. Affiliates working with adults may address career changes, career transitions, career exploration, career services, and leadership.

Use in Counseling

tHAB is intended to be used to help individuals better understand their natural abilities and how these relate to career development and planning for high school – aged students, college and university students, and adults. Counselors may also find the Battery useful in helping students understand their learning styles as one section of the instrument measures learning styles (Tavantzis, 2007). The Battery is also used to assist individuals who are in career transition, to help businesses restructure their workforce according to employee abilities, in employee team building and development, in employee training needs, and in leadership.

Interpretation of results by a trained affiliate is required by The Highlands Company. Trained affiliates are able to explain results, provide meaning to the Battery, and discuss future steps in individual and group formats. To be a trained Highlands affiliate, individuals are required to apply for application. The training consists of completing tHAB, receiving live feedback on the results, and participating in eight two-hour telephone-based training sessions. Face-to-face training is also available. Trainees are also trained to offer individual and group feedback and required to provide two practice feedback reports and two practice feedback conferences.

Written resources are also available on tHAB. Tavantzis (2007) found the *tHAB Technical Manual* to be a useful resource on the technical elements of the Battery. Two books describing tHAB have also been published by the Highlands Company entitled: *Don't Waste Your Talent* (McDonald and Hutcheson, 2005) and *Highlands: The Right Choice* (Martin and Danelo, 2006). These resources are additional tools that provide counselors a framework for understanding tHAB.

Technical Considerations

The Highlands Company has conducted several studies of tHAB since 1993. For example, in 1994 a reliability study was conducted on the Battery (Holland, 1994). This study revealed that the 19 worksamples have reliability scores ranging from .83 to .95 (Tavantzis, 2007). The study was based on a random sample of 298 test takers ranging in age between 15 and 66 and included 146 males and 152 females. Adults over 25 were mainly college graduates and those under 25 were either in college or former college students (Holland, 1994). The Highlands Company asserts that the minimum reliability scores required for all 19 worksamples of the Battery is r = .80, which is higher than the acceptable reliability range of .6 to .7 for tests of like nature (Tavantzis, 2007). This suggests the 19 worksamples are highly reliable and useful for comparison purposes.

In 2002, The Highlands Company contracted with the Chauncey Group, a subsidiary of the Educational Testing Service (ETS), to conduct a statistical audit of the CD version of the Battery (Breyer, Katz, & Duran, 2002). This study computed sample sizes, means, and standard deviations and provided norms tables for test takers in the following age categories: 15 – 21, 22 – 30, 31 – 39, and 40 and older. The researchers concluded that the CD version yielded 23 separate scores on the 19 work samples and that each score on the Battery correlated sufficiently, thus deeming them reliable for interpretation purposes.

Validity studies have also been conducted. Holland (1994) concluded that there was adequate evidence of both convergent and divergent validity when assessing individual worksamples. That is, abilities that were expected to be related (e.g., typing speed and visual speed) were in fact related. Similarly, those abilities that should not be related (e.g., time frame and writing speed) showed little relationship. This seems to suggest strong evidence of validity on tHAB.

Computer-Based and/or Online Version

tHAB is available in both CD and online formats. The CD is only compatible with PCs. Offering CD and online versions of the Battery allows test takers freedom to take the instrument at their own convenience as long as they have access to a computer and reliable Internet access. Test takers using the CD version need to complete the Battery on the same computer because scores are stored on the computer's hard drive.

Minimum software requirements include: 133 MHz processor and at least 32 MB RAM, VGA monitor, sound card with speakers (headphones recommended when in pubic settings), mouse, a reliable Internet connection (56k modem or faster), one of the following Internet browsers—Internet Explorer (version 6 or higher), Mozilla (version 1 or higher), Netscape (version 7 or higher), and/or Safari (version 1.2 or higher), Macromedia Flash Player (version 6 or higher). Users should also make sure they have Javascript and cookies enabled if they are using tHAB online.

Overall Critique

Unlike other assessment instruments such as the Strong Interest Inventory (SII) and the Myers-Briggs Type Indicator (MBTI), which require self-report and measure interests and personality, respectively, tHAB assesses natural abilities through completion of timed objective tasks. This can be helpful in assisting students with career decisions, adults who are in the midst of a life transition, and those interested in understanding how their abilities are related to leadership qualities. Another strength of tHAB has to do with technology. Both CD and online formats use voice-recorded instruction, which can be an added benefit for those who are auditory learners. Instructions, both on the screen and in the voice recording, are simple, clear, and comprehensive. Receiving results immediately upon completion of the Battery is also an added feature. In addition, Highlands affiliates are very professional and helpful in their interpretation of results.

Test takers who are not computer proficient do not have access to a computer and/or the Internet are able to use the paper and pencil test.

The time (2.5 – 3 hours) required to complete the tHAB is time-consuming when compared to other inventories. However, the benefits seem to outweigh the costs. The information provided is in-depth and can be useful for those in the midst of career exploration and decision making. Another limitation is that tHAB CD is not compatible with Macintosh computers. However, Apple users have the option of using the Internet version of the Battery—which is the most popular among the two versions. Lastly, tHAB is only available in English. The Highlands Company has discussed the idea of having it available in other languages. This would seem to be important as its use becomes more global.

References

Breyer, F. J., Katz, J., & Duran, M. (2002). *A report on the statistical characteristics of The Highlands Ability Battery CD.* Princeton, NJ: The Chauncey Group.

Holland, C. L. (1994). *Research proposal: The Highlands Ability Battery.* Atlanta: Georgia State University.

Martin, L. H., & Danelo, K. T. (2006). *Highlands: The right choice. Matching your abilities with college and career.* Leesburg, VA: Highlands Consulting Group.

McDonald, B., & Hutcheson, D. E. (2005). *Don't waste your talent: The 8 critical steps to discovering what you do best.* Larchmont, NY: The Highlands Company.

O'Connor, J. (1928). *Born that way.* Baltimore: The Williams & Wilkins Company.

Tavantzis, T. N. (2007). *A report on the organization, function, reliability, and validity of The Highlands Ability Battery (tHAB).* Philadelphia, PA: Saint Joseph's University.

KUDER CAREER PLANNING SYSTEM
KUDER SKILLS ASSESSMENT (KSA)
KUDER CAREER SEARCH (KCS)
SUPER'S WORK VALUES INVENTORY-revised (SWVI-r)
KUDER® SKILLS ASSESSMENT (KSA)

Darrell A. Luzzo, Patrick J. Rottinghaus and Donald G. Zytowski

Kuder, Inc.
302 Visions Parkway, Adel, IA 50003
www.kuder.com

Target Population: Students (grades 7 and higher) and adults.

Statement of the Purpose of the Instrument: The *KSA* assesses individual's self-reported confidence in performing a variety of tasks. Respondents rate themselves on their confidence that they can successfully perform a wide variety of tasks (e.g., "Fix a faucet that is dripping").

Titles of Subtests, Scales, Scores Provided: *KSA-6:* Outdoor/Mechanical, Science/Technical, Arts/Communications, Social/Personal Services, Sales/Management and Business Operations.

KSA-16 and *KSA-CA* are scored for States' 16 Career Clusters.

Forms and Levels Available, with Dates of Publication/Revision of Each: Three forms:

KSA-6 reporting Six *Kuder* Career Clusters, 2002

KSA-16, reporting States' 16 Career Clusters, 2004, middle school through high school

KSA-CA, 2006, reporting six or 16 clusters, college and adult.

Internet-based as components of the *Kuder Career Planning System.*

Date of Most Recent Edition of Test Manual, User's Guide, etc.: 2007. Available at http://www.kuder.com/downloads/KSA-Tech-Manual.pdf.

Languages in Which Available: English and Spanish.

Time:

Actual Test Time: *KSA-6,* on average 10 minutes, *KSA-16* and *KSA-CA,* 15 minutes.

Total Administration Time: 10 minutes

Norm Group(s) on Which Scores Are Based:

KSA-6 is normed on the same group as *KCS* and *SWVI-r:* 8785 males and females ages 14 to adult, drawn randomly and proportionately from *Kuder Career Planning System* users in 30 states.

KSA-16 is normed on 3,486 males and females ages 13 to adult drawn randomly and proportionately from nine regions of the U.S.

KSA-CA norms in development at this writing.

Note: Kuder, Inc will release a new set of norms for the *KSA* in the fall of 2008.

Manner in Which Results Are Reported for Individuals:

Types of Scores: Percentile ranks.

Report Format/Content:

BASIC SERVICE: Printable on-screen report with interpretive material includes scores in a bar graph in rank order, labeled, and color-coded to denote high, moderate and low. Interpretive material includes narrative suggesting steps for continuing career exploration and links to explore options for continuing education. Links explore occupational listings by education level within each of the clusters. Each occupation is crosswalked to additional information from the *Occupational Outlook Handbook, O*NET™* and related military occupations, for further exploration.

OPTIONS: If *Kuder Career Search* has been completed, results are presented with KSA in a combined profile, including interpretive statements suggesting possible actions keyed to various pair combinations.

Report Format/Content for Group Summaries:

Basic Service: Group summaries sorted on several variables are accessed at the administrator's site.

Scoring:

Machine Scoring Service: Not available.

Hand Scoring: Not available.

Local Machine Scoring: Not available.

Computer Software Options Available: Standard administration online.

Cost of Materials: Due to possible price changes since publication date, be sure to check with publisher web site.

Specimen Set: $19.95 (individual online purchase)
Annual license available for educational and other institutions; pricing based on enrollment or amount of uses.

Additional Comments of Interest to Users: The *KSA* is a component of the web-based *Kuder Career Planning System. (www.kuder.com)* In addition to assessments, the system offers an educational planner, college and instructional program searches and comparisons, financial aid searches, a resumé builder, and more. All online materials may be printed out or stored in user's portfolio.

Published Reviews of the Instrument in the Last 15 Years: None cited.

KUDER® CAREER SEARCH (KCS)

Frederic Kuder and Donald G. Zytowski

Kuder, Inc.
302 Visions Parkway, Adel, IA 50003
www.kuder.com

Target Population: Students (grades 7 and higher) and adults.

Statement of the Purpose of the Instrument: One form assesses interests expressed as activity preferences, reporting the test taker's similarity with employed adults in selected occupational clusters, and giving "job sketches" of a number of employed adults who most closely match the test taker's preferences.

Titles of Subtests, Scales, Scores Provided: Normative scores on occupational scales: Outdoor/Mechanical, Science/Technical, Arts/Communications, Social/Personal Services, Sales/Management, and Business Operations. Optionally scorable for States' 16 Clusters or other career cluster systems.

Forms and Levels Available, with Dates of Publication/Revision of Each: One form, 2003, middle school through adult levels, Internet-based, as a component of the *Kuder Career Planning System.*

Date of Most Recent Edition of Test Manual, User's Guide, etc.: 2003. Available at http://www.kuder.com/downloads/kcs-tech-manual.pdf.

Languages in Which Available: English and Spanish.

Time:

Actual Test Time: On average 15 minutes

Norm Group(s) on Which Scores Are Based: Cluster raw scores are developed from a pool of approximately 2,000 adults employed in a wide variety of occupations. Percentile scores are based on 8,785 males and females ages 14 though adult, drawn randomly and proportionately from *Kuder Career Planning System* users in 30 states. Note: Kuder, Inc. will release a new version of the KCS in fall of 2008, which will include a new set of norms.

Manner in Which Results Are Reported for Individuals:

Types of Scores: Percentile ranks, labeled, and color-coded high, moderate, and low.

Report Format/Content:

BASIC SERVICE: An on-screen printable report gives Kuder Career Clusters in color-coded bar graphs ranked by how closely they match test taker's interests. Clicking on a cluster name provides a description of the cluster and resources for further exploration. Several narrative paragraphs orient users to interpretation of scores, the person match system, and job sketches.

Unique to KCS are one-page job sketches—seven each in the top two career clusters—from individuals in the Person Match pool whose interests most closely match the test taker's profile. Links are provided to explore occupational listings from the Occupational Outlook Handbook, O*Net™, and related military occupations.

Options: If *Kuder Skills Assessment* has been completed, results are presented with KCS in a combined profile, with interpretive statements keyed to various high, medium, and low pair combinations.

Report Format/Content for Group Summaries:

Basic Service: Group summaries sorted on several variables may be accessed at the administrator's site.

Scoring: Scoring is instantaneous on completion of last item.

Computer Software Options Available: Standard administration online.

Cost of Materials: Due to possible price changes since publication date be sure to check with publisher web site.

Specimen Set: Individual online purchase, $19.95.
Annual license available for educational institutions; pricing based on enrollment or number of uses.

Counselee Materials: The KCS is a component of the web-based *Kuder Career Planning System.* (*www.kuder.com*) In addition to assessments, the system offers an education planner, college and instructional program searches and comparisons, financial aid searches, a resumé builder, and more. All online materials may be printed out or stored in user's portfolio.

Published Reviews of the Instrument in the Last 15 Years: None cited.

Super's Work Values Inventory – revised (SWVI-r)
Donald E. Super and Donald G. Zytowski

Kuder, Inc.
302 Visions Parkway, Adel, IA 50003
www.kuder.com

Target Population: Students (grades 7 and higher) and adults.

Statement of the Purpose of the Instrument: *Super's Work Values Inventory-revised* measures student or client preferences for an array of rewards of jobs and careers.

Titles of Subtests, Scales, Scores Provided: Achievement, Co-workers, Creativity, Income, Independence, Lifestyle, Mental Challenge, Prestige, Security, Supervision, Variety, Workplace.

Forms and Levels Available, with Dates of Publication/Revision of Each: One form, middle school student through adult levels; 2006.

Date of Most Recent Edition of Test Manual, User's Guide, etc.: 2006. Available at http://www.kuder.com/downloads/SWV-Tech-Manual.pdf.

Languages in Which Available: English and Spanish

Time:

Actual Test Time: On average 10 minutes

Total Administration Time: 10 minutes

Norm Group(s) on Which Scores Are Based: 8,785 males and females ages 14 through adult, drawn randomly and proportionately from Kuder Career Planning System users in 30 states. Note: Kuder, Inc will release a new set of norms for the SWVI-r in the fall of 2008.

Manner in Which Results Are Reported for Individuals:

Types of Scores: Percentiles, labeled high, moderate, and low.

Report Format/Content: Results presented on-screen in a rank-ordered profile, color-coded to delineate high, medium, and low scores. Definitions of each value may be obtained by clicking on the value name. Accompanying text offers suggestions for using results and steps for continuing career exploration.

OPTIONAL: Job sketches illustrate work values operating in various jobs. Users may link to the O*NET for a list of occupations in five educational levels that correspond to the user's highest work values.

Report Format/Content for Group Summaries: Group summaries of several kinds are available on an administrator's site.

Scoring:

Machine Scoring Service: Not available.

Hand Scoring: Not available.

Local Machine Scoring: Not available.

Computer Software Options Available: Standard administration online.

Cost of Materials: Due to possible price changes since publication date, be sure to check with publisher website.

Specimen Set: $19.95 (individual online purchase, includes *Kuder Career Search, Kuder Skills Assessment,* and access to numerous occupational and educational resources, plus other features.) Special annual license pricing available for educational institutions, pricing based on enrollment or amount of uses.

Counselee Materials: All online materials may be printed out or stored in user's portfolio.

Additional Comments of Interest to Users: The *SWVI-r* is a component of the *Kuder Career Planning System (www.kuder.com)*. Respondents rate themselves on their value for 12 aspects of jobs and careers, (e.g. Prestige, Independence, Security). Results link to numerous occupational (e.g.: O*NET) and educational resources through the system's online career portfolio. Administrator oversight is included in the system. The complete *Kuder Career Planning System* offers additional resources to aid college and career exploration, planning, and development.

Published Reviews of the Instrument in the Last 15 Years: None cited.

Reviewed by:

Paulette M. Schenck
Assistant Professor of Counseling
Counselor Education Program
Department of Educational Leadership,
Counseling and Special Education
Augusta State University
Augusta, GA

Description

Today's *Kuder® Career Planning System* is the legacy of Frederic Kuder's pioneering work spanning nearly 70 years. It reflects the third generation of Kuder interest inventories, "both in terms of years and in successive editions" (Zytowski, 1992, p. 245), used by an estimated 100 million worldwide over that time span. Three *Kuder* assessments are reviewed here: *Kuder Skills Assessment, Kuder Career Search with Person Match* (2003), and *Super's Work Values Inventory-revised* (2006).

Kuder Skills Assessment (KSA)

Kuder Skills Assessment (KSA) lists different activities of which test takers indicate how easily they think they can learn each task. Responses range on a four-point scale from *I don't think I could ever learn how to do this task* to *I can already do this task*. Results are reported in percentiles, labeled as high, medium, or low, and displayed in rank order of career clusters.

KSA is available in three formats. *KSA-6* (2002) contains 90 items which are based on six career clusters (Outdoor/Mechanical, Science/Technical, Arts/Communication, Social/Personal Services, Sales/Management, and Business Operations). *KSA-16* (2004) contains 175 items corresponding to the 16 federal career clusters (Agriculture, Food and Natural Resources; Architecture and Construction; Arts, A/V Technology and Communication; Business, Management, and Administration; Education and Training; Finance; Government and Public Administration; Health Science; Hospitality and Tourism; Human Services; Information Technology; Law, Public Safety, Corrections, and Security; Manufacturing; Marketing, Sales and Service; Science, Technology, Engineering, and Mathematics; and Transportation, Distribution, and Logistics) (States' Career Clusters Initiative, 2007). *KSA-16* is appropriate for middle and high school students. *KSA-CA* (2006), contains 170 items using the above six *(KSA-CA6)* or 16 career clusters *(KSA-CA16)*. It is appropriate for college students and adults.

Kuder Career Search with Person Match (KCS)

The *Kuder Career Search with Person Match* (KCS) is comprised of three components: Preference record, *Kuder* career clusters, and Person-match with job sketches. The preference record utilizes a unique format—rather than like/dislike responses to activities, test takers rank by preference 60 activity triads. Results are reported in percentiles based on norm groups, labeled as high, medium, or low, and displayed in rank order of the six or 16 career clusters stated above. The six cluster report includes 14 person matches, seven each from the top two career clusters, while the 16 cluster report includes 15 person matches, three each from the top five career clusters. These matches are based on the top 1% of matches between the interest profiles of test takers and a database of nearly 2500 job sketches from a variety of occupations (Zytowski, 2001).

Super's Work Values Inventory-revised (SWVI-r)

Super's Work Values Inventory-revised (SWVI-r), based on the work of Super (1970), uses a five-point scale response format from *not important at all* to *crucial* and compares test takers' work values to a combined norm group of males and females. Results are reported in percentiles, labeled as high, medium, or low, and displayed in rank order of 12 work values (Achievement, Challenge, Co-workers, Creativity, Income, Independence, Lifestyle, Prestige, Security, Supervision, Variety, and Workplace). The report includes 15 person matches, five each of the top three values.

Person Match

A unique feature of *Kuder* is the system of matching career interests. Rather than matching testers' responses to specific *occupations, Kuder* matches test takers' responses to similar responses of *people* in various occupations. Kuder (1980) believed "there are as many jobs as there are people" (p. 4). As a result, he concluded people seeking career information would be better served being matched to people they resemble who were enthusiastic about their work. Not only does this approach expand occupational considerations, it reflects the current changing nature of the world of work where "job seekers no longer think in terms of one career path or one job family" (Zytowski, 2001, p. 229).

A maximum pool of 2500 individual job sketches were collected and are continuously updated to reflect newly emerging professions while remaining representative of 90% of job titles in the *Occupational Outlook Handbook* (U.S. Department of Labor, 2006). Those who are profiled must be at least 25 years old, in their occupation for at least three years and, if given a choice, would select this same occupation again. Occupational narratives include a typical work day or week, occupational likes and dislikes, how the person entered the profession, and future career plans. Person matches are based on the top 1% of job profiles most similar to test takers' interests and values (Zytowski, 2001).

Use in Counseling

Two considerations when selecting any career assessment are ease of administration and availability of useful support material. *Kuder* assessments score highly in both of these areas. The new electronic format affords individual assessments to be completed usually between 10 and 15 minutes, at the test taker's own pace or convenience, and in one session or partially completed and finished at a later time. Upon completion, test-takers receive immediate feedback via the Internet, from which they can directly explore career information on the *Kuder Career Planning System* website (www.kuder.com).

These reports can also be viewed by parents or school personnel who have appropriate access codes or passwords.

From a counseling perspective, one of the greatest strengths of *Kuder* is its extensive website. With direct links to national resources such as *Occupational Outlook Handbook* (U.S. Department of Labor, 2006) and O*NET, an extensive career database (http://www. onetcenter.org), test-takers can easily navigate through a plethora of career information without having to open separate websites. Information is presented at various levels of interest, skill, and experience. Suggested occupations are grouped by three educational levels: those requiring a high school diploma or GED, one to two years of post-secondary training and education, and four or more years of college, or by pathway if using the 16 career clusters.

The *Kuder Career Planning System* website also offers comprehensive school-to-career information including planning timelines of educational and work experience from elementary school to adulthood, templates for high school educational plans, postsecondary program search, financial aid search including an online application and hints for completing the *Free Application for Federal Student Aid* (FAFSA) (U.S. Department of Education, 2007), resume builder, and job interview information. The *Develop Your Future*® curriculum series (Harris-Bowlsbey and Perry, 2005) offers auxiliary career lesson plans, mini lectures, discussion questions, and handouts for classroom activities. All of these, including the career guidelines for parents, educators, and school counselors on the *Plan for the Future* link on the *Kuder Career Planning System* website, could serve as a valuable basis for developing, refining, and supporting K – 12 career counseling programs.

While clearly designed for the younger career explorer, both in terms of focus of some support material and construct (language written to a 6th grade level and activities related to middle and high school knowledge and experience), *Kuder* assessments can be effective with adults including college students, especially those who have yet to declare a course of study, as well as adults with low reading ability (Pope, 2001). *KSA-CA* has been developed for this specific audience. *Kuder Career Planning System* website links to *Occupational Outlook Handbook, O*NET*, and state and federal job banks may make it even more appealing and relevant for the adult consumer.

Thompson (1995) in The *Twelfth Mental Measurements Yearbook* (Conoley & Impara, 1995) suggests Kuder to be valuable because of its long history, useful for initiating career exploration, and desirable because of quick and easy administration. The newest electronic versions of Kuder assessments offer even shorter administration time, quicker results, and an extensive website. This format particularly lends itself for use with individuals, small groups, or as part of an organizational comprehensive career guidance program.

In addition, the unique construction of *Kuder's* assessments offers information not available with other career assessments.

> Kuder remains the only major criterion-based inventory that employs a forced-choice format and does not employ a general reference sample as

do Campbell Interest and Skills Survey and Strong Interest Inventory. This approach offers useful information that is neither provided in other inventories nor highlighted in the RIASEC model (Savickas, Taber, & Spokane, 2002, p. 178).

While diversity exists within Kuder's norm groups in terms of geographic location, grade level, and sex, Thomson (1995) states concerns about the lack of information regarding how samples were selected and ethnic or racial composition of those samples, a concern later echoed by Pope (2001) in the fourth edition of *A Counselor's Guide to Career Assessment Instruments* (Kapes & Whitfield, 2001). As a result, caution may be suggested interpreting results of non-dominant American ethnic or racial groups.

As with any self-report format, *Kuder's* assessment results are only as accurate as test-takers' responses. This may be problematic with younger test-takers who "may not have developed conceptions of the qualities they want from work" (Rottinghaus & Zytowski, 2006, p. 220) or whether indicated vocational interests will remain stable over time for junior or high school students (Pope, 2001). Another concern with younger test-takers is the seriousness with which middle or high school students may approach completing these assessments, especially in group settings. As a result, *Kuder's* assessments, especially with younger test-takers, are most effective when used primarily for broad career exploration rather than occupation selection (Thompson, 1995).

Technical Considerations

Norms

The KSA 90 items were selected from an initial pool of 270 activities. Wanting to develop a single scale, any items showing gender bias were eliminated. From the remaining items, 15 were selected from each of the six scales (Betz, 2006). Items were specifically designed to reflect middle and high school students' experience and knowledge, including school and leisure activities.

KSA-6, KCS, and *SWVI-r* are normed on the same group (8,785 males and females, ages 14 to adult, drawn randomly and proportionally from *Kuder's* users in 30 states). *KSA-16* is normed on group of 3,486 males and females, ages 13 to adult, drawn randomly and proportionally from *Kuder's* users in nine regions in the United States. *KSA-CA* norms are in development at the time of this writing.

KCS raw cluster scores were developed from a pool of approximately 2,000 adults employed in a wide variety of occupations. Percentile scores are based on 8,787 males and females, ages 14 to adult, drawn randomly and proportionally from *Kuder's* users in 30 states.

Reliability

Kuder Skills Assessment (KSA). KSA items have internal consistency with each of the six KSA scales with a range of .91 (Social/Personal Service) to .94 (Science/Technical) (Zytowski & Luzzo, 2002).

Kuder Career Search (KCS). Based on two recent studies, the KCS internal consistency of ten activity preferences (Art, Communication, Computations, Human Services,

Mechanical, Music, Nature, Office Detail, Sales/Management, and Science/Technical) ranged from .64 (Nature) to .80 (Mechanical and Science/Technical) (Ihle-Helledy, Zytowski, & Fouad, 2004) and .65 (Nature) to .86 (Art and Human Services) (Kelly, 2002). Variances between these studies were smallest with Communication (each reporting .77) and largest with Human Services (.70 to .86). The median whole-profile test-retest reliability over a three-week interval was .81 (Zytowski, 2001). Test-retest reliability of the internal consistency of the KCS 10 activity preferences with a two-week interval ranged from .79 (Nature) to .92 (Art and Human Services) (Ihle-Helledy et al., 2004).

In the fall of 2008, Kuder, Inc., publisher of the three assessments, will release a new version of the KCS, which will include a new set of norms. Additionally, new norms will also be released for the KSA and SWVI-r at the same time.

Overall Critique

Current *Kuder* assessments stem from continuous research over a nearly 70-year period, reflecting multiple revisions and editions. Their unique format of matching work interests to people rather than occupations encourages broad career awareness. The current supplemental website with multiple internet links promotes easy navigation between information about occupations, postsecondary programs, college majors, financial assistance, and job seeking skills. They are appropriate for use in individual, small group, or organization settings. Supplemental educational materials offer additional support in using *Kuder's* as part of a comprehensive school-based career counseling program.

References

Betz, N. E. (2006). Current research on parallel measures of interests and confidence for basic dimension of vocational activity. *Journal of Career Assessment,* 14(1), 56 – 76.

Conoley, J. C., & Impara, J. C. (Eds.). (1995). *The twelfth mental measurements yearbook.* Lincoln, NE: The Buros Institute of Mental Measurements, University of Nebraska Press.

Harris-Bowlsbey, J., & Perry, N. S. (2005). *Develop your future II* (2nd ed.). Adel, Iowa: National Career Assessment Services, Inc.

Ihle-Helledy, K., Zytowski, D. G., & Fouad, N. (2004). Kuder Career Search: Test-retest reliability and consequential validity. *Journal of Career Assessment,* 12(3), 285 – 297.

Kapes, J. T., & Whitfield, E. A. (Eds.). (2001). *A counselor's guide to career assessment instruments* (4th ed.). Columbus, OH: National Career Development Association.

Kelly, K. R. (2002). Concurrent validity of the Kuder Career Search Activity Preference Scales and Career Clusters. *Journal of Career Assessment,* 10(1), 127 – 144.

Kuder, F. (1980). Person matching. *Educational and Psychological Measurement,* 40(1), 1 – 8.

Pope, M. (2001). Review of the Kuder General Interest Survey, Form E. In J. T. Kapes & E. A. Whitfield, (Eds.), *A counselor's guide to career assessment instruments* (4th ed., pp. 258 – 264). Columbus, OH: National Career Development Association.

Rottinghaus, P. J., & Zytowski, D. G. (2006). Commonalities between adolescent's work values and interests. *Measurement and Evaluation in Counseling and Development,* 38, 211 – 221.

Savickas, M. L., Taber, B. J., & Spokane, A. R. (2002). Convergent and discriminant validity of five interest inventories. *Journal of Vocational Behavior,* 61(1), 139 – 184.

States' Career Clusters Initiative (2007). Career clusters: What are career clusters? Retrieved April 9, 2007, from http://www.careerclusters.org/whatis.cfm.

Super, D. E. (1970). *Manual, work values inventory.* Chicago: Riverside.

Thompson, D. (1995). Review of the Kuder General Interest Survey. In J. C. Conoley & J. C. Impara (Eds.), *The twelfth mental measurements yearbook* (pp. 545 – 546). Lincoln, NE: The Buros Institute of Mental Measurements, University of Nebraska Press.

U.S. Department of Education (2007). *About federal student aid.* Retrieved April 4, 2007, from http://federalstudentaid.ed.gov/about/index.html.

U.S. Department of Labor (2006). *Occupational outlook handbook.* New York: McGraw Hill.

Zytowski, D. G. (1992). Three generations: The continuing evolution of Frederick Kuder's interest inventories. *Journal of Counseling & Development,* 71, 245 – 28.

Zytowski, D. G. (2001). Kuder Career Search with person match: Career assessment for the 21st century. *Journal of Career Assessment,* 9(3), 229 – 241.

Zytowski, D. G., & Luzzo, D. A. (2002). Developing the Kuder Skills Assessment. *Journal of Career Assessment,* 10(2), 190 – 199.

Motivational Appraisal of Personal Potential (MAPP)

Kenneth Neils

ZH Computer
7400 Metro Boulevard
Suite 350
Edina, MN 55439
www.Assessment.com

Target Population: All populations over age of 13 years.

Statement of the Purpose of the Instrument: MAPP provides a unique online assessment that seeks to guide, motivate, and empower people to achieve their greatest educational and career potential. MAPP identifies one's true motivations toward work and allows one to match oneself to job categories to see where one best fits.

Titles of Subtests, Scales, Scores Provided: MAPP provides a 35+ page analysis of the motivations of the individual. The data is provided in three ways: Narrative, Quantitative, and Graphical

Forms and Levels Available, with Dates of Publication/Revision of Each: MAPP is available in one level. The last revision was October 1996.

Date of Most Recent Edition of Test Manual, User's Guide, etc.: Test Manual, and Interpretation Guide are provided online. The last revision was January 2001.

Languages in Which Available: MAPP is available in eleven languages; English, French, Spanish, Swedish, Polish, Portuguese, Bulgarian, Russian, Korean, Arabic, and Chinese.

Time:

Actual Test Time: 18 – 20 Minutes

Total Administration Time: 45 Minutes

Norm Group(s) on Which Scores Are Based: Scores are based on comparison with the entire population as a whole. Over 5 million people have taken the MAPP, and the results are based on comparison within the group.

Manner in Which Results Are Reported for Individuals:

Types of Scores: Scores are given in three ways: Verbal Labels, Percentile Ranks, Standard Scores

Report Format/Content:

BASIC SERVICE: Narrative Text.

OPTIONS: Quantitative comparisons based on percentages of the entire population. Graphical comparisons based on Standard Scores.

Report Format/Content for Group Summaries: Not available.

Scoring:

Machine Scoring Service:

Cost of basic service per counselee: Narrative Only $19

Cost of options: Starter Package $29, Career Seeker Package $39, Executive Package $129

Hand Scoring: Not available.

Local Machine Scoring: Not available.

Computer Software Options Available: Computerized adaptive administration; standard administration online.

Cost of Materials: Due to possible price changes since publication date, be sure to check with publisher web site.

Specimen Set: No Cost.

Counselee Materials: No Cost.

Additional Comments of Interest to Users:

1. MAPP has over 5.2 Million users over the past four years, all online.

2. MAPP is a Member Benefit for ICF (International Coach Federation), IAC (International Association of Coaches), and CoachVille, the three leading coaching organizations in the US.

3. More than 1,500 Coaches use the MAPP in their daily practice.

4 More than 3,000 schools use the MAPP Assessment in their counseling and vocational areas.

Published Reviews of the Instrument in the Last 15 Years: None cited.

Reviewed by:

Kevin R. Kelly
Department of Educational Studies
Purdue University

Description

The Motivational Appraisal of Personal Potential (MAPP) is a comprehensive interest, personality, and aptitude measure designed to (a) enable individuals to learn more about their personality and preferences, (b) help individuals find work environments fitting their personal characteristics, and (c) improve or maximize work performance (International Assessment Network, 2007). The MAPP is intended for use by job seekers, companies, workforce and employment centers, and executive and job coaches.

The MAPP consists of 71 triads that include descriptions of three different activities (e.g., assemble and run a model railroad; assemble a large complicated jig-saw puzzle; work on a crossword puzzle from the newspaper). Test takers must designate their most and least preferred activity within each triad. The MAPP yields 19 broad vocational category scales (e.g., Education and Training) based on the Dictionary of Occupational Titles classifications (now available through O*NET, Occupational Interest Network, http://online.onetcenter.org/) and 111 specific vocational scales (e.g., Kindergarten, Elementary Education). Also, MAPP yields 72 scales in nine worker trait categories: Interest in Job Content, Temperament, Aptitude, People, Things, Data, Reasoning, Mathematical Capacity, and Language Capacity. All MAPP results are reported in percentile ranks and a five-point scale ranging from compulsive (1) to aversion (5). The MAPP is available in nine languages.

Use in Counseling

The MAPP appears to be intended for use by people in transition, such as first-time job seekers and those considering a job change, and is presented as a tool for coaching professionals and students. Further, access to the MAPP is a benefit provided for members of various coaching associations. Four general purposes are identified explicitly or implicitly on the MAPP website. First, the MAPP is intended to help test takers live a fuller life. Second, the MAPP can promote insight into personal preferences and characteristics. Third, the MAPP provides extensive feedback about vocational interests. This information can be used to make decisions regarding selection of employment and academic and training opportunities. The website identifies occupations that are congruent with MAPP profiles. Finally, the MAPP can be used by career coaches and counselors to help clients gain insight into their work successes and challenges and to plan for subsequent career development and advancement.

Technical Considerations

Norms

The MAPP does not have a traditional technical manual. Normative data are not provided on the website that administers the MAPP scales. See http://www.assessment.com/default.asp for updated information regarding the psychometric properties of this instrument.

Reliability

The results of a test-retest reliability study are reported on the MAPP website. See www.assessment.com/AboutMAPP/Reliability.asp. A group of 32 adults (12 women, 20 men, with a median age of 49) employed in professional occupations took the MAPP and were retested in a range of 152 to 496 days. The authors did not follow the typical procedure of reporting retest reliability coefficients for the MAPP scales. Instead, they reported the correlations between initial test and retest scores for the 146 MAPP scales *for each individual* and initial test and retest responses for each of the 71 MAPP items *for each individual*. The analyses demonstrated median correlations of .95 between test and retest scale scores and .71 between test and retest item scores for each individual. These correlations reflect the stability of the test takers' responses. They do not, however, reflect the stability of the MAPP scales. Also, there did not appear to be any stability data for the 19 broad vocational scales or the 111 specific vocational skill scales. No internal consistency data are reported for any MAPP scales.

Validity

A total of 133 individuals employed in technical positions were administered the MAPP and the Strong Interest Inventory (SII) to demonstrate the construct validity of the MAPP vocational scales. Correlations were calculated between the 19 broad and 111 specific MAPP scales and 25 Basic Interest Scales and 116 Occupational scales from the SII. In general, the associations between these two sets of interest scales corresponded with expectations. For example, the MAPP Craftsmanship scale had correlations of .79 and .62, respectively, with the SII Auto Mechanic and Carpenter occupational scales.

Computer-Based Versions

The MAPP is available through online administration only.

Overall Critique

The MAPP has three major assets. First, the test developers should be credited with developing scales that match the Department of Labor worker trait code system. This approach has the potential to enable job seekers and counselors make fine-grained matches between personal and work environment characteristics. Second, the matching of MAPP results with specific O*NET job titles and descriptions is a nice tool. Test takers can proceed seamlessly from receiving feedback to seeking information about jobs matching their personal characteristics. Third, test takers receive almost immediate feedback upon completion of the MAPP. This test meets the needs of those who need quick feedback, such as workers who have just lost employment and are seeking to focus their job search.

The MAPP also has six significant limitations at this stage of development. First, there is a limited amount of psychometric data available to support the use of the MAPP. Some limited reliability data are available (Gilbert, 1997). However, internal consistency data are not yet available on any MAPP scales, and stability data is not available for the 130 vocational interest scales. There is a critical need to demonstrate the stability of vocational interest scales for a test designed to assist those who are making career decisions. The validity data for the MAPP scales also are limited. The developers did provide concurrent validity data for the vocational interest scales. However, no validity data appear to be available for the 72 worker trait scales. It is difficult to interpret the interest, temperament, aptitude, people/things/data, and reasoning/math/language scales with confidence in the absence of supporting validity data.

Second, the MAPP yields an overwhelming amount of feedback. My personal report included 17 pages of narrative interpretation and feedback on 19 major vocational areas, 111 specific vocations within those 19 broad areas, 10 interest in job content scales, 12 temperament scales, 11 aptitude scales, eight people scales, eight things scales, seven data scales, six reasoning scales, six math scales, and four language scales. This is a total of 202 scales. Moreover, the MAPP provides 23 personal trait, 46 personal orientation, and 51 learning style scales for a total of 120 additional scales. This is simply too much information. It is hard to imagine how a counselor would proceed to interpret so much information within the limited time frame that is typical in career counseling. It is also difficult to imagine how an individual could understand and integrate all of this information without professional assistance (Hennen, 2001). More important, one wonders if it is necessary to provide so much feedback. There certainly must be redundancies in the total of 322 MAPP scales; test developers typically conduct factor analyses to produce a parsimonious set of variables for interpretation. Further, counselors do not have time to interpret so many scales, and it must be difficult or impossible for test takers to assimilate information about so many characteristics. It appears that the use of data reduction techniques would be beneficial to address the problem of information overload.

Third, there are questions about the content validity of the MAPP. Feedback is provided regarding mental, perceptual, and sensory/physical aptitudes and reasoning, math, and language skills although none of these skills are addressed by test items. How can one derive a manual dexterity scale score without directly testing with a tool such as the Purdue Pegboard Test (Tiffin & Asher, 1948)? How can one assess aptitude for sensing and seeing colors without providing an actual test of color perception? The MAPP provides feedback regarding skills that are not directly assessed. One must be concerned with the possibility of Barnum or Forer effects, the uncritical acceptance of generally positive narrative statement generated by computer programs (Groth-Marnat, 2003), for MAPP users. One statement of the MAPP website does explain that the test results are based on motivation rather than skill. However, it was troubling that the narrative feedback does not appear to include any explicit cautions that the skill scales were not based upon direct skill assessments. The test developers should take steps to address this problem.

Fourth, evidence is needed to demonstrate that the MAPP is free from gender, race, and ethnicity biases (National Council on Measurement in Education, 1995). The MAPP does not appear to have separate norms for women and men or for racial and ethnic minority groups. It also remains to be demonstrated that irrelevant characteristics such as race and socioeconomic status do not affect MAPP scales scores. These are important considerations for a tool that is used to help make career decisions that affect economic and psychological well-being.

Fifth, there is an expectation that Internet-based assessments have been validated for self-help use (National Career Development Assessment, 1997). Test developers must demonstrate that assessments available for use on the Internet without the involvement of a professional counselor do not cause harm and promote positive career development outcomes. This evidence remains to be provided for the MAPP.

Finally, MAPP output does not match the existing O*NET Titles. For example, there are 19 interest areas in MAPP and the O*NET has 14 interest areas. Some of the areas are quite similar, such as the MAPP Math and Science and O*NET Science, Math, and Engineering areas. However, some area labels are different, such as the MAPP Clerical and the O*NET Business Detail. Also, some MAPP areas, such as Machine Work, are not included in the O*NET and some O*NET areas, such as Plants and Animals, are not represented in the MAPP (Farr & Shatkin, 2004). It would be ideal if the MAPP could be updated to match contemporary O*NET interest, skill, and ability areas.

In summary, the MAPP is an interesting tool that shares many of the limitations typical of tests that are early in their development. More basic test development techniques, such as factor and confirmatory factor analysis and differential item functioning, should be implemented. More basic psychometric research is also needed to develop norms and to document the reliability and validity properties of this instrument. The MAPP should be considered a test in development. Until more research is available, career development professionals working with clients should be cautious in using the MAPP in place of existing personality and vocational interest measures with proven psychometric characteristics.

References

Farr, M., & Shatkin, L. (2004). *O*NET dictionary of occupational titles* (3rd ed.). Indianapolis, IN: JIST Works.

Gilbert, L. (1997). *Construct validity study.* Retrieved October 16, 2007 from the Motivational Appraisal of Personal Potential website: http://www.assessment.com/AboutMAPP/CValidity.asp.

Groth-Marnat, G. (2003). *Handbook of psychological assessment* (4th ed.). New York: Wiley & Sons, Inc.

Hennen, M. E. (2001). [Review of MAPP: Motivational Appraisal of Personal Potential.] In B. S. Plake & J. C. Impara (Eds.), *The fourteenth mental measurements yearbook* (pp. 707 – 710). Lincoln, NE: Buros Institute of Mental Measurements, The University of Nebraska.

International Assessment Network (2007). Motivational Appraisal of Personal Potential. Available online at http://assessment.com/default.asp

National Career Development Association. (1997). NCDA guidelines for the use of the internet for provision of career information and planning services. Columbus, OH: Author.

National Council on Measurement in Education. (1995). *Code of professional responsibilities in educational measurement.* Madison, WI: Author.

Tiffin, J., & Asher, E. J. (1948). The Purdue Pegboard: Norms and studies of reliability and validity. *Journal of Applied Psychology, 32,* 234 – 247.

O*NET®ABILITY PROFILER™(AP)

United States Department of Labor, Employment and Training Administration

Employment & Training Administration
USDOL, FPB Mail Stop S4231
200 Constitution Avenue, NW
Washington, DC 20210
o-net@dol.gov
www.doleta.gov/programs/onet
www.onetcenter.org

Target Population: Individuals seeking to identify their work-related abilities and use them to explore careers: high school and post secondary students as well as adults. Should be 16 years of age or older with a minimum of a sixth-grade English reading level.

Statement of the Purpose of the Instrument: The O*NET Ability Profiler was designed as part of a whole-person assessment approach. The instrument enables users to identify their ability profile to use this information to identify their occupational ability strengths. Importantly, the AP allows users to link their ability profile to occupations in the world of work through the U.S. Department of Labor's Occupational Information Network (O*NET) system at http://online.onetcenter.org, the nation's leading source of occupational information. The instrument measures nine abilities: Verbal, Arithmetic Reasoning, Computation, Spatial Ability, Form Perception, Clerical Perception, Motor Coordination, Manual Dexterity, and Finger Dexterity. The first six of these abilities are measured through six paper and pencil subtests, and the remaining three are measured by five psychomotor subtests. The instrument is appropriate for a variety of users, including students, first-time job seekers, and those individuals in occupational transition. After taking the AP, counselees receive a customized score report, which not only presents their ability profile, but presents concepts about career exploration that users will be able to use throughout their working lives.

Titles of Subtests, Scales, Scores Provided: Percentile and raw scores for nine abilities: Verbal, Arithmetic Reasoning, Computation, Spatial Ability, Form Perception, Clerical Perception, Motor Coordination, Manual Dexterity, and Finger Dexterity.

There are a total of 11 subtests: Arithmetic Reasoning, Vocabulary, Three-Dimensional Space, Computation, Name Comparison, Object Matching, Mark Making, Place, Turn, Assemble, and Disassemble.

Forms and Levels Available, with Dates of Publication/Revision of Each: O*NET Ability Profiler Form 1, released in 2001.

Date of Most Recent Edition of Test Manual, User's Guide, etc.:

Instrument Materials

O*NET Ability Profiler, Form 1 (2000):

Using Your O*NET Ability Profiler Results (2000)
Part 7 Mark Making Answer Sheet (2000)

Administration Materials

O*NET Ability Profiler User's Guide; Forms 1 and 2 (2000)
O*NET Ability Profiler Administration Manual (2000)
O*NET Ability Profiler Record of Apparatus Scores (2000)
O*NET Ability Profiler Three-Dimensional Space Cutouts (2000)

Scoring Materials

O*NET Ability Profiler Scoring Program User's Guide (2000)
O*NET Ability Profiler Envelope—Premarked Response Sheets for Scoring
Calibration (2000) O*NET Ability Profiler Scoring Program (APSP) (2000)
O*NET Ability Profiler Scoring Program User's Guide (2000)
O*NET Ability Profiler Data Entry Program (2000)
O*NET Ability Profiler Data Entry Help Files (2000)

Training Materials

O*NET Ability Profiler Administrator Training Manual (2000)
O*NET Ability Profiler Administrator Training Overhead Masters (2000)
O*NET Ability Profiler Administrator Training Participant's Guide (2000)

Languages in Which Available: English only.

Time:

Actual Test Time: Approximately 60 minutes

Total Administration Time:

Three administration options:

1. Complete Test Battery (11 individually timed subtests) — 2 ½ hours
2. 6 Paper and Pencil subtests and Mark Making paper and pencil psychomotor subtest (subtest 1 through 7) — 1 ½ to 2 hours
3. 6 Paper and Pencil subtests (subtests 1 through 6) — 1 ½ to 2 hours

Norm Group(s) on Which Scores Are Based: General working population ages 18 to 54. Supplemented with high school samples, ages 16 to 18.

Manner in Which Results Are Reported for Individuals:

Types of Scores: Percentile and raw scores (number correct/total number of questions) for each of the nine abilities measured.

Report Format/Content:

BASIC SERVICE: Counselee receives a customized computer generated 16-page score report. The score report, designed for self-interpretation, includes: (1) definitions of the abilities measured, (2) percentile and number correct scores for each of nine abilities, (3) graphical display of an individual's ability profile, (4) an exercise to select a job zone (amount of training, education, work experience the counselee currently has or wishes to pursue), (5) a set of steps describing using your ability profile and job zone to explore careers, and (6) five lists of occupations developed using the client's ability profile and each one of the five job zones. The score report also instructs the counselee in exploring occupations on his/her occupational lists in the U.S. Department of Labors' O*NET system, the nation's leading source of occupational information.

Report Format/Content for Group Summaries: Not available.

Scoring:

Machine Scoring Service: Not available

Hand Scoring: Not available.

Local Machine Scoring: Provisions/conditions/equipment required.

There are two options for scoring:

1) O*NET Ability Profiler Scoring Program (APSP). This program enables the use of answer sheets which are machine scanned. The scanned results are downloaded to a computer which produces the printed customized individual score report. Instructions and materials for using the APSP and scanner equipment are provided for free download at www.onetcenter.org/AP.html .

2) O*NET Ability Profiler Data Entry Program. This program enables data entry of clients' item responses and the creation of a file which can be downloaded to a computer. The downloaded file produces the client's customized score report. The data entry program and instructions for use are provided for free download at www.onetcenter.org/AP.html .

Equipment/configuration necessary for the O*NET Ability Profiler Scoring Software is as follows:

Computer Hardware
- Personal computer with at least an Intel Pentium family central processing unit (CPU) running at 200 MHz.
- 32 MB of random access memory (RAM).
- About 30 MB of free disk space.
- CD-ROM or DVD drive.
- Screen resolution of 800 x 600 or higher.
- Printer (optional)
- For reasonable speed you should be running at least a Pentium II 233-MHz CPU and have at least 64 MB of RAM.

Support Software
- Windows 95, 98, NT 4.0, or Windows 2000.
- Word 97 or Word 2000 (or Office 97 or Office 2000). APSP will function only if Word 97 or Word 2000 (or a later version) is available on the same machine.

Recommended Scanning Equipment and Software
- NCS scanner models: 6
- OpScan 2, 3, 4, 4xp, 5, 6, 7, 8, or 10

Note: Other scanner models may also work correctly but have not been tested. If you need to use an older NCS scanner model such as Sentry 30xx or OpScan 21 or a non-NCS model, confirm that the scanner is reading the data in a manner compatible with APSP

- Windows ScanTools software version 1.6 or higher or Windows ScanTools II software version 1.0 or higher.
- Connection cable between scanner and CPU.

Note: There are many configurations of hardware and software on the market that can be used to automatically scan the examinee response sheets and place the information in a computer file in the layout expected by the scoring program. At this time, National Computer Systems (NCS) scanners and NCS compatible scanners along with NCS ScanTools software are supported. These particular types of scanning equipment and software are not required to use the APSP.

However, if a different scanner and/or scanning software are used, someone with computer programming skills may be needed to create a new examinee test response sheet definition file that will allow your scanner to read the answer sheet.

Computer Software Options Available: Not available

Cost of Materials: Instrument and supporting materials are available free of charge at www.onetcenter.org/AP.html. The machine scorable answer sheet can be purchased in packs of 50 for approximately $43.00.

Specimen Set: All materials (instrument, demonstration version of the instrument, user's guide designed for counselors, technical development reports) are available for download free of charge at www.onetcenter.org/AP.html.

Counselee Materials: O*NET Ability Profiler Instrument, Form 1 Ability Profiler Machine Scorable Answer Sheet

Additional Comments of Interest to Users: All materials, except for the machine scannable answer sheet, including instruments, score reports, user guides, administrator training materials, and development and technical reports are available for free download at www.onetcenter.org/AP.html. Ability Profiler technical development reports are also available at this site. Additionally, customer service is available from onet@ncmail.net.

Reviewed by:

Richard T. Kinnier
Professor

Joanna Gorin
Assistant Professor

Division of Psychology
Arizona State University
Tempe, AZ

Description

The O*NET Ability Profiler is one of three new O*NET assessment tools. The other two are the Interest Profiler and the Work Importance Profiler and are reviewed separately in other chapters of this Guide. The primary goal of these tools is to provide clients with career-related information about themselves that can serve to facilitate career choice. The Ability Profiler focuses on the extent to which the test taker has (or can learn) the knowledge and skills required by numerous occupations.

The Profiler, developed by the U.S. Department of Labor, derived from Forms E and F of the General Aptitude Test Battery (GATB; U.S. Employment Service). Following considerable efforts to improve the scales qualitatively and quantitatively (e.g., a reduction of the number of items and subtests, the reduction of item bias, aesthetic and clarity improvements), those forms were the basis for the development of the Ability Profiler Forms 1 and 2. The Ability Profiler consists of 11 separately timed sections. Seven are paper and pencil tests of which six are non psychomotor and one is psychomotor. Four sections involve the manipulation of pegs and rivets. The tests are combined to measure nine basic abilities. They are: Arithmetic Reasoning (18 items), Verbal (19 items), Spatial (20 items), Computation (40 items), Clerical Perception (90 items), Form Perception (42 items), Motor Coordination (drawing lines within squares), Manual Dexterity (placing and turning pegs), Finger Dexterity (assembling and disassembling rivets).

Full administration of the test takes about 2 ½ hours according to the manual. Shorter administration options are described in the manual. Administration and scoring requires some formal training; a full one- or two-day workshop is recommended. The Administration Training Manual is 57 pages long, reflecting the many precise rules that must be followed for administering and scoring the test. Examinees must be at least 16 years old and be able to read at a 6th grade level (U.S. Department of Labor, 2002a).

Test results are presented in two ways: (1) Scores expressed as percentiles (derived from large national norms) for each of the nine ability scales, and (2) A list of occupations that "match" the examinee's ability profile. Examinees can also search for their "matches" within five specific Job Zones. Zones refer to levels of preparation needed to enter a particular job. Zones range from "little or no preparation" needed (Zone 1) to "extensive preparation" needed (Zone 5).

Use in Counseling

As with all tests in career counseling, the results of any test should be used in conjunction with other test results and the "raw data" derived from the client's life experiences and self-assessment activities. The results from the Ability Profiler can be a rich data source providing a profile of a client's abilities and a list of promising occupations. Certainly the two other O*NET tests (as well as other well-respected values and interest inventories) could further enhance the test taker's self-knowledge.

The Ability Profiler results should rarely, if ever, be used to definitively rule in or out any specific occupation. Rather, high scores can inform the client that he or she may possess a talent for succeeding in specified occupations while low scores might serve as a warning that challenges loom ahead if he or she chooses to pursue any of those occupations. That information should be considered along with other criteria relevant to career success and satisfaction.

In our opinion, the most important benefit to be derived from using the Ability Profiler (and other tests) is how the derived information is likely to inspire the client to seek more career-related information. Clients are likely to want to find out more about occupations identified as good "matches" for them. The O*NET system also provides extensive information about those and other occupations that clients might be interested in reading about.

Technical Considerations

Individual Scales

The O*NET Ability Profiler was derived from the already highly regarded GATB. Impressive attempts were made to improve the GATB scales both qualitatively and quantitatively (see Segall & Monzon, 1995; Ability Profiler User's Guide, US Department of Labor, 2002c). Qualitative revisions included aesthetic and clarity improvements as well as improvements in item wording and scoring procedures. Quantitatively, item and scale properties were examined with modern psychometric methods. Item response theory (IRT) was used to assist in the equating of the nonspeeded forms, to select optimally discriminating items, as well as to reduce cultural bias of any items. The final versions of the scales provide the most reliable information for the middle of the ability distribution. The dimensionality analyses used, which employed the most modern nonlinear factor analytic techniques, supports the hypothesized structure of most of the ability scales.

Reliability was estimated by alternate-form correlations. The alternate-form reliability coefficients for the Profiler (range = .78 to .92) were higher than the coefficients for the GATB forms. Validity was evaluated by correlating scores between the GATB scales and the Ability Profiler scales. They are highly correlated. Also, nonlinear factor analysis verified the structural validity of the scores. In our opinion, reliability and validity of the individual Profiler Scales have been well established. Validity would be further enhanced if future studies performed correlational analyses on the scales with external measures of job performance and success.

Score Profiles for Occupational "Matches"

The procedures by which the authors established "matching" test-taker score profiles with numerous occupations were psychometrically complex and ambitious (See McCloy, Campbell, Oswald, Rivkin, & Lewis, 1999). In essence, based on preexisting GATB score profiles for numerous Dictionary of Occupational Titles (D.O.T.). occupations and job analysis information, prediction equations were developed for the nine abilities of the Profiler. Profile scores for about 11,500 occupations (labeled, O*NET occupations) were standardized (M = 100, SD = 20), allowing test takers' profiles to be correlated with occupational profiles. This information is translated into a list of occupations that the test taker's pattern of abilities "match" (i.e., occupations that the test taker has the requisite skills to perform successfully).

While the procedures and analyses employed to establish match profiles for test takers and occupations is impressive, we were not able to find some information that would give us more confidence that the score profile matches are clearly valid. Based on the available information, the psychometric and statistical data reduction procedures applied likely resulted in appropriate job profiles, though evidence specifically addressing this issue would be useful. For example, while regression equations were established for ability estimates of the D.O.T. occupations, some O*NET occupations combine numerous D.O.T. occupations. Their regression equations are based on "representative" D.O.T. occupations. To what extent are these valid representatives? In spite of our concerns and questions, we think the psychometrics of the O*NET Ability Profiler probably ranks it as one of the most valid psychological tests in existence.

Computer-Based and/or Online Versions

According to David Rivkin (personal communication, March 27, 2007), one of the developers of the O*NET Ability Profiler, test takers record their answers for the paper-and-pencil portions of the instrument on a machine-scannable answer sheet. Administrators record raw scores on the answer sheets for the psychomotor portions of the instrument. The psychomotor portions are optional. Answer sheets are scanned, and a data file is created which is read by a scoring software program. The scoring software produces a customized score report for each individual test taker. If scanning equipment is not available, administrators can enter in the test takers' answers into a data entry program which then produces the customized score reports.

Overall Critique

The O*NET Ability Profiler is an impressive test. Its predecessor test, the GATB, was a widely used and well-established test. The Profiler is an improvement on an already excellent test. For test takers, the items and instructions are clear and straight-forward. The 2 ½ hour test yields much data on the test taker's career-related abilities. The psychometric procedures, including the use of IRT based methods, used to improve the test and establish reliability and validity are ambitious and impressive. Future external validity studies on the individual scales and a more clear establishment of the validity on all of the occupational matches will improve an already great measure. In the meantime, counselors should feel confident that their clients' scores are basically valid. Profiler results (like all test results) are best used in conjunction with other assessment information to guide further self exploration and occupational information seeking. Given that perspective, we highly recommend the O*NET Ability Profiler as one excellent career counseling tool.

References

McCloy, R., Campbell, J., Oswald, F., Rivkin, D., & Lewis, P. (1999). *Generation and use of occupational Ability Profiles for exploring O*NET Occupational units* (Volumes I and II). Raleigh, NC: National Center for O*NET Development.

Segall, D. O., & Monzon, R. I. (1995). *Equating forms E and F of the P&P-GATB.* San Diego, CA: Navy Personnel Research and Development Center.

U.S. Department of Labor (2002a). *O*NET Ability Profiler Administrator Training Manual.* Washington, D. C.: Author.

U. S. Department of Labor (2002b). *O*NET Ability Profiler Administration Manual.* Washington, DC: Author.

U. S. Department of Labor (2002c). *O*NET Ability Profiler User's Guide.* Washington, DC: Author.

OCCUPATIONAL APTITUDE SURVEY AND INTEREST SCHEDULE – THIRD EDITION (OASIS-3)

Randall M. Parker

PRO-ED Inc.
8700 Shoal Creek Blvd.
Austin, TX 78757-6897
info@proedinc.com
www.proedinc.com

Target Population: Grades 8 – 12 and adults.

Statement of the Purpose of the Instrument: The OASIS-3 was developed to assist individuals in their career search by providing them with information regarding their relative strengths in several aptitude areas related to the world of work. By using the OASIS-3 and related materials, students and adults may identify a list of jobs to help focus the search for further job information.

Titles of Subtests, Scales, Scores Provided: Subtests: (1) Vocabulary, (2) Computation, (3) Spatial Relations, (4) Word Comparison, (5) Making Marks.

Forms and Levels Available, with Dates of Publication/Revision of Each: OASIS-3 Aptitude Survey (2001): (1) Student Booklets, (2) Student Answer Sheets, (3) Student Profiles.

OASIS-3 Interest Schedule (2001): (1) Student Booklets, (2) Student Answer Sheets, (3) Student Profiles, (4) Scoring Forms.

OASIS-3 (AS/IS) Interpretation Workbooks.

Date of Most Recent Edition of Test Manual, User's Guide, etc.: 2001

Languages in Which Available: English only.

Time:

Actual Test Time: 35 minutes – Aptitude, About 30 minutes – Interest.

Total Administration Time: At least 1 hour, 5 minutes total.

Norm Group(s) on Which Scores Are Based: 8th – 12th grade public school students. Adults in postsecondary educational settings.

Manner in Which Results Are Reported for Individuals:

Types of Scores: percentiles, stanine, raw scores.

Report Format/Content:

Protocols – Hand scored reports.

Machine-scored service is also available, special forms must be purchased/used when administering the test. The completed machine-score forms are then shipped to PRO-ED to scan.

Report Format/Content for Group Summaries: Not available.

Scoring:

Machine Scoring Service:

COST OF BASIC SERVICE PER COUNSELEE:

Protocols, hand-scored – estimated $1.46 per protocol (Aptitude Survey), estimated $1.68 per protocol (Interest Schedule), estimated $3.14 total, if entire test is completed .

COST OF OPTIONS:

Machine scored protocols – estimated $5.10 per protocol (Aptitude Survey) , estimated $5.10 per protocol (Interest Schedule), estimated $10.20 total, if entire test is completed.

TIME REQUIRED FOR SCORING AND RETURNING: Less than a week.

Hand Scoring:

SCORED BY: Counselor.

TIME REQUIRED FOR SCORING: About 5 – 10 minutes.

Local Machine Scoring: Not available.

Computer Software Options Available: Not available.

Cost of Materials: Due to possible price changes since publication date, be sure to check the publisher's website.

Specimen Set: OASIS-3 Aptitude Survey Test Specimen Kit, $62.00, OASIS-3 Interest Schedule Test Specimen Kit, $62.00.

Counselee Materials:

REUSABLES: Aptitude Survey: Examiner's Manual, Student Booklets, Scoring Keys;

INTEREST SCHEDULE: Examiner's Manual, Student Booklets.

Reviewed by:

Patrick Akos
University of North Carolina at Chapel Hill
Chapel Hill, NC

Rebecca Spangler
Mount Saint Joseph High School
Baltimore, MD

Description

The purpose of the third edition of the Occupational Aptitude Survey and Interest Schedule (OASIS-3) is to "assist students with levels of education ranging from 8th grade through postsecondary education in self-exploration, vocational exploration, and career development" (Parker, 2002a, p .1). The OASIS-3 has two components, an Aptitude Survey (AS) and an Interest Schedule (IS). Each part can be administered separately as a means of fostering discussion and enhancing career development. The OASIS-3 Aptitude Scale (OASIS-AS) is designed to provide information about personal strengths in several aptitude areas related to the world of work. The OASIS-3 Interest Schedule (OASIS-3:IS) is designed to provide information regarding vocational interests. The OASIS was originally published in 1983. This third revision is primarily intended to improve usability and to extend norms upward to the postsecondary population. Separate examiner manuals (Parker, 2002a, 2002b) for the AS and IS have each been updated in response to recent research findings and technical modifications.

The OASIS-3:AS consists of five scales. The vocabulary test consists of 40 items given in a 9-minute time limit. Each item lists four words, two of which the test taker must identify as either synonyms or antonyms. The computation section is comprised of arithmetic and algebra problems where the answer is one of five options provided. This section is 30 items and is timed at 12 minutes. The examinee has 8 minutes to complete the third section of 20 items involving spatial relations. Each problem consists of a two-dimensional figure and the individual must choose which one of four three-dimensional figures the original could look like. The fourth section is word comparison. The examinee has five minutes to determine whether two sets of words, numbers, or nonsense syllables in each of 100 items are different or the same. Making marks is the final scale of the OASIS-3:AS. It measures how many boxes out of 160 can be marked in an "asterisk" form in two separately timed 30-second subsections. This subtest measures motor coordination. The scales were heavily influenced by the research and constructs from both the Differential Aptitude Tests (Psychological Corporation, 1992) and the General Aptitude Test Battery (U.S. Department of Labor, 1970).

The OASIS-3:IS consists of 240 items, with the first 120 job titles and the second 120 job activities. Each item is assigned to one of the following 12 scales: (1) Artistic (ART), (2) Scientific (SCI), (3) Nature (NAT), (4) Protective (PRO), (5) Mechanical (MEC), (6) Industrial (IND), (7) Business Detail (BUS), (8) Selling (SEL), (9) Accommodating (ACC), (10) Humanitarian (HUM), (11) Leading-Influencing (LEA), and (12) Physical Performing (PHY). Each scale is made up of 20 items. Of those 20 items, 10 are occupational titles and 10 are job activities related to each scale. These items are traditional or stereotypical activities associated with the occupations. Examinees rate each on item on a three point scale: *like, neutral,* or *dislike.* ART, For example includes "musician" as sample job title and "novel writer" as sample job activity). Another example is the HUM interest that includes "nurse" as a job title and "help people with medical, social, and vocational problems" as a job activity. The scales were developed from research on worker traits (Cottle, 1950) and interest research done by the United States Employment Service.

Use in Counseling

The OASIS-3:AS is designed to identify specific abilities and strengths that an individual possesses or "developed cognitive abilities" (Parker, 2002b, p. 2). Counselors can use the test to help students increase self-knowledge of vocational capabilities and further self-exploration and a focused search for career possibilities. The overall time required to administer the instrument (including orientation and instructions) could take one hour or more. The OASIS-3:AS can be machine scored or hand scored using the clear plastic scoring keys provided in the OASIS-3:AS kits. For both scoring strategies, the "Making Marks" section must be hand scored by adding up the total number of boxes filled in per section. The raw scores of the OASIS-3:AS are simply the number correct in each section. A general ability section is reported on the student profile by adding together the vocabulary and computation totals. Therefore there are six reported raw scores on the student profile. The raw scores can then be converted to percentiles and stanine scores using the normative table provided in the *OASIS-3: AS Examiner's Manual* (Parker, 2002b). In total, it takes just over an hour and a half to complete the test (60 minutes or more), to score the test (10 – 15 minutes), and to transfer information to the profile sheet (10 – 15 minutes).

The OASIS-3:IS is designed to "assist students in organizing their search for occupational information." (Parker, 2002a, p. 1). The instrument is designed to stimulate the process of self-exploration and help clients/students identify a list of jobs to help learn about future possibilities. Similar to the aptitude survey, it should be used as a catalyst for future counseling and discussion where the counselor can continue to encourage the client/student to explore other career options obtained through other sources, such as parents, hobbies, etc. For example, a client/student who scores high in Artistic may be informed about additional school art electives, community classes, or perhaps local artists to shadow or visit. Previous reviews (Remer, 1986) indicate high utility for special needs personnel in developing individual educational plan (IEP) goals in the area of transition planning, although others (Blackwell & Lutyhe, 2003) noted a need for more instructions on test administration accommodations. While the IS is not timed liked the AS, in total, it takes about one hour to finish the test (30 – 40 minutes), score the test (10 – 15 minutes), and complete the profile sheet (10 – 15 minutes).

Both instruments can be administered and interpreted individually or in a group or class setting (suggested 1:30 ratio). Raw scores are not useful in comparison to a norm group but provide the basis for identifying percentile scores and stanines. All percentile scores should be interpreted to test takers in a positive way, even those that fall below the 50th percentile ranking. Several appendices and an interpretation workbook allow comparison to norms and links to specific careers and additional resources (e.g., websites) are included.

The most important aspect of using the OASIS-3 is providing the examinee with an in-depth and analytic interpretation. During this process, the counselor should allow time for the test taker to process the information being presented. Counselor should note verbal and nonverbal reactions of the test taker in order to clarify and engage in discussion and self-exploration. It is strongly encouraged that the administrator informs students that while the OASIS-3 can be used to further occupational discovery, it is in no way a predictive tool that will tell what the test taker will, or should, pursue as a career. For example, in interpretation of the aptitude survey, it is important to note the potential influence of new experiences and learning situations on score variability. Parker (2002a, 2002b) notes about an hour is needed per test (AS and IS) for individual or group interpretation (although it seems logical that group interpretation would be longer), and previous reviews have noted the interpretation process as "cumbersome" (Blackwell & Lutyhe, 2003).

Technical Considerations

The examiner manual (Parker, 2002a) for each test devotes an entire section to technical information. Comparative data for the OASIS-3 was normed and standardized on a total of 2,005 students in 8th grade through postsecondary education (defined as through graduate school). Norms for the postsecondary population were found to differ slightly from that of the original adolescent population and therefore normed on a separate scale. The third edition includes normed data from 500 adults in postsecondary educational settings. In order to obtain a representative sample of the actual United States population (based on U.S. Census and U.S. Department of Education data), quota and purposive sampling methods were used.

No significant differences appear for gender for the AS, but a major difference was noted between genders in IS results (only for the 8th – 12th grade population). Males and females in the 8th grade through 12th grade group differed on five of the 12 IS scales: Mechanical, Business Detail, Accommodating, Humanitarian, and Physical Performing; therefore, separate norms for these scales are identified by gender in order to meet gender bias and discrimination laws and regulations and to meet the requirements and recommendations of the National Institute of Education (now the Office of Educational Research and Improvement).

Alpha, split-half, alternate forms, and test-retest reliabilities were employed for the AS, and alpha and test-retest reliabilities were used in developing the IS. For the 8th – 12th grade population, alpha coefficients for the AS all were above the low .80s, and the subtests performed equally well in other reliability testing (.70 or above). Similarly, slightly lower (.70s) alphas and comparable reliability was found for the postsecondary population. Alpha coefficients ranged from .78 (ACC) to .95 (NAT) for subgroup samples using the IS. Test-retest reliabilities of 54 students in 8th grade through 12th grade were calculated at two-week intervals and ranged from .66 (SEL) to .91 (ART) for the 12 scales. Alpha reliability for the postsecondary population ranged from .84 (LEA) to .96 (IND) for the entire norm sample group (N = 500). Test-retest results ranged from .82 (SEL) to .91 (SCI & NAT) suggesting that the IS is internally consistent.

For construct validity for the IS, factor loadings ranged from .93 (NAT) to .35 (MEC) with some similarities between the mechanical and industrial scales (Remer, 1986), which is particular problematic with the postsecondary group. Content validity of the 12 interest factors is established based on dated research (Cottle, 1950) by the US Employment Service, which has led to guides for occupational exploration based on the 12 areas (Maze & Mayhall, 1995). Internal consistency is reported as respectable, and criterion-related validity was reported in comparison to the SDS. The 12 interest areas corresponded to the Holland scale mostly as predicted (with exception of the accommodating and physical performing areas which lacks correlation to any specific Holland code). Parker (e.g., Green & Parker, 1989) also reports on a host of studies (several dissertations) that look at the OASIS-IS in relation to Kolb's learning styles (Kolb, 1984), college majors, learning disabilities, work experience, and self-ratings.

Overall Critique

The OASIS-3 is a thoughtfully designed instrument that has thorough instructions and utility for counselors working with students in high schools and postsecondary settings. The third revision of the OASIS makes an effort to improve upon the instrument by reflecting recent research findings and extending the normative population to be applicable to postsecondary students who may be seeking assistance in career exploration. The rational for this extension seems appropriate when considering that the United States job market is constantly changing and enrollment in postsecondary institutions is dramatically increasing. However, it is difficult to find abundant recent research in either the examiner manual nor in searches for recent research in academic research databases.

The OASIS-3 appears to be a useful tool for increasing self-awareness and organizing further career exploration. Parker (2000a, 2000b) is very explicit to note that the instrument is not for predictive purposes and should be used as a stimulus for further investigation. The examiner manuals provide useful guidelines that involve verbal and nonverbal interpretations by the counselor/test administrator, as well as resources for further exploration. The OASIS-3 Interpretation Workbook, for example, lists possible occupations related to each interest scale (with corresponding aptitudes) and relative salaries, educational requirements, and job growth.

While previous reviews (Remer, 1986) found IS items too stereotypical, we feel they are appropriate and overall a good stimulus for future exploration. The major questions that emerged in this review include the representativeness of the norm population for the 8th – 12th grade group, the length of time needed to administer, score, and interpret the instruments, and the availability of other computer-based tools that might more efficiently produce the self- and career-awareness goals noted for the OASIS-3. There have been several other reviews of the OASIS-3 (Blackwell & Lutyhe, 2003; Bunch, 2005; Michael, 2005). Although other reviews (Blackwell & Lutyhe, 2003) found the OASIS-3 to be time- and cost-effective, we respectfully disagree with this assessment given our orientation toward efficiency concerns as school counselors). Also, Parker (2000b) suggests that the availability of computer scoring and computer-generated interpretive reporting has "had the effect of removing students from the vocational counseling process" (p. 2). However, it seems that computer-based tools can provide more efficiency if quality interpretation is included with the use of such instruments.

References

Blackwell, T., & Lutyhe, T. (2003). Test review. *Rehabilitation Counseling Bulletin, 46*(4), 247 – 250.

Bunch, M. B. (2005) Review of Occupational Aptitude Survey and Interest Schedule (Third Edition). In R. A. Spies & B. S. Plake (Eds.), *The sixteenth mental measurements yearbook* (pp. 713 – 715). Lincoln, NE: University of Nebraska – Lincoln.

Cottle, W. (1950). A factorial study of Multiphasic, Strong, Kuder, and Bell inventories using a population of adult males. *Psychometrika, 15,* 25 – 47.

Green, D., & Parker, R. (1989). Vocational and academic attributes of students with different leaning styles. *Journal of College Student Development, 30,* 395 – 400.

Kolb, D. (1984). *Experiential learning: Experience as the source of learning and development.* Englewood Cliffs, NJ: Prentice Hall.

Maze, M., & Mayhall, D. (1995). *The Enhanced guide for occupational exploration: Descriptions for the 2,800 most important jobs.* Washington D.C.: JIST Works.

Michael, W. B.(2005) Review of Occupational Aptitude Survey and Interest Schedule (Third Edition). In R. A. Spies & B. S. Plake (Eds.), *The sixteenth mental measurements yearbook* (pp. 715 – 720). Lincoln, NE: University of Nebraska – Lincoln.

Parker, R. (2002a). *Occupational aptitude survey and interest schedule, 3rd ed. Interest schedule examiner's manual.* Austin, TX: Pro-Ed.

Parker, R. (2002b). *Occupational aptitude survey and interest schedule, 3rd ed. Aptitude survey examiner's manual.* Austin, TX: Pro-Ed.

Psychological Corporation. (1992). *Differential aptitude tests, 5th ed..* San Antonio, TX: Author.

Remer, R. (1986). Review of the Occupational Aptitude Survey & Interest Schedule (OASIS). *Journal of Counseling and Development, 64,* 467 – 468.

U.S. Department of Labor. (1970). *Manual for the USES General Aptitude Test Battery, Section III: Development.* Washington, D.C.: U.S. Government Printing Office.

System for Assessment and Group Evaluation (SAGE 2001)

Chuck Loch, Charles Kass and Joseph Kass

PESCO International, Inc.
21 Paulding Street
Pleasantville, NY 10570
www.pesco.org

Target Population: 8th grade to college, all populations except TMRs.

Statement of the Purpose of the Instrument: To screen applicants for employers, training programs, program placement, and counseling.

Titles of Subtests, Scales, Scores Provided: Reasoning, Math, Language-GED levels, General, Verbal, Numerical, Spatial, Form Discrimination, Clerical Perception, Manual Dexterity, Finger Dexterity, Eye-Hand-Foot Coordination, Color Discrimination, Motor Coordination, Vocational Interest, Learning Styles, Job Temperament, Work Ethics, Work Attitude.

Languages in Which Available: English, Spanish, Greek, Russian, Vietnamese.

Time:

Actual Test Time: 2 minutes to 22 minutes.

Total Administration Time: Time is based on the groups of tests administered.

Norm Group(s) on Which Scores Are Based: Junior High School, High School, employed worker, welfare, and vocational technical.

Manner in Which Results Are Reported for Individuals:

Types of Scores: Reports are produced by percentile—Aptitude level, verbal level.

Report Format/Content:

BASIC SERVICE: System provides more than 25 preformatted reports and allows for the creation of unlimited reports.

Scoring:

Machine Scoring Service: Computerized SAGE—Self-scoring instantly, manual SAGE—Cards fed through optical scanner in seconds.

Time required for scoring and returning (maximum): 48 hours.

Computer Software Options Available: Computerized adaptive administration; standard administration online.

Other: voice for test administration. All manipulative tests are linked to the computer. Local Area Network and Wide Area Network available for Windows 2003.

Cost of Materials: Due to possible price changes since publication date, be sure to check with publisher web site.

SAGE COMPUTERIZED ASSESSMENT SYSTEM

(Bilingual, Network with unlimited user access)

JOBS 6 PROGRAM	$15,000

CD-ROM Employer File (list of local employers)

Client Reports based on assessment & previous job history

Descriptions/Profiles of DOT/O*NET Titles

Transferability of skills

SAGE COMPUTERIZED Bi-lingual TESTING SYSTEM

Vocational Aptitude Battery	$15,995

3 Eye-Hand-Foot/Motor Testing Units

  3 Finger Testing Units

  3 Manual Testing Units

  General, Verbal, Numerical, Spatial

  Clerical, Form, Color, Work Concerns

  Reading & Math Equivalency Levels

GED Levels—Reasoning, Math & Language Skills

Vocational Interest Inventory

Job Temperaments

Assessment of Work Attitudes

Work Ethics Inventory

CITE Learning Styles

Technical Support	$700
Shipping and Handling	$100
TOTAL	$31,795
TRAINING (3 days at your facility)	$1,500
Expenses (airfare, room & board, car for 1 trainer)	$1,500

SAGE MANUAL ASSESSMENT SYSTEM

Vocational Aptitude Battery (VAB)	$20,995

- 1 Eye-Hand-Foot Testing Unit
- 1 Motor Coordination Testing Unit
- 1 Finger Dexterity Testing Unit
- 1 Spatial Aptitude Test Unit
- 1 Manual Dexterity Test Unit
- 1 Color Discrimination Test Unit
- 1 Clerical Aptitude Test Unit
- 1 Form Perception Test Unit
- 1 General, 1 Verbal, & Numerical Ability Testing Units

Cognitive & Conceptual Abilities Test (C-CAT)
Vocational Interest Inventory (VII)
Temperament Factor Assessment (TFA)
Assessment of Work Attitudes (AWA)
Cite Learning Styles Test (CITE)
Work Ethics Inventory
Full Set of SAGE Scoring Cards for 250 clients
5 Electronic Timers
An Optical Scanner for Autoscoring

JOBS 6 PROGRAM
   CD-ROM Employer File (list of local employers)
   Client Reports based on assessment & previous job history
   Descriptions/Profiles of DOT/O*NET Titles
   Transferability of skills
An IBM Compatible Computer with
   Pentium 4 processor at 2.2 GHz
   256 MB RAM
   40 GB hard drive
   Microsoft Windows XP Home
Monitor
Laser Printer

Full Technical Support for 1 Year	$350
Shipping and Handling	$225
TOTAL	$21,570

PESCO ASSESSMENT SYSTEM PROPOSAL
3 Full Days of Training are Recommended

Training Fee $500 per day	$1,500
Plus expenses (approximate)	$1,500
	$3,000

Optional System Enhancements

Automated Scoring and Prescription Program for TABE	$1,295
Scoring cards for the program	$24.50 each
1 Set of Carrying Cases (4)	$775

The entire SAGE Manual Testing system can be packed in cases for transporting.

AUDIO capacity for test to be read to client	$1,250

CAREER NAVIGATOR (Network 10 User access) $4,995

Self-administered assessment with bilingual reports and job matches printed automatically.

Career Navigator includes the following assessments:

General Learning Ability includes:

Verbal Aptitude

Numerical Aptitude

Spatial Aptitude

Clerical Perception

Form Perception

Vocational Interest Inventory

General Education Development (GED)

Reasoning

Math

Language

Technical Support $250

SAGE Components can be added to the CAREER NAVIGATOR

1 Set of Manipulatives $2,085
Manual, Finger, Eye/Hand/Foot/Motor Units

Color Discrimination $595

CITE Learning Styles $595

Job Temperament $595

Assessment of Work Attitudes $595

Reading/Math $595

Work Concerns $595

Transferability of Skills Program $750

CD-ROM Employer File $350

TRAINING (2 days at your facility) $1,000

Expenses (expenses) $1,200

Published Reviews of the Instrument in the Last 15 Years: None cited.

Reviewed by:

Bruce Thompson
Distinguished Professor
Department of Educational Psychology
Texas A&M University

Description

The SAGE 2001 (System for Assessment and Group Evaluation 2001) assessment system http://www.pesco.com is a wide-ranging, comprehensive package of protocols intended to create a "One Stop Career Center." The assessment system consists of three major elements, as well as five other substantial components.

With respect to the three major components, SAGE includes (a) a vocational aptitude battery measuring 11 vocational aptitudes (10 general, 10 verbal, 10 numerical, and one each spatial, form perception, clerical perception, motor coordination, finger dexterity, manual dexterity, eye-hand-foot coordination, and color discrimination tests), (b) a cognitive and conceptual measure evaluating General Educational Developmental (GED) reasoning, math, and language abilities directly related to the requirements in the U.S. Department of Labor (DOL) *Dictionary of Occupational Titles (1991)*, and (c) a vocational interest inventory that measures an individual's areas of interest using 20 booklets in 12 interest areas, 66 work groups, and the Holland codes used by the DOL. One form of these various protocols is a self-administered, abbreviated computerized system, Career Navigator that meets government assessment requirements, and can be completed in under 60 minutes.

Additionally, the CITE Learning Styles Inventory is an untimed measure of preferred learning styles (i.e., visual, auditory, or kinesthetic), modes of expression (i.e., oral or written), and modes of learning (i.e., solitary or group). Respondents characterize how well they are described (i.e., "most like me," "somewhat like me," "not much like me," and "least like me") by the statements in 10 booklets.

The Assessment of Work Attitudes requires evaluation of and responses to on-the-job situations. The assessment includes color pictures with written narratives that describes the various work situations. Participants respond using four-point Likert scales.

The Temperament Factor Assessment is intended to measure personal traits presumed to be related to job performance and job turnover. The traits correspond to the 11 temperaments used by the DOL in its job classifications. This untimed unit depicts various aspects of work (e.g., being given job directives) to which participants respond in a true-false format.

A Work Ethics component, consisting of 10 booklets, is intended to measure personality types thought to be related to job survival. Finally, the Jobskills component is a software product that requires participants to complete a software task in an actual software environment (e.g., Word, Word Perfect, Lotus). The Jobskills protocol also supports the creation of local benchmark tests for evaluating basic computer skills using the Jobskills question bank.

The SAGE 2001 system can be administered either individually or to multiple users, in either standalone of networked environments, using commonly available computer-operating systems. Bookmarking allows participants to enter or exit any assessment and return later, if desired. Although paper-and-pencil versions of some units are available, which can then be scanned, most contemporary users will elect to work completely in the computerized environment. In any case, computerization allows immediate scoring and report generation. The units are available in English, Spanish, large print, and Braille.

Use in Counseling

The SAGE 2001 assessment system is potentially applicable in secondary or postsecondary career counseling, vocational rehabilitation, and in employment job placement and training. The system is vast in its coverage, and indeed is among the most widereaching of the protocols reviewed in *A Counselor's Guide*. The protocol has impressive flexibility with respect to the use of assessment components and assessment units. Case management software includes the capacity to produce reports in prepackaged forms, including Individualized Education Plans and Individualized Written Rehabilitation Plans.

Assessment results can also be matched with either national or local job availability information. And individualized reports can be printed that match a given participant's comprehensive vocational profile.

Technical Considerations

The most recent technical report on SAGE 2001 score psychometrics apparently still is Loch (1999), a report available prior to Rojewski's (2001) review in *A Counselor's Guide*. It is a matter of some concern that a more recent, and a more integrated technical manual has not yet been produced.

The manual (Lock, 1999, p. 15) seems to characterize reliability as being a property of a given measure, rather than being correctly characterized as a property of a given set of scores (Thompson, 2003). The realization that score reliability fluctuates, even for a given measure, led to Vacha-Haase's (1998) development of the measurement meta-analysis method called "reliability generalization" (RG). The modern view of reliability requires on-going scrutiny of score reliability across time, and across subpopulations as well. Greater sensitivity to these dynamics might result in an updated, and a more comprehensive and systematic reporting of score psychometric features.

The SAGE 2001 manual (Loch, 1999) suggests that "a coefficient of at least +.70 or higher is usually considered adequate" with respect to reliability. By this standard, the scores produced by the protocol had reasonable reliability, at least in the prior documented applications.

Of course, score validity is also a critical psychometric consideration. Most of the evidence here is in the form of concurrent validity coefficients. Again, selected validity coefficients are presented in separate studies. One would instead expect an integrated, comprehensive presentation that makes a coherent, thoughtful argument that all the scores are indeed trustworthy.

Overall Critique

The most appealing features of the SAGE 2001 system include (a) the huge array of assessment choices, (b) which can be administered, scored, and reported with modern, flexible computerized support. A CD-ROM available from the publisher and web-based information, make comprehensible the huge array of applications and assessment choices. The ties to existing theories, databases, and measures (e.g., the DOL *Dictionary of Occupational Titles,* the GED, and Holland's codes) are positive features of the protocol. The potential to use the measure with persons with disabilities or Spanish speakers also is important.

Less positive is the limited integrated documentation of contemporary psychometric evidence that scores are reliable and especially that they are valid. Nevertheless, career counselors working in high schools, universities, corporate, or private practice settings will find the impressive flexibility and comprehensiveness of the protocol quite appealing.

References

Loch, C. (1999). *A manual of research and norm studies.* Pleasantville, NY: Pesco International.

Rojewski, J. W. (2001). Review of PESCO 2001. In J. Kapes & E. Whitfield (Eds.), *A counselor's guide to career assessment instruments* (4th ed., 158 – 163). Columbus, OH: National Career Development Association.

Thompson, B. (Ed.). (2003). *Score reliability: Contemporary thinking on reliability issues.* Newbury Park, CA: Sage.

Vacha-Haase, T. (1998). Reliability generalization: Exploring variance in measurement error affecting score reliability across studies. *Educational and Psychological Measurement, 58,* 6 – 20.

U.S. Department of Labor (1991). *Dictionary of occupational titles (4th ed.).* Washington, DC: Government Printing Office.

TESTS OF ADULT BASIC EDUCATION (TABE 9 &10)

CTB/McGraw-Hill

CTB/McGraw-Hill

20 Ryan Ranch Road
Monterey, CA 93940
www.ctb.com

Target Population: TABE can be used with a wide range of audiences: high-school equivalency or GED programs; vocational programs; certain community college programs; welfare-to-work programs; occupational or military advancement programs; alternative educational programs; and English for speakers of other languages (ESOL) programs, which may include basic education, vocational, and life skills assessment.

Statement of the Purpose of the Instrument: To provide a measurement of basic skills and abilities for adult students to show job readiness, prediction of performance on the GED, placement of students in an adult basic education program, and diagnostic information showing strengths and weaknesses.

Titles of Subtests, Scales, Scores Provided: Subtests: Reading, Mathematics, Language, Language Mechanics, Vocabulary, and Spelling.

Forms and Levels Available, with Dates of Publication/Revision of Each:

2 forms—TABE 9&10

- Form 9—November 2003 publication date
- Form 10—November 2003 publication date

5 levels—Limited Literacy, Easy, Medium, Difficult, and Advanced

Date of Most Recent Edition of Test Manual, User's Guide, etc.: The TABE Teacher's Guides were published in 2005. The date for the Test Directions is 2003.

Languages in Which Available: English only.

Time:

Actual Test Time /Total Administration Time

TABE 9&10 Levels E, M, D, and A: Item Count and Test Times*

	Complete Battery		Survey	
Locator Test	**No. Items**	**Testing Time (h:m)**	**No. Items**	**Testing Time (h:m)**
Reading	50	0:50	25	0:25
Math Comp	40	0:24	25	0:15
Applied Math	50	0:50	25	0:25
Language	55	0:55	25	0:25

Language Mech	20	0:14		
Vocabulary	20	0:15		
Spelling	20	0:10		
Total	225	3:34	100	1:30

* Allow 10 minutes for instruction, recording names on answer sheets, etc. Note that the Spelling test is optional and does not contribute to the total Battery scores.

Norm Group(s) on Which Scores Are Based: Norms from 2002 – 2003. Norming population included adult general and juvenile (ages 14 – 20).

Manner in Which Results Are Reported for Individuals:

Types of Scores: Grade equivalent, scale scores, number correct, national percentile, NCE, national stanine, % mastery, predicted GED score, NRS (National Reporting System) level.

Report Format/Content:

BASIC SERVICE: Customer scored is the only option for TABE 9&10. CTB does not provide scoring.

OPTIONS: Online scoring and reporting is available with TestMate TABE software. Hand scoring option is available with scoring stencils or by using the self-scoring Scoreze answer sheets.

Report Format/Content for Group Summaries:

Student Subtest Report—Offers a skill by skill report for each individual student

Student Pre-Post Test Report—Offers a pre-post summary for each individual student

Student Prescriptive Report—Shows individual performance by skill, then refers each student to specific lessons in the books and software.

Rank List Report—Presents (in roster listing) students in selected score order. Also allows for a "cut score" option

Group List Report—Presents a class roster, listing each student's grade equivalent, national percentile, and additional scores.

Group Report—Gives summary or pre-post scores for all students in a group, plus average scores for the group selected.

Item Analysis Report—Presents item-by–objective results for an individual. Includes individual response as well as correct answers for each item.

Scoring:

Machine Scoring Service: Not available.

Hand Scoring:

Scored by: Counselor

Local Machine Scoring: Provisions/conditions/equipment required: Requires TestMate TABE for Windows Software for scanning, scoring and reporting TABE results. Supports scanners with 48-column double-sided read-heads, including

NCS OpScan series and Scantron Scanmark series. The system requirements are 256 MB of RAM, 10 MB hard drive, Pentium III or higher, VGA monitors.

Computer Software Options Available: Standard administration online. Other TABE-PC offers a computer-based administration of TABE 9&10 that is administered on PC locally and is computer scored.

Ways in Which Computer/Online Version Differs: Computer version has real-time scoring and reporting and is administered completely online.

Cost of Materials: Due to possible price changes since publication date, be sure to check with publisher web site.

Specimen Set: Includes test books for each level for Complete Battery and Survey and test directions.

Counselee Materials:

For Each Student:

$36.00/25	1 Practice Exercise and Locator Test Book
	1 Practice Exercise and Locator Test Answer Sheet
$101.00/25	1 Complete Battery or Survey Form Test Book (order the level determined by the Locator Test score)—Reusable
$36.00/25	1 Answer Sheet for the Survey or 1 set of Answer Sheets for the Complete Battery
$16.00/25	1 Complete Battery Individual Diagnostic Profile

For Each Administrator:

$19.00/1	1 Test Directions for Complete Battery—Reusable
	1 Test Directions for Survey—Reusable
$60.00/1	1 Test Coordinator's Handbook (Guide to Administering TABE)—Reusable
$21.00/1	1 Technical Report—Reusable
$19.00/1	1 Norms Book—Reusable

Additional Comments of Interest to Users: The newest addition to the TABE family of tests is now available for English language learners. TABE Complete Language Assessment System—English (TABE CLAS-E) assesses the English language skills in adult students to provide an accurate measure of English proficiency. The assessment is available with two forms for pretesting and posttesting to show learning gains in Reading, Listening, Writing, and Speaking.

Published Reviews of the Instrument in the Last 15 Years: None cited.

Reviewed by:

Esther Prins
Assistant Professor of Education
The Pennsylvania State University

Description

The Tests of Adult Basic Education (TABE) is a norm- and criterion-referenced standardized test "designed to assess skills in contexts important to adults, such as life skills, work, and education" (CTB/McGraw-Hill, 2004, p. 2). Forms 9&10 are the updated version of 7&8 (the proportion of new content is unknown). A Locator Test determines the appropriate test level: L (grades 0 – 1.9, only available in Complete Battery), E (2.0 – 3.9), M (4.0 – 5.9), D (6.0 – 8.9), and A (9.0 – 12.9). The Complete Battery includes subtests in Reading, Language, Mathematics Computation, Applied Mathematics, Vocabulary, Language Mechanics, and Spelling. In the shorter Survey version, the latter three subtests are optional.

Test Directions provide detailed information about administering the TABE, including a framework for classifying accommodations. Student with visual disabilities may use large-print, Braille, or audio editions. Assessment results include objective mastery levels and percentile, scale, and Grade Equivalent scores, among others. Electronic reports provide additional diagnostic information.

The TABE is the most widely used standardized test in adult basic education (ABE) and GED programs in the U.S, and is also popular in correctional education, vocational education, and other adult education settings. Usage has likely increased since the National Reporting System (NRS) began requiring federally funded adult education programs to administer standardized pretests and posttests. Conveniently, NRS performance levels are linked to TABE scores.

Use in Counseling

The TABE is typically used to place students at an appropriate instructional level, to diagnose strengths and weaknesses in subject areas, to measure and report student progress, to predict GED readiness, and to guide selection of curricular materials. Because 7&8 and 9&10 are on the same scale, users can compare results from different forms. Venezky, Bristow, and Sabatini (1997) found that a previous version of the Locator Test was more effective than the Complete Battery in placing students at appropriate literacy instructional levels, but no research has examined Forms 9&10. The publisher recommends against using Locator Tests for placement.

The TABE can also serve as a screening tool for educational programs or employers requiring a certain math or reading level; however, multiple measures should be used for high-stakes decisions. Subtests may be administered separately to assess specific skills, but should not be the sole basis for important decisions. Scores near the top or bottom of a scale are less reliable, and should be interpreted cautiously. For these reasons, users should be trained to administer the TABE.

After completing the 37-minute Locator Test, examinees need approximately 2 hours to complete the Survey with Optional subtests (1.5 hours without) and 3.5 hours for the Complete Battery. Examiners should add 5 to 10 minutes *per subtest* to administer practice questions and read instructions, which may prove time-consuming for programs which admit students continuously and administer tests individually. To measure more accurately the abilities of returning adult learners, users should consider administering the TABE after enrollment.

Reviewers and researchers have identified several shortcomings of the TABE. First, Grade Equivalents are based on how children's skills develop and may not capture adults' real-world knowledge (Cumming, Gal, & Ginsburg, 1998; Kruidenier, 2002). Although the publisher states the TABE "enables examinees to demonstrate their true skills in working with real-life test stimuli" (CTB/McGraw-Hill, 2004, p. 2), many items are decontextualized (e.g., math problems with little text). Researchers suggest the TABE may not adequately reflect adults' real-life competencies or their classroom learning. The American Institutes for Research (Condelli, 2006) concluded the 9&10 math tests include few contextualized problems and do not allow for partly correct answers or assess reasoning, problem solving, or critical thinking. Finally, TABE content should not drive instruction or curricula.

Technical Considerations

Test developers employed rigorous procedures to reduce ethnic, age, and gender bias, but social class is not mentioned. Items include a mix of male and female characters and pronouns and several nontraditional gender roles. Several items cover multicultural topics, and some Latino, Asian, and traditionally African-American names are included. Prompts about famous persons feature only two nonwhite individuals.

Middle-class examinees are more likely to be familiar with the content and format of numerous problems, such as checkbook registers, bank loans, plane travel, and business letters. Strikingly, no items feature bus or subway information, money orders, receipts, job applications, or shopping lists—literacy and numeracy practices more familiar to many low-income adults. Other prompts, such as fliers, advertisements, and recipes, are widely relevant to functional contexts.

A few problems are ambiguous or inaccurate: One item is based on faulty assumptions about how round trip airfare is calculated, another presumes salads are never served after the main dish (not so in Europe), and a third item, asking examinees to predict future actions, includes two plausible answers.

Forms 9&10 were normed on 34,676 individuals age 14 years and older in 495 programs across 46 states. The Locator Test was normed on 4,000 individuals. Norms are provided for "ABE-All" and "ABE-Juvenile," comprised of 12,271 individuals age 14 to 20. Norms were pooled across TABE levels with varying numbers of cases (1,323-9,069). The publisher states the sample was "nationally representative," but does not describe the sampling rationale or procedures for institutions or individuals. Comparison of the norming group to federal data on state-sponsored adult education programs (2002 – 2003) reveals that women, Latinos, and adults over 20 were *underrepresented* in the norming group (by approximately 27%, 24%, and 19%, respectively), while men, African-Americans, and young adults were *overrepresented* (by 26%, 19%, and 13%) (http://www.ed.gov/about/offices/list/ovae/pi/AdultEd/aedatatables.html). The overrepresentation of inmates in the norming group (53%) may help explain this pattern. These demographic discrepancies raise questions about the appropriateness of comparing adult learners to the norming group.

An equating study was conducted to place TABE 9&10 on the same scale as Form 7. Correlations between subtests are .51 – .76 for Forms 7 and 9, and .52 - .74 for Forms 7 and 10 (average = .64). In his review of TABE 7&8, Beck (1998) considered .52 – .73 to be low correlations and recommended that users consider carefully the relationship between older and newer tests. No correlations between Forms 9 & 10 or between the Complete Battery and Survey are presented.

TABE developers took several steps to ensure construct validity, such as meeting with adult educators and reviewing curricula, standards, and the GED test. To align the TABE and GED, Forms 9&10 include more life- and work-related material. Overall, the *Technical Report* provides insufficient evidence to assess construct validity (e.g., alignment between subtest objectives and curricula). Correlations between related or unrelated subtests (.64 for Reading and Language, and Applied Math and Math Computation) demonstrate convergent and divergent validity. Correlations between Form 7 and the 2002 GED test (.52 – .57 for subtests, .63 for Total Battery) provide some evidence of criterion-related validity. However, significance levels are not provided, nor are correlations of Forms 9 & 10 and the GED.

Internal consistency reliability coefficients for subtests are .73 – .95. No reliability data are presented for Total Math, Total Battery, or Total Survey. I estimated average reliability coefficients for each level and form in Complete Battery and Survey (Core Tests and Total Survey). The Complete Battery (.87) is more reliable than the Survey (Core = .84, Total Survey = .83). All 26 test versions meet the standard (.60) for group reporting and decision making (Salvia & Ysseldyke, 1998). Twenty-four meet the threshold (.80) for screening and evaluation. Survey Level D (Core and Total, Form 9) tests fall just below the standard. Two tests—Level E, Complete Battery, Forms 9 & 10—meet the threshold (.90) for making high-stakes decisions about individuals.

Standard Error of Measurement (SEM) curves show that "TABE 9 & 10 and TABE 7 by level and by subtest measure accurately over the same range of the test scale" (CTB/McGraw-Hill, 2004, p. 27). SEMs are higher for the Survey than the Complete Battery, and at the high and low end of scale scores than in the mid-range.

The *Technical Report* does not explain how Grade Equivalents were established. Three statistical methods were used to establish Locator Test cut points. Little explanation, however, is provided for mastery (≥75%), partial mastery (50 – 74%), and nonmastery cut points (<50%). The publisher recommends supplementing mastery levels with additional information about student performance.

Overall Critique

TABE 9&10 materials are visually appealing, easy to use, and include more prompts simulating functional contexts. The tests are useful for measuring basic skills in reading, math, and language; placing students; conducting pretesting and posttesting; making comparisons among students; and meeting federal reporting guidelines. Given demographic incongruities between the norming group and adult learners in state-administered programs, users should exercise caution in comparing results to the reference group. Since the TABE may not accurately reflect adults' real-world competencies or what they learn through instruction, multiple measures should be used when seeking a fine-grained assessment of adults' abilities or making high-stakes decisions.

References

Beck, M.D. (1998). Review of the Tests of Adult Basic Education. In J.C. Impara & B.S. Plake (Eds.). *The thirteenth mental measurements yearbook* (1080 – 1083). Lincoln, NE: University of Nebraska.

Condelli, L. (2006). *A review of the literature in adult numeracy: Research and conceptual issues.* Washington, DC: American Institutes for Research.

CTB/McGraw-Hill. (2004). *TABE 9/10 technical report.* Monterey, CA: Author.

Cumming, J., Gal, I., & Ginsburg, L. (1998). *Assessing mathematical knowledge of adult learners: Are we looking at what counts?* Philadelphia: National Center on Adult Literacy, University of Pennsylvania.

Kruidenier, J. (2002). Literacy education in adult basic education. In J. Comings, B. Garner & C. Smith (Eds.), *Annual review of adult learning and literacy* (Vol. 3, pp. 84 – 151). San Francisco: Jossey-Bass.

Salvia, J., & Ysseldyke, J. E. (1998). *Assessment* (7th ed.). Boston: Houghton Mifflin.

Venezky, R. L., Bristow, P. S., & Sabatini, J. P. (1997). When less is more: Methods for placing students in adult literacy classes. *Adult Basic Education, 7*(1), 3 – 22.

Wonderlic Basic Skills Test (WBST)

Eliot R. Long, Victor S. Artese and Winifred L. Clonts

Wonderlic, Inc.
1795 North Butterfield Road
Suite 200
Libertyville, IL 60048-1380
mike.callans@wonderlic.com
1-800.323.3742
www.wonderlic.com

Target Population: High school students and adults.

Statement of the Purpose of the Instrument: Short form measure of adult language and math skills for job or school training readiness.

Titles of Subtests, Scales, Scores Provided: Subtests: Verbal Skills and Quantitative Skills; Scores: Test of Verbal Skills: (Word Knowledge, Sentence Construction, Information Retrieval, Total). Test of Quantitative Skills (Explicit Problem Solving, Applied Problem Solving, Interpretive Problem Solving, Total), Composite score.

Forms and Levels Available, with Dates of Publication/Revision of Each: V1, V2, Q1, and Q2, 1994.

Date of Most Recent Edition of Test Manual, User's Guide, etc.: October 1999

Languages in Which Available: English only.

Time:

Actual Test Time: 20 minutes for each test.

Total Administration Time: 5 minutes for each test.

Norm Group(s) on Which Scores Are Based: Students in high schools, junior colleges, vocational schools and adults in work settings (manufacturing financial services, fast food services, oil drilling, truck assembly, highway/construction).

Manner in Which Results Are Reported for Individuals:

Types of Scores: Scale score, Percentile distribution, GED scale, grade level.

Report Format/Content:

Basic Service: Individual score report—Summary report.

Scoring of the WBST can be through the use of the PC and the WBST Scoring Program diskette or through the Wonderlic Reporting Service. The WBST Scoring Program can provide the following reports, which can be printed: Individual Summary Report, Individual Detailed Report, Summary Listing, and Interpretation Guide. The Wonderlic Reporting Service will score and run diagnostic analyses to evaluate individual assessments. The Wonderlic Reporting Service also provides quarterly reports.

Report Format/Content for Group Summaries:

BASIC SERVICE: Local vs. National norms

Scoring

Machine Scoring Service:

COST OF BASIC SERVICE PER COUNSELEE: $55 per quarter

Hand Scoring: Not available.

Computer Software Options Available: Paper-and-pencil administration—computer diskette scoring.

Computer administration: Administration via the Internet available.

Cost of Materials: Due to possible price changes since publication date, be sure to check the publisher's website.

Specimen Set: Sample Tests: No charge.

Counselee Materials:

Verbal	pkg/25	$160
Quantitative	pkg/25	$220
Composite	pkg/25	$315

Reviewed By:

Sally J. Power
Professor of Management
University of St. Thomas
St. Paul/Minneapolis, MN

Description

The Wonderlic Basic Skills Test (WBST) is made up of two short, multiple-choice tests that determine basic levels of quantitative and verbal skills for teenagers and adults. The test is designed for those with less than a high school education and is focused on the lower three levels of the six-level General Educational Development scale. Both tests can be taken in an hour. This test is used primarily by employers to determine job readiness. It also is used to identify jobs for which an individual might have the basic skills and/or an individual's readiness for vocational training. Finally, it is approved by the Department of Education for use in assessing Title IV "ability to benefit" Federal financial aid (FR Doc. E6-7682, 5/19/06).

For example, the test might report that an individual had language skills at GED level 3, math skills at GED level 2, and composite skills at GED level 3 (the composite skills score in the WBST is used as an estimator of the reasoning skills dimension in the DOL schema according to Donlon (1998)). Such a person could expect to have the basic abilities to be a word processor since those are the levels for basic math, language and reasoning for that job in the *Dictionary of Occupational Titles, (U.S. Department of Labor, 1991)* but would need more training in basic reasoning to be able to work successfully as a supervisor, which the *Dictionary of Occupational Titles* reports needs an adequate score in reasoning at GED level 4.

There are two versions of each type of test available. They are nicely printed and come with answer sheets and a PC-compatible disk for on-site scoring. The text questions have been reviewed and analyzed statistically by independent experts to assure that the questions would be equivalent for all subgroups and free of content bias (Long, Artese, & Clonts, 2001). Hanna (1998) reports that the test items are well written, varied, and clearly relevant to the world of work without being job specific, gender specific, or subculture specific.

Scoring can be printed as summary reports or detailed reports for individuals. In addition, an interpretive guide can be printed as well as a report listing of all examinees in the current drive using the scoring software. Another scoring option is to contract with Wonderlic Reporting Service. This will provide more sophisticated analysis of individual results as well as quarterly reports of testing done at your site with comparisons to Wonderlic's national database by job title, education level, demographic classification, and recruiting source.

Use in Counseling

The test could be very useful for career counseling with individuals who have been out of school for some time, have a high school education or less, and are seeking an entry level job and/or additional vocational training. It would give quick information concerning the general levels of the basic language, math, and reasoning skills in a form that can be used to identify types of jobs they might want to pursue. Because the test also reports its results in terms of grade level, it could be used to identify the level of training materials individuals could use successfully.

This test is also an option for counselors involved in providing Title IV "ability to benefit" Federal financial aid because the test has been approved for that use. If that use is contemplated, however, the Wonderlic company must be informed and additional systems and manuals must be acquired (Jo Long, Wonderlinc, Inc. representative, personal communication, 2007).

One table in T*he Wonderlic Basic Skills Test User's Manual* may be particularly useful for career counselors who are focusing on facilitating job searches. This table reports the median WBST scores by job title and training program for jobs where Wonderlic has data from 50 or more individuals. These data were collected either in the original field studies done with the test or in their work with commercial customers (Jo Long, personal communications,2007). If one assumes that employers are likely to hire applicants with better scores, these data provide information about levels of scores needed for likely employment in specific jobs whereas The *Dictionary of Occupational Titles* and O*NET (http://online.onetcenter.org) report minimum requirements. At this point, the table contains only 86 jobs or training programs, but this list is likely to grow.

Also, the instrument reports the individual's performance on the test using subscales. For the language test, the subscales are word knowledge, sentence construction, and information retrieval. For the math test, the subscales are explicit, applied (word questions), and interpretative (use of tables, charts, and figures) subscales (Long et al., 2001). These subscales, however, are not designed to allow those interpreting the scores to identify specific areas of weakness. *The Wonderlic Basic Skills User's Manual* specifies that the subscales are designed to aid employers making hiring decisions when the scores are borderline. For example, low subscale scores would confirm a low general score. Or, a mixture of high and low subscale scores could be matched to a job's particular needs (Long et al. 2001).

The test can be administered untimed for examinees that are unlikely to have a fair assessment of their skills using the 20-minute time limit. It will indicate when the pattern of answers on the test suggests the examinee may have been skipping questions, guessing, or making careless mistakes; retesting is then suggested. Finally, the test results will indicate whether the individual's GED level is above the assessment range of the test.

Technical Considerations

The WBST used item response theory (IRT) heavily during the development of its items. IRT's guiding assumption is that only one dominant factor is being measured—in this case, basic verbal and quantitative skills. Items were tested to make sure that each progressive item was more difficult than those before and that all items have comparable capacity to separate examinees into their appropriate skill levels. Finally, the IRT methodology allows for comparing the reliability of test items (Long et al., 2001).

Test reliability was measured by doing test-retest studies with various time periods. The reliability coefficients in this series of tests are reported for same form (ranging from .83 to .91 for the quantitative skills test and from .84 to 90 for the verbal skills test) and for parallel forms (ranging from .83 to .89 for the quantitative skills test and from .89 to .93 for the verbal skills test). Finally, internal consistency was measured by calculating Chronbach alphas for all subscales comparing timed and untimed tests. The Chronbach alphas for the separate tests ranged from .77 to .90 and showed not only that all content domains were measured reliably but that the 20-minute time limit is sufficient for the tests. Hanna and Hughey (2001) note that while the variety of reliability testing is highly commendable, the samples in these studies did not include means or standard deviations and thus were difficult to interpret.

The prime method for determining validity of the tests has been through content validity. Test content was developed by subject matter experts in line with the GED levels, and the manual shows correlations with students in grades 6 – 12, which indicates that the test does, in fact, measure basic verbal and quantitative skills. As has been pointed out by other reviewers, however, the evidence of the validity of this test would be stronger if studies showing its predictive validity had been done (Donlon, 1998; Hanna, 1998). Furthermore, not testing has shown the possible effects of "test wiseness" or sensitivity to coaching (Hanna, 1998).

Overall Critique

The WBST is a very good test of basic verbal and quantitative skills. It could be particularly useful when working with adults with a high school education or less who have been out of school for a number of years. Its prime weakness from the perspective of career counseling is that it is not designed to allow a diagnosis of weaknesses within these basic skills. A potential strength is that the analysis of its commercial use which Wonderlic has made available via the table on median scores for occupations. This provides counselors with information regarding the level of basic skills possessed by people who are likely to be hired for particular jobs.

References

Department of Education, Update Notice, Federal Register, vol. 71, no. 97 (May 19, 2006) page 29135 – 29137, accessed on March 21, 2007 at www.gpoaccess.gove/fr/index.html.

Donlon, T.F. (1998). Review of the Wonderlic Basic Skills Test. In J.C. Impara and B.S. Plake (Eds.), *The thirteenth mental measurements yearbook*. Lincoln, NE: Buros. Accessed on March 19, 2007 from Mental Measurements Yearbook database.

Hanna, G.S. (1998). Review of the Wonderlic Basic Skills Test. In J.C. Impara and B.S. Plake (Eds.), *The thirteenth mental measurements yearbook*. Lincoln, NE: Buros. Accessed March 19, 2007, from Mental Measurements Yearbook database.

Hanna, G.S. & Hughey, K.F. (2001) Wonderlic Basic Skills Test Review. In J.T. Kapes and E. A. Whitfield (Eds.), *A Counselor's Guide to Career Assessment Instruments, 4th ed.*, Columbus OH: National Career Development Association.

Long, E. R., Artese, V.S., & Clonts, W.L. (2001). *The Wonderlic Basic Skills Test User's Manual.* Libertyville, IL: Wonderlic Inc.

Long, J. (2007). Personal communication, Wonderlic Inc. representative.

U.S. Department of Labor. (1991). *Dictionary of occupational titles* (4th ed.). Washington, DC: U.S. Government Printing Office.

WorkKeys Assessments (WorkKeys)

ACT, Inc.

ACT
500 ACT Drive
P.O. Box 168
Iowa City, Iowa 52243-0168
www.act.org

Target Population: Current or potential job seekers; recommended grade 10 through adult.

Statement of the Purpose of the Instrument: WorkKeys assessments are part of a job skills assessment system that links education and the workforce, offering a common language to enhance communication about job skill requirements needed to develop employees and build a better workforce. "Real world" skills that employers believe are critical to job success are measured, including communication, problem solving, critical thinking, and personal and interpersonal skills.

Titles of Subtests, Scales, Scores Provided: (12 separate content areas)

WorkKeys Applied Mathematics, level scores 3 – 7; scale scores 65 – 90

WorkKeys Applied Technology, level scores 3 – 6; scale scores 65 – 90

WorkKeys Business Writing, level scores 0 – 5, analytic scores for Focus, Organization, Development, Sentence Structure, and Mechanical Conventions

WorkKeys Listening, level scores 0 – 5

WorkKeys Locating Information, level scores 3 – 6, scale scores 65 – 90

WorkKeys Observation, level scores 3 – 6, scale scores 65 – 90

WorkKeys Reading for Information, level scores 3 – 7, scale scores 65 – 90

WorkKeys Teamwork, level scores 3 – 6, scale scores 65 – 90

WorkKeys Writing, level scores 0 – 5

WorkKeys Performance (measure of risk-taking and corporate citizenship), WorkKeys Talent (measure of various personality facets), WorkKeys Fit (measure of interest and fit to occupations), percentile rankings and categorical descriptors

Forms and Levels Available, with Dates of Publication/Revision of Each: See content areas and levels above; all assessments except Performance, Talent, and Fit have at least three forms of each available at all times. Reading, Math, Listening, and Writing were first published in 1992; Reading and Math have annual new form releases. Locating Information, Teamwork, and Applied Tech were first published in 1993; Locating has annual new form releases; a new form of Teamwork was released in 2001 and a revision is underway; new forms of Applied Tech were released in 2006. Observation was first published in 1995; it is currently being revised. Business Writing was released in 2001 and has new forms released annually. Performance, Talent, and Fit were just released in late 2006/early 2007.

Date of Most Recent Edition of Test Manual, User's Guide, etc.: There is a 2007 Technical Bulletin for the assessments included in the National Career

Readiness Certificate, Applied Mathematics, Locating Information, and Reading for Information. Other Technical Manuals, one for each content area, are under development and expected to be released Spring 2008.

Languages in Which Available: All content areas are available in English. Applied Mathematics, Applied Technology, Locating Information, and Reading for Information are also available in Spanish.

Time:

Actual Test Time: Applied Mathematics, Applied Technology, Locating Information, and Reading for Information have time limits of 45 minutes for paper-and-pencil delivery; Business Writing, Performance, Talent, and Fit have time limits of 30 minutes; Teamwork and Observation have time limits of 60 minutes; Listening and Writing have time limits of 40 minutes.

Total Administration Time: Collection of demographics, tutorials, and reading directions take up to 15 minutes

Norm Group(s) on Which Scores Are Based: WorkKeys assessments are criterion based, except for Performance, Talent, and Fit.

Manner in Which Results Are Reported for Individuals:

Types of Scores: See above for level scores for most WorkKeys assessments and percentile ranks and descriptors for Performance, Talent, and Fit

Report Format/Content:

BASIC SERVICE: Individual score reports, with description of current skills and recommendations for raising scores.

Comparison of individual score with "profile" of job requirements.

Report Format/Content for Group Summaries:

BASIC SERVICE: Roster report.

Data export for sorting and filtering by demographic and other categories.

Comparison of group scores (by individual and aggregate) with "profile" of job requirements.

Scoring:

Machine Scoring Service:

COST OF BASIC SERVICE PER COUNSELEE: Cost is per content area, averaging $5 to $20 per assessment.

COST OF OPTIONS: Not available.

Paper-and-pencil materials shipped for scoring 10 days from arrival to score

Hand Scoring: Not available.

Local Machine Scoring: Local scoring available through ACT contractual arrangement.

Provisions/conditions/equipment required: Online testing available for many content areas (see below); paper-and-pencil delivered materials on-site scoring requires license (Express Score) and specified scanning equipment and software.

Computer Software Options Available: Standard administration online.

Ways in Which Computer/Online Version Differs: Additional 10 minutes for test taking on Applied Mathematics, Applied Technology, Locating Information, Reading for Information

Performance, Fit, and Talent only available online

Listening, Writing, Teamwork, and Observation not currently available online, but projected

Cost of Materials: Due to possible price changes since publication date, be sure to check with publisher website.

Specimen Set: Website examples of all assessments.

Counselee Materials: Practice tests available both in paper and online for Applied Mathematics, Applied Technology, Locating Information, and Reading for Information; they are for individual use and not reusable.

Additional Comments of Interest to Users: WorkKeys Applied Mathematics, Locating Information, and Reading for Information are the underpinnings for ACT's National Career Readiness Certificate and System, which includes a job/talent bank.

Published Reviews of the Instrument in the Last 15 Years: None cited

Reviewed by:

Debra S. Osborn
Associate Professor
Counselor Education
Department of Psychological and Social Foundations
University of South Florida
Tampa, FL

Description

WorkKeys is an integrated, comprehensive system developed by American College Testing (ACT), that assesses "real-world" job skills and allows for comparison to skills required for positions identified specifically by an employer as being fundamental to successful performance in that job. A key purpose of the WorkKeys system is to aid employers in hiring and promotion decisions (ACT, 2005).

According to the technical manual (ACT, 2001), WorkKeys has four key components that interact with each other. These components include job profiling, assessments, instructional support, and research and reports. At the core of each of these components are skill scales that provide information about the skill levels required for jobs as compared to the actual skills individuals possess.

Job profiling is a tool for job analysis that involves four steps: Creating an Initial Task

List, Task Analysis, Skill Analysis, and Documentation. In step 1, an analyst obtains information from the employer about the company, the specific job, and identifies the tasks most relevant to that specific position in ACT's SkillPro database. During step 2, Task Analysis, the WorkKeys skills, as well as the level of specific skills required for successful performance in that job are identified. The analyst also meets with Subject Matter Experts (SMEs), who will be the supervisor of the person who is hired for the position to verify that the identified skills and skill level represents the job. They rate each identified task on factors of task importance and relevant time spent on that task in comparison to other tasks. During this process, additions and deletions of tasks may also occur. To identify the critical rating for each task, the average importance rating and the average relative time spent on each task are multiplied. By the end of the process, the tasks most critical to successful job performance are identified and weighted.

The second component (and the third step) of WorkKeys is the Skills Analysis. The assessments cover both foundational skills, which measure cognitive abilities, as well as personal skills that allow for a prediction of how an employee will perform on the job. The SME are presented with examples of problems or situations that employees in that occupation are likely to face. The SME determines the level of WorkKeys skills necessary for the job, and ranks the skills according to how critical each skill is to job performance. Preparation packages that include a practice test/answer sheet, estimated skill level, testing tips, and other information are available for several of the skill assessments. Online practice tests can also be purchased. The foundational skills assessments evaluate employability skills in ten areas:

- Applied Mathematics
- Applied Technology
* Business Writing
- Listening
- Locating Informaton

- Observation
- Readiness
- Reading for Information
- Teamwork
- Writing

The *Applied Mathematics* assessment measures one's ability to use mathematical reasoning with work-related problems. The *Applied Technology* assessment measures a person's technological problem-solving abilities. The *Listening* and *Writing* tests are usually administered at the same time, but they do measure two distinct skills. The *Locating Information* test assesses the person's ability to understand and use information presented in the test items such as diagrams, charts, floor plans, and graphs. The *Observation* test measures a person's skill in paying attention to details and following instructions. The *Reading for Information* test measures an individual's ability to read and understand instructions and policies that are work related. The Teamwork assessment examines a person's ability to make decisions that support a team and result in successful completion of the given task. The *Business Writing* test measures a person's ability to communicate in writing an original response when confronted with a work-related situation. The *Readiness* test is a screening instrument for the *Applied Mathematics* and *Reading for Information* that is self-scored to help a person decide if they are ready to complete a WorkKeys test, or if they need to complete additional training first.

The Personal Skills Assessment includes three assessments: *Performance*, *Talent* and *Fit* tests. The Performance test is used as a pretest to examine an applicants work attitudes and tendency toward unsafe work behaviors. The *Talent* assessment examines components of cooperation, discipline, influence, and stability. The *Fit* test compares an individual's interests and values to specific occupations within an organization to determine the level of "fit" between the two.

The final step of ACT's Job Profiling Process is Documentation. In this step, the profiler creates a customized Job Profile Report that identifies the tasks most critical to successful performance of the position as well as the WorkKeys skills (including the level of skill required) for job entry and effective job performance. The report shows the link between the critical tasks and WorkKeys skills. An executive summary at the beginning of the report details the individualized approach a specific job profiler took throughout the profiling process. For example, where and when the profiler talked with a supervisor, toured the facilities, met with the subject matter experts, etc. In addition to the process identified above, ACT offers two additional ways to profile jobs, including SkillMap and WorkKeys Estimator. SkillMap is a web-based program that allows the user to link job tasks to skills and skills levels of WorkKeys and claims to be compliant with the Equal Employment Opportunity Commission (EEOC). WorkKeys Estimator is a paper-and-pencil system that allows the individual to make estimates of WorkKeys skills and links to the occupational profiles in WorkKeys.

The third key component of WorkKeys is Instructional Support. This component allows for the teaching of WorkKeys skills through the use of instructional guides entitled *Targets for Instruction.* These guides were created by content specialists, experienced teachers, and curriculum experts. Each guide describes one of the WorkKeys skills, also known as a Target, and also distinguishes one level of skill from another. The guides do not specify how to teach the target, but describe the specific skill and provide strategies and resources for teaching that skill. The focus of the guides is not on general instruction, such as reading and writing, but on skills relevant to the workplace, such as workplace communications.

The fourth key element is Research and Reports. The research of WorkKeys includes information on all item level and score level analyses, estimates of reliability, the quality of alternative forms, supports for validity, and adverse impact as well as a "return on investment studies" (ACT, 2007). Report format is standard, but also may be customized. A standard package includes the Individual Reports for each examinee, a Roster Report (name, identification number, gender, ethnicity, and skill level score), the Aggregate Report that uses a chart format, and the Vocational Information Report that indicates the percentage of employees who are interested in specific jobs. Other reports include the Career Development Report, Score Labels, and the Cohort Group Report. The Career Development Report is a two-page report that compares an individual's skill scores to an occupation of interest. The first page shows the comparison and the second page lists other potential occupations of interest. Score labels are labels that provide identification and skill levels for each examinee. The cohort allows for comparison of the skills and skills levels of one group over time. Finally, there are several business reports available as well.

The format of the tests are performance-based, paper-and-pencil, with the exception of four of the tests also being available in Spanish and computer-based. These four tests include Applied Mathematics, Applied Technology, Locating Information, and Reading for Information. The actual test is comprised of items that sequentially increase in complexity and difficulty, and include sample workplace situations, problems, reading materials and messages to which the test taker must respond to or answer. Prior knowledge about the specific job is not necessary for the test taker to do well on the test; the scenarios and questions are based on general skills that can be applied across different industries. The test administrator has the option to give all components of the WorkKeys system or individual tests. A 45-page test coordinator manual (ACT, 2006b) provides detailed information for the testing coordinator on arrangements for testing, test administration guidelines, planning the test administration schedule, reporting test irregularities, etc., and includes sample schedules and tracking logs.

Six of the assessments are designed with multiple choice questions, including Applied Mathematics, Applied Technology, Locating Information, Observation, Reading for Information, and Teamwork. Two of the assessments, Listening and Writing Skills, are assessed at the same time with one set of prompts. With both the Observation and Teamwork assessments, examinees view a video and respond to related questions. Mastery of a level is responding correctly to 80% of the items representing that level. Levels contain from six to nine items, and there are four to five levels per skill. In addition, the use of scale scores can be used to make group comparisons or to show growth over a period of time (ACT, 2005).

A website created for the WorkKeys system (*www.act.org/workkeys*) includes a wealth of information on the product, the process, and support. Sample reports are provided along with demos of products such as SkillMap. In addition, multiple case studies are included that highlight how WorkKeys is being used in different environments, as well as a demonstration of sample tests within each of the assessment areas. Some of these are audio; others are video, and appear to have a good representation of various cultures.

Use in Counseling

WorkKeys can be used by employers as well as counselors. Employers can complete the profile on their positions and then compare the results of applicants to the profile to aid in hiring decisions. Or, if a company knows that they are wanting to promote from within or assign teams to projects, the WorkKeys results can be used to identify which employees are best skilled for those tasks. The thoroughness of the job profiling process and skills analysis of employees or applicants offers employers documentation for their hiring and promotion decisions that are related back to performance.

Counselors can have clients complete an assessment of their current skill level and compare those results to the skills required for their occupation of interest. Gaps can be noted and addressed in a self-improvement plan or through specific curriculum and training within the WorkKeys *Targets for Instruction* (ACT, 1997). If an employee or a student/potential employee notes areas of weakness, they can take one of 2,500 distance learning courses that focus on WorkKeys skills. These are offered through a nationwide network of ACT test centers. Or learners/clients/users can enroll in KeyTrain, a comprehensive curriculum offered face-to-face and designed to address each of the WorkKeys skills. Another option would be the WIN Instruction Solution (*http://www.act.org/workkeys/sktrain/win.html*) for WorkKeys, which has over 1,000 hours of interactive instruction and is self-directed, focusing on those who have scored below the WorkKeys scale. While WorkKeys was designed to provide a comprehensive evaluation of a job and applicants, an individual may decide to use portions of the WorkKeys system to focus on skills in a specific area.

WorkKeys can also help in the occupational knowledge aspect of career planning, in that occupational profiles can serve to inform about the typical skills they will need in a given occupation. For counselors or human resources specialists, the WorkKeys system can be used to identify gaps in knowledge and skills and thus identify potential training areas. In addition, WorkKeys can be used to develop potential partnerships between schools and businesses, in that employers can identify key skills they need and schools can provide potential employees and in some cases, specialized training.

Technical Considerations

The assessments are criterion based, meaning that each potential employee is evaluated on his or her knowledge of the WorkKey skills determined by the employer to be most necessary for success in that position, not comparing the individual to a normative group. The developers state clearly that WorkKeys is not a measure of aptitude, but of skill demonstrations. (*http://www.keytrain.com/wrk_assess.asp*). WorkKeys boasts over 10,000 job titles that have been profiled, with jobs representing many different industries and levels. Practice tests are available online for a fee.

The jobs in the Job Cluster database include occupations in Administration & Sales, Business Operations, Technical, Science & Technology, Arts, and Social Services. Information in these profiles include skill levels for an occupation across jobs, companies, or industries, as well as online occupational information by O*Net. The jobs in the database include white-collar professional jobs as well as jobs in areas such as manufacturing, health care, law enforcement, and hospitality.

The technical manual, 100 pages in length, provides information about the development of WorkKeys, as well as detailed information on the key components and the history of how the skill scales were developed. With respect to content validity, items are developed first from conversations with experts and then reviewed by a minimum of nine content reviewers and a minimum of six fairness reviewers to ensure that the items are unbiased and unoffensive to racial, ethnic, and gender groups. In addition, statistical differential item functioning analyses are conducted to ensure that items do not contain bias for specific groups.

Alternative formats of the Applied Mathematics forms based on KR20s ranged from .80 to .83.The reliability of level scores for the WorkKeys multiple choice tests range from .59 (Teamwork) to .78 (Applied Mathematics), with an average reliability of .72. The Listening and Writing assessments are constructed-response assessments, and generalizability theory (Cronbach, Gleser, Nanda, & Rajaratnam, 1972) was used to conduct two reliability studies. The first study results, using data from 24,842 examinees, showed that the effect of the rater on the listening or writing skill of the person or the task performance was minimal, while the interaction between person and task was the major source of error. Writing scores were found to be more reliable than Listening scores, and individuals scores differed more in Writing than in Listening. In the second study, the data from 7,097 examinees were examined with two raters across six tasks to determine reliability. Similar to the first study, the second study also found Writing scores to have higher reliability than the Listening scores. A study conducted on the Writing and Listening tests (Brennan, Gao, & Colton, 1995) concluded that two raters should be used to evaluate the responses with a minimum of six person-message interactions required.

While WorkKeys is not a norm-based inventory, demographic information is included in the technical manual that shows the descriptive statistics for the 1999 – 2000 sample of 179,967 records. These statistics include gender, race/ethnicity, programs of study (not majors, but college prep versus general prep, etc.), highest level of education, and the number for which English is the preferred language for the examinee. A second table breaks down the percentage of each of these groups to the skill levels for the different tests.

The WorkKeys website (*http://www.act.org/workkeys/index.html*) houses several downloadable sources of information entitled "Job Aid Series" that address technical concerns, such as *Reading for Information: Estimating Grade-Level Equivalents* (ACT, 2006a) or *When Should a Job Be Profiled Again?* (ACT, 2006c).

Overall Critique

According to the WorkKeys website, WorkKeys is defined as "A job skills assessment system measuring real-world skills." In addition, a chief purpose of WorkKeys is to connect work skills to training and testing for both employers and educators. The technical manual notes two common uses of WorkKeys related to applicant screening. It helps determine that the basic skill levels for successful job performance are present, and helps identify training needs by determining employee skill gaps.

A main strength of WorkKeys continues to be the participation from the business community on the identification of skills necessary for success in an occupation and the linking of that information to employees or potential hires. A second strength is that the high content validity of the skills assessments allows employers to base their hiring/promotion decisions on the results and to know that they have legally defensible evidence for doing so, in that the skills identified were determined to be critical for successful completion of the job. For a student who may be a year out from job searching, engaging in WorkKeys skills assessment and comparing that to the job profiles will yield incredibly useful information on areas to strengthen prior to embarking on the job search.

The Technical Handbook (Act, 2001) provides excellent, detailed information on validation procedures that will be especially useful for employers making hiring decisions for high stakes jobs. The information provided in the reports as well as the manual demonstrate the legal standing an employer has in making hiring decisions based on the outcome of the WorkKeys assessment results of an individual.

As Townsend (2001) pointed out, the main weakness of WorkKeys is that it works best as a comprehensive system. While you can select to use only certain features, by doing this, the other components are weakened. You could, for example, simply use the profiles as a way to provide career information and, while the information is very useful and specific to key skills, the power of the tool comes when comparing one's own skills to those required for a certain occupation. In addition, the amount of options available can be overwhelming. It may be difficult to determine which parts of the system, and within the parts which subparts, are going to benefit an individual the most. For example, is the WorkKeys Estimator or SkillMap the best choice? The use of various names, titles, and services can also become difficult to sort through. For example, there is WIN, KeyTrain, the skills domains, Job Profiling, SkillMap, WorkKeys Estimator, Targets for Instruction, DACUM, and many others. The technical manual (ACT, 2001) has a useful diagram demonstrating how the skill scales relate to the WorkKeys system; however, it would also be very helpful to have a diagram that demonstrates how the different services noted above work together.

When reviewing the purposes of WorkKeys and the detailed technical information provided about the assessments and the process of job profiling, it is apparent that the WorkKeys system is an excellent tool for use by both career counselors and employers. The website offers extensive information, samples, and resources. Employers, educators, counselors, and clients can all benefit from the extensive services offered by this system.

References

ACT, Inc. (1997). *Targets for instruction.* Iowa City, IA: Author.

ACT, Inc. (2001). *Technical handbook.* Iowa City, IA: Author.

ACT, Inc. (2005). *WorkKeys: Scale score interpretation guide.* Iowa City, IA: Author.

ACT, Inc. (2006a). *Reading for information: Estimating grade-level equivalents.* Iowa City, IA: Author.

ACT, Inc. (2006b). *Test coordinator manual.* Iowa City, IA: Author.

ACT, Inc. (2006c). *When should a job be profiled again?* Iowa City, IA: Author.

ACT, Inc. (2007). *The WorkKeys System.* Retrieved March 20, 2007, from http://www.act.org/workkeys/index.html.

Brennan, R. L., Gao, X., & Colton, D. A. (1995). Generalizability analyses of WorkKeys Listening and Writing tests. *Educational and Psychological Measurement, 55,* 157 – 176.

Cronbach, L. J., Gleser, G. C., Nanda, H. I., & Rajaratnam, N. (1972). *The dependability of behavioral measurement: Theory of generalizability of scores and profiles.* New York: Wiley.

Townsend, J. (2001). WorkKeys. In J. T. Kapes, & E. A. Whitfield, (Eds.), *A counselor's guide to career assessment inventories* (4th ed., pp. 186 – 191). Columbus, OH: National Career Development Association.

World of Work Inventory (WOWI)

Robert E. Ripley, Gregory P. M. Neidert, and Nancy L. Ortman

World of Work, Inc.
410 W. 1st Street, Suite 103
Tempe, AZ 85281-2874
http://www.wowi.com/
info@wowi.com

Target Population: Ages 13 – 65+.

Statement of the Purpose of the Instrument: Designed to assist individuals in identifying occupations most compatible with their unique combination of job-relevant abilities, interests, and personality. Used for career counseling, vocational rehabilitation, employee selection and development, student guidance, and adult/career education classes.

Titles of Subtests, Scales, Scores Provided: 35: *Career Interest Activities* (17 scores: Public Service, The Sciences, Engineering & Related, Business Relations, Managerial, The Arts, Clerical, Sales, Service, Primary Outdoor, Processing, Machine Work, Bench Work, Structural Work, Mechanical and Electrical Work, Graphic Arts, Mining); *Job Satisfaction Indicators* (12 scores: Versatile, Adaptable to Repetitive Work, Adaptable to Performing Under Specific Instructions, Dominant, Gregarious, Isolative, Influencing, Self-Controlled, Valuative, Objective, Subjective, Rigorous); *Career Training Potentials* (6 scores: Verbal, Numerical, Abstractions, Spatial-Form, Mechanical/Electrical, Organizing Skill).

Forms and Levels Available, with Dates of Publication/Revision of Each: The WOWI Short Form is comprised of 330 items and is available in a number of Versions and Reading Levels.

Standard Version is written at the 8th-grade reading level. Includes: North American English (last revised and published in 2007); British English (last revised and published in 2007); Australian English (last revised and published in 2006).

Modified Version is written at the 5th-grade reading level. North American English version only (last revised and published in 2007).

3G Version is written at the 3rd-grade reading level. North American English version only (last revised and published in 2007).

Spanish Version is written at the 6th-grade reading level in a universal, nonidiomatic Spanish. (last revised and published in 2005).

Date of Most Recent Edition of Test Manual, User's Guide, etc.: Interpretation Manual for the World of Work Inventory (5th edition) was last revised and published in 2001. An interpretation guide, quick reference sheet, and numerous detailed help menus are available to test administrators on the wowi.com website. These online test administration and interpretation resources were last revised in 2006.

Languages in Which Available: North American English, British English, Australian English, Spanish.

Time:

Actual Test Time – Based on 10 separate samples totaling 1,255 individuals. Career Interest Activities (10 – 15 minutes). Career Training Potentials (30 – 40 minutes). Job Satisfaction Indicators (8 – 10 minutes).

Total Administration Time (48 – 65 minutes)

Norm Group(s) on Which Scores Are Based: The norms are based on a national cross section of 169,436 individuals, including corporate executives, managers, line level employees, displaced and injured workers, students (high school, college and graduate), welfare recipients, inmates at correctional facilities (federal, state, and local), etc. The norms were last updated and published in November 2003. A new and updated set of norms will be published in Fall 2007.

Manner in Which Results Are Reported for Individuals:

Types of Scores: All of the measured scales of the World of Work Inventory provide both a numerical score and graphical representation of each score on the Profile Report. A written description and interpretation of each score is provided in the Interpretive Report. The Career Interest Activities and Job Satisfaction Indicator subscales are idiographic by design and are therefore expressed only as raw scores, between –60 and +60. The Career Training Potentials (formally named the Vocational Training Potentials) subscales are nomothetic by design and are therefore both expressed as raw and standardized scores [in standard deviation units], with separate comparisons of the test taker with those of the same age and education level.

Report Format/Content:

BASIC SERVICE: All test takers receive a three-page Profile Report, which provides both numerical scores and graphical representation of individuals' assessment results. In addition, a two to three page Summary Report provides the test taker with a brief narrative description of each measured scale. The Summary Report concludes with a listing of job recommendations that have at least an 85% match with the test takers results. The jobs are organized by levels of educational attainment and represent occupations that are stable or growing in demand.

OPTIONS: In addition, a six to eight page Interpretive Report provides the test taker with a narrative description and interpretation of each measured scale of the assessment. The Interpretive Report concludes with a listing of job recommendations that have at least an 85% match with the test takers results. The jobs are organized by levels of educational attainment and represent occupations that are stable or growing in demand. For test takers in the United States, each recommended job title has direct links to its O*NET Online, Occupational Outlook Handbook (OOH), and optionally Dictionary of Occupational Titles (DOT) descriptions. For test takers in Canada, Australia, and the United Kingdom, each recommended job title has direct links to its description in each country's respective online occupational resource.

Report Format/Content for Group Summaries: Not available.

Scoring:

Machine Scoring Service: Not available.

Hand Scoring: Not available.

Local Machine Scoring: Not available.

Computer Software Options Available: Standard administration online.

Cost of Materials: Due to possible price changes since publication date, be sure to check the publisher's website.

Specimen Set: Complimentary WOWI Online assessment provided to qualified workforce, rehabilitation, and career professionals.

Counselee Materials:

ONLINE SITE LICENSE (one-time fee) $189.00. Additional Site Licenses within the same organization $50.00 each.

ACCOUNT UPGRADES: Email notification (one-time fee) $50.00. Client View Feature (one-time fee) $50.00.

SCORING COSTS: WOWI Online—Profile Report with Summary Report (1 – 4) $25.00 each; (5 – 19) $19.00 each; (20+) $15.00 each. WOWI Online—Profile Report with Summary and Interpretive Report (1 – 4) $27.00 each; (5 – 19) $21.00 each; (20+) $17.00 each.

PAPER-AND-PENCIL ADMINISTRATION: Reusable Test Booklet $7.00; Quick Entry Answer Sheets are free, the cost for scoring is as follows:

Scoring Costs: WOWI Online—Profile Report with Summary Report (1 – 4) $25.00 each; (5 – 19) $19.00 each; (20+) $15.00 each. WOWI Online—Profile Report with Summary and Interpretive Report (1 – 4) $27.00 each; (5 – 19) $21.00 each; (20+) $17.00 each.

Additional Comments of Interest to Users: Updated norms will be published in 2007. Job recommendations continue to be regularly updated as the Department of Labor updates job information, publishes new projections, etc.

Reviewed by:

Eugene P. Sheehan
Dean, College of Education and Behavioral Sciences
University of Northern Colorado
Greeley, CO

Description

As the name suggests, the World of Work Inventory (WOWI) is an instrument designed to provide career information and advice to test takers. The WOWI collects information about the test taker's occupational interests, inclination to perform certain job tasks, aptitude in different vocational areas, and job temperament factors. Clients receive a Profile Report and also an Interpretive Report. Within these reports, they receive information on their career interests, job-related temperament factors, aptitude for learning, and academic achievement. This information is matched to occupational characteristics with a list of specific job recommendations is provided in the Interpretive Report.

There are several components to the WOWI. Test takers first indicate their choice, from a list of 12, of two general occupational areas in which they would like to work. Also from a list of 12, they select their two best-liked academic subjects.

The major components of the WOWI are the Career Interest Activities (CIAs), Vocational Training Potentials (VTPs), and Job Satisfaction Indicators (JSIs). The CIAs section contains 136 items in which respondents specify whether or not they would like, dislike, or are neutral about performing a job-related activity (e.g., "convincing people of your ideas," "planning river dams to control floods") for at least six months or more. The Interpretation Manual (Neidert & Ortman, 2001) states the "CIAs measure what job duties people like (and dislike), and how much they like (or dislike) engaging in them" (p. 44). These responses are linked to the respondent's interest in the 17 Basic Occupational Areas, as identified by the U.S. Department of Labor: public service, the sciences, engineering and related, business relations, managerial, the arts, clerical, sales, service, primary outdoor, processing, machine work, bench work, structural work, mechanical/electrical work, graphic arts, and mining. The Profile Report that is generated provides a scale score on each of these occupational areas.

The VTPs section covers a range of areas that are either aptitude or achievement based. There are six subsections: verbal, numerical, mechanical/electrical, spatial-form, clerical, and abstractions. There are 98 total items on the VTPs section: 28 on the verbal and 14 on each of the others. Each of the subsections contains fairly standard types of items. For example, in the verbal section there are items that cover vocabulary and word reasoning. The numerical section contains items that deal with addition, decimals, metrics, and series. The Report Profile allows respondents to compare their performance on each area of the VTPs with others of the same age and others of the same education.

The JSI section measures temperament factors that relate to job satisfaction and work motivation. This scale contains 96 items to which respondents indicate if they would like, dislike, or are neutral about performing job-related tasks such as "keeping things orderly and systematic," "doing work involving fine accuracy," or "facing physical dangers." Responses to these items result a scale report along 12 job satisfaction/temperament dimensions: versatile, adapt to repetitive work, adapt to performing under specific instructions, dominant, gregarious, isolative, influencing, self-controlled, valuative, objective, subjective, and rigorous.

Administration of the WOWI is quite straightforward. It can be administered via an assessment booklet or online. I took the online version of the inventory and found the web page easy to navigate and the test directions easy to follow. Completion of the inventory took under an hour, with most of the time devoted to the VTPs section (respondents need time to solve the numerical reasoning and series questions).

Use in Counseling

Respondents receive three WOWI reports: a Profile Report, an Interpretive Report and a Summary Report. The Profile Report summarizes the areas in which the respondent has demonstrated high training potential (e.g., numerical and mechanical/electrical), self-selected occupational areas (e.g., mathematics and science) and best-liked subjects (e.g., social studies or history), high measured job satisfaction indicators (e.g., subjective), and high measured career interest activities (e.g., the sciences). As mentioned earlier, this report also permits respondents to compare their performance on the VTP section with others of the same age and others of the same education. Scaled score profiles of the Job Satisfaction Indicators and the Career Interest Activities round out this report.

The Interpretive Report is a narrative explanation of the respondent's inventory profile. It goes through all of the various scales on which the respondents had high scores and provides an outline of the meaning of each dimension and the application of that dimension to work situations. The interpretive report ends with a list of career recommendations. With the online report, each of the jobs listed comes with an active link to further information. Interestingly, in my case, several of the jobs on my list were jobs I had performed prior to entering the academy.

As its name implies, the Summary Report is a brief outline of the Report Profile and the Interpretive Report.

The inventory and the three reports can provide a career counselor and a client with a good deal of information to provoke discussion about job-related strengths and weaknesses along with information about career interests, job temperament, and satisfaction factors as well as a list of potentially relevant jobs. In the hands of a competent counselor, this wealth of information could be put to good use in assisting a client narrow a career focus. There are many vocational inventories such as this and, in general and from a face validity perspective, the WOWI stands up well.

Technical Considerations

Two reviews in *The Mental Measurement Yearbook,* including one by me, have questioned some of the psychometric data supporting the WOWI (Jenkins, 2005; Sheehan, 2005). Both the manual and the website contain information on the development of the WOWI. The process of test development adhered to commonly accepted standards. Proper item analysis procedures were followed, including the use of judges to assist in item selection.

The test authors indicate the WOWI is normed on a large sample: 169,436 individuals. However, as both Jenkins (2005) and Sheehan (2005) point out, no descriptive data beyond gender, age, and education are provided. Critical information such as occupation and norming procedures is not provided, making use of the scales questionable.

Reliability and validity data are detailed. Coefficient alphas are provided for each scale and the data are favorable, with alphas for all scales over .81. For 28 of the 35 scales alphas are .85 or higher. Data on test-retest reliabilities, taken at one-week, six-week, and two-year intervals, are also favorable. For example, the one-week reliabilities are .92 for the CIAs, .89 for the JSIs and .70 for the VTPs.

As mentioned earlier, the face validity of the instrument is strong. To a respondent it is very clearly a psychometric device to be used in career guidance. Measured validity data are positive, with interitem correlations at appropriate levels of significance and in anticipated directions. Comparisons with other career counseling instruments reveal expected results.

Overall Critique

The WOWI is a comprehensive instrument designed to assist in the career guidance process. It provides information on a wide range of job-related variables that a respondent and counselor would find invaluable in the career counseling process. Test administration and scoring are easy and straightforward. The three reports provided are very helpful, with the interpretive report providing useful information in narrative format. Norming notwithstanding, the psychometric information on the WOWI indicates the instrument is constructed in a sound manner and has solid data to support its use as a career counseling tool.

References

Jenkins, J. (2005). Review of the World of Work Inventory. In R. A. Spies & B. S. Plake (Eds.), *The sixteenth mental measurements yearbook* (pp. 1172 – 1174). Lincoln, NE: University of Nebraska Press.

Neidert, G., & Ortman, N. (2001). *Interpretation manual for the World of Work Inventory.* Tempe, AZ: World of Work Inc.

Sheehan, E. (2005). Review of the World of Work Inventory. In R. A. Spies & B. S. Plake (Eds.), *The sixteenth mental measurements yearbook* (pp. 1174 – 1176). Lincoln, NE: University of Nebraska Press.

CHAPTER 9

INTEREST AND VALUES INSTRUMENTS

- Business Career Interest Inventory (BCII) (CareerLeader)

- Campbell Interest and Skill Survey (CISS)

- Career Directions Inventory (CDI) (Second Edition)

- Career Exploration Inventory (CEI)

- Hall Occupational Orientation Inventory (Fourth Edition)

- Harrington-O'Shea Career Decision-Making System-Revised (CDM-R)

- Jackson Vocational Interest Survey (JVIS) (Second Edition)

- O*NET Interest Profiler (OIP) and Computerized Interest Profiler (CIP)

- O*NET Work Importance Locator (WIL) and Work Importance Profiler (WIP)

- Self-Directed Search (SDS) (R) (E) (CP) (CE)

- Strong Interest InventoryAssessment Tool (SII) and Skills Confidence Inventory (SCI)

- Wide Range Interest and Occupation Test (Second Edition) (WRIOT-2)

Business Career Interest Inventory (BCII) (CareerLeader)

Timothy Butler and James Waldroop

Peregrine Partners
1330 Beacon Street, Suite 265
Brookline, MA 02446
www.careerleader.com

Target Population: People interested in careers in business and management, whether for-profit, non-profit, or government.

Statement of the Purpose of the Instrument: CareerLeader assesses the user's interests, abilities, and motivations, then recommends specific business careers (e.g. marketing, finance, supply chain management, human resource management) and organizational cultures that are likely to fit well with that profile.

Titles of Subtests, Scales, Scores Provided: Business Career Interest Inventory, Management and Professional Abilities Profile, Management and Professional Rewards Profile.

Forms and Levels Available, with Dates of Publication/Revision of Each: Not available.

Date of Most Recent Edition of Test Manual, User's Guide, etc.: 2005.

Languages in Which Available: English, Mandarin.

Time:

Total Administration Time Approximately 50 minutes.

Norm Group(s) on Which Scores Are Based: 100,000 business professionals, most with MBA degrees.

Manner in Which Results Are Reported for Individuals:

Types of Scores: Standard scores.

Report Format/Content: Narrative professional report.

Report Format/Content for Group Summaries: Not available.

Scoring:

Machine Scoring Service: Not available.

Hand Scoring: Not available.

Local Machine Scoring: Not available.

Computer Software Options Available: Standard administration online.

Ways in Which Computer/Online Version Differs: N/A

Cost of Materials: Due to possible price changes since publication date, be sure to check with publisher website.

Specimen Set: Free.

Counselee Materials: Cost ranges from $20.00 to $95.00 per use, depending on size of order.

Additional Comments of Interest to Users: CareerLeader is used worldwide by MBA programs, universities, and corporations. It has been validated cross-culturally (12 countries).

Published Reviews of the Instrument in the Last 15 Years: None Cited.

Reviewed by:

William F. Shuster
Clinical Professor
Department of Management

Jackie Peila-Shuster
Instructor

College of Applied Human Sciences
Colorado State University

Description

The Business Career Interest Inventory (BCII) is one of the three instruments that comprise the interactive career assessment program called CareerLeader (available via the Internet since 1998), targeting graduate business students, and CareerLeader-College (launched in 2002), which focuses on undergraduate business students. Also included in the assessment are the Management and Professional Reward Profile (focusing on work-reward values) and the Management and Professional Abilities Profile (emphasizing relative abilities necessary for success in various business careers). CareerLeader is also used by private industry, and thus is not limited to higher education.

The CareerLeader assessment is popular with business schools for numerous reasons. One of these is that the assessment is online, giving maximum flexibility for the student/client in taking the inventories. The numerous downloads that delve into practical application beyond the test results and professional profile provide a plethora of value-added knowledge to the student. Examples include a professional report, which takes the assessment results and puts it into a narrative form; career research; 360-review feedback forms; and career paths based upon the BCII. Additionally, industry sketches and profiles and helpful information on potential career opportunities and obstacles are provided.

Another reason for its popularity is the ease of administration. The assessment results can be obtained through the Internet to facilitate asynchronous communications, decreasing the lag time between the completion of the assessments and the interpretation meeting. Marketing brochures and suggestions are included to help career counselors in providing a client-focused, consistent message. Online manuals (which can be printed) are available in full-form and concise versions. In-depth training is also available for counselors, and the customer support is timely, helpful, and accurate.

According to the authors, Butler and Waldroop (2004), the BCII presents an effective way to describe the interest patterns within career occupation and the essential functional activities of that occupation. Focusing on business, and studying a large sample of business professionals over 15 years, the authors derived an eight-factor business core function model (Butler & Waldroop, 2004). These factors are:

1. Application of Technology (reengineering through technology)
2. Quantitative Analysis (running the numbers to reach solutions)
3. Theory Development and Conceptual Thinking (abstract thinking/research)
4. Creative Production (brainstorming novel ideas)
5. Counseling and Mentoring (helping others succeed)
6. Managing People and Relationships (accomplishing goals by working with others)
7. Enterprise Control (setting and executing strategy)
8. Influencing through Language and Ideas (persuading others)

These eight business core activities allow students to match their interests with specific career paths. The authors believe that an individual's pattern of interests is the single most powerful predictor of success and satisfaction in a career because they are likely to remain stable through a person's life. In addition, these factors provide the energy and effort to succeed in a career (CareerLeader, *Concise user's guide*, n.d.).

The purpose of the function-centered model is to convey the congruence between student interest patterns and the activities that are present within occupational fields. This congruence was developed on the analysis of interviews and psychological inventories given to more than 650 business professionals over a 10-year time period and working with a database that now includes testing data on more than 75,000 business professionals and business students (Butler & Waldroop, 2004).

Use in Counseling

Based upon the premise that interests will remain relatively stable throughout life, the BCII provides a baseline for business students to find language in their field of interest. Matching the life-long interests of a client with core business functions of a particular occupation provides an excellent way to proceed through the career exploration process. The use of this inventory can provide sound rationales for, and facilitate the exploration of, specific career paths. Because of the integrated nature of the entire CareerLeader system, these instruments have the potential to greatly assist students in their transitions from higher education to the working world.

Additionally, the BCII is a highly valued tool for immediacy and relevance of information, ease of administration, and high-quality supporting information. The customer support staff is strong which, in combination with the supporting slides and manual, provides the counselor/administrator with a wide array of resources to facilitate the career decision making process.

Technical Considerations

The final general business sample used for BCII normative purposes was composed of 14,400 individuals who were established in their business careers from a wide spectrum of industries and functions. The mean age was 38 years, and the sample was approximately one-third women and two-thirds men. Gender specific norms were developed (Butler & Waldroop, 2004). Although the sample came from a variety of cultures, the large majority of it was composed of professionals working in the United States, Canada, and Western Europe. However, in the years following the development of the initial scale, the database collected by the authors has grown to more than 100,000 business professionals from 84 different countries. Research since then has indicated that the degree to which national culture influences career interests accounts for only 1.5% total variance of levels of interest in the eight core business activities of the BCII (CareerLeader, *Concise user's guide,* n.d.).

Both test-retest and internal consistency studies have been conducted on the BCII. The authors indicated that the mean test-retest correlation over a six-month period was .77, with a .66 to .86 range over the eight scales. In using a time period of six years, the authors found a mean correlation of .60, with a range of .53 to .68 across the eight scales. Reported internal consistency measures revealed a mean Cronbach's Alpha of .91, with a range of .88 to .93 across the eight scales. Also reported for internal consistency was a mean split-half (Spearman Brown) correlation of .87 (CareerLeader, *Business career interest inventory: reliability and validity studies,* n.d.).

In studies investigating convergent and discriminate construct validity, positive correlations were found between business core function scales and thematically related scales from the Strong Interest Inventory. Additionally, negative correlations were found between those scales predicted to be unrelated. For further details, the reader is referred to the book *Discovering Your Career in Business,* pages 79 to 90 (Butler & Waldroop, 1997). According to the authors, factor analytic validation studies corroborated the presence of an underlying factor structure for all eight core functions, suggesting support for the eight core function model (Butler & Waldroop, 2004; CareerLeader, *Business career interest inventory: reliability and validity studies,* n.d.). Regarding criterion-related validity, the authors found that business core function profiles of highly experienced and satisfied individuals in specific business career areas (e.g., production and operation management, human resources, investment banking) discriminate between these occupational groups in a predictable manner (Butler & Waldroop, 2004). Discriminant studies of predicted differences between general occupational samples were also conducted. The four general occupational samples used were (a) students from a leading business school, (b) general business professionals (c) administrators in education, government and human services, and (d) nonbusiness workers. These studies indicated that there were business core function differences between these groups in predicted directions (Butler & Waldroop, 2004).

Overall Critique

The BCII is an important entity in the area of business career development. The quality and usefulness of the information is high and immediately relevant for a client's career planning process. Additionally, the system is user-friendly from the client and counselor perspective.

This comprehensive assessment provides an easy-to-navigate interface to assist individuals with their career pursuits by giving relevant information that can be used in a practical manner. Matching the life-long interests of a client with core business functions of a particular occupation provides an excellent baseline to proceed through the career exploration process while the specificity of the inventory allows for a rich discussion with clients on their potential futures.

References

Butler, T., & Waldroop, J. (1997). *Discovering your career in business.* Reading, MA: Addison-Wesley.

Butler, T., & Waldroop, J. (2004). A function-centered model of interest assessment for business careers [Electronic version]. *Journal of Career Assessment, 12,* 270 – 284.

CareerLeader. (n.d.). *Business career interest inventory: reliability and validity studies.* Retrieved March 18, 2007, from http://www.careerleader.com/cf/univ/add/toolsnew.html.

CareerLeader. (n.d.). *CareerLeader: The concise user's guide.* Retrieved March 18, 2007, from http://www.careerleader.com/ftpfiles/CareerLeader_ConciseGuide.pdf.

Campbell Interest and Skill Survey (CISS)

David Campbell

Pearson Assessments
5601 Green Valley Drive
Bloomington, MN 55437
www.pearsonassessments.com

Target Population: Individuals age 15 and over.

Statement of the Purpose of the Instrument: The CISS Inventory helps assess an individual's interest in occupational areas and provide a comparison to people who are happily and successfully employed in those fields. In addition, the CISS adds parallel skill scales that present an estimate of the individual's confidence in his or her ability to perform various occupational activities.

Titles of Subtests, Scales, Scores Provided: Orientation Scales, which cover seven broad themes of occupational interests and skills; Basic Interest and Skill Scales, which are detailed subscales of the Orientation Scales; and Occupational Scales, which compare interest and skill patterns with those of workers in a range of occupations.

Orientation Scales: Influencing, Organizing, Helping, Creating, Analyzing, Producing, and Adventuring.

Basic Scales: Divide the Orientation Scales into 25 categories, each with a parallel interest and skill scores.

- Influencing: Leadership, Law/Politics, Public Speaking, Sales, Advertising/Marketing
- Organizing: Supervision, Financial Services, Office Practices
- Helping: Adult Development, Counseling, Child Development, Religious Activities, Medical Practice
- Creating: Art/Design, Performing Arts, Writing, International Activities, Fashion, Culinary Arts
- Analyzing: Mathematics, Science
- Producing: Mechanical Crafts, Woodworking, Farming/Forestry, Plants/Gardens, Animal Care
- Adventuring: Athletics/Physical Fitness, Military/Law Enforcement, Risks/Adventure

Forms and Levels Available, with Dates of Publication/Revision of Each: One form.

Date of Most Recent Edition of Test Manual, User's Guide, etc.: 1992

Languages in Which Available: English, Spanish.

Time:

Actual Test Time: 25 minutes

Total Administration Time: 25 minutes

Norm Group(s) on Which Scores Are Based: Reference sample of 5,225 employed men and women representing a wide array of occupations and ethnic backgrounds.

Manner in Which Results Are Reported for Individuals:

Types of Scores: Standard Scores.

Report Format/Content: Narrative report.

OPTIONS: Report Summary.

Report Format/Content for Group Summaries: Not available.

Scoring:

Machine Scoring Service:

COST OF BASIC SERVICE PER COUNSELEE: $10.95 for 5 – 49 vouchers; $10.70 for 50 – 99 vouchers; $10.45 for 100 – 249 vouchers. Additional volume discounts are available.

TIME REQUIRED FOR SCORING AND RETURNING: instant.

Hand Scoring: Not available.

Local Machine Scoring:

Provisions/conditions/equipment required:

Q Local scoring and reporting software required (available from Pearson Assessments).

System Requirements:

- Pentium II Processor
- 350 MHz
- 128 MB RAM
- 400 MB of free hard disk space
- Operating Systems:
  Windows XP Professional, SP2
  Windows XP Home, SP2
  Windows NT Workstation 4.0 SP6a
  Windows NT Server 4.0 SP6a
  Windows NT Server 4.0 Enterprise SP6a
  Windows 98SE
  Windows 2000
  Windows ME
  Windows 2003, SP1
  Microsoft Desktop Edition (MSDE) 2000 sp3 installed with the Q Local installation. If you have a different version installed, you will have to upgrade to sp3 or sp3a

At this time, Q Local is not compatible with or support 64-bit platforms.

Computer Software Options Available: Standard administration online.

Cost of Materials: Due to possible price changes since publication date, be sure to check with publisher website.

Counselee Materials:

CISS

Test Materials and Scoring Services Price List

CISS Manual (required):

- Softcover $33.00
- Hardcover (includes transparency masters and three-ring binder): $51.50

CISS Interest/Skill Pattern Worksheets: (optional, 50 per pkg) $12.50

CISS Career Planner: Qty 1 – 249, $2.30 each; 250+, $1.55 each

Q Local Software: (for on-site personal computer test administration scoring NOT via Internet—see Internet pricing below.) $89 Annual license fee.

Q Local Scored Starter Kit with Profile Reports: Includes CISS manual (softcover), three CISS Career Planners, Interest/Kill Pattern worksheets, three answer sheets with test items, and three Q Local administration. (does not include Q Local Software.) $55.00

CISS Answer Sheets: Test items included. (25 per pkg) $21.00

Q Local Individual Profile Reports: Qty 5 – 49, $7.35 each; 50 – 99, $7.30 each; 100+, $7.10 each. Additional volume discounts available.

Mail-in Scored Starter Kit with Profile Reports: Includes CISS manual (softcover), 3 CISS Career Planners, Interest/Skill Pattern worksheets and three answer sheets with test items included; all the materials necessary to generate three reports using the mail-in scoring service. $60.00

Mail-in Scored Profile Reports: Price includes answer sheet with test items & scoring: Qty 5 – 49, $9.60 each; 50 – 99, $9.35 each; 100+, $9.10 each. Additional volume discounts available.

Internet Administration & Scoring:

CISS Vouchers (each) Includes Profile Report: Qty 5 – 49, $10.95 each; 50 – 99, $10.70 each; 100 – 249, $10.45 each; 250+, $10.10 each. Additional volume discounts available.

Published Reviews of the Instrument in the Last 15 Years:

Impara, J.C., & Plake, B.S. (Eds.) (1998). *The thirteenth mental measurements yearbook.* Lincoln, NE: Buros Institute of Mental Measurements.

Reviewed by:

Lisa E. Severy
Director of Career Services
University of Colorado at Boulder

Description

The Campbell Interest & Skill Survey (CISS) is one of three Campbell Development Surveys (CDS) published by NCS Pearson. The instrument helps individuals discover how their interests and perceived skill levels compare with the world of work (Campbell, 2002). The CISS was developed by Dr. David Campbell after his split with the publishers of the Strong-Campbell Interest Inventory in 1987. He first released the new instrument, including self-perception of skill, in 1989. The CISS is currently available in paper form, stand-alone computer software, or online at www.pearsonassessments.com/tests/ciss.htm.

The CISS contains 200 interest and 120 skill items, and takes about 25 minutes to complete. Respondents are asked to rate their level of interest or skill on six-point scales. Pairs of interest and skill scores are graphically reported in the results profile, providing guidance as to where the user might find satisfaction and success in the world of work. The CISS also provides an Interest/Skill Pattern worksheet to expand the clients' understanding by helping them to engage the results in future planning.

The CISS results include five sections: 7 Orientation Scales, 29 Basic Interest and Skill Scales, 58 Occupational Scales, 3 Special Scales, and Procedural Checks. To make the results easier to explain, the scoring scales are reported as T scores, normed so that the average of each scale is 50 with a standard deviation of 10 (Campbell, Hyne, & Nilsen, 1992).

The Orientation Scales reflect the interest content domain well established by theorists such as E.K. Strong and John Holland. Campbell felt that the titles for these categories were confusing to clients and sometimes rejected due to associated values, so he updated them for the new inventory (Campbell et al., 1992). He also expanded the original six interest categories by dividing the Realistic construct into two different categories (Campbell, 2002). The Campbell Orientation Scales include:

Campbell's Codes	
Influencing (I)	Interests in leadership, politics, public speaking, and marketing
Organizing (O)	Interests in organizing and managing people or systems as well as monitoring financial performance
Helping (H)	Interests in teaching, healing, counseling, and otherwise helping others
Creating (C)	Interests in artistic, literary, or musical production
Analyzing (N)	Interests in research, mathematics, and scientific experiments
Producing (P)	Interests in production and hands-on skill use such as construction, farming, and mechanical pursuits
Adventuring (A)	Interests in risk-taking, competition, and adventure through athletics, police, or military activities

Counselors familiar with John Holland's codes will recognize the similarities:

Holland's Codes	Campbell's Codes
Realistic	Adventuring & Producing
Investigative	Analyzing
Artistic	Creating
Social	Helping
Enterprising	Influencing
Conventional	Organizing

As with other interest inventories, the Orientation Scales on the CISS are reported in terms of a one, two, or three-letter code designed to reflect interest profiles. By comparing individual letter codes with occupational codes, clients can explore occupational areas where they are more likely to feel satisfied and confident (Campbell et al., 1992).

The Basic Interest and Skill Scales cover specific topic areas like law/politics, writing, mathematics, or animal care, and are arranged according to their intercorrelations, with those having the most in common next to each other. The Occupational Scales represent 58 specific occupations like attorney, financial planner, realtor, or media executive to which individual scales are compared. The scales reflect a sample of workers from each occupation self-described as satisfied and successful. Therefore, an individual's score on an Occupational Scale signifies the degree of similarity between that individual's preferences and satisfied workers in a particular occupation (Campbell et al., 1992).

The CISS also provides measures for three Special Scales. These scales represent interest preferences and perceived skills in Academic Focus (intellectual, scientific, and literary activities), Extraversion (attraction to and confidence in outgoing activities), and Variety (the number of diverse tasks within an occupation). The Variety Scales are experimental and are, therefore, not graphically reported on the results profile (Campbell et al., 1992).

Finally, the Procedural Checks are reported to give the user the ability to detect problems in the test administration or processing. These include the Response Percentage Check (unusual patterns to responses), Inconsistency Check (correlations between similar items), and Omitted Items Check (how many items were skipped).

Whether the test is administered on paper or online, the CISS results provide graphic illustrations of both interests and skills. Clients are encourage to *pursue* areas that indicate both a High Interest and a High Skill confidence, *develop* any areas that indicate a High Interest but Low Skill confidence, *explore* possibilities in areas with *low* Interest but High Skill confidence, and avoid areas with both a Low Interest and Low Skill confidence.

Use in Counseling

The CISS is widely used by practitioners helping clients seeking information about their occupations interests and skills, making educational or career plans, or for group activities such as team building (Campbell et al., 1992). The instrument has been designated a sixth-grade reading level and can be used with most adult populations, including higher education settings (Campbell et al., 1992). The 13-page report that describes and explains the results is geared towards the client rather than the counselor, making the report easy to understand and interpret. After reviewing results in an individual session or within a group session, clients are encouraged to take the report home for further review. With both paper and online versions of the instrument, the CISS is simple to administer, take, and interpret.

It is important for both counselors and clients to understand that the skills assessment included in the CISS is not an actual assessment of skill but rather a rating of level of self-confidence in that skill. For example, a question pertaining to mathematics is not measuring a person's actual skills in mathematics, but rather his or her self-assessment of ability to do mathematics. As such, the skill assessment may be more useful if considered a measure of self-efficacy related to a particular skill. Profiles that include low self-estimates of skill may be indicative of self-efficacy problems that should be explored further (Campbell et al., 1992).

Technical Considerations

The CISS is referenced to a norm base of self-described satisfied and successful employees spread out over 58 different occupations. The norm sample, collected in 1989, consisted of 1,790 women and 3,435 men, and was subsequently weighted to provide equal gender representation (Campbell et al., 1992). Unlike other similar inventories, the CISS compares individuals to the norm sample collectively rather than divided by gender (Campbell et al., 1992). Practitioners should be aware that 7of the 29 Basic Interest and Skill scales reflected a gender gap in terms of employment areas that they are attracted to and in which they feel confident (Campbell et al., 1992). Women scored higher on Child Development and Fashion whereas men scored higher in Financial Services, Mechanical Crafts, Woodworking, Military/Law Enforcement, and Risk/Adventure. As this gender gap occurs in almost one-quarter of the Basic Scales, those interpreting results should examine these categories closely and be aware of ways in which an individual's interest and/or skill reports may be overemphasized or underemphasized due to gender. In other words, a woman expressing a slight preference for Child Development may not have a preference at all compared only to other women. At the same time, a man who shows a slight preference for Child Development may have a significant interest when compared only to other men. Some researchers, including Betz (1993) recommend that counselors use a combination of same-sex normed inventories and sex-balanced inventories (such as the CISS) in order to balance the gender influence on interest inventory results.

The manual for the CISS includes reports on reliability as well as validity (Campbell et al., 1992). Campbell (2002) resists the concept of "statistical significance" and, as such, focuses instead on measures of magnitude, consistency, and replication (Campbell et al., 1992). Excellent estimates of reliability and validity have also been reported by independent researchers (Rottinghaus, Larson, & Borgen, 2003). In addition, Hansen and Neuman (1999) found good to excellent predictive validity of the CISS in regard to choice of college major.

As noted earlier, the Interest portion of the CISS is designed to measure the construct of interests also measured by numerous other instruments. In an interesting monograph, Savickas, Taber, and Spokane (2002) examined whether a collection of interest inventories that claim to measure the same construct actually produce scores that correspond. As a popular and well-researched instrument, the CISS was one of the instruments included. Results of the study indicated that the scales correlated moderately and demonstrated convergent and discriminant validity. In looking specifically at the CISS, however, Savickas et al. (2002) found that the CISS Adventure scale correlated significantly with the Social scale in two of the instruments and the Enterprising scale in two others. In other words, the Adventure scale seemed to have more in common with seemingly unrelated scales than with the Realistic scale as the CISS developers purport (Savickas et al., 2002). Similar problems were found with the Organizing scale. Thus, although five of the seven CISS Orientation Scales demonstrated validity in correlation with Holland's codes, the Adventuring and Organizing Scales did not (Savickas et al., 2002). While these discrepancies do not change the validity of the test itself, practitioners should be aware of these discrepancies when interpreting the CISS using Holland's constructs or when referring clients to subsequent materials such as the Holland Dictionary of Occupational Codes.

Overall Critique

The CISS is a widely used and accepted measure of interest preferences and self-reported skills. Whether in the paper version or online application, it is easy to administer and easy for clients to engage. The generated Individual Profile Report provides both appropriate narrative explanation and graphic illustrations that make the results easy to understand. Both practically and historically, it is a well-built inventory with an established base of users. As with other career inventories, careful interpretation is necessary when reviewing the specific career titles as clients must understand those titles are representative of a diverse range of jobs. There is always some danger of clients taking these results too literally and selecting exact job titles based upon these results.

While careful attention has been paid to item bias and sensitivity to the issues of diversity with the CISS, this has mainly focused on the avoidance of potentially-offensive language. In that significant differences were found between genders within the norm group, it is reasonable to assume that some ethnic or racial gaps would also be found within some items. Other similar instruments report such differences and advise interpreters accordingly (Harmon, Hansen, Bore, & Hammer, 1994). In a study by Lauver and Jones (1991), ethnic and gender differences were found in various measures of self-efficacy, especially with American Indian respondents. As not much information is readily available regarding the CISS and ethnicity directly, counselors must take extra care in interpreting results for clients whose backgrounds may be significantly different from the norm sample. Future research should focus on the demographics of the original norm sample as well as any significant differences in item responses.

References

Betz, N.E. (1993). Issues in the use of ability and interest measures with women. *Journal of Career Assessment, 1,* 217-232.

Campbell, D.P (2002). The history and development of the Campbell Interest and Skill Survey. *Journal of Career Assessment, 10,* 150 – 168.

Campbell, D.P., Hyne, S.A. & Nilsen, D.L. (1992). *Manual for the Campbell Interest and Skill Survey (CISS).* Minneapolis: NCS Pearson, Inc.

Hansen, J-I.C. & Neuman, J.L. (1999). Evidence of concurrent prediction of the Campbell Interest and Skill Survey (CISS) for college major selection. *Journal of Career Assessment, 7,* 239 – 247.

Harmon, L.W., Hansen, J-I.C., Bore, F.H., & Hammer, A.L. (1994). *Strong Interest Inventory: Applications and technical guide.* Palo Alto, CA: Consulting Psychologists Press.

Lauver, P.J., & Jones, R.M. (1991). Factors associated with perceived career options in American Indian, White, and Hispanic rural high school students. *Journal of Counseling Psychology, 38,* 159 – 166.

Rottinghaus, P.J., Larson, L.M., & Borgen, F.H. (2003). The relations of self-efficacy and interests: A meta-analysis of 60 samples. *Journal of Vocational Behavior, 62,* 221 – 236.

Savickas, M.L., Taber, B.J., & Spokane, A.R. (2002). Monograph: Convergent and discriminant validity of five interest inventories. *Journal of Vocational Behavior, 61,* 139 – 184.

CAREER DIRECTIONS INVENTORY (CDI)
(SECOND EDITION)

Douglas N. Jackson

SIGMA Assessment Systems, Inc
P.O. Box 610984
Port Huron, MI 48061-0984
www.SigmaAssessmentSystems.com

Target Population: Age: 14+. Groups: schools, colleges, university counseling services, employment offices and agencies, business and industry, vocational rehabilitation, adult counseling centers.

Statement of the Purpose of the Instrument: The Career Directions Inventory (CDI) is designed to facilitate educational and career exploration. It matches an individual's interests with related career and academic paths. The CDI is suitable for a wide spectrum of the population, not only for those who are headed for postsecondary school or a professional career.

Titles of Subtests, Scales, Scores Provided: Administrative, Assertive, Food Service, Health Service, Personal Service, Sales, Systematic, Writing, Art, Clerical, Industrial Arts, Outdoors, Persuasive, Science, Teaching/Social Service.

Forms and Levels Available, with Dates of Publication/Revision of Each: N/A

Date of Most Recent Edition of Test Manual, User's Guide, etc.: 2003.

Languages in Which Available: English and French.

Time:

Actual Test Time: 30 minutes.

Total Administration Time: 30 minutes.

Norm Group(s) on Which Scores Are Based: Norms are based on a sample of 2500 individuals (1250 men and 1250 women). Separate norms are available for males and females and for six age groups (15 years or less, 16 to 17 years, 18 to 19 years, 20 to 30 years, 31 to 40 years, and 41 or greater).

Manner in Which Results Are Reported for Individuals:

Types of Scores: Percentiles.

Report Format/Content: Extended Report: The CDI Extended Report includes a basic interest profile, a profile for seven general occupational themes, scores of similarity to 27 broad occupational clusters with narrative summaries of the three most similar clusters, sample occupations and a lengthy profile of similarity to more than 100 educational/occupational groups. Lists of sample occupations are included with the O*NET or Canadian National Occupational Classification (NOC) codes for each given occupation. (www.hrsdc.gc.ca)

Options: The Extended Report is available online at www.SigmaTesting.com as well as through Software and mail-in scoring.

Report Format/Content for Group Summaries: Not available.

Scoring:

Mail-in Scoring Service:

Cost of basic service per counselee: CDI Extended Reports: Price includes machine scorable question and answer document and computer-generated report.

Item No. 9033   1 report $15.00*

Item No. 903

    1-3 packages (10 reports/pkg) $100.00*

    4+ packages (10 reports/pkg) $90.00*

Time required for scoring and returning (maximum): 48 hours

* Prices are based on 2008 catalog.

Hand Scoring: Not available.

Computer Software Options Available: Computerized adaptive administration, standard administration online.

Ways in Which Computer/Online Version Differs: Computer software must be administered on-site, wherever the computer is located. Online scoring can be administered on any computer with Internet access.

Cost of Materials: $27*. Due to possible price changes since publication date, be sure to check with publisher web site.

Specimen Set: CDI Examination Kit.

Counselee Materials: Kit includes manual (CD-ROM) and one mail-in Extended Report.

Published Reviews of the Instrument in the Last 15 Years: None Cited.

Reviewed by:

Kenneth F. Hughey
Professor

Aaron H. Carlstrom
Assistant Professor

Department of Special Education, Counseling, and Student Affairs
College of Education
Kansas State University

Description

The Career Directions Inventory (CDI), second edition, is an interest inventory, originally published in 1986, "designed to identify areas of greater or lesser interest from among a wide variety of occupations" (Jackson, 2003, p. 9). According to Jackson

(2003), the CDI "is appropriate for a very wide spectrum of the general population, not only those headed for a university education or a professional career" (p. 10). At the publisher's website, it is noted that the CDI can be used with high school students, college/university students, and adults (www.sigmaassessmentsystems.com/assessments/cdi.asp). The manual, however, provides five case summaries; four of high school students and one of an adult.

The CDI consists of 100 forced-choice triads of statements associated with job-related activities. For each of the triads, respondents are to select both the activity most liked and the one least liked (on the machine-scorable version). On the Internet version, the respondent is instructed to "choose the one statement that describes you MOST accurately, as well as the one statement that is LEAST accurate in describing you." Even though these directions are different, the assumption, it seems, is that respondents are able to differentiate equally between the three options for each item. Jackson (2003) stated, "Low scale scores on the CDI represent rejected activities" (p. 14), and added that these are activities that are disliked or detested. We concur with Sabers (1994) who stated, "A more accurate statement, because of the forced-choice nature of the task, is that these are relatively less attractive activities for the individual" (p. 153). From our perspective, taking into account both high and low CDI scores is important.

The CDI items are written at the sixth-grade reading level and can be completed in approximately 30 minutes (Jackson, 2003). The CDI is available in three formats: a machine-scorable booklet, a software package, and an Internet version.

The CDI computerized report is an in-depth report, approximately 20 pages, and includes a two-page Counselor's Summary Report. Included are the CDI results relating to 15 Basic Interest Scales (BIS), 7 General Occupational Themes (GOT), a comparison of one's scores to 27 Job Clusters, and a profile showing the similarity of one's interests to those of students in 100 educational fields. In addition, administrative indices, Infrequency Score and Reliability Index, are provided to assess inconsistent or problematic responding. Percentile scores are reported; however, standard scores and raw scores are referred to on p. 40 of the manual.

The BIS (e.g., Administration, Clerical, Science, Writing, Assertive) scores "are indicative of the degree to which respondents will be interested in activities within the domain of each of the named basic interests" (Jackson, 2003, p. 40). The GOT are similar to Holland's (1997) types. Based on research for the CDI, a seventh theme, Serving, is included. While the Holland type names are used (e.g., Realistic/Practical), the order of the themes in the manual and the report varies from Holland's work. Jackson (2003) stated, "Many jobs will combine the expression of two or more of these occupational themes" (p. 20); however, this idea does not seem to be developed for respondents' use with their results.

Use in Counseling

According to the publisher's website, the CDI "is designed to facilitate educational and career exploration." Jackson (2003) stated, the CDI "is particularly appropriate for use in educational and career counseling, educational and occupational decision making, and for research in vocational interest, job satisfaction, and personnel classification" (p. 9).

The CDI report is presented in an organized, informative manner. We believe the applicability and relevance of CDI results for respondents' career and educational planning are enhanced with solid interpretations by knowledgeable counselors/professionals.

The CDI report includes a list of resources (i.e., O*NET listings, Suggested Readings, Organizations, Activities) for three job clusters that most closely match respondents' interest pattern. The use of O*NET, a database on a website at http://www.onetcenter.org, is commendable; however, for our results, the *Occupational Outlook Handbook (OOH)* (U.S. Department of Labor, 2006) was not noted as a resource. Given the availability of the OOH, reference to it would have been helpful. In addition, under Suggested Readings for each of the occupation groups, there were some resources with publication dates in the early 1990s. The provision of relevant, timely information is essential to facilitate career exploration and planning. Under the final set of activities intended to help students explore their career options, it would seem helpful to include the involvement of parents and school counselors in career and educational planning.

Jackson (2003) presented cautions to professionals using the CDI. He noted that the CDI is not intended to be an aptitude or achievement test, and stated, "an interest in an area does not necessarily imply ability to succeed in that area" (p. 40). In addition, he cautioned about its use for employee selection. Also, he stated, "it is unreasonable to expect that interest measures will yield 100% accuracy in predicting career satisfaction" (p. 10) and "It would be incorrect to assume that the purpose of vocational interest assessment is to recommend only one ideal occupation" (p. 60).

Technical Considerations

Jackson (2003) stated that in standardizing the CDI a "broad representation from a wide geographic area, diverse specialty groups, and a wide sampling of educational institutions" was sought. To develop the "initial normative sample" 12,846 individuals (roughly equal numbers of males and females) were drawn from "several appropriate occupationally-oriented programs" (p. 94) that offered the different educational specialty groups identified. A subsample of 1,000 individuals (500 males, 500 females) was selected from the original group and used to develop the original norms for the first edition of the CDI. A new sample of 2,500 individuals (1,250 males, 1,250 females), drawn from the United States and Canada, was used to develop the profiles for the current CDI. The new norms were presented in six age groups: 15 years and younger, 16 – 17 years, 18 – 19 years, 20 – 30 years, 31 – 40 years, and 41 years and older. No rationale was provided for the age groupings.

It is commendable that the new sample was drawn from both the United States and Canada, and included age groupings. However, age (for the new norm group) and gender are the only demographic information provided. Other demographic information relevant to career development (e.g., race/ethnicity, socioeconomic status, and region beyond reporting that the new norm group was sampled from both the United States and Canada) was not reported. Based on the information presented in the manual, it would be challenging for counselors to assess the relevance of the norm sample for the individuals and groups with whom they work. Additionally, the ability to assess the representativeness of the norm sample to any external population is limited. This is a concern since CDI scores are presented as percentiles; without the ability to assess the relevance of the norm group, percentiles lack meaning.

Means and standard deviations for the 15 BIS are provided for the age groups for the new norms, and for gender and total sample for both the new and old norms. However, no mean comparison data are provided regarding potential differences by age, norm group, or gender.

Reliability and validity evidence does not appear to have been updated for the second edition of the CDI. Test-retest reliability and internal consistency reliability are reported for the various scales. Test-retest reliability coefficients were (a) .72 – .94, with a median coefficient of .87 for the BIS; (b) .86 – .95, with a median coefficient of .90 for the GOT; (c) .76 – .92, with a median coefficient of .875 for the Occupational Clusters; and (d) .67 – .96, with only 10 reliability coefficients falling below .80 for the Educational Specialty Groups. These reliability coefficients are satisfactory to good; however, the test-retest reliability is based on a sample of 70 high school students, with a time between sessions that averaged four weeks. Having test-retest reliability data representative of groups targeted by the CDI would be helpful and informative.

Internal consistency reliability evidence is based on a sample of 1000 individuals from the original norm sample. Internal consistency reliability coefficients ranged from (a) .62-.91 (median = .80) for the BIS; (b) .85 – .91 (median = .87) for the GOT; (c) .74 – .91 (median = .855) for the Occupational Clusters; and (d) .62 – .92, with only 8 reliability coefficients falling below .70 for the Educational Specialty Groups.

Jackson's (2003) description of the construction of the CDI indicates techniques (e.g., factor analysis, item analysis) associated with building valid tests were used. From this description, it also appears that items of the BIS are relevant and representative. Additionally, Jackson (2003) noted that the use of the forced-choice format removes a significant response bias associated with interest measures and, thus, contributes to increased discriminant validity.

Further validity evidence for the CDI was assessed by comparing "people in general" (i.e., the 1,000 individuals from the original norm group) and the individuals in different specialty groups (i.e., individuals in relevant specialty groups from the original sample of 12,846 not included in the 1,000-person norm group). Comparisons were made between the groups on the distribution of scores of educational specialty group scales and cluster scales. For example, individuals in the Electrical Engineering Technology specialty group were compared with "people in general," on the Electrical Engineering Technology Scale and the Electronic/Technology Cluster Scale. A greater percentage of people in the Electrical Engineering Technology specialty group had higher scores on both of the scales than "people in general" which appeared to be offered as concurrent validity for those two scales. Additionally, a comparison of cumulative percentiles for the Electrical Engineering Technology Scale and Electronic/Technology Cluster Scale between "people in general" and persons in the Electrical Engineering Technology specialty group was provided. As predicted, the same score was associated with a lower cumulative percentage of individuals in the specialty group, which again demonstrated that the specialty group had greater interest in areas connected with their specialty than people not in their specialty group.

Validity evidence was not provided for every Educational Specialty Group or Occupational Cluster. Additionally, validity evidence was presented only graphically. Potential significance of group mean differences was not reported. No evaluation of concurrent validity with other interest inventories was reported. We echo Sabers' (1994) comment that there is not a lack of validity data, but that the validity evidence is of poor quality. Also, Maddux (2007) noted that validity of the CDI "has not been satisfactorily established."

In general, there are two primary psychometric concerns relative to the CDI. First, percentile scores, as opposed to percentile bands are used. A potential drawback in the use of a single number in interpretation is the possible misperception about the level of accuracy of the instrument in measuring the construct under consideration. A Reliability Index is provided; however, this is first reported in the Administrative Indices, found on page 19 of the CDI Extended Report. Second, the description of the normative sample lacks clarity which can lead to interpretive difficulties when using norm-referenced scores. Related to this point is the lack of a description of the racial/ethnic composition of the normative samples.

Overall Critique

Based on feedback from graduate students and colleagues who completed the CDI and our review of the CDI, we believe it can be useful in facilitating students' career exploration and planning. Thoughtful, professional interpretation and integration of the results are strongly recommended to maximize the usefulness of the CDI. The utility of the CDI for various groups may vary, depending on their career development and educational status. As noted in this review, there are technical and interpretive issues that, from our perspective, need to be considered with respect to the CDI. In addition, we concur with Goldman (2007) that "With the exception of new norms from which little technical data are compiled, the addition of four new job clusters, and the division of one job cluster into two, the second edition of the CDI and its accompanying manual appears to be identical to the first edition, which was published in 1986." Including a section in the manual that clarified the enhancements in the second edition of the CDI would have been helpful.

References

Goldman, B. A. (2007). Review of Career Directions Inventory (2nd ed.). In K. F. Geisinger, R. A. Spies, J. F. Carlson, & B. S. Plake (Eds.), *Seventeenth mental measurements yearbook.* Retrieved January 22, 2007, from the Buros Institute's Test Reviews Online website: http://www.unl.edu/buros

Holland, J. L. (1997). *Making vocational choices: A theory of vocational personalities and work environments* (3rd ed.). Odessa, FL: Psychological Assessment Resources.

Jackson, D. N. (2003). *Career Directions Inventory manual.* Port Huron, MI: Sigma Assessment Systems.

Maddux, C. D. (2007). Review of Career Directions Inventory (2nd ed.). In K. F. Geisinger, R. A. Spies, J. F. Carlson, & B. S. Plake (Eds.), *Seventeenth mental measurements yearbook.* Retrieved January 22, 2007, from the Buros Institute's Test Reviews Online website: http://www.unl.edu/buros

Sabers, D. L. (1994). Review of the Career Directions Inventory. In J. T. Kapes, M. M. Mastie, & E. A. Whitfield (Eds.), *A counselor's guide to career assessment instruments* 3rd ed. (pp. 151 – 155). Alexandria, VA: National Career Development Association.

U.S. Department of Labor. (2006). *The occupational outlook handbook.* Washington, DC: U.S. Government Printing Office.

CAREER EXPLORATION INVENTORY (CEI)

John J. Liptak

JIST Publishing
8902 Otis Avenue
Indianapolis, IN 46216
www.jist.com

Target Population: Junior High School and above.

Statement of the Purpose of the Instrument: The CEI helps individuals explore and plan three major areas of their lives—work, leisure activities, and learning. A career exploration tool, it asks users to reflect on 128 activities and consider their past, present, and future interest in them. Scores are then connected to 16 career interest areas (based on the Department of Education career clusters), with related jobs, education and training options, and leisure activities listed for each one. Test can be self-administered, self-scored, and self-interpreted.

Titles of Subtests, Scales, Scores Provided: Scores into 16 career interest areas based on Department of Education career clusters: Agriculture and Natural Resources; Architecture and Construction; Arts and Communication; Business and Administration; Education and Training; Finance and Insurance; Government and Public Administration; Health Science; Hospitality, Tourism, and Recreation; Human Service; Information Technology; Law and Public Safety; Manufacturing; Retail and Wholesale Sales and Service; Scientific Research, Engineering, and Mathematics; Transportation, Distribution, and Logistics

Forms and Levels Available, with Dates of Publication/Revision of Each: Career Exploration Inventory Assessment (2006), Career Exploration Inventory Administrator's Guide (2006), Career Exploration Inventory Professional Resources CD-ROM (2006), Career Exploration Inventory EZ (2007)

Date of Most Recent Edition of Test Manual, User's Guide, etc.: 2006.

Languages in Which Available: English and Spanish.

Time:

Actual Test Time 20 – 40 minutes

Total Administration Time 20 – 40 minutes

Norm Group(s) on Which Scores Are Based: For the original CEI, adult norms were generated from sample populations of 104 unemployed/underemployed adults participating in Job Training Partnership Programs offered by the Private Industry Council of Westmoreland/Fayette, Inc., and 106 adults who previously participated in seminars and workshops sponsored by the Employee Career Development Program at Virginia Tech. This adult population ranged in age from 18 to 65 and was chosen because they had a variety of work and leisure interests. Since that time, new data for 834 more adults have been collected. In addition, norms for a college student population are currently being calculated and will be available with the next edition of the CEI.

Manner in Which Results Are Reported for Individuals:

Types of Scores: The CEI yields content-referenced scores in the form of raw scores. The CEI measures developmental interests by asking respondents to identify whether they enjoyed doing the activity in the past 5 to 10 years (P), if they currently enjoy doing the activity (C), and if they think they would enjoy doing the activity 5 to 10 years in the future (F). Because the CEI measures interests over time, respondents can circle interest in up to three time frames. Therefore, a raw score in this case is the total of the numbers circled for each of the eight self-report interest statements for the 16 scales. The performance of individual respondents or groups of respondents can only be evaluated in terms of the mean scores on each of the scales.

For each of the scales on the CEI: Scores from 0 – 5 are in the low range and indicate that the respondent does not have much interest in the types of occupations, leisure activities, and educational programs represented by that interest area. Scores from 6 – 18 are in the average range and indicate that the respondent has average interest in the types of occupations, leisure activities, and educational programs represented by that interest area. Scores from 19 – 24 are in the high range and indicate that the respondent has a great deal of interest in the types of occupations, leisure activities, and educational programs represented by that interest area.

Report Format/Content: Assessment is self-scoring and self-interpreting. Work, Leisure and Learning Activities Guide and multiple exploration and planning worksheets are included with each assessment. Respondents follow a series of eight steps to complete the CEI. Assessment is a 12-panel foldout.

Report Format/Content for Group Summaries: Not available.

Scoring:

Machine Scoring Service: Not available.

Hand Scoring:

Scored by: Counselee.

Time required for scoring: 5 minutes.

Computer Software Options Available: Computerized adaptive administration.

Ways in Which Computer/Online Version Differs: Automated scoring and automated report generation.

Cost of Materials: Due to possible price changes since publication date, be sure to check with publisher web site.

Specimen Set: $36.95/package of 25—Includes free Administrator's Guide

Professional Resources CD-ROM: $29.95 (Reusable).

Additional Comments of Interest to Users: New EZ version shortens administration time and makes it easier for individuals to score and interpret their results.

Published Reviews of the Instrument in the Last 15 Years:

Pletcher, K.T. (2001) Review of the *Career Exploration Inventory.* Alexandria, VA: The Association for Assessment in Counseling and Education. http://aac.ncat.edu/ newsnotes/y00spr.html

Impara, J.C., & Plake, B.S. (Eds.) (1998). Review of the Career Exploration Inventory. *The thirteenth mental measurements yearbook.* Lincoln, NE: The Buros Institute of Mental Health.

Reviewed by:

Jeff Powell
Dean of Students
Touro University
Henderson, Nevada

Description

The Career Exploration Inventory (CEI) is a career interest test that can be self-scored and interpreted. In addition to measuring interests in major occupational interest areas, the CEI is unique in measuring past, present, and future interests in both leisure and learning activities.

The Career Exploration Inventory, revised in 2006 to reflect changes in how occupations are classified, uses the 16 career clusters used by the Department of Education and the New Guide for Occupational Exploration (Liptak, 2006). The CEI also incorporates the O*NET (Occupational Information Network) job titles and job groups in the Work, Leisure, and Learning Activities Guide. Some inventory items were revised to reflect changes in society, technology, and the world of work (Liptak, 2006).

The Career Exploration Inventory consists of eight sequential steps:

Step 1 asks the test taker to identify past, current, and future work, leisure, and learning interests. Past activities are defined as activities done in the past 5 to 10 years. Current activities are those in which one is now involved, and future activities are those that one would like to do in the next 5 to 10 years.

After test takers identify the activities, they are asked to consider four points. These include how their work, leisure, and learning interests are similar; how those interests influence one another; which interests have stayed the same over time; and which three activities they enjoy the most and would want to include in a career.

The second step is completing the CEI Work, Leisure, and Learning Inventory. The inventory is comprised of 128 items that are ultimately grouped into 16 interest areas.

In Step 3, test takers add up their total score on the CEI Work, Leisure, and Learning Inventory. Test takers are asked to write the number of circled responses in the "Subtotal" column for each row. When all subtotals are obtained, 16 pairs of subtotals are added together to get a total for each pair. This is recorded in the "Total" column. The totals are numbered 1 through 16 for each of the interest areas.

Step 4 is called "Interpreting Your CEI Scores." This indicates how much interest one has in each of the 16 interest areas on the Career Exploration Inventory.

Step 5 provides the test taker with an interpretation of what the scores on the interest profile mean. Step 6 is a Work, Leisure and Learning Activities Guide that provides information for each of the 16 interest areas. This includes related occupations, typical leisure activities, related education, and training, and the related O'NET job groups. Step 6 also includes a Work, Leisure and Learning Activities Worksheet to identify the activities of most interest.

Step 7 of the CEI gives test takers additional sources of information. Step 8 allows test takers to create an action plan based on what they learned from taking the Career Exploration Inventory.

Uses in Counseling

The CEI aids in career exploration and career planning. It helps individuals identify their work, leisure, and educational interests. The Inventory uses a holistic, comprehensive approach to career development by showing test takers how their work, leisure, and learning activities combine over a lifetime to influence their career choices.

The Career Exploration Inventory identifies individuals' work-leisure patterns. By studying their scores on each of the scales, individuals can gain insight into how their leisure activities affect or are affected by the work they do. The CEI also assists people who have limited or no work experience. Individuals identify leisure experiences that can be turned into viable employment opportunities.

The Career Exploration Inventory helps individuals identify areas of interest that can lead to a satisfying career. An awareness of interests will have a positive influence on a person's work and personal life. The CEI assists test takers in examining their developmental interests by asking them to identify their past, present, and future interests. Although many career counselors use a developmental approach, no other existing interest inventory has a format to measure developmental interests according to Liptak (1996).

The CEI can be used individually or in a group setting with a variety of clients. These can include welfare-to-work clients, people planning for retirement, students transitioning to work, college students, offenders and ex-offenders, outplaced employees, unemployed adults, and rehabilitation clients (Liptak, 1996).

Technical Considerations

The Career Exploration Inventory is based on two theoretical constructs that have not been previously utilized as the basis for an interest inventory. These are Super's (1980) Life Span, Life Space theory of career development and McDaniels' (1984) concept of Career Equals Work Plus Leisure (C = W + L). The life span aspect of Super's theory was instrumental in constructing the unique developmental item response format. As stated by Super (1984), "It is important to obtain three time perspectives: the past from which one has come, the present in which one currently functions, and the future toward which one is moving" (p. 192).

The CEI uses a free-response format comprised of P for past interest, C for current interest, and F for interest anticipated for the future. This differs from the traditional response format of L for like, I for indifferent, and D for dislike. This format allows the test-taker to identify sustained interest, not solely interest at the time of testing.

The Career Exploration Inventory provides scores for both males and females. As inventory scales were developed, standardization groups were sex-balanced to the greatest extent possible. The CEI uses an item pool that reflects experiences and activities that are equally familiar to both females and males. Items that imply an activity that might be more appropriate for one gender or the other (e.g., policeman, stewardess) were eliminated. The CEI also presents occupational titles in gender-neutral terms. Separate norms for males and females still need to be developed.

The CEI was field-tested to gather quantitative data about its validity and reliability. The final form was given to 104 unemployed and underemployed adults participating in a Job Training Partnership Act (JTPA) program in southwestern Pennsylvania and to 106 employees who had attended program activities offered by the Employee Career Development Program (ECDP) at a southeastern land grant university.

The 104 subjects participating in the JTPA program included 40 females and 64 males, ranging in age from 18 to 73, who volunteered to participate in this study. The sample of 106 employees from the ECDP included 85 females and 21 males ranging in age from 23 to 62. The total sample of 210 subjects consisted of 85 males and 125 females ranging in age from 18 to 73.

Construct validity was established by determining the number of times the Career Exploration Inventory accurately measured sustained interests from the past, in the present, and anticipated for the future. For example, a "hit" was recorded if a person listed gardening as a leisure interest in the past, present, and future.

Test retest reliability was obtained by re-administering the CEI to a portion of the original sample approximately three months after the initial testing in order to get an estimate of the stability of the scales; 55 subjects were tested.

The Career Exploration Inventory's internal consistency measures range from .56 to .84. These are comparable to existing interest inventories including the Strong-Campbell Interest Inventory (Campbell and Hansen, 1981), Vocational Interest Inventory (Lunneborg, 1981) and the Life Interest Survey (Frisbie, 1982).

The CEI most accurately measured leisure interests in the present (79%) and leisure interests in the past (77%). The instrument also accurately recorded subjects' past work experience (72%). While present work interests were the lowest percentage (69%) measured by the CEI, this percentage is still relatively high as a large portion of the sample were unemployed and enrolled in a job-search program at the time of testing.

Past leisure interests of subjects were accurately identified 51% of the time, while present leisure interests correctly identified 49% of the time. The CEI accurately measured subjects' past work interests 43% of the time and present work interests 44% of the time.

Construct validity for the Career Exploration Inventory was measured by the number of times the instrument accurately predicted a subject's developmental, sustained interests. The CEI accurately identified 54% of the subjects' sustained work interests (i.e., past, present, and future work interests). It also successfully identified 67% of the subjects' sustained leisure interests (i.e., past, present, and future leisure interests). Because the CEI is the first interest inventory to measure sustained interests over the life span, no existing instrument can provide comparable data.

Overall Critique

The Career Exploration Inventory test materials include a Workshop Manual and a Professional Manual for administrators contained on a CD-ROM. Both are well organized and to the point. Administration and scoring procedures are clearly stated in the directions provided on the CEI. The time necessary to take the inventory is approximately 30 minutes.

The CEI is very user-friendly. It can be administered to both individuals and groups. Test takers need only the testing booklet to take the test, making it easy to self-administer, self-score, and self-interpret. Directions are clearly stated and easy to read.

The sample of subjects used to standardize the Career Exploration Inventory was small (N = 210). Also, information is not provided on either the ethnic composition or the socioeconomic status of the entire sample. In terms of test-retest reliability, the CEI was found to have acceptable correlation coefficients for the interest areas. However, the inventory was re-administered to only 55 of the 210 participants. In addition, internal consistency comparisons were made to inventories that were published 20- 3 years ago.

Since the Career Exploration Inventory was standardized on both unemployed/underemployed and employed adults, this instrument is effective when used with these populations. The CEI might also prove to be effective in helping secondary students and college students identify and explore the interaction between work and leisure interests, according to Liptak (2006). This instrument could potentially facilitate career development in other populations such as retirees, non-English-speaking subjects, and individuals with disabilities. However, for this to be the case, norms should be established for each of these populations.

References

Campbell, D. P., & Hansen, J. C. (1981). *Manual for the SVIBSCII.* Stanford, CA: Stanford University Press.

Frisbie, G. R. (1982). Development of a career (leisure/work) interest inventory. *Dissertation Abstracts International 44,* 73A.

Liptak, J. J. (1996). *User's guide for the Barriers to Employment Success Inventory.* Indianapolis, IN: JIST.

Liptak, J. J. (2006). *Professional manual for the Career Exploration Inventory: A guide for exploring work, leisure and learning,* 3rd ed. Indianapolis, IN: JIST Works.

Lunneborg, P. W. (1981). *Vocational interest inventory manual.* Los Angeles: Western Psychological Services.

McDaniels, C. (1984). Work and leisure in the career span. In N.C. Gysbers, (Ed.), *Designing Careers.* San Francisco: Jossey-Bass.

Super, D. E. (1980). A life-span, life-space approach to career development. *Journal of Vocational Behavior 16,* 282 – 298.

Super, D. E. (1984). Leisure: What it is and might be. *Journal of Career Development 11(2),* 71 – 80.

HALL OCCUPATIONAL ORIENTATION INVENTORY (FOURTH EDITION)

Lacy G. Hall

Scholastic Testing Service, Inc. (STS)
480 Meyer Road
Bensenville, IL 60106-1617
www.ststesting.com

Target Population: Young adult/College/Adult.

Statement of the Purpose of the Instrument: To provide career, leisure, and lifestyle planning assistance that goes far beyond that of most tests. Also provides a verbal picture of one's interests, work values, and needs for satisfaction in one's chosen career instead of prescribing what a person should choose as a career.

Titles of Subtests, Scales, Scores Provided: Provides a rating scale so that test takers can determine their fields of greatest interest from 22 different areas of interest, needs, and values.

Forms and Levels Available, with Dates of Publication/Revision of Each: Form II (2000) and Young Adult/College/Adult Form (2000) for middle school and beyond.

Date of Most Recent Edition of Test Manual, User's Guide, etc.: 2000.

Languages in Which Available: English only.

Time:

Actual Test Time: Time varies. Typically less than 45 minutes.

Norm Group(s) on Which Scores Are Based: No norms. The Hall is an inventory not a test. The Hall allows for interpretation based on reviewing the overall responses on 22 different scales, and then reviewing each sentence that was marked for the interests, needs, and work values.

Manner in Which Results Are Reported for Individuals:

Types of Scores: The verbal labels include areas such as need for security, risk, and relationships toward people, data or things.

Report Format/Content: Individuals take the inventory and mark on a self-marking, self-scored response sheet. Once the response sheet is complete, directions are provided to profile the interests, needs, and work values of the individual.

Report Format/Content for Group Summaries: Not available.

Scoring:

Machine Scoring Service: Not available.

Hand Scoring:
SCORED BY: Counselee; Counselor.

Local Machine Scoring: Not available.

Computer Software Options Available: Not available.

Cost of Materials: Due to possible price changes since publication date, be sure to check with publisher website.

Cost of basic service per counselee: Sample set is $16.50. Set includes one Inventory Booklet, one Interpretive Manual, and one Response Sheet.

Cost of options: Pkg. of 20 Inventory Booklets ($41.30/Pkg.), Pkg. of 20 Response Sheets (28.00/Pkg.) and Pkg. of 20 Self-Interpretive Folders (29.35/Pkg.), Choosing: Your Way and Counselor/User's Manual ($42.20).

Specimen Set: $16.50 postage paid.

Counselee Materials: The Counselor/User's Manual and *Choosing Your Way* are reusable.

Published Reviews of the Instrument in the Last 15 Years: Other reviews of this product are available in *Tests in Print VII* printed in 2006 by the Buros Institute of Mental Measurements.

Geisler, J.S. (2005) Review of the Hall Occupational Orientation Inventory. In R.A. Spies & B.S. Plake (Eds.) *The sixteenth mental measurement yearbook (425 – 427).* Lincoln, NE: Buros Institute of Mental Measurements.

Law, J.G. (2005). Review of the Hall Occupational Orientation Inventory. In R.A. Spies & B.S. Plake (Eds.), *The sixteenth mental measurements yearbook (427 – 428).* Lincoln, NE: Buros Institute of Mental Measurement.

Reviewed by:

Bryan J. Dik
Assistant Professor

Brandy M. Eldridge
Doctoral Student
Counseling Psychology

Department of Psychology
Colorado State University

Description

The Hall Occupational Orientation Inventory (The Hall) is a self-report measure consisting of 175 items. Testing materials include a reusable inventory booklet and one-time use scoring response forms, as well as a counselor's manual. The Hall is intended to be self-scored and can be self-interpreted with the assistance of the companion booklet *Choosing: Your Way, A Supplementary Career Reader* (Hall, 2000a). The Hall reports scores for 35 homogenous scales arranged into five categories. First, the Hall includes scores for nine scales designed to measure needs and values (Creativity-Independence; Information-Knowledge; Belongingness; Security; Aspiration; Esteem; Self-Actualization; Personal Satisfaction; and Routine-Dependence) based on Roe's

(1956) theory of occupational choice and Maslow's (1954) personality-need theory. Next, scores for six career interest scales (People-Social-Accommodating; Data-Information; Things-Physical; People-Business-Influencing; Ideas-Scientific; and Aesthetic-Arts) and six corresponding ability scales (which use the same labels) are reported. The dimensions these scales measure are derived from a model of interests adapted by Hall from the twelve interest areas in the U.S. Department of Labor's *Guide for Occupational Exploration* (U.S Dept. of Labor, 1979) and bear a strong resemblance to those in Holland's theory of vocational types. The HALL also includes eight job characteristic scales (geographic location; abilities; monetary compensation; workplace; coworkers; time; qualifications; and risk). Finally, six scales corresponding to Hall's choice styles (Subjective External Authority; Objective External Authority; Subjective Internal Authority; Shaping, Autonomy and Self-Empowerment; Interdependent; and Procrastination) are reported. Hall's career choice model posits that decision-making progresses in stages that correspond loosely to those in Piaget's (1930) and Kohlberg's (1984) models of cognitive and moral development.

A variety of continuous and weighted response formats are used for items on the Hall. For Needs-Values, Career Interest, and Job Characteristics scales, anchors are: 4 = Most Desirable, 3 = Desirable, 2 = Not Important, 1 = Undesirable, and 0 = Very Undesirable. Choice Style scales use the following anchors: 4 = Very Like Me, 2 = Like Me, 1 = Not Like Me; finally, for Ability scales, anchors are 4 = Strong, 3 = Above Average, 2 = Average, 1 = Weak. In the inventory booklet, these options are presented using single-letter abbreviations of the anchor descriptions (e.g., Most Desirable = M). These are converted to numeric values and summed to produce raw scores that are transferred to a self-interpreted profile sheet (contained in a separate booklet) which classifies raw scores as Low, Average, or High. This booklet also contains written interpretations for the 35 scales and urges respondents to use the supplemental *Career Reader* for further assistance in interpreting scores on the Hall profile.

Use in Counseling

The Hall can be used in both individual and group counseling settings, although group procedures are described in much greater detail in the *Counselor/User's Manual* (Hall, 2000b). Hall recommends using the first group interpretation session to draw clients' attention to items eliciting *a very desirable or very undesirable response* and relating this item-level information to his choice model. Clients are encouraged to make use of self-interpretation tools on their own time, allowing subsequent group sessions to focus on in-depth application of scores using Hall's model.

The *Counselor/User's Manual* provides suggestions for using assessment information effectively with various population groups for which use of the Hall is recommended. The author suggests using the inventory with individuals as young as junior high age, for whom the Hall can assist in the process of "identifying and exploring their 'innerselves' and relating this to the external world of career and occupational information" (p. 21). With high school seniors and college students, the inventory is described as useful in assisting with the crystallization of life goals, the identification of major and career possibilities, and with building self-efficacy for various tasks in the career choice process. For adults considering a career change, counselors are encouraged to use the Hall as an aid in reexamining values, needs, interests, and other occupational concerns. Finally, Hall proposes that the nonthreatening nature of the results presented on the Hall makes the inventory useful in teambuilding and conflict resolution interventions in organizations, such as in initiating conversations among employees in which interpersonal differences are explored. Job dissatisfaction can be explored by using the Hall to isolate sources of discomfort or providing a vocabulary for discussing them.

Technical Considerations

Scales on the Hall originated with a pool of more than 1,000 items. First, items that correlated higher with another scale's total score than with its own, or at a level below .55, were eliminated. Each of the remaining items was selected by the test author according to the extent to which it had "a singular and logical relationship to the one scale for which it was written" (Hall, 2000b, p. 5). The Hall was designed to report raw scale scores for use in ideographic interpretation; thus, no normative data are reported in the *Manual*.

Evaluating evidence for reliability and validity of scale scores on the Hall is difficult, given the extremely limited scope of psychometric information reported in the *Manual*. A survey of 2,200 individuals for the purpose of examining the item response distribution is reported, but no demographic data for the sample are cited and no reference is cited to help the reader gather more information about the survey. Similarly, brief descriptions of results from surveys of 225 college students, 288 workers from various occupations, 75 professional counselors, and an unspecified number of college seniors were reported. These results were described as providing evidence of validity using traditional criteria (e.g., "comprehensiveness" or content validity, "relevancy" or predictive validity, and "occupational differences" or concurrent validity) and unconventional criteria (e.g., attitudes of acceptance toward taking the inventory, evidence of appropriate use by practitioners), the latter of which, although interesting, do not represent useful information for evaluating the extent to which the inventory meets the claims made for it. All descriptions of these studies lack information related to the demographics of the samples, methods used to collect the survey data, or any test statistics obtained, and no publication references were cited. Limited validity data are available in the form of correlations among Hall's interest types, which were compared to correlations found among the six types in Holland's interest model. Intercorrelations among interest types as measured by the Hall range from r = .16 to r = .52 and generally vary in expected directions based on relative degrees of similarity among interest types. Finally, results from an experimental study of 160 college freshman found that participants in a group counseling intervention incorporating the Hall reported a larger increase in levels of self-awareness than did participants in a group counseling intervention incorporating the Strong Vocational Interest Blank (SVIB). However, no information about the method of the study, the composition of the sample, or the size of the effect was reported, and no publication references were cited.

The author states that because the characteristics measured by the Hall are dynamic and continually changing, traditional benchmarks for assessing reliability are not relevant. Thus, reliability data reported in the *Manual* consists only of item-scale correlations for each of the inventory's 175 items. By design, these are all larger than .55.

Overall Critique

Some users may find merit in using the Hall as a vehicle for conversation with clients, and the inventory's basis in a humanistic career choice model makes it somewhat unique. However, the Hall continues to suffer from the considerable limitations identified in earlier reviews. Most notably, very little data are reported from the scale development efforts, and evidence supporting the reliability and validity of scale scores is both extremely limited and insufficiently reported. The test author reports that the Hall is not subject to the standards of traditional reliability criteria because the inventory measures dynamic personality variables that are constantly changing. However, strong evidence exists to suggest a high level of stability in at least some of the constructs (e.g., vocational interests) measured by the Hall. The test author reiterates at several points in the *Manual* that the inventory is designed for exploration, not prediction. Yet compelling rationale is not provided to suggest that these apparently competing purposes are in fact distinct. As with any inventory used for career exploration purposes, when assessment information is used to inform career decisions that potentially have long-term implications, evidence for predictive validity always is relevant. The nonnormative, nonpredictive model on which the HALL was based is described by the author as a "new psychometric paradigm" that "has perhaps become a preeminent standard used throughout the United States and numerous foreign countries" (Hall, 2000b, p. xi). This claim simply is not supported.

References

Hall, L. G. (2000). *Hall Occupational Orientation Inventory* (4th ed.). Bensenville, IL: Scholastic Testing Service.

Hall, L. G. (2000a). *CHOOSING: YOUR WAY, A supplementary career reader for the HALL Occupational Orientation Inventory* (4th ed.). Bensenville, IL: Scholastic Testing Service.

Hall, L. G. (2000b). *Counselor/user's manual for the HALL Occupational Orientation Inventory* (4th ed.). Bensenville, IL: Scholastic Testing Service.

Kohlberg, L. (1984). *The psychology of moral development: Essays on moral development* (Vol. 2). San Francisco: Harper & Row.

Maslow, A. H. (1954). *Motivation and personality.* New York: Harper and Brothers.

Piaget, J. (1930). *The child's conception of physical causality.* London: Routledge & Kegan Paul.

Roe, A. (1956). *The psychology of occupations.* New York: John Wiley & Sons.

U.S. Department of Labor, Employment and Training Administration. (1979). *Guide for occupational exploration.* Washington, D.C.: Government Printing Office.

HARRINGTON-O'SHEA CAREER DECISION-MAKING SYSTEM – REVISED (CDM)

Thomas F. Harrington and Arthur J. O'Shea

Pearson Assessments
5601 Green Valley Drive
Bloomington, MN 55437
http://ags.pearsonassessments.com

Target Population: Middle school through adult.

Statement of the Purpose of the Instrument: A multidimensional systems approach to career decision-making that uses an individual's self-knowledge of interests, stated career choices, school subjects, work values, and future training plans to suggest career options for further exploration.

Titles of Subtests, Scales, Scores Provided: Scales: Crafts Interest Area, Scientific Interest Area, The Arts Interest Area, Social Interest Area, Business Interest Area, Office Operations Interest Area.

Scores: Crafts Interest Area Score, Scientific Interest Area Score, The Arts Interest Area Score, Social Interest Area Score, Business Interest Area Score, Office Operations Interest Area Score.

Forms and Levels Available, with Dates of Publication/Revision of Each: CDM Level 1 (Middle School and Low Level Readers), 1982: CDM-R. 1993, 2000; CDM Level 2 (High School through Adult), 1982: CDM-R, 1993 2000. Both Levels 1 and 2 had small revisions in 2005.

Date of Most Recent Edition of Test Manual, User's Guide, etc.: 2000.

Languages in Which Available: Hand-scored editions (Level 1 Booklet, Level 2 Survey Booklet and Interpretive Folder) are available in English and Spanish. Computer-scored edition (Level 2) is available in English; there are English and French Canadian editions, latest 2008.

Time:

Actual Test Time: 20 – 40 minutes.

Total Administration Time: 25 – 45 minutes.

Norm Group(s) on Which Scores Are Based: No derived scores. Standardization samples 1991: Level 1 – 965; Level 2 – 996. Sample defined based on 1990 U.S. Census data.

Manner in Which Results are Reported for Individuals: Hand-scored (Levels 1 and 2).

Types of Scores: Interest Area Raw Scores; percentile Rank Norms, by gender, for Interest Area Raw Scores.

Report Format/Content: Level 1: Interest Area Results and Interpretive Information included in Survey Booklet (i.e., survey results and student self report of career choices, work values, preferred school subjects, abilities, and future plans). Level 2: Summary Profile and Interpretive Folder which includes survey results and student self-report of career choices, work values, preferred school subjects, abilities, and future plans.

Report Format/Content for Group Summaries: Not Available

Scoring:

Machine Scoring Service: Not Available.

Hand Scoring:

SCORED BY: Counselee

TIME REQUIRED FOR SCORING: About 5 – 10 minutes.

Cost of Materials: Due to possible price changes since publication date, be sure to check with publisher web site.

Specimen Set: Yes.

CDM Manual: $33.

Counselee Materials:

Level 1 Booklet (25 per pkg) 1 – 4 $62; 5 – 19 $60.55; 20+ 57.50; Level 2 Survey Booklet and Interpretive Folders (25 per pkg) $62; 20+ $57.50; Audiocassette $17.00; CDM Career Video Series, *Tour of Your Tomorrow* $220.45

CDM-Level 1 – Career Exploration Classroom set includes CDM Level 1 Booklets (25), BCES Workbooks (25); Teacher's Guide; and *Tour of Your Tomorrow* Video Series $437.75

CDM Level 2 – Career Exploration Classroom Set includes CDM Level 2 Booklets and Interpretive Folders (25); BCES Workbooks (25); Teacher's Guide, and *Tour of Your Tomorrow* Video Series $437.75

For other updated information about material costs:

http://ags.pearsonassessments.com/group.asp?nGroupInfoID=a12633

Additional Comments of Interest to Users: New computer-related and engineering job opportunities are included, as are rapidly growing nontechnical positions. Career Clusters cover between 90% and 95% of all current U.S. jobs. Color changes, new typography, and a contemporary design make CDM easier to use. The RIASEC equivalent for the six Career Interest Areas is provided. CDM's school subject listings match today's curricular offerings. There are new sources of career information and a direct link to the Internet. An Annotated Bibliography of recently published research is now included in the CDM Manual.

The CDM Career Video Series, *Tour of Your Tomorrow,* is a six-tape series that helps students see how the CDM's interest areas relate to job clusters, college majors, and training programs. Career areas covered are Crafts (Realistic), Sciences (Investigative), The Arts (Artistic), Social (Social), Business (Enterprising), and Office Operations (Conventional). Dreams, goals, and personal passions are explored in illuminating detail as enthusiastic people engaged in real-world experiences give insider views of more than 100 careers. This series is recommended for middle school students to adults-in-transition who want to accelerate their career exploration, gain feedback about their career plans, and hear from real workers who have turned their strengths into career satisfaction.

Published Reviews:

Neubert, D. (1995). Review of the Harrington-O'Shea Career Decision-Making System Revised. In J.C. Conoley & J.C. Impara (Eds.). *Twelfth mental measurements yearbook*. Lincoln, NE: Buros Institute of Mental Measurements.

Pope, M. L. (2005). Review of the Harrington-O'Shea Career Decision-Making System Revised. In R.A. Spies & B.S. Plake (Eds.). *Sixteenth mental measurements yearbook*. Lincoln, NE: Buros Institute of Mental Measurements.

Kelly, K.R. (2005).). Review of the Harrington-O'Shea Career Decision-Making System Revised. In R.A. Spies & B.S. Plake (Eds.). *Sixteenth mental measurements yearbook*. Lincoln, NE: Buros Institute of Mental Measurements.

Shaffer, M.B. (1995). Review of the Harrington-O'Shea Career Decision-Making System Revised. In J.C. Conoley & J.C. Impara (Eds.). *Twelfth mental measurements yearbook* (p. 457). Lincoln, NE: Buros Institute of Mental Measurements.

Reviewed by[1]

Vicki L. Campbell
Associate Professor

Gretchen W. Raiff
Graduate Student

Department of Psychology
University of North Texas

Description

The 2000 revision of the Career Decision-Making System (CDM-R) is well designed to present the components of career planning. The "system surveys not only interests, but also stated career choices, school subjects, work values, abilities, and future training plans" (Harrington & O'Shea, 2000, p. 1). The interest survey is based on Holland's theory of vocational types, renamed for occupational relevance (Crafts, Scientific, The Arts, Social, Business, Office Operations). Added to the basic hexagonal structure are 18 "career clusters" that fall within the six career interest areas and provide a useful way to conceptualize job themes.

The 2000 CDM-R makes few changes from the 1991 version. Revisions center on adding emerging jobs and careers to the career clusters (e.g., in high technology),

---

[1] This review is a reprint from the fourth edition of *A Counselor's Guide to Career Assessment Instruments*. The test publisher informed the editors that the instrument is being revised. It is reprinted for readers' convenience. Check publisher's web site for updates.

improving readability, and adding a link to the Internet. Broad changes were made to the CDM in the 1991 revision, which split the test into Level 1 for younger students (7th through 10th grade) and Level 2 for senior high school students and adults. A Spanish translation of Level 1 and Level 2 has been available since 1993.

Using the CDM-R encourages users to integrate their interests, abilities, and values, and prepares them to "approach the career advisor as a professional resource person" (Harrington & O'Shea, 2000, p. 2). Level 1 is an introduction to career planning, and Level 2 helps advanced planners take steps to facilitate decisions about college majors, career training, or select an occupation. Although the order and means for collecting data vary between the two levels, both guide users to self-administer an interest survey and select their most preferred work values, abilities, school subjects, future educational plans, and possible career choices.

Interpretive materials help users examine career areas identified by the interest survey in relation to self-report information (values, abilities, etc.). Actual job titles grouped with corresponding values, school subjects, and abilities help users evaluate how well their career plans hold together. The Level 1 summary page, and the color-coded, user-friendly Level 2 Interpretive Folder offer a big-picture view of the user's top three career clusters, preferences, and corresponding career information. Job titles are labeled with abbreviations for growth outlook and education and training required. Administration time is 30 to 45 minutes but does not include time for interpretation, which will vary depending on how the materials are used. For example, the Interpretive Folder lists seven steps, and the manual describes a sample career workshop with five meetings.

Use In Counseling

The CDM-R is suitable for junior high school students through adults. Level 1 can introduce younger students to career planning, help them make appropriate school course choices, give them basic occupational information, and help them explore how their interests and values can apply to the world of work. For advanced students and adults, the Level 2 Interpretive Folder provides an opportunity to clarify job requirements and focus interests on specific careers.

The CDM-R manual offers several excellent tools to help school guidance counselors or career counselors plan a career development program. In addition to steps for individual administration, a Group Exploration Program offers a workshop format. Case examples nicely illustrate key career development concepts, such as ideas for working with individuals who demonstrate unrealistic career goals, and looking out for possible gender stereotyping.

Technical Considerations

The 2000 edition of the CDM-R relies primarily on psychometric information for the 1991 revision and the 1981 CDM that has been reviewed previously (Neubert, 1995; Shaffer, 1995; Vansickle, 1994). Most of the information addresses the interest scales, with some evaluation of the self-report sections.

The system uses interest scale raw scores that are described as domain referenced. The authors note the benefits of raw scores and make their case for the necessity of looking to "one's personal hierarchy of interests" (Harrington & O'Shea, 2000, p. 39). Nonetheless, percentile rank norms are reported for Level 1 and 2 interest scale raw scores for the 1991 standardization sample. Use of these norms will raise the issue of gender differences on the scales; however, this topic is clearly addressed in the manual.

The CDM-R interest scales are very internally consistent (median .90 Level 1; .93 Level 2). Test-retest reliability is slightly lower, and the only information for the CDM-R (Level 1) is for a group of 45 unemployed adults after one month (median .79). The stability of CDM codes and self-report information is reported, with percentages of agreement demonstrating "general consistency over the five-month interval" (Harrington & O'Shea, 2000, p. 68). The equivalence of interest scores for the CDM-R Level 1 and 2 and the CDM-R and the CDM is supported, which is important because of the reliance on CDM data. Hand-scoring errors have been reduced for the CDM-R (4% Level 1, 1% Level 2) in comparison to the CDM (6%). Other studies showed that the transparent scoring system and description of expressed interests prior to filling out the interest survey had little influence on scores.

All validity information discussed in the body of the manual uses the 1981 CDM. An annotated bibliography includes 19 additional articles, four of which use the CDM-R. Evidence for the construct, concurrent, and predictive validity of the interest scales, and to some extent, the self-report information, is provided. The intercorrelations of the interest scales (English and Spanish language) in different samples are discussed as support for the construct validity and cross-cultural validity of the instrument. The authors conclude that there is support for the cross-cultural relevance of the CDM; however, others have questioned whether the hexagonal structure proposed by Holland holds up across cultures or even among ethnic groups within the U.S. (Rounds & Tracey, 1996).

"Exploration validity" is an important concept for the CDM-R, given that the primary objectives are to help users learn about themselves and progress in career decision making. Tittle (1978) coined the term, pointing out that whether career instruments stimulate client exploration may be more important than traditional forms of validity. The CDM-R manual does little to address exploration validity with the exception of two studies included in the bibliography. These showed use of the CDM-R can result in increased vocational identity and decreased career indecision (Caligiuri, 1996, cited in Harrington & O'Shea, 2000), and increased knowledge of career decision-making (Luzzo & Taylor, 1995, cited in Harrington & O'Shea, 2000).

Computer-Based Version

Computer software is available for the CDM-R Level 2 English version. The survey items can be administered online, data can be entered directly into the program, or a scannable survey booklet can be used. A computer-based version is also available as a part of the Guidance Information System, from Riverside Publishing Company. Computer-scoring generates a report of the individual's interest scale scores, self-reports, and suggested career clusters and, for the career advisor, a breakdown of interest survey responses. A Group Summary Report summarizes career goals, interests, and school subjects as a possible aid to curriculum planners and administrators. Research has found that the computer-based CDM was slightly more reliable than the paper-and-pencil version.

Overall Critique

As a career exploration and planning system, the CDM-R offers several benefits. It provides broad exposure to career information inexpensively, the system has been carefully developed, and its psychometric characteristics compare favorably to similar instruments. The strength of the CDM lies in the attractive way it encourages exploration and career planning. The Interpretive Folder (Level 2) and overall attention to ease of use appear extremely engaging.

Another strength is the extensive, well-written CDM-R manual. It is a solid instruction to the system and a benchmark for career assessment systems seeking to educate a broad audience about career development concepts, theory, and counseling. Past critiques about scoring errors, the transparency of a self-scoring system, and problems with assessing one's own abilities are readily addressed.

The primary criticism of the CDM-R is the limited psychometric evaluation of this version and the sparse research addressing the primary purpose of career exploration. Most information uses the 1981 CDM and has not been updated, although there is support for the equivalence of the CDM-R. The authors' use of the CDM in a variety of cultures is to be applauded, but the relevance and usefulness to different cultural and socioeconomic groups need further investigation. An examination of materials suggests the CDM-R's greatest strength is encouraging exploration. However, research supporting this view is just beginning. More studies of this type would be useful to those deciding whether to select the CDM-R for a career decision-making program.

References

Harrington, T. F., & O'Shea, A. J. (2000). *The Harrington-O'Shea Career Decision-Making System-Revised Manual.* Circle Pines, MN: American Guidance Service.

Neubert, D. (1995). Review of the Harrington-O'Shea Career Decision-Making System Revised. In J. C. Conoley & J. C. Impara (Eds.), *The twelfth mental measurements yearbook* (pp. 456 – 457). Lincoln, NE: Buros Institute of Mental Measurements, University of Nebraska – Lincoln.

Rounds, J., & Tracey, T. J. (1996). Cross-cultural structural equivalence of RIASEC models and measures. *Journal of Counseling Psychology, 43,* 310 – 329.

Shaffer, M. B. (1995). Review of the Harrington-O'Shea Career Decision-Making System Revised. In J. C. Conoley & J. C. Impara (Eds.), *The twelfth mental measurements yearbook* (pp. 457). Lincoln, NE: Buros Institute, University of Nebraska – Lincoln.

Tittle C. K. (1978). Implications of recent developments for future research in career interest measurement. In C. K. Tittle & D. G. Zytowski (Eds.), *Sex-fair interest measurement: Research and implications* (pp. 123 – 128). Washington, DC: National Institute of Education.

Vansickle, T. R. (1994). Review of the Harrington-O'Shea Career Decision-Making System Revised. In J. T. Kapes, M. M. Mastie, & E. A. Whitfield (Eds.). *A counselor's guide to career assessment instruments* (3rd ed., pp. 174 – 177). Alexandria, VA: National Career Development Association.

Jackson Vocational Interest Survey (JVIS) (Second Edition)

Douglas N. Jackson

SIGMA Assessment Systems, Inc
P.O. Box 610984
Port Huron, MI 48061-0984
www.SigmaAssessmentSystems.com

Target Population: Age: 14+. Groups: schools, colleges, university counseling services, employment offices and agencies, business and industry, vocational rehabilitation, adult counseling centers.

Statement of the Purpose of the Instrument: The JVIS was developed to create an efficient hand or machine scorable vocational interest measuring device to appraise the interests of males and females along a common set of dimensions. As a technique to aid in vocational counseling and decision making, it will find its greatest utility in settings where such decisions are made. The format and scales for the JVIS were designed to combine an optimal amount of information relevant to vocational interests with ease of interpretation.

Titles of Subtests, Scales, Scores Provided:

Creative Arts, Performing Arts, Mathematics, Physical Science, Engineering, Life Science, Social Science, Adventure, Nature-Agriculture, Skilled Trades, Personal Service, Family Activity, Medical Service, Dominant Leadership, Job Security, Stamina, Accountability, Teaching, Social Service, Elementary Education, Finance, Business, Office Work, Sales, Supervision, Human Relations Management, Law, Professional Advising, Author Journalism, Academic Achievement, Technical Writing, Independence, Planfulness, Interpersonal Confidence.

Forms and Levels Available, with Dates of Publication/Revision of Each: N/A

Date of Most Recent Edition of Test Manual, User's Guide, etc.: 2000.

Languages in Which Available: English, French, and Spanish.

Time:

Actual Test Time: 45 minutes

Total Administration Time: 55 minutes

Norm Group(s) on Which Scores Are Based: The most recent normative sample of JVIS profiles was collected in 1999. These consist of the responses of 1,750 males and 1,750 females from Canada and the U.S. This sample of 3500 individuals includes the responses of 2380 secondary school students (1,190 males and 1,190 females) and 1,120 adults (560 males and 560 females). The adult sample consists of university and college students as well as adults seeking career interest assessment. The total sample of 3,500 profiles is used to generate the JVIS Extended and Basic Reports as well as the profile sheets for hand scoring.

Manner in Which Results Are Reported for Individuals:

Types of Scores: Raw Scores, Percentiles.

Report Format/Content: Extended Report: The JVIS Extended Report includes the basic interest profile, a profile for 10 general occupational themes, a profile of similarity to 17 educational major field clusters, a ranking of 32 occupational group clusters, validity scales, an academic satisfaction score and other information. A narrative summary of the three highest ranked educational and occupational clusters is particularly useful.

BASIC SERVICE: The JVIS Basic Report contains the basic interest scales profile and data similar to the Extended Report but with preprinted interpretative information rather than the personalized narrative summaries.

OPTIONS: The Basic Report is only available through mail-in scoring. The Extended Reports are available online at www.SigmaTesting.com or www.JVIS.com, as well as through mail-in scoring. Other options of administration include hand scoring and Software scoring.

Scoring:

Mail-in Scoring Service:

COST OF BASIC SERVICE PER COUNSELEE: JVIS Extended Reports: Mail-in answer sheet and laser printed report.

Item No. 1077	1 report	$15.00*
Item No. 107		
1 – 3 packages (10 reports/pkg)		$100.00*
4+ packages (10 reports/pkg)		$90.00*

JVIS Basic Reports: Mail-in answer sheet and laser printed report.

Item No. 1088	1 report	$12.00*
Item No. 108		
1 – 3 packages (10 reports/pkg)		$70.00*
4+ packages (10 reports/pkg)		$60.00*

Time required for scoring and returning: 48 hours

* Prices based on 2008 catalog.

Hand Scoring:

SCORED BY: Clerk, Counselor

TIME REQUIRED FOR SCORING: 10 minutes

Local Machine Scoring: Not available.

Computer Software Options Available: Computerized adaptive administration; standard administration online.

Ways in Which Computer/Online Version Differs: Computer software must be administered onsite, wherever the computer is located. Online scoring can be administered on any computer with Internet access.

Cost of Materials: Due to possible price changes since publication date, be sure to check with publisher website.

Specimen Set: JVIS Examination Kit.

Counselee Materials: Kit includes manual on CD, JVIS Applications Handbook, JVIS Occupations Guide, machine scorable answer sheet for Extended Report, reusable test booklet, hand scorable answer sheet, profile sheet, and JVIS.com password.

Cost: $100.00*

Additional Comments of Interest to Users: Marc Verhoeve, author of the JVIS Applications Handbook, offers a free, 90-minute teletraining session discussing the best practices in counseling and how to get the most out of the JVIS. Upcoming dates are listed on the company's website.

Published Reviews of the Instrument in the Last 15 Years: None cited.

Reviewed by:[1]

Eleanor E. Sanford-Moore
Vice-president for Research and Development
MetaMetrics, Inc.
Durham, North Carolina

Description

The *Jackson Vocational Interest Survey* (JVIS) was developed by Douglas Jackson as a means to describe the vocational interests of males and females across a common set of dimensions during career exploration and planning. The research for the JVIS began in 1969. The second edition (Jackson, 1999) of the JVIS is a result of (1) renorming the instrument, (2) conducting additional studies with the instrument (reliability, validity, and other areas of research), and (3) revising and updating reports and interpretative materials. The JVIS booklet consists of 289 pairs of statements describing occupational activities that are used to represent interests (work roles) and preferences (work styles) relevant to work.

Regardless of ability, the respondent is asked to determine which of the two statements he or she prefers.

The JVIS reports the following scores: 34 Basic Interest Scales that examine work roles and work styles, 10 Occupational Themes, Academic Satisfaction Scale, similarity to 17 clusters of educational majors, similarity to 32 job groups, and three administrative indices (number of unscorable responses, Response Consistency Index, and the Infrequency Index). Once converted to percentiles, the scores are used to develop a profile of the respondent's vocational interests and preferences.

---

[1] Portions of this review are adapted, by permission, from the author's original review in the Fifteenth Mental Measurements Yearbook

The JVIS can be administered either individually or in a group setting by paper and pencil, on the computer (using the *SigmaSoft JVIS for Windows* computer software), and over the Internet. The JVIS will take the respondent about 45 – 60 minutes to complete, and it may be scored by hand or by computer.

Use in Counseling

Marc Verhoeve (2000) describes a job as just one aspect of an individual's career, albeit a central aspect. The JVIS can be used to interpret career transition points that range from career starters (adolescents completing high school) to career transitioners (adults considering job changes, promotions, job loss, or retirement) to blended-career pathers (dual professional spouses) to team management in the work place.

Before interpreting the JVIS profile, the results from the three administrative indices should be examined to determine the validity of the situation and examine the respondent's test-taking behavior. The respondent's profile can be interpreted in relation to combined norms or gender-specific norms. The manual suggests that gender-specific norms are more appropriate for some scales (e.g., Engineering, Elementary Education) because the use of separate norms can encourage the diminishment of traditional occupational roles.

The assessment manual provides extensive information and case studies to help counselors and other test administrators interpret the results of the JVIS. There is a section that describes recurring counseling problems and situations with suggestions and solutions: a flat JVIS Basic Interest profile, measured interests that are discrepant with career plans, abilities and interests appear to conflict, low reliability index for an individual machine-scored profile, Basic Interest Scales appear to conflict with Similarity to Job Groups, and the client is considering an occupation which appears unrelated to any of the 32 job groups. In addition, the *JVIS Applications Handbook* (Verhoeve, 2000) provides extensive case studies that can be used during training.

The *JVIS Applications Handbook,* (Verhoeve, 2000) presents a methodology to interpret the results of the JVIS based on over 20 years of interpretation and analysis of profiles and the tracking of career paths of these individuals. Verhoeve (2000) presents the Career Constellation Model to work with clients to "explain the stress of career transition, and for dramatically improving the power of the Jackson Vocational Interest Survey as a computerized career snapshot" (p. 11). This model consists of eight dimensions that describe a person's career: education, fitness, religion, personal space, community activities, hobbies, family, and job (at the center). This model can be used during the interpretation of JVIS profiles to help the client understand how the various aspects of his or her life impact career choices.

To help clients better understand the General Occupational Themes, Verhoeve presents a more dynamic method—the Career Ergonomic Decagon. This model portrays the relationship of the individual with the environment by examining the personality fit between the person and the job environment. Verhoeve has found that this model facilities more discussion with the client about the whole person and shows how the General Occupational Themes are interrelated. This model also works very well in spousal and team-management situations where the individuals can see how the skills of the various people can complement each other.

Technical Considerations

Development. The JVIS has undergone an extensive development process. The conceptual foundation of the JVIS is related to the work of David Campbell (Campbell, Borgen, Eastes, Johansson, & Peterson, 1968 and Campbell, 1971) with the Strong Vocational Interest Blank (SVIB). The SVIB examined the relationship of vocational interests to specific occupations. Jackson departed from this way of thinking to instead relate vocational interests to work roles and work styles (occupational clusters). Thus, the focus of the results is more for career exploration and planning (examining many occupations), rather than seeing how well an individual's interests match a specific occupation. Jackson began by identifying a large set of work roles and work styles and then selecting dimensions within these work roles and work styles to measure.

Initially more than 3,000 statements were developed and administered in multiple forms to 2,203 respondents. The results were examined by first suppressing response bias resulting from the initial item format (the respondent was asked to indicate whether he or she "liked" or "disliked" the activity in the statement). The residual score matrix was then factor analyzed to identify statements that were related to each of the Basic Interest Scale dimensions. Based on these results, the final items were selected for each scale such that the relationship of the item to other items on the scale was maximized and the relationship of the item to other scales for which it was not related was minimized.

The JVIS was renormed in 1999 with 3,500 secondary school students and adults. The sample was equally split between males and females. Raw score means and standard deviations and percentiles are provided for each scale for males, females, secondary students, adults, and the combined sample.

Reliability. In the JVIS manual, test-retest and coefficient alpha correlation coefficients are presented for the Basic Interest scales (generally in the mid .70s to low .80s) and for the General Occupational Themes (generally in the mid to upper .80s).

Validity. The internal structure of the JVIS is examined by correlating the scales. Generally, the scales are independent for samples of females and males (N = 1,250 in each sample) with the mean interscale correlation coefficient of .28 for males and .24 for females. In another study, a factor analysis was conducted with 1,163 male and 1,292 female high school students. Two conclusions were drawn from the results of the factor analysis: (1) there are characteristic patterns of JVIS scores and the counselor can expect to see these patterns, and (2) the emergence of the patterns permitted the development of the 10 Occupational Themes for reporting results. Also, the manual contains studies showing how the JVIS can be used in other areas of research: relationship to academic major, genetic and environmental influences on career interests, choice of academic college, classification of occupational groups, structure of interests, and the career assessment of groups of individuals (individuals with disabilities, women, minorities, and different age groups).

Computer-Based and/or Online Versions

If the JVIS is scored by computer, the report contains a comparison of the individual's profile with various educational groups and occupational clusters. The JVIS website (www.jvis.com) contains information and links for students, parents, school counselors, and career changers. Information is provided about the assessment and basic interpretive frameworks (with suggestions to discuss the results with a career counselor). The information comes in various forms including a Career Exploration Guide, a University Exploration Guide, and a career links section. Each section contains practical information, case studies, and links to numerous websites with specific information.

Overall Critique

The JVIS takes a different approach to the assessment of vocational interests by examining the relationship of interests and preferences to occupational clusters. By focusing on occupational clusters rather than specific occupations, respondents are more likely to explore careers that they may not have considered previously. The respondent can then take into consideration other information related to career choice: the availability of opportunities, interest in higher education or training, individual abilities and interpersonal skills, and individual values in relation to work satisfactions. The JVIS is a well-developed test for examining occupational interests for career planning and has adequate validity and reliability for this use. The JVIS website provides information that can be tailored to the informational needs of each examinee.

References

Campbell, D. P. (1971). *Handbook for the Strong Vocational Interest Blank.* Stanford, CA: Stanford University Press.

Campbell, D. P., Borgen, F. H., Eastes, S. H., Johansson, C. B., & Peterson, R. A. (1968). A set of basic interest scales for the Strong Vocational Interest Blank for men. *Journal of Applied Psychology* (Monograph), *52(6).*

Jackson, D. N. (1999). *Jackson Vocational Interest Survey (JVIS) manual.* Port Huron, MI: SIGMA Assessment Systems, Inc.

Sanford, E.E. (2003). Review of the Jackson Vocational Interest Inventory (1999 Revision). In B.S. Plake, J.C. Impara, & R.A. Spies, *The fifteenth mental measurements yearbook.* Lincoln, NE: Buros Institute of Mental Measurements.

Verhoeve, M.A. (2000). *JVIS Applications Handbook.* London, ON: Research Psychologists Press Division, SIGMA Assessment Systems, Inc.

O*NET® INTEREST PROFILER™ (IP)

United States Department of Labor, Employment and Training Administration

Employment & Training Administration
USDOL, FPB S4231
200 Constitution Avenue, NW
Washington, DC 20210
o-net@dol.gov
www.doleta.gov/programs/onet
www.onetcenter.org

Target Population: Individuals seeking to identify their work related interests and use them to explore careers, high school and postsecondary students as well as adults. Should be 14 years and older with a minimum of a sixth-grade reading level.

Statement of the Purpose of the Instrument: The O*NET Interest Profiler was developed as a self-assessment instrument as part of a whole person assessment approach. The instrument was designed to help individuals identify their work-related interests and use them to explore the world of work. The instrument is appropriate for a variety of users including students, first-time job seekers, and those individuals in occupational transition. In addition to receiving scores that identify their most salient work-related interests, users receive a list of occupations based on their results. Users can further explore these occupations in the U.S. Department of Labor's Occupational Information Network (O*NET) system at http://online.onetcenter.org, the nation's leading source of occupational information.

Titles of Subtests, Scales, Scores Provided: Interest results are provided in a format compatible with Holland's R-I-A-S-E-C constructs; Realistic, Investigative, Artistic, Social, Enterprising, and Conventional. A numerical raw score is provided for each interest area.

Forms and Levels Available, with Dates of Publication/Revision of Each: Version 3.0 is available. Released in 2001.

Date of Most Recent Edition of Test Manual, User's Guide, etc.: O*NET Interest Profiler User's Guide, designed for workforce development professionals. Released in 2001.

Languages in Which Available: English only.

Time:

Actual Test Time: 15 – 30 Minutes (Assessment is not timed)

Total Administration Time: Designed for Self-administration, 15 – 30 minutes.

Norm Group(s) on Which Scores Are Based: Not norm referenced; however, tryout and validity/reliability information was collected from more than 2,000 subjects from across the country. Participants included high school students, college students, workers in transition, and employed and unemployed workers. Additionally, during the tryout of the O*NET Interest Profiler, the Interest Finder, a well-established interest measure, was also administered to compare the psychometric characteristics of the instruments.

Manner in Which Results Are Reported for Individuals:

Types of Scores: Raw numerical scores associated with each interest area label: Realistic, Investigative, Artistic, Social, Enterprising, and Conventional.

Report Format/Content:

BASIC SERVICE: Clients receive a 24-page preprinted score report. Clients transfer their six numerical interest scores from the instrument to the first page of the score report. The score report walks the client through several phases that enables the client to use their primary and/or secondary interest score to explore careers: (1) The score reports defines the interest areas for the client. (2) The client selects a job zone (level of education, training, and work experience they have now our wish to pursue) which they will use to help select occupations to explore. (3) Six steps are presented that enables the client to use their top interest areas and job zone to select occupations to explore. (4) If the client is not satisfied with their results, alternatives are presented to help the client continue his/her career exploration. (5) Lists of occupations sorted by interest area and job zone are presented. Clients can explore occupations in these lists by going to the U.S. Department of Labor's O*NET system at http://online.onetcenter.org, the nation's leading source of occupational information. Additionally, clients are directed towards expanded lists of occupations to explore.

Report Format/Content for Group Summaries: Not available.

Scoring:

Machine Scoring Service: Not available. Instrument can be self-scored.

Hand Scoring:

SCORED BY: Counselee

Time required for scoring: *Less than five minute*s— Counselee counts number of "Ls" (work activities they would like to perform) marked for each of the six interest areas measured (R, I, A, S, E, C). Counselee records each of the six scores on the instrument.

Local Machine Scoring: Not available.

Computer Software Options Available: standard administration online.

Other: A computerized version of the instrument, the O*NET Computerized Interest Profiler (CIP) is available for download, free of charge. The CIP can be downloaded to individual computers or network systems from www.onetcenter.org/CIP.html. The items presented in the CIP are the same as those presented in the paper and pencil O*NET Interest Profiler. The CIP scores the instrument for the client, and uses all six RIASEC scores the client received and the job zone the client selected to identify occupations to explore.

Ways in Which Computer/Online Version Differs: See above.

Cost of Materials: Print shop files of all materials can be downloaded free of charge at www.onetcenter.org/IP.html

Specimen Set: O*NET Interest Profiler, O*NET Interest Profiler Score Report, O*NET Interest Profiler User's Guide.

All materials are available for free download at www.onetcenter.org/IP.html. An O*NET Interest Profiler Demo also is available for free download.

Counselee Materials:
O*NET Interest Profiler
O*NET Interests Profiler Score Report
O*NET Occupations Master List (expanded list of occupations to explore)
O*NET Occupations Combined List: Interests and Work Values (Counselees can use their O*NET Interest Profiler Results and their O*NET Work Importance Locator Results in combination to identify occupations to explore)

Additional Comments of Interest to Users: All materials including instruments, score reports, user guides, development and technical reports are available for free download at www.onetcenter.org/IP.html . Additionally, customer service is available at onet@ncmail.net.

Published Reviews of the Instrument in the Last 15 Years:

Eggerth, D. E., Bowles, S. M., and Andrew, M. E. (2005). Convergent validity of O*NET Holland code classifications. *Journal of Career Assessment, 13,* 150 – 168.

Pope, M. (2005). Review of the O*NET Career Interests Inventory: Based on the 'O*NET Interest Profiler' developed by the U.S. Department of Labor. In R.A. Spies, & B.S. Plake, (Eds.), *The sixteenth mental measurements yearbook.* Lincoln, NE: The Buros Institute of Mental Measurements.

COMPUTERIZED O*NET® INTEREST PROFILER™ (CIP)

United States Department of Labor, Employment and Training Administration

Employment & Training Administration
USDOL, FPB S4231
200 Constitution Avenue, NW
Washington, DC 20210
o-net@dol.gov
www.doleta.gov/programs/onet
www.onetcenter.org

Target Population: Individuals seeking to identify their work related interests and use them to explore careers, high school and postsecondary students as well as adults. Should be 14 years and older with a minimum of a sixth-grade English reading level.

Statement of the Purpose of the Instrument: The Computerized O*NET Interest Profiler (CIP) was developed as a self-assessment instrument as part of a whole person assessment approach. The instrument was designed to enable users to identify their six score profiles of work-related interests and use their entire interest profile to identify occupations to explore in the world of work. The instrument is self-scoring, and presents multiple options for linking results to occupations for career exploration. The instrument is appropriate for a variety of users, including students, first-time job seekers, and those individuals in occupational transition. In addition to receiving their interest profile of work-related interests, users can identify their most salient work-related interests. They also receive lists of occupations to explore which match their interest profile and the level of education, training, and work experience they currently have or wish to pursue. Users can further explore selected occupations in the U. S. Department of Labor's Occupational Information Network (O*NET) system at http://online.onetcenter.org, the nation's primary source of occupational information.

Titles of Subtests, Scales, Scores Provided: Interest results are provided in a format compatible with Holland's R-I-A-S-E-C constructs: Realistic, Investigative, Artistic; Social, Enterprising, and Conventional. A numerical raw score is provided for each interest area.

Forms and Levels Available, with Dates of Publication/Revision of Each: Version 3.0 is available. Released in 2001.

Date of Most Recent Edition of Test Manual, User's Guide, etc.: O*NET Computerized Interest Profiler User's Guide, designed for workforce development professionals. Released in 2001.

Languages in Which Available: English only.

Time:

Actual Test Time: 15 – 30 Minutes (Assessment is not timed)

Total Administration Time: Designed for Self-administration

Norm Group(s) on Which Scores Are Based: Not norm referenced, however, tryout and validity/reliability information was collected from more than 500 subjects from across the country. Participants included high school students, college students, workers in transition and employed and unemployed workers. During the administration of the O*NET Computerized Interest Profiler, the O*NET Interest Profiler was also administered for comparison purposes.

Manner in Which Results Are Reported for Individuals:

Types of Scores: Raw numerical scores associated with interest area label. Six numerical scores are provided, one for each interest area. Users can print out their interest profile, consisting of six individual scores, as well as definitions for each interest area.

Report Format/Content:

BASIC SERVICE: Counselee results are presented on several screens in the O*NET

CIP. In addition to viewing their results, counselees can print out their six score interest profiles, definitions of the six individual interest areas, and the definitions of the job zone (level of education, training, and work experience they have or wish to pursue) they selected to use to help select occupations to explore. Counselees can also print out the list of occupations that best match their interest profile and job zone. These occupations can be found in the U.S. Department of Labor's O*NET system, the nation's leading source of occupational information. Counselees have several other options within the CIP in identifying occupations to explore. They have the flexibility of identifying and printing occupations based on a single interest area and a selected job zone. Whether they are using their entire interest profile or a single interest area, counselee may also select a different job zone to identify a new set of occupations to explore.

The client is presented with several screens that explain the next steps in career exploration. Additionally, screens are presented that describe alternative options if the counselee is not happy with their results. The client can print out all of these screens.

Report Format/Content for Group Summaries: Not available.

Scoring:

Machine Scoring Service: Not available. Instrument is self-scoring.

TIME REQUIRED FOR SCORING AND RETURNING: Less than two minutes.

Hand Scoring: Not available.

Local Machine Scoring: Not available.

Computer Software Options Available: Not available.

Cost of Materials: Instrument and supporting materials are available free of charge at www.onetcenter.org/CIP.html.

Specimen Set: All materials (instrument, demonstration version of the instrument, user's guide designed for counselors, technical development reports) are available for download free of charge at www.onetcenter.org/CIP.html

Counselee Materials: O*NET Computerized Work Importance Profiler

Additional Comments of Interest to Users: All materials including instruments, score reports, user guides and development and technical reports are available for free download at www.onetcenter.org/CIP.html. Additionally, customer service is available through onet@ncmail.net.

Published Reviews of the Instrument in the Last 15 Years:

Eggerth, D. E., Bowles, S. M., and Andrew, M. E. (2005). Convergent validity of O*NET Holland code classifications. *Journal of Career Assessment, 13,* 150 – 168.

Pope, M. (2005). Review of the O*NET Career Interests Inventory: Based on the 'O*NET Interest Profiler' developed by the U.S. Department of Labor. In R.A. Spies, & B. S. Plake (Eds.), *The sixteenth mental measurements yearbook.* Lincoln, NE: The Buros Institute of Mental Measurements.

Reviewed by:[1]

Mark Pope
Professor and Chair
Division of Counseling and Family Therapy
University of Missouri – Saint Louis

Description

The O*NET Interest Profiler (OIP), Version 3.0, is a new vocational interest assessment instrument that helps individuals identify their work-related interests (National Center for O*NET Development, 2000). It is one of five instruments that are part of the U.S. Department of Labor's O*NET Career Exploration Tools (OIP, O*NET Computerized Interest Profiler (OCIP), O*NET Work Importance Profiler, O*NET Work Importance Locator, O*NET Ability Profiler). They are further identified as "a group of career counseling tools" (p. 1).

A reformatted commercial version of the OIP, Version 3.0 (O*NET Career Interest Inventory), is also available through JistWorks and has been reviewed previously (Pope, 2005). The OCIP is the computer version of the OIP paper and pencil version.

This review focuses on the OIP and OCIP only. Almost all statements are applicable to both instruments, except in the special section in this review on "Computer-based and/or Online Versions."

Use in Counseling

There were four primary goals in the development of the OIP/OCIP: (1) develop an instrument that has strong technical characteristics that provides clients with accurate and useful information, (2) develop an unbiased instrument that can serve the needs of clients from a variety of ethnic, cultural, and socioeconomic backgrounds, (3) develop an instrument that includes items representing the entire world of work to insure that it would provide useful information to individuals with different work-related goals and interests, and (4) develop an instrument that can be used as a self-assessment tool that individuals can self-administer, self-score, and self-interpret to empower clients to take control of their career exploration efforts.

In the User's Guide, the authors state explicitly that the "O*NET Interest Profiler results should be used for career exploration and vocational counseling purposes only .... (These) results should not be used for employment or hiring decisions ... (as) the relationship between results ... and success in particular jobs or training programs has not been determined" (p. 3).

The OIP Instrument is a 12½-page consumable question booklet that can be self-scored, self-administered, and self-interpreted. It was designed for clients who are 14 years of age or older and have a minimum of a sixth-grade reading level. It takes 20 – 60 minutes to complete and it is recommended that clients complete the OIP in one

---

[1] Portions of this review are adapted, by permission, from the author's original review in the Sixteenth Mental Measurements Yearbook

session. It is expected that three-quarters of that time will be spent taking the instrument with one-quarter on scoring. After that time (and potentially at a different session), more time is needed for reading and using the OIP Score Report which "helps clients interpret their results and explore occupations presented in O*NET Online" (p. 7).

The OIP instrument is divided into four functional sections: getting started, how to complete the interest profiler, items, and here's how to score your interest profiler, along with a full page devoted to the "user's agreement." In using a four-step process rather than simply a conventional inventory format, it is similar to the Self-Directed Search (Holland, 2003) and other self-scored career interest inventories.

The items consist of 180 statements regarding work activities (e.g. "buy and sell stocks and bonds). The response format requires the client to darken one of three check boxes placed vertically in the larger box containing the statement. Those check boxes contain an "L", "D", or "?" — "L" if the person would like that work activity, "D" if the person would dislike it, and "?" if the person is unsure.

In the "here's how to score your interest profiler" section, the client is given explicit instructions on how to score the responses along with a scoring example and a scoring grid, all color-coded. The client is also warned that "(i)t is important to make sure you count the number of LIKES correctly. Double-check your totals." The result of this process is a frequency distribution of like responses categorized by the six RIASEC interest areas.

The explicitness of the instructions and their focus on the requisite response set of the individual who is taking the instrument will go a long way to ensure that responses are accurate. This special control for response set is a strength of the instrument and enhances accuracy. Further, the items have a currency to them (e.g. "develop a spread sheet using computer software), and are easily understood.

Scores are then reported on the OIP Score Report (v. 3.0), a 30-page consumable interpretive report form that guides the client through a process to understand the results from the OIP instrument. The OIP Score Report addresses recording the results from the individual's OIP (into the six RIASEC interest areas). Using an ipsative methodology, interest areas are then rank ordered for use in this interpretative step. Information is also provided for each of the six interest areas as well as each of the five "job zones" (i.e., these job zones are U.S. Department of Labor categories based on ordered levels of training, education, and experience) where "1" corresponds to "little or no preparation needed" to "5" described as "extensive preparation needed."

The Score Report also addresses "exploring your career using interests and job zone" information, along with a section on what to do if you are "not really sure you agree with your results," a page to record occupations that match the interest areas and job zones of the client, and a 12-page list of some occupations categorized by the six interest areas by the five job zones (with the majority of categories containing 15 – 20 occupations and with instructions to refer to the "O*NET Occupations Master List" for the remaining categorized occupations).

The O*NET Occupations Master List (v. 3.0) is a 20-page booklet containing a list of occupations categorized by the six RIASEC interest areas by the five job zones. All of the occupations included in the O*NET Standard Occupational Classification are included on this list except for 74 of the total 812 where data were not available.

Another important part of the OIP Tools is the O*NET Occupations Combined List: Interests and Work Values (v. 3.0, 2000). This 60-page booklet consists of a list of all occupations (categorized by the six RIASEC interest areas by the five job zones) included in the O*NET Occupations Master List (v. 3.0) above along with a categorization by work values from the Work Importance Locater (another instrument in the O*NET collection). This is a very useful document for career counselors and their clients; however, several of the job zones in each interest area do not contain any occupations, for example, job zone 1—enterprising (interest area) —independence (work value). This may have substantial face validity and be intuitively obvious that a lower level job would have little independence, but it is an issue for users of these instruments.

The OIP User's Guide, (National Center for O*NET Development, 2000, v. 3.0) is a 60-page booklet that was developed for the paper- and-pencil version of the OIP to assist user's of the instrument to administer, interpret, and understand the development of the instrument. The OIP User's Guide is divided into those three chapters and further subdivided many times using a question format for ease of use. For example, the "Self-Administration" subsection is organized around sub-subsections (even listed in the table of contents) such as: "What age levels was the O*NET Interest Profiler designed for?" The User's Guide is designed for the career counselor or other professional who is administering and interpreting this instrument to others. This type of format is very user-friendly as it is simple, well-organized, and direct, yet comprehensive.

Technical Considerations

In the OIP User's Guide, there is a lengthy explanation of the development of the OIP. That explanation leaves a knowledgeable reader feeling quite secure about the initial rationally derived item and scale development as well as the research used to validate the completed item selection and scale development. The development chapter is especially simple and well organized. This is not always the case with such instruments.

In the OIP User's Guide, the authors addressed the issues of bias in the instrument in a straightforward way and provide evidence of reducing bias at each step in the development of the instrument. One of the primary goals in the development of the OIP was to "develop an unbiased instrument that would serve the needs of clients from a variety of ethnic, cultural, and socioeconomic backgrounds" (National Center for O*NET Development, 2000, p. 31). The U.S. Department of Labor developers made a substantive effort to meet this goal by first training item writers and item reviewers to write items that would "reduce spurious gender and race/ethnic endorsement rate differences" (p. 34). In the first pilot study, items with large gender differences or large race/ethnic differences were removed. Next, the remaining items underwent a seven-step screening process that included the elimination of items that would be offensive to particular segments of the user population. A panel representing diverse ethnic and racial groups reviewed each item for possible bias against or offensiveness to racial, ethnic, or gender groups. Next, the pool of remaining items was piloted using a large representative sample that included approximately equal numbers of males and females, a high degree of ethnic diversity, a broad distribution of age groups, and represented a variety of education and employment situations. Also, there were other procedures that were employed to reduce bias.

An important issue for any consumer of these materials is the stability of vocational interests over time because, if interests change substantially, it would limit the application of the scores received on any career interest measure. In the User's Guide, the authors address such issues including the research supporting the reliability and validity of the OIP. In a section titled "Phase 6: Evaluation of Reliability, Validity, and Self-Scoring," a summary of these data is presented.

On page 4 of the User's Guide, the authors state that "(c)lients receive an accurate, reliable profile of their vocational interests ...." This is a very strong statement. Even with the substantial amount of reliability and validity data that are presented, a better statement that there is strong "evidence" of reliability and validity would be more appropriate and more accurate. This recommended format is already used in other sections of the User's Guide, just not this one place.

In the User's Guide, internal consistency data are reported in text for the Interest Area scales ranging from .93 to .96, but the only data reported by individual scale in a table indicate the range of alphas is .95 to .97. In Rounds, Walker et al. (1999) this is clarified when the authors state that the first range is for "coefficient" alphas, while the second range is for "Cronbach" alphas. The table makes no distinction, and user's should not have to search for this information.

The User's Guide also reports that the correlation to the RIASEC scales suggests a problematic Enterprising scale, since it correlates too closely to the Artistic scale, likely due to the instrument's inclusion of many low-level jobs that were not in Holland's original RIASEC model. The authors explain that it may be a result of adding items to address lower level "job zone" occupations that "are not consistently perceived as Enterprising activities by assessment takers" (p. 43).

Further, the authors have been forthright in addressing reliability and validity issues. For example, in the "psychometric characteristics" section (p. 39), the authors directly address discrepancies between the OIP and the instrument used to provide evidence of validity of the OIP, the Interest-Finder, part of a previous ASVAB Career Exploration Program. There is also a substantive "gender and race/ethnic bias" section that identifies important issues when the OIP is used with women and with African-Americans.

Nowhere in the OIP User's Guide was there an explanation of how occupations were categorized into RIASEC classes. Only in Rounds, Smith et al. (1999a) was this addressed and, although this study was available on the O*NET website, it also should be addressed in the User's Guide as part of the development of the OIP.

In too many places in the User's Guide, statements are made without providing the detailed evidence upon which the statement is based. Instead readers are left to ferret out that evidence in the volumes of data that are available on the website (McCloy,

Campbell, Oswald, Lewis, & Rivkin, 1999; Oswald, Campbell, McCloy, Rivkin, & Lewis, 1999; Rounds, Mazzeo, et al., 1999; Rounds, Smith, Hubert, Lewis, & Rivkin, 1999b, 1999c; Rounds, Walker, et al., 1999). Two examples illustrate this issue.

In the OIP self-scorable format (as with any self-scorable format with large numbers of items), there remains substantial room for error as large numbers of items increase simple counting errors. The OIP User's Guide, however, directly addressed this issue and stated that "an examination of client's ability to self-score the instrument revealed a low percentage of scoring errors and, more importantly, a minimal presence of individuals identifying the wrong top interest due to scoring errors" (p. 42). The User's Guide did not, however, provide any specific data on error rates associated with the instrument; these data were found in Rounds, Walker et al. (1999).

Test-retest reliability values are reported to range from .81 to .92 for a "short period of time." No specific time frames were reported in the User's Guide, but Rounds, Walker et al. (1999) reported that there was approximately one month between administrations.

Computer-Based and/or Online Versions

The OCIP is the computer-based version of the OIP and was developed to include all of the items and many of the instructions from the original OIP. A 75-page OCIP User's Guide is available which details the development, administration, and use of the OCIP. It also retains many of the previously cited instructions and sections which are quite helpful to users (e.g., a section on what to do if you are "not really sure you agree with your results).

There is no web-based version of the OIP, but the OCIP is available for download at http://www.onetcenter.org/tools.html. The downloaded file is, however, only available in Windows format (.exe) and will not run on a Mac. The installation process is fully automated with no difficult technical decisions required.

All instructions to the test taker are bold and clear, fully using the graphics capabilities of the computer in an extremely user-friendly and ergonomic way. Decision screens are simple and clear. For example, at the query "Is this your first time taking the Interest Profiler?", you can get detailed instructions (with the "yes" response) or you can retake or start where you left off (with the "no" response).

Taking the OCIP and changing responses to items is easy and always allowed up to the very last item, where a one-page summary page of your responses in RIASEC format along with a 2 – 4 sentence summary of each of the six RIASEC categories is provided.

The OCIP is more than simply an interest assessment system. After taking the interest profile and generating the RIASEC report, users are taken to a section that allows them to integrate their inventories interest scores with stated job zones (described in "Use in Counseling" section of this review) and generate a list of occupations that match their responses in a four-page report.

The OCIP has a very well-designed computer-human interface that provides valuable information in an easily understandable and accessible format.

Overall Critique

The OIP/OCIP have substantial reasons to recommend their use with junior high and high school students and with adults as part of a comprehensive career assessment program. They are no to low cost instruments that are up-to-date and supported by substantial research providing good evidence of validity and reliability. The OIP User's Guide is a substantial, accessible, and moderately comprehensive interpretive guide and technical manual; however, it needs additional development detail. Such details are included in various research reports on the website, but it is difficult to find all of the development research when it is spread all over the website in separate electronic files. It is important to give the users the data in one place, not just a summary or an interpretation of that data, and let them make the decisions if the evidence is sufficient. That is what a user's guide is for.

It is hoped that the reliability and validity research with this instrument continues and grows. The evidence of validity is tied to one instrument (the Interest-Finder, formerly part of the ASVAB Career Exploration Program),[2] which had some well documented problems of its own (Rogers, 2001). Further, test-retest reliability research needs to be conducted over longer periods of time to provide additional evidence of such reliability, especially six month, one year, two year, and even longer follow-up studies. One month is insufficient evidence of this type of reliability.

The OIP is also more likely to be a better measure of career interests since it does not include items that are self-estimates of competencies, such as are included in the Self-Directed Search. Although items that are self-estimates of competencies can be useful as measures of confidence in the use of certain skills, they are suspect as interest measures.

It is recommended that a Mac version of the OCIP be developed as it is only available in Windows format (.exe). This is problematic for use in many secondary schools where Apple computers are a mainstay.

Finally, it is also hoped that the program does not fall out of favor with federal lawmakers and lose it's funding because the OIP and really all of the O*NET Career Assessment Tools are an important contribution to the workforce development of our nation.

References

Holland, J. (2003). Self-Directed Search. Odessa, FL: Psychological Assessment Resources.

Lewis, P., & Rivkin, D. (1999) Development of the O*NET Interest Profiler. Raleigh, NC: National Center for O*NET Development.

McCloy, R., Campbell, J., Oswald, F. L., Lewis, P., & Rivkin, D. (1999). Linking client assessment profiles to O*NET occupational profiles. Raleigh, NC: National Center for O*NET Development.

---

[2] Editors' note: The current ASVAB CEP is reviewed in Chapter 8 of this book. A new, 90-item interest inventory, Find Your Interest (FYI) for the ASVAB CEP, was developed and implemented a few years ago.

National Center for O*NET Development. (2000). *O*NET Interest Profiler user's guide*. Raleigh, NC: Author.

Oswald, F., Campbell, J., McCloy, R., Rivkin, D., & Lewis, P. (1999). *Stratifying occupational units by specific vocational preparation*. Raleigh, NC: National Center for O*NET Development.

Pope, M. (2005). Review of the O*NET Career Interest Inventory. In R.A. Spies, & B.S. Plake (Eds.), *The sixteenth mental measurements yearbook*. Lincoln, NE: The Buros Institute of Mental Measurements. (Also published in *Test Reviews Online* at www.unl.edu/buros.)

Rogers, J. E. (2001). Review of the Armed Services Vocational Aptitude Battery Career Exploration Program. In J.T. Kapes & E.A. Whitfield (Eds), *A counselor's guide to career assessment instruments* (4th ed.) (pp. 93 – 101). Columbus, OH: National Career Development Association.

Rounds, J., Mazzeo, S. E., Smith, T. J., Hubert, L., Lewis, P., & Rivkin, D. (1999) *O*NET Computerized Interest Profiler: Reliability, validity, and comparability*. Raleigh, NC: National Center for O*NET Development.

Rounds, J., Smith, T., Hubert, L., Lewis, P., & Rivkin, D. (1999a). *Development of occupational interest profiles for O*NET*. Raleigh, NC: National Center for O*NET Development.

Rounds, J., Smith, T., Hubert, L., Lewis, P., & Rivkin, D. (1999b). *Development of the occupational interest profiles for O*NET (Volume I: Report)*. Raleigh, NC: National Center for O*NET Development.

Rounds, J., Smith, T., Hubert, L., Lewis, P., & Rivkin, D. (1999c). *Development of the occupational interest profiles for O*NET (Volume II: Appendices)*. Raleigh, NC: National Center for O*NET Development.

Rounds, J., Walker, C. M., Day, S. X., Hubert, L., Lewis, P., & Rivkin, D. (1999). *O*NET Interest Profiler: Reliability, validity, and self-scoring*. Raleigh, NC: National Center for O*NET Development.

Wall, J. E., & Baker, H. E. (1997). The Interest-Finder: Evidence of validity. *Journal of Career Assessment, 5*, 255 – 273.

O*NET® Work Importance Locator™ (WIL)

United States Department of Labor, Employment and Training Administration

Employment & Training Administration
USDOL, FPB S4231
200 Constitution Avenue, NW
Washington, DC 20210
o-net@dol.gov
www.doleta.gov/programs/onet
www.onetcenter.org

Target Population: Individuals seeking to identify their work values and use them to explore careers; high school and postsecondary students as well as adults. Should be 16 years and older with a minimum of a sixth-grade reading level.

Statement of the Purpose of the Instrument: The O*NET Work Importance Locator (WIL) was developed as a self-assessment instrument as part of a whole person assessment approach. This work values assessment was designed to help individuals identify aspects or conditions of work that are important to them in a job or career. Counselees use a simple card-sorting format to rank order the importance of 20 cards, each describing an aspect of work that satisfies one of six broad work values. Based on the theory of work adjustment by Dawis & Lofquist, (1984), the WIL helps clients accurately identify their highest work values from a group of six: Achievement, Independence, Recognition, Relationships; Support, and Working Conditions. Counselees can use their work values to help improve their self-awareness and identify important aspects of work that they want to find in a career. Counselees can link their results directly to the world of work through the U.S. Department of Labor's Occupational Information Network (O*NET) system at http://online.onetcenter.org, the nation's primary source of occupational information. The instrument is appropriate for high school and postsecondary students, adults new to the work force, and workers in career transition.

Titles of Subtests, Scales, Scores Provided: Work Values are reported as: Achievement, Independence, Recognition, Relationships, Support, and Working Conditions.

Forms and Levels Available, with Dates of Publication/Revision of Each: Version 3.0 is available, released in 2001.

Date of Most Recent Edition of Test Manual, User's Guide, etc.: O*NET Work Importance User's Guide designed for workforce development professionals, released in 2001.

Languages in Which Available: English only.

Time:

Actual Test Time: 15 – 30 Minutes (Assessment is not timed)

Total Administration Time: Designed for self-administration.

Norm Group(s) on Which Scores Are Based: Not norm referenced. Extensive tryouts and evaluations conducted. See User's Guide, development and technical reports at www.onetcenter.org for more information.

Manner in Which Results Are Reported for Individuals:

Types of Scores: Raw numerical scores associated with each work value label. Six numerical scores are provided, one for each work value area.

Report Format/Content:

BASIC SERVICE: Clients receive a 24-page preprinted score report. Clients transfer their top two (highest scoring) work values from the WIL to the score report. The score report walks the client through several phases that enable the client to use their top two work values to explore careers: (1) The score report defines the work values for the client. (2) the client selects a job zone—level of education, training, and work experience they have now our wish to pursue—which they will use to help select occupations to explore. (3) Six steps are presented that enable the client to use their top work values and job zone to select occupations to explore. (4) If the client is not satisfied with their results, alternatives are presented to help the client continue his/her career exploration. (5) Lists of occupations sorted by work values area and job zone are presented. Clients can explore occupations in these lists in the O*NET system. Additionally, clients are directed towards expanded lists of occupations to explore.

Report Format/Content for Group Summaries: Not available.

Scoring:

Machine Scoring Service: Not available.

Hand Scoring:

SCORED BY: Counselee

TIME REQUIRED FOR SCORING: Takes under 5 minutes

Local Machine Scoring: Not available.

Computer Software Options Available: Not available.

Cost of Materials: Instrument and supporting materials are available free of charge at www.onetcenter.org.

Specimen Set: All materials (instrument print-shop files, score report, demonstration version of the instrument, user's guide designed for counselors, technical development reports) are available for download free of charge at www.onetcenter.org/WIL.html.

Counselee Materials: All materials: instrument print-shop files, score report, demonstration version of the instrument, user's guide designed for counselors, technical development reports are available for download free of charge at www.onetcenter.org/WIL.html.

O*NET Work Importance Locator Instrument (includes: Instrument booklet, Work Importance Locator Cards; Work Importance Locator Card Sorting Sheet).

O*NET Work Importance Locator Score Report

Additional Comments of Interest to Users: All materials including instruments, score reports, user guides, and development and technical reports are available for free download at www.onetcenter.org/WIL.html . Additionally, customer service is available at onet@ncmail.net.

Published Reviews of the Instrument in the Last 15 Years:

Green, K. (2005). Review of the O*NET Career Values Inventory: Based on the 'O*NET Work Importance Locator' developed by the U.S. Department of Labor. In R.A. Spies, & B. S. Plake (Eds.) *The sixteenth mental measurements yearbook*. Lincoln, NE: Buros Institute of Mental Measurements, The University of Nebraska.

Kelley, K. N. (2005). Review of the O*NET Work Importance Locator. In R.A. Spies, & B. S. Plake, (Eds.) *The sixteenth mental measurements yearbook*. Lincoln, NE: Buros Institute of Mental Measurements, The University of Nebraska.

Reference:

Dawis, R.V. & Lofquist, L.H., (1984). *Psychological Theory of Work Adjustment*. Minneapolis, MN, University of Minnesota Press.

O*NET® WORK IMPORTANCE PROFILER (WIP)

United States Department of Labor, Employment and Training Administration

Employment & Training Administration
USDOL, FPB S4231
200 Constitution Avenue, NW
Washington, DC 20210
o-net@dol.gov
www.doleta.gov/programs/onet
www.onetcenter.org

Target Population: Individuals seeking to identify their work values and use them to explore careers; high school and postsecondary students as well as adults. Should be 16 years and older with a minimum of a sixth-grade reading level.

Statement of the Purpose of the Instrument: The O*NET Work Importance Profiler (WIP) is a computerized self-assessment career exploration tool that allows customers to focus on what is important to them in a job. Based on the theory of work adjustment by Dawis & Lofquist (1984), the WIP helps counselees identify occupations that they may find satisfying based on the similarity between their work values (such as achievement, autonomy, and conditions of work) and the characteristics of the occupations. There are four major sections of the instrument. In the first section, counselees rank order 21 need statements (each related to a particular work value) by comparing them to one another and ordering them according to their relative importance. In the second section, they rate the work needs by indicating whether or not the need is important to them, independent of the other work needs. In the third section the counselee identifies a job zone (the level of training, education, and work experience they have now or wish to pursue). In the final section of the instrument, the counselee receives his/her work values profile, as well as lists of occupations that match their work values profile and job zone. Counselees can explore these occupations in the U.S. Department of Labor's O*NET system at http://online.onetcenter.org, the nation's leading source of occupational information. The instrument is appropriate for high school and postsecondary students, adults new to the work force, and workers in career transition.

Titles of Subtests, Scales, Scores Provided: Work Values are reported as: Achievement, Independence, Recognition, Relationships, Support, and Working Conditions.

Forms and Levels Available, with Dates of Publication/Revision of Each: Version 3.0 is available. Released in 2001.

Date of Most Recent Edition of Test Manual, User's Guide, etc.: O*NET Work Importance Profiler User's Guide, designed for workforce development professionals. Released in 2001.

Languages in Which Available: English only.

Time:

Actual Test Time: 15 – 30 Minutes (Assessment is not timed)

Total Administration Time: Designed for self-administration. Takes 30 – 45 minutes to complete.

Norm Group(s) on Which Scores Are Based: Not norm referenced. Extensive tryouts and evaluations conducted. See User's Guide and development and technical reports at www.onetcenter.org/WIP.html for more information.

Manner in Which Results Are Reported for Individuals:

Types of Scores: The counselee's top two work values are identified. A 21-need profile consisting of numerical raw scores is also available for printing.

Report Format/Content:

Basic Service: Counselee results are presented on several screens in the O*NET Work Importance Profiler. In addition to viewing their results, counselees can print out their top two work values, their 21-need score profile, definitions of the work values and needs, and the definitions of the job zone (level of education, training, and work experience they have or wish to pursue) they selected to use to help identify occupations to explore. Note, for ease of use, the score report focuses on the counselees top two work values rather than their 21-need score profile. Counselees can also print out the list of occupations that best match their 21-need score profile (work values) and selected job zone. These occupations can be found in the U.S. Department of Labor's O*NET system, the nation's leading source of occupational information.

Counselees have several other options within the WIP in identifying occupations to explore. They have the flexibility of printing occupations based on a single work value area and a selected job zone. Whether they are using their entire need profile (e.g., work values) or a single work value, a counselee may also select a different job zone to identify a new set of occupations to explore.

The client is presented with several screens that explain the next steps in career exploration. Additionally, screens are presented that describe alternative options if the counselee is not satisfied with their results. The client can print out all of these screens.

Report Format/Content for Group Summaries: Not available.

Scoring:

Machine Scoring Service: Not available.

Hand Scoring: Not available.

TIME REQUIRED FOR SCORING: Instrument is self scoring. Under 5 minutes

Computer Software Options Available: Not available.

Other: Stand alone and network versions of the instrument are downloadable free of charge, from www.onetcenter.org/WIP.html

Cost of Materials: All materials (instrument, demonstration version of the instrument, User's Guide designed for counselors, technical development reports) are available for download free of charge at www.onetcenter.org/WIP.html)

Specimen Set:

O*NET Work Importance Profiler

O*NET Work Importance Profiler User's Guide

O*NET Work Importance Profiler Demonstration Version

Counselee Materials:

O*NET Work Importance Profiler

Additional Comments of Interest to Users: All materials including instrument, demonstration version, user guide, and development and technical reports are available for free download at www.onetcenter.org/WIP.html. Additionally, customer service is available at onet@ncmail.net.

Reference:

Dawis, R.V. & Lofquist, L.H., (1984). *Psychological Theory of Work Adjustment.* Minneapolis, MN, University of Minnesota Press.

Reviewed by:

Joseph C. Ciechalski
Professor, Department of Counselor Education
East Carolina University

Description

According to McCoy, Waugh, Medsker, Wall, Rivkin, & Lewis (1999a) the Occupational Information Network (O*NET) is a comprehensive system for collecting, organizing, describing, and disseminating data on occupational characteristics and worker attributes. O*NET is the replacement for the Dictionary of Occupational Titles (DOT; U.S. Department of Labor, 1991).

The Work Importance Profiler – Computer (WIP-C) and the Work Importance Locator – Paper and Pencil (WIL-P&P) versions will be reviewed. The WIL-P&P will be reviewed in this section while the WIP-C will be reviewed in the Computer-Based and/or Online Version section of this review.

Both versions were modeled on the Minnesota Importance Questionnaire (MIQ). The original form of the MIQ consisted of 20 scales of five items, each of which required individuals to rate the importance of specific aspects of work on a five-point Likert scale. Although the MIQ was an important basis of the development of the O*NET work values assessment instruments, it was not selected as one of the tools for direct use in the O*NET program because of the complexity of the MIQ. An instrument that could be self-scored, self-administered, and self-interpreted was needed. Thus, the O*NET system was developed.

The research design for developing the WIL-P&P and the WIP-C involved three studies: (1) a Prepilot Study; (2) a Pilot Study, and (3) a Main Study. Data for these studies were collected at four points in time (referred to as Time 1, Time 2, Time 3, and Time 4). Prior to the Prepilot Study at Time 1, a draft version of the WIL-P&P and the WIP-C was developed using items from the MIQ. The purpose of the Pilot Study (Time 2) was to get feedback and information for refinement of the WIL- P&P and the WIP-C. Data for the Main Study on the WIL-P&P and the WIP-C were collected at times 3 and 4. In the Main Study, the WIL-P&P, WIP-C, and the MIQ were administered to employment center clients and junior college students.

The WIL-P&P is a self-scored measure of work values. Instead of using a booklet with test items, the WIL-P&P version of the Work Importance Locator uses 20 work value cards and a booklet containing directions for administering the instrument. Each of the cards contains information about different aspects of work.

In step 1, the individual is required to read all 20 cards before going to step 2. In step 2, using the Work Value Card Sorting Sheet, the individual places each card in one of five columns from 5 (Most Important) to 1 (Least Important). The four most important statements are placed in column 5, the next four important statements are placed in column 4, and so on until you place the final four statements in column 1. In step 3, individuals must determine their work value scores. Work value scores are groups of related work needs of the individual: Achievement, Independence, Recognition, Relationships, Support, and Working Conditions. This is accomplished by using the worksheet on page 5 in the Work Importance Locator (WIL-P&P) booklet. The score for each card is the number of the column the card was placed in. For example, the cards in column 5 each receive a score of 5. The cards in column 4 each receive a score of 4, and so on until the test taker reaches column 1. In step 4, the individual must find his/her highest work values and place them in the spaces provided on page 5 in the WIL-P&P booklet. After completing step 4, the individual takes his/her scores to the *Work Importance Locator Score Report* (U.S. Department of Labor Employment & Training Administration, 2000) to determine what these scores mean and how to use them in exploring careers. For example, each work value is divided into five job zones. Job zones are based on the overall experience, education, and job training required by a particular occupation. Zone 1 requires the least amount of preparation and zone 5 the most amount of preparation. In addition to the above information, the *Work Importance Locator Score Report* provides information on what the scores mean.

Use in Counseling

The WIL- P&P and the WIP-C are useful for individuals from a variety of ethnic, cultural, and socioeconomic backgrounds. The instruments give individuals a starting point in exploring various occupations. Both instruments are very easy to administer, score, and interpret.

According to the *User's Guide,* "...the use of the O*NET Career Exploration Tools is authorized for career exploration, career planning, and career counseling purposes only. Each O*NET Career Exploration Tool must be used consistent with its own *User's Guide.* No other use of these tools or any part of the tools is valid or authorized" (U.S. Department of Labor Employment & Training Administration, 2002, p. i). This is a rather strict caution coming from the publisher.

It is also important to note that the U.S. Department of Labor has also developed other career exploration materials useful in counseling. These instruments include but are not limited to the O*NET Interest Profiler, the O*NET Ability Profiler, and the Workplace Literacy Tests. These instruments are also available in computer and paper-and-pencil formats.

Technical Considerations

A MANOVA was done on the instruments to determine if the level of education affected the magnitude of work value scores. The results indicated that those with a two-year or four-year college degree scored higher on the Achievement and Autonomy values than those with a high school diploma or less. Those with a two- or four-year college degree scored lower on Comfort and Safety values than those with a high school diploma.

A two-way MANOVA was done to determine if racial/ethnic group or gender affected the magnitude of the work value scores. Only Whites, African-Americans, and Hispanics were included in the analysis because of the small number of individuals in the other racial/ethnic groups. The results indicated that level of education was related to differences on the values of Achievement, Autonomy, Safety, and Comfort. African-Americans and Hispanics tended to express their values for status more than did Whites. Females tended to express their values for Safety and Altruism more than males.

Test-Retest Reliability—The WIP-C was administered in junior college classes and then re-administered in the same classes 4 – 8 weeks later. Each participant completed both the WIP-C and the WIL-P&P at each administration. The correlations between the Time 1 and Time 2 results were computed for each need and value measured in the WIP-C. The correlations for the individual needs were moderate, ranges from .53 to .76 with a median of .63. The correlations for the values were less variable than the needs with a range of .59 to .66 and a median of .62. Correlations of time 1 and time 2 scores were .77 and .72 for both the needs and work values, respectively.

Alternate Form Reliability—The WIP-C and the WIL-P&P were developed to be alternative measures to each other. To analyze the similarity among the participants' MIQ, WIP-C, and WIL-P&P profiles, correlations were computed for both the need and value profiles of each participant. The median correlations between the profiles for each instrument pair ranged from .66 to .77. The profile correlations were .05 to .10 higher for the needs than for the work values. Overall, the WIP-C showed respectable correspondence with the MIQ and somewhat less correspondence with the WIL-P&P.

Internal Consistency Reliability – The internal consistency reliabilities of the six work value scales were estimated using coefficient alpha. The alphas reported for the WIP-C ranged from .50 to .86 for Time 1 and .46 to .84 for Time 2.

Validity—The WIP-C was designed to measure the same constructs as the original MIQ. Based on the results of the construct validity analyses, the MIQ and WIP-C appear to have very similar factor structures. The data also provide moderate support for the present six-factor work values model.

Computer-Based and/or Online Versions

According to McCoy et al. (1999b) and the *Work Importance Profiler - User's Guide* (2002) U.S. Department of Labor Employment and Training Administration), the O*NET WIL-C is the automated version of the Work Importance Locator. This computerized version, like the WIL-P&P version, was designed to assist participants in identifying their most important work values and the possible occupations that correspond with those work values.

In step 1 (ranking phase), the individual is required to rank the five work need statements by indicating how important each is to the individual's ideal job. To rank the statement on each screen, the individual selects the most important work need from the list. Then the individual selects his/her second most important statement, and so on until all statements are ranked to reflect the individual's order of importance.

In step 2, the individual will again see the work need statements. The computer in this step displays all 21 work need statements on a single screen. An individual is required to indicate whether each need is or isn't important by indicating a "Y" for "Yes" or "N" for "No." Then the computer combines the ranking and rating scores to create the Work Importance Profiler Results. These results are presented as "Work Values" which were described in the description section of this review.

In step 3, the computer presents the WIP-C results. The two most important work values appear in order of importance in red while the remaining four work values appear underneath in black. Because the work values are presented in order of importance, the WIP-C results will usually be different for each person. The WIP-C results are used to generate a list of possible occupations that the individual may find satisfactory. On another screen, the individual can click on a square button next to the individual value to obtain more information about their work values. Directly linked to the WIP-C is the O*NET database which lists occupations which corresponds to the individual's most important work values.

In step 4, the individual selects a job zone. The computer screen has five job zones selected, and the individual is asked to click on the folder to see each of the five job zones that correspond to his/her career goals. After selecting a job zone, the computer program will generate a list of possible occupations which are based on the individual's WIP-C results along with the job zone selected.

In step 5, the computer screen presents a list of possible occupations to consider on the O*NET Work Importance Profiler Occupational Report. This report also provides the O*NET Standard Occupational Classsification (SOC) (Social—Working Conditions) Code and O*NET Title for each occupation.

Overall Critique

The WIL-P&P and the WIP-C are well-constructed instruments. Both are very easy to administer, score, and interpret. However, a counselor is needed to assist the individual in administering, scoring, and interpreting the instruments. Both instruments may be administered individually or to a group. Individuals with at least an eighth-grade reading level should have no problem with it. Both instruments were carefully developed and standardized, and the results are provided in several technical manuals. A web address (http:// online.onetcenter.org) is also provided for those who have questions, concerns, or suggestions about the instruments. In conclusion, I recommend the use of the WIL-P&P or WIP-C for career exploration, career planning, and career counseling.

References

McCloy, R., Waugh, G., Medsker, G., Wall, J., Rivkin, D., & Lewis, P. (1999a). *Development of the O*NET Paper-and-Pencil Work Importance Locator.* Raleigh, NC: National Center for O*NET Development – Employment Security Commission.

McCloy, R., Waugh, G., Medsker, G., Wall, J., Rivkin, D., & Lewis, P. (1999b). *Development of the O*NET Computerized Work Importance Profiler.* Raleigh, NC: National Center for O*NET Development - Employment Security Commission.

U.S. Department of Labor Employment and Training Administration (2000). *Work Importance Locator Score Report.* Washington, DC: U. S. Government Printing Office.

U.S. Department of Labor Employment and Training Administration (2002). *O*NET Work Importance Profiler User's Guide.* Washington, DC: U.S. Government Printing Office.

U.S. Department of Labor (1991. *Dictionary of occupations titles* (Rev. 4th ed.). Washington, DC: U.S. Government Printing Office.

Self Directed Search-R: (SDS-R) (4th Edition)

John L. Holland

Psychological Assessment Resources, Inc.
16204 N. Florida Avenue
Lutz, FL 33549
www.parinc.com/

Target Population: High school students, college students, and adults.

Statement of the Purpose of the Instrument: The SDS-R is an easy-to-use, self-administered test that helps individuals find the occupations that best suit their interests and skills.

Titles of Subtests, Scales, Scores Provided: Holland Code, numerical scores in six Holland (RIASEC) categories (Realistic, Investigative, Artistic, Social, Enterprising, Conventional), Aspirations code.

Forms and Levels Available, with Dates of Publication/Revision of Each: Professional User's Guide; Technical Manual; Form R Assessment Booklet; Form R Occupations Finder; Form R Alphabetized Occupations Finder; Dictionary of Holland Occupational Codes (DHOC), 3rd Edition; The Self-Directed Search and Related Holland Career Materials: A Practitioner's Guide. All Qualification Level A. Publication date for all: August 24, 1994, except DHOC, (December 17, 1996) and Practitioner's Guide, (February 27, 1998).

Date of Most Recent Edition of Test Manual, User's Guide, Etc.: August 24, 1994 (except DHOC, December 17, 1996 and Practitioner's Guide, February 27, 1998).

Languages in Which Available: English, English-Canadian, French-Canadian, Spanish (also translated into over 20 other languages).

Time:

Total Administration Time: 35 – 45 minutes.

Norm Group(s) on Which Scores Are Based: 2,602 students and working adults: 1,600 females and 1,002 males, ranging in age from 17 – 65 years, with 75% Caucasians, 8% African- Americans, 7% Hispanics, 4% Asian-Americans, 1% Native Americans, and 5% from other ethnic backgrounds; data were collected in 10 high schools, nine community colleges, 19 colleges or universities, and a variety of other sources throughout the U.S.

Manner in Which Results Are Reported for Individuals: Holland Code.

Types of Scores: Percentile ranks for high school students, college students, and adults.

Report Format/Content: Form R Windows Computer Version or Interpretive Report (10 – 15 page report): includes careers and educational programs that match the person's Holland Code. Report also describes the RIASEC system and provides concrete suggestions for further exploration.

Report Format/Content for Group Summaries: Not available.

Scoring:

Machine Scoring Service: SDS-R Professional Report Service.

COST OF BASIC SERVICE PER COUNSELEE: $7.60 in quantities of 250

TIME REQUIRED FOR SCORING AND RETURNING (MAXIMUM): Within 24 hours of receipt, on next business day.

Hand Scoring:

SCORED BY: Counselee; Clerk.

TIME REQUIRED FOR SCORING: 5 – 10 minutes.

Local Machine Scoring: Not available.

Computer Software Options Available: Standard administration online. Other: SDS-R on the Internet (www.self-directed-search.com).

SDS-R: CV (computer version) on-screen administration and report.

SDS-R: IR (interpretive report).

SDS-R: Software System DOS-based (online administration and report).

Requirements: Windows 95/NT 4.0 with Internet Explorer 4.0 or higher, Windows 98/Me/2000/XP; CD-ROM drive for installation; Internet connection or telephone for software activation and counter update

Ways in Which Computer Version Differs: A report is generated automatically based on the individual's responses to the test. An 8 – 16 page personalized report will appear on the computer screen when the test is completed.

Cost of Materials: Due to possible price changes since publication date, be sure to check with publisher website.

Professional User's Guide, $30; Technical Manual & Professional User's Guide, $54; Form R Assessment Booklets (pkg/25), $36; Form R Alphabetized Occupations Finder, (pkg/25) $38; Form R You and Your Career Booklets, (pkg/25) $30.

The cost for the online test (at http://www.self-directed-search.com/) is $9.95 per test completion.

Specimen Set: SDS Form R Introductory Kit which includes SDS Professional User's Guide, Technical Manual, 25 Assessment Booklets, 25 Occupations Finder, and 25 You and Your Career Booklets, $148.00

Counselee Materials: Form R Assessment Booklet (not reusable); Occupations Finder (reusable); Form R Alphabetized Occupations Finder (reusable); Form R You and Your Career Booklet (reusable); Educational Opportunities Finder (reusable); Leisure Activities Finder (reusable).

Additional Comments of Interest to Users: The SDS family of career products provides a set of self-assessment tools for a variety of populations, available in paper-and-pencil, computer, and professional report service versions. An audiotape version is also available for individuals with reading limitations.

Published Reviews:

Conneran, J. M., & Hartman, B. W. (1993). The concurrent validity of the Self Directed Search in identifying chronic career indecision among vocational education students. *Journal of Career Development, 19,* 197 – 208.

Dumenci, L. (1995). Construct validity of the Self-Directed Search using hierarchically nested structural models. *Journal of Vocational Behavior, 47,* 21 – 34.

Spokane, A. R., & Holland, J. L. (1995). The Self-Directed Search: A family of self-guided career interventions. *Journal of Career Assessment, 3,* 373 – 390.

SELF-DIRECTED SEARCH-E: (SDS-E) (FOURTH EDITION)

John L. Holland

Psychological Assessment Resources, Inc.
16204 N. Florida Avenue
Lutz, FL 33549
www.parinc.com

Target Population: Adults and older adolescents with lower educational levels (fourth grade reading level).

Statement of the Purpose of the Instrument: Assess career interests among individuals with limited reading skills.

Titles of Subtests, Scales, Scores Provided: Holland Code, RIASEC scores, Aspirations Code.

Forms and Levels Available, with Dates of Publication/Revision of Each: Professional User's Guide; Technical Manual; Form E Assessment Booklet; Form E Jobs Finder; Form E You and Your Job Booklet. All Qualification Level A. Publication date for all July 23, 1996.

Date of Most Recent Edition of Test Manual, User's Guide, Etc.: July 23, 1996.

Languages in Which Available: English, English-Canadian, Spanish.

Time:

Total Administration Time: 35 – 45 minutes.

Norm Group(s) on Which Scores Are Based: 719 individuals 15-72 years of age from a variety of ethnic and educational backgrounds.

Manner in Which Results Are Reported for Individuals: Two-letter Holland Code.

Report Format/Content for Group Summaries: Not available.

Scoring:

Machine Scoring Service: Not available.

Hand Scoring:

SCORED BY: COUNSELEE.

TIME REQUIRED FOR SCORING: 10 minutes.

Local Machine Scoring: Not available.

Computer Software Options Available: Not available.

Cost of Materials: Due to possible price changes since publication date, be sure to check with publisher website.

SDS Form E Introductory Kit (includes SDS Professional User's Guide, Technical Manual, 25 Assessment Booklets, 25 Jobs Finders, and 25 You and Your Job Booklets) $150

SDS Form E Sets of Assessment Booklets and Jobs Finders (pkg/25 each), $66

Form E Assessment Booklets $36 (pkg/25)

Form E Jobs Finder $36 (pkg/25)

Form E You and Your Job Booklets $29 (pkg/25)

Specimen Set: One of each: Form E Assessment Booklet, Form E Jobs Finder, Form E You and Your Jobs Booklet, Educational Opportunities Finder, Leisure Activities Finder—cost $10 plus shipping.

Counselee Materials:

Form E Assessment Booklets (not reusable).

Form E Jobs Finder (reusable).

Form E You and Your Job Booklet (reusable).

Additional Comments of Interest to Users: Audiotape is available—individual still has to fill in answers on the paper-and-pencil booklet. Print size in booklet is larger size to help people who have reading difficulties.

Published Reviews:

Conneran, J. M., & Hartman, B. W. (1993). The concurrent validity of the Self Directed Search in identifying chronic career indecision among vocational education students. *Journal of Career Development, 19,* 197 – 208.

Dumenci, L. (1995). Construct validity of the Self-Directed Search using hierarchically nested structural models. *Journal of Vocational Behavior, 47,* 21 – 34.

Spokane, A. R., & Holland, J. L. (1995). The Self-Directed Search: A family of self-guided career interventions. *Journal of Career Assessment, 3,* 373 – 390.

SELF DIRECTED SEARCH CAREER PLANNING: (SDS-CP)

John L. Holland

Psychological Assessment Resources, Inc.
16204 N. Florida Avenue
Lutz, FL 33549
www.parinc.com

Target Population: Individuals on the career development track.

Statement of the Purpose of the Instrument: Developed to answer the demands of the many SDS organizational users, the SDS-CP focuses exclusively on occupations at upper levels of career responsibility and their corresponding educational requirements. Also helps employees plan for future professional advancement, helps individuals affected by organizational changes make career transitions, and helps employees reentering the workforce to establish new career foundations.

Titles of Subtests, Scales, Scores Provided: Holland Code, RIASEC Scores.

Forms and Levels Available, with Dates of Publication/Revision of Each: Professional User's Guide; Technical Manual; Form CP Assessment Booklet; Form CP Career Options Finder; Exploring Career Options booklet. All Qualification Level A. Publication date for all January 15, 1991.

Date of Most Recent Edition of Test Manual, User's Guide, etc.: January 15, 1991.

Languages in Which Available: English only.

Time:

Total Administration Time: 15 – 25 minutes.

Norm Group(s) on Which Scores Are Based: Regular Form R sample. Pairwise correlations of section and summary code scores for Form R and Form CP.

Manner in Which Results are Reported for Individuals: Three-letter Holland Code.

Types of Scores: SDS Manual provides percentile ranks for adults.

Report Format/Content:

BASIC SERVICE: 15 – 24 page report generated by either the Form CP IR (Interpretive Report) or Professional Report Service lists careers that match the individual's Holland Code.

Report Format/Content for Group Summaries: Not Available.

Scoring:

Machine Scoring Service: SDS-CP Professional Report Service.

COST OF BASIC SERVICE PER COUNSELEE: SDS Form CP Assessment Booklets/ Answer Sheets (pkg/10)—Prices for mail-in Answer Sheets include scoring, interpretive report, and return postage), $116

TIME REQUIRED FOR SCORING AND RETURNING: Within 24 hours, on the next business day.

Hand Scoring:

SCORED BY: Counselee.

TIME REQUIRED FOR SCORING: 5 – 10 minutes.

Local Machine Scoring: Not Available.

Computer Software Options Available: SDS-CP Interpretive Report.

Ways in Which Computer Version Differs: Counselor enters scores from a paper-and-pencil administration and the IR software automatically generates a report.

Cost of Materials: Due to possible price changes since publication date, be sure to check with publisher website.

SDS Form CP Introductory Kit (includes SDS Professional User's Guide, Technical Manual, 25 Assessment Booklets, 25 Career Options Finders, and 25 Exploring Career Options Booklets), $188

SDS Form CP Sets of Assessment Booklets and Career Options Finders (pkg/25 each), $88

Form CP Assessment Booklets (pkg/25), $46.00

Form CP Career Options Finder (pkg/25), $46.00

Form CP Exploring Career Options Booklet (pkg/125), $46.00

Specimen Set: One of each: Form CP Assessment Booklet, Form CP Career Options Finder, Form CP Exploring Career Options Booklet, Educational Opportunities Finder, Leisure Activities Finder—cost $10.00 plus shipping

Counselee Materials: Form CP Assessment Booklets (not reusable).

Form CP Career Options Finder (reusable).

Form CP Exploring Career Options Booklet (reusable).

Published Reviews:

Conneran, J.M., & Hartman, B.W. (1993). The concurrent validity of the Self Directed Search in identifying chronic career indecision among vocational education students. *Journal of Career Development, 19*, 197 – 208.

Dumenci, L. (1995). Construct validity of the Self-Directed Search using hierarchically nested structural models. *Journal of Vocational Behavior, 47*, 21 – 34.

Spokane, A.R., & Holland, J.R. (1995). The Self-Directed Search: A family of self-guided career interventions. *Journal of Career Assessment, 3*, 373 – 390.

Self-Directed Search Career Explorer: (SDS-CE)

John L. Holland and Amy B. Powell

Psychological Assessment Resources, Inc.
16204 N. Florida Avenue
Lutz, FL 33549
www.parinc.com

Target Population: Middle or junior high school students (third grade reading level).

Statement of the Purpose of the Instrument: Helps students assess and explore interests for future education and career planning.

Titles of Subtests, Scales, Scores Provided: Holland Code, RIASEC Scores, Aspirations Code.

Forms and Levels Available, with Dates of Publication/Revision of Each: Professional User's Guide; Technical Manual; Career Explorer Self Assessment Booklet; Career Explorer Careers Booklet; Career Explorer Exploring Your Future with the SDS Booklet. All qualification Level A. Publication date for all January 31, 1994.

Date of Most Recent Edition of Test Manual, User's Guide, Etc.: January 31, 1994.

Languages in Which Available: English only.

Time:

Total Administration Time: 35 – 45 minutes.

Norm Group(s) on Which Scores Are Based: 102 sixth, seventh, and eighth grade students.

Manner in Which Results Are Reported for Individuals: Two-letter Holland Code.

Report Format/Content:

Basic Service: 8 – 12 page report generated by either the IR (Interpretive Report) software or the mail-in Professional Report Service provides general educational and vocational information to junior high and middle school students who are beginning to think about potential careers.

Report Format/Content for Group Summaries: Not available

Scoring:

Machine Scoring: SDS Explorer Professional Report Service

Cost of basic service per counselee: $6.50.

Time required for scoring and returning (maximum): Within 24 hours, on next business day.

Hand Scoring:

SCORED BY: Counselee.

TIME REQUIRED FOR SCORING: 5 – 10 minutes.

Local Machine Scoring: Not available.

Computer Software Options Available: SDS Career Explorer: Interpretive Report.

Ways in Which Computer Version Differs: Counselor enters the individual's two-letter code from a paper-and-pencil administration and the software generates the 8 – 12 page report to help the individual begin his or her educational and vocational exploration.

Cost of Materials:

Due to possible price changes since publication date, be sure to check with publisher website.

SDS Career Explorer Introductory Kit (includes User's Guide, Technical Manual, Technical Information Booklets, Teacher's Guide, 35 Self-Assessment Booklets, 35 Careers Booklets, and 35 Exploring Your Future with SDS Booklets), $230

SDS Career Explorer Combination Package (includes 35 Self-Assessment Booklets, 35 Careers Booklets, and 35 Exploring Your Future with the SDS Booklets), $158

Career Explorer Self Assessment Booklet, $56 (pkg/35).

Career Explorer Careers Booklet, $56 (pkg/35).

Career Explorer Exploring Your Future with the SDS Booklet, $56 (pkg/35).

Specimen Set: One of each: Career Explorer Self Assessment Booklet, Career Explorer Careers Booklet, Career Explorer Exploring Your Future with the SDS Booklet, Teachers Guide—cost $10 plus shipping.

Counselee Materials:

Career Explorer Assessment Booklets (not reusable).

Career Explorer Careers Booklet (reusable).

Career Explorer Exploring Your Future with the SDS Booklet (reusable).

Published Reviews: None cited.

Reviewed by:[1]

Joseph C. Ciechalski
Professor
Department of Counselor & Adult Education
East Carolina University

Description

The Self-Directed Search (SDS) is an easy-to-use self-administered, self-scored, and self-interpreted interest inventory that assists individuals in finding occupations that are similar to their interests. It is based on John Holland's theory of vocational choice, which assumes that most people can be categorized into one of six personality and environmental types. The six personality and environmental types are: Realistic (R), Investigative (I), Artistic (A), Social (S), Enterprising (E), and Conventional (C). Currently, there are four forms of the SDS: Form R, Form E, Form CP, and the Career Explorer. Each of these forms is designed for use with specific and distinct populations.

The Self-Directed Search (SDS) Form R: 4th Edition was revised in 1994. Form R is the original or regular form of the SDS and is designed for use with high school students, college students, and adults. This form of the SDS consists of the *Assessment Booklet, The Educational Opportunities Finder, You and Your Career, The Occupations Finder,* and the *Leisure Activities Finder.*

Like the 1985 edition, Form R of the *Assessment Booklet* is divided into five scales: Occupational Daydreams, Activities, Competencies, Occupations, and Self-Estimates. Only 67 of the 228 items contained in the Assessment Booklet were revised in the current version. The *Assessment Booklet* is used by the examinees to determine their three-letter Summary Code. Except for the Occupational Daydream scale, all of the remaining scales are used to calculate the examinee's three-letter Summary Code.

The examinee's three-letter Summary Code is used with *The Occupations Finder* to identify occupations that match this code. Revised in 1996, *The Occupations Finder* lists over 1,300 occupations arranged according to Holland's "RIASEC" system. *The Occupations Finder* also lists the nine-digit DOT number as well as the educational level of the occupation.

The *You and Your Career Booklet* was revised in 1994 and helps the examinees to better understand their three-letter Summary Code using six easy-to-follow steps. This booklet concludes with a most informative section on Making Career Decisions. In addition to the above booklets, *The Educational Opportunities Finder and the Leisure Activities Finder* were included with Form R.

Formerly called the *College Majors Finder, The Educational Opportunities Finder* (EOF) was revised in 1997. The EOF contains over 750 programs to assist individuals in locating educational opportunities consistent with an individual's Summary Code. Also

---

[1] This review is a reprint from the fourth edition of *A Counselor's Guide to Career Assessment Instruments.* The test publisher informed the editors that the instrument is unchanged since the last edition of the Guide. It is reprinted for readers' convenience. Check publisher's website for updates.

revised in 1997, *The Leisure Activities Finder* lists over 750 leisure activities (hobbies, sports, and avocations) according to the first two letters of the Summary Code.

The Self-Directed Search (SDS) Form E: 4th Edition contains 198 items written at the sixth-grade reading level whereas the directions are written at the fourth-grade level. Form E of the SDS consists of the *Assessment Booklet, The Jobs Finder,* and *You and Your Job.*

Like Form R, the *Assessment Booklet* consists of five scales, but these are divided as follows: Jobs You Have Thought About, Activities, Skills, Jobs, and Rating Your Abilities. Instead of calculating a three-letter Summary Code, Form E requires one to find a two-letter Summary Code. *The Jobs Finder,* like *The Occupations Finder* of Form R, is used to classify over 800 job titles using the two-letter Summary Code.

The revised *You and Your Job* booklet, like the *You and Your Career* booklet of Form R, is used to help individuals better understand their scores and to use The Job Finder. In an earlier review of Form E, Ciechalski (1998) stated that, "The 1990 Revision of Form E reflects the author's dedication to improving on an already popular and well established instrument" (p. 892). The same statement applies to this revision of Form E.

The Self-Directed Search (SDS) Form CP: Career Planning focuses on long-term career planning and occupations that require high levels of education and training. Form CP of the SDS was specifically designed for professionals and adults in career transition. It differs from Form R in three ways: (1) it contains new items focusing only on adult workers, (2) there are no Daydreams or Self-Estimates scales in the *Assessment Booklet,* and (3) *The Career Options Finder* contains over 1,300 occupational titles exclusively at the upper levels of career responsibility. This form also consists of the *Assessment Booklet, The Career Options Finder* (COF), and the interpretive booklet, *Exploring Career Options.*

The Self-Directed Search (SDS) Form CE Career Explorer was designed for middle and junior high school students. It consists of the *Self-Assessment Booklet,* The Careers Booklet, and the interpretive booklet, *Exploring Your Future. The Assessment Booklet* contains 204 items. Of the 204 items, 30 items are new and 174 items came from other forms of the SDS.

The SDS Career Explorer is written at the third-grade reading level. It was designed to introduce middle and junior high school students to vocational planning and to suggest ways of obtaining additional information about careers. Like Form E, the Career Explorer form yields a two-letter Summary Code. *The Careers Booklet,* a shorter version of the *Occupations Finder,* lists over 400 job titles according to Holland's code. Unlike the other forms of the SDS, this form focuses more on vocational exploration rather than on choosing a career.

The SDS has been adapted in over 25 countries. In addition, there are English Canadian (Form R & Form E), French Canadian (Form R), Spanish (Form R & Form E), and Vietnamese (Form E) versions of the SDS. For those who are visually impaired, there is a Braille edition of the SDS available.

Use In Counseling

The *SDS Professional User's Guide* (Holland, Powell, & Fritzsche, 1997) combines information on all four forms of the SDS into one comprehensive volume. This guide is a most valuable resource for both veteran and new users of the SDS.

According to the *SDS Professional User's Guide* (1997), the SDS has a number of uses. The SDS may help those individuals who are not certain about which career to pursue or those individuals who are considering a second career. It may be used for diverse populations. For example, the SDS has been used in middle schools, high schools, adult centers, employment offices, and correctional institutions and has met with satisfaction. It may also be used in placement and staff development in both business and industry. The SDS is a useful research tool as evidenced by the numerous studies cited in the *SDS Professional User's Guide* (1997).

In addition to the suggested uses and applications of the SDS mentioned above, the *SDS Professional User's Guide* (1997) contains well-written chapters on administering and scoring the SDS. To address the concerns of some former reviewers dealing with the errors encountered in scoring the SDS, the authors of the *SDS Professional User's Guide* state that, "The scoring of the SDS should be supervised and checked because test takers do make scoring errors"(p.15).

Information to assist counselors in the interpretation of the SDS is included in chapter 5, Interpretive Ideas, of the *SDS Professional User's Guide.* Chapter 5 not only describes the content and structure of the SDS, but also includes a number of SDS profiles which provide counselors with illustrative examples for using and interpreting the SDS with individuals.

Technical Considerations

The *SDS Technical Manual* (Holland, Fritzsche, & Powell, 1997) is completely revised and contains valuable information about the history, development, research, and technical aspects of the SDS. Like the *SDS Professional User's Guide* (1997), the *SDS Technical Manual* combines information about all four forms of the SDS. The manual contains a total of 105 tables (66 in the text and 39 in the appendices).

Normative data were developed by administering the 1994 edition of Form R to a sample of 2,602 students and adults. There were 1,600 females and 1,002 males ranging in age from 17 to 65 years of age. This sample consisted of 47% white, 8% African-American, 7% Hispanics, 4% Asian-Americans, 1% Native Americans, and 5% from other groups. Demographic variables by gender, age, and ethnic background and education are contained in separate tables in the technical manual.

Internal consistency coefficients (KR-20) for the Activities, Competencies, and Occupations scales ranged from .72 to .92 and the summary scale coefficients ranged from .90 to .94. Correlation coefficients between the two Self-Estimates ratings per scale ranged from .37 to .84. According to the authors of the *SDS Technical Manual,* these coefficients indicate that the ratings contain shared variance and that each contributes some variance.

Test-retest reliability was tested over 4 – 12 week time intervals. The resulting coefficients ranged from .76 to .89 indicating stability.

The concurrent validity of the 1994 SDS, like earlier editions of the SDS, was found by assessing the "percentage of hits." According to the authors of the technical manual, "The percentage of hits equals the percentage of a sample whose high point code and one-letter aspiration or occupational code agree" (p. 23). The range of hit rates for most interest inventories is 40% to 55%. For the 1994 SDS sample, the overall hit rate was 54.7% (the high end of the range).

Technical information on the alternate forms (Forms E, CP, and Career Planning) are included in Chapter 4 of the technical manual. Chapter 4 describes the development of the alternate forms as well as validity and reliability information. The results cited in the technical manual indicate that all four forms are equivalent.

Computer-Based Versions

Computer-based versions of the SDS are available for Forms R and CP. The computer versions administer, score, and interpret the SDS. A narrative report based on an individual's score is generated by the computer. In addition, the computer-based version includes, *My Vocational Situation,* a two-page questionnaire that provides an indication of the level of career assistance a client may need.

Interpretive Reports (IRs) are available for Forms R, CP, and the Career Explorer. These software reports are unlimited use programs which interpret the client's SDS scores and produce a narrative report. To use this service, counselors must key the scores into the computer and the software program generates a 10 – 15 page Interpretive Report based on the information keyed in from the *Assessment Booklet.*

Professional report services are available for Form R, Form CP, and the Career Explorer. Prepaid mail-in answer sheets are sent to the publisher. A 15 – 24 page report, which includes an explanation of Holland's theory, individual's scores, Summary Code, and a list of matching careers are returned by the publisher to the counselor.

Form R of the SDS is available on the Internet (www.self-directed-search.com). Regardless of which computer-based form one uses, this reviewer believes that examinees should see a counselor for assistance in interpreting their results.

Overall Critique

In summary, the Self-Directed Search (SDS) Form R: 4th Edition and all of the alternate forms reflects the authors' continuing work and dedication to improving on an already outstanding instrument. It is a well-developed instrument with numerous studies to support its use. As Daniels (1994) stated in an earlier review of the SDS, "Its popularity among practitioners and researchers alike is testimony to its perceived utility and effectiveness" (p. 211). The SDS is and continues to be an excellent interest inventory.

References

Ciechalski, J.C. (1998). Review of the Self-Directed Search, Form E—1990 Revision. In J.C. Impara & B.S. Plake (Eds.), *The thirteenth mental measurements yearbook* (pp. 893 – 894). Lincoln, NE: Buros Institute, University of Nebraska – Lincoln.

Daniels, M.H. (1994). Review of the Self-Directed Search, In J.T. Kapes, M.M. Mastie, & E.A. Whitfield (Eds.), *A counselor's guide to career assessment instruments* (3rd ed. p. 208 – 212). Alexandria, VA: National Career Development Association.

Holland, J.L., Fritzsche, B.A., & Powell, A.B. (1997). *The Self-Directed Search technical manual*. Odessa, FL: Psychological Assessment Resources, Inc.

Holland, J.L., Powell, A.B., & Fritzsche, B.A. (1997). *The Self-Directed Search professional user's guide*. Odessa, FL: Psychological Assessment Resources, Inc.

STRONG INTEREST INVENTORY ASSESSMENT TOOL®

E.K. Strong

Consulting Psychologist Press, Inc. (CPP, Inc.) and Davies-Black Publishing
1055 Joaquin Road, 2nd Floor
Mountain View, CA 94043
Tel: (650) 969-8901
Toll free: (800) 624-1765
Fax: (650) 969-8608
www.cpp.com

Target Population: 14 years and up.

Statement of the Purpose of the Instrument: The Strong Interest Inventory assessment tool measures a client's interests in a broad range of occupations, work activities, leisure activities, and school subjects.

Titles of Subtests, Scales, Scores Provided: General Occupational Themes: Realistic, Investigative, Artistic, Social, Enterprising, Conventional; Basic Interest Scales (30); Occupational Scales (244); and Personal Style Scales (5).

Forms and Levels Available with Dates of Publication/Revision of Each: Profile (2004). Interpretive Report (2004);, Career Report with the MBTI instrument (2005), Strong and Skills Confidence Inventory Profile (2004).

Date of Most Recent Edition of Test Manual, User's Guide, etc.: 2005.

Languages in Which Available: English, Korean, Portuguese, Argentian Spanish, Anglicized adaptation.

Time:

Actual Test Time: 35 – 40 minutes.

Total Administration Time: 35 – 40 minutes

Norm Group(s) on Which Scores Are Based: More than 55,000 people from across the United States representing age, gender, and ethnic percentage based on U.S. census data.

Manner in Which Results are Reported for Individuals: Profile, interpretive.

Types of Scores: Standard scores and verbal labels.

Report Format/Content:

BASIC SERVICE: Strong Profile, Standard Edition; Strong Profile, High School Edition; Strong Profile, College Edition.

OPTIONS: Strong Interpretive Report, Strong and MBTI Career Report, Strong and Skills Confidence Inventory Profile.

Report Format/Content for Group Summaries: Not Available.

Scoring:

Machine Scoring Service: Mail-in software, web administration site.

Cost of basic service per counselee (2008 prices): $8.20

Cost of options: Interpretive, $14.20; Strong & MBTI®Career, $11.20; Skills Confidence, $11.20

For Mail in: Combined Item Booklet/Answer Sheets, for the reports cited above are available in pkg of 10at the same prices as above. Discounts apply for packages of 50. Contact the publisher for details.

Hand Scoring: Not Available.

Local Machine Scoring:

Provisions/conditions/equipment required: Mail-in scoring.

Computer Software Options Available: Standard administration and CPP Web Administration Site. The newly revised Strong assessment is available via SkillsOne.com, CPP's state-of-the-art online assessment delivery system, as well as for mail-in scoring.

Ways in Which Computer Version Differs: Ability to keep client date electronically; ability to keep client notes electronically.

Option: Ability to administer over the Internet.

Cost of Materials: Due to possible price changes since publication date, be sure to check the publisher's website.

Published Reviews: None cited.

Skills Confidence Inventory (SCI)

SCI: Nancy E. Betz, Fred H. Borgen, and Lenore W. Harmon

Consulting Psychologist Press, Inc. (CPP, Inc.) and Davies-Black Publishing
1055 Joaquin Road, 2nd Floor
Mountain View, CA 94043
Tel: (650) 969-8901
Toll free: (800) 624-1765
Fax: (650) 969-8608
www.cpp.com

Target Population: People 15 years old and above. Use the inventory with college students and adults entering the workforce or exploring new careers.

Statement of the Purpose of the Instrument: The instrument measures clients' perceived level of confidence in performing skills related to the six General Occupational Themes (GOTs). The report shows whether a client has very little, little, moderate, high, or very high confidence in skills related to the six GOTs. It opens discussion of the client's confidence level in his or her skills, a factor that could be preventing the client from considering high-interest careers.

Titles of Subtests, Scales, Scores Provided: Results are prioritized into: High Priority; High Confidence, High Interest; Possible Options If Interest Develops; High Confidence, Little Interest, Good Option If Confidence Increases; Little Confidence, High Interest, Low Priority; Little Confidence, Little Interest.

Forms and levels Available, with Dates of Publication/revision of Each: Level B, published since 1996, and re-issued in 2004 for use with the Newly Revised Strong Interest Inventory.

Date of Most Recent Edition of Test Manual, User's Guide, etc.: 2005

Languages in Which Available: English and Canadian French.

Time:

Actual Test Time: Less than 30 minutes.

Total Administration Time: 40 – 50 minutes.

Norm Group(s) on Which Scores Are Based: Percentiles are based on 1,147 working adult participants and the return rate across gender/occupation combinations ranged from 50%. The normative sample of college students consisted of 706 enrolled in introductory psychology courses at Ohio State University and Iowa State University.

Manner in Which Results Are Reported for Individuals:

Types of Scores: Approximate percentile equivalents based from 1.0 to 5.0.

Report Format/Content:

BASIC SERVICE: Includes Holland's Hexagon and the General Occupations. Included as a one-page report at the end of the nine-page Strong Profile. The report shows whether a client has very little, moderate, high, or very high confidence in skills related to the six GOTs.

OPTIONS: The Skills Confidence Inventory is available only in combination with materials for the Strong Interest Inventory. The Skills Confidence Inventory Profile may be paired with the Strong Profile, the Strong Interpretive Report, or the Strong College Profile.

Report Format/Content for Group Summaries: Not available.

Scoring:

Pre-Paid, Mail-in Scoring Service:

COST OF BASIC SERVICE PER COUNSELEE: The publisher offers mail in scoring that has a five-day turnaround period. It is a one-page report that follows the nine-page Strong Profile, or any of the reports identified in "Options" above. The price of scoring is included in the original ordering price.

Hand Scoring: Not available.

Local Machine Scoring: Not available.

On-line Scoring: Available through the publisher's Skills One ® Website (www.skillsone.com). Set-up fees and annual maintenance fees apply. Contact the publisher for details and prices.

Cost of Materials: Due to possible price changes since publication date, be sure to check the publisher's website.

Additional Comments of Interest to Users: Lack of experience may lead to lower skills confidence scores, rendering the scores somewhat less meaningful. Lower levels of confidence should be considered to indicate areas where new learning might be attempted.

Reviewed by:

Jeffrey A. Jenkins
Associate Professor
School of Justice Studies
Roger Williams University

Description

Few psychological assessment tools of any type possess the measurement pedigree of the Strong Interest Inventory (SII). Since 1927, when Edward K. Strong, Jr., first developed the Strong Vocational Interest Blank (SVIB), the SII has maintained a standard of excellence nearly without peer in the measurement of career and vocational interests. The same can be said of the current (2004) revision of the instrument.

With its 80-year history, the SII is well-known and has been extensively used and studied. It measures career interests, that is, the preferences of individuals for those aspects of occupations that most appeal to them. Although the primary use of the SII is in career counseling, the revised *SII Manual* notes that the SII may also be useful for other decisions, such as identifying "preferences for activities and situations that are not specifically work related—for example, interests in recreational activities or preferences for types of people that may guide decisions about leisure time or living arrangements." (Donnay, Morris, Schaubhut, & Thompson, 2005, p. 2).

Briefly, the SII consists of 291 items presented as statements relating to the world of work and other life activities. Respondents indicate the extent of their preference for each item on a five-point Likert scale (Strongly Like, Like, Indifference, Dislike, and Strongly Dislike). In prior editions, a three-point scale was used. Examples include "Being your own boss," "Reading a book," and "Security guard." These reported preferences are compared to patterns of responses by people working in various occupations. Item responses are summarized as scores on six General Occupational Themes (GOT; Realistic, Investigative, Artistic, Social, Enterprising, and Conventional) based largely on Holland's vocational classification system, 30 Basic Interest Scales (BIS; e.g., Computer Hardware and Electronics, Athletics, Social Sciences), 122 Occupational Scales (OS; e.g., Accountant, Firefighter, Respiratory Therapist), and five

Personal Style Scales (PSS; Work Style, Learning Environment, Leadership Style, Risk Taking, and Team Orientation).

The newly revised 2004 version of the SII, while unchanged in overall format and approach, is improved and updated in significant ways. The first involves the addition or revision of numerous items resulting in fewer items overall (291 items, down from 317 in the 1994 version). The fewer items resulted in six, rather than the former eight, sections of the SII. Item responses were also changed from a three-point Likert format to a five-point scale for all items, improving variability of response choice and making response choices consistent for the entire instrument. The second involves revisions of and additions to the Basic Interest Scales. These include renaming ten of the scales, eliminating four, and adding ten new scales. The changes better reflect career choices available today. The third type of revision relates to the Occupational Scales, which have been increased from 211 to 244, expanding the range of occupational interests available to users. The fourth type of revision includes the addition of a PSS, Team Orientation, intended to measure the extent to which respondents prefer to work independently or with others. Other changes in the PSSs were also made, most importantly revision of the Risk Taking PSS to better measure a range of risk taking behavior. Finally, revisions in the Administrative Indexes in the report profile were made. The most important of these are the removal of the infrequent responses index and replacing it with a "typicality" index that reveals inconsistent response patterns.

The SII may also be used with a companion instrument, the Skills Confidence Inventory (SCI), developed in 1996. Although a revised *SCI Manual* was published in 2005 (Betz, Borgen, & Harmon, 2005), the SCI has not been revised since its initial development. The revised *SCI Manual* updates research using the instrument and its relationship and use with the revised SII.

Use in Counseling

The SII is intended to assist career counselors and their clients as they engage in an exploration of the client's interests. Understanding these interests may assist the client in decision making across the life span. In this regard, the SII is useful for a accomplishing a number of beneficial counseling activities, including identifying the client's specific interests, choosing a field of study in the college years, considering occupations in which those interests may best be pursued, changing careers, or remaining active in retirement. Along with the SCI, the SII offers the career counselor both a practical and a theoretical basis for issues explored in the counseling session.

As the *SII Manual* recommends, the SII is most useful when the client has been oriented toward its administration and interpretation. As with any psychological assessment, the purpose of the SII should be clarified prior to administration and the meaning of each of the specific scales found in the profile explained and discussed. (See American Educational Research Association, American Psychological Association & National Council on Measurement in Education, 1999). Perhaps most important is emphasizing the distinction between "interests" and "abilities," since, without guidance, clients may confuse what they "like" with what they "are good at." The *SII Manual* also recommends that clients are given an explanation of Holland's (1997) theory of vocational choice and the six general occupational interests.

The SCI is used in conjunction with the SII by helping the client to understand how good they believe themselves to be at various activities. As noted above, the SCI Profile provides a comparison of the client's interests and perceived confidence in their abilities in each of the six GOT. This is a useful tool for helping the client explore high interest/ high confidence areas for vocational and occupational choices, as well as addressing areas of high interest where clients have low confidence.

Technical Considerations

Norms for the SII consist of a sample of 2,250 working men and women. These were randomly selected from a pool of more than 20,000 online respondents to be generally representative of the U.S. workforce in terms of occupation, ethnicity, and gender. The specific rates of inclusion in the sample are reported in the SII Manual, as are other demographic characteristics. Development of the norm sample for the 2004 SII marked a departure from prior norm group data- gathering methods. For the first time, the majority of respondents included in the norm group responded to the web-based version of the SII, in part due to difficulties in obtaining mailed responses because of national security concerns in 2001 – 2002. The norm group, previously referred to as the General Reference Sample, is now called the General Representative Sample (GRS) to reflect a greater attempt to achieve representativeness through proportional selection based on gender and ethnicity. Unless indicated otherwise, the GRS was also the sample used for reliability and validity studies of the new version.

As has been true of past versions, reliability estimates for the SII are high for all scores reported. Chronbach's alpha for all six of the GOT scales is .90 or greater, and test-retest reliabilities average .85 over the six scales. This represents a modest improvement over the 1994 GOTs, and continues to exhibit one of the more remarkable characteristics of these useful scales.

The BIS scales exhibit a similar degree of reliability. Coefficient alpha ranges from .80 to .92 across the 30 BIS scales, with some scales showing a marked improvement from the 1994 version. Test-retest values show similar improvement. This reflects the care taken in the extensive revision of BIS items in 2004.

Test-retest reliability over a 2 to 23 month period was examined for the OS scales and was reported to range from .71 to .93.

Finally, the Personal Style Scales showed a high degree of reliability, as was true in 1994 (the year in which PSSs were introduced), with Cronbach's alpha ranging from .82 to .87. Test-retest reliabilities were similarly high (.74 to .91). Reliability for the SCI is unchanged from 1994, with Cronbach's alpha ranging from .84 to .88 (based on the original normative group).

While the aforementioned reliability estimates are based on adequate research samples of varying sizes, it is worth noting that the *SII Manual* also reports reliabilities separately for males and females. For the majority of scales, these estimates do not differ greatly and allow a greater degree of confidence in the use of the SII with both genders.

It is also worth noting that reliability as high or higher than the 1994 version was accomplished with fewer items in the 2004 version (317 and 291 items, respectively), while increasing the number of subscale scores reported.

Evidence of the validity of past versions of the SII is available (for the GOTs, see Donnay & Borgen, 1996, Savickas, Taber, & Spokane, 2002;; for the BISs, see Borgen & Lindley, 2003; Donnay & Borgen, 1996; for the OSs see Dik & Hansen, 2004; Strong, 1935; Zarrella & Schuerger, 1990; and for the PSSs, see Kahn, Nauta, Gailbreath, Tipps, & Chartrand, 2002; Lindley & Borgen, 2000). To add to this body of work, the 2004 edition was subjected to additional tests to examine its validity. This was of particular importance given the number of item revisions and additions and other changes this newest version represents. This review focuses only on additional support based on data using the 2004 edition.

For the GOTs, three sources of validity evidence were examined: scale intercorrelations, concurrent validity, and construct validity. Based on the GRS of 1,125 women and 1,125 men, intercorrelations among the six scales provide support for Holland's (see Cole, Whitney, & Holland, 1971) hexagonal structure of the GOT dimensions, showing stronger correlations between adjacent scales and weaker correlations between opposing scales. Concurrent and construct validity was supported by computing correlations between the GOTs and OSs, which showed high correlations between GOTs and their expected occupational counterparts (e.g, the correlation between the Artistic GOT and the Editor OS was .89 for both men and women). In addition, differences between mean GOTs for students in different fields found differences across majors in the predicted direction for each of the GOTs.

For the BISs, three sources of evidence are reported: correlations with the 1994 scales, concurrent validity, and construct validity. Although technological changes in the workforce led to significant changes in the BISs in 2004, strong relationships (ranging from .80 to .98) between substantially similar items comprising the same BISs in the newer and older versions support the validity of the revised scales. Concurrent validity was demonstrated by correlating the OSs with each BIS, which allowed examination of the highest and lowest correlating BISs of people in different occupations. This analysis also supports the construct validity of the revised BISs, along with the scale construction methods employed.

The concurrent validity of the OSs was examined using the degree of overlap between occupational samples and the GRS using the Q statistic (Tilton, 1937) and Cohen's (1988) d statistic. This analysis provided support for many, but not all, of the OSs. In addition, intercorrelations among OSs were examined to provide evidence of the scales' discriminant validity. Evidence of validity exists when intercorrelations among OSs within a GOT are greater than intercorrelations overall. Based on a study of these correlation in the GRS, the publisher found that higher median intercorrelations existed among within-theme OSs (ranging from .39 to .58) than median overall intercorrlations across all OSs for females (.05) and males (.07). This pattern of intercorrelations lends support to the scales' validity.

The construct, concurrent, and discriminant validity of the PSSs was examined in three different ways. First, the relationship between each PSS and the six GOTs, as well as their relationship to the specific BISs within each theme, were examined in the GRS. This analysis demonstrated a pattern of relationships showing fairly high consistency among themes, interests, and personal styles. For example, the PSS "Leadership Style" was highly correlated with the Enterprising theme (female = .69, male = .71) and the "Management" BIS (female = .61, male = .65), whereas it had a weak relationship to the "Realistic" theme (female = .13, male = .17) and the BIS "Mechanics and Construction" (female = .08, males = .09).

Second, PSS differences among occupational groups in the GRS were examined. Specifically, differences in the correlations between each PSS and the OSSs for various occupations would indicate support for the validity of the PSSs. Generally, this analysis revealed a pattern of correlations between OSS and occupations consistent with the validity of the scales.

Third, PSS mean differences among educational majors for a sample of 879 college students were examined. Rank ordering of means for each PSS revealed that students with high scores on certain PSSs tended to major in fields reflected by those personal styles. For example, those students scoring highest on "Learning Environment" tended to prefer majors such as literature and history, whereas those scoring lower preferred majors in law enforcement and computer technology. These results, while not determinative, lend support to the validity of the PSSs.

As noted earlier, the SCI has not been revised since it was first published in 1996. Therefore, the norm group for the SCI consists of the 1,853 participants in its original development (1,147 adults and 706 college students). Summaries of the instrument's development, norms, and technical characteristics are available elsewhere (Harmon, Borgen, & Berreth, 1996; Betz, Borgen, & Harmon, 2005). Additional studies of the SCI's reliability and validity since 1996, as well as its use with the 2004 SII, are discussed here.

The SCI was initially found to be quite reliable, with internal consistency reliabilities for the scales ranging from .84 to .88. Later studies have confirmed both the internal consistency (Betz & Gwilliam, 2002) and test-retest (Parsons & Betz, 1998) reliability of the instrument, reporting scale reliabilities in the .80 to .90 range.

Concurrent validity of the SCI was examined by Betz, Borgen, Kaplan, & Harmon (1998) by examining gender differences in skills confidence within occupations. Based on a large national sample of adults, they found only minimal differences in confidence within occupations, consistent with the theoretical expectation that women and men within occupations should have the same degree of confidence in their skills. Similar results were reported by Robinson & Betz (2004). Further, Betz et al. (1998) were able to predict Holland job family based on SCI scores.

Online Version

In addition to paper administration with mail-in scoring, web-based administration of the SII and SCI is available via www.skillsone.com. The internet offers a preferable way of administering the SII in many instances since it allows the respondent to more quickly work sequentially through items on the instruments, records responses, and provides immediate scoring and report generation. Other than administration format, there are no differences between the online and paper versions.

Overall Critique

A consistent strength of the SII has been its ability to assist respondents in understanding their interests in terms of both their personal activities and the demands of the workplace. These beneficial characteristics are improved in the revised SII. The revisions, while extensive, were well-planned and address only those aspects of the instrument that make it more user-friendly, more consistent with its goals, and more technically sound. Particularly commendable are reducing the number of items while maintaining or improving reliability, better aligning the BISs with today's occupational environment, and improving the PSSs. Also noteworthy are the integration of the SCI with the SII and the organized and well-formatted interpretive profiles and reports. In addition, it should be noted that the resources available to counselors, including classroom training, website information, and test manuals are extensive and particularly useful.

If a weakness in the revised version exists, it lies in the manner in which data in the GRS were gathered. The GRS was largely made up of respondents identified by their web-surfing for career information using online search engines. As noted earlier, while more than 20,000 responses were obtained from this source, approximately 10% eventually became members of the norm group. This self-selected and publisher-limited group may be a sufficient basis for comparison, but it may not. Moreover, by selecting respondents who surf the web for career information, the sample is further limited to those with potentially greater interests and abilities in computer technologies. Such individuals may differ in important ways from the general population for whom the instrument is designed. The publisher has carefully reported some demographic characteristics of the group, which is helpful in making this determination, but given uncertainties about the manner in which these data were collected, further study of the revised instrument in a variety of populations may be needed before full confidence in interpretation exists.

Nonetheless, the SII should rightfully maintain its position as a premier inventory in the measurement of career interests. Its history, its regular revision, its solid technical characteristics, and its interpretive reports make it a tool that every career counselor should understand and use.

References

American Educational Research Association, American Psychological Association, & National Council on Measurement in Education. (1999). *Standards for educational and psychological testing*. Washington, DC: American Educational Research Association.

Betz, N. E., Borgen, F. H., & Harmon, L. W. (2005). *Skills confidence inventory manual* (revised ed.). Mountain View, CA: CPP, Inc.

Betz, N. E., Borgen, F. H. Kaplan, A. & Harmon, L. W. (1998). Gender and Holland type as moderators of the validity and interpretive utility of the Skills Confidence Inventory. *Journal of Vocational Behavior, 53,* 281 – 299.

Betz, N. E., & Gwilliam, L. (2002). The utility of measures of self-efficacy for the Holland themes in African American and European American college students. *Journal of Career Assessment, 10,* 283 – 300.

Borgen, F. H., & Lindley, L. D. (2003). Optimal functioning in interests, self-efficacy, and personality. In W. B. Walsh (Ed.), *Counseling psychology and optimal human functioning* (pp. 55 – 91). Hillsdale, NJ: Lawrence Erlbaum Press.

Cohen, J. (1988). *Statistical power analysis for the behavioral sciences* (2nd ed.). Hillsdale, NJ: Lawrence Erlbaum Press.

Cole, N. S., Whitney, D. R., & Holland, J. L. (1971). A spatial configuration of occupations. *Journal of Vocational Behavior, 1,* 1 – 9.

Dik, B. J., & Hanson, J. C. (2004). Development and validation of discriminant functions for the Strong Interest Inventory. *Journal of Vocational Behavior, 64,* 182 – 197.

Donnay, D. A. C., & Borgen, F. H. (1996). The incremental validity of vocational self-efficacy: An examination of interest, self-efficacy, and occupation. *Journal of Counseling Psychology, 46,* 432 – 447.

Donnay, D. A. C., Morris, M. L., Schaubhut, N. A., & Thompson, R. C. (2005). *Strong interest inventory manual* (revised ed.). Mountain View, CA: CPP, Inc.

Harmon, L.W., Borgen, F.H., & Berreth, J.M. (1996). The Skills Confidence Inventory: A measure of self-efficacy. *Journal of Career Assessment, 4,* 457 – 477.

Holland, J. L. (1997). *Making vocational choices: A theory of vocational personalities and work environments* (3rd ed.). Odessa, FL: Psychological Assessment Resources.

Kahn, J. H., Nauta, M. M., Gailbreath, R. D., Tipps, J., & Chartrand, J. M. (2002). The utility of career and personality assessment in predicting academic progress. *Journal of Career Assessment, 10,* 3 – 23.

Lindley, L. D., & Borgen, F. H. (2000). Personal style scales of the Strong Interest Inventory: Linking personality and interests. *Journal of Vocational Behavior, 57,* 22 – 41.

Parsons, E., & Betz, N. E. (1998). Test-retest reliability and validity studies of the Skills Confidence Inventory. *Journal of Career Assessment, 6,* 1 – 12.

Robinson, C.H., & Betz, N.E. (2004). Test-retest reliability and concurrent validity of the expanded Skills Confidence Inventory. *Journal of Career Assessment, 12,* 407 – 422.

Savickas, M. L., Taber, B. J., & Spokane, A. R. (2002). Convergent and discriminant validity of five interest inventories. *Journal of Vocational Behavior, 61,* 139 – 184.

Strong, E. K., Jr. (1935). Predictive value of the Vocational Interest Test. *Journal of Educational Psychology, 26,* 332.

Tilton, J. W. (1937). The measurement of overlapping. *Journal of Educational Psychology, 28,* 656 – 662.

Zarrella, K. L., & Schuerger, J. M. (1990). Temporal stability of occupational interest inventories. *Psychological Reports, 66,* 1067 – 1074.

Wide Range Interest and Occupation Test (Second Edition) (WRIOT-2)

Joseph J. Glutting and Gary S. Wilkinson

PRO-ED Inc.
700 Shoal Creek Blvd.
Austin, TX 78757-6897
info@proedinc.com
www.proedinc.com

Target Population: Individuals between the ages of 9 through 80 years; individuals or groups, wide range of literacy levels and languages including: individuals who are English dominant and have college educations, people with limited English proficiency or little formal education, individuals with learning disabilities and/or reading problems.

Statement of the Purpose of the Instrument: To help people choose a satisfying career. The WRIOT-2 is an important tool for career selection because it provides participants with a better understanding of themselves, the types of occupations they prefer, their pattern of likes and dislikes among work-related activities, and the intensity and consistency of their response pattern.

Titles of Subtests, Scales, Scores Provided: There are 39 scales in all and each is organized according to three broad clusters: the Occupational Cluster, the Interest Cluster, and the Holland Type Cluster. Scales in the Occupational Cluster show the extent to which participants like 17 types of careers. The Interest Cluster has 16 scales and evaluates the needs, motives, and values that influence a participant's occupational choice. (The Interest Cluster is further arranged according to whether the scale provides information about the Functional Duties of Work, Chosen Skill Level, Social Rewards, Conditions of Work, and data about a participant's Response Pattern. The Holland Type Cluster (new to the WRIOT-2) offers scores at the most global level of analysis and the scores are supplementary. The Holland Type Cluster describes performance according to six occupational themes: Realistic, Investigative, Artistic, Social, Enterprising, and Conventional.

Forms and Levels Available, with Dates of Publication/Revision of Each: WRIOT-2 Picture Book and Response Form (paper-and pencil-form) and WRIOT-2 Software Program.

Date of Most Recent Edition of Test Manual, User's Guide, etc.: 2003

Languages in Which Available: English only.

Time:

Actual Test Time: 30 minutes.

Total Administration Time: 40 minutes individually, or 50–60 minutes to groups.

Norm Group(s) on Which Scores Are Based: Norms for the WRIOT-2 are based on a nationally-stratified sample and are representative of individuals across the United States ages 9 through 80 years. Unlike the 1979 edition of the WRIOT, norms for the WRIOT-2 are no longer gender based.

Manner in Which Results Are Reported for Individuals:

Types of Scores: Derived scores for the WRIOT-2 are expressed as percentiles that help participants make sense of their own performance. (The WRIOT-2 adds to the interpretive process by presenting descriptive labels for each range of percentiles.) Percentiles may also be converted to standard scores using the manual. The WRIOT-2 software program also produces a score profile for the participant and test examiner.

Report Format/Content:

BASIC SERVICE: Results are presented in a graphic portrayal of the individual's strengths and weaknesses in each of the 17 Occupational, 16 Interest, and 6 Holland-type scales. Occupations range from unskilled labor to the highest levels of technical, managerial, and professional training.

OPTIONS: The software package that comes with the WRIOT-2 provides the following features: Test administration on the computer, Data entry of responses when the WRIOT-2 is administered using the pencil-and-paper format, Test scoring, Report generation, Report writing assistance by providing narrative options to WRIOT-2 findings, Scored and unscored data storage, Information on purchase and installation of additional scoring uses.

Report Format/Content for Group Summaries: Not available.

Scoring:

Machine Scoring Service: Not available.

Hand Scoring: Not available.

Local Machine Scoring: Not available.
  Provisions/conditions/equipment required: For the WRIOT-2, the only option is to use computer software for scoring.

Computer Software Options Available: Computerized adaptive administration.

Other: The Counselor may use the computer software for scoring after administering the paper-and-pencil test.

Cost of Materials: Due to possible price changes since publication date, be sure to check the publisher's website.
WRIOT-2 Complete Kit, $365
WRIOT-2 Computer Administration program/25-use CD, $200
WRIOT-2 Response forms, pkg of 25, $47
WRIOT-2 Scoring CD, 25 uses, $100
Specimen Set: Picture Book, Administration CD, 25-use Scoring CD and a Manual.

Additional Comments of Interest to Users: The WRIOT-2 is a pictorial interest test which does not require reading or language understanding. It provides a level of self-projected ability, aspirations, and social conformity to help coordinate instruction/therapy plans with interest/attitude patterns. Ideal for use with educationally and culturally disadvantaged, learning disabled, mentally retarded, and deaf individuals. Picture titles can also be read to the blind.

Reviewed by:[1]

Albert M. Bugaj
Professor of Psychology
University of Wisconsin–Marinette

Description

A revision of the *Wide Range Interest-Opinion Test* of 1979, the Wide Range Interest and Occupation Test, second edition (WRIOT-2) is a nonverbal test meant to assist people in choosing careers. It is intended for individuals ages 9 to 80, and can be administered via computer or by paper and pencil with an accompanying picture book. When administered as a paper-and-pencil test, the data must be entered into the WRIOT-2 software program for scoring.

Consisting of 39 scales organized into three clusters, the WRIOT-2 asks individuals "to indicate whether they like, dislike, or are undecided about work situations illustrated in 238 pictures" (Glutting & Wilkinson, 2003, p.1). The Occupation Cluster shows the extent to which test takers like 17 career areas. The Interest Cluster consists of 16 scales evaluating needs, motives, and values that influence occupational choice. The final cluster, based on Holland's (1966, 1997) theory of occupation choice, identifies a person as a Realistic, Investigative, Artistic, Social, Enterprising, or Conventional type.

Use in Counseling

The manual says the test is suitable for individuals who are English dominant and have college educations, or those who have limited English proficiency or little formal education, as well as people with learning disabilities and/or reading problems, and individuals with mental retardation. The authors of the test feel that the WRIOT-2 may be used to study changes in a person's interests during periods of growth, decline, and/or life crises. The Occupational and Holland Type scales can be used in career planning. The manual suggests the test can be used by counselors in elementary school through college, employment counselors, rehabilitation counselors, and clinical psychologists, to name a few. WRIOT-2 scores are expressed as percentile ranks and reported in comparison to general norms, with no breakdown according to gender or group.

Technical Considerations

A preliminary set of 300 pictures was developed by revising items from the test's previous edition. A panel of judges placed each picture into what they felt were appropriate occupational categories. Seventeen occupational categories matching twelve occupational areas specified by the Division of Testing of the U.S. Employment Service (U.S. Department of Labor, 1965) and other publications including the *Complete Guide for Occupational Exploration* (JIST, 1993) were used. Items were retained only if inter-rater agreement yielded Kappa coefficients of reliability of.80 or higher, and only if their item-total point-biserial correlations were.30 or higher during pretesting of the

---

[1] Note: Portions of this review were adapted from the author's original review in the *Sixteenth Mental Measurement Yearbook* with permission of the Buros Institute.

items, and again following standardization. A similar three-step process determined the content validity of the Interest and Holland-type clusters, resulting in the final 238 items. Comparison of the pictures in the Holland-type scales to similar listings in the *Dictionary of Holland Occupational Codes* (Gottfredson & Holland, 1996) resulted in a high rate of agreement as to each items appropriate category (K +.88).

The manual states that approximately 92% of the pictures in the WRIOT-2 were rated as clear and unambiguous by a panel of judges. Neither the nature of the scale used in the ratings nor the number of judges (referred to as "experts and users") is provided. Although the ratings of the pictures for clarity are an improvement over the earlier edition, and the occupations illustrated might appear unambiguous to "experts and users," it cannot be ascertained if they are unambiguous to the range of individuals who are potential test takers.

The normative sample of the WRIOT-2 consisted of 1,286 participants. The sample closely matched the U.S. population on age, gender, race/ethnicity, education, and geographic distribution as reported by the U.S. Census Bureau (2001). Minor weightings applied to various groups in the sample brought the sample into alignment with census figures. No norms exist for the specialized groups for whom the test is said to be suitable (e.g., individuals with mental retardation).

Internal consistency of the WRIOT-2 was determined by calculating Cronbach's alpha for each scale for six different age groups (total n = 1,286), the youngest ranging from 9 to 14, the oldest being 50 and above. With the exception of the scale measuring inconsistent response patterns, Cronback's alpha was above .82 for all scales. On the Inconsistency scale, the average alpha across age groups was .68.

Test-retest reliability was determined for two age groups: adolescents (n = 67) and adults (n = 49). Median time between administrations was 23 days. Test-retest reliability was lowest for the inconsistency scale (.68 for adolescents, .44 for adults). Other test-retest reliabilities generally ranged from .61 to .91, being somewhat higher for adults. These measures were not obtained on specific groups such as individuals with limited English proficiency.

Convergent validity was determined by intercorrelating each scale on the WRIOT-2. Most intercorrelations (ranging between .50 and .87) proved to be logically consistent. However, because the same pictures are used for all three "clusters" on the test, inflated correlations between scales could result.

Several methods were used to determine the criterion and construct validity of the WRIOT-2. First, using a contrasted-groups approach, 503 individuals from the standardization sample were placed into a Holland-type classification on the basis of their occupations. Analysis of variance indicated participants received significantly higher scores for their own type in comparison to highly incongruent types.

In another study, the WRIOT-2 and the Strong Interest Inventory (SII) were administered to 72 adults. The criterion validity of the Holland-type scales was strongest, with each scale on the WRIOT-2 correlating significantly only with its SII counterpart (r ranging from .56 to .68). Correlations for occupational scales ranged from .40 to .73.

The occupational scales of the WRIOT-2 were also subjected to a discriminant function analysis, resulting in five functions that were logically related to Holland types, although item overlap may have affected the results.

Computer-Based Version

The manual (Glutting & Wilkinson, 2003) is well written and informative. The computer program loads without difficulty and is easy to navigate. The instructions to the test taker are straightforward. Both the computerized or paper-and-pencil formats of the test are easy to administer. The computer-generated report provides a brief description of each scale and extended paragraph-length descriptions of the three highest scores on the Occupational cluster. Extended descriptions for additional scales in the Occupation Cluster and the Interest and Holland career areas assessed can also be printed. This information is also available in the test manual. A "travel disc" allows the administration of the test on computers on which the full program has not been installed. This disc allows the collection of responses to test items, but scoring must be performed on a computer on which the entire program has been installed.

Overall Critique

While the WRIOT-2 can be recommended for use with general population, its use with specific populations (e.g., those with learning disabilities or limited reading ability) must be called into question. The test's norms are appropriate for the general population, a group for whom rigorous methods were used in development. For more specific groups no norms were developed, nor were validity and reliability data collected. Further, it cannot be ascertained if groups such as individuals with mental retardation would perceive the stimulus materials as unambiguous.

Of the WRIOT-2 "clusters," the Holland-type Cluster seems to be the most robust, with scores correlating with their counterparts on the SII. Individuals already established in specific occupational areas also received appropriate scores on this cluster. The Occupational Cluster appears somewhat weaker. Although many of the scales correlate with their SII counterparts, no data using a known-groups procedure are provided (i.e., data that could document strong criterion validity). Measures of convergent and divergent validity analyzing the relationships between the scales on the WRIOT-2 may also have been affected by item overlap.

The WRIOT-2 does appear to have strong internal consistency, as measured by Cronbach's alpha. Test-retest reliability is high. However, additional testing of specific scales is needed. For example, the "Likes scale" is designed to measure social desirability by counting the number of times a test taker selects "like" as an option. However, social desirability bias could best be assessed by instructing a group of research participants to attempt to "fake good" on the test, using their response pattern as a criterion, or by examining the relationship of this scale to other tests measuring social desirability. Despite a lack of research on non–English-speaking populations or on exceptional individuals, the WRIOT-2 should prove a useful research tool for studying the career interests of such individuals. However, it cannot be recommended as a counseling tool for those groups, although it is highly suitable for the general population.

References

Glutting, J. J., & Wilkinson, G. S. (2003). *WRIOT-2 (Wide Range Interest & Occupation Test Second Edition).* Wilmington, DE: Wide Range Inc.

Gottfredson, G. D., & Holland, J .L. (1996). *Dictionary of Holland Occupational Codes—Third edition.* Odessa, FL: Psychological Assessment Resources.

Holland, J. L. (1966). *The psychology of vocational choice.* Waltham, MA: Blaisdell.

Holland, J .L. (1997) *Making vocational choices: A theory of vocational personalities and work environments.* (3rd ed.). Odessa, FL: Psychological Assessment Resources.

JIST. (1993). *Complete guide for occupational exploration.* Indianapolis, IN: JIST Works.

U.S. Census Bureau. (2001).Washington, DC: US Government Printing Office.

U.S. Department of Labor. (1965). *Dictionary of occupational titles.* (3rd ed.; Vol. II: Occupational Classification). Washington, DC: U.S. Government Printing Service.

CHAPTER 10

CAREER DEVELOPMENT / CAREER MATURITY MEASURES

- Barriers to Employment Success Inventory (Second Edition) (BESI)

- Career Attitudes and Strategies Inventory (CASI)

- Career Decision Self-Efficacy Scale (CDSE) and CDSE Short Form

- Career Factors Inventory (CFI)

- Career Thoughts Inventory (CTI)

- Career Transitions Inventory (CTI)

- Childhood Career Development Scale (CCDS)

- Job Search Attitude Inventory (JSAI) (Third Edition)

- Job Survival and Success Scale (JSSS)

- Quality of Life Inventory (QOLI)

Barriers to Employment Success Inventory (Second Edition) (BESI)

John J. Liptak

JIST Publishing, Inc.
8902 Otis Avenue
Indianapolis, IN 46216
www.jist.com

Target Population: Ages 14 and up.

Statement of the Purpose of the Instrument: The Barriers to Employment Success Inventory (BESI) helps individuals identify the barriers that keep them from getting a good job or from getting ahead in their career. It then offers strategies for overcoming those barriers.

Titles of Subtests, Scales, Scores Provided: Scores in five categories representing the most common barriers job seekers face: Personal and Financial, Emotional and Physical, Career Decision-Making and Planning, Job-Seeking Knowledge, and Training and Education

Forms and Levels Available, with Dates of Publication/Revision of Each: Barriers to Employment Success Inventory Assessment; Barrier to Employment Success Inventory Administrator's Guide. No special qualifications required. Second Edition, 2002.

Date of Most Recent Edition of Test Manual, User's Guide, etc.: 2002

Languages in Which Available: English only.

Time:

Actual Test Time: 20 – 30 minutes (50 items)

Total Administration Time: 20 – 30 minutes (self-administered)

Norm Group(s) on Which Scores Are Based: The primary norm group for the BESI was male and female adults. The adults used in the norm group were college students, long-term unemployed, offenders and ex-offenders, and welfare-to-work clients.

Manner in Which Results Are Reported for Individuals: Scale scores are profiled into three score ranges with easy-to-understand interpretations for each scale (raw scores between 10 and 19 indicate that the respondent has fewer barriers than most unemployed adults, raw scores between 20 and 30 indicate that the respondent has a similar amount of barriers as most unemployed adults, and scores between 31 and 40 indicate that the respondent has more barriers than most unemployed adults). Self-scoring and self-interpreting.

Types of Scores: Raw scores are calculated for each of the five scales (Personal and Financial, Emotional and Physical, Career Decision-Making and Planning, Job-Seeking Knowledge, and Training and Education) on the BESI.

Report Format/Content:

Basic Service: Assessment is self-scoring and self-interpreting. Interpretation Guide and Action Plan are included with each assessment. Respondents follow a series of five steps to complete the BESI.

Report Format/Content for Group Summaries: Not available.

Scoring:

Machine Scoring Service: Not available.

Hand Scoring: Counselee.

Time required for scoring: Less than 5 minutes. Included in administration time above.

Local Machine Scoring: Not available

Computer Software Options Available: Computerized adaptive administration

Ways in Which Computer/Online Version Differs: Automated scoring and automated report generation

Cost of Materials: Due to possible price changes since publication date, be sure to check publisher website

Specimen Set: $39.95 for a package of 25. Each package includes a free Administrator's Guide. Administrator's Guide also available for free download from jist.com.

Additional Comments of Interest to Users: Barriers to Employment Success Inventory, Third Edition available 2007, includes updated research, validity, and reliability data, and an enhanced interpretation guide. Check publisher website for details.

Published Reviews of the Instrument in the Last 15 Years:

Spies, R.A., & Plake, B.S. (Eds.) (2005). *The sixteenth mental measurements yearbook.* Lincoln, NE: Buros Institute of Mental Measurements.

Cavan, D.E. (2001). Review: Barriers to Employment Success Inventory. *Association for Assessment in Counseling and Education Newsnotes.* http://aac.ncat.edu/

Reviewed by:[1]

Kathy E. Green
Professor,
Morgridge College of Education,
University of Denver

Description

The Barriers to Employment Success Inventory (BESI) is a 50-item paper-and-pencil or online measure intended to assess individuals' perceived barriers to getting a job,

---

[1] Note: Portions of this review were adapted from the author's original review in the Sixteenth Mental Measurement Yearbook with permission of the Buros Institute.

keeping a job, or succeeding in a job. The BESI can be self-administered and self-interpreted; it is also self-scored via adding responses to obtain subtotals. Results, which are obtained immediately, are used to initiate a dialogue between the job seeker and counselor about barriers to job or career success and how barriers might be addressed (Liptak, 2002).

The BESI takes 10 – 15 minutes to complete. It is written for adolescents and adults with an eighth-grade or above reading level. Responses are written directly on the nonreusable booklet. Color coding is used to indicate which responses are to be added together and transferred to a profile and interpretation guide. Examples of barrier interpretation and strategies for overcoming barriers are provided. The BESI was developed from case studies, reported needs of unemployed adults, interviews with unemployed adults, literature review, and consultation with employment and career counselors. The primary basis for the BESI was Miller and Oetting's (1977) identification of employment barriers. A pool of 100 items was reviewed by professional counselors for appropriateness and category placement, and the pool ultimately reduced to 50 items.

Use in Counseling

The author describes the BESI as a counseling tool whose purpose is to open a dialogue about the client's perception of employment barriers and how barriers could be addressed. The BESI seems to be oriented to clients with lower educational levels. The author implies the BESI aligns with the National Employment Counseling Association's competencies related to recognition of "special needs and barriers of minorities, women seeking nontraditional occupations, culturally different immigrants, the disabled, older workers, and persons with AIDS" (Liptak, 2002, p. 5) with four pages of the 12-page administrator's guide devoted to discussion of changes and challenges in the workplace.

Five scale scores with 10 items each are used to summarize more than 30 barriers. These five scales are described as follows: P (Personal and Financial) measures concerns about resources for basic survival (e.g., health care, money, childcare). E (Emotional and Physical) measures self-esteem, insecurity, physical issues, anger, and depression. C (Career Decision-Making and Planning) measures concerns about goal setting, finding information, identifying interests and values, and small and home-based business opportunities. J (Job-Seeking Knowledge) measures concerns about effective job search skills and communication skills. T (Training and Education) addresses concerns about lack of knowledge and skills related to education or training. After completion of closed-response items, clients are provided items that ask for open-ended self-report of their most troublesome barriers in each of the five areas. Suggestions for overcoming barriers are provided with space for client comments.

The BESI seems to be most useful as a preliminary intake measure for career counselors to promote discussion or to get initial ideas about how services might be directed. Client self-interpretation of results may not be advisable for clients with limited job search skills. Suggestions for overcoming barriers are listed; however, these suggestions are simplistic and possibly impractical to implement without the assistance of a counselor. While some normative interpretation is provided in the test booklet, it is not clear how norm values were obtained and so counselors accustomed to translating inventory scores with reference to similar groups may not find this information useful. The vocational counselor could use the BESI to identify dominant client concerns about job skills and employment barriers. If clients answer the open-ended questions asking for identification of the most troublesome barrier, the counselor could use this along with scale scores as a starting point for a directed conversation. In-depth information about skills, values, and attitudes might subsequently be obtained through qualitative interview or through use of measures with strong support for validity (Krumboltz, 1994; Nevill & Super, 1989).

Technical Considerations

Internal consistency and test-retest reliability were assessed for each score category in the development study, with values ranging from .87 to .92 for coefficient alpha ($n = 135$) and from .79 to .90 for stability ($n = 95$, six months between tests). The participants were more than 150 adults participating in government-sponsored job training programs. Although it seems the 10 items comprising each score category were the basis for calculating internal consistency, this was not made clear. A split-half coefficient is also provided even though no total score is calculated. Internal consistency was high, and so were the test-retest correlations. A second, larger sample is noted in the manual, but no reliability results were provided for that sample.

The author cites low scale intercorrelations as evidence of concurrent validity. Scale intercorrelations of .45 to .70 were moderate rather than low. These intercorrelations would be support for validity if scales were derived from theory or from a confirmed factor structure. Neither theory nor a proposed factor structure were noted, thus scale intercorrelations cannot be taken as support for validity. No validity information aside from content validity taken from professional counselors' review of inventory items was provided. The effects of job training on perceived barriers would be of interest.

The sample used to estimate reliability was described as adults in job training. A more complete description of the sample with the distribution of participants by race, gender, ethnicity, age, educational level, and marital status is needed.

After clients calculate category scores, they place scores on a profile, which has boundaries for "fewer than average", "average", and "more than average" barriers for most adults. No explanation is provided of how these boundaries were determined. The administrator's manual lists category means for the development sample and for another larger sample, and it seems the boundaries were roughly determined by adding and subtracting one standard deviation from the category mean. However, the means differ across categories by up to about four points and standard deviations differ as well, but the boundaries for low, average, and high are shown as the same. This profile would likely be interpreted as normative, but normed data are not provided. Also, the reference group in the profile is listed as "most adults," which is misleading because the data referenced are a sample of unemployed adults participating in job training who may not be representative of most adults.

Online Versions

The BESI is available for online administration, however details were not provided in the administrator's manual. Counselors open an account for use of clients and test results are then provided to the counselor in PDF format. More information may be available from the publisher at www.jist.com.

Overall Critique

This instrument is similar to other self-administered assessments but lacks sufficient technical information on development, norming, and validation. Its strength is its brevity, availability of immediate feedback, and ease of use. Also, it is inexpensive. While both internal consistency and stability reliability are high, support for validity other than content validity, in particular criterion-related validity, is lacking. Since there is a clear intended outcome resulting from BESI use and job counseling—that is, getting and keeping a job—future validation studies could profitably address whether the BESI and subsequent counseling predict this outcome. The lack of validation information limits the instrument's use to being a tool to promote discussion rather than a predictor of employment counseling and job training outcomes. The BESI will not provide validated scores for any of its subscales. However, its stated purpose is to help individuals identify major barriers to employment and the BESI seems useful for this purpose.

For additional reviews of this instrument see Green (2005) and Camara (2005).

References

Camara, W. J. (2005). Review of *Barrier to Employment Success Inventory* (2nd ed). In R. A. Spies & B. S. Plake (Eds.), *The sixteenth mental measurements yearbook.* (pp. 90 – 93) Lincoln, NE: Buros Institute.

Green, K. E. (2005). Review of *Barrier to Employment Success Inventory* (2nd ed). In R. A. Spies & B. S. Plake (Eds.), *The sixteenth mental measurements yearbook.* (pp. 93 – 94) Lincoln, NE: Buros Institute.

Krumboltz, J. D. (1994). The Career Beliefs Inventory. *Journal of Counseling and Development,* 72, 424 – 428.

Liptak, J. J. (2002). BESI: *Barrier to Employment Success Inventory Administrator's Guide* (2nd ed.). Indianapolis, IN: JIST Works.

Miller, C. D., & Oetting, G. (1977). Barriers to employment and the disadvantaged. *Personnel and Guidance Journal,* 56, 89 – 93.

Nevill, D. D., & Super, D. E. (1989). *The Values Scale—Theory, applications, and research.* Palo Alto, CA: Consulting Psychologists Press.

CAREER ATTITUDES AND STRATEGIES INVENTORY (CASI)

John L. Holland and Gary D. Gottfredson

Psychological Assessment Resources
16204 N. Florida Avenue
Lutz, FL 33549
custserv@parinc.com
http://www3.parinc.com/

Target Population: Adults.

Statement of the Purpose of the Instrument: This instrument helps to identify and clarify career problems and stimulates constructive discussion of these areas.

Titles of Subtests, Scales, Scores Provided: (1) Job Satisfaction, (2) Work Involvement, (3) Skill Development, (4) Interpersonal Abuse, (5) Family Commitment, (6) Risk-Taking Style, (7) Dominant Style, (8) Career Worries, (9) Geographical Barriers. Interpretive Summary Booklet provides three score ranges with easy-to-understand interpretation for each scale.

Forms and Levels Available, with Dates of Publication/Revision of Each: Manual; Inventory Booklet; Hand-Scorable Answer Sheet; Your CASI Interpretive Summary Booklet. All Qualification Level A. Publication date for all: July 22, 1994.

Date of Most Recent Edition of Test Manual, User's Guide, etc.: July 22, 1994.

Languages in Which Available: English only.

Time:

Actual Test Time: Self-administered.

Total Administration Time: 35 minutes.

Norm Group(s) on Which Scores Are Based: 747 (36% men, 64% women), 17 – 77 years old, mixed educational background, six ethnic groups.

Manner in Which Results Are Reported for Individuals: Raw scale scores are transferred to interpretive summary booklet, which provides three score ranges with easy-to-understand interpretation for each scale.

  Types of Scores (e.g., standard scores, percentile ranks, verbal labels): 9 scale scores: (Job Satisfaction, Work Involvement, Skill Development, Dominant Style, Career Worries, Interpersonal Abuse, Family Commitment, Risk-Taking Style, Geographical Barriers, plus a Career Obstacles checklist).

Report Format/Content: None.

Report Format/Content for Group Summaries: None.

Scoring:

Machine Scoring Service: Not available.

  TIME REQUIRED FOR SCORING AND RETURNING (MAXIMUM): 5 minutes to score and profile.

Hand Scoring:

SCORED BY: Clerk; Counselor.

TIME REQUIRED FOR SCORING: 5 minutes to score and profile.

Local Machine Scoring: Not available.

Computer Software Options Available: Not available.

Cost of Materials: Due to possible price changes since publication date, be sure to check with the publisher website.

CASI Introductory Kit (includes CASI Manual, 25 Inventory Booklets, 25 Hand-Scorable Answer Sheets, and 25 Your Interpretive Summary Booklets), $124; Manual, $32; Inventory Booklet (pkg/25), $34; Hand-Scorable Answer Sheets (pkg/25), $34; Your CASI Interpretive Summary Booklet (pkg/25), $34.

Specimen Set: One each: Inventory Booklet, Hand-Scorable Answer Sheet, Your CASI Interpretive Summary Booklet. No Charge.

Counselee Materials: Inventory Booklet, reusable; Hand-Scorable Answer Sheet, not reusable; Your CASI Interpretive Summary Booklet, not reusable.

Reviews:

Donohue, R. (2003). An evaluation of the Career Attitudes and Strategies Inventory and Holland's propositions in terms of predicting career change and career persistence. *Australian Journal of Psychology, 55,* 121 – 122.

Reviewed by:[1]

Michael B. Brown
Professor of Psychology
East Carolina University

Description

The Career Attitudes and Strategies Inventory (CASI) is a self-scored, self-profiled, and self-interpreted inventory developed to identify the attitudes, feelings, and obstacles that affect the careers of adults. The nine scales of the CASI survey areas related to career adaptation, and taken together are intended to provide an assessment of the client's job stability. The scales include Job Satisfaction, Work Involvement, Skill Development, Dominant Style, Career Worries, Interpersonal Abuse, Family Commitment, Risk-Taking Style, and Geographical Barriers. The resulting score profile provides an overview of the positive and negative aspects of a client's career adjustment.

---

[1] Portions of this review are adapted, by permission, from the author's original review in the Thirteenth Mental Measurements Yearbook. This review is a reprint from the fourth edition of A Counselor's Guide to Career Assessment Instruments. The test publisher informed the editors that the instrument is unchanged since the last edition of the Guide. It is reprinted for readers' convenience. Check publisher's web site for updates.

Following in the tradition of the *Self-Directed Search* (Holland, 1994), the inventory is intended to be completed and scored by the client. The CASI consists of three parts: The 130-item questionnaire, a self-scoring answer sheet, and an Interpretive Summary. The materials are attractively done. The four-page test booklet is well-designed and easy to read. The assessment procedure is relatively straight forward. For each item on the inventory the client chooses whether a statement is True, Mostly True, Mostly False, or False. Examples of statements include "I don't like change in my life" and "I listen to advice about how I should do my job." Responses are indicated by circling the appropriate response on the answer sheet. The two true responses are each designated by an upper case letter "T"; the lighter colored T is circled for Mostly True and the darker T for True. A similar system using upper case letters "F" indicates Mostly False or False. The answer sheet also includes a separate checklist of 21 potential career obstacles.

The carbonless answer sheet automatically transfers the answers to a scoring grid. The client adds up his or her raw scores and transfers them to a profile sheet on the Interpretive Summary which provides a visual representation of the relative strength of each of the aspects of the client's career. Each scale has three potential interpretations, each corresponding to one of three raw score ranges. The interpretive summaries are succinct and clearly written.

The 46-page manual, while brief, is clearly written and organized. Practical applications of the CASI and scoring procedures are concisely described. Interpretive information includes a brief description of each scale along with 14 case profiles. The illustrative profiles are helpful and include persons with a range of ages and occupations, although occupations which require more education and training predominate. The major limitation of the illustrative profiles is the brevity of case material and corresponding interpretations.

While the CASI is not an overly complex instrument, the authors suggest that the user should read and become familiar with literature on vocational identity (such as Holland, Johnston, & Asama, 1993). An article by Gottfredson (1996) provides an additional discussion of the CASI. The manual has a very useful section on becoming a competent user of the inventory. There is a even short "test" to help the user assess understanding of the basic concepts of the CASI.

Use in Counseling

The authors believe that the CASI is most useful for evaluating job dissatisfaction, job changing, work adjustment, or work dysfunction. They view it as an effective way to identify and gather information about career problems and promote discussion, and recommend its use as a way for professionals to broaden their assessments to include relevant aspects of career adjustment.

The CASI is also recommended for use on an organizational level. It may be used as a needs assessment tool, providing information about sources of worker dissatisfaction or identifying potential areas of need to be addressed by training and development programs. The authors suggest the use of the CASI as a program evaluation tool, comparing pre- and post-intervention scores to identify changes resulting from organizational interventions. They also view the inventory as a helpful tool in assessing the outcomes of individual counseling.

The CASI may be most useful to the career counselor when used as a checklist to obtain a client's self-rating in a number of areas that are relevant to career adjustment. As such it can be used to rapidly "screen" for client opinions and attitudes and generate information for discussion between client and counselor. I would certainly find it useful as a pre-interview survey, a device to generate discussion or to identify potentially problematic areas that would benefit from further exploration. The suggestion that the CASI be used by counselors providing personal counseling as a broad assessment device to gather information about the client's career issues is appealing, although counselors reading this book are not likely to overlook the career domain in counseling.

The CASI was developed as a supplement to other measures of aptitudes, interests, and specific career-relevant characteristics, and additional instruments must be administered if the counselor is interested in these domains.

Technical Considerations

The current inventory is the third version in the development of the CASI. The first version was developed by the authors based on theoretical concepts, clinical experience and the use of a 135-person exploratory analysis group. The second version was created from item analyses using both data derived from the first version and new data collected from an additional 266 individuals. Many new items were added to improve the scale. The third version is derived from further refinement of the second version.

The normative sample consists of persons who participated in the research on the second and third versions. The resulting group of 747 persons range in age from 17 to 77 years of age. Women are overrepresented in the norm group (64% women, 26% men, 11% unreported), although the manual points out that there appears to be only small differences in the scores of men and women. The majority of the group is composed of persons with some education beyond high school (only 10% of the sample had 12 or fewer years of education). It is difficult to ascertain the actual ethnic composition of the norm group, as over one-third of the group were not asked to provide an ethnic identification. There is no indication of the geographic representation or socioeconomic status of the sample. Normative data provided for career obstacles are considered "approximate" as identical instructions were not given to each of the two groups used in the norming process.

Internal consistency reliability coefficients for the CASI scales ranged from .76 to .92, which is adequate for this type of inventory. Test-retest reliability was assessed using a small sample ("N = 38 – 40") of working adults between the ages of 25 and 54. The average interval was 13 days, and test-retest reliabilities of the scales ranged from .66 to .94. This sample is too small to adequately determine test-retest reliabilities.

Validity is inferred through a number of methods. One of the difficulties in assessing the validity of the CASI is that different versions were used at different points during its development to determine validity. For instance, data on some aspects of concurrent validity were obtained by using 112 – 134 persons who completed Version 2 of the CASI. Note that this is a rather small group, and that Version 3 is likely to be somewhat different from Version 2. Caution is suggested when interpreting the validity data, since both the norm group and the CASI itself appear to have undergone substantial changes from the first to the third version.

Concurrent validity is addressed through correlation of the CASI and the Hoppock Job Satisfaction Blank, a two-item indicator of general happiness, career search activities, and measures of vocational identity and personality type. Correlation coefficients are provided for the correlations between various scales and the measures of concurrent validity. Correlations for each of these comparisons are said to be in the expected direction. For example, persons with low scores on Job Satisfaction and high scores on Career Worries, Interpersonal Abuse, and Family Commitment report being involved in a number of job search activities. The CASI and the Hoppock Job Satisfaction Blank have a correlation of .86, while the CASI and the measure of general happiness have a correlation of .71, which is consistent with a positive relationship between the two measures of job satisfaction and positive disposition.

Construct validity is inferred through an examination of the intercorrelations between various CASI scales. As an example, the Job Satisfaction Scale is negatively correlated with the Career Worries and Interpersonal Abuse Scales. Correlations range between .60 for Job Satisfaction and Career Worries to .53 for Career Worries and Interpersonal Abuse Scales. Correlations are all said to "appear predictable from the scale titles."

Overall Critique

The lack of adequate norms and limitations in the determination of its validity presents serious drawbacks for the CASI. In addition, there are no data that illuminate the extent, if any, of ethnic differences on the CASI. The structure and appearance of the materials give it a look of psychometric sophistication that exceeds its present technical state. This is of particular importance when clients self-score and interpret their results, as there is a danger that the client would consider the results to be more exact than warranted by its technical characteristics. I recommend that the use of the CASI be preceded by a discussion of the limitations of the instrument and the meaning of its scale scores.

The answer system, combined with the compact layout of the answer sheet, may prove confusing for some clients. Counselors who use the CASI will need to ensure that clients understand the directions for answering and are able to maintain their place as they complete the survey. Some clients may need more guidance to follow the directions for self-scoring, or the counselor may decide to do the scoring for the client. The interpretations may require more detailed explanation and integration by the counselor, particularly for clients who are less sophisticated or have lower verbal ability.

Given these substantial limitations, is there a use for the CASI? I think that there is, provided the counselor use the results as one broad source of career information about the client. It may be a useful tool to stimulate client self-exploration and further discussion in the counseling session. It should be used in an ipsative rather than normative fashion until better psychometric data is produced which would allow the user to make normative comparisons with confidence.

References

Gottfredson, G. D. (1996). The assessment of career status with the Career Attitudes and Strategies Inventory. *Journal of Career Assessment, 4(4)*, 363 – 381.

Holland, J. L. (1994). *The Self-Directed Search.* Odessa, FL: Psychological Assessment Resources.

Holland, J. L., Johnston, J. A., & Asama, N. F. (1993). The Vocational Identity Scale: A diagnostic and treatment tool. *Journal of Career Assessment, 1,* 1 – 12.

CAREER DECISION SELF-EFFICACY SCALE (CDSE) AND (CDSE-SHORT FORM)

Nancy E. Betz and Karen M. Taylor

Nancy E. Betz and Karen M. Taylor
478 Whitney Avenue
Worthington, OH 43085

Target Population: Students representing racial ethnic minority groups, adults experiencing work adjustment concerns, women.

Statement of the Purpose of the Instrument: Measures an individual's degree of belief that he/she can successfully complete tasks necessary to making career decisions.

Titles of Subtests, Scales, Scores Provided: Subtests: The five subscales included behaviors pertinent to: (1) accurate self-appraisal, (2) gathering occupational information, (3) goal selection, (4) making plans for the future, and (5) problem solving.

Scales: Responses are obtained on a 10-point scale ranging from Complete Confidence (9) to No Confidence (0). The item can range from 0 to 9, with larger numbers reflecting "easier" items. An alternative five-level confidence continuum (ranging from No Confidence at All, scores 1, to Complete Confidence, scores 5) has also been instituted.

Scores Provided: A total score reflecting self-efficacy expectations with regard to all 50 career decision-making tasks is calculated by summing the confidence ratings for the 50 items. The maximum score on the Career Decision Self-Efficacy Scale (CDSE) is 250 or 450. Confidence scores for each of the five subscales are calculated from the sum of responses to the 10 scale items; the maximum subscale score is 90 when the 10-level response is used.

Forms and Levels Available, with Dates of Publication/Revision of Each: CDSE-SF (short form): 1996. The CDSE short form (CDSE-SF) consists of five 5-item scales, or a total of 25 items. Responses are again obtained using a 10-level confidence continuum, ranging from No Confidence at All (1) to Complete Confidence (10). The short form was developed by eliminating five of the ten items from each of the five CDSE scales.

Levels available: Adapted the CDSE for use with middle school students in 1996.

A revision of the CDSE for high school students was undertaken in 1992.

Date of Most Recent Edition of Test Manual, User's Guide, Etc.: Manual for the Career Decision Self-Efficacy Scale and CDMSE—Short Form by Nancy E. Betz and Karen M. Taylor, February, 2001.

Languages in Which Available: English, and Hebrew version, using 6-item subscales.

Norm Group(s) on Which Scores Are Based: The CDSE was initially validated in sample of 346 college students, 156 students (68 males and 88 females) attending a private liberal arts college and 193 students (60 males and 130 females) attending a large state university. Both schools were located in the Midwest.

Manner in Which Results Are Reported for Individuals:

Types of Scores: Means and standard deviations for gender and ethnicity subgroups are available from Nancy Betz. Percentiles corresponding to CDSE-SE subscale scores and total score are also available.

Scoring Instructions (CDSE)

The 50 items are distributed among five subscales, indicated on the scoring key. Each subscale score is the sum of the responses given to the ten items on that subscale. Thus, total subscale, scores can range from 0 to 90. A total score is the sum of the five subscale scores or, alternatively stated, the sum. across all 50 items. The maximum is 450.

Scoring Instructions (CDSE)-SF

The 25 items are rationally distributed among five subscales, as indicated on the scoring key. Each subscale score is the sum of the responses given to the five items on that subscale. Thus, total subscale scores can range from 5 to 25. A total score is the sum of the five subscale scores or, alternatively stated, the sum across all 25 items. The maximum is 125.

Scoring:

Machine Scoring Service: Not available

Cost of Materials: Due to possible price changes since publication date, be sure to check with author/publisher address below.

Counselee Materials:

Manual: $20.00

Purchasing the rights entitles the user to the CDSE or CDSE-SF and scoring keys. The cost is $100.00 per 150 administrations, and $75.00 per each additional 150 administrations. (User does copying and obtaining of own scoring sheets or setting up on computer).

Graduate students wishing to use the CDSE or CDSE-SF in a thesis or dissertation may receive a 50% discount on scale use (not the manual) by supplying the following:

> Name, department and university affiliation, mailing address, and email
> Thesis or dissertation proposal title
> Name of thesis or dissertation adviser
> Adviser's address and email
> Time frame for data collection and number of CDSE or CDSE-SF planned to administer

For ordering information contact:
Nancy E. Betz, Ph.D.
478 Whitney Avenue
Worthington, OH 43085

Published Reviews of the Instrument in the Last 15 Years:

Plake, B. S., & Impara, J. C. (Eds.). (2001). *The fourteenth mental measurements yearbook.* Lincoln, NE: Buros Institute of Mental Measurements.

Reviewed By:[1]

James K. Benish
Adjunct Faculty Member
Department of Education
Carroll College
Helena, Montana

Description

Both the standard and short forms of the Career Decision Self-Efficacy Scale were originally published in 1983 by Nancy E. Betz and Karen M. Taylor at Ohio State University. The current version (revised August 2006) has changed very little from the 1983 edition. The authors made note that "due to trade marking of the term 'career decision making' by" another party, the original title of the scale was changed from "Career Decision Making Self-Efficacy Scale" to the present title. The acronym for this new scale and the short form version is CDSE and CDSE-SF respectively. The CDSE contains 50 item questions and the CDSE-SF contains 25 items.

"The Career Decision Self-Efficacy Scale (Taylor & Betz, 1983) measures an individual's degree of belief that he/she can successfully complete tasks necessary to making career decisions" (CDSE Manual p. 6). According to the authors, their development of the CDSE was heavily influenced by Bandura's (1977) studies, along with Crites (1978) model of Career Choice Competencies (CDSE Manual, 2006). Further research by the authors included a significant change in the latest version of the CDSE by reducing the ratings of each item from a ten-level confidence continuum to a five-level rating. Over 20 years of research on career decision making and self-efficacy have been devoted toward the development of this instrument.

The CDSE is comprised of five subscales that measure behaviors in: (1) Self-Appraisal, (2) Occupational Information, (3) Goal Selection, (4) Planning, (5) Problem Solving.

Each subscale contains ten questions in the CDSE, while the CDSE-SF (short form) each contains five questions. Accordingly, the authors developed normative data for each subscale.

A major change in this instrument was the reduction of the response choices from a ten-point scale to a five-point scale. The authors indicated (p. 7) this change as equally reliable and valid, although the test users were given the option to continue with a ten-point rating if that were their preference. The only other change that appeared noteworthy was a minor revision to bring this instrument into the computer age. The item "Use the Internet to find information about occupations that interest you" was substituted for "Find information in the library about occupations you are interested in" (p. 9).

Although user qualifications were not discussed in the manual, some graduate level

---

[1] Portions of this review are adapted, by permission, from the author's original review in the *Fourteenth Mental Measurements Yearbook*.

training would be needed in order to interpret test outcomes for both research and as a tool in real world counseling. An awareness of career development and background knowledge of theories governing career decision making would be advantageous.

No time limits were stated for either the CDSE or the CDSE-SF. With the reduction in response choices from ten to five for both of these scales, individuals might be able to complete either scale in even less time than before. The CDSE (both forms) may be administered either individually or to a group.

Use in Counseling

This instrument continues to serve primarily as a research tool for the authors, but has practical application for career counseling. Having been normed at both a small private college and a large public university, the CDSE could provide useful information for postsecondary career centers and the students using those services. Further application could extend to employment and rehabilitation agencies as a tool during intake or for individuals seeking training in another field. Since age norms were not specified, the CDSE might possibly be useful for guidance counselors at the secondary level, although some questions obviously pertain to college students. In 1997, Fouad, Smith, and Enochs actually adapted the CDSE for middle school students by selecting 12 items that could be asked of a young adolescent (p. 20). Other revisions were developed (p. 20), and administered to high-school – age students. Generally, however, most applications would presume that an individual plans to graduate from college and/or receive graduate training. There was no mention by the authors of revising the CDSE for other than college-age students.

Technical Considerations

Interestingly, both the CDSE and the CDSE-SF were validated from a population of 346 college students back in 1983 (p. 7). Of this sample, 128 were males and 218 were females. As noted above, the normative data was comprised of students from both a small private and a large state university in the Midwest. The five-point response continuum was recommended by the authors in 2005, and relied on other studies to support the recommendation that the CDSE would be as reliable and valid as previously reported. The CDSE test manual contains well-organized, easy-to-read tables containing item analysis, gender comparisons, and statistical data such as mean and standard deviation. Other data gathered by well over twenty years of research was less accessible because it was subsumed within the text of the manual.

Both versions of the CDSE appeared highly reliable. According to the test manual, internal consistency reliability coefficients were expressed with the following values for Self-Appraisal (.88), Occupational Information (.89), Goal Selection (.87), Planning (.89), and Problem Solving (.86). Total reliability was .97 (test manual, p. 9). It was unknown whether the change to a reduction in response choices might impact reliability values. The above mentioned reliability coefficients were standardized from a 1983 Taylor and Betz study test manual, p. 9). CDSE Short Form reliability values were similar, with a total reliability of .93 (test manual, p. 9). An older version discussed in the test manual suggested test-retest reliability to be .83.

As with reliability studies, the authors of the CDSE have conducted numerous ongoing and exhaustive validity research studies to support good content, concurrent, and construct validity. Over the course of the evolution and metamorphosis of both the CDSE and the CDSE Short Form, the authors, and others using this instrument in research, have supported adequate validity in most areas.

An interesting notation by the authors was their premise that "perhaps the most consistent, and important, correlate of career decision self-efficacy is career indecision" (test manual, p. 13). Other works were cited and a focus on career indecision was discussed as a common predictor of CDSE results. From this topic, the authors discussed how the CDSE was related to test instruments such as My Vocational Situation (test manual, p. 14).

Overall Critique

The CDSE and the CDSE Short Form offer a credible tool for both research and application within a counseling setting. There is much research conducted on this instrument both by its authors and by others involved with vocational counseling and theory. This latest version of the original 1983 instrument has been updated and revised in obviously subtle ways. A question was reworded in order to add the use of online computer resources as a way students might search out career information. The original ten-point response choice was reduced to a five-point response. Discussion was presented to justify this as an added convenience without compromising the intent and strength of the instrument. There appears to be a real value in considering this instrument because of the 23 years of study and research involved with the CDSE.

From a pragmatic stance, both versions of the CDSE might be better aligned with research studies. Comparing an earlier version with this 2006 edition, I felt that little had changed as far as preparing the CDSE as a marketable published test. There is no question that both versions of the CDSE can be used in community and school counseling settings. Valuable information for individuals can be obtained. Discussions about possible career indecisions and career options can be held. However, the current CDSE versions are no more than typed pages with accompanying questions and answer keys. There are no copyrighted protocols or manuals printed and marketed for consumers to purchase either online or from a catalog. The Manual for the Career Decision Self-Efficacy Scale and CDSE-Short Form can be obtained by contacting the author, Nancy E. Betz, Ph.D., Department of Psychology, The Ohio State University, 1835 Neil Avenue Mall, Columbus, OH 43210-1222 and through e-mail: betz.3@osu.edu. In my opinion, if the authors intend to market this test, a professional publisher should be considered, and it should be presented in a manner that would interest counselors working in the field.

References

Bandura, A. (1977). Self-efficacy: Toward a unifying theory of behavioral change. *Psychology Review, 84*, 191-215.

Betz, N.E., Hammond, M., & Multon, K. (2005). Reliability and validity of response continuua for the CDSE. *Journal of Career Assessment, 13*, 131-149.

Crites, J. O. (1978). *Career Maturity Inventory.* Monterey, CA: CTB/McGraw Hill.

Fouad, N. A., Smith, P. L., & Enochs, L. (1997). Reliability and validity evidence for the Middle School Self-Efficacy Scale. *Measurement and Evaluation in Counseling and Development, 30*, 17-31.

Taylor, K.M. & Betz, N.E. (1983). Applications of self-efficacy theory to the understanding and treatment of career indecision. *Journal of Vocational Behavior, 22*, 63-81. Original CDMSE.

CAREER FACTORS INVENTORY (CFI)

Judy M. Chartrand, Steven B. Robbins and Weston H. Morrill

Consulting Psychologists Press, Inc. (CPP, Inc.) and Davies-Black Publishing
1055 Joaquin Road, 2nd Floor
Mountain View, CA 94043
Tel: (650) 969-8901
Toll free: (800) 624-1765
Fax: (650) 969-8608
www.cpp-db.com

Target Population: 13 years and up. (eighth-grade reading level).

Statement of the Purpose of the Instrument: The CFI is designed to help people identify their own difficulties in the career-planning and decision-making process.

Forms and Levels Available with Dates of Publication/Revision of Each: Self-scorable booklet and interpretation Internet accessible via skillsone website.

Languages in Which Available: English only.

Time:

Actual Test Time: 10 minutes.

Total Administration Time: 10 minutes.

Manner in Which Results Are Reported for Individuals: Self-scoring booklet

Basic Service: Self-scoring covering results or each of the scales

Options: Internet accessible via www.skillsone.com. Narrative text is provided.

Report Format/Content for Group Summaries: Not available.

Scoring:

Machine Scoring Service: Via website

COST OF BASIC SERVICE PER COUNSELEE: Self-scorable, $1.65; Internet career package including five other assessments, $24.95.

TIME REQUIRED FOR SCORING AND RETURNING (MAXIMUM): Internet results are immediate.

Hand Scoring:

SCORED BY: Counselee.

TIME REQUIRED FOR SCORING: 5 minutes.

Local Machine Scoring: Not available.

Computer Software Options Available: Internet administration available via www.skillsone.com

Cost of Materials: Due to possible price changes since publication date, be sure to check with the publisher website.

Specimen Set: CFI Applications and Technical Guide (A), $46.75

Reviewed by:[1]

Ayres D'Costa
Associate Professor of Education
The Ohio State University

Description

The *Career Factors Inventory (CFI)* is "designed to help people determine whether they are ready to engage in the career decision-making process" (Chartrand & Robbins, 1997, p. 1). Materials made available to this reviewer were a Technical Guide (Chartrand & Robbins, 1997), along with a Self-Scorable Test Booklet and Interpretation (Chartrand, Robbins, & Morrill, 1997). This review updates the original review presented in Buros' *Fourteenth Mental Measurement Yearbook* (D'Costa, 2001). Luzzo (2001) also presents a detailed review of the CFI.

A recent revision allows the CFI to be self-administered online. The Report and Interpretation are also provided online. This is a great convenience and a welcome addition.

The CFI consists of 21 items requiring Likert-type response, using five rating levels ranging from Strongly Disagree (1) to Strongly Agree (5). The CFI can be administered conveniently by a counselor to clients, on an individual or group basis, in about 5 to 10 minutes. It provides scores on four scales (*Need for Career Information, Need for Knowledge, Career Choice Anxiety,* and *Generalized Indecisiveness*). A good feature of the CFI is that it is self-scorable. There also is good assistance in the Inventory itself for plotting an Individual Profile based on these four scores, and for interpreting this Profile.

A sample item provided in the Technical Manual is:

1. Before choosing or entering a career area, I need to gather more information about one or more occupations.

Strongly Disagree 1 2 3 4 5 Strongly Agree

Use in Counseling

The CFI is a counseling tool that assesses readiness for career decision making in terms of its four scales (Need for Career Information, Need for Knowledge, Career

---

[1] Note: Portions of this review were adapted from the author's original review in the Fourteenth Mental Measurement Yearbook with permission of the Buros Institute.

Choice Anxiety, and Generalized Indecisiveness). It also can help undecided persons uncover the source of their indecision. Two sources of indecision obstacles, *Information Needs* and *Decision Needs,* are specifically addressed. The *Applications and Technical Guide* (Chartrand & Robbins, 1997) claims that the CFI "has been used successfully in a variety of educational, business, and counseling settings" (p. 15). Now that the CFI is available online, it is a very flexible tool that can be used by students both in and out of school/college environments. Counselors can direct students to the CFI, help them understand their assessment report and, most importantly, help them remedy their information/knowledge deficiencies. This last step could take the form of personal counseling and pointing out or providing access to critical career information.

Technical Considerations

Career choice is a critical challenge in vocational counseling, and the CFI, which claims to address career indecision, therefore has the potential to be an important counseling tool. The CFI does well in addressing two important causes for career indecision, namely a lack of information about oneself or about careers, and poor decision-making approaches due to anxiety or general indecisiveness. However, it does not address counseling challenges related to diagnosing or following up bad career choices.

While the CFI's inherent simplicity makes it obvious and vulnerable to faking, it is a remarkable tool with respect to its construct definition effort, which has implications for its validity. The Guide indicates that 31 items were initially written to represent five constructs associated with career decision making, based on a review of literature. Principal components factor analyses, including confirmatory factor analysis, were used to decide on the current four constructs.

The goodness-of-fit results for the four constructs, as well as the other discriminant/convergent validity studies, appeared reasonably convincing to me. The validity of the four scales, based on correlations with similar scales from other instruments, appear to be supportive of the authors' claims, although there are some glaring exceptions. Several of the correlations are low (below .30), and a couple appear to be in a direction opposite to that ordinarily expected. One table that is noteworthy is the change in CFI scores following counseling intervention. In other words, assuming the intervention was indeed effective, the CFI was able to document it, although one wishes statistical tests of significance also were conducted and made available.

Gender differences were noted only for *General Indecisiveness,* with females reporting greater indecisiveness. No ethnic group differences were noted. Again, no statistical tests of significance were conducted.

In order to enhance the utility and interpretation of the test, the administration instructions recommend that, before taking the CFI, students be helped to understand its purpose and the four scales it measures. Although this clarifies the CFI's intent, it also makes this self-report instrument extremely easy to fake.

With regard to reliability considerations, it should be noted that the individual item error variances reported are quite high, indicating a serious problem for this item style.

The test-retest (two-week and three-month administration intervals) and internal consistency reliability indexes range in the 60s and 80s, the higher values occurring for the only trait measure among the four scales, *General Indecisiveness*. The other reliability indexes are modest.

The norms used in interpreting CFI scores are based on convenience samples of college students in general psychology courses at two universities. No justification is provided for extending the interpretation beyond these limited samples, other than "career decision making was deemed salient for these individuals" (Chartrand & Robbins, 1997, p. 7). To judge other more diverse clients, such as high school students and special adult groups, using the distribution of scores obtained by this select college group, appears inappropriate. No attempts are apparent in the Guide to pool data for more diverse norms given the wide variety of clients claimed to have been successfully tested using the CFI.

The interpretation of scores identifies three regions using two arbitrary statistical cutoffs, "Mean" and the "Mean plus one Standard Deviation," and assumes a normal distribution of scores. No justification, theoretical or empirical, is provided for these assumptions or interpretations.

The Guide also recommends plotting the four scale scores and joining these points to obtain a polygon-like profile. This approach, while commonly used, can lead to over interpretation. There is no rationale for the sequence of the four scales, other than they belong together in pairs to two major constructs, *Lack of Information and Difficulty in Decision-making*.

Nevertheless, I was impressed by the very practical Interpretation Model and the clinical counseling approach presented in chapter 4 of the Guide. The case studies presented with the relevant CFI profiles should be very helpful to counselors.

Computer-Based Online Version

This version has recently been provided and constitutes a definite improvement of the original CFI. Students can now administer the CFI to themselves at their own personal convenience and in complete privacy. Scoring, while it has been a simple process, is now automatic, since it is handled completely by computer. This includes a detailed Report, with some explanations, which can be printed and kept in one's personal records for future reference and follow-up.

Overall Critique

Despite its overarching and therefore inappropriate title, the CFI must be recognized as a quick and simple tool designed to do a limited job, namely determine readiness for career decision making in terms of four factors assumed to be the key problems. It should not be expected to do any more than that. The term "Career Factors Inventory" used in the title may be misleading because it is too broad. The CFI is not a typical career decision-making tool in that clients are not enabled to make good career decisions. Nor is it an inventory of all factors related to careers or the choice thereof. It merely addresses readiness to make decisions, and that, too, in a very simplistic way.

A major problem in the CFI is an inherent weakness in the wording of several of the items, which, in my mind, poses a serious validity concern. The phrase, *"Before choosing or entering a particular career area, I need to . . . ",* is intended by the authors to reflect a compelling feeling, which is then scored as a deficit or need. Students who agree are deemed to indicate a deficit, therefore, a lack of readiness for career decision making. Unfortunately, this choice of phrasing can also be understood as asking a student to reflect a belief about what is appropriate to do in the particular circumstance. It is quite reasonable to agree to the special "need" as an appropriate or wise step you believe you should first take. For example, it is wise to need to talk to, or recognize the importance of talking to, engineers before choosing engineering as a career. Therefore, scoring this response as a deficit could add to the item error variance and also adversely impact the validity (interpretation) of the CFI scores. The high item error variance and low validity coefficients reported in the guide might be reflections of this problem.

Assuming that the confusing phrase mentioned above can be clarified in the CFI administration process, this reviewer believes that the CFI is a limited but reasonable counseling tool. A change in title would also be in order to more accurately reflect what this Inventory is designed to do. With these limitations recognized and corrected, I applaud the authors' efforts to meet the psychometric standards appropriate to this potentially useful counseling instrument.

References

Chartrand, J. W., & Robbins, S. B. (1997). *Career Factors Inventory: Applications and technical guide.* Palo Alto, CA: Consulting Psychologists Press.

Chartrand, J. W., Robbins, S. B. & Morrill, W. H. (1997). *Career Factors Inventory: Self-scorable booklet and interpretation.* Palo-Alto, CA: Consulting Psychologists Press.

D'Costa, A. (2001). Review of the *Career Factors Inventory.* In B. S. Plake & J. C. Impara (Eds.), *The fourteenth mental measurements yearbook* (pp. 219 – 221), Lincoln, NE: Buros Institute of Mental Measurements, The University of Nebraska.

Luzzo, D. A. (2001) Review of *Career Factors Inventory.* In J. T. Kapes & E. A. Whitfield (2001). *A counselor's guide to career assessment instruments 4th ed.,* (pp. 331 – 335) Columbus, Ohio: National Career Development Association.

Career Thoughts Inventory (CTI)

James P. Sampson, Jr., Gary W. Peterson, Janet G. Lenz, Robert C. Reardon, and Denise E. Saunders

Psychological Assessment Resources, Inc.
16204 North Florida Avenue
Lutz, FL 33549
www.parinc.com

Target Population: Adults, college students, and high school students

Statement of the Purpose of the Instrument: The CTI is a self-administered and objectively scored measure of negative career thinking designed to improve the quality of career decisions and the quality of career service delivery.

Titles of Subtests, Scales, Scores Provided: (1) Decision-making Confusion; (2) Commitment Anxiety; (3) External Conflict; and CTI Total Score as well as scores on the three construct scales.

Forms and Levels Available, with Dates of Publication/Revision of Each: Professional Manual; Workbook; Test Booklet. All qualification Level B. Publication date for all: July 24, 1996.

Date of Most Recent Edition of Test Manual, User's Guide, etc.: July 24, 1996.

Languages in Which Available: English only.

Time:

Actual Test Time: Self-administered.

Total Administration Time: 7–15 minutes.

Norm Group(s) on Which Scores Are Based: National sample of more than 1,650 adults, college students, and high school students.

Manner in Which Results Are Reported for Individuals: The CTI yields a CTI Total Score as well as scores on three construct scales.

Types of Scores: Raw scores to T score conversions for adults, college students, and high school students.

Report Format/Content: Exercises in the CTI Workbook help individual improve career thinking and develop an Individual Action Plan.

Report Format/Content for Group Summaries: Not available.

Scoring:

Machine Scoring Service: Not available.

Hand Scoring:

Scored by: Counselee; Clerk; Counselor.

Time required for scoring: About five minutes.

Local Machine Scoring: Not available.

Computer Software Options Available: Not available.

Cost of Materials: Due to possible price changes since publication date, be sure to check with publisher web site.

CTI Introductory Kit (includes Manual, five Workbooks, and 25 Test Booklets),	$99
CTI Professional Manual	$30
CTI Workbook	$8
CTI Workbooks (pkg/10)	$65
CTI Test Booklets (pkg/25)	$41

Specimen Set: None. Option: purchase manual; one free copy of each component; manual may be returned.

Counselee Materials: Workbook (not reusable), Test Booklet (not reusable).

Additional Comments of Interest to Users: CTI is a self-help instrument that is ideal for use in career counseling centers and career development programs.

Published reviews of the Instrument in the Last 15 Years: None cited.

Reviewed by:[1]

Rich W. Feller
Professor

Joe Daly
Professor

Colorado State University

Description

The Career Thoughts Inventory (CTI) is a 48-item inventory designed to provide a measure of dysfunctional thinking related to career decision making. It is used, in conjunction with a 36-page workbook, with adults considering a career change, and college and high school students choosing a field of study, an occupation, or employment. The goal of the CTI is to improve the quality of career decisions and the quality of career counseling. Part of a new genre of assessment tools that move beyond basic assessment to provide an instructional stimulus within the delivery of career services, the CTI offers value-added features to counselors, evaluators, and researchers. By integrating the assessment function with a comprehensive theory-based model (Peterson, Sampson & Reardon, 1991) on intervention, clients can immediately do something with the results. It uniquely purports to engage the clients and make more efficient use of their time and

---

[1] This review is a reprint from the fourth edition of A Counselor's Guide to Career Assessment Instruments. The test publisher informed the editors that the instrument is unchanged since the last edition of the Guide. It is reprinted for readers' convenience. Check publisher's web site for updates.

the time of their human service practitioner, while more effectively incorporating the assessment concepts into intervention strategies for change (Sampson, Peterson, Lenz, Reardon, & Saunders, 1996, p.1).

The primary use of the CTI within direct client service is to serve as (1) a screening device identifying those most likely to express problems in making career choices because of dysfunctional thinking; (2) a needs assessment identifying the nature of dysfunctional thinking and needs related to decision making confusion, commitment anxiety and external conflict; (3) a readiness assessment (Sampson, Peterson, Reardon, & Lenz, 2000) used to make preliminary decisions about the level of practitioner support required in relation to individual needs; and (4) a learning resource to be used with various counseling interventions.

The CTI's goals for utility can be seen as a client takes 7–15 minutes to indicate a level of agreement with 48 statements describing thoughts that some people have when considering career choices. Many of these thoughts are negative. A two-layer answer sheet can be hand scored in 5–8 minutes and provides raw scores in four areas: CTI Total (a single global indicator of dysfunctional career thinking), Decision Making Confusion (14 items such as "I'll never understand myself well enough to make a good career choice"), Commitment Anxiety (10 items such as "My interests are always changing"), and External Conflict (five5 items such as "I know what job I want, but someone's always putting obstacles in my way"). Profiles for adults, college students, and high school students appear on the back of the test booklet where raw scores can be converted to standard scores and to percentiles.

The CTI also has demonstrated its value in research, evaluation, and theory development. It can be used to measure learning outcomes of interventions that involve identifying, challenging, and altering cognition. It has been used as the dependent variable in at least eight dissertations (Dipeolu, 1997; Kilk. 1997; Osborn, 1998; Railey, 1997; Saunders, 1997; Slatten, 1999; Strausberger, 1998; Voight, 1999) related to career problem solving and decision making. It should also prove to be useful as a tool "to further validate theory and to create new theoretical constructs associated with career problem solving and decision making" (Sampson et al., 1996, p. 2).

Although the CTI is self-administering and self-scoring (Gilbert, 1997), we observed that students can have difficulty with the scoring because of limited test-taking support information on the test booklet. Some discussion of what to expect and how to score the inventory proved to be very helpful. Our sample also reacted to the negative phrasing of the statements, which the authors explain is necessary to make use of the *CTI Workbook*. A discussion prior to taking the CTI of what to expect and how to score the inventory proved to be very helpful. Thus, the CTI's intended use with a side-by-side practitioner relationship or group supervision as advised by the authors is necessary.

Use In Counseling

Tests often allow counselors to label traits, compare clients, and identify differences that are useful to institutions but that are of limited use in helping clients take action. Tools that help clients learn what to do next offer positive advantages to the counseling process. The CTI stands out by addressing the relationship between specific dysfunctional career thinking and exploratory behavior. The substance and level of specific interaction between client and counselor can be very rich and specific as a result of the inventory items. The three construct scales also bring a needed language to almost any decision-making challenge.

The CTI offers a sound model to drive counselor action and practitioner instruction. By offering a client-counselor collaborative model and a comprehensive system, it can get clients "talking back" to specific dysfunctional thoughts which will lead to new actions. Although this may require new thinking about how to conduct their work, a counselor's study of the comprehensive and easy-to-learn model from the *Professional Manual* (Sampson et al., 1996) adds a new dimension to practice.

Technical Considerations

The Professional Manual is clear and thorough in presenting the information related to the technical qualities of the CTI. Norms are provided for "adults" (N = 571), "college students" (N = 595), and "high school students" (N = 396). The normative samples were geographically well distributed and generally representative in terms of gender and ethnicity. The authors recommend the development of local norms to further enhance the usefulness of the Inventory.

Both internal consistency (alpha coefficients) and stability (test-retest) measures of reliability are reported. Internal consistency coefficients are shown for each scale for all three groups. Alpha coefficients for the CTI total (.93–.97) and DMC (.90–.94) were high across all groups. Alpha coefficients for CA (.79–.91) and EC (.74–.81) were lower. As one would expect, the shorter the scale the lower the reliability.

Test-retest correlations over a four-week period are shown for college and high school students. Stability data for the adult population were not reported. Total score test-retest reliability was .89 for college students, but dropped to .69 for high school students. Reliabilities for the subscales ranged from .82 to .74 for college students and from .72 to .52 for the high school students. Given the nature of the constructs being measured by the CTI, one would not expect the test-retest correlation to be as high as the measures of internal consistency. The high school coefficients are low, especially for the EC scale. Increasing the number of EC items would help address the low reliability of this scale.

Item and construct development for the CTI is based on the cognitive information processing theory of career development. Factor analysis of CTI items resulted in the three constructs scales (DMC, CA and EC) of the inventory. Intercorrelations of the CTI scales with the content dimensions of CPI range from .62 to .92.

Convergent validity data for the CTI shows good relationships between the CTI total score, DMC, CA, and EC scale scores and scores on My Vocational Situation, Career Decision Scale, Career Decision Profile, and the NEO Personality Inventory. Analysis of Variance studies showing significant differences in CTI scores of client and nonclient populations at Florida State University and Ohio State University provided good evidence of the criterion-related validity of the instrument.

Technically, the CTI is a well-developed inventory with good reliability and validity that does a good job of doing what it says it does. The exception to this statement is the EC scale of the inventory. The low reliability of this subscale raises questions as to its usefulness, especially with high school students.

Overall Critique

The CTI reflects the daily action research being conducted at the Career Center at Florida State University, where the authors test their ideas with clients as they build theory and transform traditional career services. This gives credibility to the CTI and its continued development. This model may find some resistance from those who might question a cognitive approach, yet its clarity can be easily appreciated.

The CTI should not be considered a self-help inventory. The authors state in the *Professional Manual* (Sampson et al., 1996, p. 22) that practitioners and professionals using the CTI should have experience and training in career development, career service delivery, and cognitive-behavioral theory. They should also be very familiar with the *Professional Manual* and all components of the CPI. As Gilbert (1997) suggests, this is not a typical assessment found in employment agencies or college and high school career centers. Counselors in these settings would need to have the background and training mentioned and be willing to meet the demands of the CTI on both the counselor and the client. The client needs to understand the purpose of the CTI and to have some understanding of the four content domains that are being measured. The counselor needs to understand the inventory and the workbook, and how to facilitate the clients use of both. The CTI covers a lot of ground in a short time. Although it demands much from users, its returns are great for the client, the quality of the process, and structure of delivering career services.

References

Dipeolu, A. O. (1997). A study of the relationship between learning disabilities, dysfunctional career thoughts, and adjustment to disability (decision-making confusion, commitment, conflict, anxiety, career thoughts inventory). (Doctoral dissertation, Florida State University, 1997). *Dissertation Abstracts International, 58* (07), 3938B.

Gilbert, H. B. (1997, January). *Career Thoughts Inventory: A review and critique.* Paper presented at the annual meeting of the Southwest Educational Research Association, Austin, TX. (ERIC Document Reproduction Service No. ED 408 526).

Kilk, K. L. (1997). The relationship between dysfunctional career thoughts and choosing an academic major. (Doctoral dissertation, University of Northern Colorado, 1997). *Dissertation Abstracts International, 58* (08), 3038A.

Osborn, D. S. (1998). The relationships among perfectionism, dysfunctional career thoughts, and career indecision. (Doctoral dissertation, Florida State University, 1998). *Dissertation Abstracts International, 58* (08), 3746A.

Peterson, G. W., Sampson, J.P., Jr., & Reardon, R. C. (1991). *Career development and services: A cognitive approach.* Pacific Grove, CA: Brooks/Cole.

Railey, M. G. (1997). The relationship between dysfunctional career thoughts and career interests with respect to offender status of female inmates and probationers. (Doctoral dissertation, Florida State University, 1997). *Dissertation Abstracts International, 58* (06), 3325B.

Sampson, J. P., Jr., Peterson, G. W., Lenz, J. G., Reardon, R. C., & Saunders, D.E. (1996). *Career Thoughts Inventory: Professional manual.* Odessa, FL: Psychological Assessment Resources.

Sampson, J.P., Jr., Peterson, G.W., Reardon, R.C., & Lenz, J.G. (2000). Using readiness assessment to improve career services: A cognitive information processing approach. *The Career Development Quarterly, 49,* 146-174.

Saunders, D. E. (1997). The contribution of depression and dysfunctional career thinking to career indecision. (Doctoral dissertation, Florida State University, 1997). *Dissertation Abstracts International, 58* (07), 3953B.

Slatten, M. L. (1999). *Dysfunctional career thoughts and self-appraised problem-solving ability among substance abusers.* Unpublished doctoral dissertation, Florida State University.

Strausberger, S. J. (1998). The relationship of state-trait anger to dysfunctional career thinking and vocational identity. (Doctoral dissertation, Florida State University, 1998). *Dissertation Abstracts International, 59* (10), 3747A.

Voight, L. (1999). *Parental attachment and ego identity as antecedents of career identity.* Unpublished doctoral dissertation, Florida State University.

The Career Transitions Inventory (CTI)

Mary J. Heppner, Ph.D.

Mary J. Heppner, Ph.D.
201 D Student Success Center
University of Missouri-Columbia
Columbia, MO 65211

Target Population: The inventory was developed and is most appropriate for adults in career transition.

Statement of the Purpose of the Instrument: The purpose is to assess psychological strengths and barriers for adults in career transition.

Titles of Subtests, Scales, and Scores Provided: Five factors: Confidence, Readiness, Control, Social Support, and Decision Independence.

Forms and Levels Available, with Dates of Publication/Revision of Each: One form is available.

Date of Most Recent Edition of Test Manual, User's Guide, etc.: Just the psychometric article about the development of the scale which appeared in Heppner, M. J., Multon, K. D., & Johnston, J. A. (1994). Assessing psychological resources during career change: Development of the Career Transitions Inventory. *Journal of Vocational Behavior, 44,* 55–74.

Languages in Which Available: English, Chinese, Japanese, and French.

Time:

Total Administration Time 15 minutes.

Norm Group(s) on Which Scores Are Based: Adults in career transition.

Manner in Which Results Are Reported for Individuals:

Types of Scores: High, medium, and low scores based on adults in career transition norm group — with the highest and lowest 20% indicating the highs and lows and 60% in the middle.

Report Format/Content:

BASIC SERVICE: Self scoring and interpretive materials about what a high, medium, and low score means included.

Report Format/Content for Group Summaries: Not available.

Scoring:

Machine Scoring Service: Not available.

Hand Scoring:

SCORED BY: COUNSELEE; CLERK; COUNSELOR

TIME REQUIRED FOR SCORING: 5 minutes

Local Machine Scoring: Not available.

Computer Software Options Available: Not available.

Cost of Materials:

Specimen Set: Free

Counselee Materials: Due to possible price changes since publication date, be sure to check with the author for current costs.

One packet of 25 instruments with interpretive booklet and *Journal of Vocational Behavior* article describing the CTI's development is $30.00 plus shipping of $3.00 for 1–2 packets and $6.00 for 3 or more packets.

Reviewed by:

Jean Powell Kirnan
Professor and Chair
Psychology Department
The College of New Jersey

Description

The Career Transitions Inventory (CTI) is designed as a measure of the psychological resources and barriers that operate during a time of adult career change. This measure of career adjustment yields five subscales designed to measure Confidence, Readiness, Control, Social Support, and Decision Independence. While career counselors have for years used measures of interest and ability, little work has been conducted on the process of the career transition. This instrument is aimed at filling that void by providing a measure of the factors which can enhance or inhibit one's career transition.

The 72 items in the original CTI were written to reflect current literature and theory on career counseling. Small groups of adults in transition as well as counselors provided feedback and recommendations for item rewording in the early stages of the CTI's development. A group of experts successfully sorted the items into the original six constructs that the CTI aimed to measure. A factor analysis of these items resulted in the current instrument of 40 items that measure the five distinct constructs listed above.

The CTI has a single form developed in 1991 that is available in paper-and-pencil format only. This self-report instrument can be self-administered and self-scored in about 15 minutes. Clients respond to statements about their current career transition process using a six-point Likert agreement scale. Items represent a mix of positively worded statements (e.g., "People whom I respect have said they think I can make this career transition successfully") and negatively worded statements (e.g., "I don't feel that I have the talent to make a career transition that I will feel good about"). A few items are worded awkwardly, and some are conjunctions making it difficult to answer if the respondent agrees with one part of the sentence but not the other. As with many personality and interest inventories, the items are transparent and thus susceptible to faking. The accuracy of the CTI scores depends upon the client's willingness to respond honestly. Responses are recorded on a separate answer sheet that has carbon paper which conceals the scoring key. The answer sheet is difficult to complete as the item numbers, while running from left to right in rows, often skip columns. This is done on purpose as it facilitates scoring the attached carbon sheet, but it is confusing to the respondent who has to search for the next answer space, skipping over empty cells.

Use in Counseling

After clients have identified their career interests and assessed relevant job skills, they may still encounter difficulty in the career transition process. The CTI was designed to measure psychological processes such as locus of control and self-efficacy that may work to help or hinder this change. However, rather than using existing measures, the author constructed a multidimensional scale with items specifically framed to reflect the career transition process. The goal of the CTI then would be to identify for clients both the resources as well as the barriers that they face when it comes to career change. This knowledge will also be useful to the counselor in devising interventions to assist clients in using resources and overcoming impediments.

Heppner (1998) provided detailed suggestions for the use of the CTI in a counseling setting. The CTI should be used in conjunction with traditional measures of interests and abilities. Clients should be assisted in the interpretation of CTI scores to understand the meaning of the scores both compared to adult norms but also on an individual basis as clients explore the relative importance of each construct in their own lives. Counselors should aid clients not only in overcoming barriers, but in maximizing the strengths that they bring to the career transition process. Finally, the CTI should act as a means of integrating personal issues with career issues by opening a dialog that extends beyond the traditional career- planning process.

Technical Considerations

Score interpretation is accomplished by an interpretive guide. Each of the five subscales has a high, medium, and low category which are defined by raw score intervals. For example, one can reference a raw score of 67 on Readiness and see that it is in the high score category (scores of 66 to 78). There is also an interpretive narrative that accompanies each of the categories. The high score on Readiness is described as a person who is highly motivated and more likely to expend the effort to pursue the career transition at this time. The development of the categories is not detailed in the materials provided to users. In a separate communication, the author describes how percentile ranks from the normative group were used to derive the categories of high (top 20%), medium (middle 60%), and low (bottom 20%). However, no rationale was provided as to how these cutoffs were selected.

Both internal and external measures of reliability are reported for the CTI. Cronbach's coefficient alphas were strong for Readiness (.87) and Confidence (.83), but somewhat weaker for Control (.69), Perceived Support (.66), and Decision Independence (.67). Test-retest reliabilities were acceptable for Readiness (.74), Confidence (.79), Perceived Support (.77), and Decision Independence (.83), but considerably weaker for Control

(.55). Given that the Control subscale is weak on both measures of reliability suggests that this scale be reviewed for possible improvement or modification.

Appropriate construct validity is demonstrated through the accumulation of evidence that an instrument is in fact measuring the construct(s) that it purports to measure. The development of the CTI points to several indications of construct validity. Various demographic variables as well as responses to a series of career-transition coping items demonstrated appropriate relationships with CTI total and subscale scores. Additionally, convergent and divergent validity were demonstrated between the CTI scores and scores on My Vocational Situation (MVS) and the Hope Scale.

There is no formal manual to answer questions regarding cost, reliability, validity, administration, or scoring. Instead, individuals who purchase the CTI are provided with a copy of a published article which details the instrument's development (Heppner, Multon, & Johnston, 1994). This is insufficient and should be remedied by the author. A second article (Heppner, 1998), which is not provided to purchasers, provides a case study along with specific suggestions of how to use the CTI in a counseling setting. This information is very useful and would fit well into a manual for potential users of the instrument.

In the original article on the development of the CTI (Heppner, Multon, & Johnston, 1994), the authors noted that the initial normative group, while diverse in terms of socioeconomic status, was largely Midwestern and Caucasian. The exact size of the normative group is unclear as three distinct samples are discussed in the article. Regardless of size (which conceivably could range from 300 to 447), none of the samples were diverse. They advised the need for a larger and more diverse normative sample so that the CTI could be used with confidence in a diverse client pool. To date, this has not been accomplished as no additional normative information is available.

Heppner et al. (1994) also called for additional research to explore the stability of the five constructs over time and the impact of intervention on the constructs. One research study by Heppner, Fuller & Multon (1998) explored the relationship between the CTI and the Five Factor Model of personality as measured by the NEO-FFI. The study used a Midwestern, predominantly Caucasian sample of involuntarily laid-off workers. The results indicated many appropriate relationships between subscale scores on the two instruments. This research is meaningful for counselors as personality traits are considered stable across the lifetime whereas the measures of the CTI are much more transitory. The ability to identify certain personality characteristics that facilitate or inhibit career transition will prove quite useful in assessment and intervention. In addition to this article, several unpublished studies of the CTI (such as dissertations) have been undertaken.

Overall Critique

The greatest shortcoming of the CTI is the small and geographically and racially restricted normative group that both the factor analysis and scoring interpretations are based upon. It is reasonable to hypothesize that individuals from other geographical regions and, in particular, different racial and cultural groups will face distinct barriers due to variations in family values, accepted work roles, educational opportunities, and employment discrimination. The author emphasizes the importance of the normative data and the need for clients to interpret their scores relative to other adults in career transition. This seems overconfident given these restrictions. It is disappointing that more than 10 years have passed and there is no evidence that this issue has been addressed.

The CTI reveals a strong developmental base. The instrument is a product of theory, expert review, and empirical analysis. The CTI demonstrates acceptable reliability and validity. It is recommended that the author develop a separate users manual and expand the normative database to increase both size and diversity which would increase the utility of this instrument. In the author's own words, the CTI is best used as a "... tool of discovery and exploration. The instrument was designed to help establish a dialog between the client and counselor" (Heppner, 1998, p. 140). This is an appropriate use of the CTI: not as a means to make decisions about one's career transition, but as a method of developing self understanding and providing a focus for counseling discussions.

References

Heppner, M. J. (1998). The Career Transitions Inventory: Measuring internal resources in adulthood. *Journal of Career Assessment, 6,* 135–145.

Heppner, M. J., Fuller, B. E., & Multon, K. D. (1998). Adults in involuntary career transition: An analysis of the relationship between the psychological and career domains. *Journal of Career Assessment, 6,* 329–346.

Heppner, M. J., Multon, K. D., & Johnston, J. A. (1994). Assessing psychological resources during career change: Development of the Career Transitions Inventory. *Journal of Vocational Behavior, 44,* 55–74.

CHILDHOOD CAREER DEVELOPMENT SCALE (CCDS)

Donna E. Schultheiss and Graham B. Stead

Donna E. Schultheiss and Graham B. Stead
Counseling, Administration, Supervision and Adult Learning
Cleveland State University
2121 Euclid Avenue, Cleveland, OH, 44115
Phone: (216) 687-5063
Fax: (216)687-5378
d.schultheiss@csuohio.edu

Target Population: Grades 4, 5, and 6.

Statement of the Purpose of the Instrument: The purpose of the CCDS is to measure childhood career progress. The CCDS is based on Super's 1990 theoretical model of childhood career development.

Titles of Subtests, Scales, Scores Provided: The CCDS has the following eight scales: Planning, Self-concept, Information, Interests, Locus of Control, Curiosity / Exploration, Key Figures, Time Perspective.

Forms and Levels Available, with Dates of Publication/Revision of Each: Childhood Career Development Scale (2004).

Date of Most Recent Edition of Test Manual, User's Guide, etc.: 2004

Languages in Which Available: English only.

Time:

Actual Test Time 20 minutes.

Total Administration Time 25 minutes.

Norm Group(s) on Which Scores Are Based: Students in Grades 4, 5, and 6.

Manner in Which Results Are Reported for Individuals:

Types of Scores: Percentiles and T scores

Report Format/Content for Group Summaries: Not available.

Scoring:

Machine Scoring Service: Not available.

Hand Scoring:

SCORED BY: Counselor.

TIME REQUIRED FOR SCORING: 10 minutes

Local Machine Scoring: Not available.

Computer Software Options Available: Not available.

Cost of Materials: Due to possible price changes since publication date, be sure to check with the test author/publisher.

Additional Comments of Interest to Users: There also is a South African version of the Childhood Career Development Scale for students in grades 4 to 7.

Reviewed by:

Cass Dykeman
Associate Professor
Teacher and Counselor Education
Oregon State University

Description

The Childhood Career Development Scale (CCDS) represents an important advancement in the measurement of this domain of childhood development. There has been little research on this domain (Schultheiss, Palma, & Manzi, 2005). Moreover, the few instruments that previously have attempted to measure this domain have lacked theoretical and/or psychometric soundness (Schultheiss & Stead, 2004). With the CCDS, Donna Schultheiss and Graham Stead have made great progress in addressing a dire need in the career measurement field.

The CCDS is an operationalization of Donald Super's (1990) theory of childhood career development dimensions. To date, there have been four iterations of this instrument (Schultheiss & Stead, 2004). There is parallel South African version as well (Stead & Schultheiss, 2003).

The CCDS is a pencil-and-paper test. Children are asked to respond to 52 items using the following fully anchored Likert-type scale: "SA — Strongly Agree (I agree a lot)," "A — Agree," "U — Uncertain (I am not sure)," "D — Disagree," and "SD — strongly disagree (I do not agree at all)." The CCDS contains eight scales. See Table 1 for an example item from each scale.

Table 1: Scale Examples

Scale	Number of Items	Example Item
Curiosity/Exploration	7	I wonder about things I learned in school
Information	6	I wonder about different jobs
Interests	6	I know what games I like to play
Key Figures	5	I want to do the same job as someone I look up to
Locus Of Control	7	I have control over the things I do
Planning	11	It is important to plan for the future
Self-Concept	6	I know what kind of friend I am
Time Perspective	4	I think about where I will work when I'm grown up

Scoring of the CCDS is straightforward (Schultheiss & Stead, 2005a). For each scale, the scores from the scale's items (score range: 1–5) are added together for a total scale raw score. The total scale raw score ranges vary from 4–20 (Time Perspective) to 11–55 (Planning).

Use in Counseling

Schultheiss and Stead designed the CCDS to both measure career programming effectiveness and provide a vehicle to research childhood career development. I will address each of these purposes in order.

Measure career programming effectiveness. From the U.S. president on down, there have been strong demands to hold K-12 educators more accountable for the effectiveness of their professional work (U.S. Department of Education, 2005). Elementary school counselors have not been immune from these demands. Yet, in one major dimension of their responsibilities, career development, they lack a scientifically sound instrument to measure the impact of their work. The CCDS represents progress in addressing this measurement dearth. However, for psychometric reasons that will be addressed in the *Technical Considerations* section, I cannot yet recommend the CCDS to my fellow school counselors as a summative program evaluation (i.e., a formal evaluation outlining the impact of a program [NWREL, 2007b]) tool . High-stakes decisions (e.g., position funding) are made with summative evaluations, and the present psychometric unknowns outweigh the potential benefits of CCDS use.

I can recommend the use of the CCDS for formative program evaluation (i.e., to gather information about a program to fine-tune its implementation [NWREL, 2007a]). Elementary school counselors have far more task demands than time to accomplish them. As such, any tool that could help a school counselor focus the limited time they have for career development work would be helpful. For example, a school counselor could administer the CCDS to their 5th graders. If that school counselor found that the T score for Key Figures was much lower than the T scores for the other scales, the school counselor could choose to put their limited career development time into implementing a mentorship program. Thus, a school counselor's career development programming efficiency can be enhanced by identifying group and/or grade level needs of elementary school students.

For the same psychometric reasons I mentioned earlier, I cannot recommend the CCDS for clinical use at present. An individual's CCDS results should not be used to make high-stakes career intervention decisions for that individual.

Research childhood career development. Among the myriad of career interventions that an elementary school counselor can employ, which ones can "deliver the most bang for the buck?" Also, how much of a dosage of a high-leverage intervention is needed to make a positive impact on a child's career development? These are just some of the critical questions that career development experts have no answers to give to inquiring school counselors. The CCDS presents the first sound instrument to address critical questions like those just presented.

Technical Considerations

There exist American norms for the CCDS (Schultheiss & Stead, 2005b). In this section, I will report on norming, reliability, and validity issues.

Norming issues. The norming group was drawn from one urban school in the Midwestern U.S. This group contained 447 students (52% males, 47% females, 1% missing data) with ages ranging from 8 to 13 years (M = 10.51, SD = 0.80). The percentage breakdown by grade was 10% fourth grade, 48% fifth grade, and 42% sixth grade. The racial/ethnic composition was 58% African American, 37% European American, 3% multiracial, and 2% other (i.e., Native American, Asian, or Hispanic). For each CCDS scale, a norm table provides percentiles and T scores for each raw score. The extent to which the norms from this group can be generalized to the entire population of fourth to sixth grade students is unknown.

Reliability issues. Scale internal consistency (Cronbach's α) ranged from.66 to.84. Table 2 contains the complete information on scale internal consistency. When examining the psychometrics of a measure, another important thing to examine is test-retest reliability (i.e., an indication of the stability of results). Test-retest reliability for the CCDS is unknown at present.

Table 2: Scale Internal Consistency

Scale	Cronbach's α
Curiosity/Exploration	.66
Information	.72
Interests	.68
Key Figures	.68
Locus of Control	.79
Planning	.84
Self-Concept	.84
Time Perspective	.69

Validity issues. Donna Schultheiss and Graham Stead followed the best practices in measurement development (Downing & Haladyna, 2006) in establishing the CCDS's content (via expert panel) and construct validity (via principal components analysis). As noted by the authors themselves (Stead & Schultheiss, 2003), research on the concurrent and predictive validity of the CCDS is needed.

Overall Critique

Donna Schultheiss and Graham Stead have taken the first major steps forward in the sound measurement of childhood career development. Both elementary school counselors and childhood career development researchers should commend them for their work. I recommend the use of the CCDS for both formative program evaluation and research. For the CCDS to reach its full potential as a clinical, evaluation, and research tool, the following must be generated: (1) test-retest reliability information, (2) concurrent validity information, and (3) predictive validity information.

References

Downing, S. M., & Haladyna, T. M. (2006). Handbook of test development. London: Routledge.

NWREL. (2007a). Formative evaluation: Assistance developing, implementing, and documenting educational programs. Retrieved on August 1, 2007 from http://www.nwrel.org/evaluation/formative.shtml

NWREL. (2007b). Summative evaluation: Measurement and documentation of program impacts. Retrieved on August 1, 2007 from http://www.nwrel.org/evaluation/summative.shtml

Schultheiss, D. E. P., & Stead, G. B. (2004). Childhood Career Development Scale: Scale construction and psychometric properties Journal of Career Assessment, 12, 113–134.

Schultheiss, D. E. P., & Stead, G. B. (2005a). *Childhood Career Development Scale and Scoring Key* (52-item U.S. Version). Cleveland, OH: Authors.

Schultheiss, D. E. P., & Stead, G. B. (2005b). *Norm Table for Childhood Career Development Scale* (52-item U.S. Version). Cleveland, OH: Authors.

Schultheiss, D. E. P., Palma, T. V., & Manzi. A. J. (2005). Career development in middle childhood: A qualitative inquiry. *Career Development Quarterly, 53,* 246–262.

Stead, G. B., & Schultheiss, D. E. P. (2003). Construction and psychometric properties of the Childhood Career Development Scale. *South African Journal of Psychology, 33,* 227–235.

Super, D. E. (1990). A life-span, life-space approach to career development. In D. Brown. & L. Brooks (Eds.), *Career choice and development* (2nd ed.; pp. 197–261). San Francisco: Jossey-Bass.

U.S. Department of Education. (2005). *10 facts About K-12 education funding.* Washington, DC: Author.

Job Search Attitude Inventory (JSAI) (Third Edition)

John J. Liptak

JIST Publishing, Inc.
8902 Otis Avenue
Indianapolis, IN 46216
www.jist.com

Target Population: High school to adult.

Statement of the Purpose of the Instrument: The Job Search Attitude Inventory (JSAI) helps individuals identify their key attitudes about looking for a job and consider suggestions for improvement and for becoming more self-directed in the job search.

Titles of Subtests, Scales, Scores Provided: Scores in four categories representing key attitudes, beliefs, and approaches regarding the job search process: Luck vs. Planning, Uninvolved vs. Involved, Help from Others vs. Self-Help, Passive vs. Active.

Forms and Levels Available, with Dates of Publication/Revision of Each: Job Search Attitude Inventory Assessment; Job Search Attitude Inventory Administrator's Guide. No special qualifications required. Third Edition, 2006.

Date of Most Recent Edition of Test Manual, User's Guide, etc.: 2006

Languages in Which Available: English only.

Time: Actual Test Time: 15–25 minutes (32 items).

Total Administration Time: 15–25 minutes (self-administered).

Norm Group(s) on Which Scores Are Based: For the JSAI, four groups were used to develop norms that are included in the Administrator's Guide: Youth between the ages of 12 and 18, College and Community College Students, Welfare-to-Work clients, and Offenders.

Manner in Which Results Are Reported for Individuals: Raw Scale scores are profiled into three score ranges (scores between 8 and 16 indicate that the respondent is other-directed, scores between 17 and 23 are average, and scores between 24 and 32 indicate that the respondent is self-directed in searching for and finding employment). The JSAI includes easy-to-understand interpretations for each scale. Self-scoring and self-interpreting.

Types of Scores: Four raw scale scores (Luck vs. Planning, Uninvolved vs. Involved, Help from Others vs. Self-Help, Passive vs. Active) are included on the JSAI.

Report Format/Content:

BASIC SERVICE: Assessment is self-scoring and self-interpreting. Interpretation Guide and Improvement Plan are included with each assessment. Respondents follow a series of five steps to complete the JSAI.

Report Format/Content for Group Summaries: Not available.

366

Scoring:
MACHINE SCORING SERVICE: Not available.
HAND SCORING:
Scored by: Counselee
Time required for scoring: Less than 5 minutes. Included in administration time above.
LOCAL MACHINE SCORING: Not available.

Computer Software Options Available:
Computerized adaptive administration; standard administration online.

Ways in Which Computer/Online Version Differs:
Automated scoring and automated report generation.

Cost of Materials: Due to possible price changes since publication date, be sure to check with publisher website.
SPECIMEN SET: $42.95 for a package of 25. Each package includes a free Administrator's Guide. Administrator's Guide also available for free download from jist.com

Additional Comments of Interest to Users: New third edition contains updated research data, simplified scoring, and a list of resources for individuals to further enhance their job search.

Published Reviews of the Instrument in the Last 15 Years:
Spies, R.A., & Plake, B.S. (Eds.) (2005). *The sixteenth mental measurements yearbook.* Lincoln, NE: Buros Institute of Mental Measurements.

Reviewed by:[1]

John W. Fleenor
Group Director, Research and Innovation
Center for Creative Leadership
Greensboro, NC

Description

According to its author (Liptak, 2006), the *Job Search Attitude Inventory* (Third Edition) provides a brief (10–15 minute) assessment of the motivation level of individuals who are in the process of searching for a job. The purpose of the *Job Search Attitude Inventory* (JSAI) is to provide these individuals with a snapshot of their attitudes towards the job search process, and to make suggestions to job seekers as to how they can be more motivated to find a job. The JSAI yields scores on four scales: (a) Luck vs. Planning, (b) Uninvolved vs. Involved, (c) Help from Others vs. Self-Help, and (d) Passive vs. Active.

The JSAI is based on the premise that increasing individuals' self-esteem can enhance their self-directed motivation to search for a job. Helwig (1987) indicates that the most

---

[1] Note: Portions of this review were adapted by permission from the author's original review in the *Sixteenth Mental Measurements Yearbook.*

important factor in finding a job is the individual's attitudes towards unemployment and the job search process itself. According to Helwig, personal motivation to find a job can be more important than job search skills themselves. Individuals who fail to display self-directed motivation in the job search often exhibit tendencies of learned helplessness (Abramson, Seligman, & Teasdale, 1978).

Additionally, Goleman (2000) suggests that, in order to be successful, job seekers must have the emotional intelligence necessary to perform in a variety of job-related situations. Goleman defines emotional intelligence as key skills and competences that, unlike conventional intelligence (i.e., IQ), can be learned. Competencies related to emotional intelligence include being able to motivate oneself, being persistent in the face of obstacles, and planning for the future. The self-directed job search skills measured by the JSAI are examples of competencies related to emotional intelligence that are critical to conducting an effective job search.

The JSAI can be administered individually or in groups. Respondents should be informed of the purpose of the assessment. There is no time limit for the instrument — the average administration time is 20 minutes, depending on factors such as age and reading ability. The items are written at or below the eighth-grade reading level. Respondents indicate their level of agreement on 32 items using a four-point Likert scale, ranging from strongly agree to strongly disagree. Test takers respond to each item directly in the test booklet. They then self-score their responses and copy these scores to a graphic profile, which presents the test taker's score on the four dimensions measured by the JSAI. Step-by-step scoring instructions are included in test booklet. Higher scores indicate the likelihood that individuals will find their own jobs.

The current JSAI represents the third edition of the instrument. In the third edition, the following enhancements were made to the instrument: (a) items from each of the four scales were grouped together so that scoring and interpretation are easier, (b) the profile was revised so that it is easier for respondents to read and respond to the items, and (c) in the scoring, steps 3 and 4 were combined to make administration and interpretation easier.

In addition to the enhancements made to the third edition, the following improvements had been previously made to the second edition of the JSAI (Liptak, 2002): (a) simplified language and instructions, and a six-panel design, which makes it easier for users to read, complete, and score the instrument; (b) concrete suggestions for job seekers on how to be motivated to find work; (c) new research on learned helplessness; (d) better documentation of the estimates of reliability and validity; and (e) additional research by Liptak indicating that self-directed attitudes are likely to result in individuals finding jobs in less time.

Use in Counseling

The instrument is designed to make job seekers more aware of their attitudes toward the job search. The attitudes measured by the JSAI were identified by a review of the literature, case studies, and interviews with unemployed adults. Liptak (2006) suggests that the instrument will be useful for (a) predicting who will be more likely to find a job, (b) determining who will better benefit from job search services, and (c) for use as a pre- and post-test to measure the effectiveness of job-search training programs. Because self-motivated individuals can benefit from relatively inexpensive services (e.g., job search assistance), the JSAI is touted as a cost-effective method for determining which services a job seeker should receive.

Possible uses of the JSAI include outplacement counseling, employment counseling, job search assistance, career counseling, rehabilitation counseling, and correctional counseling. For example, the JASI can be used as a pretest to uncover attitudes that may be a hindrance to the job-search process. By identifying these attitudes in advance, counselors can better direct their energies in the counseling process. The JSAI can be used as the first step in assessing an individual's job search needs. Additionally, it can be used as a motivational tool for encouraging individuals to become more self-directed by providing ways to do so.

Technical Considerations

An eight-page manual, which was written by the test author (Liptak, 2006), presents information on the theory, development, reliability and validity, administration, scoring, and interpretation of the JSAI. Guidelines for interpreting the scores are also presented in the manual.

The manual presents the means and standard deviations for a sample of 135 adults (70 males and 65 females). Descriptive statistics are also presented for 521 convicted offenders, 235 welfare-to-work clients, 325 college students, and 285 youths (ages 12 to 18).

A rational-empirical method (Crites, 1978) was used in the development of the instrument. The author employed a review of the literature, case studies, and interviews with unemployed adults to develop the scales and the item content. The resulting pool of 50 items was reviewed by professional counselors, who assigned the items to one of the four scales. Intercorrelations among the four scales were calculated using the sample of 135 adults described above. These intercorrelations were in the acceptable range.

The author reports the usual estimates of reliability, including split-half, coefficient alpha, and test-retest reliabilities. These reliabilities were calculated using the scores of the sample of 135 adults described above. The reliabilities were generally in the acceptable range; however, the split-half reliability of the Uninvolved vs. Involved scale was somewhat low (.53).

In general, the instrument was validated using content validation strategy. No evidence of criterion-related validity is presented in the manual; therefore, the test results should be interpreted with caution.

Online Version

The instrument can be administered online at www.jist.com. According to the website, the benefits of using the online version of the JSAI include:

- Considerable savings in administration time

- The ability to purchase and administer only the needed number of tests
- Price break for quantity purchases
- Can be administered where ever internet access is available
- Test security — results can be accessed only by the test administrator

Overall Critique

The JSAI appears to have utility as a measure of the attitudes of job seekers. The test is a short, self-scored instrument for which the interpretation is relatively straightforward. A strength of the instrument is that test takers and counselors receive immediate feedback, which is presented graphically. The reported reliabilities are acceptable, with the exception of the split-half reliability of the Uninvolved vs. Involved scale.

The instrument was validated using a content validation procedure; therefore, no evidence of criterion-related validity is provided in the manual. A criterion-related validity study would require an investigation of the relationship between test scores and actually finding a job. It is not known, therefore, if the instrument is able to predict accurately how well an individual will actually do in the job search process. Because the instrument is not a normative measure, no norms are available for comparison purposes. Before the instrument can be recommended without reservation, some evidence of criterion-related validity is necessary. Additionally, all estimates of reliability and validity should be based on larger sample sizes.

References

Abramson, L., Seligman, M., & Teasdale, J. (1978). Learned helplessness in humans: Critique and reformulation. *Journal of Abnormal Psychology, 87*, 49–74.

Crites, J. (1978). *Theory and research handbook for the Career Maturity Inventory* (2nd ed.). Monterey, CA: CB/McGraw-Hill.

Fleenor, J.W. (2005). Review of the Job Search Attitude Inventory (Second Edition). In R. A. Spies & B. S. Plake (Eds.), *The sixteenth mental measurements yearbook* (pp. 503–505). Lincoln, NE: University of Nebraska-Lincoln.

Goleman, D. (2000). *Working with emotional intelligence.* New York: Bantam Books.

Helwig, A. (1987). Information required for job hunting: 1,121 counselors respond. *Journal of Employment Counseling, 24*, 184–190.

Liptak, J. J. (2002). *Job Search Attitude Inventory (Second Edition): Administrator's Guide.* Indianapolis: JIST Works.

Liptak, J. J. (2006). *Job Search Attitude Inventory (Third Edition): Administrator's Guide.* Indianapolis: JIST Works.

O'Neill, T.R. (2005). Review of the Job Search Attitude Inventory (Second Edition). In R. A. Spies & B. S. Plake (Eds.), *The sixteenth mental measurements yearbook* (pp. 505–506). Lincoln, NE: University of Nebraska-Lincoln.

Job Survival and Success Scale (JSSS)

John J. Liptak

JIST Publishing, Inc.
8902 Otis Avenue
Indianapolis, IN 46216
www.jist.com

Target Population: High school to adult.

Statement of the Purpose of the Instrument: The Job Survival and Success Scale (JSSS) is designed to help individuals identify their most and least effective job survival and success skills, including the key "soft skills" that employers desire most. It then guides them to create a "Success Plan" for improving those skills.

Titles of Subtests, Scales, Scores Provided: Scores in five categories representing the most desirable skills and traits for the world of work: Dependability, Responsibility, Human Relations, Ethical Behavior, and Getting Ahead.

Forms and Levels Available, with Dates of Publication/Revision of Each: Job Survival and Success Scale; Job Survival and Success Scale Administrator's Guide. No special qualifications required. 2005.

Date of Most Recent Edition of Test Manual, User's Guide, etc.: 2005

Languages in Which Available: English only.

Time:

Actual Test Time: 20–30 minutes (60 items).

Total Administration Time: 20–30 minutes (self-administered).

Norm Group(s) on Which Scores Are Based: The Job Survival and Success Scale was developed using three norms groups: high school students from ages 16 to 18; college students from ages 17 to 23; and adult noncollege students from ages 20 to 67.

Manner in Which Results Are Reported for Individuals: Raw scores for each of the scales are profiled into three score ranges (High, Average, and Low) with easy-to-understand interpretations for each scale. Self-scoring and self-interpreting.

Types of Scores: Five raw scale scores (Dependability, Responsibility, Human Relations, Ethical Behavior, and Getting Ahead.) can be compared to the norms developed for the population taking the JSSS.

Report Format/Content:

BASIC SERVICE: Assessment is self-scoring and self-interpreting. Profile Interpretation and Success Plan are included with each assessment. Respondents follow a series of five steps to complete the JSSS.

Report Format/Content for Group Summaries: Not available.

Scoring:

Machine Scoring Service: Not available.

Hand Scoring:

Scored by: Counselee

Time required for scoring: Less than 5 minutes. Included in administration time above.

Local Machine Scoring: Not available.

Computer Software Options Available: Not available.

Cost of Materials: Due to possible price changes since publication date, be sure to check with publisher website.

Specimen Set: $37.95 for a package of 25. Each package includes a free Administrator's Guide. Administrator's Guide also available for free download from jist.com.

Additional Comments of Interest to Users: The JSSS is the only work-related assessment to measure Emotional Intelligence skills used in the workplace. The JSSS has been used in recent research studies to identify the Emotional Intelligence of today's workforce. The JSSS can be used to improve job retention rates of employees. The JSSS can be used in conjunction with the Job Search Attitude Inventory (JIST Publishing) and Barriers to Employment Success Inventory (JIST Publishing) in a comprehensive employment counseling approach.

Published Reviews of the Instrument in the Last 15 Years: None cited.

Reviewed by:

William I. Sauser, Jr.
Professor of Management
College of Business
Auburn University

Description

The *Job Survival and Success Scale* (JSSS) is one of several instruments published by JIST Works (an imprint of JIST Publishing, Inc.) designed to help job seekers and their vocational counselors explore various occupations and the job seeker's interests and abilities with respect to the duties those jobs require. For other recent reviews of the JSSS, see Austin and Tischendorf (2007) and Johnson (2007). The JSSS is attractive, colorful, and engaging. It is easy to complete within roughly 20 minutes, can be administered to groups or individuals, is self-scoring (with easy-to-follow instructions), and contains useful interpretive information directly on the instrument itself. It is well designed for use within a one-hour counseling session. Normative tables are provided for high school students, college students, and adults (ages 20–67), thus the JSSS is designed for use with a wide variety of job seekers. None of the items is gender specific.

John Liptak (2005b), the author of the instrument, states on p. 1 of the *Manual,* "Although job-related knowledge is critical to being a successful employee, other skills are needed to prepare college students and others to be successful in the workplace." He cites a number of references (Calvert, 2002; Goleman, 1995, 1998; National Association of Colleges and Employers, 2005; Shivpuri & Kim, 2004; Wolf-Wendel & Ruel, 1999) to indicate that "soft" social skills (in addition to "hard" job-related knowledge and skills) are necessary for success in the employment setting; such "soft" skills include "interpersonal and communication skills, honesty and integrity, continuous learning, strong work ethic, teamwork skills, and motivation and initiative" (Liptak, 2005b, p. 1). Liptak recommends that both sets of skills be taught (and assessed) in a holistic manner within colleges and universities, school-to-work programs, rehabilitation agencies, and employee training programs. His purpose in creating the JSSS thus was to provide an assessment device that would aid counselors and other educators in evaluating the level of "soft" skills possessed by the job seeker.

The JSSS consists of 60 items grouped into five categories (12 items each): Dependability, Responsibility, Human Relations, Ethical Behavior, and Getting Ahead. A sample item is, "On the job I would ... follow the dress code set by others in the organization" (Liptak, 2005a, p. 2). Each item is rated on a four-point scale: 4 — A lot like me, 3 — Somewhat like me, 2 — A little like me, 1 — Not like me. (Reverse-scored items are rated 1 through 4 and are mixed throughout the instrument.) Scores for the five categories are calculated simply by summing the scores for the 12 items within each category. The job seeker is then asked to "profile your scores" by plotting them on a colorful graph, and interpretations are given for low, average, and high scores as indicated by the plots on the graph. In further steps the job seeker is asked to "interpret your profile" by studying suggestions for improvement provided in interpretive sections of the instrument, then to devise "my success plan" by setting some goals to better prepare the job seeker for success in the workplace.

Use in Counseling

The instrument states clearly on its cover that the JSSS "is not a test," and I heartily concur. It is not designed for fine measurement, can easily be faked, and (as noted below) does not possess the psychometric quality one would desire in a testing instrument. It is designed instead as a device to guide job seekers and their counselors in a fruitful mutual exploration of "soft" skills, their importance for success in the workplace, a rough idea of the job seeker's current self-reported level of those skills, and a focused discussion on how to enhance the job seeker's "soft" skills to better prepare him or her for success in the workplace. The real value of the instrument, in my opinion, is dependent on the degree to which the job seeker engages in this exercise and the counselor provides insight and guidance. In other words, what a person gains from the JSSS is highly dependent on the effort he/she makes to understand the importance of dependability, responsibility, ethical behavior, and the other "soft" skills essential for success in the modern workplace.

As a guide for discussion, I find the items useful (if a bit narrow in scope, especially with respect to ethics), the scoring instructions clear, the profiling graph simplistic, the interpretive comments very helpful, and the success planning section a good start but not well enough developed. This reviewer wishes the instrument put even more emphasis on the need for the job seeker to take a proactive approach to building these skills. Both the job seeker and his or her vocational counselor will find a wealth of ideas in the books, pamphlets, and (free) online aids provided through the publisher's web site, www.jist.com. While the JSSS may provide the job seeker with some useful information for career preparation, it is the depth of discussion between the job seeker and the counselor — perhaps supplemented with some of the publications listed on the web site — that will truly provide the holistic approach to job preparation called for by Liptak (2005b) in the JSSS *Manual.*

Technical Considerations

The process used to develop the JSSS is described briefly in the Manual (pp. 5–6). After reviewing literature relating to job readiness and retention and determining the five "soft" skills to be assessed, the author generated a large pool of items designed to tap each of the five categories represented on the instrument. This pool of items was subjected to a form of item analysis: weak items "which did not correlate well" (Liptak, 2005b, p. 5) were culled; the remaining items were reviewed, edited, and clarified; the 12 best items for each category were selected; and the entire instrument was carefully reviewed "to eliminate any reference to sex, race, culture, or ethnic origin" (p. 5).

Norms were then developed using very small samples of high school students (n = 98), college students (n = 52), and adults (n = 51). Coefficient alpha (a measure of internal consistency or reliability) was calculated (n = 110) for each scale; these fall within an acceptable range of.87 (Human Relations) to.92 (Responsibility). Likewise, test-retest reliability for the five scales (n = 75) was found to be acceptable, ranging from.79 (Human Relations) to.89 (Getting Ahead).

Validity evidence for the JSSS is very weak. Liptak (2005b) presents an interscale correlation table (n = 65) which he claims as evidence for concurrent validity, since "the highest correlation, .39, is found between Dependability and Human Relations" (p. 6). As evidence of construct validity, the author simply presents the three norms tables; this is inadequate evidence in my opinion. No evidence is presented to show that the five scales actually predict job success. This glaring weakness must be addressed through further research if the JSSS is to gain respect as a trustworthy measurement device. As noted above, the instrument can easily be faked by any job seeker who desires to appear stronger or weaker in "soft" skills than is really the case. For these reasons, it would be irresponsible to use this instrument for employee selection or performance prediction, uses for which the JSSS clearly was not designed.

Computer-Based and/or Online Versions

The Job Survival and Success Scale is currently available in print form only.

Overall Critique

The Job Survival and Success Scale is an engaging, easy to administer, self-scoring instrument designed to assess a job seeker's self-reported "soft" skills in five categories deemed important for success in the modern workplace: Dependability, Responsibility, Human Relations, Ethical Behavior, and Getting Ahead. It does not possess the psychometric quality one would desire of a selection instrument or psychological test, but it was not designed for such use. It does appear useful in a holistic vocational counseling context where the focus is on "hard" job-related abilities *and* those interpersonal and job readiness "soft" skills necessary to succeed in today's workplace. In the hands of a skilled vocational counselor, the instrument could be used to help the job seeker gain greater insight into what is needed to advance in the workplace, and to plan and implement a proactive program to build those skills. Even in a "self administered, self-interpreted" context the JSSS might prove to be a valuable tool for use by highly motivated job seekers.

References

Austin, J. T., & Tischendorf, S. D. (2007). Review of the Job Survival and Success Scale. In K. F. Geisinger, R. A. Spies, J. F. Carlson, & B. S. Plake (Eds.), *The seventeenth mental measurements yearbook* (pp. 447–449). Lincoln, NE: Buros Institute of Mental Measurements.

Calvert, R. (2002). Soft skills: A key to employment today. *Career Opportunity News, 20(3)*, 6.

Goleman, D. (1995). *Emotional intelligence.* New York: Bantam Books.

Goleman, D. (1998). *Working with emotional intelligence.* New York: Bantam Books.

Johnson, S. B. (2007). Review of the Job Survival and Success Scale. In K. F. Geisinger, R. A. Spies, J. F. Carlson, & B. S. Plake (Eds.), *The seventeenth mental measurements yearbook* (pp. 449–451). Lincoln, NE: Buros Institute of Mental Measurements.

Liptak, J. J. (2005a). *Job Survival and Success Scale.* Indianapolis, IN: JIST Works.

Liptak, J. J. (2005b). *Job Survival and Success Scale administrator's guide.* Indianapolis, IN: JIST Works.

National Association of Colleges and Employers (2005). *Job outlook 2005.* New York: NACE.

Shivpuri S., & Kim, B. (2004). Do employees and colleges see eye-to-eye? *NACE Journal, Fall 2004*, 37–46.

Wolf-Wendel, L. E., & Ruel, M. (1999). Developing the whole student: The collegiate ideal. *New Directions for Higher Education, 105*, 35–46.

QUALITY OF LIFE INVENTORY (QOLI)

Michael B. Frisch

Pearson Assessments
5601 Green Valley Drive, 4th Floor
Bloomington, MN 55437
www.pearsonassessments.com

Target Population: Individuals 18 years and older.

Statement of the Purpose of the Instrument: The QOLI test is a measure of positive psychology and mental health, Brief but comprehensive, the QOLI test provides an overall score and a profile of problems and strengths in 16 areas of life such as love, work, and play.

Titles of Subtests, Scales, Scores Provided: The 16 areas addressed in the QOLI assessment are Health, Self-Esteem, Goals and Values, Money, Work, Play, Learning, Creativity, Helping, Love, Friends, Children, Relatives, Home, Neighborhood, Community.

Date of Most Recent Edition of Test Manual, User's Guide, etc.: 1994

Languages in Which Available: English only.

Time:

Actual Test Time: Approximately 5 minutes to administer.

Norm Group(s) on Which Scores Are Based: Normative data were collected from the nonclinical population in 12 states in the Northeast, South, Midwest and West.

Manner in Which Results Are Reported for Individuals:

Types of Scores: The QOLI Profile Report graphically presents the overall quality of life score and a weighted satisfaction profile for the 16 areas assessed. It also provides a brief narrative description of the person's overall classification and lists areas of dissatisfaction that may need further exploration.

Report Format/Content: Profile Report, Hand-scoring Report.

Report Format/Content for Group Summaries: See above.

Scoring:

Machine Scoring Service:

COST OF BASIC SERVICE PER COUNSELEE: The QOLI test can be administered by paper-and-pencil answer sheet or administered locally on Q Local software. The assessment is scored via Q Local software. Each profile report is approximately $2.30 per report. Paper/pencil answer sheets are sold for 21.50 per package of 25. The Q Local software is an $89 annual license fee. Time required for scoring and returning: 5 minutes

Hand Scoring:

SCORED BY: Counselee

TIME REQUIRED FOR SCORING: 10 minutes

Local Machine Scoring:

PROVISIONS/CONDITIONS/EQUIPMENT REQUIRED: This is the Q Local option.

Computer Software Options Available: Q Local is the computer scoring option.

Cost of Materials: Due to possible price changes since publication date, be sure to check with publisher website.

Hand-scoring Starter Kit includes QOLI manual, 50 answer sheets and 50 worksheets for $101.50

Q Local Profile Reports are approximately $2.30 per administration

    (Q Local software is an $89 annual license fee)

QOLI Answer Sheets (25 per package) is $21.50

QOLI Test Manual is $41.50

Published Reviews of the Instrument in the Last 15 Years: None cited.

Reviewed by:

Laurie A. Carlson
Associate Professor
Counseling and Career Development
Colorado State University

Description

The *Quality of Life Inventory (QOLI)* is an easily used assessment tool based upon Quality of Life Theory (Frisch, 1994), a melding of cognitive therapy and positive psychology. The basic premise behind the theory and *QOLI* is that an individual's quality of life is equated with life satisfaction, an objective and subjective determination of the gap between the importance of life areas and perceived attainment of those needs. The *QOLI* examines 16 constructs identified in the literature to be unique contributors to life satisfaction (Frisch, 1994). These 16 constructs are "Health, Self-Esteem, Goals-and-Values, Money, Work, Play, Learning, Creativity, Helping, Love, Friends, Children, Relatives, Home, Neighborhood, and Community" (Frisch, 1994, p. 6). It is interesting to note that recent factor analytic procedures with results from a clinical sample of 217 indicated that the 16 scales loaded into a two-factor solution: self-oriented and other-oriented (McAlinden & Oei, 2006).

Each of the 16 constructs are measured with two items; the first requires the individual to indicate importance of the construct (0 – not important to 2 – extremely important), and the second asks the individual to indicate level of current satisfaction (3 – very dissatisfied to +3 – very satisfied). The satisfaction scores are then multiplied by the importance scores yielding a "weighted satisfaction score" (ranging from –6 to +6) for each area. These weighted scores are then added together and divided by the number of areas that were rated important or extremely important to yield a total raw score. The manual provides tables for converting the total raw score to T-scores or percentiles.

Items include a general description of the construct to aid in understanding, and the entire instrument is written at the sixth-grade reading level. The layout of the instrument is intuitive and friendly. The QOLI is appropriate for individuals 17 years of age or older and may be administered individually or in groups (Frisch, 1994). The instrument takes about five minutes to complete and is available for either paper-and-pencil or computer administration. Hand scoring of the paper-and-pencil version is clearly outlined in the test manual using step-by-step instructions and should generally take no longer than several minutes to score (Johnson, 2001). The advantage to using the hand-scored version is that the instrument includes opportunity for the client to add narrative reflection regarding the nature of concerns or problems in each of the 16 areas.

Use in Counseling

The *QOLI* is grounded in positive psychology and adheres to the precept that life satisfaction and subjective well-being are inextricably intertwined with psychological and physical health. Frisch (1994) identifies a broad range of literature that supports the premise that reduced quality of life leads to a greater degree of psychological distress and disease. The *QOLI* has been successfully used in measuring treatment outcome, treatment planning, and screening individuals who are at risk for health problems. Specifically, Frisch (1994) indicates that the instrument can be used to (a) gain a more complete view of the client's mental status, (b) gain a more complete view of the client's physical health status, (c) predict future health problems, (d) aid in measuring medical health outcomes, (e) aid in developing new treatments, and (f) provide a integrative construct for understanding and treating mental disorders.

The *QOLI* has been used successfully with geriatric clients (Bourland, Stanley, Snyder, Novy, Beck, Averill, & Swann, 2000). In a rather cursory search, however, no literature emerged related to the use of the *QOLI* with culturally or ethnically diverse clients. The electronic and hand-scored versions differ in that the hand-scored version includes a section that allows the client to provide a narrative explanation of their responses to each of the 16 quality of life indicators. The narrative response area of the hand-scored version serves to strengthen the applicability of the instrument and provides material for discussion with the client. It is this characteristic that indicates use of the hand-scored version with populations that might not be clearly represented in the standardization sample.

Use of the *QOLI* is facilitated by rather comprehensive and well-written sections in the manual regarding test interpretation and treatment guidance. Each of these topics constitutes a separate section in the manual and provides strong guidance for the test user. The nature of the construct, quality of life, indicates that the instrument is appropriate for a multitude of settings (i.e., clinical, school, and career).

Technical Considerations

The standardization sample of 798 from 12 states across the country roughly matches the 1992 census data with respect to racial/ethnic characteristics and gender (Frisch, 1994), but the demographic data included in the manual do not clearly describe the sample with regards to other pertinent demographic characteristics (Barnes, 2001). The manual reports that the standardization sample was nonclinical and that the instrument was primarily administered in groups (Frisch, 1994). Barnes (2001) points out that the sampling procedure is not clearly articulated in the manual and that some of the participants were paid.

Reliability for the *QOLI* was measured using both a two-week test-retest and coefficient alpha. The test-retest study included only 55 participants and yielded a rather weak reliability coefficient of .73 (Frisch, 1994). Although statistically significant at $p < .01$, this coefficient is markedly smaller than those reported in the earlier version of the *QOLI* ($r = .91$ over 33 days and $r = .80$ over 18 days [Johnson, 2001]). Internal consistency analyses yielded a coefficient alpha of .79 using the sum of the weighted satisfaction ratings instead of the raw score. Frisch (1994) indicates that using the weighted score was appropriate as the process or computing the raw score is not the same for all individuals and, in correlation analysis, the correlation between the sum of the weighted scales and the *QOLI* raw score was .99.

The manual for the *QOLI* outlines the process used for examining convergent and discriminant validity as well as sensitivity to clinical treatment. Validity coefficients for *QOLI* T scores with scores from the Satisfaction With Life Scale (SWLS) and the Quality of Life Index are .56 and .75, respectively. The *QOLI* yielded a statistically significant, yet small, coefficient of .25 with the Marlowe-Crowne Social Desirability Scale. Frisch (1994) presents data supporting sensitivity to clinical treatment through a rather small (N = 13) study of bibliotherapy with a sample of clinically depressed individuals. Predictive and treatment validity has been supported in work with college students (Frisch, Clark, Rouse, Rudd, Paweleck, Greenstone, & Kopplin, 2005), older adults with generalized anxiety disorder (Bourland et al., 2000), and patients with anxiety and depression (McAlinden & Oei, 2006).

Overall Critique

The *QOLI* presents a theoretically sound instrument that aids in working with a multitude of clients through the positive psychology approach. The instrument is comprehensive, yet concise enough to be highly useful for practitioners in multiple settings. The time of administration and scoring is minimal (generally 10-20 minutes for both), and generates not only a "score," but also material for further work with the client. The manual is intuitive, easy to use, and generally comprehensive. The "Hand-Scoring Starter Kit" includes the manual as well as 50 administrations, making the instrument rather economical for the practitioner.

The true strength of the instrument lies in the way that the practitioner uses the information gathered. Certainly, the narrative comment portion of the hand-scored version provides further insight into the client's quality of life and material for discussion in treatment planning and implementation. This feature also lends to a more culturally sensitive application of the instrument. One can certainly use the instrument for the purpose of quantifying client perception of quality of life or treatment outcomes, yet it seems that one would then not be fully using all that the instrument has to offer.

References

Barnes, L. L. B. (2001). Test review of the Quality of Life Inventory. In B. S. Plake & J. C. Impara (Eds.), *The fourteenth mental measurements yearbook* [Electronic version]. Retrieved January 27, 2007 from the Buros Institute's *Test Reviews Online* website: http://www.unl.edu/buros.

Bourland, S. L., Stanley, M. A., Snyder, A. G., Novy, D. M., Beck, J. G., Averill, P. M., & Swann, A. C. (2000). Quality of life in older adults with generalized anxiety disorder. *Aging & Mental Health, 4,* 315–323.

Frisch, M. B. (1994). *Quality of life inventory: Manual and treatment guide.* Minneapolis, MN: NCS Pearson Assessments.

Frisch, M. B., Clark, M. P., Rouse, S. V., Rudd, M. D., Paweleck, J. K., Greenstone, A., & Kopplin, D. A. (2005). Predictive and treatment validity of life satisfaction and the quality of life inventory. *Assessment, 12,* 66–78.

Johnson, R. W. (2001). Test review of the Quality of Life Inventory. In B. S. Plake & J. C. Impara (Eds.), *The fourteenth mental measurements yearbook* [Electronic version]. Retrieved January 27, 2007 from the Buros Institute's *Test Reviews Online* website: http://www.unl.edu/buros.

McAlinden, N. M., & Oei, T. P. S. (2006). Validation of the quality of life inventory for patients with anxiety and depression. *Comprehensive Psychiatry, 47,* 307–314.

CHAPTER 11

PERSONALITY ASSESSMENTS

- California Psychological Inventory (CPI 434)

- Clifton StrengthsFinder or StrengthsFinder 2.0

- Jackson Personality Inventory – Revised (JPI-R)

- Myers-Briggs Type Indicator (MBTI) Form M

- NEO Personality Inventory – Revised (NEO PI-R)

- Student Styles Questionnaire (SSQ)

CALIFORNIA PSYCHOLOGICAL INVENTORY
(CPI 434)

Harrison Gough

Consulting Psychologists Press (CPP, Inc.) and Davies-Black Publishing
1055 Joaquin Road, 2nd Floor
Mountain View, CA 94043
Tel: (650) 969-8901
Toll free: (800) 624-1765
Fax: (650) 969-8608
www.cpp.com

Target Population: CPI 434: Adults (people aged 13 years and older), reading level is fourth grade. Individual assessments of adolescents and adults.

Statement of the Purpose of the Instrument: Designed to evaluate interpersonal behavior and social interaction within normal individuals in order to help promote teamwork, build leadership competencies, and find and develop employees destined for success.

Titles of Subtests, Scales, Scores Provided: The inventory contains 434 items and 20 folk scales.

Forms and Levels Available, with Dates of Publication/Revision of Each: Revised 3rd edition. CPI 260 (short form): The CPI 260 assesses normal adult personality. It differs from the CPI 434 in that it was developed specifically for the work and organizational setting. It was updated with newer language, revised scales, and new interpretive material. The CPI 260 has a focus on leadership development and is often used as a selection tool.

Date of Most Recent Edition of Test Manual, User's Guide, etc.: 1996

Languages in Which Available: English, French, German, Italian, Japanese, Spanish.

Time:

Actual Test Time: 45 minutes.

Total Administration Time: 50 minutes.

Norm Group(s) on Which Scores Are Based: Norms are available for males only, females only, and male/female data combined. The CPI was developed and normed on nonpsychiatric or nonclinical populations. Normative sample of 6,000 men and women.

Manner in Which Results Are Reported for Individuals:

Types of Scores: Standard scores.

Report Format/Content:

BASIC SERVICE: Profile, narrative, and configural supplement available.

(Comparative profiles based on both gender-specific and combined male/female norms)

Report Format/Content for Group Summaries:

Basic Service: Available by request.

Scoring:

Machine Scoring Service: Available. Time required for scoring and returning: 24 hour turnaround + mail time. Scoring centers in Minneapolis, MN; Washington, DC; Palo Alto, CA.

Hand Scoring:

SCORED BY: Clerk; Counselor

TIME REQUIRED FOR SCORING: 60 minutes

Local Machine Scoring: Provisions/conditions/equipment required: 640-K memory, 80-column printer, DOS 2.0 or greater, IBM PC /IBM-XT/IBM PC-AT or IBM PC compatible . ½-size expansion card slot.

Computer Software Options Available: Five or ten year leases $600–$800.

Cost of Materials: Due to possible price changes since publication date, be sure to check with the publisher website.

Specimen Set: Test Booklet, Profile Answer Sheet prepaid, Administrator's Guide.

Counselee Materials:

CPI Manual (A), reusable, $87.50

A Practical Guide to CPI Interpretation (A), reusable, $76.50

CPI Item Booklets, $37.75 for pkg of 10

The CPI Applications Guide (A), reusable, $139.50

Prepaid CPI Profile Answer Sheets, $155.50 pkg of 10

Prepaid CPI Narrative Report Answer Sheets, $168.00 pkg of 5

Prepaid CPI Configural Analysis Report Answer Sheets, $209.00 pkg of 5

Published Reviews of the Instrument in the Last 15 Years:

None cited.

Reviewed by:

Robert C. Chope
Professor and Chair
Department of Counseling
San Francisco State University

Description

The self-administered California Psychological Inventory 434 (CPI 434) consists of 434 true-false items written at an eighth-grade reading level that ask for information pertaining to personal attributes and feelings, opinions, attitudes, adherence to rules, and social and familial issues. First published in 1957, revised in 1987, this third edition was released in 1996. It can be administered both online and with paper-and-pencil answer sheets that can be either mailed in or scored in house with appropriate scanning equipment. There is no hand scoring. Three different protocols are available for users to choose from: a profile report, narrative report, or configural analysis report.

The items yield standard scores on three vector scales, the original 20 folk concept scales (everyday common dimensions of personality), and seven special purpose scales. Six of the original 13 special purpose scales have been dropped from all of the protocols although they can be hand scored with scoring keys available in the appendix of the manual (Gough and Bradley, 1996, p.182). Interestingly, 171 items were taken from the *Minnesota Multiphasic Personality Inventory* (MMPI; Hathaway and McKinley, 1943) and 158 items are concurrently in use on the MMPI-2 (Butcher, Dahlstrom, Graham, Tellegen, & Kaemmer, 1989).

The profile report offers the vector scales scores, folk scales scores with gender specific and combined gender norms, and the seven special purpose scales scores, all of which are given greater articulation below.

The broader narrative report enlarges on the scales scores that are presented graphically in the profile report and, in addition, includes 100 California Q-sort items based on Block's (1961) California Q-set. These are presented in nine categories which move from "extremely characteristic or salient" to "extremely uncharacteristic or negatively salient."

The configural analysis report contains the five components of the narrative report but adds an interpretation based upon combinations of two or more scales originally conceived by McAllister (1996). There are two types of interpretations, one empirically based and the other more speculative.

The three vector scales, derived from factor analysis, form a cuboid typology reflecting how an individual scores on three dimensions. Vector one is reminiscent of the aged introversion, extroversion orientation (internality/externality), while vector two focuses upon an orientation to authority (norm questioning/norm favoring). Together these two vectors structure four lifestyle quadrants or types, titled Alpha, Beta, Gamma, and Delta. Alphas are productive joiners and good leaders, Betas tend to be more ancillary followers and preservationists, Gammas are social skeptics and social change advocates, while Deltas are self-reflecting innovators. Vector three (self-realization) speaks to individual self actualization, ego integration, and potential.

These dimensional scales are presented first on the different reports as a "classification for type and level" and help to guide further interpretation of the original 20 folk concept scales (Dominance, Capacity for Status, Sociability, Social Presence, Self-Acceptance, Independence, Empathy, Responsibility, Socialization, Self-Control, Good Impression, Communality, Well-Being, Tolerance, Achievement via Conformance, Achievement via Independence, Intellectual Efficiency, Psychological-Mindedness, Flexibility, Femininity/Masculinity). The 20 folk concept scales are presented in four different classes. The scales have common, easily understood, everyday names and descriptors.

The seven special purpose scales are related to occupational issues (Managerial Potential, Work Orientation, Law Enforcement Orientation) and personal characteristics (Creative Temperament, Leadership Potential, Amicability, Tough-Mindedness). All appear to be useful in coaching or counseling people with work-related issues. The six scales that have been eliminated from the protocols (Baucom Scales for Masculinity and Femininity, Anxiety, Narcissism, Dicken Social Desirability, and Dicken Acquiescence) can be scored with keys made available in the appendix of the manual (Gough and Bradley, 1996, p.182).

Use in Counseling

Before proceeding with counseling, the protocol should be reviewed by the counselor for consistency and possible faking (good or bad) by noting extreme scores on the Good Impression, Communality, and Well-Being scales. The protocol also is reviewed electronically for any evidence of invalidity. Thereafter, the protocol can be classified via the cuboidal model and then considerations can be made for the highest and lowest elevations on the 20 folk scales. The special purpose scales and patterns of scales that have particular meaning can also be discussed.

Counselors can be well served by following the protocol interpretation with a clinically focused discussion. This may include exploring whether or not the client has realized his or her potential and has a life that is congruent with former expectations, current circumstances, and the data presented in the protocol.

The CPI 434 is not designed to be useful in the assessment of psychopathology, although early on research demonstrated that very low scores on the folk scales can demonstrate poor personal adjustment (Higgens-Lee, 1990). The CPI 434 can be used as a stand-alone instrument, but it is quite useful in consort with other measures. It has been brought into team-building exercises and is an effective, practical tool for exploring career and managerial alternatives. The mostly positive, unassuming scale names allow clients to understand themselves while they also look at their lifestyle, relationship, and career choices. Counselors have been known to use the instrument to assist people in understanding why they communicate as they do.

To aid with interpretation, there are eight illustrative cases in the CPI 434 manual that can help to guide counselors in interpreting/using the CPI. A skilled counselor should be able to integrate the protocol data with clinical information to develop a potent profile of a client.

Technical Considerations

The CPI 434 manual provides extensive reference tables for comparative purposes. The normative samples are large (3,000 for each gender) but are heavily weighted toward young and well-educated individuals. While there are some data for special populations (e.g., Irish entrepreneurs), there is a lack of data for any multiethnic, multicultural, and diversified populations.

Reliability and validity data are comparable to other measures of personality. Retest reliability data are presented in 1-, 5-, and 25-year intervals, useful for demonstrating long-term stability in scale traits but not necessarily useful in demonstrating shorter term changes (Atkinson, 2003). Internal consistency estimates for the vector scales and most of the folk and special scales are above .70 (Gough, 1987).

Extensive criterion-related and construct validity are also presented in the manual supporting the strong validity of empirical scales even when they may be factorially complex. Speaking to the practical orientation of the instrument, there is a robust focus on predictive validity. Construct validity evidence is on the order of .4 to .8 for the folk and vector scales (Atkinson, 2003). Still, there are criticisms regarding the lack of construct validity for the instrument and the justifications for the criteria used in developing the folk scales (Hattrup, 2003).

Computer-Based Versions

Computers are involved in all of the scoring mechanisms. Web administration is available with the online delivery system established by the publisher, Consulting Psychologists Press.

Overall Critique

The CPI 434 has been available in one form or another for more than 50 years. It has a well-established track record among clinicians even with criticisms from researchers concerned about the lack of purity and complexity of some of the scales. Moreover, items continue to have a middle class bias regarding education and lifestyle.

Nevertheless, the inventory has strong representation in the career counseling and coaching arena. It can assist in recruitment, team building, assessing leadership, exploring appropriate employment alternatives, and motivation. In fact so much attention has been given to the potential career and leadership use of the inventory that the CPI 260 has been developed to capitalize on the needs of career counselors, coaches, and trainers focusing on strengths and areas for needed improvement. This instrument may prove to be more relevant and efficient for training purposes than the CPI 434.

References

Atkinson, M. J. (2003). Review of the California Psychological Inventory Third Edition. In B. S. Plake, J.C . Impara, and R.A. Spies (Eds.), *The fifteenth mental measurements yearbook.* (pp. 159–161). Lincoln, NE: Buros Institute of Mental Measurements.

Block, J. (1961). The Q-sort method in personality assessment and psychiatric research. Springfield, IL: Charles C. Thomas.

Butcher, J. N., Dahlstrom, W. G., Graham, J. R., Tellegen, A., & Kaemmer, B. (1989) *Manual for the restandardized Minnesota Multiphasic Personality Inventory: MMPI-2. An administrative and interpretative guide.* Minneapolis: University of Minnesota Press.

Gough, H.G. (1987). *California Psychological Inventory: Administrators guide. Palo Alto, CA: Consulting Psychologists Press.*

Gough, H.G., & Bradley, P.B. (1996). *CPI Manual* (3rd ed.). Mountain View, CA. Consulting Psychologists Press.

Hathaway, S. R., & McKinley, J. C. (1943). *Minnesota Multiphasic Personality Inventory.* Minneapolis: University of Minnesota Press.

Hattrup, K. (2003). Review of the California Psychological Inventory Third Edition. In B. S. Plake, J.C . Impara, and R.A. Spies (Eds.), *The fifteenth mental measurements yearbook.* (pp. 161–163). Lincoln, NE: Buros Institute of Mental Measurements.

Higgens-Lee, C. (1990). Low scores on the California Psychological Inventory as predictors of psychopathology in alcoholic patients. *Psychological Reports, 67,* 227–232.

McAllister, L. W. (1996). *A practical guide to CPI interpretation* (3rd ed.). Mountain View, CA: CPP, Inc.

CLIFTON STRENGTHSFINDER
OR STRENGTHSFINDER 2.0
Gallup Organization

Gallup Organization

1001 Gallup Drive
Omaha, NE 68102
www.strengthsfinder.com

Target Population: Ages 15 and above. Adolescents and adults with a reading level of tenth grade or higher, businesses, schools, community groups, individuals; the tool has been used by consultants in the workplace to promote employee development and associated productivity. In addition, the Clifton StrengthsFinder (CSF) has been administered on more than 400 campuses. Career counselors have used the measure in conjunction with interest and personality inventories. StrengthsFinder is an omnibus assessment based on strengths psychology. Its main application has been in the work domain, but it has been used for understanding individuals in a variety of settings — families, executive teams, and personal development. It is not intended for clinical assessment or diagnosis of psychiatric disorders.

Statement of the Purpose of the Instrument: Since its development, the CSF has been used primarily by consultants in the workplace to promote employee development and associated productivity. In the last few years, with the development of StrengthsQuest, a set of guidance tools designed to help college students use their strengths to pursue their academic and social goals, the CSF has been administered on more than 200 campuses. The web-based talent assessment tool measures a person's talent within 34 themes that are indicative of success.

The 34 talent themes are: Achiever, Activator, Adaptability, Analytical, Arranger, Belief, Command, Communication, Competition, Connectedness, Consistency, Context, Deliberative, Developer, Discipline, Empathy, Focus, Futuristic, Harmony, Ideation, Includer, Individualization, Input, Intellection, Learner, Maximizer, Positivity, Relator, Responsibility, Restorative, Self-Assurance, Significance, Strategic, and Woo

It reports the five most dominant themes or "Signature Themes" from the entire sequence of 34 themes in order of dominance. Its purpose is for personal development and growth, not selection, placement, or screening for mental health.

Titles of Subtests, Scales, Scores Provided: Top 5 Talent Themes are identified without raw or normative data.

Date of Most Recent Edition of Test Manual, User's Guide, etc.: 2007. StrengthsFinder 2.0 (2007) by Tom Rath (book which accompanies the online assessment, details the ways to apply an individual's results).

Languages in Which Available: 24 languages including Dutch, German, Arabic, Swedish, Thai, Japanese, Korean, Italian, Portugese, Bulgarian, English, Spanish (Latin American), Spanish (Spain), French, Hebrew, Polish, Romanian, and others.

Time:

Total Administration Time 30–45 minutes.

Norm Group(s) on Which Scores Are Based: Score report is based on the relative intensity ratings and a proprietary scoring formula.

Manner in Which Results Are Reported for Individuals:

Types of Scores: Summary scores are not given. Instead a report listing the individual's top five talent themes based on intensity are provided along with "action items" for each theme. The 34 themes are available through indepth client engagements including consulting sessions, Gallup University programs like Great Manager Program, Demands of Leadership, etc.

Report Format/Content:

BASIC SERVICE: Students receive a report describing their top five "signature themes" that represent their most intense themes of talent, rather than themes that have been compared to the responses of other people.

Scoring:

Hand Scoring: Not Available.

Local Machine Scoring: Not Available.

Computer Software Options Available: Standard administration online.

Cost of Materials: Due to possible price changes since publication date, be sure to check with publisher website.

CSF codes are typically sold as part of a Gallup Press book. Books typically sell for $20 to $25

Counselee Materials:

StrengthsFinder 2.0 by Tom Rath (2007)

StrengthsQuest: Discover and Develop Your Strengths in Academics, Career, and Beyond by Donald O. Clifton, Ph.D. and Edward "Chip" Anderson, Ph.D. (2006)

Published Reports of the Instrument in the Last 15 Years:

Lopez, S. J., Hodges, T., & Harter, J. (2005). *Clifton StrengthsFinder technical report: Development and validation.* Omaha, NE: The Gallup Organization.

Plake, B. (1999). *An investigation of ipsativity and multicollinearity properties of the Strengthsfinder Instrument [technical report].* Lincoln, NE: The Gallup Organization.

Schreiner, L.A. (2005). *Executive summary: Psychometric properties of the Clifton StrengthsFinder within a college student sample.* Omaha, NE: The Gallup Organization.

Reviewed by:

Shane J. Lopez
Associate Professor of Counseling Psychology

Heather A. Tree
Doctoral Candidate in Counseling Psychology

Psychology and Research in Education
The University of Kansas

Description

The *Clifton StrengthsFinder* is grounded in over three decades of studying success across a wide variety of functions in business and education and in the principles of positive psychological science. It was developed by Gallup, under the direction of Donald O. Clifton. His mission was to select and develop the right people for the right jobs and to help people reach their potential through strengths development. At the heart of his strengths work was a simple decree: That great organizations must not only accommodate the fact that each employee is different, they must capitalize on these individual differences (Buckingham & Clifton, 2001). Leaders must watch for clues to each employee's natural talents, and then position and develop each employee or student so that his or her talents are transformed into bona fide strengths. By changing the way it selects, measures, and develops its people and channels their careers, a strengths-based organization builds its entire enterprise around the strengths of each person (Buckingham & Clifton, 2001).

Clifton believed that these talents were naturally recurring patterns of thought, feeling, or behavior that can be productively applied. Strengths were viewed as developed talents. Specifically, a strength was defined as a talent that was honed with the knowledge and skills that were needed to achieve excellence (Schreiner, 2005). Clifton and his Gallup colleagues developed hundreds of structured interviews to help schools, businesses, and government agencies select for talent. Based on the knowledge gained from selection interviews, the Clifton StrengthsFinder was created to identify the raw talents that could then be developed into strengths. This assessment was not designed or validated for use in employee selection or mental health screening. It is meant to be used as a development tool, to help individuals discover how to build upon his or her talents to develop strengths within his or her role (Asplund, Lopez, Hodges, & Harter, 2007; Lopez, Hodges, & Harter, 2005).

The CSF is an online assessment, appropriate for administration to adolescents and adults with a reading level of tenth grade or higher. Through a secure Internet connection, the CSF web page presents a demographic questionnaire (tapping country of residence, age, and gender) and the 180-item pairs chosen from a pool of 5,000 items. A recent revision of the instrument (Clifton StrengthsFinder 2.0) reduced the number of item pairs to 177 in the preferred language of the user. Each item lists a pair of potential self-descriptors, such as "I read instructions carefully" and "I like to jump right into things." The descriptors are placed as if anchoring polar ends of a continuum. From each pair, the participant is then asked to choose the descriptor that best describes him or her, and also the extent to which it does so. The participant is given 20 seconds to respond to an item before the system moves on to the next item. (Research showed that the time limit resulted in a negligible item noncompletion rate.) The estimated time of completion is 40 minutes.

Summary scores are not given to each participant. In most cases, an individual will receive a report listing only their top five talent themes based on intensity along with "action items" for each theme. They may request a full list of all 34 themes, but this must be done through a personal feedback session with a Gallup consultant.

Use in Counseling

Since its development, the CSF has been used primarily by consultants in the workplace to promote employee development and associated productivity. In the last few years, with the development of *StrengthsQuest* (Clifton & Anderson, 2002; Clifton, Anderson, & Schreiner, 2006), a set of guidance tools designed to help college students use their strengths to pursue their academic and social goals, the CSF has been administered on more than 200 campuses. Career counselors have used the measure in conjunction with interest and personality inventories. The University of Missouri has integrated the CSF into its career development courses and into its individual and group career counseling (Eric Smitherman and Joe Johnston, personal communication, December 18, 2006). In a Career Explorations course offered to freshmen and sophomores, students consider their strengths and interests while learning more about the world of work. In a College-to-Career course, juniors and seniors use their strengths results to prepare for life after graduation. Specifically, the CSF results are used in conjunction with a mock interview assignment to better communicate students' employability. Finally, in the Career Center, Career Specialists work with clients to develop an understanding of how personal strengths will promote success in school and in a chosen career.

The CSF also has been used in university counseling centers and in student advising offices. Strengths Mentoring (SM); (Lopez, Tree, Bowers, & Burns, 2004, 2006), a three-session manualized approach, promotes the intentional use of strengths (as measured by the CSF) in students' daily lives. Used in counseling and advising centers, is a student development strategy designed to capitalize on the common factors of change and to boost agency for academic goals. Over the course of SM, trained mentors and student mentees identify salient academic goals that could be attained over the course of a semester. Using microcounseling skills and narrative and hope-enhancing techniques, the mentor helps mentees move through three stages (Naming, Nurturing, and Navigating) of strengths development.

In SM, students are assigned to mentors based on schedule availability. Before arriving for the Naming session, mentees complete the CSF and print off their feedback. During the structured session, the mentor works to develop academic goals and to help the mentee understand the feedback and how it relates to school-related goals and to incorporate the five strengths into personal descriptions. The mentor walks the mentee through a Strengths Imagery activity toward the end of the session. As homework given at the end of the first session, mentees are asked to share their feedback with people close to them (via email or by phone) and to craft stories about how the strengths are used. In the Nurturing session, mentees are encouraged to complete narrative exercises designed to create a catalog of critical events that have been and could be resolved through intentional use of strengths or "doing what you do best." Nurturing homework involves completing additional story-telling exercises (which are emailed to the mentor upon completion) about using strengths to attain goals. During the last session, focused on Navigating, mentees are challenged to create pathways that would help resolve several academic challenges or overcome real or perceived obstacles that might get in the way of academic success. Finally, the mentor and mentee discuss success experiences associated with using strengths and concerns about future strengths development and academic pursuits.

Technical Considerations

Reliability

Reliability of the CSF is adequate for the intended purposes of the assessment (i.e., strength development programs in the workplace and on campus). Internal consistency meets expectations for measures used in psychology research and practice (coefficient alpha = .70; American Educational Research Association, American Psychological Association, National Council on Measurement in Education, 1999). The alpha for the majority of the themes (23 of them) is at or above .70, whereas only three have alphas below .65 (i.e., Context, .62; Connectedness, .58; and Restorative, .55) (Asplund et al., 2007; Lopez et al., 2005).

Since respondents are only provided with their five top themes, their stability is an important issue. Almost all of the themes have a test-retest reliability over a six-month interval between .60 and .80. An initial study conducted in the 1990s revealed an average correlation coefficient of .76 for the theme score after a three-week test-retest period (during which the participants had been given their feedback reports) (Asplund et al., 2007; Lopez et al., 2005). A study by Schreiner (2005) looked at a college sample with a 12-week test-retest interval (during which they received no test feedback) and found a reliability estimate of .70.

Another important aspect of reliability is the degree to which the top five themes remained the same over time. When the CSF contains 278,256 possible unique combinations of signature themes and a change in the response to even one item on some scales can move a theme in or out of the top five, the likelihood of retaining exactly the same themes in the same order is very small. However, 52% of the students in a college sample had at least three themes that remained among their top five themes both times. Another 35% retained two of their top five themes over time, 11% retained only one of their themes, and 2% did not retain any of the same five themes from time 1 to time 2.

Validity

Average item correlations were computed for each of the 34 themes using 601,049 respondents (i.e., laypersons, businesspeople, and students) in the CSF database (Asplund et al., 2007; Lopez et al., 2005). Overall, the results suggest that items relate to their respective themes in a consistently positive manner (Asplund et al., 2007; Lopez et al., 2005). It also appears that the average item cross-total correlations have a higher positive relationship with their assigned themes rather than with other themes. This suggests the absence of redundancy among themes.

Research provided by Gallup suggests that the CSF does not vary across demographic variables or culture. The standard deviation of the correlations across countries is 0.03 and ranges from .01 to.04 (Asplund et al., 2007; Lopez et al., 2005). A similar result was found across languages and age groups.

Evidence of the construct validity of the measure also was obtained in a correlational study of participants' scores on each of the 34 themes with their scale scores on three personality instruments since certain themes were expected to be at least moderately related to scales on these other instruments (Schreimer, 2005). According to Schreiner, the theme of Achiever appears to measure a strong need for achievement, as well as stamina, hard work, and productivity. Thus, it ought to be related to the Achievement scales on the California Personality Inventory (CPI-260) (Gough & Bradley, 1996) and, in fact, this was the case ($r = .47$). Woo, described as characteristic of those who enjoy the challenge of meeting new people, was expected to correlate with the Extraversion scale score on the 16PF (Cattell, 1993) and did so significantly ($r = .62$). In the same manner, 137 different predicted relationships between specific CSF theme scores and their counterparts on the CPI-260 and 16PF were explored. A total of 128 (93.4%) of these predictions were confirmed by significant correlation coefficients, providing strong evidence for the construct validity of the CSF. Finally, a study correlating talent themes with the Big 5 constructs (McCrae et al., 2000) provided initial evidence for the measure's convergent and discriminant validity (Asplund et al., 2007; Lopez et al., 2005). That is, the CSF and personality variables were not redundant and were generally associated as hypothesized.

Overall Critique

The Clifton StrengthsFinder has been administered more than two million times, making it one of the most used psychological measures. Despite this, due to the propriety nature of the measure and of its scoring formula, few external psychometric examinations have been conducted. The psychometric reports that have been made available (Asplund et al., 2007; Lopez et al., 2005; Schreiner, 2005), focusing on employee and college student samples, are quite thorough though more information is needed about construct validity. Generally, the 34 scales measuring the talent/strength themes are internally consistent and stable. Validity examinations reveal a lack of redundancy in the 34 themes and expected relationships with scales on established personality scales.

References

American Educational Research Association, American Psychological Association, National Council on Measurement in Education. (1999). *Standards for educational and psychological testing.* Washington, D.C.: American Educational Research Association.

Asplund, J., Lopez, S. J., Hodges, T., & Harter, J. (2007). *Technical report: Development and validation of the Clifton StrengthsFinder 2.0.* The Gallup Organization.

Buckingham, M., & Clifton, D. O. (2001). *Now, discover your strengths.* New York: Free Press.

Cattell, R. B. (1993). *The 16PF fifth edition.* Champagne, IL: Institute for Personality and Ability Testing, Inc.

Clifton, D. O., & Anderson, E. C. (2002). *Discover and develop your strengths in academics, career, and beyond.* New York: Gallup Press.

Clifton, D. O., Anderson, E. C., & Schreiner, L. (2006). *Discover and develop your strengths in academics, career, and beyond.* New York: Gallup Press.

Gough, H., & Bradley, P. (1996). *CPI manual (3rd edition).* Palo Alto, CA: CPP, Inc.

Lopez, S. J., Hodges, T., & Harter, J. (2005). *Clifton StrengthsFinder technical report: Development and validation.* Omaha, NE: The Gallup Organization.

Lopez, S. J., Tree, H., Bowers, K., & Burns, M. E. (2004). *KU Strengths Mentoring Protocol.* Unpublished mentoring protocol, University of Kansas, Lawrence.

Lopez, S. J., Tree, H., Bowers, K., & Burns, M. E. (2006, October). Positive psychology on campus: Discovering students' strengths. In S. J. Lopez (Chair), *Positive psychology on campus.* Symposium at the 5th Gallup International Positive Psychology Summit, Washington, DC.

McCrae, R., Costa, P., Ostendorf, F., Angleitner, A., Hrebickova, M., Avia, M., Sanz, J., Sanchez-Bernardos, M., Kuddil, M., Woodfield, R., Saunders, P., & Smith, P. (2000). Nature over nurture: Temperament, personality, and life span development. *Journal of Personality and Social Psychology, 78,* 173–86.

Schreiner, L.A. (2005). *Executive summary: Psychometric properties of the Clifton StrengthsFinder within a college student sample.* Omaha, NE: The Gallup Organization.

Jackson Personality Inventory – Revised (JPI-R)

Douglas N. Jackson

SIGMA Assessment Systems, Inc.
P.O. Box 610984
Port Huron, MI 48061-0984
www.SigmaAssessmentSystems.com

Target Population: Age: 16+ Groups: Counseling and clinical settings, business and industrial settings, psychological research.

Statement of the Purpose of the Instrument: The Jackson Personality Inventory was developed to provide, in one convenient form, a set of measures of personality reflecting a variety of interpersonal, cognitive, and value orientations likely to have important implications for a person's functioning.

Titles of Subtests, Scales, Scores Provided: Analytical: Complexity, Breadth of Interest, Innovation, Tolerance; Extroverted: Sociability, Social Confidence, Energy Level; Emotional: Empathy, Anxiety, Cooperativeness; Opportunistic: Risk Taking, Social Astuteness; Dependable: Organization, Traditional Values, Responsibility.

Forms and Levels Available, with Dates of Publication/Revision of Each: N/A

Date of Most Recent Edition of Test Manual, User's Guide, etc.: 1994

Languages in Which Available: English and French.

Time:

Actual Test Time: 45 minutes.

Total Administration Time: 55 minutes.

Norm Group(s) on Which Scores Are Based: Norms include the responses of 1,107 individuals (367 males and 740 females) drawn from educational institutions in North America. A second set of norms is based on the responses of 893 (629 males and 264 female) blue-collar workers. A third set of norms is derived from the responses of 555 senior executives. These sets of norms are representative of scale scores from three relatively large and unique segments of the population.

Manner in Which Results Are Reported for Individuals:

Types of Scores: Raw Scores, Percentiles.

Report Format/Content:

BASIC SERVICE: The JPI-R Basic Report consists of a profile of the 15 JPI-R scale scores, description of high and low scores for each scale, a profile of the five JPI-R cluster scores, administrative indices and a table of raw responses.

OPTIONS: The JPI-R is available for administration online at www.SigmaTesting.com, through hand scoring, mail-in service, and Software scoring.

Scoring:

Mail-in Scoring Service:

COST OF BASIC SERVICE PER COUNSELEE:

JPI-R Basic Reports: Mail-in answer sheet and Basic report coupon.

Item No. 3088   1 report $12.00*

Item No. 308

    1–3 packages (10 reports/pkg) $70.00*

    4+ packages (10 reports/pkg) $60.00*

Time required for scoring and returning: 48 hours

* Prices based on 2008 catalog.

Hand Scoring:

SCORED BY: Clerk; Counselor

TIME REQUIRED FOR SCORING: 10 minutes

Local Machine Scoring: Not available.

Computer Software Options Available: Computerized adaptive administration; standard administration online.

Ways in Which Computer/Online Version Differs: Computer software must be administered onsite, wherever the computer is located. Online scoring can be administered on any computer with Internet access.

Cost of Materials: Due to possible price changes since publication date, be sure to check with publisher website.

Specimen Set: $85*, JPI-R Examination Kit.

Counselee Materials: Kit includes manual on CD, five reusable tests, five Quick Score answer sheets, five profile sheets, and one JPI-R Basic Report for mail-in scoring.

Published Reviews of the Instrument in the Last 15 Years: None cited.

Reviewed by:[1]

Peter Zachar
Professor of Psychology
Auburn University at Montgomery

Description

The Jackson Personality Inventory–Revised (JPI-R) is the second edition of a test designed to measure personality functioning for use in schools, universities, and industry. The instrument measures 15 bipolar scales that are organized into five conceptually

---

[1] Portions of this review are adapted, by permission, from the author's original review in the *Thirteenth Mental Measurements Yearbook*.

integrated clusters termed Analytic (A), Emotional (E), Extroverted (Ex), Opportunistic (O), and Dependable (D). The 15 scales are as follows: Complexity (A), Breadth of Interest (A), Innovation (A), Tolerance (A,) Empathy (E) Anxiety (E), Cooperativeness (E), Sociability (Ex,) Social Confidence (Ex), Energy Level (Ex), Social Astuteness (O), Risk Taking (O), Organization (D), Traditional Values (D), Responsibility (D).

Created by Douglas Jackson, a prominent developer of psychological tests, the constructs measured were derived from research in personality and social psychology plus Jackson's professional experience. The test can be given and scored in paper-and-pencil formats, mail-in computer formats, and web-based formats. It can also be administered in groups.

Use in Counseling

This JPI-R is intended for use in counseling, particularly career counseling. The manual (Jackson, 1998) specifically discourages drawing inferences about psychiatrically relevant personality traits based on test results. Although an examinee's fit for a wide range of careers might be usefully explored with this test, careers in the business world would be particularly appropriate. Because it is also designed for use by industry as a selection instrument, the JPI-R lends itself to discussion of personal and career maturity for college-age students. For example, a student low on organization and responsibility may be encouraged to further explore her plans for a managerial career. A student scoring low on extroversion and social astuteness who plans to enter sales may also benefit from a discussion of typical behaviors and criteria for success in his intended field. A test such as this can serve as an impetus for exploration, and is probably more useful in counseling when there is a mismatch between reported dispositions and intended occupation and/or vocational interests.

Diversity has become a major focus in counseling psychology in the past 20 years. Although marketed for counseling psychology settings, there is limited information available for its use with diverse populations. The primary nod to diversity in the manual is a claim that a middle-aged person employed in an occupation with allegiance to conservative political opinions should not be labeled as low on tolerance if he or she is not low on tolerance relative to other middle-aged people working in conservative settings. This is a very puzzling argument. Almost any high or low score can be defined as "normal" if the right comparison group was chosen. In reality, no relevant information on minority populations is presented in the manual.

Technical Considerations

The strengths of Jackson's approach to scale development include high internal consistencies, scales that do not overlap with each other, minimization of socially desirable response biases, and efficiency. These features, as expected, can be attributed to the JPI-R. The manual is written for experts in psychological measurement more than for counselors, although some useful administration guidelines are provided early on. One helpful addition is a listing of items by scale in Appendix A. For example, all the items on the complexity scale are presented together. Studying these lists is important for understanding what a scale measures because scale names can be misleading. Users should also study what a scale is correlated with to further understand what it measures. Correlates of the various scales with other instruments are also presented in the manual, although they would be interpretable only to someone who is already familiar with the other instruments.

Norms are available for college students, blue collar workers, and business executives. The manual reports Cronbach's alphas for the 15 basic scales. They appear to be reasonably adequate (i.e., most alphas are in the .70s and .80s). One of the unusual aspects to this test is that it bucks the current trend toward dimensionally pure constructs in favor of more heterogeneous constructs. To assess these broader constructs, the manual reports Bentler's theta coefficients – which are higher for those scales with alphas in the .60s such as tolerance and social astuteness.

Internal consistency indices are not presented for the five clusters. Given that they were derived from a factor analysis of the basic scales and they have a larger number of items, these reliability coefficients should be high, and their absence is a curious omission.

Surprisingly, no test retest correlations were presented. This is a serious omission. Without evidence of temporal stability, the existence of personality "traits" has not been demonstrated. Interpretations should therefore be made cautiously.

Reflecting its emphasis on careers in business, this revised edition of the test eliminates the kinds of questions placed on clinical validity scales that are often experienced by test takers as irrelevant during personnel selection. One of the advantages of the computer-based and web-based version of this test is that they calculate an infrequency score and a response consistency index. Despite the reasons given for eliminating the original JPR infrequency scale (i.e., it shortened the test), assessing profile validity may still be important in career and personnel settings. Unfortunately these two scales were not validated in a systematic way, and cutoffs for rejecting profiles were not appropriately evaluated.

The manual includes a lengthy discussion of *modal profile* analysis, which is an attempt to derive a typology based on measure of personality dimensions. Ten male personality types and ten female personality types are presented. Unfortunately, not enough information to actually use a modal profile analysis is provided, nor is its application demonstrated in any meaningful way.

Overall Critique

Douglas Jackson has a good reputation among those in the counseling profession. Students should find the test attractive for theses and dissertations. Counselors will be attracted to the nonpsychiatric focus, and examinees will find the test easy to take. Its psychometric properties are adequate, but the whole test package is at best partially developed. Although the manual is not written for career counselors, the test is potentially relevant to career counseling and personnel selection. More information about use in specific industries is needed. In relation to the current dominance of tests derived from factor analysis that offer coherent structural models of personality, the constructs in the JPI-R seem to be cobbled together in an idiosyncratic way. It would be useful for the publisher to demonstrate what kind of incremental validity this test has relative to the more unidimensional tests related to the five factor model and its various siblings. At present, the claim that this test measures something additional is argued for but not actually demonstrated.

References

Jackson, D. N. (1998). *Personality Research Form manual* (3rd ed.). Port Huron, MI: Sigma Assessment Systems.

Myers-Briggs Type Indicator (MBTI)

Isabel Briggs Myers and Katherine C. Briggs

Consulting Psychologists Press, Inc. (CPP, Inc.), and Davies-Black Publishing
1055 Joaquin Road, 2nd Floor
Mountain View, CA 94043
Tel: (650) 969-8901
Toll free: (800) 624-1765
Fax: (650) 969-8608
www.cpp-db.com

Target Population: 14 years and up. Seventh-grade reading level.

Statement of the Purpose of the Instrument: The MBTI instrument helps counselor/ career professionals/consultants improve work and professional relationships, increase productivity, and identify leadership and interpersonal communication preferences for clients.

Titles of Subtests, Scales, Scores Provided: Extraversion-Introversion, Sensing-Intuition, Thinking-Feeling, Judging-Perceiving. Additional scales called "Facets" are provided for Form Q of the assessment (5 facets for each dichotomy, 20 facets in total).

Forms and Levels Available, with Dates of Publication/Revision of Each:

Current Forms:

MBTI®Complete: based on Form M and includes interactive interpretive sessions online that provides verified type

Form M: Profile, Interpretive Report, Interpretive Report for Organizations, Team Report, Career Report, Work Styles Report.

Form Q: Profile, Interpretive Report.

Combined: Newly Revised Strong and MBTI Career Report, Leadership Report Using Firo-B & MBTI, Strong and MBTI Career Report, Strong and MBTI Entrepreneur Report.

Older Forms:

Form G, Form K, Form J

Date of Most Recent Edition of Test Manual, User's Guide, etc.: 1998 MBTI Manual, Third Edition.

Languages in Which Available: English, Spanish, German, French, Dutch, Canadian French, Italian, Korean, Portuguese, Danish, Norwegian, Chinese, Swedish, Russian, Anglicized adaptation. (Available in 21 languages.)

Time:

Actual Test Time: 15–25 minutes.

Total Administration Time: Approximately one hour.

Norm Group(s) on Which Scores Are Based: 3,009 adults 18 years and older from across the US. Percentages of age, gender, and ethnic group matched 1990 US census percentage.

Manner in Which Results Are Reported for Individuals:

Types of Scores: Verbal labels. MBTI uses ipsative scores and provides ipsative scoring along four dimensions, each corresponding to a verbal label.

Report Format/Content:

BASIC SERVICE: Self-scorable booklet, hand-scorable, template scored, software scoring or mail-in scoring.

OPTIONS: Interpretive Report for organizations, Team Report, Career Report, Expanded Interpretive (Step II), Leadership Report with FIRO-B, Career Report with Strong, Entrepreneur Report with Strong. (Additional reports are listed above under "forms and levels available.")

Report Format/Content for Group Summaries:

Basic Service: MBTI Team Report or MBTI Work Styles Report (for groups of 2).

Scoring:

Online scoring and report administration service: SkillsOne.com offers real-time scoring and report generation.

FORM M PROFILE: 1 – 9 for $10.95 each; 10 – 99 for $10.15 each; 100+ for $9.30 each

FORM M INTERPRETIVE REPORT: 1 – 9 for $17.60 each; 10 – 99 for $16.30 each; 100+ for $14.95 each

FORM Q PROFILE: 1 – 9 for $20.75 each; 10 – 99 for $19.20 each; 100+ for $17.65 each

FORM Q INTERPRETIVE REPORT: 1 – 9 for $31.00 each; 10 – 99 for $28.70 each; 100+ for $26.35 each

INTERPRETIVE REPORT FOR ORGANIZATIONS: 1 – 9 for $21.55 each; 10 – 99 for $19.95 each; 100+ for $18.30 each

TEAM REPORT: 1 – 9 for $21.20 each; 10 – 99 for $19.60 each; 100+ for $18.00 each

WORK STYLES REPORT: 1 – 9 for $23.40 each; 10 – 99 for $21.65 each; 100+ for $19.90 each

CAREER REPORT: 1 – 9 for $13.25 each; 10 – 99 for $12.25 each; 100+ for $11.25 each

Note: When not specified reports can be generated from Form M or Form Q. All Form M reports can be generated from Form Q.

Machine Scoring Service: Mail-in, Scoring Software, Network Software, Web Accessible via CPP software.

TIME REQUIRED FOR SCORING AND RETURNING: Mail-in: 48 hours plus mail; Software: immediate.

PROVISIONS/CONDITIONS/EQUIPMENT REQUIRED: CPP software system, Web administration on-site—PC only, Windows 95, 98, or Windows NT 4.0, 20-MB free hard disk space.

FORM M PROFILE Combined Item Booklet/Answer Sheets, Prepaid (for mail-in scoring): $109.50 for package of 10

Self-scorable and Hand Scoring:

Scored by: Counselee; Counselor.

Time required for scoring: 10 minutes.

Form M Self-scorable: $90.75 for package of 10

Form M Scoring Templates, PrePaid: $79.95 for set of 8

MBTI®Complete is a new offering that, for the first time, brings together the Form M assessment and a basic interpretation of a client's verified type—all delivered online. Cost for 1–10 administrations is $53.95 each, 11–99 administrations is $47.95 each, and more than 100 administrations is $41.95 each.

Computer Software Options Available: Computerized adaptive administration; standard administration online; Internet service via career professionals website.

New software is available for $1100 for initial set-up. Renewals are $275 per year.

Ways in Which Computer Version Differs: None.

Cost of Materials: Due to possible price changes since publication date, be sure to check the publisher's web site.

Specimen Set: MBTI Manual, Third Edition, $99.00

Counselee Materials:

Introduction to Type® booklets: $13.25 each, $99.00 for a pack of 10

MBTI® Type Overviews: $31.95 for package of 10, $42.75 for set of 16 (one of each type)

Additional Comments of Interest to Users: The MBTI assessment tool was revised in 1998. The new Form M is the most current form for Step I of the instrument. Form Q was revised in 2000 and is the most current form for Step II of the instrument.

Published Reviews:

Healy, C. (2001) Review of the Myers-Briggs Type Indicator. In J.T. Kapes. & E.A. Whitfield (Eds.). *A counselor's guide to career assessment instruments* (4th ed.). Columbus, OH: National Career Development Association

Reviewed by:[1]

Paul M. Mastrangelo
Senior Consultant
Director of New Service Development
Genesee Survey Services
Rochester, NY

Description

The Myers-Briggs Type Indicator® (MBTI®) dates back to 1943 when Katherine Cook Briggs and her daughter Isabel Briggs Myers published two forms of the Briggs-Myers

[1] Note: Portions of this review were adapted with permission from the author's original review in *The Fourteenth Mental Measurements Yearbook.*

Type Indicator Test (University of Florida George A. Smathers Libraries, 2003) under a slightly different name. The authors relied heavily on the observations and writings of Carl Jung, a colleague of Sigmund Freud in the early 1900s. The most recent version, Form M, features 93 items, each with two response options. Indeed, unlike most modern personality measures, the MBTI does not provide scores on a continuum; there is no middle ground. Rather, the MBTI identifies a person as having either one preference or the other for each of the four "dichotomies." Thus, a person is classified into one of the 16 "types" based on a preference for Extraversion (E) vs. Introversion (I), Sensing (S) vs. Intuition (N), Thinking (T) vs. Feeling (F), and Judging (J) vs. Perceiving (P). The most common type (modal type) for men is ISTJ (16.4% of a representative US sample), and the most common type (modal type) for women is ISFJ (19.4% of a representative US sample).

Use In Counseling

The *MBTI® Manual* (Briggs Myers, McCaulley, Quenk, & Hammer, 1998) does devote a chapter (Uses of Type in Career Counseling, Chapter 12) toward career counseling. However, what seem like impressive tables that validate the use of the instrument for career preferences can be misleading without closer examination. For example, the first four tables are not based on empirical data; rather, they display aspects of the work environment that two of the *Manual's* coauthors "believed were associated with each preference." The fifth table is based on actual data, but from a small sample of 98 university employees, who apparently were not seeking career counseling. This table displays matches between "Ideal Work Environment Characteristics" and preferences on the MBTI, but the actual correlations are not reported. While the table note states that the correlations are greater than .20, this magnitude is hardly strong enough to suggest a strong association between Work Environment Scale subscales and MBTI preferences. The most helpful breakout of different career preferences by type comes from table 12.9, which suggests that occupational trends vary mostly by the "function pairs, ST, SF, NF, and NT." The *Manual* also refers to research suggesting that the J-P scale is least likely to be associated with career choice. As I explain in the next section, such findings undermine the basic assumptions of the MBTI. In other words, occupational trends seem *not* to vary across all 16 types, but on just two of the preferences. Based on the *Manual's* emphasis on holistic interpretation of the types, these empirical findings would suggest the MBTI's use in career counseling is not substantively warranted. Chapter 12 in the *MBTI Manual* essentially states that the purpose of the MBTI in career counseling situations is to assess the person and his/her ability to "create work environments to better fit with their personal preferences" (p. 286). Psychometric research in the *Manual* suggests that the MBTI lacks the precision necessary to reliably and validly assess a person and, therefore, the fit between that person and his or her work environment. Even though tables and numbers abound in the Manual, there is little support for the accuracy of the MBTI type format in determining occupational preferences and work environments.

Technical Considerations

Although it is true that responses from the four MBTI scales show very high levels of internal consistency (typically >.90) and test-retest reliability (.83–.97 for a four-week interval), these analyses are irrelevant in testing the consistency of dichotomous classifications. Furthermore, the MBTI is meant to identify a person's whole type (e.g., ENTP) rather than four separate scale scores. Therefore, the true test of the MBTI's reliability is its ability to indicate the same four preferences consistently for any individual. Amazingly, only one such study is reported in the *Manual* for Form M (p. 163- 164). After only four weeks, just 65% of the 424 respondents in the retest sample received the same type classification. Adhering to holistic interpretation of the type suggests any career guidance/counseling based on the MBTI would be wrong for 35% of the recipients.

In reviewing the MBTI's validity (the degree to which the MBTI scores measure the concepts they were designed to measure), the assumptions on which the MBTI is based such as dichotomous preferences, seem to be ignored . For example, a traditional approach to estimating construct validity is to correlate the MBTI scores with other measures of personality. Studies using this approach tend to use a continuous score for the four MBTI scales rather than the standard dichotomous scores. Such studies suggest that the four MBTI scales correspond to four of the "Big Five" personality domains, representing the dominant framework for modern personality assessment. The E-I scale corresponds with Extroversion (E = high, I = low), the S-N scale corresponds with Openness (N = high, S = low), the T-F scale corresponds with Agreeableness (F = high, T = low), and the J-P scale corresponds with Conscientiousness (J = high, P = low).

However, the demonstrations of validity for whole type scores (not continuous numeric scores) do *not* support the underlying principles of the MBTI's types. As Mastrangelo (2001) reports:

> The best test of the purported interaction among the four dichotomies was the calculation of the F-test for four-way interactions to predict various variables such as work preferences, job satisfaction, and values (p. 202). If a person's type is really more than just the sum of four dichotomies, then this four-way interaction term should predict many variables — certainly more than the four separate dichotomous scores. In fact, the four-way interaction term predicted only 3 of 73 dependent variables while the four main effects predicted 16 to 36 variables. To make matters worse, there is no listing of specific dependent variables or specific p-values that were significantly predicted in this table (9.19), which is very misleading as it preys on less sophisticated consumers of statistical results. The dearth of significant four-way interactions directly contradicts the fundamental assumption that the combination of the four preference scores is more important than the individual scores (p. 819).

Computer-Based and/or Online Version(s)

The MBTI can be administered via on-site software and the Internet.

Overall Critique

The MBTI is a popular personality instrument because it provides a simple, easily memorable score, but this simplicity is exactly why the MBTI should not be used in career counseling settings unless the instrument's results are tempered by the perspective of an experienced professional counselor and the desires of the client. Consider the overly simple notion of either being introverted or extroverted. Are all of your extroverted friends *equally* extroverted? Would they all feel comfortable introducing themselves to a room of strangers the way a salesman or politician might do? It seems more likely that there are degrees of extroversion and introversion. Failure to consider that some people have only a weak preference could explain why the MBTI provided contradicting types for 35% of a sample just four weeks removed from their initial completion of the instrument. In using psychological measures to predict behavior, you have to have consistency in order to have validity. If one out of three of your clients will have a different MBTI type four weeks from now, then how accurate can your career counseling and client's decisions be, based on their current MBTI scores?

Even if continuous scores were introduced and the test-retest consistency were higher for the MBTI, it still does not provide subscale scores for each of the four personality domains. While the MBTI only classifies a person as an extrovert or introvert, most established personality measures will assess "lower order" facets of the person's extroversion score, such as friendliness, gregariousness, assertiveness, activity level, excitement-seeking, and cheerfulness (Goldberg, 1999; International Personality Item Pool, 2007). A recent study demonstrates the usefulness in using precise personality facet scores to correspond with preferences on Holland's RIASEC types (Sullivan & Hansen, 2004). Again, the simplicity of the MBTI reduces its ability to pinpoint the elements of someone's personality that could more precisely match to career preferences than a two-letter dichotomous score.

While it is true that the MBTI does synthesize the four dichotomies to create the 16 types, there is little evidence that these holistic combinations correspond to career preferences or any other behavior. For all these reasons, the MBTI simply cannot provide the consistent, specific measurement needed to help clients make decisions about their future.[2]

References

Briggs Myers, I., McCaulley, M. H., Quenk, N. L., & Hammer, A. L. (1998). MBTI manual: *A guide to the development and use of the Myers Briggs type indicator.* (3rd ed). Palo Alto, CA: Consulting Psychologists Press.

Goldberg, L. R. (1999). A broad-bandwidth, public domain, personality inventory measuring the lower-level facets of several five-factor models. In I. Mervielde, I. Deary, F. De Fruyt, & F. Ostendorf (Eds.), *Personality psychology in Europe,* Vol. 7 (pp. 7–28). Tilburg, The Netherlands: Tilburg University Press.

---

[2] Editors' Note: The test publisher has recently added a "Career Report" to the interpretive materials available to users of the MBTI

International Personality Item Pool (2007). *A scientific collaboratory for the development of advanced measures of personality traits and other individual differences.* Available at http://ipip.ori.org.

Mastrangelo, P. M. (2001). Review of the Myers-Briggs Type Indicator, Form M. In B. S. Plake & J. C. Impara (Eds.). *The fourteenth mental measurements yearbook.* Lincoln, NE: The Buros Institute of Mental Measurements.

Sullivan, B. A. & Hansen, J. C. (2004). Mapping associations between interests and personality: Toward a conceptual understanding of individual differences in vocational behavior. *Journal of Counseling Psychology, 51,* 287–298.

University of Florida George A. Smathers Libraries (2003). *Guide to the Isabel Briggs Myers Papers.* Available at http://www.uflib.ufl.edu/spec/manuscript/guides/Myers.htm.

NEO Personality Inventory-Revised (NEO PI-R)

Paul T. Costa and Robert R. McCrae

Psychological Assessment Resources, Inc. (PAR)
16204 N. Florida Avenue
Lutz, FL 33549
www.parinc.com

Target Population: Ages 17 years and older. Individual or group administered.

Statement of the Purpose of the Instrument: Obtain a detailed assessment of normal personality.

Titles of Subtests, Scales, Scores Provided: Five Domains: Neuroticism, Extraversion, Openness, Agreeableness, Conscientiousness, with six facets per domain. T scores and percentiles scores provided for each domain and facet raw score.

Forms and Levels Available, with Dates of Publication/Revision of Each:

NEO PI-R Reusable Form S Item Booklets.

NEO PI-R Reusable Form R Item Booklets (Men and Women Versions).

NEO PI-R Form HS (Hand-Scorable) Answer Sheets.

NEO PI-R Form S Adult Profile Forms (designed for self-reports, it is appropriate for use with adult men and women, including individuals of college age).

NEO PI-R Form R Adult Profile Forms (designed for observer reports, it is written in the third person for peer, spouse, or expert ratings; use as an alternative measure or as a supplement to self-reports from adult clients).

NEO PI-R College Student Profile Forms.

Your NEO Summary Feedback Sheets (gives clients easy-to-understand information about the five domains of personality).

Date of Most Recent Edition of Test Manual, User's Guide, etc.: April 29, 2003.

Languages in Which Available: Arabic, Bulgarian, Chinese, Croatian, Dutch, Farsi, Filipino, Finnish, French, Hindi, Hmong, Hungarian, Icelandic, Indonesian, Italian, Japanese, Lithuanian, Malay, Marathi, Norwegian, Peruvian, Polish, Portuguese, Romanian, Russian, Serbian, Swedish, Taiwanese, Telugu, Thai, Tigrignan, Turkish, Urdu.

Time:

Actual Test Time: 35 – 45 Minutes.

Total Administration Time: Self-Administered.

Norm Group(s) on Which Scores Are Based: 1,000 adults, matched to the age and ethnic percentages of the 1995 US Census.

Manner in Which Results Are Reported for Individuals:

Types of Scores: T scores and percentiles, using college age or adult norms.

Report Format/Content:

Basic Service: Profiles based on T scores, Summary.

Options: Software provides T scores, profiles, interpretive text, and circumplexes, using college age or adult norms.

Scoring:

Machine Scoring Service:

Cost of basic service per counselee: 2006 Prices: Answer sheets are $112 for a pkg of 10: item booklets are $36.00 for pkg of 10.

Cost of options: Cost of scoring, interpretive report, and return postage is included in cost of forms above.

Time required for scoring and returning: Answer Sheets are scanned within 24 hours of receipt. Add time for mail to and from PAR.

Hand Scoring:

Scored by: Counselee, Clerk, Counselor.

Time required for scoring: 10–15 minutes.

Local Machine Scoring:

Provisions/conditions/equipment required: Requires OpScan pencil reading scanner and NEO On Site Scanning Software.

Computer Software Options Available: Computerized adaptive administration.

Cost of Materials: Due to possible price changes since publication date, be sure to check with publisher website.

Specimen Set: 2006 Prices: NEO PI-R Comprehensive Kit, $245.00

Counselee Materials: 2006 Prices:

Professional Manual – 40.00

Reusable Form S or Form R Item Booklets (pkg/10) – 36.00

Hand Scorable Answers Sheets (pkg/25) – 38.00

Profiles- specify Form S or Form R, Adult or College (pad/25) – 38.00

Summary Feedback Sheets (pad/25) – 30.00

Published Reviews of the Instrument in the Last 15 Years: None cited.

Reviewed By:[1]

Michael Stebleton
Faculty/Counseling
Inver Hills Community College
Inver Grove Heights, MN

Description

The Revised NEO Personality Inventory (NEO PI-R) is the most current version of Paul Costa and Robert McCrae's personality instrument (1992). It takes the place of the first edition that was published in 1985. The instrument is based on the extensively researched five-factor model (FFM) of personality. According to the Revised NEO manual, the instrument "is a measure of normal personality traits that has demonstrated its utility in both clinical and research settings" (Costa & McCrae, 1992, p. 1).

The Revised NEO measures five major areas or domains of personality according to the FFM. The five domains are Neuroticism (N), Extraversion (E), Openness to Experience (O), Agreeableness (A), and Conscientiousness (C). There are six lower level facets measured by the inventory. They include (1) Neuroticism facets: Anxiety, Angry Hostility, Depression, Self-Consciousness, Impulsiveness, and Vulnerability; (2) Extraversion facets: Warmth, Gregariousness, Assertiveness, Activity, Excitement-Seeking, and Positive Emotions; (3) Openness to Experience facets: Fantasy, Aesthetics, Feelings, Actions, Ideas, and Values; (4) Agreeableness facets: Trust, Straightforwardness, Altruism, Compliance, Modesty, and Tender-Mindedness; and (5) Conscientiousness facets: Competence, Order, Dutifulness, Achievement Striving, Self-Discipline, and Deliberation.

There are two forms of the Revised NEO. Form S is a self-report booklet containing 240 items. Form R contains the same questions, but is presented in the third person used for observer reports for peers, spouses/partners, or expert ratings. The instrument can be hand scored or computer scored. The response options are organized on a five-item scale ranging from strongly disagree to strongly agree. Example items include statements such as "I am not a methodical person" (item #70) and "If I don't like people, I let them know" (item #109). The NEO Software System is an online modular system that allows participants to complete the tool on screen via counter serial numbers.

Use in Counseling

The Revised NEO has a variety of uses and applications including: counseling, clinical psychology, and psychiatry. Other applications could include: behavioral medicine, health psychology, educational research, and career counseling and organizational psychology. It was not designed to measure psychopathology or assess psychiatric disorders.

The Revised NEO can be used as a complement to other vocational interest assessments, such as the Strong Interest Inventory (SII), the Self-Directed Search (SDS),

---

[1] Portions of this review were adapted from the *Twelfth Mental Measurements Yearbook* (1995) with permission of the Buros Institute, Lincoln, NE.

and the Campbell Interest and Skill Survey (CISS). The Revised NEO should not take the place of these other well-validated instruments specifically designed to assess career interests. Industrial organizational psychologists may find the instrument useful for screening and placement since the Revised NEO does help to point towards individuals' strengths through the Conscientiousness (C) domain.

Furthermore, career development practitioners who are working with undecided clients may find the Revised NEO to be relevant. In a study of college undergraduates that completed the NEO, results indicated that career decidedness was positively and significantly related to life satisfaction, agreeableness (A), and conscientiousness (C) as well as negatively related to neuroticism (N) (Lounsbury, Tatum, Chambers, Owens, & Gibson, 1999). Many career development practitioners use the Myers-Briggs Type Indicator (MBTI) in individual appointments and life-career planning courses. The Revised NEO may be used as a complement to the MBTI or as an alternative to assess personality preferences (McCrae & Costa, 1989).

The manual is well-written and organized. It includes a comprehensive overview of practical, user-friendly information plus scholarly sections on directions for future research, development and validation, and an extensive reference section.

Technical Considerations

The technical aspects of the Revised NEO are especially strong and impressive – including norms, reliability, and validity. Norms: The normative sample for NEO PI-R Adult Form S are based on three subsamples: (1) 405 men and women in the Augmented Baltimore Longitudinal Study of Aging who were part of earlier studies and completed new items for the revised version, (2) 329 ABLSA participants who did a computerized version between 1989 and 1991, and (3) 1,539 volunteers (men and women) who participated in a national sample of job performance. In order to establish a diverse normative sample, 500 men and 500 women were selected from the above group. The sample was stratified to match the U. S. Census projections for 1995; this was a major improvement over the previous version. College norms profile forms were added in 1991.

The reliability and stability measures of the Revised NEO are solid. Domain-level reliabilities range from .86 to .95 for both self and observer ratings Facet reliabilities range from .56 to .81 in self reports and from .60 to .90 in observer ratings according to the manual (pp. 44–45). Retest reliability ranged from .66 to .92. Costa and McCrae, (1992), stress that the NEO-PI is one of the few instruments that measures enduring traits over time assessed by both self report and by the ratings of others.

Validity measures are equally as impressive. The manual includes a comprehensive overview of studies conducted on validity, including consensual, convergent, divergent, and construct. Consensual validity between self and peer/spouse rating correlations are from .35 to .54. Convergent, divergent, and construct validity correlates were all relatively high. Studies conducted on NEO-PI facet scales found relationships between constructs on a variety of career assessments, including Holland's Self-Directed Search (SDS) and the Myers-Briggs Type Indicator (MBTI) Jungian types. For example, Holland's Investigative Types were most closely connected to O5: Openness to Ideas, and Artistic Interests were most highly correlated to O2: Aesthetics (Costa, McCrae, & Holland, 1984).

More recently, Sullivan and Hansen (2004) found relationships between the Revised NEO and results from the Strong Interest Inventory (SII) and the Campbell Interest and Skill Survey (CISS). Correlates of the NEO PI-R Form S facet scales indicated relationships with scales on other personality instruments such as the Minnesota Multiphasic Personality Inventory (MMPI), the Revised California Personality Inventory (CPI), the State-Trait Personality Inventory (STPI), the Personality Research Form (PRF), and others.

Finally, the NEO PI-R appears to have cross-cultural application. According to McCrae, Costa, Del Pilar, Rolland, and Parker (1998), the five-factor model is a biologically based human universal. For example, the Revised NEO has demonstrated cross-cultural replicability of the FFM, including data from French and Filipino translations (p. 171).

Overall Critique

The NEO PI-R is a well-researched instrument that can be used as complement to other vocational interest inventories. There are several strengths and weaknesses of the instrument.

Strengths:

1. Validity and Reliability: As indicated, the Revised NEO is a solid tool that has been validated against other personality measures. Additionally, the reliability including the retest reliability is an advantage.

2. Ease of Use: It only takes about one hour to complete and self-score. Clients can complete in one session and get immediate results with interpretive assistance from a career counselor. The directions are well-written and easy to follow.

3. Supported by Comprehensive Research: There is extensive research done on the big five personality measures and the NEO. Career counselors can easily access additional literature about the assessment.

Weaknesses:

1. Item format and content criteria: According to one review in the Twelfth Mental Measurements Yearbook (Juni, 1995), the item format and content criteria are not well developed. I agree. Some of the questions included double negative statements and proved to be difficult to interpret. Despite the instrument's cross-cultural applicability, the wording of certain items may present a challenge to clients where English is not the first language. I work with recent immigrants at a community college, and many of these students would have trouble interpreting some of the items (see item #238: "I believe that the 'new morality' of permissiveness is no morality at all").

2. Lack of supplemental interpretative materials for participants: Two

colleagues who completed the inventory expressed a need for a more comprehensive explanation of the domains and facets. The document Your NEO Summary is brief and concise, but does not thoroughly explain the meaning of the domains and facets. Furthermore, one colleague stated a need for more applied suggestions, including areas for individual development, based on his individual scores.

3. Possible limited clinical utility: Butcher and Rouse (1996) contended that the Revised NEO may have limited clinical use due to variation with facet scores within the domain. They argued that a personality assessment should provide more useful information about a person's psychological functioning (p. 94). Costa and McCrae countered this critique by arguing that personality at the domain level is a beginning point, and the Revised NEO serves this function.

In summary, career development practitioners will want to use the tool as a complement and not a replacement for other career assessments. I would recommend the Revised NEO for this purpose. Likewise, career counselors in academic settings may find the Revised NEO to be useful when working with undecided students who are engaged in the life-career planning process.

References

Butcher, J. N., & Rouse, S. V. (1996). Personality: Individual differences and clinical assessment. *Annual Review Psychology, 47,* 87–111.

Costa, P. T., Jr., & McCrae, R. R. (1992). *Revised NEO Personality Inventory and NEO Five-Factor Inventory: Professional manual.* Lutz, FL: Psychological Assessment Resources.

Costa, P. T., Jr., McCrae, R. R., & Holland, J. L. (1984). Personality and vocational samples in an adult sample. *Journal of Applied Psychology, 69,* 390–400.

Juni, S. (1995). Review of the Revised NEO Personality Inventory. In J. C. Conoley & J. C. Impara (Eds.), *The twelfth mental measurements yearbook* (pp. 863–868). Lincoln, NE: University of Nebraska Press.

Lounsbury, J., Tatum, H. E., Chambers, W., Owen, K. S., & Gibson, L. W. (1999). An investigation of career decidedness in relation to 'Big Five' personality constructs and life satisfaction. *College Student Journal, 33,* 646–651.

McCrae, R. R., & Costa, P. T., Jr. (1989). Reinterpreting the Myers-Briggs Type Indicator from the perspective of the five-factor model of personality. *Journal of Personality, 57,* 17–40.

McCrae, R. R., Costa, P. T., Jr., Del Pilar, G. H., Rolland, J. P., & Parker, W. D. (1998). Cross-cultural assessment of the five-factor model: The Revised NEO Personality Inventory. *Journal of Cross-Cultural Psychology, 29,* 171–188.

Sullivan, B. A., & Hansen, J. C. (2004). Mapping associations between interests and personality: Toward a conceptual understanding of individual differences in vocational behavior. *Journal of Counseling Psychology, 51,* 287–298.

Student Styles Questionnaire (SSQ)

Thomas Oakland, Joseph Glutting, and Connie Horton

The Psychological Corporation
19500 Bulverde Road
San Antonio, Texas 78259
1-800-872-1726
http://harcourtassessment.com

Target Population: Grades 3–12, ages 8–17.

Statement of the Purpose of the Instrument: Measures learning, relating, and working styles of students.

Titles of Subtests, Scales, Scores Provided: Extroverted/Introverted, Thinking/Feeling, Practical/Imaginative, Organized/Flexible.

Forms and Levels Available, with Dates of Publication/Revision of Each: One form, 1996.

Date of Most Recent Edition of Test Manual, User's Guide, etc.: Manual, 1996; Classroom Applications Booklet, 1996.

Languages in Which Available: English only.

Time:

Actual Test Time: Untimed.

Total Administration Time: Can be completed in less than 30 minutes.

Norm Group(s) on Which Scores Are Based: Approximately 8,000 students in standardization sample, stratified by age, sex, race/ethnicity, geographic region, and school type.

Manner in Which Results Are Reported for Individuals:

Types of Scores: Prevalence-based T scores.

Report Format/Content: The professional report sections include: General Description; Personal Styles—Imported Beliefs, Social Factors, Family Factors; Educational Styles—Attitudes Toward School, Relationships with Teachers, Relationships with Classmates, Learning Styles, Instructional Styles, Curriculum Content; Occupational Styles; Room for Growth; Summary.

Report Format/Content for Group Summaries: Not available.

Scoring:

Machine Scoring Service: Not available.

Hand Scoring:

Scored by: Clerk; Counselor.

Local Machine Scoring:

Provisions/conditions/equipment required: Record Forms, Windows Kit.

Computer Software Options Available: Not available.

Cost of Materials: Due to possible price changes since publication date, be sure to check the publisher's website.

Specimen Set: Complete Kit (Includes Manual, Classroom Applications Booklet, package of five Ready Score Answer Documents, Question Booklet), $69.

Counselee Materials:

Question Booklets (pkg/25), $79 (reusable)

Ready Score Answer Documents (pkg/25), $42

Manual, $95

Record Forms (for computer scoring/reporting) (pkg/25), $22

Classroom Applications Booklet, $29 (reusable)

Reviewed by:

Michelle L. Bruno

Assistant Professor
Department of Counseling
Indiana University of Pennsylvania

Description

The Student Styles Questionnaire (SSQ) is a self-report instrument designed to detect individual differences in student's (ages 8–17) personal learning styles, temperaments, and preferences (Oakland, Glutting, & Horton, 1996). The instrument shares some of the same philosophical views of temperament as Carl Jung (1971), who conceptualized that individuals possess psychological types along several continuums: introverted/extroverted, sensation/intuition, and thinking/feeling. Modifications of this theory resulted in a fourth continuum labeled judging/perceiving (Myers & Myers, 1980). The SSQ reflects the views of Jung through its intent to examine student's preferences along similar dimensions.

The SSQ began test development with 245 items. Five national experts on temperament reviewed the items for construct validity purposes, resulting in 120 items. These items were examined for consistency with the intended third-grade reading level and were piloted on 1,300 students. Subsequent statistical analyses confirmed the four-scale temperament model. Finally, the test authors used factor analysis and item statistics to identify the best 100 test items for implementation in the national standardization procedure. Based on the 1990 U.S. Census data, the standardization sample was stratified by age, sex, race/ethnicity, geographic region, and school type.

Currently, the SSQ is comprised of 69 items intended to assess a student's personal learning style. Items encompass eight personal style dichotomies or dimensions:

introverted/extroverted, practical/imaginative, thinking/feeling, and organized/flexible. Each item is formatted with a partial statement reflecting everyday situations, followed by two mutually exclusive response options, representing each extreme of the particular dimension assessed. For example, one item that examines the organized/flexible dimension reads: "I like to work on _____" and students choose from (a) one thing at a time or (b) many things at the same time. The instrument takes approximately 30 minutes to complete and can be administered individually or in groups.

The SSQ can be hand scored using a carbon scoring sheet or electronically scored through manual data entry into a software program. The program compiles scores and produces two interpretive reports, one for the student and another for the test giver. Scoring by either method uses prevalent-based T-scores. Oakland et al. (1996) explain that this nontraditional method was chosen because mean scores on the four scales differ from one another in the general population; thus, reliance on one set of means for all scales is not reflective of the general population. For example, it is estimated that about 65% of people in the general population prefer the extroverted style versus 35% introverted. On other dimensions, the base rate in the population varies from 35% to 65% (Oakland et al., 1996).

As stated, each item on the SSQ represents a continuum of preferred learning styles with two extreme contrasting styles. The items are scaled such that for each question, a student could score from, "1" (lowest preference) to "3" (highest preference) on either of the two dimensions (i.e., extroverted or introverted). Scores of "3" are weighted more heavily as they indicate "more idealized responses in each of the styles" (Schraw, 2001, p. 1197). Responses on each style are summed to achieve the raw scores. The manual provides instructions on converting raw scores to prevalence-based scores through a series of simple steps.

There are three methods of test interpretation in the SSQ: (1) analysis of the eight basic scales by pairs, (2) analysis of Keirseian combinations (Keirsey & Bates, 1984), and (3) analysis of the 16 possible interactions between the four dichotomies. Each of the methods offers increasing complexity in the interpretation. The first method requires the test giver to examine how students scored on each of the four pairs of preferences (introverted/extroverted, practical/imaginative, thinking/feeling, and organized/flexible) and is the recommended starting point in interpretation (Oakland et al., 1996). The overall scoring groupings by preference are as follows: mild (T-scores ranging from 50 to 54), moderate (55 to 64), strong (65 to 74), and very strong (75 and above). The second method addresses how combinations of two styles can be indicative of children's temperament. It represents four specific combinations of styles including practical-organized, practical-flexible, imaginative-thinking, and imaginative-feeling. This interpretation style is designed to explain scores for students with at least moderate preference (i.e., T-scores at least 55). Similar to the scoring of the Myers-Briggs Type Inventory (MBTI; Myers & McCaulley, 1985), this method examines interactions of one's preferences on all four dichotomies. Validity and reliability hold for the first scoring method only.

Use in Counseling

Oakland et al. (1996) summarize the primary uses of the SSQ into eight categories: identification of talent, adjusting for possible weaknesses, enhancing personal and social development, promoting understanding of others, assessing learning styles, promoting educational development, exploring prevocational interests, and facilitating research and evaluation studies.

The SSQ manual is structured in such a way that for each of the three scoring methods (see chapters 4–6 of Oakland et al., 1996, for complete information), readers have access to general characteristics of students based on scores, typical roles they have in social interactions, familial relationships, and in academic settings. Additionally, each scoring method highlights potential occupations for specific personal style types as well as potential barriers to success. Finally, case examples are provided.

The SSQ can serve several purposes in school counseling. Counselors can collaborate with teachers to use the SSQ to help improve the environment for all students. In its national model, the American School Counselor Association (ACSA) national model (American School Counselor Association, n.d.) emphasizes academic, personal/social, and career development as key areas of emphasis for every student. The SSQ could be used in each of these areas. For instance, academic and personal development could be focused on by conducting classroom guidance that helps students learn more about their preferences as learners. Doing so can help students gain insight into their personal learning, ways of interacting, and decision-making styles. These skills can carry over into other areas, such as gaining interpersonal skills, identifying unique assets, and learning to view them as strengths. Further, emphasizing individual differences can contribute to an environment that embraces diversity among students, fostering a more positive environment for all students. The SSQ could also contribute to enhancing career development of students by helping them identify subject areas and fields that are congruent with temperament and interest. Through collaboration with teachers, school counselors can use results from the SSQ to create guidance lessons that address all three areas emphasized by the ASCA model.

Technical Considerations

The SSQ was standardized on a representative sample of 7,902 individuals. Norms are based on the first interpretation method mentioned above. It has been used with students across various cultures including Caucasian, African-American, and Hispanic students. This is useful as the student body in today's schools is increasingly diverse.

Reliability scores for the SSQ were achieved using internal consistency indices and test-retest strategies. Internal consistency calculations were conducted using Cronbach's (1951) alpha coefficient resulting in the following: .79 (Practical-Imaginative), .80 (Thinking-Feeling), and .87 (Organized-Flexible and Extraversion-Introversion). Given that the SSQ is designed with the developmental level of youth in mind, the instrument is intended to be as concise as possible; however, this likely produces a lower estimate of internal consistency (Oakland et al., 1996). To augment these figures, test-retest reliabilities were conducted with a seventh-month interval and resulted in reliability coefficients ranging from .67 to .80, with an average of .74 for the four scales ($n = 137$). The authors failed to report statistical power for these findings.

The support for internal validity is offered through item analysis, expert consensus, and factor analysis. Initially, the authors used theoretical considerations to place each item within a scale. This set of items then underwent review by a panel of experts. Factor analysis, including parcel analysis, was then conducted. Oakland and colleagues argue that this approach was necessary because of the dichotomous nature of the SSQ items. Detailed tables of item and parcel scores are provided in the manual and support a four factor structure (Rounds & McKenna, 2001). Intercorrelations between the four scales range from −.03 (Practical-Imaginative and Extroverted-Introverted) to .24 (Organized-Flexible and Practical-Imaginative). As none of the four dimensions were highly correlated, independence among the scales is likely (Oakland et al., 1996; Rounds & McKenna, 2001).

In establishing external validity, the authors provide comprehensive information. Using several research studies, the SSQ scores were compared concurrently to other variables (i.e., reported preferences). For example, students' activity preferences were examined in relation to answers on the SSQ. Correlations between activity preferences (e.g., parties, quiet time alone, reading, school) and SSQ styles indicate significant correlations for 10 of the 16 pairs. Using convenience samples, Oakland and colleagues conducted two additional studies to examine concurrent validity by comparing students' scores on the SSQ (predictors) with responses on the Values Inventory (VI; Oakland, 1990) and the MBTI (criterion). In study one, multivariate correlations were significant for the relationships between SSQ scores and both the helpfulness domain (.54) and the loyalty domain (.38). In study two, multivariate correlations indicated significant relationships between scores on the SSQ and three of the four MBTI scales in the expected direction.

Further evidence of external validity is offered through four additional studies that examine divergent validity by comparing the SSQ to each of the following instruments: Weschler Intelligence Scale for Children–Third Edition (WISC-III; Weschler, 1981), California Achievement Test (CAT; CTB/McGraw-Hill, 1985), and the Metropolitan Achievement Test–Sixth Edition (MAT6; Prescott et al., 1985). Overall, results from these studies indicate that style preferences as measured by the SSQ are independent of achievement and ability scores (Schraw, 2001).

Overall Critique

The SSQ is a user-friendly scale of personal style preferences and temperament. The SSQ supports a nonpathological framework for discussing student's strengths, limitations, and problematic areas (Joyce & Oakland, 2005). The emphasis on strengths and unique attributes is congruent with the approach used by school counselors. It has been used among a diverse group of students, which lends itself for use in a multicultural society. Investing resources into additional validity studies (e.g., predictive validity) may contribute to the aforementioned benefits of the SSQ, particularly if it can be linked to increased personal, social, and academic success.

Psychometric properties warrant further exploration. Although the SSQ appears to be a reliable measure, only 137 participants were included in the test-retest sample, which likely indicates weak statistical power. With regard to validity, Schraw (2001) identifies weaknesses due to the multiple methods of interpretation and the lack of relationship with achievement and intelligence tests. Specifically, he argues that the instrument strives to produce matches between student learning styles, teachers, and programs, yet fails to produce evidence of such a relationship. Further, there is no available information regarding statistical power in the validity studies. In some cases, significant correlations were omitted to avoid spurious significant relationships; however, conducting power analysis and including the results along with the details can overcome this problem.

There is a paucity of information on whether individuals with mental health concerns comprised the standardization sample. As Stewart (2001) asserts, individuals with mental health disorders could impact the results; although, a recent study among children with defiant disorders (Joyce & Oakland, 2005) indicated minimally significant differences among children with Oppositional Defiant Disorder, Conduct Disorder, and the general population. More work of this kind can elucidate utility in school settings, where such struggles are not uncommon.

When considered in its entirety, the SSQ offers promise as a useful instrument for school counselors and/or teachers seeking to learn more about student preferences. Consumers of this instrument should be cognizant of the limitations of the SSQ as a typed-based measure and consider its use to help build a more substantial body of research.

References

American School Counselor Association (n.d.). *The ASCA national model: A framework for school counseling programs.* Retrieved September 9, 2007, from www.schoolcounselor.org.

Cronbach, L. J. (1951). Coefficient alpha and the internal structure of tests. *Psychometrika*, 16, 297–334.

CTB/McGraw-Hill. (1985). *California Achievement Test.* Monterey, CA: Author.

Joyce, D., & Oakland, T. (2005). Temperament differences among children with conduct disorder and oppositional defiant disorder. The California School Psychologist, 10, 125-136.

Jung, C. G. (1971). *Psychological types.* (R. F. C. Hull, Revision of Trans, by H. G. Baynes). Princeton, NJ: Princeton University Press. (Original work published 1921).

Keirsey, D. & Bates, M. (1984). Please understand me: Character and temperament types, (5th ed.). Prometheus Nemesis Book: Del Mar, CA.

Myers, I. B., & McCaulley, M. H. (1985). *Manual: A guide to the development and use of the Myers-Briggs Type Indicator.* Palo Alto, CA: Consulting Psychologists Press.

Myers, I. B., & Myers, P. B. (1980). *Gifts differing.* Palo Alto, CA: Consulting Psychologists Press.

Oakland, T. (1990). *The Values Inventory.* Austin, TX: Author.

Oakland, T., Glutting, J., & Horton, C. (1996). *Student Styles Questionnaire.* San Antonio, TX: The Psychological Corporation.

Prescott, G. A., Balow, I. H., Hogan, T. P., & Farr, R. C. (1985). *Metropolitan Achievement Tests, Sixth Edition.* San Antonio, TX: The Psychological Corporation.

Rounds, J., & McKenna, M.C. (2001). Student Styles Questionnaire (SSQ). In J.T. Kapes, & Whitfield, E. A. (Eds.). *A counselor's guide to career assessment instruments* (4th ed.). Columbus, OH: National Career Development Association.

Schraw, G. (2001). Review of the Student Styles Questionnaire. In B.S. Plake & J.C. Impara (Eds.). *The fourteenth mental measurements yearbook* (pp.1197–1198)). Lincoln, NE: Buros Institute of Mental Measurements.

Stewart, J. R. (2001). Review of the Student Styles Questionnaire. In B.S. Plake & J.C. Impara (Eds.). *The fourteenth mental measurements yearbook* (pp. 1198–1199). Lincoln, NE: Buros Institute of Mental Measurements.

Weschler, D. (1981). *Weschler Intelligence Scale for Children – Revised.* San Antonio, TX: The Psychological Corporation.

CHAPTER 12

INSTRUMENTS FOR SPECIAL POPULATIONS

- Ashland Interest Assessment (AIA)

- Becker Work Adjustment Profile Second Edition (BWAP: 2)

- BRIGANCE Diagnostic Life Skills Inventory (LSI) and BRIGANCE Diagnostic Employability Skills Inventory (ESI)

- Geist Picture Interest Inventory (GPII) (Revised Eighth Printing)

- Life Centered Career Education Competency Assessment: Knowledge and Performance Batteries (LCCE)

- Reading-Free Vocational Interest Inventory Second Edition (R-FVII:2)

- Transition Planning Inventory – Updated Version (TPI-UV)

- Valpar Test of Essential Skills in English and Math (VTES)

Ashland Interest Assessment (AIA)

Douglas N. Jackson and Connie W. Marshall

SIGMA Assessment Systems, Inc.
P.O. Box 610984
Port Huron, MI 48061-0984
www. SigmaAssessmentsSystems.com

Target Population: Ages 15+.

Groups: The AIA may be employed for educational and career exploration counseling, and decision making, and for conducting research concerning vocational interest, job satisfaction, and personal classification.

Statement of the Purpose of the Instrument: The AIA is an inventory of career interests, especially designed to be appropriate and easily understood by persons faced with a variety of barriers to employment. Accordingly, the language level, content, and potential career options of the AIA were carefully chosen to address conditions that restrict a person's ability to make use of other widely used inventories. By design, the AIA may be used by all segments of the population, but specifically, it addresses a need for an assessment tool that will accommodate individuals with restricted abilities, due directly or indirectly to any one or a combination of educational, physical, emotional, cognitive, or psychiatric conditions.

Titles of Subtests, Scales, Scores Provided: Arts and Crafts, Sales, Mechanical, Personal Service, Construction, Food Service, Protective Service, Clerical, Plant or Animal Care, Health Care, Transportation

Forms and Levels Available, with Dates of Publication/Revision of Each: N/A

Date of Most Recent Edition of Test Manual, User's Guide, etc.: 1997.

Languages in Which Available: English and French.

Time:

Actual Test Time: 35 minutes

Total Administration Time: 45 minutes

Norm Group(s) on Which Scores Are Based: Norms were collected from employment agencies, schools, learning centers, psychiatric hospitals, and mental health associations. The AIA was normed on 725 females and 725 males.

Manner in Which Results Are Reported for Individuals:

Types of Scores: Raw scores, percentiles.

Report Format/Content:

BASIC SERVICE: AIA Extended Report consists of a profile of the scores on the 12 Basic Interest scales, as well as a description of these scales. A profile of Similarity to 12 Occupational Groups and a narrative summary of the three highest-ranked Occupational Groups with links to the DOT codes are also included. A summary report is provided for the counselor.

Scoring:

Machine Scoring Service:

COST OF BASIC SERVICE PER COUNSELEE:

AIA Extended Reports: Mail-in question/answer sheet and printed Extended Report

Item No. 9688 1 report	$15.00*
Item No. 9608	
1 – 3 pkgs (10 reports/pkg)	$80.00*
4+ pkgs (10 reports/pkg)	$70.00*

Time required for scoring and returning (maximum) 48 hours

* Prices based on 2008 catalog

Hand Scoring:

SCORED BY: Clerk; Counselor

TIME REQUIRED FOR SCORING: 10 minutes

Local Machine Scoring: Provisions/conditions/equipment required.

Computer Software Options Available: Computerized adaptive administration.

Cost of Materials: Due to possible price changes since publication date, be sure to check with publisher website.

Specimen Set: AIA Examination Kit.

Counselee Materials: Kit includes manual, five question/answer booklets for hand scoring, five profile sheets, five scoring sheets, one set of templates (reusable), one question/answer document for an Extended Report (mail-in scoring).

Published Reviews of the Instrument in the Last 15 Years: None Cited.

Reviewed by:

Ann Herrmann
Career Counselor

Cori Shaff
Career Counselor/Outreach Specialist

University of Colorado at Boulder

Description

The Ashland Interest Assessment (AIA) was developed in 1997 to serve as an assessment for individuals who experience barriers to employment. Examples of barriers experienced by the target population include: limited access to education;

limited English proficiency; emotional, cognitive, mental or physical handicap; learning or developmental disabilities; and chronic unemployment. (Jackson & Marshall, 1997; McCowan & McCowan, 2001). The AIA was designed to support individuals with such barriers because "factors, and other handicapping conditions, can create obstacles for persons attempting to ascertain their job interest and develop realistic career goals" (Jackson & Marshall, 1997, p. 4).

The AIA can be taken utilizing various formats (pencil and paper, mail-in, or computer) and can be hand or computer scored by the counselor or publisher. Typically, the AIA takes between 20 and 90 minutes to complete, with a 30-minute completion time as the average. The instructions for the AIA are simple, readable, and easy to understand as the AIA was written at a third-grade level. The AIA questions, answer booklets, and extended reports have been translated into French. The AIA consists of 144 pairs of work-related tasks, which require the participant to choose between one of two possible options. The instructions indicate that the choice should be made based on the more desirable of the two activities; the AIA does not take into account a person's ability to complete the specified task. The tasks correspond with 12 Basic Interest Scales (arts and crafts, sales, clerical, protective services, food service, personal service, health care, general service, plant/animal care, construction, transportation, and mechanical).

The Extended Report includes a description of the 12 Basic Interest Scales, a profile graph of scores on the scales (a high score indicates an interest in the activities in that area, and a low score indicates less interest in the activities in that area), and a summary report for the counselor. Additionally, the report also provides information about how a client's scores compare to people from different occupational group. A high score means the client's Basic Interest Profile is very similar to people working in that occupation, while a low score indicates they are dissimilar. The Extended Report also includes a description of the client's reported top three occupational groups and an average of 15 sample jobs with their corresponding *Dictionary of Occupational Titles* (DOT) numbers. Since the DOT is no longer in use and has been replaced by O*NET OnLine (Occupational Information Network), we suggest using this internet resource to gain information about occupations.

Use in Counseling

One of the strengths of the AIA is its ease of use. Step-by-step directions in the form of a script are provided in the manual. While the manual mentions that the AIA may be administered in group settings (Jackson & Marshall, 1997), hand-scoring multiple assessments would take some additional time. Therefore, the counselor is advised to plan time between administration and interpretation to allow for this step.

The counselor informs the client that the purpose of the AIA is to understand his/her interests in specific types of work activities (e.g., sort clothes to be washed vs. sell shoes) and that it does not measure abilities. The counselor guides the client through the instructions, checking in regularly to ensure that he/she understands the instructions and how to select which of two activities would be most interesting. No time limit is set so that the client knows he/she has plenty of time to complete the questionnaire.

The results are easy to understand as well, as they are presented in both raw score and graph form (percent scores), with clear descriptions of the Basic Interest Scales and Occupational Groups, as described above.

Connie Marshall, in collaboration with Douglas Jackson, developed the assessment when, as a rehabilitation counselor working with clients with disabilities, she could not find an interest assessment that met her clients' needs. "Driven by need" (C. Marshall, personal communication, December 11, 2006), she set out to create an instrument appropriate for her clients.

As one source of assessment information among a collection of multiple sources, the AIA can serve as a helpful starting point for clients interested in exploring interests and developing a course of action. The manual (Jackson & Marshall, 1997) cautions against using the AIA profile results as the only source of information when exploring career interests with a client. Instead, the counselor needs to consider the client's "career values, work and educational experiences, abilities, academic achievement, personality traits, knowledge about career alternatives, and previous career plans" (Jackson & Marshall, 1997) as well as the client's overall satisfaction with the results themselves (C. Marshall, personal communication, December 11, 2006). This approach is supported in the literature. Smart & Smart (2006) urge counselors to "recognize that disability is never entirely a personal, subjective and idiosyncratic experience." Thus, the counselor must note that while the AIA is a useful tool for individuals with employment barriers, used alone it may negatively impact an individual due to the simplicity of the assessment questions.

Technical Considerations

The AIA went through four phases of development that spanned several years to determine validity and reliability. During these phases, the creators determined the activities and Basic Interest Scales to measure and how to format the questions. Additionally, the authors used the following criteria to maintain a high level of validity: p-values, item-scale correlations, and item-efficiency index. During the second phase, the authors used a forced-choice test format in the final version to avoid a response bias from test takers and to increase validity. The target population consisted of Canadian citizens within a wide age range that also experienced one or more barriers to employment. The authors do not mention ethnicity or race. The authors collected norms from mental health agencies, hospitals, educational facilities, employment agencies, and mental health agencies.

The authors consulted the Canadian Classification, the Dictionary of Occupations, and the National Occupational Classification to choose occupations and job activities for the assessment. Additionally, the authors considered familiar occupations and work tasks that would properly represent the broad and varied world of work in a comprehensive manner. While the norm group did consist of only Canadian citizens, the work tasks are comparable to those in the United States.

The norm group was made up of 1,450 Canadian representatives between 15 – 64 years of age who resided in household settings. In a separate process, data for the occupational groups were determined from Canadians working or training in the 12 Occupational Groups. Of the normative group, 949 representatives reported having one or more disabilities.

While there was careful planning throughout the development of the assessment, no independent research has been done on the AIA. Additional research on the concurrent validity and test-retest reliability is recommended. Concurrent validity data may be limited, as the authors of this critique did not find a similar interest assessment specifically designed for individuals with disabilities. Typically, other interest inventories have a higher reading grade level and were developed for individuals preparing for postsecondary education, and thus would not be similar enough to gather data for concurrent validity.

Computer-Based Version

Like the paper and pencil version, the computer version of the AIA is in large print and easy to understand. The counselor installs the software for a registration fee and purchases coupons to generate reports.. Once the client has completed the assessment, a report (Extended, Basic, or Data) may be generated with using coupons . An Extended Report costs five coupons and provides the most useful and comprehensive information for the client. It includes the client's profile scores, a description of the 12 Basic Interest Scales, and summary report for the counselor. Additionally, it provides information about the client's top three Occupational Groups, different activities people in this group can complete, examples of work places, and a list of some of the jobs found in the DOT. The Basic Report requires three coupons, and provides the same information as the Extended Report but does not include information about the client's top three Occupational Groups. The Data Report costs two coupons and provides information useful only to the counselor.

Overall Critique

The AIA is a helpful tool for clients who are interested in exploring their career interests and may have limited options in the work world. It fills a gap in career counseling interest assessments by providing appropriate activities and occupational choices for clients who experience barriers to employment as a result of disabilities, and will likely not be pursuing postsecondary education.

C. Marshall (personal communication, December 11, 2006) uses the assessment regularly, and finds that it is especially helpful for clients who do not have any work experience, do not plan to pursue education past high school, and for those who are seeking volunteer work. The work tasks are simple, and many of them do not require previous experience or advanced education.

While the AIA can be useful for many clients, it may not be appropriate for just anyone with a barrier to employment. For example, an immigrant worker with limited familiarity with English meets the definition set by the authors as a member of the appropriate client population for which the assessment is designed. This particular client may not be interested in pursuing postsecondary education, but may have capabilities well beyond the clientele for which the assessment is most useful. This would not be an appropriate use of the AIA, and could negatively impact his/her experience with the assessment, as well as with the counselor. Additionally, if the norm group consisted of mostly White/Caucasian Canadian citizens, the counselor may need to be careful about interpreting results with clients of different ethnicities.

Further research needs to be done to assess the AIA's validity and reliability as well as its use across ethnicities. Additionally, we found the assessment difficult and tedious to score due to lack of clear and specific instructions and a counterintuitive scoring technique.

References

Jackson, D.N. & Marshall, C.M. (1997). *Ashland interest assessment manual.* Port Huron, MI: Sigma Assessment Systems, Inc.

McCowan, R.J. & McCowan, S.C. (2001). Review of the Ashland Interest Assessment. In B. S. Plake & J.C. Impara (Eds.), *The fourteenth mental measurements yearbook* [Electronic version]. Retrieved November 3, 2006, from the Buros Institute's *Test Reviews Online* website: http://www.unl.edu/buros.

Smart, J.F. & Smart, D.W. (2006). Models of disability: Implications for the counseling profession. *Journal of Counseling and Development, 84,* 2 – 40.

Becker Work Adjustment Profile Second Edition (BWAP:2)

Ralph L. Becker

Elbern Publications
P.O. Box 9497
Columbus, OH 43209
ebecker@insight.rr.com

Target Population: Individuals who are school age to adult (ages 13–69) with mental retardation, learning disability, physical disability, emotionally disturbed, economically disadvantaged, or developmentally disabled (autistic, cerebral palsied, epileptic, etc.).

Statement of the Purpose of the Instrument: To assess the vocational competency and needed work supports of individuals who are classified with special needs to be successful in the workplace or related areas of work. The instrument assesses the vocational competence of individuals for work placement or training in five levels: Day Care, Work Activity, Extended Workshop, Transitional, and Community-Competitive. Work supports are listed/assessed from least to most supports for an individual as Limited, Low, Moderate, High, and Extensive.

Titles of Subtests, Scales, Scores Provided: The subtests are listed as Work Habits & Attitudes, Interpersonal Relations, Cognitive Skills, Work Performance and Skills, and a composite score called Broad Work Adjustment. Raw scores are converted to Standard scores, percentiles, and levels of vocational competency and supports.

Forms and Levels Available, with Dates of Publication/Revision of Each: A single form is used for males and females. This second edition was revised and published in 2005.

Date of Most Recent Edition of Test Manual, User's Guide, etc.: Test forms and the Manual were revised in November 2005.

Languages in Which Available: English only.

Time:

Actual Test Time: 10 minutes or less.

Total Administration Time: 15 minutes or less.

Norm Group(s) on Which Scores Are Based: (1) Mentally Retarded, (2) Learning Disabled, (3) Physically Disabled, (4) Emotional Disturbed, and (5) Economically Disadvantaged.

Manner in Which Results Are Reported for Individuals:

Types of Scores: Standard scores, Percentiles, and Levels of Vocational Competency and Supports as descriptive ratings.

Report Format/Content:

BASIC SERVICE: A two-page report of client performance completed by the examiner includes a graphic profile of performance for each examinee.

Report Format/Content for Group Summaries: Not available

Scoring:

Machine Scoring Service: Not available.

Hand Scoring:

SCORED BY: Counselor.

TIME REQUIRED FOR SCORING: 15 minutes.

Local Machine Scoring: Not available.

Computer Software Options Available: Not available.

Cost of Materials: Due to possible price changes since publication date, be sure to check with he test publisher.

Specimen Set: $41.00 (two test booklets + one manual).

Counselee Materials:

Manual, $40.00 (reusable)

Pkg. of 25 test booklets, $33.75 (nonreusable)

Pkg. of 50 test booklets, $31.75 per set of 25 (nonreusable)

Value Kit: 25 test booklets + one manual, $70.75 (only manual is reusable).

Additional Comments of Interest to Users: The publisher is considering developing separate norms for special populations of people with the following disabilities: (1) cerebral palsy, (2) autism, and (3) multiple sclerosis as this relates to training and employment.

Published Reviews of the Instrument in the Last 15 Years: This is a new version and no publications are available.

Reviewed by:

Patricia L. Sitlington
Professor
Department of Special Education
University of Northern Iowa

Heather L. Trilk
Classroom Teacher
Cedar Rapids (IA) Public Schools

Description

The *Becker Work Adjustment Profile: 2* (Becker, 2005) is a revision of the Becker Work Adjustment Profile (Becker, 1989). It is an observer rating scale designed to assess work habits, attitudes, and skills and to measure vocational competency of individuals with special needs, ages 12 to adult. Vocational competency should be evaluated by persons such as vocational evaluators, rehabilitation counselors, occupational therapists, work-study specialists, teachers, psychologists, and other professionals who interact with the individual with disabilities during the workday. The rating scale was designed to evaluate work behavior and not ability of the individual.

The *BWAP:2* contains 63 items that measure work behavior on a five-point descriptive graphic rating scale that has multiple units that range from "0" (least skill) to "4" (most skill). Each item is written behaviorally and descriptively. A sample item is: "Changes in routine: Response to change in work routine or job assignment. 0: Actively refuses; Becomes upset; 1: Displays reluctance; Grudgingly accepts; 2: Accepts change, but needs encouragement; 3: Accepts change; 4: Willingly accepts change."

The content of *BWAP:2* is divided into four domains and a composite score called Broad Work Adjustment (BWA). The *Work Habits/Attitudes* domain (10 items) assesses attendance and punctuality, personal hygiene, motivation, and posture as well as the individual's attitude toward these elements. The *Interpersonal Relations* domain (12 items) assesses the individual's social interaction, emotional stability, and cooperation. This domain assesses overall emotional behavior and employer-worker relations. The *Cognitive Skills* domain (19 items) assesses skills in knowledge of abilities in reasoning, judging, perceiving, thinking, and recognizing. It also rates functional reading, writing, and computational skills; time and time concepts; job-related knowledge; and management of daily situations in independent living. The *Work Performance Skills* domain (22 items) assesses skills in gross and fine motor, communication, job responsibility, and work efficiency. It also measures proficiency involving finger dexterity, manual dexterity, communication of basic needs and problems, verbal expression, capacity to learn a job task using new or old skills, and the quality and quantity of work produced. The *Broad Work Adjustment* summarizes the worker's performance across the variety of work and social activities. The BWA score is used in helping determine the individual's placement in a program or the amount of support needed.

The individual's work placement level is then identified as *community-competitive, transitional, high sheltered, low sheltered, work activity,* or *day care,* based upon the scores in each respective domain and the BWA score. The community-competitive level is unskilled, semi-skilled, or technical nonsheltered work that is community-based competitive employment following a limited training time. The transitional work level is a short-term training program of individual instruction and practical application in occupational skills and personal-social adjustment training. The sheltered work level is a program of vocational training, work, and adjustment therapy in a sheltered work environment. The work activity level is a program combining therapeutic activity and structured work skills training. The focus is to provide the basic meaning of work. The day care level is a program of basic skills for individuals with severe of profound disabilities. The individual's level of work support needs is also identified as *limited, low, moderate, high, extensive.*

The *BWAP:2* provides two different options for responding to the items in the Questionnaire Booklet. The first option is first person assessment, in which the evaluator independently scores each item based on observation of the individual's work behavior. If the evaluator has not had the opportunity to observe all behaviors or if the individual has not performed a particular activity, the evaluator is asked to estimate the individual's performance based on previous observations of similar tasks. The second option is third party assessment, in which the evaluator requires another person to adequately complete the rating scale. This is usually an employer or a parent/guardian who knows the individual well. The cover page of the Questionnaire Booklet provides space for descriptive information regarding the individual being evaluated. A scoring summary sheet labeled the Individual Profile Form provides space for the raw score, T-score, percentile, work placement level, and work support needs for each respective domain, as well as the BWA.

Use in Counseling

The main use of this instrument with individuals with and without special needs should be with a focus on the ratings from the individual items. It may be useful to have the individual independently rate himself or herself and compare the ratings with the evaluator and possibly other independent raters who have directly observed the individual's work. These comparisons have the potential for prompting rich discussion and focusing the individual on his or her strengths and areas in need of improvement.

For reasons cited in the Overall Critique section of this review, we do not feel that the work placement ratings should be used in the counseling process. The level of work support needs may be of some use, but will require the use of the norm tables, whose weaknesses are also discussed in the Overall Critique section. As with all assessment approaches, this profile should be used as only one measure of the individual's work habits/attitudes, interpersonal relations, cognitive skills, and work performance.

Technical Considerations

Norming data were obtained from 4,019 subjects in special education and regular classrooms in public and private schools, sheltered work centers, state-operated vocational rehabilitation centers, and community training and job placement programs in 20 states, Canada, and the territory of Puerto Rico. Categories represented in the standardization sample included mental retardation, learning disabled, physically disabled, emotionally disturbed, and economically disadvantaged. The largest category represented in the sample was mental retardation. A normative table is provided for each category; each normative table applies to individuals of all ages.

Reliability estimates are reported in the manual for each domain and the total score for each categorical subgroup of the standardization sample. Internal consistency ranged from .83 to .91. Test-retest coefficients (over a two-week interval) ranged from .85 to .96. The Standard Error of Measurement ranged from .91 (Interpersonal Relations — Emotionally Disturbed Category) to 5.84 (Broad Work Adjustment — Emotionally Disturbed Category). Interrater reliability data were collected on 117 adults in three midwestern sheltered workshops. Indices ranged from .82 for Work Habits/Attitudes to .89 for Cognitive Skills.

Content, criterion-related, and construct validity are described in the manual. High internal consistency coefficients and a factor analysis supporting the basic domains of the instruments are cited as support for content validity. Intercorrelations between the *BWAP:2* and the *AAMR Adaptive Behavior Scale* (Nihira, Leland, & Lambert, 1993) for 167 persons with mental retardation from the standardization sample are cited as support for criterion-related validity. Six testable hypotheses related to the *BWAP:2* are listed to support construct validity.

Overall Critique

The main strength of the *BWAP: 2* lies in the actual items included in the scale. The items focus on observed work behaviors, not perceived ability. The responses for each item are clearly written statements, which describe the behavior associated with a score from 0 to 4 for each item. The behaviors measured by the items are key behaviors needed in the workplace. A second strength of this instrument is the user's manual. For the most part, it is clearly written and provides case studies illustrating how to interpret sample test scores.

The main weakness of the *BWAP: 2* lies in the use of work placement levels (community competitive, transitional, extended sheltered, work activity, day care). Although the author describes the process of associating specific T-score and percentile ranges with these levels, it is unclear how many individual scores were used in this process. It is also difficult to understand how the scores from one instrument can be used to determine placement for any individual. Even more importantly, these levels place little emphasis on community-based employment, which should be the focus of preparation for all youth and adults.

A second weakness relates to the norm tables included in the user's manual. Each norm table provided covers all ages — from age 12 through adulthood. In addition, there is no opportunity to compare an individual's score to individuals without special needs. (There is a group described as "economically disadvantaged," but no further information could be found on this population.)

References

Becker, R. L. (1989). *Becker Work Adjustment Profile.* Columbus, OH: Elbern Publications.

Becker, R. L. (2005). *Becker Work Adjustment Profile: 2.* Columbus, OH: Elbern Publications.

Nihira, K., Leland, H., & Lambert, N. (1993). *AAMR Adaptive Behavior Scales — Residential and community version.* (2nd ed.). Austin, TV: Pro-Ed.

BRIGANCE SYSTEM
BRIGANCE DIAGNOSTIC LIFE SKILLS INVENTORY (LSI)
BRIGANCE DIAGNOSTIC EMPLOYABILITY SKILLS INVENTORY (ESI)

BRIGANCE DIAGNOSTIC LIFE SKILLS INVENTORY (LSI)

Albert H. Brigance

Curriculum Associates, Inc.
153 Rangeway Road
North Billerica, MA 01862-0901
e-mail: info@cainc.com
www.CurriculumAssociates.com

Target Population: Transitional, secondary special education, vocational, ESL programs.

Statement of the Purpose of the Instrument: The Life Skills Inventory is an authentic assessment of basic skills and functional life skills in the context of real-world situations. The criterion-referenced instrument determines present level of performance, assesses strengths and weaknesses, and aids in developing instructional plans and monitoring progress.

Titles of Subtests, Scales, Scores Provided: The 168 criterion-referenced assessments span nine areas: Speaking and listening, functional writing, words on common signs and warning labels, telephone, money and finance, food, clothing, health, and travel and transportation.

Forms and Levels Available, with Dates of Publication/Revision of Each: N/A

Date of Most Recent Edition of Test Manual, User's Guide, etc.: 1994

Languages in Which Available: English only.

Time:

Actual Test Time: N/A

Norm Group(s) on Which Scores Are Based: N/A

Manner in Which Results Are Reported for Individuals:

Report Format/Content: Assessors record student's responses in a Student Record Book which becomes an ongoing record of skills assessed, skills mastered, and objectives established.

Report Format/Content for Group Summaries: An optional Class Record Book forms a matrix of skills assessed, mastered, and objectives established for up to 15 students.

Computer Software Options Available: Browser-based Data Management Service provides online record book, exportable goals and objectives for IEPs, and progress reporting feature. Exportable goals and objectives are also available on CD-ROM.

Ways in Which Computer/Online Version Differs: Same method of assessment. Service facilitates record keeping and reporting.

Cost of Materials: Due to possible price changes since publication date, be sure to check with the publisher website.

Inventory, $89.95. Record Book 10-pack, $24.95; 100 pack, $229.00. Class Record Book, $12.95. Goals and Objectives CD, $59.95. Subscription-based Management System based on number of users — contact Web Services at 800-225-0248 for a quote.

Additional Comments of Interest to Users: The Life Skills Inventory is being revised for release in late 2007.

BRIGANCE® DIAGNOSTIC EMPLOYABILITY SKILLS INVENTORY (BRIGANCE® ESI)

Albert H. Brigance

Curriculum Associates, Inc.
153 Rangeway Road
North Billerica, MA 01862-0901
e-mail: info@cainc.com
www.CurriculumAssociates.com

Target Population: Transitional, secondary special education, vocational, ESL programs.

Statement of the Purpose of the Instrument: The Employability Skills Inventory is an authentic assessment of basic skills and employability skills in the context of job seeking and employment. The criterion-referenced instrument determines present level of performance, assesses strengths and weaknesses, and aids in developing instructional plans and monitoring progress.

Titles of Subtests, Scales, Scores Provided: The 124 criterion-referenced assessments span these areas: Speaking and listening, reading grade placement, reading skills, preemployment writing, math skills and concepts, career awareness and self-understanding, job-seeking skills and knowledge. Ratings Scales are provided for subjective skills — self-concept and attitudes, job interview preparation, trainee's worth experience, and others.

Forms and Levels Available, with Dates of Publication/Revision of Each: N/A

Date of Most Recent Edition of Test Manual, User's Guide, etc.: 1995

Languages in Which Available: English only.

Time:

Actual Test Time: N/A

Norm Group(s) on Which Scores Are Based: N/A

Manner in Which Results Are Reported for Individuals:

Report Format/Content: Assessors record student's responses in a Student Record Book which becomes an ongoing record of skills assessed, skills mastered, and objectives established.

Report Format/Content for Group Summaries: An optional Class Record Book forms a matrix of skills assessed, mastered, and objectives established for up to 15 students.

Computer Software Options Available: Browser-based Data Management Service provides online record book, exportable goals and objectives for IEPs, and progress reporting feature.

Exportable goals and objectives are also available on CD-ROM.

Cost of Materials: Due to possible price changes since publication date, be sure to check with the publisher website.

Inventory, $89.95. Record Book 10-pack, $24.95; 100 pack, $229.00. Class Record Book, $12.95. Goals and Objectives CD, $59.95. Subscription-based Management System based on number of users — contact Web Services at 800-225-0248 for a quote.

Additional Comments of Interest to Users: The Employability Skills Inventory is being revised for release in late 2007.

Published Reviews of the Instrument in the Last 15 Years:

Carlson, J. V. (2001). Review of the BRIGANCE Employability Skills Inventory. In B.S. Plake & J. C. Impara (Eds.), *The fourteenth mental measurements yearbook.* Lincoln, NE. Buros Institute of Mental Measurements.

Tierre, W. C. (2001). Review of the BRIGANCE Employability Skills Inventory. In B.S. Plake & J. C. Impara (Eds.), *The fourteenth mental measurements yearbook.* Lincoln, NE. Buros Institute of Mental Measurements.

Reviewed by:[1]

JoEllen V. Carlson

Director & Associate Professor
Institute for Instructional Research and Practice
Institute for At-Risk Infants, Children & Youth, and Their Families
University of South Florida

Description

The BRIGANCE® Diagnostic Life Skills Inventory (LSI) and the BRIGANCE® Diagnostic Employability Skills Inventory (ESI) are two sets of assessments in the BRIGANCE System. The system, which the publisher advertises in its catalog as

---

[1] Portions of this review are adapted, by permission, from the author's original review in the *Fourteenth Mental Measurements Yearbook.*

providing "consistent assessment from birth through secondary level" (Curriculum Associates, 2006, p. 1), consists of a series of inventories purporting to assess "more than 500 developmental, readiness, academic, life, and employability skills" (Curriculum Associates, 2006, p. 1). The format of the inventories, the process for administration, and the record keeping are identical across the series.

The Inventory of Early Development II and Comprehensive Inventory of Basic Skills–Revised are used primarily in special or alternative education with children from birth to grade 9 with special needs, such as disabilities or limited English proficiency. Both assessments provide normed/standardized diagnostic data. The life skills and employability skills inventories, the secondary-level instruments in the series, are used for those students and also in school-to-work programs for students working toward basic, entry-level employability. The life skills inventory is intended to assess basic and functional life skills in the context of real-world situations, and the employability skills inventory is intended to assess basic and employability skills in the context of job seeking and on the job. Each inventory also includes a Quick Screen, which contains a sample of items from each skill area, to help determine whether the assessments in the inventory are appropriate for a particular learner. The Screens are used in Head Start Programs. These inventories are more appropriate in this context.

The life skills inventory (LSI) consists of assessments in Speaking and Listening Skills, Functional Writing Skills, Money and Finance, Food, Clothing, Health, and Travel and Transportation. It also includes five optional rating scales: Speaking Skills, Listening Skills, Health Practices and Attitudes, Self-Concept, and Auto Safety. Learners may complete the rating scales as self-ratings, and/or teachers, parents, or both may complete them.

The employability skills inventory is designed to complement the life skills inventory. In addition to a Quick Screen and Reading Grade-Placement assessments, the inventory includes six assessments: Career Awareness and Understanding, Job-Seeking Skills and Knowledge, Reading Skills, Speaking and Listening Skills, Preemployment Writing, and Math Skills and Concepts. Also, rating scales are included for Self-concept and Attitudes, Responsibility and Self-discipline, Motor Coordination and Job Requirements, Thinking Skills/Abilities and Job Requirements, Job-Interview Preparation, Job Interview, and Trainee's Work Experience. If needed, additional lists of items are provided to supplement the rating scales. In both inventories, all reading, listening, and speaking skills are presented in the context of specific functional areas. The content of the life skills inventory is based on areas such as money recognition and use, money and finance writing skills, lists, simple messages, maps, telephone use, clothing labels, catalog ordering, transportation schedules and signs, and many others. The content of the employability inventory is based on preemployment and employment-related situations and includes time concepts, simple measurements, money concepts, information signs, safety signs, directions from common employment forms, an application for a social security card, simple and complex employment applications, and other job-related situations.

Materials include the examiner's manual, a Learner Record Book, and a Class Record

Book. The manuals are thorough and efficiently organized, and they seem easy to use. With individual administration, responses can be oral or written and are recorded in the Learner Record Book. Some parts can be given to groups, and materials are provided for reproduction as needed.

The manual states that administering the inventories does not require special training and specifically states that, with professional supervision, tutors and paraprofessionals can administer the inventory. Administration time varies, depending on the needs of the learner and the program. Once there is sufficient information to plan instruction or other follow-up, testing can be stopped and resumed later to gather additional information and monitor progress. The same protocol can be used several times to monitor progress for an individual by using a different color pencil each time and dating the record book.

These instruments yield skill-by-skill inventories. All sections have guides and directions for using the results as an educational tool. Sample instructional objectives and detailed task/skills breakdowns are included in each section. For each of the inventories, there is an optional CD that assists in developing goals and objectives based on learner results.

Use in Counseling

The primary purpose of the instruments is to identify a learner's specific skills and deficits to support development of appropriate goals and objectives. These inventories give specific feedback that assists with planning, monitoring, and assessing individual learning and growth. Suggestions for Individualized Educational Plan (IEP) goals are given in the manual for all skills tested. The CD assists in creating lists of goals and objectives that can be saved, edited, and printed or exported to the school's own IEP forms.

The results of these inventories also can help in communicating with learners themselves and helping them to develop realistic goals and objectives. The Rating Scales are self-evaluated and intended to aid the learner in becoming more aware of traits, behaviors, attitudes, or skills to be developed for better life and/or workplace adjustment. Also, results can assist in discussions with parents/guardians about a learner's specific strengths and weaknesses.

These inventories are repeatedly cited by educational agencies as appropriate for transition planning. Appendices of the manuals demonstrate the relationships between both inventories and P.L. 94-142, and, in the employability skills inventory, relationships with the JTPA, Perkins Act, Americans with Disabilities Act, Fair Employment Law, and the Immigration Reform and Control Act of 1986. The employability skills inventory also is cross-referenced with CASAS standards and SCANS foundation skills, and supports the objectives of the Workforce Investment Act. The cross-referencing is presented in a manual appendix.

Technical Considerations

Unfortunately, no technical data are provided with these instruments. The developer and publisher seem to indicate that such data are not needed because the instruments are criterion-referenced. To the contrary, criterion-referenced instruments need evidence of reliability and validity of several types. For instruments of this sort from which curricular and program objectives are being developed, content validity and representativeness are of great concern. In the case of life skills and employability skills, evidence of predictive and criterion-related validity also is needed.

Although the manual states that the inventory assesses "the major skills viewed as prerequisites to employability," there is no discussion of the qualifications of those making this judgment, little of the process by which it was determined, and no empirical evidence to support it. A brief history cites reliance on responses and critiques from users of the Inventory of Essential Skills and other BRIGANCE inventories, review of publications, and the author's knowledge and experience. Although it appears that the inventories were developed over more than ten years of experience, it is impossible to tell the extent to which they have been administered to appropriately composed samples of the target populations. A few field test locations are named and the personnel are thanked for their ideas, recommendations, and constructive criticism, but no other description of their involvement is given.

Overall Critique

Despite the lack of empirical information, these instruments enjoy widespread use. The U.S. Department of Education, many state departments of education, and many school districts include these inventories on their lists of instruments that may be used for transition assessment under IDEA and to meet other federal and state requirements. Both inventories seem to be popular with teachers as well.

The popularity of these instruments would seem to attest to their utility. They do appear to be comprehensive in coverage, flexible, convenient to administer, and easy to score. The method of recording results and monitoring progress is appealing. The apparent ease and flexibility of administration without special training, however, lead to a caution. In the absence of evidence to the contrary, it would seem that reliability and validity could be negatively affected by certain variations in administration.

Albert Brigance, the author of these instruments, is commended for cautioning in the manuals against overreliance on the results of a single instrument and encouraging the use of multiple assessments and all data available in making judgments about a learner. Also noteworthy is his admonition to check to be sure that a learner who can perform certain skills during the assessment can apply those skills to daily activities. If these cautions are heeded, the utility of the life skills and employability skills inventories is enhanced.

Given the impressive scope, detail, apparent efficiency, and potential utility of these instruments, a program of psychometric research should certainly be undertaken. Information about the instrument's objectivity, reliability, and validity — particularly documentation of content validity and investigation of concurrent and predictive validity — are essential to broaden its utility.

References

Carlson, J. V. (2001). Review of the BRIGANCE Employability Skills Inventory. In B.S. Plake & J.C. Impara (Eds.), *The fourteenth mental measurements yearbook.* Lincoln, NE. Buros Institute of Mental Measurements.

Curriculum Associates, Inc. (2006). *BRIGANCE diagnostic inventories, screens · data management.* [Catalog] North Billerica, MA: Author.

Geist Picture Interest Inventory (GPII) (Revised Eighth Printing)

Harold Geist

Western Psychological Services
12031 Wilshire Blvd.
Los Angeles, CA 90025-1251
www.wpspublishers.com

Target Population: Students with disabilities, Students of low reading ability or nonreaders, Educationally deprived students, Eighth grade through adult populations, Individual and group administrations, Adults with developmental disabilities, Deaf individuals, Youth involved in the juvenile justice system, Young children who lack verbal and reading abilities.

Statement of the Purpose of the Instrument: The purposes of this inventory are to (1) assess quantitatively 11 male and 12 female general interest areas, (2) identify motivating forces behind occupational choice, (3) provide an interest inventory for working with those having limited verbal abilities, (4) provide possible additional information through projective uses, and (5) further research.

Titles of Subtests, Scales, Scores Provided: Subtests: Picture Triad booklet (for male and female) and Motivation Questionnaire (for male and female)

Scales:

> Motivational Areas: 1. Could not Say 2. Family 3. Prestige 4. Financial 5. Intrinsic and Personality 6. Environmental 7. Past experience

> Interest Areas: 1. Persuasive (A), 2. Clerical (B), 3. Mechanical (C), 4. Musical (D) 5. Scientific (E), 6.Outdoor (F), 7. Literary (G), 8. Computational (H), 9. Artistic (I), 10. Social Service (J), 11. Dramatic (K), 12. Personal Service (L) (only for females).

Scores provided: Two basic groups of scores are obtained from the GPII.

> 1. Interest: 11 for males, 12 for females.

> 2. Motivation: 7 for males, 7 for females.

> The T score which corresponds to the raw score in each interest area is entered in the "T score" column. If the Counselor wishes, the T scores can be plotted to form the GPII Interest Profile.

> In general, a T score over 70 indicates the examinee has a high interest in an area, while a T score under 30 indicates he/she does not like or enjoy activities in the interest area as compared with other interest areas.

Forms and Levels Available, with Dates of Publication/Revision of Each: Geist Picture Interest Inventory: Male and Female, Eighth printing, September 1988.

Date of Most Recent Edition of Test Manual, User's Guide, etc.: The most current version of the GPII was updated in 1971 and consists of 27 items for female examinees and 44 items for male examinees. The GPII is currently in its eighth printing, September 1988.

Languages in Which Available: English only.

Time:

Actual Test Time: 10 – 20 minutes.

Total Administration Time: 30 – 50 minutes.

* The GPII has no time limit but examinees are encouraged to work rapidly.

Norm Group(s) on Which Scores Are Based: Geist's initial instrument was piloted on 1,500 boys in grades 4 – 12 from four different communities in California. A female form was developed for the 1964 revision.

Norms are provided for an extensive array of groups for both men and women, including U.S. mainland in grades 8-12, trade school, and university; social workers, artists, librarians, and physical education instructors; and vocational rehabilitation clients and those diagnosed with schizophrenia.

Manner in Which Results Are Reported for Individuals:

Types of Scores: Scores are collected as raw scores and converted into T scores in order to be able to make standard comparisons.

The T score which corresponds to the raw score in each interest area is entered in the "T score" column. If the Counselor wishes, the T scores can be plotted to form the *GPII Interest Profile.* In general a T score over 70 indicates the examinee has a high interest in an area while a T score under 30 indicates he does not like or enjoy activities in the interest area as compared with other interest areas. (GPII Manual)

Report Format/Content:

BASIC SERVICE: The GPII is a self-administering, pencil-and-paper instrument.

Males are provided with Form M, females with Form F, and told to complete the Picture Triad Booklet according to directions. When there is a server reading disability, directions and questions under the triads are read aloud to the examinee, who circles the drawings of his or her choice. A sample triad of drawings is part of the instructions. After the examinee reads the cover page, he or she can respond to GPII items properly.

Report Format/Content for Group Summaries:

BASIC SERVICE: The group administration procedure is the same as individual administration except that the examiner asks if directions are clear and if not, he/she clarifies and illustrates responses to items by reading the directions and discussing the sample item.

Scoring:

Machine Scoring Service: Not available.

Hand Scoring: Counselor

Local Machine Scoring: Not available.

Computer Software Options Available: Not available.

Cost of Materials: Due to possible price changes since publication date, be sure to check with publisher website.

Specimen Set: $78.50 (kit includes test booklets for males and females, and manual)

Counselee Materials:

Manual— describes the GPII (reusable).

Picture Triad booklet: Male (Form M)—contains 44 triads of drawings, representing major vocations and avocations. Also included is the GPII interest profile. (not reusable).

Picture Triad booklet: Female (Form F)—contains 27 triads of drawings based on the rationale operating in Form M. Also included is the GPII interest profile, initial directions, and information concerning the counselee. (not reusable).

Motivation Questionnaire: Male (Form M)—contains the GPII Motivating Forces Profile (not reusable, optional for counselee to complete).

Motivation Questionnaire: Female (Form F)—used with the female test booklet. (not reusable, optional for counselee to complete).

Published Reviews of the Instrument in the Last 15 Years: None cited.

Reviewed by:

Tammi Vacha-Haase

Serena Enke

Psychology Department
Colorado State University

Description

The GPII is a pictorial interest inventory best known for its use with populations having limited verbal ability. The first version of the Geist Picture Interest Inventory (GPII) was developed in the 1950s by Harold Geist with the goal of creating a measure of vocational interest that was less dependent on verbal ability than the existing or more traditional interest measures (Geist, 1959). Geist's initial instrument was piloted on 1,500 boys in grades 4 – 12 from four different communities in California. A female form was developed for the 1964 revision. The most current version of the GPII was updated in 1971 and consists of 27 items for female examinees and 44 items for male examinees. The GPII is currently in its eighth printing and can be ordered from Western Psychological Services (www.wpspublishers.com).

Instead of answering a verbal question, examinees completing the GPII choose one of three pictures portraying either a person (men on the male form and women on the female form) in an occupation or activity, or a tool associated with an occupation. For example, female examinees choose between a waitress, a physical therapist, and an elevator operator. Male examinees choose from picture triads such as potter, cellist, and medical doctor. Sets of pictures are accompanied by a question such as "Which would you rather do?" or "Which are you most interested in doing?"

Each picture is associated with at least one of 11 interest areas: Persuasive, Clerical, Mechanical, Musical, Scientific, Outdoor, Literary, Computational, Artistic, Social Service, and Dramatic (the first ten match those suggested by G. F. Kuder in 1956). The test is scored by adding the number of marks in each interest area column. An examinee's profile displays the T scores for each area.

For a more in-depth understanding of examinee interests, the GPII includes an optional measure that explores the motivations behind each of the examinee's answers. After completing the primary instrument, examinees choose one of 35 reasons for each selected career choice on a grid checklist. The motivators combine to form seven categories: Could Not Say, Family, Prestige, Financial, Intrinsic and Personality, Environmental, and Past Experience. Little guidance is offered regarding the scoring or interpretation of this optional measure, and no norms are provided. However, Geist recommends that motivations which the examinee chooses over 60% of the time should be "considered carefully" in interpretation, as the examinee was "influenced" by this category in occupational choices (Geist, 1959).

Use in Counseling

The GPII is a self-administering, pencil-and-paper instrument, generally requiring 10 – 25 minutes to complete, with an additional 20 – 40 minutes needed to complete the optional checklist. This instrument is appropriate for a variety of populations and can be administered individually or in groups. After administration, the pictures can be used to gather additional projective information from the examinee.

The pictorial nature of the GPII makes it ideal for use with young children who may not have the verbal ability to complete other types of interest inventories. This instrument is also appropriate for populations with a decreased verbal ability and/or those whose first language is not English. The GPII is often used for specialized populations, such as deaf individuals whose primary language is signed, with separate norms available for deaf individuals (Geist, 1962a) as well as other groups. Other potential uses include the learning disabled or populations with higher percentages of learning disabilities, such as juvenile delinquents (Kronenberger & Quatman, 1968). The GPII can be used with the developmentally disabled, although Burg and Barrett (1965) found it necessary to both show the picture and give an oral description, in addition to reading the questions out loud.

Technical Considerations

Norms are provided for an extensive array of groups for both men and women, including U.S. mainland in grades 8 – 12, trade school, and university; social workers, artists, librarians, and physical education instructors; and vocational rehabilitation clients and those diagnosed with schizophrenia.

The reliability and validity of the GPII tend to be acceptable, but are not without criticism (Tiedeman, 1960). Research suggests that test-retest reliability of the GPII over a six-month interval varies considerably depending on the sample used (e.g., .62 for eighth graders in Puerto Rico; .87 for the U.S. mainland sample.) Correlations with the Kuder scales are generally statistically significant, and Geist (1959) suggested "that the GPII scores may be more valid than the Kuder scores for examinees with reading handicaps" (p. 422.) A five-year follow-up on the norming samples used in the original GPII indicated that most examinees were employed in professions that matched the interests they indicated on the GPII (Geist, 1962b).

Overall Critique

The GPII is a short, simple approach to gathering information about vocational interests, being easy to score and relatively simple to interpret, especially for those familiar with the Kuder scales. Because it requires minimal verbal ability, it offers practitioners the opportunity to provide vocational information to populations that might otherwise be overlooked.

The most salient criticism of the GPII is that it is outdated, having last been revised 35 years ago. Clothing and instruments are clearly dated (e.g., nurses wearing pointed paper caps and people using typewriters), and several pictures represent vocations that may no longer be viable (e.g., switchboard operator or television repairman). In addition, many of the more recent or fastest growing occupations available today are not represented (e.g., computer software engineer, chiropractor, translator, or hazardous materials removal worker.)

Questions also exist regarding the accuracy of Geist's basic premise that pictures better represent an occupation than do verbal descriptions or job titles (Geist, 1959). Each drawing represents only a small portion of the job, whereas a job title may bring to mind a more complete picture. It is unclear whether the intention of the GPII is for the examinee to choose *activities* or *occupations* that are of interest. Additional concern exists regarding the ambiguity or confusing nature of pictures, as a number of drawings are not easily recognizable.

Finally, the current revision appears to perpetuate gender stereotypes. For example, the medical pictures on the female form overwhelmingly depict nurses rather than physicians. Rather than gender specific norms in different occupations, norms representing how similar an examinee's scores are to a typical or satisfied person in a particular occupation may be more useful during interpretation.

References

Burg, B.W., & Barrett, A.M. (1965). Interest testing with the mentally retarded: A bi-sensory approach. *American Journal of Mental Deficiency,* 69(4), 548 – 552.

Geist, H. (1959). The Geist Picture Interest Inventory: General form: Male. *Psychological Reports, 5,* 413 – 438.

Geist, H. (1962a). Occupational interest profiles of the deaf. *Personnel and Guidance Journal. 51(1),* 50 – 55.

Geist, H. (1962b). A five year follow-up of The Geist Picture Interest Inventory. *California Journal of Educational Research, 13(5),* 195 – 208.

Kronenberger, E.J., & Quatman, G.L. (1968). Performance of institutionalized juvenile delinquents on the Geist Picture Interest Inventory. *Psychological Reports, 22,* 185 – 186.

Tiedeman, D.V. (1960). Geist Picture Interest Inventory. *Personnel and Guidance Journal, 38,* 506 – 507.

Life Centered Career Education Competency Assessment: Knowledge and Performance Batteries (LCCE)

Donn E. Brolin

The Council for Exceptional Children
1110 North Glebe Road
Arlington, VA 22201
www.cec.sped.org

Target Population: The test was standardized and developed for students in grades 9–12 with mild mental retardation and specific learning disabilities. It can also be used (with caution) with lower grades and other populations such as students at risk, adults, and students with emotional/behavior disorders.

Statement of the Purpose of the Instrument: The primary purpose of this criterion-referenced battery is to identify areas of strengths and weaknesses in 20 of the 22 competencies comprising the Life Centered Career Education curriculum, and to gauge effectiveness of the instructional program. Together with its companion, the LCCE performance battery can be used to provide a comprehensive career/life skills assessment.

Titles of Subtests, Scales, Scores Provided: Subtests: "Daily Living Skills Questions;" "Personal Social Skills Questions;" "Occupational and Guidance Questions." Scores are recorded by administrator on form called the Student Competency Assessment Record (SCAR).

Forms and Levels Available, with Dates of Publication/Revision of Each: The Knowledge Battery (KB) comes in two forms, A and B. The original publication date is 1992. Minor revisions were made in 1997. The KB is written at a fourth-grade reading level. It is presented in a multiple-choice format.

Date of Most Recent Edition of Test Manual, User's Guide, etc.: D. E. Brolin, *Life Centered Career Education: A Competency Based Approach,* 5th Edition (1997).

Languages in Which Available: English only.

Time:

Actual Test Time: 2–4 hours depending on abilities of students taking test.

Norm Group(s) on Which Scores Are Based: The test is not norm referenced. Standardized on students in grades 9–12 who have mild mental retardation or specific learning disabilities.

Manner in Which Results Are Reported for Individuals:

Types of Scores: The scores are reported as a total number correct out of a total of ten questions. There are 10 questions for each of the first 20 competencies. A score of 8 is considered "competent" (i.e., passing).

Scores are provided at both the competency and domain level. The Student Competency Assessment Record (SCAR) is used to record student's knowledge scores.

Report Format/Content:

BASIC SERVICE: None available.

Test administrator records scores on SCAR.

Report Format/Content for Group Summaries: Not available.

Scoring:

Machine Scoring Service: Not available.

Hand Scoring:

Scored by: Clerk; Counselor.

Time required for scoring: 5–10 minutes.

Local Machine Scoring:

PROVISIONS/CONDITIONS/EQUIPMENT REQUIRED: If a scoring machine is available and students are able to successfully use Scantron-type answer sheets, a 200-item sheet can be used. The test administrator will need to create an answer sheet for the machine available.

Computer Software Options Available: Not available.

Cost of Materials: Due to possible price changes since publication date, be sure to check with publisher website.

Specimen Set: Complete set (included three CD ROMs covering DLS, PSS, and OGP; a teacher's copy of each of the three accompanying student workbooks; performance batteries; knowledge batteries; a copy of LCCE teacher's guide), $1,424.95

Counselee Materials: Test booklets sell for $20 per pack of 10. If separate answer sheets are used, the booklets are reusable. It is illegal to photocopy the test booklets.

Additional Comments of Interest to Users: CD-ROMs are now available for purchase.

The Knowledge Battery is part of the complete curriculum package and can also be purchased separately. A Pictorial Knowledge Battery for the Modified Curriculum is under development.

Also, there is now an LCCE Performance Battery. The performance batteries were designed to go a step beyond ascertaining students' knowledge of the LCCE competencies, and to actually assess students' ability to apply the LCCE competencies in their lives. Like the knowledge battery, the performance battery is curriculum based.

The PB consists of two alternate forms for each of the 21 competency units. The majority of the items are performance based. It is composed of open-ended questions, role-playing scenarios, card-sorting, and other hands-on activities.

Published Reviews: None cited.

Reviewed by:

Steven R. Sligar
Assistant Professor

Rebecca Burke
Research Assistant

Department of Rehabilitation Studies
East Carolina University

Description

The *Life Centered Career Education: A Competency Based Approach* (LCCE) contains three independent though interrelated instruments: the LCCE Competency Rating Scale (CRS) and the LCCE Competency Assessment Batteries, which has two separate instruments, the LCCE *Knowledge Battery* (KB) and *Performance Battery* (PB) (Brolin, 1997). All three are screening instruments based in and used with the LCCE curriculum. The primary target group is seventh- through twelfth-grade students in special education, specifically those who have mild intellectual and severe learning disabilities, though Brolin (1997) notes that other groups may benefit from this approach to career education. The complete LCCE includes the screening instruments and three CDs (Council for Exceptional Children, 2004) containing the Daily Living Skills, Personal Social Skills, and Occupational Guidance and Preparation Skills lesson plans. Also included are forms and materials for assessment or instruction that may be duplicated.

The LCCE was first published in 1978 and has served the same purpose since its inception, which is to infuse career education into the academic curriculum. Brolin (1997) envisioned an integration of classroom instruction with community-based experiences to foster transition (from school to work or further training),to provide an outcomes-based educational program and to promote self-determination efforts. The content of the LCCE is grounded in three domains: Daily Living Skills (DLS), Personal-Social Skills (PSS), and Occupational Guidance and Preparation (OGP), all situated on a supportive base of Academic Skills. The LCCE curriculum is comprised of 22 competencies (DLS-9, PSS-7 and OGP-6) (see Table 1) with 97 subcompetencies (DLS-41, PSS-28, and OGP-28).

The *Competency Rating Scale* (CRS) was designed to insure a consistent evaluation of a student's mastery of the LCCE content domains. The assessment consists of 87 observations of student behaviors across all 97 subcompetencies. The four sections of the CRS Manual describe evaluation of student performance. Section I contains the observational ratings: *0 = Not Competent* (unable to perform any of the criteria); *1 = Partially Competent* (performs at least one of the criteria); *2 = Competent* (performs all of the criteria); and *NR = Not Rated.* These are conducted at the time the student enters middle or high school and competed at the end of each school year until graduation. Section II describes how to complete the recording form. Section III lists the Behavioral Criteria for Rating Subcompetencies. Example content from each domain follows: calculate balances of debts (DLS); write basic physical needs (PSS); and name jobs of interest (OGS). Section IV — Interpretation suggests that users identify areas of strengths and weaknesses to assist with IEP development and as aggregate data to identify curriculum development needs.

Table 1.

LCCE Competencies by Curriculum Area		
Daily Living Skills	**Personal-Social Skills**	**Occupational Guidance & Preparation**
1. Managing personal finances	10. Achieving self-awareness	17. Knowing & exploring occupational choices
2. Selecting & managing a household	11. Acquiring self-confidence	18. Selecting & planning occupational choices
3. Caring for personal needs	12. Achieving socially responsible behavior	19. Exhibiting appropriate work-habits behavior
4. Raising children & meeting marriage responsibilities	13. Maintaining good interper-sonal skills	20. Seeking, securing, and maintaining employment
5. Buying, preparing, & consuming food	14. Achieving independence	21. Exhibiting sufficient physical-manual skills
6. Buying & caring for clothing	15. Making adequate decisions	22. Obtaining specific occupational skills
7. Exhibiting responsible citizenship	16. Communicating with others	
8. Utilizing recreational facilities & engaging in leisure		
9. Getting around the community		

The *Knowledge Battery* (KB) is a standardized, criterion-referenced instrument comprised of 200 multiple-choice questions spread across the DLS, PSS, and OGP domains. There are ten questions representative of each of the instructional objectives from 20 competency areas. Competencies from two areas were not included because they require demonstration of specific manual or vocational skills that cannot be evaluated in a knowledge test. Equivalent forms (A & B) are provided for test-retest. Example test content follows: identify the correct value of a drawn picture of a coin (DLS); identify feelings and consequences of actions (PSS); and identify payroll deductions (OGS). The KB was standardized on simultaneous oral/visual presentation of the instructions, test items, and four possible answers; instructions for student self-administration are included but it is not recommended. Administration time is approximately 2–4 hours for the entire battery, which may be given all at once or spread over several days. Group administration is allowed for up to 15 students with a proctor. The manual notes that the cultural or ethnic values of the student may require modification of 15 questions for Form A and 17 for Form B. Student scores are recorded in the Student Competency Assessment Record (SCAR).

The *Performance Battery* (PB) is a nonstandardized, criterion-referenced instrument comprised of two forms (A & B). Items include performance (57%), simulated performance (33%), and performance-related knowledge (10%) spread across the DLS, PSS, and OGP domains. Example test content follows: plan a budget (DLS); use personal hygiene products (PSS); and list four things to find a job (OGS). The items are presented orally or on paper with either individual or group activities. The PB is to be given in approximately 22–24 classes (hours) with scores reported on the Student Competency Assessment Record along side the KB scores.

Use in Counseling

The results provide a functional description of the student and may be used to determine placement and progress within the LCCE. The information may be used to develop goals and objectives for Individual Education Plans (IEP) or Individualized Transition Plans (ITP). In addition, the LCCE conceptual framework combines three developmental stages (readiness, career exploration, and career preparation) with four career roles (work done at home, volunteer work, work as an employee, and other productive avocational activities) (Brolin & Gysbers, 1989). This framework may serve as a useful heuristic for counseling. However, we caution against using the results solely to determine vocational and life skills knowledge; other information must be incorporated in the interpretation of the results.

Technical Considerations

After field testing from 1984 to 1991, test-retest reliability (.68–.85) was determined on special education students from Missouri, Wisconsin, California, West Virginia and Michigan (N = 177) on both forms (A & B) separately and together. According to the 1992 version of the Knowledge Battery, validity of the final 200 item version had not yet been established (Brolin, 1992). No technical information for either the CRS or the PB was given.

Overall Critique

We received three curriculum CDs (Council for Exceptional Children, 2004) and the *Knowledge Battery* (KB) manual for review (Brolin, 1992). We secured the *Performance Battery* (PB) and the *Competency Rating Scale* (CRS) (Brolin, 1997) from an outside source. The *Knowledge Battery* and *Performance Battery* are unique as assessments of life and occupational skills for students with disabilities. Both assessment instruments can be used as stand-alone assessments. The *Knowledge Battery* is primarily a screening instrument for the LCCE. The *Performance Battery* is useful as an assessment of students' learned skills after they have completed the LCCE curriculum. Users of the LCCE can link the assessment with instruction and can receive further day-long training from the Council for Exceptional Children (CEC) in Arlington, Virginia. We had problems opening the Adobe file on the CD. The problem was resolved with a downloaded patch for Microsoft Windows. The need for this patch was not explained in the materials sent to us from the CEC, although the information is available on the LCCE web page that describes the product. The information is on the bottom of the page and is a link to an Adobe PDF file (LCCE MS Hot Fix), which is a statement from the marketing manager about the technical problem and resolution (see http://www.cec.sped.org/Content/NavigationMenu/ProfessionalDevelopment/ProfessionalTraining/LCCE/).

Potential users of the LCCE need to be aware that some of the items (from the version we received) are out of date with references to typing a letter, playing a tape, or purchasing a soda for 50 cents. Other items may not be culturally relevant, for example, references to clothing worn to school, selection of healthy foods, and ways of dealing with grief. There are no references to the Internet or other learning tools commonly used in schools today. The items need to reference worker rights, especially in light of the Americans with Disabilities Act, and the overall LCCE needs to include linkages with the No Child Left Behind Act and other legislation enacted since 1997.

References

Brolin, D. E. (1992). *Life centered career education: knowledge and performance batteries.* Arlington, VA: Council for Exceptional Children.

Brolin, D. E. (1997). *Life center career education* (5th ed.). Arlington, VA: Council for Exceptional Children.

Brolin, D. E., & Gysbers, N. C. (1989). Career education for students with disabilities. *Journal of Counseling and Development, 68,* 155–159.

Council for Exceptional Children. (2004). *Life centered career education (CD-ROM).* Arlington, VA.

THE READING-FREE VOCATIONAL INTEREST INVENTORY SECOND EDITION (R-FVII:2)

Ralph L. Becker

Elbern Publications
P.O. Box 9497
Columbus, OH 43209
ebecker@insight.rr.com

Target Population: Ages 13 to adult. Mentally Retarded, Learning Disabled, Disadvantaged, Regular Classrooms.

Statement of the Purpose of the Instrument: A nonreading inventory to realistically measure the vocational interests of special-needs students and adults: people who are mentally retarded, learning disabled, or educationally disadvantaged, as well as students in regular classrooms.

Titles of Subtests, Scales, Scores Provided: 11 Scales: Animal Care, Automotive, Building Trades, Clerical, Food Service, Horticulture, Housekeeping, Laundry Service, Materials Handling, Patient Care, & Personal Service. Scores are provided for 11 scales and 5 clusters.

Forms and Levels Available, with Dates of Publication/Revision of Each: One form is available for males and females. Separate norms are available by gender and type of disability (i.e. MR, LD, etc.).

Date of Most Recent Edition of Test Manual, User's Guide, etc.: 2000. The test booklet was also revised in 2000.

Languages in Which Available: English only.

Time:

Actual Test Time: 20 minutes or less.

Total Administration Time: 20 minutes.

Norm Group(s) on Which Scores Are Based: Mentally retarded, learning disabled, educationally disadvantaged, regular classrooms.

Manner in Which Results Are Reported for Individuals:

Types of Scores: Standard Scores, Percentiles, Descriptive Ratings (i.e. High Average, etc), for scales and cluster scores.

Report Format/Content:

BASIC SERVICE: A "Record of Interest and Cluster Scores" Format reports on an individual's scores in 11 areas and 5 clusters. A graphic profile of interests is produced that visual represents the rage of vocational interest for each area as High, Above Average, to Low interest in the measured scales.

Report Format/Content for Group Summaries: Not available.

Scoring:

Machine Scoring Service: Not available.

Hand Scoring:

SCORED BY: Clerk; Counselor

TIME REQUIRED FOR SCORING: approximately 10 minutes

Local Machine Scoring: Not available.

Computer Software Options Available: Not available

Cost of Materials: Due to possible price changes since publication date, be sure to check with the Test Publisher.

Specimen Set: $55.75 (including Test Booklets and one Manual).

Counselee Materials:

Pkg/20 Test Booklets, $38.00

Manual, $40 each

Examination Set (1 test booklet & 1 manual), $40.50

Occupational Title lists, $32.00

Additional Comments of Interest to Users: The Occupational Titles List (OTL:2, 2001) is a supplement to the R-FVII:2. It includes more than 900 realistic job titles for people who have mental or physical disabilities.

Published Reviews of the Instrument in the Last 15 Years : None cited.

Reviewed by:[1]

Zandra S. Gratz
Professor of Psychology
Kean University
Union, New Jersey

Description

The Reading-Free Vocational Interest Inventory Second Edition (R-FVII:2) began as a Project on Vocational Interest at the Columbus State School and published by the American Association on Mental Deficiency. When published in 1975, separate test booklets were used for males and females. The 1981 revision used one booklet for both genders; an effort was made to balance gender across job tasks and vocational interest areas. The most current revision was directed at updating pictures, adding contemporary tasks, and expanding normative data.

The R-FVII:2 makes use of simple, black-and-white drawn pictures in order to assess the vocational interests of individuals who have been diagnosed as mentally

---

[1] Portions of this review are adapted, by permission, from the author's original review in the *Fifteenth Mental Measurements Yearbook.*

retarded, disabled, and/or disadvantaged. The R-FVII:2 generates 11 interest area scores: Automotive, Building Trades, Clerical, Animal Care, Food Service, Patient Care, Horticulture, Housekeeping, Personal Service, Laundry Service, and Materials Handling. Five cluster scores are generated by combining two or more interest area scores; these include Mechanical, Outdoor, Mechanical/Outdoor, Food Service/Handling Operations, and Clerical/Social Service.

The test is considered suitable for persons age 12 to 61. Although there is no time limit, it can be administered individually or in a group setting within a 45-minute class period. It is suggested that choice of administration paradigm (individual or group) should be made in consideration of the abilities of the potential test taker to work independently in a group setting.

The test booklet presents 55 triads of line drawings of individuals in job-relevant activities. A forced choice format requires respondents to circle the picture they like the best. Scoring requires the examiner to transfer respondent's selections to an answer sheet. The layout of the answer sheet facilitates the summing of scores to generate each interest area and cluster score. R-FVII:2 interest area raw scores can be transformed into T-scores, percentiles, and descriptive ratings, which range from Below Average to Above Average. Record and profile forms are provided on which to record scores and support score interpretation. The manual provides extensive information on the SEMs for each interest area score and subpopulation. Also presented in the manual are completed forms and interpretations for four sample clients.

Use In Counseling

The R-FVII:2 requires Level B training, as defined by the American Psychological Association (Becker, 2000). The authors caution further that although the R-FVII:2 could be administered by trained clerical or paraprofessional staff, interpretation of results should only be effected by persons who have expertise in both counseling and assessment. Similarly, it is important for the test administrator to garner confirmation that the test taker is able to comprehend and interpret the verbal instructions and pictures of the R-FVII:2. That is, valid assessments require that response choices be based on the test taker's understanding of the activity presented in each picture. In deciding the applicability of the R-FVII:2, reading limitations may not be the sole issue to consider.

Exacerbating issues relative to being able to comprehending the pictures, as noted by another reviewer (Pope, 2003), the clarity of the pictures may be of concern. That is, some pictures, albeit simple in nature, many not convey the essence of the task at hand. For example, the bellboy example, in which the word "hotel" is printed on the desk, may appear as a sales clerk in the absence of awareness as to what "hotel" indicates.

What may be of particular interest to the vocational counselor is the R-FVII:2 companion piece, *The Occupational Title Lists, 2nd ed.* (OTL) (Becker, 2001). The OTL provides the vocational counselor with 954 specific occupations as related to each of the 11 occupational scales of the R-FVII:2. In addition to listing jobs by interest area, the OTL presents the U.S. Department of Labor Occupational Information Network code and DOT (Dictionary of Occupational Titles) number. These codes, listed by job, delineate worker functions (data, people, things) by complexity, which are likely to provide the vocational counselor useful information when advising clients. Client scores, in concert with counselor knowledge of the client's ability, are likely to help identify potential jobs. Although linkages between job titles and R-FVII: 2 scores are logically based, data supportive of these linkages are not offered.

Technical Considerations

As described in the manual (Becker, 2000), more than 15,000 examinees participated in the normative sample. Norms are stratified by gender, age (12 to 15, and 16 and over), and classification (mental retardation, learning disabled, regular classroom, adult disadvantaged, and adult work sheltered). The number of examinees in each sample ranged from 765 to 1,140. As previously noted (Gratz, 2003), although for most categories the sample appears sufficient, some concern is noted for data concerning adult disadvantaged. All adult disadvantaged subjects were from one geographic area (distressed Appalachian counties). and the extent to which the data are applicable to adult disadvantaged of other regions, such as inner cities, is questionable (Gratz, 2003).

Internal consistency estimates of reliability are presented for a sample of more than 1,600 subjects diagnosed as mentally retarded. The sample, stratified by age and gender, yielded KR20 estimates ranging from .72 to .94. Most scales sported reliability estimates of .80 or higher; the exception to this was in Materials Handling, for which estimates ranged between .72 and .78. As noted by Gratz (2003), in that the KR20 estimates were generated from normative sample data, the lack of KR20 coefficients for other subgroups (e.g. learning disabled) is curious.

Test-retest estimates with two-week interval were obtained from a subsample of the original standardization sample. Samples stratified by gender, age, and classification were included in the test-retest studies and ranged in size from 41 to 76 subjects. For most samples and scales, test-retest reliability estimates were .80 or higher. The exception to this was Materials Handling, for which test-retest reliability estimates were between .70 and .79. As noted by Gratz (2003), across all samples, test-retest reliability estimates for Automotive and Building Trades based on males were .90 or higher, whereas for females, test-retest reliability estimates for these scales ranged between .72 and .86. Thus, for the traditionally male occupations, female test takers demonstrated less dependability over time than males.

Content validity was first established rationally and then revised in concert with empirical data. The articulation of jobs and interests for the 1975 edition was based on a guide for jobs for persons with mental retardation (Peterson and Jones, 1964). The manual describes revisions in content for the 1981 version to include jobs appropriate for the learning disabled student and adults in sheltered workshops. Item analysis using the extreme groups method indicated sufficient discrimination of items relative to each interest scale. Extreme groups data were also used to identify items which loaded on more than one item.

Concurrent criterion related validity was established through correlations with the Geist Picture Interest Inventory (Geist, 1988). Stratified by age, gender and classification, correlations ranged from .07 to .79. With the exception of the Materials Handling scale, most correlations were statistically significant. In generating these data, as noted by Gratz (2003), the manner in which scales on the Geist were matched to that of the R-FVII:2 is not clear. Beyond this, the manual's explanation for differences in the magnitude of the correlations across scales as being the result of group differences is not persuasive.

Also presented in the manual are the R-FVII:2 scale scores of employed persons with mental retardation. Graphs presented confirm that the mean interest scale standard score was highest for the interest areas in which the subject worked. However for a number of occupations, several interest area scores appear very close to that of the occupation of the subjects. Neither descriptive nor inferential data are presented to allow for further examination of the distance between interest area scores within each occupation. As noted in an earlier review (Gratz, 2003), no predictive criterion related validity was presented in the manual.

Overall Critique

The manual reports to "furnish information for individuals engaged in a wide range of occupations and job tasks at the range of occupations and job tasks at the unskilled, semiskilled, and skilled levels" (Becker, 2000, p.3). As noted by Gratz (2003), the manual does not present detailed content validity data to assess the extent to which a systematic review of jobs likely to be available to the target population was completed. The extent to which jobs depicted in the R-FVII:2 depict unskilled, semiskilled, and skilled occupations is questionable. Beyond this, the original basis for the development of the R-FVII scales is dated (Peterson & Jones, 1964). For this reason, jobs described within the manual and depicted within the inventory may not do justice to jobs in such areas as information technology which may be suitable for the target populations. This limitation puts more onus on the counselor interpreting the scores to recognize clients whose interests may be in such fields as technology.

Although the psychometric qualities of the R-FVII:2 are substantial, some concerns exist. In particularly, relatively low levels of reliability and validity for the Materials Handling interest scale place into question interpretation of this scale to guide vocational choice. In addition, as is typical of many interest inventories, gender differences in scale properties appear to exist and should be examined further. Also, although the manual depicts how to compute cluster scores and the resultant definitions, it does not detail how or why one would use them.

Given that the purpose of an interest inventory is to help in vocational planning, predictive criterion related validity is important. Therefore, as noted by Gratz (2003), it is a concern that the R-FVII:2 does not provide evidence of predictive validity.

Summary. The R-FVII:2 has a long history of providing data to support its use as a measure of interests for individuals who have limited reading ability. As noted earlier

(Gratz, 2003), vocational counselors, knowledgeable in the range of jobs available for persons with disabilities, are likely to find the R-FVII:2 a useful addition to their assessment paradigms.

References

Becker, R.L. (2000). *Reading-free vocational interest inventory: 2 manual* (2nd ed.). Columbus OH: Elbern Publications.

Becker, R.L. (2001). *Reading-free vocational interest inventory: 2 occupational title lists* (2nd ed.). Columbus OH: Elbern Publications.

Geist, H. (1988). *Geist picture interest inventory.* Los Angeles: Western Psychological Service.

Gratz, Z. (2003). Review of the Reading Free Vocational Interest Inventory: 2. In B. S. Plake, J.C. Imparta, & R.A. Spies (Eds.). *The fifteenth mental measurements yearbook* (pp. 718–719). Lincoln, NE: University of Nebraska Press.

Peterson, R.O., & Jones, E.M. (1964). *Guide to jobs for the mentally retarded.* Pittsburgh: American Institutes for Research.

Pope, M. (2003). Review of the Reading Free Vocational Interest Inventory: 2. In B.S. Plake, J.C. Impara, & R.A. Spies (Eds.). *The fifteenth mental measurements yearbook* (pp. 719–722). Lincoln, NE: University of Nebraska Press.

Transition Planning Inventory – Updated Version (TPI-UV)

Gary M. Clark and James R. Patton

PRO-ED Inc.
700 Shoal Creek Blvd.
Austin, TX 78757-6897
info@proedinc.com
www.proedinc.com

Target Population: General age range: 14–22.

Statement of the Purpose of the Instrument: The Transition Planning Inventory (TPI) is an instrument for identifying and planning for the comprehensive transitional needs of students. It is designed to provide school personnel a systematic way to address critical transition planning areas that are mandated by the Individuals with Disabilities Education Act (IDEA) of 2004 and that take into account the individual student's needs, preferences, interests, and strengths. Information on transition needs is gathered from the student, parents or guardians, and school personnel.

Titles of Subtests, Scales, Scores Provided: Transition Domains: (1) Employment, (2) Further Education, (3) Daily Living, (4) Leisure Activities, (5) Community Participation, (6) Health, (7) Self-Determination, (8) Communication, Interpersonal Relationships, and (9) Other.

Scores provided: none

The TPI-UV is criterion referenced; normative/standard scores are not yielded in this test.

Forms and Levels Available, with Dates of Publication/Revision of Each:

TPI Profile and Further Assessment Recommendation Form (1997, 2006)

TPI School Form (1997, 2006)

TPI Home Form (1997, 2006)

TPI Student Form (1997, 2006)

TPI Home Form (Spanish Version) (1997, 2006)

Date of Most Recent Edition of Test Manual, User's Guide, etc.: TPI-UV Administration and Resource Guide, 2006.

Languages in Which Available: English, Spanish, Chinese, Japanese, and Korean.

Time:

Total Administration Time: Estimated 15–30 minutes

Norm Group(s) on Which Scores Are Based: The TPI-UV is criterion referenced; a normed group is not included.

Manner in Which Results Are Reported for Individuals:

Types of Scores: Not reported.

Report Format/Content:

BASIC SERVICE: Protocols – Hand-scored reports

OPTIONS: A computerized version of the TPI-UV is available as a separate product. The system and forms are electronic; data is entered and reports are generated through the computer.

Report Format/Content for Group Summaries: Not available.

Scoring:

Machine Scoring Service: Not available.

Hand Scoring:

SCORED BY: Counselor.

TIME REQUIRED FOR SCORING: About 10 minutes.

Local Machine Scoring: Not available.

Computer Software Options Available: Computerized adaptive administration sold as a separate product, called TPI–Computer version.

Ways in Which Computer/Online Version Differs: The system is entirely run through a computer.

Cost of Materials: Due to possible price changes since publication date, be sure to check the publisher's website.

Specimen Set: TPI-UV Test Specimen Kit, $25.00.

Counselee Materials: Reusables: TPI-UV Administration and Resource Guide, Informal Assessment in Transition Planning, Case Studies in Assessment for Transition Planning.

Reviewed by:

John S. Wadsworth
Associate Professor
Rehabilitation Counselor Education
The University of Iowa

Description

The Transition Planning Inventory–Updated Version is designed "to provide a comprehensive way to identify the strengths and needs of students who were preparing to move from high school to any number of available jobs" (Clark & Patton, 2006, p. vii). The purposes of the TPI-UV are to offer a framework and generate information that will assist school-based professionals in creating comprehensive school-to-work transition plans that comply with the Individuals with Disabilities Education Act

(IDEA). The instrument is not designed to provide a comparison of the student with peers or normative data. The TPI-UV material provided by the publisher Pro-Ed Inc. consists of the three manuals: *Administration and Resource Guide* (Clark & Patton,, 2006), *Case Studies in Assessment for Transition Planning* (Trainor, Patton, & Clark, 2005), *Informal Assessments for Transition Planning* (Clark, Patton, & Moulton, 2000); as well as a *Modified Student Form for Students with Significant Disabilities, a Planning Notes Form*, and reproducible copies of the *Home Form* in Spanish, Mandarin Chinese, Japanese, and Korean. Copies of the evaluation forms for use by students, parents, teachers, and transition planning teams are included with the TPI-UV administration materials and are available separately.

Developed by Gary M. Clark and James R. Patton, the TPI was first published in 1996. The 2006 TPI-UV is designed for all disability groups; a modified version for students with significant or multiple disabilities is included in the TPI administration materials. The TPI also is available as the TPI Computer Version, which is a stand-alone electronic alternative to the printed assessment materials. The TPI-UV consist of three paper-and-pencil evaluation forms: *Student Form, Home Form*, and *School Form*. These self-report measures request that the student, parents, and teachers rate their level of agreement on a five-point scale anchored at *strongly disagree* (0) and *strongly agree* (5) with each of 46 transitional planning statements. In addition, the *Student Form* includes a section with 15 open-ended questions designed to elicit self-report information regarding interests and activity preferences. A fourth form, *Profile and Further Assessment Recommendation Form*, is used to summarize the self-report data using three general domains: (a) areas that require additional assessment, (b) the skills to be acquired, and (c) the service and support needs.

The TPI-UV includes a pool of items that capture information in nine categories: Employment, Further Education/Training, Daily Living, Leisure Activities, Community Participation, Health, Self-Determination, Communication, and Interpersonal Relationships. Each item in the *Student, Home,* and *School* forms measures the same traits or behaviors across all forms. Each form words the item differently to meet the needs of the intended respondent. For example, Employment Question 2 states, "I can choose a job that fits my interest and abilities" in the *Student Form;* "Can chose a job that fits his/her interests and abilities" in the *Home Form;* "Makes informed choices among occupational alternatives, based on his/her own interests, preferences, and abilities" in the *School Form;* and "Makes informed choices" in the *Profile and Further Assessment Recommendations Form*, which is the summary document. Example items of each of the eight remaining categories (as taken from the *Student Form*) are as follows: "I know how to get into a community employment training program that meets my needs" (item 6) from Further Education/Training, "I can find a place to live" (item 12) from Daily Living, "I go to different places for entertainment" (item 19) from Leisure Activities, "I am an active citizen" (item 21) from Community Participation, "I know how reproduction works" (item 30) from Health, "I set personal goals" (item 35) from Self-determination, "I have the writing skills I need" (item 40) from Communication, and "I can make friends wherever I go" (item 43) from Interpersonal Relationships. The ratings from the three data collection forms are compiled in columns on the *Profile and Further Assessment Recommendations Form.* The response to each item is then compared across the three forms.

Although the TPI-UV has no time limits, self-administration time is reported to be 15 to 20 minutes, with special needs administration ranging from 20 to 30 minutes or more. The *Student* and *School Forms* are provided in English. The *School Form* is self-administered and completed by school personnel who have a direct working knowledge of the student. The *Administration and Resource Guide* indicates that a school representative should explain the forms to the student and parent(s) before they complete the instrument. Clark and Patton (2006) caution that individuals who have receptive or expressive limitations may require interpreters, adapted materials, or oral administration. Specific adaptations to administer the instruments (e.g., translators or interpreters for non-English speaking or hearing impaired individuals; large-print, Braille, or audiotape versions for persons with visual deficits) may be needed. According to the administration manual (Clark & Patton) both the *Parent* and *Student Forms* can be administered using one of three different methods: (a) independent self-administration, (b) guided self-administration, and (c) oral administration.

Guidelines and scripts that are provided for items describe the skill or ability in detail in order to assist individuals who experience difficulty understanding the meaning of an item. For example, question 28 on the *Student Form* (Health domain) asks the student to rate the level of agreement to the statement "I am emotionally healthy". If the student does not understand the meaning, the provided script indicates that the meaning of the item is "Student performs those actions that contribute to a healthy emotional and mental lifestyle and prevents unhealthy states" (Clark & Patton, 2006 p. 72).

The ratings for each of the individual items in the three forms are then transferred to the *Profile and Further Assessment Recommendations Form* so comparisons can be made across the three forms. If a difference in ratings is found, then it is recommended that the item be discussed among the three participants and consensus reached regarding the level of performance.

Use in Counseling

The TPI-UV can identify strengths and service needs as perceived by the student, parent(s), and school personnel. The TPI-UV also facilitates identification of strengths in academic and community environments. Through comparison of the student's self-report, parent report, and school report, transition teams and counselors can identify areas in which there is agreement and discrepancies in the perception of transition readiness. Disagreements between students, parents, and teachers with regard to service needs are often barriers to completion of the Individual Education Plan (IEP). The TPI-UV provides a systematic framework to identify these discrepancies and facilitate discussion of the service needs of the student.

Additionally, the TPI-UV is useful in career counseling and career planning. Counselors can make use of the ratings to help the students consider career opportunities that match strengths and to use the ratings to target barriers to successful career development. Counselors can use the data from the TPI-UV to identify students who are unable to perform an activity and would better benefit from skill building activities as compared to interpersonal or group counseling. The strength-based approach of the TPI-UV also can assist counselors in identifying domains in which esteem-building activities can be best implemented.

The greatest strength of the TPI-UV is the ability to insure that counselors and other members of transitions team do not inadvertently overlook important domains and factors that contribute to transition success. For example, the instrument guides the team to consider reproductive education, wellness, and decision making as factor in the transition process.

Technical Considerations

All three forms of the instrument use the same item format:

	Not Appropriate	Strongly Disagree	Strongly Agree	Don't Know
3. Knows how to get a job.	NA	0 1 2 3 4 5		DK

(Example from *Parent Form*)

This format provides the student, parent, or teacher a method of indicating if the item is relevant or if the rater has no knowledge of the student's performance on this item. Items scored as NA or DK are not scored. Clark and Patton (2006) caution that if the "don't know" or "not applicable" response is used too frequently, then the instrument becomes less powerful.

Reliability for the TPI-UV was determined using content sampling and test-retest methods across a sample of 310 individuals with a variety of mental and physical disabling conditions. The authors provide content sampling reliability coefficients for the total group, persons identified as having a learning disability, and persons identified as having mental retardation. Internal consistency reliability (Coefficient alpha) for the total group across the nine categories ranged from.83 to.94 on the *School Form*, .79 to .92 on the *Parent Form*, and .70 to .87 on the Student Form. Test-retest reliability across the nine categories ranged from .87 to .98 on the *School Form*, .70 to .91 on the *Parent Form*, and .70 to .84 on the *Student Form.*

Validity was assessed using content and criterion-related methods. The authors solicited expert judgments on an initial pool of 250 items drawn from the literature. The process of revising items and submitting item revisions for review lead to the 49 items that were selected and then rated for relevancy by direct service staff, school administrators, and educators. A high degree of agreement was reported by Clark and Patton (2006). A test of concurrent validity was conducted by correlating the TPI with the *Wechsler Intelligence Scale for Children–Third Edition* (Wechsler, 1991) and the *Vineland Adaptive Behavior Scales* (Sparrow, Balla, & Cicchetti, 1984) on a sample of 48 students. The authors report that "Due to the small number of cases (48) and the absence of a truly appropriate comparison of psychological constructs, many correlations were not significant" and "Additional studies involving the TPI and other related measures are being conducted" (Clark & Patton, 2006, p. 66).

Overall Critique

The TPI–UV was designed to provide a systematic assessment and planning tool for use in individualized educational planning with students with disabilities and to provide school personnel with a systematic way to comply with the federal mandate for addressing transition services planning and to use recommended practices in IEP planning. The instrument provides a framework to insure that data are collected using an organized strategy that permits a comparison of perceived strengths in nine domains by stakeholders in the transitional process.

The lack of data to support the predictive and concurrent validity of the TPI-UV is a concern. This instrument is designed to assist students, parents, and school personnel with the creation of an individual plan that addresses future needs. The predictive validity of the summary data generated by comparison of the three report instruments needs to be addressed before users can assume that the summary data are a valid method of identifying strengths that lead to transition success.

The TPI is a strength-based assessment that can assist transition teams in developing strength-based IEP plans. However, because there are no internal methods of ascertaining the accuracy of self-reports and each observer reports on only one environment the outcome easily may be subject to observer biases. Thus the instrument is most useful in conjunction with observational data obtained from neutral third party observers.

Clark and Patton are to be commended for providing the Home Form in multiple languages and for proving a modified version of the Student Form in a form adapted to students with more significant disabilities. The authors' note that care should be taken to insure respondents understand the items. Although scripts are provided to assist in the explanation of items, persons with severe receptive language or severe intellectual disabilities may not be able to gain insight into the authors' intended interpretation of each question. Items are subject to interpretation by respondents who do not ask for clarification.

As a part of a multimodal evaluation that includes self-report, observational data, and artifacts of accomplishment the TPI-UV can assist professionals in systematically collecting and interpreting self-report data in an organizational framework that facilitates the IEP process. In this reviewer's opinion, the TPI-UV is very useful in identifying discrepancies among stakeholders in the IEP process; these discrepancies often are the seeds of failure and disagreement in the transition process. Counselors and others can easily use the data generated by the TPI-UV to identify areas in which consensus building is necessary and to identify perceptions of the students' abilities by any of the parties involved.

References

Clark, G. M., & Patton, J. R. (2006). *Administration and Resource Guide: Transition Planning Inventory–updated version.* Austin, TX: PRO-ED.

Clark, G. M., Patton, J. R, & Moulton, L. R. (2000). *Informal assessments for transition planning.* Austin, TX: PRO-ED.

Sparrow, S. S., Balla, D. A. & Cicchetti, D. V. (1984). *Vineland Adaptive Behavior Scales: Survey form.* Circle Pines, MN: American Guidance Service.

Trainor, A. A., Patton, J. R., & Clark, G. M. (2005). *Case studies in assessment for transition planning.* Austin, TX: PRO-ED.

Wechsler, D. (1991). *Wechsler Intelligence Scale for Children* (3rd ed.). New York: Psychological Corporation.

Valpar Test of Essential Skills in English and Math (VTES)

Bryan B. Christopherson and Alex Swartz

Valpar International Corporation, Inc.
2440 N. Coyote Drive, Suite 127
Tucson, AZ 85745
www.valparint.com
valparbbc@aol.com

Target Population: People of working age (15 and above).

Statement of the Purpose of the Instrument: The tests are designed to help examinees demonstrate in a relatively short period of time important basic English and math skills that are required of workers in most of the occupations or training programs in the United States and Canada.

Titles of Subtests, Scales, Scores Provided: English, Section 1: Vocabulary (synonyms, synonyms fill in the blank, antonyms), Spelling (pick correctly spelled word), Usage and Capitalization; Section 2: Reading Comprehension. Math, Section 1: Computation; Section 2: Usage.

Forms and Levels Available, with Dates of Publication/Revision of Each: Two parallel forms (A and B) for both English and Math tests.

Date of Most Recent Edition of Test Manual, User's Guide, etc.: 1998

Languages in Which Available: English only.

Time:

Actual Test Time: 45 minutes each, English and Math.

Total Administration Time: Approximately 1 hour each, English and Math.

Norm Group(s) on Which Scores Are Based: Criterion referenced to scholastic curricula and U.S. Department of Labor's General Levels of Educational Development, Language and Math.

Manner in Which Results Are Reported for Individuals:

Types of Scores:

English: Grade levels (below sixth through above tenth); GED-Language (below second through above fourth); Raw scores by section, subsection, and total test; Percent scores by section and total.

Math: Grade levels (Computation: below fourth through above eighth; Usage: below sixth through above tenth. Total: below fourth through above tenth). Raw scores by test section, total, grade level, and GED level. Percent cores by section total, total test, grade level, and GED level.

Report Format/Content:

Basic Service: Reports are automatically generated by scoring software.

Options: Reports may be customized to suit user needs.

Report Format/Content for Group Summaries: Not available.

Scoring:

MACHINE SCORING SERVICE: The scoring software scores individual tests and produces a variety of reports. Test response data can be entered by hand or via an appropriate Scantron scanner. Optionally, users may send answer sheets to Valpar for scoring and report writing.

Cost of basic service per counselee: If a user does not have access to a computer, he or she may send scores to Valpar for scoring/reporting for a nominal fee.

Cost of options: Contact Valpar for current price for this service.

Time required for scoring and returning: 24 hours.

HAND SCORING: Not available.

LOCAL MACHINE SCORING: Provisions/conditions/equipment required: Scantron and computer or computer only.

Computer Software Options Available: Not available.

Cost of Materials: Due to possible price changes since publication date, be sure to check the publisher's website.

SPECIMEN SET: Called "Evaluation Kit," cost is $50. Includes one manual, 10 answer sheets (good for both Math and English tests), two English test booklets, two Math test booklets, scoring software.

PURCHASED SEPARATELY: manual, $30; package of 25 answer sheets, $75; Package of 10 Math test booklets form A, $50 (same for Math form B and both forms of the English test booklets).

COUNSELEE MATERIALS: Answer sheets, one per evaluee, accommodate both Math and English test responses. Booklets are reusable.

Additional Comments of Interest to Users: It is not necessary to use both Math and English tests; if user is interested in either math or English only, appropriate scoring and reporting are included. Or, users may administer the English test one day and the Math test another time, or vice versa.

Published Reviews of the Instrument in the Last 15 Years:

Ellen, A. S. (2005) Review of Valpar Test of Essential Skills. In R.A Spies & B.S. Plake, (Eds.). *The sixteenth mental measurements yearbook*. Lincoln, NE: Buros Institute of Mental Measurements, The University of Nebraska.

Powell, S. & Bulter, M. (2005) Review of Valpar Test of Essential Skills. In R.A Spies & B.S. Plake, (Eds.). *The sixteenth mental measurements yearbook*. Lincoln, NE: Buros Institute of Mental Measurements, The University of Nebraska.

Reviewed by:[1]

Michelle A. Butler
United States Air Force Academy

Shawn Powell
University of Northern Colorado

Description

The Valpar Test of Essential Skills in English and Math (VTES) assesses "important basic English and math skills required of workers in most occupations or training programs" (Christopherson & Swartz, 1998, p. 1). It is a criterion-referenced, timed test of English and mathematics skills linked to the Department of Labor's (DOL) General Levels of Educational Development (GED) and job standards from the *Dictionary of Occupational Titles* (U.S. Department of Labor, 1991). Through this comparison, VTES results are intended to represent an individual's capability to successfully perform various occupations.

The VTES was developed to assess basic English and mathematics skills to assist organizations in making occupational decisions. It measures academic skills required for the majority of occupations contained in the *Dictionary of Occupational Titles*. The VTES was designed to measure occupational skills related to GED mathematics levels 1 to 4 and GED language levels 2 to 4. It has two forms, A and B, and is intended to be administered to individuals 15 years of age and older.

The VTES assesses the following areas: vocabulary, spelling, grammar/usage, reading, mathematics computation, and mathematics usage. Scores in the form of GED levels and scholastic grade levels are provided for each area the VTES evaluates. Additionally, a total English score and a total mathematics score are given. Both VTES versions use multiple-choice formats with test items arranged from easy to more difficult.

The English tests consist of 50 items designed to measure language skills commonly taught in grades 6 to 10. The vocabulary test includes 10 synonym knowledge items, 10 items that require a synonym to be chosen to complete a short sentence, and five items measuring antonym knowledge. The spelling section consists of five items. The grammar/usage section consists of 10 items, and the reading comprehension section has 10 items.

The mathematics test has 41 items. These items include 20 mathematics computation items and 21 mathematics usage items. The mathematics computation section is intended to evaluate arithmetic skills routinely taught in grades 4 to 8. The mathematics usage section is designed to assess arithmetic skills taught in grades 4 to 10+.

Use in Counseling

The VTES can be used to assist clients make career decisions. Organizations can use it to assist in making employment selection, training, and placement decisions. Clients

---

[1] Portions of this review are adapted, by permission, from the authors' original review in the *Sixteenth Mental Measurements Yearbook*.

who complete the VTES can obtain information regarding future employment choices and suitable vocational training options. As it is linked to the DOL's job standards, it provides realistic information regarding suitable occupations and can be used for career counseling.

The VTES can be administered by anyone who can serve as a test proctor. Interpretation of the VTES report requires specific training in testing and knowledge of the VTES, GED levels, scholastic grade levels, and the *Dictionary of Occupational Titles* (DOL, 1991).

Computer-Based and/or Online Version

Although the VTES does not have an online or computer-based version, it must be computer scored. A software program produces a computer-generated report containing scores an individual achieves and occupational information related to the Department of Labor's GED levels in English and mathematics. The software program required to score the VTES is easy to install and has a straightforward technical manual. Technical support from Valpar is readily available.

Technical Considerations

The VTES manual indicates two different samples were used for its reliability and validity studies. One sample had 50 participants and the other had 228 participants. The larger sample's African-American/Black representation was 31%, compared to 12.3% African-American/Black representation in the U.S. population (U.S. Census Bureau, 2000). The smaller sample's Hispanic representation was 32%, compared to 12.5% Hispanic representation reported in the 2000 census. The larger sample was drawn from six states (i.e., Florida, Indiana, Missouri, Oklahoma, South Dakota, and Texas).

For internal consistency the K-R 20 reliability coefficient formula was used. The correlations for the English sections range from .56 to .71. Internal consistency for forms A and B's total English score is .95. The mathematics sections' internal consistency ranges from .61 to .83, and the total mathematics scores internal consistency are .88 for Form A and .82 for Form B. The reliability correlations for alternate forms range from .40 to .78. Reported means for Forms A and B are similar with small standard deviations suggesting both forms produce similar results. As the VTES is criterion referenced, evidence of its reliability is also presented in the form of P and agreement indexes. The VTES P indexes range from .76 to 1.00. The VTES agreement indexes show a high level of concurrence.

In developing the VTES, efforts were taken to have the content of the tests represent typical school curriculum. To accomplish this goal, VTES items were developed based on samples of English and mathematics educational materials from eight states (i.e., Alabama, Arizona, California, Florida, Kansas, New York, North Carolina, and Texas). The VTES authors further addressed content validity by following a thorough process for choosing words for the vocabulary portions that adequately reflected the grade level content they were developed to measure. This procedure involved making alphabetical grade level lists of "several thousand potentially suitable words" (Christopherson & Swartz, 1998, p. 24) from The Living Word Vocabulary (Dale & O'Rourke, 1976). Potential subject words paired with their synonyms or antonyms and distractors were randomly selected from these grade-level lists. Spelling test items were selected from the same word lists used for the vocabulary tests. The VTES grammar or language usage items were selected to measure the ability to discern various types of errors in capitalization or sentence construction. To measure reading comprehension, 10 short passages were chosen using two items per grade level from grades 6 to 10.

The VTES mathematics test items were specifically selected to measure arithmetic skills directly related to the DOL's GED levels. The mathematics computation items are intended to correspond to skills taught in grades 4 to 8 and GED levels 1 to 2+. These items range from adding whole numbers without carryover to dividing fractions. The mathematics usage items were developed to represent skills ranging from single-step whole number addition to simple trigonometry ordinarily taught in grades 4 to 10+ and GED levels 2 to 4+. Content validity correlations between reported years of education and obtained VTES scores range from .07 to .64.

Evidence of construct validity for the VTES is provided through comparisons of the VTES to other educational tests. However, it should be noted these comparisons reflect data collected over the course of a year. Criterion validity is not discussed.

Overall Critique

The VTES offers a quick assessment of an individual's basic English and mathematics skills. Its intended use in making occupational decisions is readily apparent as the skills it measures are linked to DOL's job standards. It is easy to administer, score, and interpret and it can be given in either individual or group settings. While the VTES is purportedly linked to DOL occupational standards, its psychometric properties are problematic. In particular, this test requires an adequate normative group and evidence of criterion validity.

The first concern is the absence of a large normative group representative of the U.S. population. For reliability and validity purposes, two samples are reported. However, due to their small sizes, both samples are inadequate. Additionally, neither sample reflects the current U.S. population's racial/ethnic demographics.

The second concern is the lack of criterion validity data comparing VTES results to actual job performance. The method in which construct validity data was obtained is also troubling. The comparisons of the VTES to other educational achievement tests are based on test results accumulated over a year. This is problematic as the VTES measures basic academic skills, and a person's level of achievement would be expected to change over the course of a year, especially for individuals involved in training programs.

The content of the VTES English tests is limited as it only reflects curriculum materials from eight states, thus the English skills being tested are especially problematic. The mathematics portion of the VTES is more robust in this regard as schools across the U.S. tend to follow similar curriculums for mathematics instruction compared to language arts. The mathematics tests appear to have a good representation of various problems to assess a person's skill level.

Nonetheless, as a criterion-referenced test linked to the DOL occupational standards, the VTES offers a solid addition to the assessment of job related academic skills. However, it is advised that the counselor be mindful of the limitations of the psychometric properties at the current time.

References

Christopherson, B. B., & Swartz, A. (1998). *Valpar Test of Essential Skills in English and Math.* Tucson, AZ: Valpar International Corporation.

Dale, E., & O'Rourke, J. (1976). *The living word vocabulary.* Chicago: World Book–Childcraft International. Inc.

U.S. Department of Labor, Employment, and Training Administration. (1991). *Dictionary of occupational titles,* (4th rev. ed.). Washington DC: U.S. Government Printing Office.

U.S. Census Bureau. (2000). *Census 2000.* Retrieved November 20, 2003, from http://factfinder. census.gov/servlet/QTTable?ds_name=DEC_2000_SF1_U&geo_id=01000US&qr_name=DEC_2000_SF1_U_DP1.

CHAPTER 13

ADDITIONAL
CAREER ASSESSMENT
INSTRUMENTS

- Multiple Aptitude, Achievement, and Comprehensive Measures

- Specific Aptitude and Achievement Measures

- Interest Instruments

- Measures of Work Values, Satisfaction, and Environments

- Card Sorts

- Career Development/Maturity Measures

- Personality Measures

- Instruments for Special Populations

CHAPTER 13

ADDITIONAL CAREER ASSESSMENT INSTRUMENTS[1]

Chris Wood
Department of Counseling
& School Psychology
College of Education
Seattle University

Edwin A. Whitfield
Associate Director – Retired
Office of Supportive Learning Environments
Office of Assessment
Ohio Department of Education

Brenda Gerhardt
Sibyl Cato
Doctoral Students
The Ohio State University

In previous chapters of this book, 71 major career assessment instruments are described and reviewed. In this chapter, additional instruments are briefly described and essential information such as publisher, date of publication, intended populations, and published reviews is provided. The entries for each instrument are grouped into logical categories that are parallel, but are not identical to, those used to organize the major instrument reviews. However, there are instruments not included that may be useful for some career assessment applications. For example, types of instruments usually not included are those which primarily assess educational achievement, general intelligence, specific aptitude measures without broad applications, and abnormal personality and adjustment. Also, although each instrument is included under only one category, in many cases it can be argued that it could also fit into one or more other categories. The User's Matrix, provided in Appendix D, attempts to reflect this overlap of categories.

---

[1] This chapter is a continuation and update of work done in previous editions of this Guide by Jerome T. Kapes and Linda Martinez at Texas A &M University and Tammi Vacha-Haase at Colorado State University.

To facilitate the use of this chapter, the following key to the categories of information presented is provided:

- **Type of Instrument.** The categories used to organize the instruments in the order presented are –

  a. Multiple Aptitude, Achievement, and Comprehensive Measures
  b. Specific Aptitude and Achievement Measures
  c. Interest Instruments
  d. Measures of Work Values, Satisfaction, and Environments
  e. Card Sorts
  f. Career Development/Maturity Measures
  g. Personality Measures
  h. Instruments for Special Populations

- **Name.** The name of the instrument is listed first in boldface print. Common acronyms, when used, are provided in parenthesis immediately following the name.

- **Publisher.** Only the name of the publisher is provided. The addresses and, when available, phone numbers, e-mail addresses, and Web page of the publishers are listed in Appendix B. Additional information about the instruments can be obtained by contacting the publisher.

- **Date.** The date given refers to the initial date the instrument was published and/ or when it was last revised. A range of dates, (e.g., 1960-1993) signifies ongoing development and revision of the instrument during that time span. "No Date" indicates that the date of publication was unavailable.

- **Population.** The population refers to the group or groups of individuals for whom the publisher indicates the instrument is appropriate.

- **References.** Several of the major sources of instrument reviews are cited in an abbreviated form. An annotated bibliography of each source is presented in Appendix A. The key to the abbreviations is as follows.

  a. CG refers to *A Counselor's Guide to Vocational Guidance Instruments* – First Edition (1), *A Counselor's Guide to Career Assessment Instruments* – Second Edition, (2), *A Counselor's Guide to Career Assessment Instruments* – Third Edition, (3), or *A Counselor's Guide to Career Assessment Instruments* – Fourth Edition (4).

  b. MY refers to the *Mental Measurements Yearbooks.* The number immediately following denotes the volume number The number following the colon refers to the test number.

c. TC is the abbreviation for *Test Critiques.* The number following the colon is the page number.

d. TP5, or TP6 for example, are the abbreviation for *Tests in Print V* or *VI.* The number following the colon is the test number.

e. T3 or T4 is the abbreviation for Tests-Third or Fourth Edition. The number following the colon is the page number.

f. AT:98 refers to *Assessment for Transitions Planning: A Guide for Special Education Teachers and Related Service Personnel* (Clark, 1998).

g. MG and MD refer to *Measurement and Evaluation in Guidance* and *Measurement and Evaluation in Counseling and Development,* respectively. Now published by the Association for Assessment in Counseling and Education (AACE) The number following the colon refers to the month and year of the issue in which the review is found (e.g., 10/92 denotes October, 1992).

h. B:93 refers to *Vocational Evaluation Systems and Software: A consumer's Guide* (Brown et al., 1993).

- **Brief Description.** This section provides an overview of what is measured and includes the titles of some of the scales associated with each instrument. Additional comments are included for some instruments (e.g., to indicate a major use, special reports or support materials available, or training required for administration).

A. MULTIPLE APTITUDE, ACHIEVEMENT, AND COMPREHENSIVE MEASURES

Name of Test/Publisher/Date/Population	Reference(s)	Brief Description
ACCU Vision – Workplace Success Skills Learning Resources http://www.learning-resources.com/index.cfm 1990 - 1999 High School to Adults		Designed to identify & measure workplace skills. Consists of 5 video modules divided into the following sections: Interpersonal Skills, Listening, Structuring Work Activities, Trainability, & Graphs & Charts. "Keyed to the SCANS foundational skills for entry level positions." Individual or group administration.
Activity Vector Analysis (AVA) Bizet Human Asset Management http://www.bizet.com/ 1948 - 1994 Prospective Employees		Designed to determine if an individual is a match for the job. Consists of 5 separate parts: Activity Vector Analysis, Job Rating Scale, Job Expectations, Behaviorally Based Interview Questions, & Job Model. Paper/Pencil or Computer administered; must be interpreted by a certified person.
Basic Skills Locator Test (BSLT) Piney Mountain Press http://www.pineymountain.com/ 1998 Age 15 to Adults	TP5:259	Designed to assess math & language skill levels of individuals functioning at the 12th grade level or below. Results provided in terms of GED & grade levels. Results correlated to DOL job classifications, OOH, DOT, & GOE. Computer scored, machine scored, or publisher scored. Computer version available.
Career and Vocational Form of the SOI-LA Basic Test SOI Systems http://www.soisystems.com/ 1975 Adolescents to Adults	T3:787	Measures 24 cognitive abilities which predict career & vocational options. Consists of subtests taken from the SOI-LA Basic Test. Paper/pencil tests. Suitable for groups. Instructions for self-administration. Computer analysis available.
Career IQ and Interest Test (CIQIT) Advantage Learning Solutions http://advantagelearningsolutions.com/ 1997 Age 13 to Adults		Assists individuals in identifying possible job choices. Consists of a CD-ROM that includes: vocational aptitude test, interest measure, & recent OOH information. Aptitude survey measures 6 factors such as: general ability & manual dexterity. Interest schedule measures 12 factors such as: artistic & nature.
Career Profile Assessment LIFECORP http://www.life-corp.com/ 1998 Junior and Senior High School		Assesses 10 aptitudes & 12 interests using a computer-based system. Aptitudes include: reasoning, mathematics, language, learning, numerical, spatial, & color discrimination. Interest assessment covers the 12 GOE categories. Output tied to DOT Worker Qualification Profile & New Concepts career information.
Career Programs Assessment Test (CPAT) ACT, Inc. http://www.act.org/ 1981 - 1994 Adults	T4:189	Measures both the entry-level & academic skills important to success in educational programs offered by career schools, colleges & other post-secondary institutions. Basic skills test include: Language, Reading, & Numerical.
Career Technical Assistance Program (C-Tap) WestEd http://www.wested.org/cs/we/print/docs/we/home.htm 1998 Grade 9 to Adults		Designed to assist students in learning/refining career-technical skills & to assess readiness for entry-level jobs and/or post-secondary training. Consists of 3 parts: portfolio, project, & written scenario. Referenced to standards in career areas, such as: agriculture, business, & health careers.
COIN Basic Skills and Career Interest Survey COIN Educational Products http://www.coinedu.com/ 1996 High School to Adults		Provides aptitude and interest information for career planning. Basic skills component uses Wonderlic Basic Skills Test to assess math & language skills used in the workplace. Survey assesses activities in 7 areas of interest. Scores are combined & linked to matching occupations & reported in GED levels.
Comprehensive Ability Battery (CAB) Institute for Personality and Ability Testing (IPAT) http://www.ipat.com/ 1975 - 1982 Grade 10 to Adults	MY9:255 MY8:484 TP7:647 TP5:644 T4:486	Consists of 4 test booklets containing 20 subtests, each designed to measure a primary ability factor related to performance in industrial settings. Examples of scores reported are: verbal & numerical ability, clerical speed & accuracy, memory span, etc.
Employee Aptitude Survey (EAS) Psychological Services PSI http://corporate.psionline.com/ 1952 - 1995 Adults	CG3 TP7: 937 MY14:137 MY6:769 MY5:607 TP5:937 T4:488	Designed as a diagnostic tool for employee selection & vocational guidance. Consists of 10 ability tests such as: Verbal Comprehension, Numerical Ability, Space Visualization, Visual Speed & Accuracy, Manual Speed & Accuracy, & Symbolic Reasoning. Machine or hand scored.

Name of Test/Publisher/Date/Population	Reference(s)	Brief Description
Flanagan Aptitude Classification Test (FACT) Vangent, Inc. http://www.vangent.com/ 1951 - 1994 High School to Adults, Prospective Employees	MY7:675 TP7:1033 TP5:1042 T4:506	Designed to predict success in various occupational fields via composite occupational scores. Consists of 16 subtests such as: inspection, coding, memory, precision, assembly, scales, coordination, judgment & comprehension, arithmetic, patterns, components, tables, etc.
Flanagan Industrial Tests (FIT) Vangent, Inc. http://www.vangent.com/ 1960 - 1996 Adults	MY8:981 TC2:282 TP7:1034 TP5:1043 T4:506	Measures 18 aptitudes or job tasks involved in supervisory, technical, office, skilled, & entry-level job demands. Designed for selection, placement, reassignment, or reclassification of employees.
Hay Aptitude Test Battery Wonderlic, Inc. http://www.wonderlic.com/ 1947 - 1997 Adults	MY12:179 MY9:470 TP7:1153 TP5:1180 T4:600	Assesses clerical & numerical aptitude through 4 paper/pencil tests. Tests include: warm-up (which is not scored), number perception, name finding, & number series completion. Designed to aid in the selection of clerical workers. Hand scored.
Industrial Reading Test (IRT) Harcourt Assessment, Inc. http://www.harcourtassessment.com/ 1976 – 1978 Grade 10 to Adults	MY9:504 TP7:1233 TP5:1256 T4:507	Contains 9 readings passages & 38 test items on work-relevant topics to assess reading comprehension. Some passages depict sections of technical manual; others are written in the form of company memoranda. All passages are at the secondary reading level.
IPI Aptitude-Intelligence Test Series Industrial Psychology International (IPI) http://www.metritech.com/IPI/ipi_home.htm 1982 - 1986 Adults	TC2:363 TP5:1323 T4:579	Consists of various aptitude & personality tests such as: dexterity, blocks, parts, numbers, tools, judgement, fluency, sales, etc. Aids in employee selection in 28 job fields such as: computer programmer, dental technician, sales, clerk, etc.
Job Skills Tests (See also Basic Skills Tests) Ramsay Corporation http://www.ramsaycorp.com/ 1981 - 1991 Job Applicants and Industrial Workers	MY9:551 TP5:1353	Designed to measure abilities expected of all job applicants, such as reading, arithmetic, measurement, inspection, process monitoring, problem solving, and checking accuracy.
LOMASelect:Entry Level (formerly Job Effectiveness Prediction System; JEPS) Life Office Management Association http://www.loma.org/ 1986 Adults	T4:627	Paper/pencil test which measures a variety of skills required for a wide range of clerical & technical/professional positions. Examples of subtests include: Numerical Ability, Mathematical Skill, Spelling, etc. Used for selection/place-ment of employees in insurance companies.
Making a Terrific Career Happen (MATCH) EdITS http://www.edits.net Middle to High School		MATCH is a self-evaluation questionnaire that uses student's interests, abilities, and values to find careers. Scores help to find sample jobs, lists of classes and college majors, related skills and abilities, and activities useful for experience in those jobs.
Multidimensional Aptitude Battery (MAB) MAB II Sigma Assessment Systems http://www.sigmaassessmentsystems.com/ 1982 - 1999 Grade 10 to Adults	MY10:202 TC2:501 TP7:1688 TP5:1731 T4:45	Assesses aptitudes & intelligence through 5 verbal & 5 performance subtests. Yields a profile of scores. Can be individually or group administered using paper/pencil or IBM compatible disk. Mail-in scoring generates narrative report.
NOCTI Occupational Competency Tests National Occupational Competency Testing Institute http://www.nocti.org/ 1986 Students in Vocational and Technical Programs	TP5:1792	Multitude of competency tests in 3 categories: Experienced Workers, Industrial Assessments, Job Ready Assessments. Occupations include: Accounting, Appliance Repair, Carpentry, Commercial Art, Die Making, Electronics Technology, Mechanical, Medical Assistant, Pipefitter, Retail Trades, & many more.
Professional Employment Test Psychological Service PSI http://corporate.psionline.com/ 1986 - 1988 Potential Employees	MY12:312 TP7:2038 TP5:2072 T4:497	Assesses reading comprehension, reasoning, quantitative problem solving, & data interpretation. Consists of 40 items and yields one total score. Provides a sample item for each area with an explanation of the correct response. Individual or group administration.

Name of Test/Publisher/Date/Population	Reference(s)	Brief Description
PSI Basic Skills Test (BST) Psychological Services, Inc. http://corporate.psionline.com/ 1982-1986 Potential Employees	CG4 MY9: 1010 T5:2105	To assess abilities and skills that are important for successful performance in clerical, administrative and customer service jobs.
Revised Beta Examination-Third Edition (BETA-III) Harcourt Assessment, Inc. http://www.harcourtassessment.com/ 1931 - 1999 Adults	MY9:1044 TP5:2212 T4:498	Assesses mental abilities in individuals having limited or no reading skills. Consists of 6 tests: mazes, coding, paper form boards, picture completion, clerical checking, & picture absurdities. Can be group administered. Available in Spanish.
Scholastic Level Exam (SLE) Wonderlic, Inc. http://www.wonderlic.com/ 1937 - 1988 Age 15 to Adults	MY14:421	A 50 question, 12 minute timed test of cognitive ability or aptitude for learning. Measures students' ability to understand instructions, keep up with classroom pace, solve problems & use occupational training on the job.
Schubert General Ability Battery (GAB) Slosson Educational Publications, Inc. http://www.slosson.com/ 1986 Grade 10 to Adults	MY7:386 TC3:579 TP7: 2264 TP5:2324 T4:47	Assesses intellectual abilities including verbal, arithmetic, & syllogistic measures of reasoning ability. The 4 subtests are designed to indicate individuals' levels of success and/or placement in school, college, & business.
Success Skills 2000 Employment Technologies Corp. http://www.etc-easy.com/ 1991 - 1997 High School to Adults		A video-based, computer-scored test for corporate recruiting & development of entry-level professionals in 4 major categories: engineering, professional/finance, supervision, & sales & marketing. Measures critical skills in 3 broad categories: applied problem solving, interpersonal effectiveness, & accountability.
Technical Test Battery (TTB) SHLAmericas http://www.shl.com/shl/americas 1992 Adults	T4:638 TP7: 2264	Consists of 4 separate instruments: Mechanical Comprehension designed to assess understanding of basic mechanical principles, Numerical Computation designed to assess numerical ability in a technical setting, Spatial Recognition to measure spatial ability, & Visual Estimation of spatial perception.
Training House Assessment Kit The Richardson Co. Training Media http://www.rctm.com/ 2000 Supervisors and Managers		Designed to offer smaller organizations a wide range of reproducible assessments for managers to use to identify & target development needs. Consists of 25 instruments such as: Proficiency Assessment Report, Self-Awareness Profile, Dealing with Groups, The Apt Inventory, & Analytical Thinking Test.
Valpar Aviator Valpar International http://www.valparint.com/ 1998 Age 15 to Adults		Computerized instrument that measures GED Reasoning, Math, & Language. Tests 7 aptitude factors such as: general learning ability, verbal, numerical, & spatial perception. Includes 2 pictorial interest surveys. Matches the interest & aptitude results with its internal occupational database. Computer administered.
Valpar Pro 3000 Valpar International http://www.valparint.com/ 1999 Age 15 to Adults		Windows based version of Valpar's System 2000 modular software package. Consists of a required system manager & optional modules, such as: Career Planner, Compass (computerized assessment), Compass Lite (without work samples), DOT, OOH, & Spatial/Nonverbal assessment.
Vocational Evaluation System (See Career Profile Assessment) LIFECORP http://www.life-corp.com/ 1971 - 1997 Middle School to Adults		Audiovisual programs that assess individual's interest & ability for performing routine tasks. Activities encompass a number of job titles such as: Air Conditioning & Refrigeration, Cook & Baker, Diesel Engine Repair, Machine Trades, Drafting, & Masonry. Formerly known as the Singer Evaluation System.
VOC-TECH Quick Screener (VTQS) CFKR Career Materials http://www.cfkr.com/ 1984 - 1990 Grade 10 to Adults	MY12:411 TP5:2822	A screening tool that assesses career aptitudes, interest, & training plans. Aids in matching career goals with jobs, & identifies job options & training. Designed for non-college bound persons. Computer version available.

Name of Test/Publisher/Date/Population	Reference(s)	Brief Description
V-TECS Assessments Vocational-Technical Education Consortium of States http://www.v-tecs.org/ 1986 - 1999 High School to Adults		V-TECS is a consortium of agencies that provide occupational skills training in business/industry, education, & the military. Criterion-referenced item banks for 31 occupations are available, consisting of 3 types of items: written, performance & scenario. Tests tied to curriculum materials.
Watson-Glaser Critical Thinking Appraisal (WGCTA) Harcourt Assessment, Inc. http://www.harcourtassessment.com/ 1942 - 1994 Adults	MY13:358 T4:227 TC3:682 TP5:2857 TP7: 2742	Measures 5 aspects of critical thinking: drawing sound inferences, recognizing assumptions, deductive reasoning, drawing conclusions, & evaluating arguments. The 80 items contain content that may be controversial, thereby providing a measure of the extent of bias effect on the ability to think critically.
Wesman Personnel Classification Test (PCT) Harcourt Assessment, Inc. http://www.harcourtassessment.com/ 1946 - 1965 Adults	MY7:400 TC3:711 TP7: 2764 TP5:2871 T4:500	Measures 2 major aspects of mental ability: verbal reasoning & numerical ability. Verbal items are analogies & numerical items include basic math skills & understanding of quantitative relationships. Aids in the selection of sales people & middle management personnel.
Wonderlic Personnel Test Wonderlic, Inc http://www.wonderlic.com/ 1939 - 1998 Adults	MY14: 421 MY11:475 TC1:769 TP7: 2793 TP5:2899 T4:500	Yields a single score that predicts job applicants' ability to learn on the job, understand directions, innovations, & routine tolerance. Available in 6 equivalent forms & 13 languages. Individually or group administered by a trained clerk. Includes recommended cut-off scores for various occupations.
Workplace Skills Survey MetriTech http://www.metritech.com/Metritech/met_home.htm 1999 High School to Adult Employees		The Workplace Skills Survey provides information on basic work ethics and employment skills. Test takers respond to questions related to workplace scenarios and common business information. Results are on six scales: Communication, Adapting to Change, Problem Solving, Work Ethics, Technological Literacy, and Teamwork.

B. SPECIFIC APTITUDE AND ACHIEVEMENT MEASURES

Name of Test/Publisher/Date/Population	Reference(s)	Brief Description
Bennett Hand Tool Dexterity Test (BHTDT) Harcourt Assessment http://harcourtassessment.com 1981 High School to Adults		Designed to measure manual dexterity & gross motor coordination. Subject removes 12 bolts from one vertical board & places them on another. Task requires the use of four tools: two open end wrenches, one adjustable wrench, & one screwdriver.
Bennett Mechanical Comprehension Test (BMCT) Harcourt Assessment http://harcourtassessment.com 1940 - 1994 Adults	MY16:31 MY11:41 TC8:4 TP7:312 TP5:302 T4:484	Assesses ability to understand physical & mechanical principles. The 68 test items can be group administered by company personnel or by optional tape recordings. Two equivalent forms available. Correlates score with DOT job categories.
Career and Life Explorer, Second Edition JIST Publishing, Inc. http://www.jist.com 2007 Grades 6-10		Designed to help students explore interests, hobbies, talents and values. Students review over 250 occupations from the Occupational Outlook Handbook job titles arranged in six categories. The interest inventory portion is based on the RIASEC occupational coding system.
Clerical Abilities Battery (CAB) Harcourt Assessment http://harcourtassessment.com 1985 - 1987 Adults	MY11:71 TP7:532 TP5:532 T4:596	Measures filing, proofreading, & mathematical skills. Tests ability to copy & compare information, use tables, & reason with numbers. The 7 tests can be administered separately or as a total battery. Available in 2 forms: A-industry, B-schools.

Name of Test/Publisher/Date/Population	Reference(s)	Brief Description
Clerical Skills Test Series Walden Personnel Testing and Training http://www.waldentesting.com 1990 Adults	MY16:51 TP7:537 T4:597	Designed to measure clerical skills. A series of tests that measures proficiency in 20 areas such as: attention to detail, problem solving, spelling, alphabetizing & filing, PC graphics, bookkeeping, electronic knowledge, & mechanical com-pre-hension. Hand scored.
Computer Operator Aptitude Battery (COAB) Vangent, Inc. http://www.vangent-hcm.com 1973 - 1974 Computer Operator Applicants and Trainees	TP7:672 TP5:669 T4:614	Consists of 3 subtests: sequence recognition, format checking, & logical thinking. Scores from subtests combine to predict job performance of computer operators & to identify those applicants with the potential to succeed as a computer operator.
Computer Programmer Aptitude Battery (CPAB) Vangent, Inc. http://www.vangent-hcm.com 1964 - 1993 Computer Programmer Trainees	TP7:673 MY11:85 TP5:670 T4:614	Designed to assess an individual's potential to succeed as a computer programmer. Consists of 5 aptitude subtests: verbal meaning, reasoning, letter series, number ability, & diagramming. Oriented for both computer-experienced & inexperienced students.
Crawford Small Parts Dexterity Test (CSPDT) Harcourt Assessment http://harcourtassessment.com 1946 - 1981 High School to Adults	MY5:871 TP7:725 TP5:722 T4:632	Measures eye-hand coordination & fine finger dexterity in two parts. Part I-Subject uses tweezers to insert pins in close-fitting holes, & then places collars on the pins. Part II-Subject places small screws in holes by hand, & then uses a screwdriver to screw them down.
Customer Service Skills Assessment Program Employment Technologies http://www.etc-easy.com/ 1989 - 1997 High School to Adults		A video-based, computer scored diagnostic system that focuses on the key functions of the customer service job. Includes a series of multiple choice questions that are job-relevant & that provide a standardized assessment of a candidate's ability to do the job.
Dvorine Color Vision Test Harcourt Assessment http://harcourtassessment.com 1944 - 1958 General Population	TP7:864 TP5:862 MY6:955 T4:476	Designed to identify defective color vision. Consists of 2 parts that determine type & degree of vision defect. Each plate features a design of colored dots against a background of contrasting dots which appear shapeless to the colorblind.
General Clerical Test (GCT) Harcourt Assessment http://harcourtassessment.com 1944 - 1988 Adults	MY12:158 TC3:296 TP7:1065 TP5:1078 T4:599	Assesses abilities needed for many higher level administrative & paraprofessional positions. Consists of 9 tests which yield 3 ability scores: clerical speed & accuracy, numerical ability, & verbal ability.
Group Test of Musical Ability NFER-Nelson Publishing Co., Ltd (England) http://www.assessmentcentre.com 1988 Ages 7 - 14	MY12:173 TP7:1132	Designed to measure musical ability. Consists of 2 tests: a 24 item Pitch Test requiring the respondent to identify the higher of 2 notes & a 10 item Pulse Test requiring the respondent to compute number of pulses in a series of tempos. All test items & directions are on a cassette tape.
Intuitive Mechanics Vangent, Inc. http://www.vangent-hcm.com 1956 - 1984 Adults	MY9:523 T4:633 TP7:1271 TP5:1299	Paper/pencil test that measures the ability to understand mechanical relationships or to visualize internal movement in a mechanical system. Used in vocational counseling or personnel selection to identify individuals with high mechanical interest & ability.
Job Skills PESCO, Inc. http://www.pesco.org 1998 Prospective Employees		Designed to measure individual's proficiency with various software applications. Consists of 50 tests such as: Word, Access, Medical Secretary, Excel, Word Perfect, & Internet Basics. Three levels of testing in every standard test: basic, intermediate, & advanced skills. Companion to PESCO 2001 System.
Mechanical Aptitudes Vangent, Inc. http://www.vangent-hcm.com 1947 - 1996 Grade 12 to Adults	T4:637	Measures ability to learn mechanical skills in 3 areas: mechanical knowledge, space relations, & shop arithmetic. Designed for assistance in selection of entry-level applicants & trainees.
Mechanical Movements Vangent, Inc. http://www.vangent-hcm.com 1984 Adults	T3:1067 TP7:1582 TP5:1636	Measures finger dexterity, eye-hand coordination, & visualization abilities required in office & factory tasks. May also be used by special educators to evaluate motor skills. Contains 7 subtests which can be used separately or in combination.

Name of Test/Publisher/Date/Population	Reference(s)	Brief Description
Minnesota Clerical Test (MCT) Harcourt Assessment http://harcourtassessment.com 1933 - 1979 Clerical Applicants	MY9:713 MY6:1040 TP7:1649 TP5:1693 T4:603	Designed to measure clerical aptitude. Focus is on perceptual speed & accuracy in 2 tasks: name comparison & number comparison. Each part consists of 100 pairs that the subject must identify as identical or dissimilar. Screens entry-level positions such as typists, clerks, etc.
Minnesota Paper Form Board-Revised The Psychological Corporation http://harcourtassessment.com 1970 - 1995 Adults	MY9:1045 TP5:2217 T4:637	Consists of 64 two-dimensional diagrams which assess spatial perception & mechanical-spatial ability as they relate to artistic & mechanical aptitudes. Aids in employee selection for occupations such as drafting, engineering, & electrical work.
Minnesota Rate of Manipulation Test (MRMT) American Guidance Service/Pearson http://ags.pearsonassessments.com 1931 - 1969 Grade 7 to Adults	MY7:1046 MY6:1077 TP5:1700 T4:635	Measures arm-hand dexterity using a form board with 60 round holes & 60 cylinders that fit into the holes. Consists of 5 different manipulative activities: placing, turning, displacing, one-hand turning, & two-hand turning. Also provides norms & instructions for the blind.
Minnesota Spatial Relations Test (MSRT) American Guidance Service/Pearson http://ags.pearsonassessments.com 1930 - 1979 Grade 10 to Adults	MY9:723 TP5:1703 T4:478	Assesses spatial visualization ability & the ability to manipulate three-dimensional objects. This timed test consists of the transfer of blocks from one board to their proper place in the connected board as quickly as possible.
Musical Aptitude Profile The Riverside Publishing Co. http://www.riverpub.com 1965 - 1995 Grades 4 - 12	MY12:251 MY16:157 TP7:1707 TP5:1752	Designed to measure an individual's musical aptitude. Assesses 3 basic factors: tonal, rhythmic, & expressive/aesthetic. Yields 11 scores such as: melody, har-mony, tempo, meter, balance, & style. Directions & testing items are admini-stered via an audiocassette tape.
O'Conner Finger Dexterity Test Lafayette Instrument Company http://www.lafayetteinstrument.com 1920 - 1926 Age 14 to Adults	MY6:1078 T3:1069	Designed to measure motor coordination, & finger & manual dexterity. Consists of plate containing 100 holes arranged in 10 rows. Subject's task is to insert small metal pins, in groups of three, as rapidly as possible.
O'Conner Tweezer Dexterity Test Lafayette Instrument Company http://www.lafayetteinstrument.com 1920 - 1928 Age 14 to Adults	MY6:1079 T3:1069	Designed to measure motor coordination, & finger & manual dexterity. Consists of plate containing 100 holes arranged in 10 rows. Subject's task is to insert small metal pins, one by one, into each of the holes, using metal tweezers.
Office Skills Test Vangent, Inc. http://www.vangent-hcm.com 1977 - 1984 Entry Level Applicants in the Business Field	MY9:857 TP7: 1789 TP5:1836 T4:603	Designed to measure clerical ability of entry level job applicants via 12 subtests: checking, coding, filing, form completion, grammar, numerical, oral directional, punctuation, reading comprehension, spelling, typing, & vocabulary.
Pennsylvania Bi-Manual Worksample American Guidance Service http://ags.pearsonassessments.com 1943 - 1945 Age 16 to 39	T4:635	Measures manual dexterity & eye-hand coordination in two parts: Assembly requires manually assembling bolts & nuts, & then placing them in a hole in the board, & Disassembly-requires removing the assemblies from the hole, taking them apart, & returning the parts to their bins.
Perceptual Speed Vangent, Inc. http://www.vangent-hcm.com 1987 Adults	T4:604 TP7:1884 MY15:185	Measures the ability to quickly identify similarities & differences in visual configuration. This 5 minute timed test can be used to aid in selecting personnel for occupations requiring rapid perception of inaccuracies in written material, numbers, or diagrams.
Pictorial Reasoning Test (PRT) Vangent, Inc. http://www.vangent-hcm.com 1967 - 1973 Age 14 to Adults	T4:498	Provides a general measure of the learning potential of individuals from diverse backgrounds with reading difficulties. Helpful in identifying an individual's potential for training & employment.
Purdue Pegboard Vangent, Inc. http://www.vangent-hcm.com 1941 - 1992 Grade 9 to Adults	TP7:2093 TP5:2125 T4:514	Measures gross movement of hands, fingers, & arms, & tip of finger dexterity. Consists of pegboard containing 2 rows of 25 holes into which pins are inserted individually with the right hand, left hand, & both hands.

Name of Test/Publisher/Date/Population	Reference(s)	Brief Description
Short Employment Tests (SET) The Psychological Corporation http://harcourtassessment.com 1972 - 1993 Adults	MY13:287 T4:611 TP7:2332 TP5:2406	Designed to measure verbal, numerical, & clerical aptitudes via 3 tasks: recognize synonyms, perform arithmetic computations, & locate proper names in an alphabetical list & assign codes to the amount associated with each name.
Short Tests of Clerical Ability (STCA) Vangent, Inc. http://www.vangent-hcm.com 1959 - 1997 Applicants for Office Positions	MY13:287 MY8:1039 TP7:2333 TP5:2408 T4:611	Measures 7 clerical aptitudes & abilities: arithmetic, business vocabulary, checking, coding, directions-oral & written, filing, & language. Useful for selection & placement in various office jobs such as: secretary, stenographer, office clerk, etc.
Space Relations (Paper Puzzles) Vangent, Inc. http://www.vangent-hcm.com 1984 Adults	MY15:236 TP7:2383 T4:498	Used in vocational counseling or personnel selection to identify individuals with mechanical ability & experience. Consists of 30 items that measure an indivi-dual's ability to visually select a combination of flat pieces which fit together to cover a given two-dimensional space.
Space Thinking (Flags) Vangent, Inc. http://www.vangent-hcm.com 1959 - 1984 Adults	TP7:2384 TP5:2460 T4:498	Measures the ability to visualize a rigid configuration when it is moved into different positions. This 5 minute timed test may be used to aid in identifying individuals with mechanical interest & ability.
Stromberg Dexterity Test (SDT) Harcourt Assessment http://harcourtassessment.com 1945 - 1981 Trade School & Adults	MY4:755 TP7:2444 TP5:2515 T4:638	Designed to aid in choosing workers for jobs requiring speed & accuracy of arm & hand movement. Test consists of 54 red, blue, & yellow discs & a durable board containing 54 holes on one side. Subject is timed sorting discs by color, & placing them in the holes.
Technology and Internet Assessment H & H Publishing Company http://www.hhpublishing.com 1999 Middle School to Adult	TP7:2552	Designed to assess an individuals strengths & weaknesses in basic computer knowledge, the Internet, & information technology skills. Scores yielded in 8 areas such as: use of computer, specific computer skills, basic Internet know-ledge, & ethics of technology. Administered & scored via the Internet.
Test of Mechanical Concepts Vangent, Inc. http://www.vangent-hcm.com 1976 - 1986 Grade 8 to Adults	MY8:1045 T4:637	Measures an individual's ability to visualize & comprehend basic mechanical & spatial interrelationships. Reports 4 scores: mechanical interrelationships, mechanical tools & devices, spatial relations, & total.
Valpar 300 Series Dexterity Modules (VDM) Valpar International http://www.valparint.com 1995 Age 15 to Adults		Designed to measure motor coordination, & manual & finger dexterity. Five modules are currently available: Small Parts Assembly, Asymmetric Pin Place-ment, Tool Manipulation, Bi-Manual Coordination, & Angled Pin Placement. Modules are criterion referenced to DOL standards.
Wiesen Test of Mechanical Aptitude (WTMA) Psychological Assessment Resources http://www3.parinc.com 1999 Age 18 to Adult	MY14:419 TP7:2780	Designed to assess mechanical aptitude. Consists of simple drawings that cover broad mechanical/physical concepts such as: basic machines, movement, gravity/center of gravity, basic electricity/electronics, transfer of heat, & basic physical properties. Individual or group administration.

C. INTEREST INSTRUMENTS

Name of Test/Publisher/Date/Population	Reference(s)	Brief Description
Career Assessment Battery Piney Mountain Press http://www.pineymountain.com 2005 High School to Adults		40 minute live action video and multimedia format. The participants see and hear live-action occupational situations and make choices based on the Department of Labor's worker trait groups. Scoring can be by computer, batch or publisher.
Career Assessment Inventory (CAI) Pearson Assessments http://www.pearsonassessments.com 1986 High school to Adults	CG4 MY8:993 MY10:43 T3:367	Designed to measure one's occupational interests for use in career exploration and career decision making. The Enhanced Version provides a mixture of occupations that require various amounts of postsecondary education. The Vocational Version focuses on occupations requiring up to 2 years of postsecondary education.

Name of Test/Publisher/Date/Population	Reference(s)	Brief Description
Career Compass Career Voyages http://www.careervoyages.gov/careercompass-main.cfm 1988 - 1996 Junior High to High School		Covers general career clusters, major work groups & specific occupations based on student responses to 70 work activity questions. Program printouts provide a career interest profile, additional information & a listing of related sample occupations for top 3 interest clusters.
Career Key (CK) Career Key http://www.careerkey.org/ 1993 High School to Adults	MD:7/90	Self-administered instrument that assesses Holland codes & directs users to occupations related type. Provides explanation of Holland's theory & gives vol-ume/page number of identified occupations in the Encyclopedia of Careers & Vocational Guidance. Only available online:http://www.careerkey.org/index.asp
Chronicle Career Quest Chronicle Guidance Publications, Inc. http://www.chronicleguidance.com 1991-1993 Middle School to Adult	CG4	A group-administered career guidance instrument that includes three components: an Interest Inventory, a self-scoring Inter-pretation Guide and a Career Paths occupational profile. For the interest inventory, Form S (short form) totals 108 items, while Form L (long form) includes 144 items both are scored across 12 interest areas based on United States Employment Service Guide for Occupational Exploration.
COIN Career Targets COIN Educational Products http://www.coinedu.com 1990 - 1993 Middle School to High School		Provides assessment, career exploration & individual career plans. Includes: a self-scored, self-administered inventory link-ing students' interests to 14 career clusters, an exploration of the world of work, & activities that emphasize the importance of education & the development of a high school plan.
COIN Educational Inventory COIN Educational Products http://www.coinedu.com 1994 Grades 11 and 12		Designed to provide an interest assessment to be used in post-secondary educational planning. Consists of 4 parts: Assessing Interests, Exploring Personal Interests & Post-Secondary Education & Training, Selecting Post-Secondary Training, and Choosing a Post-Secondary School.
Explore the World of Work (E-WOW) CFKR Career Materials, Inc. http://www.cfkr.com 1989 - 1991 Adults	TP5:993 TP7:984 T3:821	Designed as a quick assessment using 36 graphics: 24 work activities & 12 work values. Developed for adult retraining & reentry programs. This instrument is a pictorial form of JOB-O to accommodate low reading levels. Available in Spanish.
Guide for Occupational Exploration Inventory (GOE) II JIST Publishing, Inc. http://www.jist.com 1996 Grade 6 to Adults	T4:316 TP71134	Explores career, education, & lifestyle options. Yields a graphic interest profile with 7 factors such as: leisure, home, & educa-tion/school. Eighth grade reading level. Cross-referenced to standard occupational information sources. Map with GOE information provided. Group or individually administered.
High School Career-Course Planner CFKR Career Materials, Inc. http://www.cfkr.com 1983 - 1990 Adolescents	MY12:181 TP7:1173 TP5:1200 T3:824	Used to evaluate career interest & develop a course plan that is consistent with self-assessed career goals. Measures interests in 6 occupational areas: working with tools, working with people, creating new things, solving problems, & doing physical work.
Interest Explorer Riverside Publishing http://www.riverpub.com 1998 Middle School to Adults	CG4	Designed to help students and adults make educational and career-planning decisions about their futures. It provides information about students' interests in 14 career areas that are linked to publications of the Department of Labor.
Interest Determination, Exploration and Assessment System (IDEAS) Pearson Assessments http://www.pearsonassessments.com 1977-2000 Middle School to Adults	CG4 MY9:516	Designed as an introduction to career planning. It provides scores on 16 basic interest scales that help students and adults identify and explore occupational areas of interest.
Judgement of Occupational Behavior-Orientation 2000 + (JOB-O 2000) CFKR Career Materials http://www.cfkr.com 1978 - 1999 Grade 4 to Adults	CG1 MY12:200 MY10:16 MY9:560 TP5:1350	Uses a 9-item questionnaire to yield 9 scores: education, inter-est, inclusion, control, affection, physical activity, hands/tool/machinery, problem solving, and creating ideas. Scores are compared to 120 job titles. Designed to emphasize job aware-ness and promote job exploration. Three versions: grades 4-6, 7-10, and 10-adult.

Name of Test/Publisher/Date/Population	Reference(s)	Brief Description
Occupational Interest Profile (OIP) Beilby http://www.beilby.com.au/ 2006 Adults		Designed to assess an individual's personal preferences for varying types of work based on the following categories; artistic, practical, scientific, administrative, caring, logical, and persuasive.
Pictorial Inventory of Careers (PIC) Talent Assessment, INC http://www.talentassessment.com/ 2006 Middle to High School		Students respond to live action video segments of real work situations. By rating each segment, students determine what career/vocational area they like best. Assessment results identify areas of strong interest, dislikes, and areas which they have little or no knowledge.
School-to-Work Career Survey Piney Mountain Press http://www.pineymountain.com/ 2005 Middle to High School		Designed to assist students in identifying career options in 5 career pathways: Art & Humanities, Agricultural & Environmental, Business & Marketing, Health & Human Services, & Engineering & Industrial. Consists of a 75 item survey delivered via a video, worksheets or on a computer.
UNIACT IV ACT, Inc. http://www.act.org 1973 - 1984 High School to Young Adults	MY9:43 TC:1	A unisex interest inventory designed to eliminate sex-role stereotyping. A component of the ACT Educational Planning and Assessment System (EPAS) and the Career Planning Survey (CPS). Students respond to 90 activities grouped into 6 areas: science, creative arts, social service, business contact, business detail, and technical.
Values Scale (VS) Consulting Psychologists Press, Inc. http://www.cpp.com/ 1986 8th grade reading level and higher	CG4 MY10:379 T4:2876	Designed to help people achieve career goals by identifying important extrinsic and intrinsic values. A self-report inventory of 106 scored items yielding 21 separate scales for the individual assessment of upper elementary school and middle school students as well as adult members of semi-skilled, skilled, clerical, managerial, and professional occupations.
Vocational Interest Exploration System (VIE) McCarron-Dial Systems http://mccarrondial.com 1991 Age 14 to Adults	T4:340	Computer-assisted interest assessment program designed to assess an indivi-dual's preferences for type of work & working conditions. Yields scores in 3 areas: selection of jobs based on work preferences, occupational exploration, & job review comparison. Individual administration.
Vocational Interest Inventory and Exploration Survey (VOC-TIES) Piney Mountain Press http://www.pineymountain.com 1994 Age 13 to Adults	MY12:408 T5:2832	Designed for 3 major purposes: "to enable students to discover what vocational training entails; to determine student's vocational preferences; and to promote the concept of career equity by showing students in nontraditional roles." A Non-reading test that presents 15 training programs by video. A selection of short-term career objectives is provided.
Work Exploration Checklist Finney Company http://www.finney-hobar.com 1993 - 2000 Grade 7 to Adult		Designed to assess an individual's interests in past, present, & future activities. Consists of a 4 page checklist yielding results in GOE codes & RIASEC themes. An electronic version is also available as part of the Occupational Guidance CD-Rom.

D. MEASURES OF WORK VALUES, SATISFACTION, AND ENVIRONMENTS

Name of Test/Publisher/Date/Population	Reference(s)	Brief Description
Campbell Organizational Survey (COS) Vangent http://www.vangent-hcm.com 1988 - 1994 Working Adults	MY12:60 TP5:382 T4:525	Designed to assess individual's attitudes about aspects of work. Provides scores on 17 scales such as: supervision, benefits, job security, and an index of overall satisfaction within the organization. Scores provided in individual profile report with charts and graphs. May be taken online via the Internet.
Career Anchors: Discovering Your Real Values Jossey-Bass Pfeiffer and Company, International http://www.pfeiffer.com 1990 Adults	MY13:46 TP5:396 T4:572	Identifies career anchors, uncovers real values to help make better career choices. Yields 8 scores, such as: technical/functional competence, general managerial competence, service/dedication to a cause, pure challenge, & lifestyle. Includes orientation & career anchor interviews. Group administered.

Name of Test/Publisher/Date/Population	Reference(s)	Brief Description
Career Values Scale Psychometrics Canada Ltd. http://www.psychometrics.com 1987 - 1991 Adults		Aids in evaluation of career interests, goals, needs, & aspirations. The questionnaire consists of 80 items of preference alternatives in 4 categories: work environment, employment position, ambition, & career introspection.
Fleishman Job Analysis Survey (F-JAS) Management Research Institute, Inc. http://www.managementresearchinstitute.com 1992 - 1996 Adults	TP5:1044	A 74 item questionnaire used to determine ability requirements of jobs. Users respond to statements on a 7 point Likert-scale. Covers the full range of human abilities such as: cognitive, psychomotor, etc. Self-scored.
Individual Style Survey (ISS) Psychometrics Canada Ltd. http://www.psychometrics.com 1989 - 1990 Grade 9 to Adults	MY13:144 TP5:1253	Provides a structured activity for self & interpersonal development, with an emphasis on the unique way in which individuals respond to events & people in the environment. Includes a self-perception form & 3 forms to give to others to assess the user's style.
Job Descriptive Index (JDI) Bowling Green State University http://showcase.bgsu.edu/IOPsych/jdi/index.html 1969 - 1997 Adults	MY12:199 TC9:319 TP5:1348 T4:531	Provides an assessment of job satisfaction in any occupational field. Measures the following 5 components of satisfaction: work on present job, present pay, opportunities for promotion, supervision on present job, & people on present job.
Job Style Indicator (JSI) Consulting Resource Group International http://www.crgleader.com 1988 - 1993 Adults	MY13:164 TP5:1355 T4:509	Contains 16 items which compare perceptions of a particular job with an individual's personal style. Reveals the preferred work style of a specific job & is useful in exploring the person-job match. Designed to complement the Personal Style Indicator.
Minnesota Importance Questionnaire (MIQ) Vocational Psychology Research http://www.psych.umn.edu/psylabs/vpr 1967 - 1981 Age 16 to Adults	CG1,2,3 MY11:243 TC2:481 TP5:1694	"Designed to measure 20 (21) psychological needs (and their underlying values) found relevant to work satisfaction." Scores yielded include: ability utilization, achievement, recognition, supervision-technical, variety, altruism, & autonomy. Can be used with the MSQ. Part of Minnesota Work Adjustment Project.
Minnesota Job Description Questionnaire (MJDQ) Vocational Psychology Research http://www.psych.umn.edu/psylabs/vpr 1967 - 1968 Adults	MY8:1050 TC6:350 TP5:1695 T3:1012	Measures the working environment in terms of a profile of need-satisfaction characteristics. Aids in the person-job match of jobs along 21 reinforcer dimen-sions such as variety, creativity, security, recognition, authority, independence, etc.
Minnesota Satisfaction Questionnaire (MSQ) Vocational Psychology Research http://www.psych.umn.edu/psylabs/vpr 1963 - 1977 Age 16 to Adults	CG3 MY9:721 TC5:1701	Designed to measure an employee's satisfaction with his/her job. Long form consists of 100 items; short form consists of 20 items. Scores yielded on 20 scales such as: authority, company policy, social service, & human relations. Can be used with the MIQ. Part of Minnesota Work Adjustment Project.
Personal Style Indicator (PSI) Consulting Resource Group International http://www.crgleader.com 1988 - 1989 Adults	MY13:228 TP5:1952	A 16 item questionnaire that reveals personality & work style. Yields scores on behavioral, cognitive, affection & interpersonal dimensions. Contains detailed descriptions of 21 behavioral patterns. Self-administered & self-scored.
Position Analysis Questionnaire (PAQ) PAQ Services http://www.paq.com 1969 - 1992 Adults	MY12:299 TC5:326 TP5:2016 T4:513	Contains 189 job elements sampling what employees do to get their jobs done. Focus is on 6 behavioral areas: information input, mediation processes, work output, interpersonal activities, work situation & job context, & miscellaneous aspects.
Position Classification Inventory (PCI) Psychological Assessment Resource http://www3.parinc.com 1991 Adults	T4:513	Uses Holland Codes to classify positions/occupations to assess person-job fit. Employees & supervisors complete an inventory which describes demands & skills required in a job by rating items on a 3 point scale. Both scores are compared to aid in determination of job fit.
Salience Inventory (SI) Vocopher: The Online Career Collaboratory http://www.vocopher.com 1985 - 1987 Grade 6 to Adults	CG3 MY11:339 TP5:2282	Designed "to assess the relative importance of the work role in the context of other life roles." Consists of 170 items divided into 3 scales: commitment, parti-pation, & value expectation. Five major life roles are assessed under each of the 3 scales: homemaker, worker, student, citizen, & leisurite.

Name of Test/Publisher/Date/Population	Reference(s)	Brief Description
Rokeach Value Survey Consulting Psychologists Press (CPP) http://www.cpp.com/ 1967 - 1983 Age 11 to Adults	MY12:334 TP5:2246 TC1:549 T3:250	A self-scoring survey which contains items related to life-style & behavioral values. Utilizes a list of 18 terminal values & 18 instrumental values to aid in the determination of value priorities & assist in making life choices. A value's score is its rank.
Survey of Interpersonal Values (SIV) Vangent http://www.vangent-hcm.com 1960 - 1993 Adolescents to Adults	TC2:759 TP5:2581 T4:152	Measures 6 values involving relationships between people: support, conformity, recognition, independence, benevolence, & leadership. The 90 items are arranged in sets of 3 with each item ranked from "most" to "least" important.
Survey of Personal Values (SPV) Vangent http://www.vangent-hcm.com 1964 - 1997 Grade 10 to Adults	MY10:354 TC2:773 TP5:2588 T4:586	Measures 6 values: practical mindedness, achievement, variety, decisiveness, orderliness, & goal orientation. This self-report consists of 90 items. Each item contains 3 of the 6 values which are ranked by selecting "most" or "least" important.
Survey of Work Values Bowling Green State University http://showcase.bgsu.edu/IOPsych/jdi/measures.html 1975 - 1976 Employees	MY12:383 TP5:2593 T4:541	Designed to identify individual's attitudes towards work. Consists of 54 items yielding scores in 6 areas: social status, activity preference, upward striving, attitude toward earnings, pride in work, & job involvement. Individual or group administration.
Values Preference Indicator (VPI) Consulting Resource Group International http://www.crgleader.com 1990 Adults	TP5:2804 T4:542	Designed to assess personal value preferences. Consists of 3 parts: Identifying Key Values, Prioritizing Your Values, & Time Test. Yields 21 scores in areas, such as: accomplishment, acknowledgement, challenge, friendship, organization, expertise, & tranquility. Individual or group administration.
Work Environment Scale (WES) Consulting Psychologist Press (CPP) http://www.cpp.com 1974 - 1989 Employees and Supervisors	MY12:417 TP5:2917 T4:594	Designed to assess the social climate of various work settings. Consists of 90 items yielding scores on 10 scales including: involvement, supervisor support, peer cohesion, autonomy, task orientation, work pressure, clarity, control, physical comfort, & innovation. Individual or group administration.
Workmate Piney Mountain Press http://www.pineymountain.com 1998 6th Grade to Adults		Designed to identify & examine work related values, attitudes, and tempera-ments. Graphical printouts generated for 15 job related areas such as: risking, competing, helping, persuading, receiving recognition, working with others, physical, & routine. Group or individual administration.
Work Motivation Inventory (WMI) Teleometrics International http://www.teleometrics.com 1967 - 1973 Adults	MY8:1189 TP5:2921 T4:554	Yields 5 work maturation scores: basic creature comfort, safety & order, be-longing & affiliation, ego-status, actualization, & self-expression. Separate measures are designed for managers & employees. Self or group administered.

E. CARD SORTS

Name of Test/Publisher/Date/Population	Reference(s)	Brief Description
Deal-Me-In http://www.careersystemsintl.com/dealmin.htm Career Systems 1985 - 1992 High School to Adults	CG3	A deck of 52 color-coded playing cards divided into suits that correspond to 4 interest categories: people, data, things, ideas. Can be used with a companion guide (It's in the Cards) that covers 22 job situations in 4 work areas: job search, job orientation, performance & reputation, & enrichment & enhancement.
Knowdell Career Values Card Sort CareerTrainer http://www.careertrainer.com/ 1998 Adults	CG4 MY13:	Designed to allow clients to prioritize their career values in as little as five minutes and then to use their knowledge of their values to improve career decision making.
Knowdell Motivated Skills Card Sort CareerTrainer http://www.careertrainer.com/ 1981 - 1994 Grade 7 to Adults	CG3 MY13:204 TP5:1719 TP7:1671	Provides assessment of proficiency in, & motivation to use 48 skills. Primarily used to identify skills important to an individual's career satisfaction & success. Contains 48 skill cards & 8 category cards.

Name of Test/Publisher/Date/Population	Reference(s)	Brief Description
Knowdell Occupational Interests Card Sort CareerTrainer http://www.careertrainer.com/ 1981 - 1994 Grade 7 to Adults	CG3 MY13:213 TP5:1819 TP7:1776	Designed to assist individuals in identifying & clarifying pre-ferred occupa-tions. Contains 113 occupation cards, 5 category cards, & 9 supplementary activities designed to stimulate career exploration. Occupation cards are sorted into 5 levels of interest.
Knowdell Leisure & Retirement Activities Card Sort CareerTrainer http://www.careertrainer.com/ 1992 - 1994 Retired Adults or Adults Planning to Retire	MY13:262 TP5:2207 TP7:2156	Designed to assess adults in planning retirement & understan-ding the process of change. Consists of 48 common pastimes such as: meditation, cultural events, group leadership, & entertaining. Cards are organized & classified to help individuals determine personal criteria related to retirement.
Kolb Learning Skills Profile (LSP) Hay Group – Hay Resources Direct http://www.haygroup.com/ 1993 Junior High School to Adults	MY13:179 TP7:1431 TP5:1467	Designed to measure skills critical to job performance. Assesses the following skill groups: interpersonal, information, analytical, & behavioral. The partici-pant uses one or both decks of cards to rate his/her skills or the skill demands of his/her job. Self-administered. Learning Agenda worksheet is provided.
Missouri Occupational Card Sort University of Missouri Career Center http://career.missouri.edu/generalinfo/ 1993 Grade 11 & 12, College, & Adults	CG3 MG:10/81	An interest card sort designed to broaden knowledge of self

F. CAREER DEVELOPMENT/MATURITY MEASURES

Name of Test/Publisher/Date/Population	Reference(s)	Brief Description
Adult Career Concerns Inventory (ACCI) Vocopher http://www.vocopher.com 1988 Adults		A 61 item instrument designed to measure an individual's cur-rent level of concern related to career activities conceptualized within Donald Super's stages of career development: Explora-tion, Establishment, Maintenance, and Disengagement.
Career Action Inventory Career Systems http://www.careersystemsintl.com 1988 Adults		A 75 question self-assessment inventory to determine what an individual is doing now about career planning & professional development. Includes a comprehensive discussion of inven-tory results & offers specific ideas for taking action to improve chances for success.
Career Beliefs Inventory (CBI) Consulting Psychologists Press, Inc. http://www.cpp.com 1991 8th Grade Reading Level and Older	CG4 MY12:	Designed to help people identify career beliefs that may be preventing them from achieving their career goals. The BCI can help counselors initiate explorations of the career assumptions on which their clients operate.
Career Decision Scale (CDS) Psychological Assessment Resources http://www3.parinc.com 1976 - 1987 High School to Adults	CG2,3 MY9:194 TP5:404 TP7:412 T4:526	Provides estimates about students status in the career-decision making process; also used to judge the effectiveness of career development interventions. Consists of 19 items, yielding per-centile scores on certainty & indecision scales. Hand scored.
Career Development Inventory (CDI) Vocopher http://www.vocopher.com 1981 High School to Adults	CG4 MY9:195 T4:391	An 8 subscale instrument assessing career planning, career exploration, knowledge of the world of work, career deci-sion-making, knowledge of preferred occupation, and three composite scales. Designed to assess the career maturity of individuals.
Career Leverage Inventory Career Systems http://www.careersystemsintl.com 1983 - 1994 Adults		A 35-question survey designed to help employees identify & as-sess their realistic career options. Provides new ways to think about career growth, how to prioritize & set career goals, & how to build back-up plans so individuals always have options.
Career Maturity Inventory (CMI) http://www.vocopher.com 1995 Middle School to Adult	CG4	Career readiness assessment that measures attitudes and competencies necessary for youth and adults to make effective career decisions.

Name of Test/Publisher/Date/Population	Reference(s)	Brief Description
COIN Clue COIN Educational Products http://www.coinedu.com/ 1996 Grades 5 and 6		Provides activities in career exploration, assessment and plan-ning. Content in-cludes activities to answer questions, such as: What is work?, Why is work important?, and How do I get the work I want? Jobs are grouped into 7 categories, including: Designers & Builders, Helpers & Healers, and Transportation.
Minnesota Satisfactoriness Scales (MSS) Vocational Psychology Research http://www.psych.umn.edu/psylabs/vpr 1965 - 1982 Employees	MY8:1050 TP5:1702 TP7:1657	Designed to measure an employee's job satisfactoriness. Yields scores in 5 areas: performance, conformance, dependabil-ity, personal adjustment, & general satisfactoriness. Usually completed by supervisor judging employee's behavior. Part of Minnesota Work Adjustment Project.
My Vocational Situation (MVS) Consulting Psychologists Press (CPP) http://www.cpp.com 1980 - 1987 Grade 9 to Adults	CG2 MY9:738 TC2:509 TP5:1754 TP7:1708	Designed to identify 3 possible difficulties in making career decisions: lack of vocational identity, need for information or training, & environmental or personal barriers. Self-adminis-tered & hand-scored.

G. PERSONALITY MEASURES

Name of Test/Publisher/Date/Population	Reference(s)	Brief Description
Adult Personality Inventory (API) Institute for Personality and Ability Testing (IPAT) http://www.IPAT.com 1982 - 1996 Age 16 to Adults	MY12:20 MY14:12 TC6:21 TP5:86 TP7:93 T4:98	Assesses individual differences in personality, interpersonal style, & career/ life-style preferences. Consists of 324 items that measures 21 scales. The self report inventory is computer sco-red. Designed for employee selection, coun- seling, & personal development programs.
Applicant Review IntegriView, LLC http://www.integriview.com 1983 - 1996 Job Applicants		Designed to measure honesty & emotional stability. Consists of 102 items with 7 subscales, such as: personal honesty, honesty of others, punishment, past behavior, & moral reasoning. Scores are combined to form an honesty score. There are built in controls for faking & social desirability response bias.
Comprehensive Personality Profile (CPP) Wonderlic, Inc. http://www.wonderlic.com 1996 Employers and human resource personnel	CG4 T4:617	Designed to help organizations effectively match candidates whose personality characteristics are most compatible with the demands of the job.
Employee Reliability Inventory (ERI) Bay State Psychological Associates, Inc. http://www.eri.com 1986 - 1998 Adults and Job Applicants	MY12:137 TP7:943 TP5:944 T4:575	Assesses various dimensions of pre-employment reliability and work behavior. Consists of 81 true-false items assessing beha-vior in 7 areas such as: freedom from disruptive alcohol & sub-stance abuse, emotional maturity, long term job commitment, & safe job performance. Available in Braille and 5 languages.
Fundamental Interpersonal Relations Orientation-Behavior (Firo-B) Consulting Psychologists Press (CPP) http://www.cpp.com/ 1967 - 1996 High School to Adults	MY9:416 MY15:104 T4:114	Measures interpersonal dynamics for building productive professional relationships & enhancing productivity & career potential. Based on a model that identifies 3 interpersonal expressed & wanted needs: inclusion, control & affection.
Gordon Personal Profile-Inventory (GPP-I) Harcourt Assessment http://harcourtassessment.com 1951 - 1998 Grade 10 to Adults	MY13:133 TP7:1087 TC2:326 TP5:1101 T4:115	Combines 2 measures to assess 8 aspects of personality. The profile examines ascendancy, responsibility, emotional stability & sociability to yield a measure of self-esteem. Assesses cau-tiousness, original thinking, personal relations, & vigor.
Guilford-Zimmerman Temperament Survey (GZTS) Pearson Assessments http://www.pearsonassessments.com 1949 - 1978 Age 16 to Adults	MY9:460 TC8:251 TP5:1158 T4:115	Identifies strengths & weaknesses associated with personality & temperament. The 10 traits measured are: activity, restraint, ascendancy, sociability, emotional stability, objectivity, friendli-ness, thoughtfulness, personal relations, & masculinity/femini-nity. A computer-generated report is also available.

Name of Test/Publisher/Date/Population	Reference(s)	Brief Description
Insight Inventory Insight Institute http://www.insightinstitute.com/insight-inventory.html 1990 - 1995 Ages 16 to Adults	MY13:149 MY14:179 TP5:1273 TP7:1248	Designed to measure the ways a person uses his/her individual personality. Measures 4 personality styles: getting one's way (direct or indirect), responding to people (outgoing or reserved), pacing activity (urgent or steady), & dealing with details (unstructured or precise). Describes behavior at home & at work.
Keirsey Character Sorter Prometheus Nemesis Book Company 1978 – 1997 Adults	TP7:1351	Designed to assess temperaments. Consists of 36 items yielding scores as 2 letter MBTI type codes: Guardian (SJ), Artisan (SP), Idealist (NF) & Rational (NT). Each code is described & examples are given. Used with the book, "Please Understand Me". Only available online at http://www.keirsey.com/.
Keirsey Temperament Sorter II Prometheus Nemesis Book Company www.keirsey.com 1978 – 1997 Adults		Designed to assess temperaments. Consists of 70 items similar to the MBTI form of questions (more indirect) & yields 16 four letter codes such as: ESTI, ENFJ, & ENTP. Used with the book, "Please Understand Me". Available in 5 languages. Can be completed on-line at http://www.keirsey.com/.
Occupational Personality Questionnaire (OPQ32) SHL Americas (Saville & Holdsworth, Ltd.) http://www.shl.com/shl/en-int 1984 - 1990 Adults	MY11:267 TP5:1822 TP7:1777	Designed to measure personality & motivational characteristics relevant to the world of work. OPQ32 explores 32 personality characteristics in multiple dimensions. Available in 28 languages.
Occupational Stress Inventory – Revised (OSI-R) Sigma Assessment Systems http://www.sigmaassessmentsystems.com Adult Workers	CG3 MY11:279 MY14:260 TP7:1778 TP5:1825 T4:536	Designed to measure occupational adjustment. Consists of 3 questionnaires: Occupational Roles, Personal Strain, & Personal Resources. Raw scores & standard scores are provided for 14 scales. Administration available online.
Personality Research Form (PRF) Sigma Assessment Systems http://www.sigmaassessmentsystems.com 1965 - 1996 Age 11 to Adults	CG3 TP7:1928 MY10:282 TP5:1965 T4:134	Designed to measure personality within a normal range. Forms AA & BB consist of 440 items yielding scores on 22 scales; Forms A & B consist of 300 items yielding scores on 15 scales. Scores reported as standard (T) scores. Also available in French & Spanish. Hand or machine scored.
Sales Attitude Checklist Vangent, Inc. Creative Organizational Design http://www.creativeorgdesign.com/ 1960 - 1992 Individuals Interested in Sales Positions	MY9:1066 TP7:2205 TP5:2267 T4:647	Designed to assess sales attitudes & habits via 31 self-descriptive, forced-choice items. Specifically intended for use in identifying potentially successful salespeople.
Singer-Loomis Inventory of Personality (SLIP) Moving Boundaries http://www.movingboundaries.com 1984 - 1996 Grade 9 to Adults	MY10:334 MY9:1131 TP5:2411 T3:221	Contains 15 situations, each followed by 8 items which the individual responds to using a 5 point Likert scale. Describes the user's personality from a Jungian perspective by providing the individual with a description of thought patterns & how situations or problems are approached.
Sixteen Personality Factor Questionnaire (16PF) Institute for Personality and Ability Testing, Inc. http://www.IPAT.com 1967-1969 Ages 16 and Older	CG4 MY9:1136 MY8:679 T4:2470	Measures five global factors (extraversion, stability, receptivity, accommodating, and self-control) and sixteen personality factors (warmth, reasoning, emotional stability, dominance, liveliness, rule-consciousness, social boldness, sensitivity, vigilance, abstractedness, privateness, apprehension, openness to change, self-reliance, perfectionism, and tension).
Strategic Assessment of Readiness for Training (START) H & H Publishing Co. http://www.hhpublishing.com 1994 Adults	T4:499 MY14:369	Diagnoses learning strengths & weaknesses in work settings. Consists of 56 multiple-choice items measuring: anxiety, attitude, motivation, concentration, identifying important information, knowledge acquisition strategies, monitoring learning, & time management. Computer version available.
Strength Deployment Inventory Personal Strengths Publishing http://www.personalstrengths.com 1973 - 1996 Adults	MY14:371 TP7:2436 TP5:2507	Designed to assess individual's ability to relate to others under two conditions: when things are going well & when there is a conflict. Scores are yielded on 7 motivational value systems such as: altruistic-nurturing, assertive-directing, & flexible-cohering. Also, yields 13 scores relating to stages of conflict.

Name of Test/Publisher/Date/Population	Reference(s)	Brief Description
Styles of Teamwork Inventory (STI) Teleometrics International http://www.teleometrics.com 1963 - 1995 Adults in Work Teams	MY11:392 MY8:1048 TP7:2475 TP5:2549 T4:590	Assesses individual's attitudes & behaviors concerning work-team situations. Consists of 80 items, yielding scores in 5 areas: synergistic, compromise, win-lose, yield-lose, & lose-leave. Inventory results in an overall preferred style. Individual or group administration.
SureHire Harcourt Assessment http://harcourtassessment.com 1998 Job Applicants		Designed to assess the competencies necessary for individuals seeking employ-ment in convenience stores. Yields a graphical representation of percentile scores in 4 areas, including: problem solving, work orientation, customer service orientation, & a composite total. Individual or group administration.
Survey of Work Styles (SWS) Sigma Assessment Systems http://www.sigmaassessmentsystems.com 1987 - 1993 Adults	MY13:311 TP5:2592 TP7:2510	A computerized personality assessment which gathers information on 4 factors, (self-awareness, centeredness, perceptions, & decision making). Identifies individuals as having 1 of 8 work styles such as: forecaster, enthusiast, organizer, precisionist, caretaker, purist, etc.
Thurstone Temperament Schedule Vangent http://www.vangent-hcm.com/Home/ 1949 - 1991 Grade 9 to Adults	MY6:192 TP7:2652 TC2:815 TP5:2757 T4:586	Consists of 120 short questions that yield temperament profile scores for 6 personality traits: active, impulsive, dominant, stable, sociable, & reflective. Hand-scored carbon insert (answers transfer to scoring key on inside of test booklet). Appraisal/selection of applicants.
Viewpoint Psychological Services Inc. (PSI) http://www.psionline.com 1997 Job Applicants	MY16:259 TP7:2706	Available in 5 different instruments or combinations of instruments: Workview- 4 measures conscientiousness, trustworthiness, managing work pressure & get-ting along with other; Workview-6, measures the above plus drug & alcohol avoidance & safety orientation; Serviceview measures people-related attitudes.
Vocational Implications of Personality (VIP) Talent Assessment http://www.talentassessment.com/ 1986 Grade 7 to Adults		A computerized personality assessment that gathers information on four factors (self-awareness, centeredness, perceptions, & decision making) & then identifies individuals as having 1 of 8 work styles such as: forecaster, enthusiast, organizer, precisionist, designer, etc.
Vocational Preference Inventory (VPI) Psychological Assessment Resources http://www3.parinc.com 1953 - 1985 Grade 10 to Adults	MY10:382 TP7:2728 TP5:2835 T4:325	Designed to assess an individual's personality in areas, such as: interpersonal relations, values, self-concept, & coping behaviors. Consists of 160 occupational titles yielding scores on 11 scales including 6 Holland types & additional scales such as: acquiescence, masculinity-femininity, status, & self-control.

H. INSTRUMENTS FOR SPECIAL POPULATIONS

Name of Test/Publisher/Date/Population	Reference(s)	Brief Description
ARC Self-Determination Scale (ARC-SDS) The Beach Center on Disability http://www.beachcenter.org/ 1995 Adolescents	CG4	The ARC's Self-Determination Scale (ARC-SDS) is a 72 item self-reporting, paper-and-pencil instrument measuring four areas: autonomy, self-regulation, psychological empowerment, and self-realization.
Barsch Learning Styles Inventory – Revised Psychtest/ M.D. Angus & Associates Limited http://www.psychtest.com 1980 - 1996 Grade 9 to Adults	MY9:11 TP5:244 TP7:248	Designed to measure learning through sensory channels. Self-report instrument consisting of 24 items yielding raw scores in 4 areas: auditory, visual, tactile, & kinesthetic. Completed in 5-10 minutes. Study tips component is provided to maximize individual's learning style.
C.I.T.E. Learning Styles Inventory Piney Mountain Press http://www.pineymountain.com/ 1988-98 Age 7 to Adults	MY12:218 TP5:1476 T3:780	Assesses 9 areas: auditory language, visual language, auditory numerical, visual numerical, auditory-visual-kinesthetic, group learner, social learner, oral expressive, & written expressive. Vocational version considers environmental & working conditions. Audiovisual presentation available.

Name of Test/Publisher/Date/Population	Reference(s)	Brief Description
Endorle-Seversen Transition Rating Scales J-R (ESTRS) ESTR Publications http://www.estr.net/publications.cfm 1991 Ages 14 to 21 with a Disability	AT:98	Designed to provide information concerning transition for individuals with disabilities. Form J for students with mild disabilities consists of 84 items. Form R for students with moderate to severe disabilities consists of 136 items. Both forms have 5 subscales such as: jobs & job training, & home living.
Learning Styles Inventory Price Systems http://www.pricesystems.com/ 1976-96 Grades 3 to 12 – Special Populations	T4:243	Designed to assess individual learning preferences in the following areas: sociological needs, immediate environment, emotionality, & physical needs. Computerized summary of results is provided with suggested strategies for instructional and environmental alternatives to individual learning situations.
Learning/Working Styles Inventory (LWSI) Piney Mountain Press, Inc. http://www.pineymountain.com/ 1994 Grade 8 to Adult, Special Populations	CG4	For teachers and students to better understand the physical, social, environmental and working conditions under which an individual prefers to learn and work. The presentations are available in video and multimedia formats in order to meet the needs of special learners.
McCarron-Dial System McCarron Dial System http://www.mccarrondial.com/ 1973 - 1986 Special Populations	CG2,3 MY11:231 TP7:1555 TP5:1610 T4:327	Designed to provide a comprehensive assessment to be used in educational & vocational planning. Assesses 5 factors: verbal-spatial-cognitive, sensory, motor, emotional, & integration coping. Includes 7 tests such as: Peabody Picture Vocational Test-R, Behavior Rating Scale, & Emotional Behavior Checklist.
Microcomputer Evaluation of Career Areas (MECA) The Conover Company, Ltd. http://www.conovercompany.com/Index.html 1986 - 1992 Grade 7 to 12, Disadvantaged & Disabled	B:93	Designed for vocational exploration via 15 work samples containing 3 tasks each, such as: automotive, building maintenance, cosmetology, graphic design, custodial housekeeping, electronics, small engines, food service, health care, business & office, manufacturing, distribution, & computers.
Personnel Tests for Industry--Oral Directions Test (PTI-ODT) Harcourt Assessment www.harcourtassessment.com/ 1946 - 1974 Bilingual Persons with English as a Second Language	TP5:1974 TP7:1939 T4:497	A wide-range assessment of general mental abilities & an individual's comprehension of verbal, numerical & oral directions. English test requires 15 minutes & is hand scored. Used as a screening device for vocational trainees & industrial personnel.. May be used with persons of limited English proficiency.
Pictorial Inventory of Careers (PIC) Talent Assessment http://www.talentassessment.com/ 1992 Middle School to Adults - Special Populations	CG2,3	Reading free instrument designed to measure vocational interests. Consists of 119 real-life pictorials depicting vocational technical careers from 17 vocational clusters, & 11 career cluster definitions. Each cluster is represented by 7 scenes emphasizing the work environment, not the individual. Hand or machine scored.
Practical Assessment Exploration System (PAES) Talent Assessment http://www.talentassessment.com/ 1991 Special Populations		A Curriculum Based Vocational Assessment Program that provides hands-on evaluation. Evaluation & transition data includes job skill, quality of performance, work rate, interests, & behavioral barriers to employment & training.
Prevocational Assessment Screen (PAS) Piney Mountain Press http://www.pineymountain.com/ 1985 - 1994 Grades 9 to 12 - Special Populations	CG3 MY12:305 TP5:2054 TP7:2023	Assesses motor & perceptual abilities for requirements of local vocational training programs. Yields 16 time & error scores in 8 areas: alphabetizing, etch a sketch maze, calculating, small parts, pipe assembly, o rings, block design, & color sort. Individual administration.
Responsibility and Independence Scale for Adolescents (RISA) Riverside Publishing http://www.riverpub.com/ 1990 - 1992 Ages 12 to 20 - Special Populations	MY12:325 TP5:2204 TP7:2152 T4:238 AT:98	Norm-referenced instrument designed to measure adolescents' adaptive behavior in the areas of responsibility and independence. Consists of 9 subscales in functional areas such as: self management, social maturity, social communication, domestic skills, money management, citizenship, personal organization, transportation skills, & career skills.
Skills Assessment Module (SAM) Piney Mountain Press http://www.pineymountain.com/ 1981 - 1994 Age 13 to 18 - Special Populations	MY11:364 TP5:2421 T4:328 B:93	Assesses general aptitude, specific work behavior, & learning styles via 3 paper/pencil tests & 12 work samples such as: mail sort, payroll, computation, patient information memo, pipe assembly, block design, small parts, color sort, circuit board, etc.

Name of Test/Publisher/Date/Population	Reference(s)	Brief Description
Street Survival Skills Questionnaire (SSSQ) Harcourt Assessment http://harcourtassessment.com 1979-1993 Age 9 to Adult –Special Populations	CG4	Designed to assess community relevant adaptive skills in a comprehensive fashion. Specifically, it provides an objective and reliable method of assessing various aspects of adaptive behavior, a baseline behavioral measure to gauge the effects of training, and a prediction of the individual's potential for success in adapting to community living conditions and vocational placement.
Talent Assessment Program (TAP) Talent Assessment, Inc. http://www.talentassessment.com/ 1988 Middle School to Adult - Vocationally Disabled	CG3	Reading-free assessment of functional aptitudes. Consists of 10 hands-on tests, such as: Form Perception, Ability to Follow Patterns, Color Discrimination, & Tactile Discrimination. Results are compiled into a profile that can be compared with job requirements in the DOT and OOH.
Transition Behavior Scale, 2nd edition (TBS-2) Hawthorne Educational Services, Inc. http://www.hes-inc.com/hes.cgi 1991 - 1999 High School - Special Populations	MY16:253 TP7:2669 TP5:2779 T4:323	Designed to assess the readiness of an individual to enter the world of employ-ment & independent living. Consists of 62 items, yielding scores in 3 areas: work related behavior, inter-personal relations, & social/community expecta-tions. Manual includes IEP goals, objectives, & interventions.
Transition to Work Inventory Harcourt Assessment http://harcourtassessment.com 1996 Middle School to Adult	MY14:	Designed to 1.) ascertain the precise job-related challenges imposed by an individual's disability, 2.) assess worker-job fit for individuals with disabilities across a diverse set of jobs, and 3.) serve as a means of determining accommodation/job redesign needs for individuals with disabilities.
Valpar Component Work Sample Series Valpar International http://www.valparint.com/ 1974 - 1993 General Population & Industrially Injured Persons	CG1	Consists of 22 work samples designed to measure broad worker traits, such as: use of small tools, vocational readiness, upper extremity range of motion, simulated assembly, etc. Yields scores & clinical observations that can be used for job training & placement & for constructing programs.
Vocational Adaptation Rating Scales (VARS) Stoelting Co. http://www.stoeltingco.com/ 1980 Mentally Retarded Persons Age 13 to Adults	MY9:1334 TP5:2824 T4:467	Uses parents', teachers', & professionals' ratings to measure maladaptive behaviors likely to hinder vocational adjustment. Provides frequency & severity scores in 17 areas such as: verbal manners, communication skill, respect for property, rules & regulations, etc.
Vocational Decision Making Interview Jist Works, Inc http://www.jist.com/shop/web 1993 Special Populations	TP5:2828 MY14:409 TP7:2723	Assesses the vocational decision-making capacities of individuals with disabili-ties. Consists of 54 items, yielding scores in 4 areas: decision-making, readiness, employment readiness, self-appraisal, & a total. Uses an interview format that is orally administered to individuals.
Vocational Interest Temperament and Aptitude System (VITAS) Vocational Research Institute http://www.vri.org/ 1979 Educationally Disadvantaged	CG1 T3:658 B:93	Contains 21 independent work samples based on 16 Work Groups. Samples include: laboratory, engineering & craft technology, production work, quality control, financial detail, oral communications, etc. Requires training to administer.
Vocational Training Inventory and Exploration Survey (VOC-TIES) Psychological Assessment Ressources (PAR), Inc. Piney Mountain http://www.pineymountain.com/ 1986 - 1991 Disadvantaged & Mildly Handicapped Youth	T3:840	A multi-media kit used to identify vocational interests, enhance vocational awareness, & promote sex equity by showing persons in non-traditional rolls. Includes a video for 15 commonly available vocational programs. Apple/IBM program provides printout of interests.
Wide Range Achievement Test (WRAT3) PAR Inc http://www3.parinc.com/ 1940 - 1993 Age 5 to Adult - Special Populations	MY12:414 TP7:2775 TP5:2879 T4:210	Designed to assess the skills necessary to learn how to read, spell, & perform basic arithmetic operations. Provides absolute, standard, & grade scores on each of the 3 subtests: Reading, Spelling, & Arithmetic. Individual administration. Two equivalent forms are available.
Work Adjustment Inventory (WAI) Psychological and Educational Publications http://www.psych-edpublications.com/ 1994 Adolescents and Young Adults - Special Populations	MY13:365 TP7: 2806 TP5:2912 T4:326	A norm-referenced assessment of 6 work-related temperaments: activity, empathy, sociability, assertiveness, adaptability, & emotionality. Provides age & gender based scores that can be displayed graphically. Third grade reading level. Useful for transition planning for students with disabilities & at-risk youth.

Name of Test/Publisher/Date/Population	Reference(s)	Brief Description
Work Performance Assessment (WPA) National Clearinghouse of Rehabilitation Training Materials (NCRTM) http://www.ncrtm.org/ 1987 - 1988 Job Trainees - Special Populations	MY13:367 TP7:2816 TP5:2923	Designed to assess work-related social/interpersonal skills. Consists of 19 assessment situations involving supervisors, workers, & co-workers. Yields scores on 19 supervisory demands, such as: greet each trainee, explain supervi-sory error, provide detailed instructions, & socialize with each trainee.
Work Personality Profile (WPP) National Clearinghouse of Rehabilitation Training Materials (NCRTM) http://www.ncrtm.org/ 1986 Vocational Rehabilitation Clients	MY11:476 TP7: 2818 TP5:2924	Designed to assess fundamental work role requirements that are essential to achievement and maintenance of suitable employment. Consists of ratings on 58 items, yielding 16 scores such as: acceptance of work role, ability to profit from instruction or correction, & ability to socialize with co-workers.
Work Readiness Cognitive Screen (WCS) HeadMinder, Inc. http://www.headminder.com/site/home.html 2001 Adults		Designed for professionals who assess vocational potential in clients with known or suspected cognitive problems, the HeadMinder Work-Readiness Cognitive Screen tests memory, attention, and other key functions and integrates the results with pertinent information about the client's vocational experience, interests, and aptitudes.
Work Temperament Inventory (WTI) National Clearinghouse of Rehabilitation Training Materials (NCRTM) http://www.ncrtm.org/ 1993 Workers - Special Populations	MY13:368 TP7:2827 TP5:2928	Designed to identify an individual's traits & match those traits to occupations. Yields scores on 12 scales including: directive, repetitive, influencing, variety, expressing, judgements, alone, stress, tolerances, people, & measurable. Indivi-dual or group administration.

SOURCES OF INFORMATION ABOUT TESTING AND CAREER ASSESSMENT

Rich W. Feller

Professor, Counseling and Career Development

Jackie Peila-Shuster

Instructor, Counseling and Career Development

Colorado State University

INTRODUCTION

Information sources about assessment instruments and their use in enhancing career development are critical to the professional development of counselors and career specialists. This section includes an annotated bibliography of a representative selection of standards useful to publishers and tests users. Similarly, a selection of recent psychometric and career development textbooks, reference books, and monographs are included because their content has application to career assessment and career development issues.

A collection of materials useful in serving special populations is presented along with familiar test bibliographies and reviews to enhance the work of students, practitioners, researchers, and counselor educators. A list of periodicals that publish reviews and research articles involving career assessment instruments complements a very brief list of online review sites followed by a sampling of assessment websites. This set of resources is not intended to be exhaustive, but it is our hope that readers can find sufficient information in these sources to answer most questions about career assessment instruments and their application to the career development process.

STANDARDS FOR PUBLISHERS AND USERS OF TESTS

American Educational Research Association. (1999). *Standards for educational and psychological testing.* **Washington, DC: Author.**

These standards were developed jointly by the American Educational Research Association, the American Psychological Association, and the National Council on Measurement in Education. They address professional and technical concerns of test development and use in education, psychology, and employment. The contents are divided into an Introduction and 15 chapters which are organized into three parts: Part 1 — Test Construction, Evaluation, and Documentation; Part II — Fairness in Testing; and Part III — Testing Applications.

American Psychological Association (APA).

Its Web site includes information on testing issues at http://www.apa.org/topics/topictest.html

Association for Assessment in Counseling. (2003). *Responsibilities of users of standardized tests (RUST)* (3rd ed.). Alexandria, VA: Author.

The purpose of this document is to advance accurate, fair, and responsible use of testing by the counseling and education communities. It includes test user responsibilities in the areas of (a) qualifications of test users, (b) technical knowledge, (c) test selection, (d) test administration, (e) test scoring, (f) interpreting test results, and (g) communicating test results.

Association for Assessment in Counseling. (2003). *Standards for multicultural assessment* (2nd ed.). Alexandria, VA: Author.

This revised compilation of professional standards addresses the many challenges related to assessment of multicultural populations. The 68 standards contained in this report were identified from five source documents that address testing and/or multicultural standards in the education, counseling, and/or psychology fields.

Joint Committee on Testing Practices. (2004). *Code of fair testing practices in education.* Washington, DC: Author.

This revised code was developed by the Joint Committee that involved seven professional associations. It provides guidance to test developers and users in the four critical areas of (a) developing and selecting appropriate tests, (b) administering and scoring tests, (c) reporting and interpreting test results, and (d) informing test takers.

Joint Committee on Testing Practices. (1998). *Rights and responsibilities of test takers: Guidelines and expectations.* Washington, DC: Author.

These guidelines were developed by the Joint Committee with the intent of specifying and clarifying rights and responsibilities for test takers, developers, and administrators of psychological and educational tests. There are listings of rights and responsibilities for the test takers as well as guidelines for testing professionals regarding these rights and responsibilities.

National Association of School Psychologists. (NASP).

Its Web site includes information on testing at http://www.nasponline.org/publications/cq/cq341protocols.aspx

National Association of Test Directors (NATD).

The purpose of the organization is to share information about testing in educational settings. NATD publishes a newsletter two to four times per year. Monographs of NATD/NCME sessions presented at the annual meeting and "occasional papers" are published and mailed to members. These publications are also available for purchase. An NATD directory including mailing addresses, phone numbers, fax numbers, and e-mail addresses is distributed to members annually. Its Web site is at http://www.natd.org

National Council on Measurement in Education (NCME).

This organization encourages scholarly efforts to advance the science of measurement in the field of education; improve measurement instruments and procedures for their administration, scoring, interpretation, and use; and improve applications of measurement in assessment of individuals and evaluations of educational programs. It also disseminates knowledge about theory, techniques, and instrumentation available for measurement of educationally relevant human, institutional, and social characteristics; procedures appropriate to the interpretation and use of such techniques and instruments; and applications of educational measurement in individual and group evaluation. Its Web site is at http://www.ncme.org

PSYCHOMETRIC TEXTS AND MONOGRAPHS

Aiken, L. R., & Groth-Marnat, G. (2006). *Psychological testing and assessment* (12th ed.). Boston: Pearson Education.

This edition, like its predecessor, was designed primarily as a textbook for college students, but it also serves as a useful reference and review source for professionals involved in psychological assessment. Part III is devoted to vocational assessment, and Part IV covers assessment of personality, including a few instruments often used by career professionals.

Drummond, R. J., & Jones, K. D. (2006). *Assessment procedures for counselors and helping professionals* (6th ed.). Upper Saddle River, NJ: Pearson Education.

A systems approach is used to organize the knowledge, skills, and competencies needed by test users. Among other things, it includes chapters on assessment of abilities and intelligence, aptitudes, interest, personality, and career and employment. It also presents information on the use of computers in testing.

Hood, A. B., & Johnson R. W. (2007). Assessment in counseling: *A guide to the use of psychological assessment procedures* (4th ed.). Alexandria, VA: American Counseling Association.

This textbook about psychological assessment procedures discusses the use of more than 100 instruments as applied to counseling. Case examples help illustrate use of tests. A four-chapter section covers career and life planning assessment.

Lopez, S. J., & Snyder, C. R. (Eds.). (2003). Positive psychological assessment: A handbook of models and measures. Washington, DC: American Psychological Association.

This handbook helps support the movement away from relying solely on deficit-based models and towards explaining things in terms of positive perspectives. It demonstrates that positive personality characteristics can be measured as readily as negative ones. This volume contains 25 chapters that provide resources to assess strengths, healthy process, and well-being in a variety of domains, including career and vocational-related assessment.

Prince, J. P., & Heiser, L. J. (2000). *Essentials of career interest assessment.* New York: John Wiley & Sons.

Detailed guidance is provided in interpreting the *Strong Interest Inventory,* the *Campbell Interest and Skill Survey,* and the *Self-Directed Search.* A case report is also used to accentuate the similarities and differences between these instruments and to illustrate the value of using an assortment of measures. Additionally, a number of less traditional interest assessment tools are reviewed.

Walsh, W. B., & Betz, N. E. (2001). *Tests and assessment* (4th ed.). Englewood Cliffs, NJ: Prentice-Hall.

One of six parts in the text covers the assessment of interests and career development. Interest inventories, work values inventories, measures of career development and career maturity, and measures of career indecision are described and illustrated. The book is written specifically for a counselor audience.

Watkins, C. E., Jr., & Campbell, V. L. (Eds.). (2000). *Testing in counseling practice* (2nd ed.). Hillsdale, NJ: Lawrence Erlbaum.

This edition includes the same tests and assessment procedures as in the previous edition, but was updated according to test developments, revisions, refinements, and extensions. Several chapters covering various assessments include test background, conceptual foundations, test administration and scoring, test information, case examples, research, and evaluative comments.

Whiston, S. C. (2005). *Principles and applications of assessment in counseling* (2nd ed.). Belmont, CA: Brooks/Cole.

The goals of this book are to provide counseling students and counselors a comprehensive foundation in assessment and to expose them to a variety of assessment areas and issues. Section I focuses on the underlying principles of psychological assessment including basic concepts of measurement and fundamental assessment methods. Section II builds on those foundations by exploring specific methods and areas of client assessment, including chapters involving assessment of aptitudes, personality, couples and families, and career.

Zunker, V. G., & Osborn, D. S. (2006). *Using assessment results for career development* (7th ed.). Pacific Grove, CA: Brooks/Cole.

Three introductory chapters are comprised of assessment interpretation and use of results in counseling, and a review of measurement concepts. The following 10 chapters then cover many different types of career assessments. Descriptions of specific instruments are found within each of these chapters, and case studies are used to illustrate interpretations of some of the instruments. The final chapter is devoted to information on how to combine assessment results.

CAREER DEVELOPMENT TEXTS

Andersen, P., & Vandehey, M. (2006). *Career counseling and development in a global economy.* Boston: Lahaska Press.

This textbook provides a chapter on assessment and career counseling, and embeds various instruments within the text to facilitate an emphasis on viewing assessment instruments as a tool rather than the focus of counseling. It also includes a section designed to help guide practitioners in interpreting assessments.

Brown, D. (2007). *Career information, career counseling, and career development* (9th ed.). Boston: Allyn & Bacon.

This edition contains a stronger emphasis on technology and on cross-cultural issues, and has an increased emphasis on application. As in previous editions, career development theory, career information, career counseling practice, and career development programming are all covered in extensive detail. The text carefully describes the process of finding and securing jobs in an electronic era and presents students with the trends that are shaping the workplace today—and those that will continue to influence their careers over the next decade. However, this edition has a decided emphasis on multicultural career counseling. Also, the chapter on schools has been totally rewritten to correspond to the ASCA National Model. A single chapter on testing and assessment is included.

Brown, S. D., & Lent, R. W. (Eds.). (2000). *Handbook of counseling psychology* (3rd ed.). New York: John Wiley & Sons.

In this edition, chapters on career topics are distributed throughout the text rather than being confined to one section, as in the prior two editions. There is also a chapter on psychometrics.

Brown, S. D., & Lent, R. W. (Eds.). (2005). *Career development and counseling: Putting theory and research to work.* Hoboken, NJ: John Wiley & Sons.

Coverage of career-related theories, research, and career counseling for a variety of populations is provided in this text. A chapter on assessment highlights and discusses only tools that have acquired some scientific support.

Capuzzi, D., & Stauffer, M. D. (Eds.) (2006). *Career counseling: Foundations, perspectives, and applications.* Boston: Pearson Education.

This text provides a comprehensive view of career counseling from a variety of perspectives and authors. The chapter devoted to individual and group assessment and appraisal includes assessments developed to support theories, and those developed to measure specific career-related constructs. Readers are also provided with the description and availability of the assessments.

Duggan, M. H., & Jurgens, J.C. (2007). *Career interventions and techniques: A complete guide for human service professionals.* Boston: Allyn & Bacon.

This text provides detailed information on career development interventions appropriate to use with some of the most common populations with whom entry-level human service professionals often work. Each chapter includes a case study, a description of the population, barriers to career success, interventions, programs, a career counseling program model, and services specific to the population.

Gysbers, N. C., Heppner, M. J., & Johnston, J. A. (2003). *Career counseling: Process, issues, and techniques* (2nd ed.). Boston: Allyn & Bacon.

This textbook emphasizes the process of career counseling. Several chapters cover techniques and instruments for gathering client information, including a chapter on standardized tests and inventories. Whole chapters are devoted to card sorts and genograms.

Harris-Bowlsbey, J., Dikel, M. R., & Sampson, Jr., J. P. (2002). *The Internet: A tool for career planning.* Tulsa, OK: National Career Development Association.

This NCDA publication provides counselors with a valuable tool to help their clients engage in effective career planning. It gives annotations of Web sites, highlights potential problems and ethical concerns, presents models for integrating the use of Web sites, and provides information on how to develop a virtual career center.

Appendix A provides the *NCDA Guidelines for Use of the Internet for Provision of Career Information and Planning Services.*

Herr, E. L., Cramer, S. H., & Niles, S. G. (2004). *Career guidance and counseling through the life-span: Systematic approaches* (6th ed.). New York: Harper Collins

This text provides a comprehensive treatment of career guidance and counseling for all ages. One chapter addresses assessment and considers four major uses of assessment procedures: prediction, discrimination, monitoring, and evaluation. Within these sections, numerous instruments are described briefly.

Luzzo, D. A. (Ed.). (2000). *Career counseling of college students: An empirical guide to strategies that work.* Washington, D.C.: American Psychological Association.

This book includes chapters that help determine when career choice assessment is appropriate and ways to make assessment data more useful for college students. It also discusses principles of test selections and presents information on designing a system of career assessment intervention for large college-student groups.

Niles, S. G., & Harris-Bowlsbey, J. (2005). *Career development interventions in the 21st century* (2nd ed.). Upper Saddle River, NJ: Pearson Education.

This comprehensive textbook on career development devotes a chapter to assessment and career planning. It covers the relationship of assessment to the career planning process, its purposes, the responsibilities and competencies of counselors, and information on informal and formal assessments.

Peterson, N., & González, R. C. (2005). *The role of work in people's lives: Applied career counseling and vocational psychology* (2nd ed.). Belmont, CA: Brooks/ Cole.

This extensive revision of the first edition is a text designed for use in graduate-level classes. It contains information on measurement concepts and intersperses throughout assorted chapters assessments that can be used with various populations. Assessment with diverse populations is addressed. It also includes a "Tests and Publishers" appendix.

Reardon, R. C., Lenz, J. G., Sampson, J. P., & Peterson, G. W. (2000). Career development and planning: A comprehensive approach (2nd ed.). Belmont, CA: Wadsworth/Brooks/Cole.

This text, which is designed for use in an undergraduate career development course, uses a cognitive psychology approach to solving career problems and making career decisions. It includes a chapter on improving self-knowledge that describes various approaches to assessing values, interests, and skills.

Sampson, J. P., Jr., Reardon, R. C., Peterson, G. W., & Lenz, J. (2004). *Career counseling & services: A cognitive information processing approach.* Pacific Grove, CA: Brooks-Cole.

The authors describe career development and career counseling from a unique cognitive information-processing framework. They include one chapter on how to select and interpret career assessment procedures that elaborates on self and career schemata. A few instruments are described as examples.

Sharf, R. S. (2006). *Applying career development theory to counseling* (4th ed.). Belmont, CA: Thomson Wadsworth.

This undergraduate textbook was designed to help relate career theory and research to the actual practice of counseling. Various tests and inventories are integrated with the theories throughout the book.

Walsh, W. B., & Savickas, M. L. (Eds.). (2005). *Handbook of vocational psychology* (3rd ed.). Mahwah, NJ: Lawrence Erlbaum Associates.

This comprehensive text on the field of vocational psychology includes information to familiarize readers with various techniques, procedures and theories available for vocational assessment. Two chapters on assessment include the integration of career assessment and counseling as well as a critical review of the empirical literature regarding the use of various measures and assessments with culturally diverse individuals.

Zunker, V. G. (2006). *Career counseling: A holistic approach* (7th ed.). Pacific Grove, CA: Brooks/Cole.

This comprehensive career counseling text is intended for use in graduate level career counseling courses. It includes a chapter on using standardized assessments, and a chapter on self-assessment and nonstandardized methods of using assessment results. Many of the prominent standardized instruments that address various assessment goals are described. Additionally, publisher addresses are provided.

MATERIALS FOR SPECIAL POPULATIONS

Boer, P. M. (2001). *Career counseling over the Internet: An emerging model for trusting and responding to online clients.* Mahwah, NJ: Lawrence Erlbaum Associates.

This book discusses and attempts to clarify the link between career counseling and testing by defining assessment terms and using client examples to demonstrate implementation of online assessment. The author also includes NCDA ethical guidelines for online assessment.

Bolton, B. F. (Ed.). (2001). *Handbook of measurement and evaluation in rehabilitation* (3rd ed.). Gaithersburg, MD: Aspen Publishers.

This comprehensive revision of prior editions includes a review of measurement principles and assessment strategies in rehabilitation. It is divided into three parts that include fundamentals of measurement, review of instruments, and application in rehabilitation.

Harrington, T. F. (Ed.). (2003). *Handbook of career planning for students with special needs* (2nd ed.). Austin, TX: PRO-ED.

This is a guide for practitioners that comprehensively covers career planning with youth and adults who have special needs, based on the career competencies identified by the National Occupational Information Coordinating Committee (NOICC). Topics range from identifying goals to planning for transition. The Harrington-O'Shea Career Decision-Making System Revised (CDM-R) is addressed specifically.

Podmostko, M. (2007). *Tunnels and cliffs: A guide for workforce development practitioners and policymakers serving youth with mental health needs.* Washington, DC: National Collaborative on Workforce and Disability for Youth, Institute for Educational Leadership.

This guide was developed as part of the U.S. Department of Labor's Office of Disability Employment Policy's (ODEP's) work to help workforce development practitioners, administrators, and policymakers increase their understanding of youth with mental health needs and the supports necessary to help those youth transition into the workforce successfully. This guide provides practical information and resources for youth service practitioners. In addition, it provides policymakers from the program level to the state level with information to help them address system and policy obstacles in order to improve service delivery systems for youth with mental health needs. It can be downloaded for no cost from http://www.ncwd-youth.info/resources & Publications/mental health.html

Power, P. W. (2000). *A guide to vocational assessment* (3rd ed.). Austin, TX: PRO-ED.

This book is written for those who counsel clients with disabilities. This edition considers the assessment needs of multicultural populations and progressively recognized disability groups. Various interest, personality, intelligence, and educational achievement instruments are discussed in reference to people with disabilities.

Suzuki, L. A., Ponterotto, J. G., & Meller, P. J. (Eds.). (2001). *Handbook of multicultural assessment: Clinical, psychological, and educational applications* **(2nd ed.). San Francisco: Jossey-Bass.**

This text provides a comprehensive view of various multicultural assessment issues as well as updated information pertaining to particular testing issues and instruments. It includes sections on vocational assessment and personality assessment across cultures.

Venn, J. J. (2004). *Assessing students with special needs* **(3rd ed.). Upper Saddle River, NJ: Pearson Education.**

This text covers the assessment of students with special needs from preschool into adulthood. It includes a chapter specifically on career and vocational assessment that covers assessment of interests, and prevocational and employability skills; work sample evaluation; and situational and on-the-job assessment.

TEST BIBLIOGRAPHIES AND REVIEWS

Educational Testing Service (ETS). (2007). *Test link.* **Princeton, NJ: Author.**

The Test Collection at ETS is a library of more than 25,000 tests and other measurement devices that makes information on standardized tests and research instruments available. Collected from the early 1900s to the present, the Test Collection at ETS is the largest such compilation in the world. Vocational interest inventories and aptitude tests, work samples, attitude assessments, measures of career development, certification tests, measures for use with persons with disabilities, and instruments to measure organizational climate and managerial styles are included. Information provided for each test includes name, descriptors, availability, length of test and administration time, and a brief description.

Geisinger, K. F., Spies, R. A., Carlson, J. F., & Plake, B. S. (Eds.) (2007). *The seventeenth mental measurements yearbook.* **Lincoln, NE: Buros Institute of Mental Measurements.**

This is the most recent volume of the most well-known source of test reviews. It contains reviews of tests that are new or significantly revised. Reviews, descriptions, and references associated with many older tests can be located in previous editions. One or two critical reviews are printed for each instrument. Each test is described, and technical and practical issues are addressed. Most career-related instruments have been reviewed in one or more volumes of the MMY series. This volume contains reviews of more than 40 tests classified for vocations.

Keyser, D. J. (Ed.). (2005). *Test critiques—volume XI.* **Austin, TX: PRO-ED.**

Volumes I–XI of this series contain descriptive and critical reviews of measurement instruments that were determined to be frequently used. Included in this volume under the category of Student Evaluation and Counseling are 30 instruments used in vocational guidance and various instruments measuring interests. There are more than 100 assessments included under the category of Business and Industry, including those assessing aptitudes, interests, skills, and attitudes.

Maddox, T. (Ed.). (2003). *Tests: A comprehensive reference for assessments in psychology, education and business* (5th ed.). Austin, TX: PRO-ED.

The purpose of Tests is to provide a quick reference for tests available in English. Its coverage is narrower than Tests in Print, but there is generous overlap. Information is provided under the headings Title, Author, Copyright Date, Population, Purpose, Description, Format, Scoring, Cost, and Publisher. Five indices cover Titles, Tests not in 5th Edition, Publishers not in 5th Edition, Authors, and Publishers.

Murphy, L. L., Spies, R. A. & Plake, B. S. (Eds.). (2006). *Tests in print VII.* Lincoln, NE: Buros Institute of Mental Measurements.

Nearly all commercially published tests in English are listed here in alphabetical order by test title. Information provided includes Title, Purpose, Population, Publication Date, Acronym, Scores, Administration, Forms, Manual, Restricted Distribution, Price, Languages, Time, Comments, Author, Foreign Adaptations, Sublistings, and Cross-references. Seven indices are also provided for Title, Tests Out of Print, Acronyms, Subject, Publisher, Names, and Scores.

Thomas, J. C., & Hersen, M. (Eds.) (2004). *Comprehensive handbook of psychological assessment: Volume 4 – Industrial and organizational assessment.* Hoboken, NJ: John Wiley & Sons.

This series includes four volumes covering a broad range of psychological assessment. The fourth volume is dedicated to assessment in organizations and includes information regarding tests, inventories, interviews, simulations, and performance appraisal. It also includes assessment of work groups or teams, the employee's reaction to the workplace, and assessment for research purposes.

PERIODICALS THAT PUBLISH TEST RESEARCH AND REVIEWS
(Websites change frequently, please search for journal name on the Internet.)

Assessment. Sage Publications, Inc., 2455 Teller Road, Thousand Oaks, CA 91320 (4/yr.). www.sagepub.com

The Career Development Quarterly. National Career Development Association, 305 North Beech Circle, Broken Arrow, OK 74012 (4/yr.). http://www.ncda.org/membersonly/cdq.htm (Formerly: The Vocational Guidance Quarterly.)

The Counseling Psychologist. Sage Publications, Inc., 2455 Teller Road, Thousand Oaks, CA 91320 (6/yr.). http://tcp.sagepub.com/

Counselor Education and Supervision. American Counseling Association, 5999 Stevenson Avenue, Alexandria, VA (4/yr.). http://ohiou.edu/che/ces/

Educational and Psychological Measurement. Sage Publications, Inc., 2455 Teller Road, Thousand Oaks, CA 91320 (6/yr.). http://epm.sagepub.com/

Journal of Applied Psychology. American Psychological Association, 750 First Street NE, Washington, DC 20002-4242 (6/yr.). http://www.apa.org/journals/apl/

Journal of Career Assessment. Psychological Assessment Resources, Inc., P.O. Box 998, Odessa, FL 33556 (4/yr.). http://jca.sagepub.com/

Journal of Career Development. Sage Publications, Inc. 2455 Teller Road, Thousand Oaks, CA. 91320 (4/yr.). http://jcd.sagepub.com/ (Formerly: Journal of Career Education.)

Journal of Counseling and Development. American Counseling Association, 5999 Stevenson Avenue, Alexandria, VA 22304 (6/yr.). http://www.counseling.org/Publications/Journals.aspx

Journal of Counseling Psychology. American Psychological Association, 750 First Street NE, Washington, DC 20002-4242 (4/yr.). http://www.apa.org/journals/cou/

Journal of Educational Measurement. National Council on Measurement in Education, 1230 17th St. NW, Washington, DC 22304 (4/yr.). http://www.blackwellpublishing.com/journal.asp?ref=0022-0655

Journal of Personality Assessment. Society for Personality Assessment, Inc., 6109H Arlington Boulevard, Falls Church, VA 22044 (6/yr.). http://ejournals.ebsco.com/Journal2.asp?JournalID=103474

Journal of Psychoeducational Assessment. The Psychoeducational Corporation, 505 22nd Street, Knoxville, TN 37916 (4/yr.). http://jpa.sagepub.com/

Journal of Vocational Behavior. Elsevier, The Boulevard, Langford Lane, Kidlington, Oxford (6/yr.). http://www.elsevier.com/wps/find/journaldescription.cws_home/622908/description#description

NewsNotes. Association for Assessment in Counseling and Education, 5999 Stevenson Avenue, Alexandria, VA 22304 (4/yr.). http://aac.ncat.edu/notes.html (Formerly: AACE Newsnotes, AMECD Newsnotes, and AMEG Newsnotes.)

Measurement and Evaluation in Counseling and Development. American Counseling Association, 5999 Stevenson Avenue, Alexandria, VA 22304.(4/yr.). http://www.periodicals.com/html/ihp_e.html?em12713

Professional School Counseling. American School Counselor Association, 5999 Stevenson Avenue, Alexandria, VA 22304 (5/yr.). http://www.schoolcounselor.org/content.asp?contentid=235 (Includes what was formerly published as The School Counselor and Elementary School Guidance and Counseling.)

Psychology in the Schools. John Wiley & Sons, Inc., 606 Third Avenue, New York, NY 10158 (6/yr.). http://www.wiley.com/WileyCDA/WileyTitle/productCd-PITS.html

School Psychology Review. National Association of School Psychologists, 4340 East West Highway, Suite 402, Bethesda, MD 20814 (4/yr.). http://www.nasponline.org/publications/spr/sprmain.aspx

ADDITIONAL CAREER ASSESSMENT WEB SITES

AACE Reviews Online: Association for Assessment in Counseling and Education http://www.theaaceonline.com/resources.htm — A database of reviews are available which have been previously included within NewsNotes, the AACE division newsletter.

Achieve: http://www.achieve.org/ — Created by the nation's governors and business leaders to assist states in raising achievement so that students graduate ready for college and work.

America's Career Resource Network (ACRN): http://www.acrnetwork.org — Consists of federal and state organizations that provide information and training on career and college opportunities. Provides information, resources, and guidance to students, parents, teachers, and counselors. Products include a career toolkit, The National Career Development Guidelines, and other career decision-making tools.

American Psychological Association: http://www.apa.org/science/testclearinghs. html — Testing information clearinghouse. Publications available include finding information about tests, prediction of trustworthiness in pre-employment selection decisions, test user qualifications, and assessment-related references for women, people with disabilities, and cultural/ethnic/linguistically diverse populations.

Assessment Book: http://wadsworth.com/counseling — Listings of assessment instruments and assessment resources.

Association of Computer-Based Systems for Career Information (ACSCI): www.acsci.org/standards.asp — ACSCI promotes the use and improvement of career information technology and related services and products through standards, professional development opportunities and public information.

ATP Test Publishers: www.testpublishers.org — Listings of tests available with access to test publishers' web sites.

Buros Test Reviews Online: http://buros.unl.edu/buros/jsp/search.jsp — Publisher of the Mental Measurement Yearbook series, Test in Print, and other assessment references and monographs. Reviews are available online as they appear in the Mental Measurements Yearbook series.

Impact Publications: http://impactpublications.com — Resources on assessments instruments, career exploration, life skills, résumés, and applications.

National Alliance for Secondary Education and Transition: http://nasetalliance.org/about/index.htm — Transition Tool Kit for current research on effective schooling, career preparation, youth development, and leadership.

National Collaborative on Workforce and Disability: http://www.ncwd-youth.info/ A source of information about employment and youth with disabilities. Extensive review of literature, demonstration projects, and effective services.

O*NET Resource Center: http://www.onetcenter.org/ — A national source of occupational information and O*NET products, assessments, tools, and reports.

Sage Journals Online: http://jca.sagepub.com — Research and reports concerning career assessments and career development topics.

U.S. Department of Education: www.ed.gov — Under "Information Centers", click on "Research & Statistics". A user friendly guide to identifying and implementing practices supported by evidence.

VRI Career Planning Solutions: www.vri.org — Community-based assessment and employment planning software, resources for workplace mentoring, replacement parts for Apticom, and work samples.

APPENDIX B

PUBLISHER*
ADDRESSES – PHONE NUMBERS – WEB PAGES

ACT, Inc.
500 ACT Drive
P.O. Box 168
Iowa City, IA 52243-0168
319-337-1000
http://www.act.org

Advantage Learning Solutions
5512 NE 109th Ct. Suite A-1
Vancouver, WA 98662
http://advantagelearningsolutions.com

American Guidance Service, Inc. (AGS)
[See Pearson Assessments for AGS assessment products]

Assessment.com
7400 Metro Blvd. Suite #350
Edina, MN 55439
952-921-9368
Fax: 952-844-9025
http://www.Assessment.com
E-mail: support@assessment.com

Bay State Psychological Associates, Inc.
225 Friend Street
Boston, MA 02114
800-438-2772
Fax 888-375-5636
http://www.eri.com/contact.html
E-mail: sales@eri.com

Beach Center on Disability
University of Kansas
Haworth Hall, Room 3136
1200 Sunnyside Avenue
Lawrence, KS 66045-7534
785-864-7600
Fax: 785-864-7605
http://www.beachcenter.org

Beilby
2 Brook Street
East Perth WA 6004
Australia
+61 8 9323 8888
Fax: +61 8 9323 8899
http://www.beilby.com.au
E-mail: perth@beilby.com.au

Bizet Human Asset Management
11221 Boyce Road
Building 2 Suite 700
Pittsburgh, PA 15241
800-328-3847
http://www.bizet.com
E-mail: contactus@bizet.com

Bowling Green State University
JDI Office
Department of Psychology
Bowling Green, OH 43403
419-372-8247
Fax: 419-372-6013
http://showcase.bgsu.edu/IOPsych/jdi/index.html
E-mail: jdi_ra@bgnet.bgsu.edu

Career Consulting Corner
1492 Cloud Lane
New Braunfels, Texas 78130
830-625-9515
http://www.careercc.com
E-mail: career30@careercc.com

Career Education Readiness Measurement and Research
University of Southern Illinois
Edwardsville, Il 62025
618-650-3708

* Addresses and, when available, phone numbers, fax numbers, web pages and email addresses are provided for all instruments included in either the review or additional instruments chapters. All information provided here was compiled by Sibyl Cato, Rich W. Feller, Brenda Gerhardt, Edwin A. Whitfield, and Chris Wood.

Career Key
http://www.careerkey.org
E-mail: lawrencejonesphd@earthlink.net

Career Passports, Inc.
4747 Table Mesa Drive, Suite 200
Boulder, CO 80303
800-321-9381

Career Systems International, Inc.
2300 Stafford Avenue Suite 500
Scranton, PA 18505
800-577-6916
Fax: 570-346-8606
http://www.careersystemsintl.com/
E-mail: HQ@scibka.com

Career Trainer
10725 Ellis Ave. #D
Fountain Valley, CA 92708
800-888-4945
714-965-7698
Fax: 714-965-7697
http://www.careertrainer.com
E-mail: service@careertrainer.com

Career Vision
800 Roosevelt Road
Suite E-200
Glen Ellyn, IL 60137
800-469-8378
http://www.careervision.org
E-mail: info@careervision.org

Career Voyages
877-872-5627
http://www.careervoyages.gov/
E-mail: career.voyages@dol.gov

Careerware
38465 NYS Rt. 12
P.O. Box 129
Clayton, NY 13624
800-267-1544
E-mail: siobhan@ca.ibm.com

CASAS, Comprehensive Adult Student Assessment Systems
5151 Murphy Canyon Road, Suite 220
San Diego, CA 92123
800-255-1036
http://www.casas.org
E-mail: casas@casas.org

CFKR Career Materials, Inc.
P.O. Box 99
Meadow Vista, CA 95722
800-525-5626
Fax: 800-770-0433
http://www.cfkr.com/
E-mail: order@cfkr.com

Chronicle Guidance Publications, Inc.
66 Aurora Street
Moravia, NY 13118-3569
Phone: 800-899-0454
FAX: 315-497-0339
http://www.chronicleguidance.com/
E-mail: customerservice@ChronicleGuidance.com

COIN Educational Products
3361 Executive Parkway, Suite 302
Toledo, Ohio 43606
800-274-8515
Fax: 419-536-7056
http://www.coinedu.com
E-mail: customerservice@coinedu.com

The Conley Group, Inc.
2867 104th Street
Des Moines, IA 50322
800-383-6813
Fax: 515-277-7275
http://www.theconleygroup.com/
        products_available.htm

The Conover Company
1789 North Oakwood Rd
Oshkosh, WI 54904
800-933-1933
Fax 920-231-4809
http://www.conovercompany.com
E-mail: conover@execpc.com

Consulting Psychologists Press, Inc. (CPP, Inc.) and Davies-Black Publishing
1055 Joaquin Road, Second Floor
Mountain View, CA 94043
650-969-8901
Fax: 650-969-8608
http://www.cpp.com
E-mail: custserv@cpp.com

Consulting Resource Group International
PO Box 418 Main
Abbotsford, BC V2T 6Z7
800-852-4347
Fax: 604-850-3003
www.crgleader.com
E-mail: info@crgleader.com

Council for Exceptional Children (CEC)
1110 North Glebe Road
Arlington, VA 22201
888-232-7733
703-264-9451 (LCCE)
Fax: 703-264-9494
http://www.cec.sped.org/
E-mail: service@cec.sped.org

Creative Organizational Design
116 College St.
Kitchener, ON N2H 5A3
519-745-0142
Fax 519-745-9185
http://www.creativeorgdesign.com
E-mail: info@creativeorgdesign.com

CTB McGraw Hill
20 Ryan Ranch Road
Monterey, CA 93940
800-538-9547
Fax: 800-282-0266
http://www.ctb.com/
E-mail: tmsupport@ctb.com
E-mail: astreetman@ctb.com

Curriculum Associates, Inc.
153 Rangeway Road
North Billerica, MA 01862-0901
800-225-0248
Fax: 800-366-1158
http://www.curriculumassociates.com/
E-mail: info@cainc.com

Education Associates, Inc.
P.O. Box 23308
Louisville, KY 40223
866-427-5543
Fax: 502-244-9144
http://www.educationassociates.com/

Educational and Industrial Testing Service (Edlts)
P.O. Box 7234
San Diego, CA 92167
800-416-1666
Fax: 619-226-1666
http:// www.edits.net
E-mail: customerservice@edits.net

Educational Technologies/Invest Learning Computer Curriculum Corporation
P. O. Box 3711
Sunnyvale, CA 94088-3711
800-927-9997
http://www.ccclearn.com
E-mail: info@cccpp.com

Educational Testing Service (ETS)
Rosedale Road
Princeton, NJ 08541 USA
609-921-9000
Fax: 609-734-5410
http://www.ets.org/
E-mail: etsinfo@ets.org

Educators'/Employers' Tests and Services Associates
P.O. Box 327
St. Thomas, PA 17252
717-369-4222
Fax: 717-369-2344
E-mail: psb@epix.net

Elbern Publications
P. O. Box 9497
Columbus OH 43209
614-235-2643
No Web Page
E-mail: ebecker@insight.rr.com

Employment Technologies Corporation
532 South New York Avenue
Winter Park, FL 32789
800-833-3279
Fax: 407-788-1496
http://www.etc-easy.com/
E-mail: Info@etc-easy.com

ESTR Publications
1907 18th St. S.
Moorhead, MN 56560
218-287-8477
Fax: 218-236-5199
http://www.estr.net/
E-mail: transition@estr.net

Finney Company
8075 215th Street West
Lakeville, MN 55044
800-846-7027
Fax: 800-330-6232
http://www.finney-hobar.com/
E-mail: feedback@finney-hobar.com

Gallup Organization
1001 Gallup Drive
Omaha, NE 68102
402-951-2003
Fax: 888-500-8282
www.strengthsfinder.com

GIA Publications, Inc.
7404 South Mason Avenue
Chicago, IL 60638
800-GIA-1358 (442-1358)
708-496-3800
Fax: 708-496-3828
http://www.giamusic.com
E-mail: custserv@giamusic.com

H & H Publishing Co., Inc.
1231 Kapp Drive
Clearwater, Florida 33765-2116
800-366-4079
Fax: 727-442-2195
http://www.hhpublishing.com
E-mail: HHService@HHPublishing.com

Harcourt Assessment, Inc.
19500 Bulverde Road
San Antonio, TX 78259
Attn: Customer Service
800-872-1726
Fax: 800-232-1223
http://www.harcourtassessment.com
E-mail: customercare@harcourt.com

Hawthorne Educational Services, Inc.
800 Gray Oak Drive
Columbia, MO 65201
573-874-1673
Fax: 800-442-9509
http://www.hes-inc.com
E-mail: info@hes-inc.com

Hay Group - Hay Resources Direct
116 Huntington Avenue
Boston, MA 02116
800-729-8074
Fax: 617-927-5008
http://www.hayresourcesdirect.haygroup.com
E-mail: haytrg@haygroup.com

HeadMinder, Inc.
15 Maiden Lane, Suite 205
New York, NY 10038
212-349-2007
Fax: 212-766-9637
http://www.headminder.com/
E-mail: info@headminder.com

The Highlands Company
1328 Boston Post Road
Larchmont, NY 10538
914-834-0055 / 800-373-0083
http://www.highlandsco.com
E-mail: info@highlandsco.com

Human Resource Development Press
22 Amherst Road
Amherst, MA 01002
800-822-2801
Fax: 413-253-3490
http://www.hrdpress.com
E-mail: info@hrdpress.com customerservice@
hrdpress.com

Human Sciences Research Council
Private Bag X41
Pretoria   0001
[+27 (0) 12] 302 2999
http://www.hsrc.ac.za/
www@ludwig.hsrc.ac.za

Human Synergistics International
39819 Plymouth Rd. C8020
Plymouth, MI 48170-8020
800-622-7584
Fax: 734-459-5557
http://www.humansynergistics.com/
E-mail: info@humansynergistics.com

Impact Publications
9104 Manassas Drive, Suite N
Manassas Park, VA 20111-5211
703-361-7300
Fax: 703-335-9486
http://impactpublications.com
E-mail: query@impactpublications.com

Industrial Psychology International (IPI)
4106 Fieldstone Road Box 6479
Champaign, IL 61822 61826-6479
217-398-468
800-747-1119
Fax: 217-398-5798
http://www.metritech.com/
E-mail: ipi@metritech.com

Insight Institute, Inc.
7205 NW Waukomis Drive
Kansas City, MO 64151
800-861-4769
816-587-3881
Fax: 816-587-5119
http://www.insightinstitute.com
E-mail: customerservice@insightinstitute.com

Institute for Personality & Ability Testing (IPAT)
1801 Woodfield Drive
Savoy, IL 61874
800-225-4728
Fax: 217-352-9674
http://www.IPAT.com
E-mail: custserv@ipat.com

Instructional Technology, Inc.
P.O. Box 2056
Easton, MD 21601
800-274-6832
Fax: 410-822-0842
http://www.intecinc.net
E-mail: bchapman@IntecInc.net

IntegriView, LLC
460 N. University Avenue, Suite 201
Provo, UT 84601
800-470-6160
Fax: 801-373-8861
http://www.integriview.com
E-mail: sales@integriview.com

JIST Publishing, Inc.
875 Montreal Way
St. Paul, MN 55102
800-648-5478
Fax: 800-547-8329
http://www.jist.com
E-mail: info@jist.com

Jossey-Bass/Pfeiffer
989 Market Street
San Francisco, CA 94104-1741
415-433-1740
Fax: 415-433-0499
http://www.Pfeiffer.com
E-mail: webperson@jbp.com
E-mail: support@Learning-Resources.com
E-mail: fmcdermo@pfeiffer.com

Keirsey.com
1900 O'Farrell Street, Suite 310
San Mateo, CA 94403
www.personalityzone.com
www.keirsey.com

Kuder, Inc.
302 Visions Parkway
Adel, IA 50003
800-314-8972
www.kuder.com

Lafayette Instrument Company
P.O. Box 5729
3700 Sagamore Parkway North
Lafayette, IN 47903
800-428-7545
Fax: 765-423-4111
http://www.lafayetteinstrument.com
E-mail: lic@lafayetteinstrument.com

Learning Resource, Inc.
700 Canal Street
Stamford, CT 06902-5921
203-637-5047
Fax: 203-637-2786
http://www.learning-resources.com/
E-mail: support@Learning-Resources.com

Learning Resources, Inc.
1117 E. Putnam Avenue, # 260
Riverside, CT 06878
Phone: 203-637-5047
Fax: 203-637-2786
E-mail: support@Learning-Resources.com

Life Office Management Association (LOMA)
2300 Windy Ridge Parkway, Suite 600
Atlanta, Georgia 30339
770-984-6450 (JEPS)
Fax: 770-984-0441
http://www.loma.org/jeps.htm
E-mail: empselect@loma

LIFECORP
P.O. Box 13853
Tucson, AZ 85732
http://www.life-corp.com/

Management Research Institute
11304 Spur Wheel Lane
Potomac, MD 20854
301-299-9200
Fax: 301-299-9227
http://www.managementresearchinstitute.com/
E-mail: mrieaf@aol.com

McCarron-Dial Systems
PO Box 35285
Dallas, TX 75235-0285
214-634-2863
Fax: 214-634-9970
http://www.mccarrondial.com
E-mail: mds@mccarrondial.com

Measurement for Human Resources
83 Rougeau Avenue
Winnipeg, Manitoba CANADA R2C 3X5
204-661-6438
E-mail: mhr@escape.ca

Meridian Education Corporation
90 MacCorkle Ave., SW, Dept. WEB
South Charleston, WV 25325
800-727-5507
Fax: 888-340-5507
http://www.meridianeducation.com/
E-mail: meridian@meridianeducation.com

Metritech
4106 Fieldstone Road
P.O. Box 6479
Champaign, Illinois 61826-6479
http://www.metritech.com
E-mail: mtinfo@metritech.com

Moving Boundaries
1375 Southwest Blaine Court
Gresham, OR 97080
888-661-4433
503-661-4126
Fax: 503-661-5304
http://www.movingboundaries.com
E-mail: info@ movingboundaries.com

National Clearinghouse of Rehabilitation Training Materials (NCRTM)
Utah State University
6524 Old Main Hill
Logan, UT 84322-6524
866-821-5355
Fax 435-797-7537
http://ncrtm.org/
E-mail: ncrtm@cc.usu.edu

National Occupational Competency Testing Institute (NOCTI)
500 North Bronson Avenue
Big Rapids, MI 49307
800-334-6283
Fax: 231-796-4699
http://www.nocti.org/
E-mail: nocti@nocti.org

Nelson Canada Limited
Measurement and Guidance Department
1120 Birchmont Road
Scarborough, Ontario, Canada M1K5G4
800-268-2222
800-430-4445
http://www.nelson.com/
E-mail: rstrana@nelson.com

NFER-Nelson Publishing Co., Ltd.
2 Oxford Road East
Windsor, Berkshire SL4 1DF
44(0)1753 858961
http://www.assessmentcentre.com/
E-mail: edu&hsc@nfer-nelson.co.uk

PAQ Services, Inc.
11 Bellwether Way, Suite 107
Bellingham, WA 98225
800-292-2198
Fax: 877-395-0236
http://www.paq.com/
E-mail: paginfo@paq.com

Pearson Assessments (American Guidance Services)
5601 Green Valley Drive
Bloomington, MN 55437
800-627-7271
Fax: 800-632-9011
http://ags.pearsonassessments.com
E-mail: agsinfo@pearson.com

Peregrine Partners (CareerLeader, LLP)
1330 Beacon Street
Suite #265
Brookline, MA 02446
617-738-8819
Fax: 617-738-9783
E-mail: help@careerleader.com

Performance Assessment Network (A TALX Company)
11590 N. Meridian Street, Suite 200
Carmel, IN 46032
877-449-TEST
http://www.panpowered.com
E-mail: info@pantesting.com

Personal Strengths Publishing, Inc.
P.O. Box 2605
Carlsbad, CA 92018-2605
800-624-7347
Fax: 760-602-0087
http://www.personalstrengths.com/
E-mail: mail@personalstrengths.com

PESCO International, Inc.
21 Paulding Street
Pleasantville, NY 10570
800-431-2016
Fax: 914-769-2970
http://www.pesco.org
E-mail: pesco@pesco.org

Piney Mountain Press, Inc.
P.O. Box 986
Dahlonega, GA 30533
800-255-3127
Fax: 800-905-3127
http://www.pineymountain.com/
E-mail: cyberguy@alltel.net

Price Systems, Inc.
P. O. Box 1818
Lawrence, KS 66044-8818
800-574-4441
http://www.proedinc.com
E-mail: info@proedinc.com

Previsor
1805 Old Alabama Road
Suite 150
Roswell, GA 30076
800-367-2509
http://www.previsor.com/

Pro-Ed, Inc.
8700 Shoal Creek Blvd
Austin, TX 78757-6897
512-451-3246
800-897-3202
Fax: 512-451-8542
http://www.proedinc.com
E-mail: info@proedinc.com

Program Development Associates
P. O. Box 2038
Syracuse, NY 13220-2038
800-543-2119
Fax 315-452-0710
http://www.disabilitytraining.com
E-mail: info@disabilitytraining.com

Prometheus Nemesis Book Company
P.O. Box 2748,
Del Mar, CA 92014
800-754-0039

Psychological and Educational Publications
PO Box 520
Hydesville, CA 95547
800-523-5775
Fax: 800-447-0907
http://www.psych-edpublications.com/

Psychological Assessment Resources, Inc. (PAR)
16204 N. Florida Avenue
Lutz, FL 33549
800-331-8378
Fax: 800-727-9329
http://www3.parinc.com
E-mail: custserv@parinc.com

Psychological Corporation (PsyCorp) (see Harcourt Assessment, Inc)
19500 Bulverde Road
San Antonio, TX 78259-2498
800-872-1726
Fax: 800-232-1223
http://harcourtassessment.com
E-mail: customer_service@harcourt.com

Psychological Services, Inc. PSI
2950 N Hollywood Way, Suite 200
Burbank, CA 91505
818-847-6180
Fax: 818-847-8701
Toll Free: 800-367-1565
www.corporate.psionline.com/assessment/

Psychologists and Educators, Inc.
P.O. Box 513
Chesterfield, MO 63006
314-536-2366
Fax: 314-434-2331
E-mail: Psychologistseduc@earthlink.com

Psychometrics Canada Ltd.
7125-77 Avenue
Edmonton, Alberta, Canada T6B 0B5
800-661-5158
Fax: 780-469-2283
http://www.psychometrics.com/
E-mail: info@psychometrics.com.

Psychtest/M.D. Angus & Associates Limited
115 First Street P.O. Box 1477
Sumas, WA 98295
604-464-1466
Fax: 604-357-3113
http://www.psychtest.com
E-mail: mdangus@psychtest.com

Ramsay Corporation
Boyce Station Offices
1050 Boyce Road
Pittsburgh, PA 15241-3907
412-257-0732
Fax: 412-257-9929
http://www.ramsaycorp.com
E-mail: sales@ramsaycorp.com

R.B. Slaney
Department of Counseling Psychology
327 Cedar Building
Pennsylvania State University
University Park, PA 16803
814-865-8304
No Web Page
E-mail: trx@psu.edu

Research Psychologists Press
P.O. Box 610984
Port Huron, MI 48061-0984
800-265-1285
Fax: 800-361-9411
http://www.sigmaassessmentsystems.com
E-mail: inforeq@sigmaassessmentsystems.com

The Richardson Co. Training Media
13 Creekwood Ln SW
Lakewood, Washington 98499
800-488-0319
Fax: 253-588-0815
http://www.rctm.com
E-mail: rctm@rctm.com

Riverside Publishing
3800 Golf Road, Suite 100
Rolling Meadows, IL 60008
800-323-9540
Fax: 630-467-7192
http://www.riverpub.com
E-mail: rpcwebmaster@hmco.com
E-mail: rpcsupport@hmco.com

Scholastic Testing Service, Inc. (STS)
480 Meyer Road
Bensenville, Illinois 60106-1617
800-642-6787
Fax: 866-766-8054
http://www.ststesting.com/
E-mail: sts@mail.ststesting.com

SHL Americas (Saville & Holdsworth, Ltd.)
Flatiron Park West
2555 55th Street Suite 201D
Boulder, CO 80301
303-442-5607
Fax: 303-442-1184
http://www.shl.com/SHL/americas
E-mail: shl.boulder@shlgroup.com

SIGMA Assessment Systems, Inc
511 Fort St., Suite 435
PO Box 610984
Port Huron, MI 48061-0984
800-265-1285
Fax: 800-361-9411
http://www.sigmaassessmentsystems.com
E-mail: inforeq@sigmaassessmentsystems.com
SIGMA@sigmaassessments.com

Slosson Educational Publications, Inc.
P.O. Box 544
East Aurora, NY 14052-0544
888-756-7766
Fax: 800-655-3840
http://www.slosson.com
E-mail: slosson@slosson.com

SOI Systems
45755 Goodpasture Road, Box D
Vida, Oregon 97488
541-896-3936
Fax: 541-896-3983
http://www.soisystems.com/
E-mail: info@soisystems.com

Steck-Vaughn Rigby Steck-Vaughn
(Harcourt Achieve)
6277 Sea Harbor Drive
Orlando, FL 32887
800-531-5015
Fax: 800-699-9459
http://steckvaughn.harcourtachieve.com/en-US/
steckvaughn.htm
E-mail: eha@harcourt.com

Stoelting Company
620 Wheat Lane
Wood Dale, IL 60191
630-860-9700
Fax: 630-860-9775
http://www.stoeltingco.com
E-mail: psychtests@stoeltingco.com

Stout Vocational Rehabilitation Institute
The Rehabilitation Source
University of Wisconsin-Stout
Menomonie, WI 54751
715-232-2475
http://svri.uwstout.edu/
E-mail: luij@uwstout.edu

Talent Assessment, Inc. VIP
P.O. Box 5087
Jacksonville, Florida 32247-5087
800-634-1472
Fax: 904-292-9371
http://www.talentassessment.com
E-mail: talenta@bellsouth.net

Talico, Inc.
P.O. Box 3658
Ponte Vedra, FL 32004-3658
4375-4 Southside Blvd, Suite 157
Jacksonville, FL 32216
904-285-7757
Fax: 904-285-7306
http://www.talico.com/
E-mail: info@talico.com

Teleometrics International
4567 Lake Shore Drive
Waco, TX 76710
800-527-0406
Fax: 254-772-9588
http://www.teleometrics.com/
E-mail: teleo.info@teleometrics.com

University of Missouri
Career Center
909 Lowry Hall
Columbia, MO 65211
573-882-2351
Fax: 573-882-5440
http://career.missouri.edu/
E-mail: coatsl@missouri.edu

US Book Distributors
11000 Wilshire Blvd.
P.O. Box 24009
Los Angeles, CA 90024
Fax: 818-884-8079
http://www.usbookdistributors.com
E-mail: info@usbookdistributors.com

U.S. Department of Defense
Defense Manpower Data Center (ASVAB)
Personnel Testing Division
DoD Center Monterey Bay
400 Gigling Rd
Seaside CA 93955
831-583-2400 (Ext. 4282)
www.asvabprogram.com
E-mail: webmaster@osd.pentagon.mil

U.S. Department of Labor
Employment and Training Administration
200 Constitution Avenue, N.W.
Washington, D.C. 20210
202-219-7161
www.doleta.gov/programs/onet
www.onetcenter.org
E-mail: o-net@dol.gov

Valpar International
2450 West Ruthrauff Road, Suite 180
Tucson, AZ 85705
520-293-1510
800-528-7070
Fax: 520-292-9755
www.valparint.com
E-mail: valparbbc@aol.com

Vangent
1 North Dearborn Street
Suite 1600
Chicago, IL 60602
Phone 800-922-7343
Fax: 312-242-4400
http://www.vangent-hcm.com
E-mail: HCM_info@vangent.com

Vocational Psychology Research
University of Minnesota-Twin Cities
N612 Elliott Hall
75 East River Road
Minneapolis, MN 55455-0344
612-625-1367
Fax: 612-626-0345
http://www.psych.umn.edu/psylabs/vpr
E-mail: vpr@tc.umn.edu

Vocational Research Institute (VRI)
1528 Walnut Street, Suite 1502
Philadelphia, PA 19102
800-874-5387
215-875-7387
Fax: 215-875-0198
http://www.vri.org/
E-mail: info@vri.org

Vocational-Technical Education Consortium of States (V-TECS)
1866 Southern Lane
Decatur, GA 30037-4097
800-248-7701 Ext. 543
Fax: 404-679-4556
http://www.vtecs. org
E-mail: info@vtecs.org

Vocopher
http://www.vocopher.com/CareerTests.cfm
E-mail: kglavin@vocopher.com

Walden Personnel Testing and Training, Inc.
1445 Lambert-Closse, Suite 301
Montreal, Quebec, Canada H3H 1Z5
800-361-4908
Fax: 514-989-9934
http://www.waldentesting.com/
E-mail: Natalie@waldentesting.com

WestED
730 Harrison St.
San Francisco, California 94107-1242
415-565-3000
Fax: 415-565-3012
http://www.WestEd.org/
E-mail: customerservice@wested.org

Western Psychological Services (WPS)
12031 Wilshire Blvd.
Los Angeles, CA 90025-1251
310-478-2061
800-648-8857
Fax: 310-478-7838
http://www.wpspublish.com/
E-mail: customerservice@wpspublish.com

Wide Range, Inc
P. O. Box 3410
Willingtom, DE 19804-4184
302-658-4184
800-221-9728
Fax: 302-652-1644
http://www.widerange.com/
E-mail: widerange@widerange.com

Wintergreen/Orchard
2 LAN Drive, Suite 100
Westford, MA 01886
978-692-9708
Fax: 978-692-2304
http://www.wintergreenorchardhouse.com/
E-mail: info@wintergreenorchardhouse.com

Wonderlic, Inc.
1795 N. Butterfield Ave. Suite 200
Libertyville, Illinois 60048
800-323-3742
Fax: 847-680-9492
http://www.wonderlic.com
E-mail: info@wonderlic.com

World of Work, Inc.
410 W. 1st Street, Suite 103
Tempe, AZ 85281
480-966-5100
Fax: 602-966-6200
http://www.wowi.com/
E-mail: info@wowi.com

ZH Computer
7400 Metro Boulevard
Suite 350
Edina, MN 55439
952-844-0915
Fax: 952-844-9025
www.assessment.com or www.zhcomputer.com

APPENDIX C

TEST STANDARDS
AND CODES

- Responsibilities of Users of Standardized Tests (RUST) (3rd Edition)

- Code of Fair Testing Practices in Education

- Rights and Resposibilities of Test Takers: Guidelines and Expectations

- Standards for Multicultural Assessment

RESPONSIBILITIES OF USERS OF STANDARDIZED TESTS (RUST)

(3rd Edition)

Prepared by the Association for Assessment in Counseling (AAC)

Many recent events have influenced the use of tests and assessment in the counseling community. Such events include the use of tests in the educational accountability and reform movement, the publication of the *Standards for Educational and Psychological Testing* (American Educational Research Association [AERA], American Psychological Association [APA], National Council on Measurement in Education [NCME], 1999), the revision of the *Code of Fair Testing Practices in Education* (Joint Committee on Testing Practices [JCTP], 2002), the proliferation of technology-delivered assessment, and the historic passage of the *No Child Left Behind Act* (HR1, 2002) calling for expanded testing in reading/language arts, mathematics, and science that are aligned to state standards.

The purpose of this document is to promote the accurate, fair, and responsible use of standardized tests by the counseling and education communities. RUST is intended to address the needs of the members of the American Counseling Association (ACA) and its Divisions, Branches, and Regions, including counselors, teachers, administrators, and other human service workers. The general public, test developers, and policy makers will find this statement useful as they work with tests and testing issues. The principles in RUST apply to the use of testing instruments regardless of delivery methods (e.g., paper/pencil or computer administered) or setting (e.g., group or individual).

The intent of RUST is to help counselors and other educators implement responsible testing practices. The RUST does not intend to reach beyond or reinterpret the principles outlined in the *Standards for Educational and Psychological Testing* (AERA et al., 1999), nor was it developed to formulate a basis for legal action. The intent is to provide a concise statement useful in the ethical practice of testing. In addition, RUST is intended to enhance the guidelines found in *ACA's Code of Ethics and Standards of Practice* (ACA, 1997) and the *Code of Fair Testing Practices in Education* (JCTP, 2002).

Organization of Document: This document includes test user responsibilities in the following areas:

- Qualifications of Test Users
- Technical Knowledge

- Test Selection
- Test Administration
- Test Scoring
- Interpreting Test Results
- Communicating Test Results

Qualifications of Test Users

Qualified test users demonstrate appropriate education, training, and experience in using tests for the purposes under consideration. They adhere to the highest degree of ethical codes, laws, and standards governing professional practice. Lack of essential qualifications or ethical and legal compliance can lead to errors and subsequent harm to clients. Each professional is responsible for making judgments in each testing situation and cannot leave that responsibility either to clients or others in authority. The individual test user must obtain appropriate education and training, or arrange for professional supervision and assistance when engaged in testing in order to provide valuable, ethical, and effective assessment services to the public. Qualifications of test users depend on at least four factors:

- Purposes of Testing: A clear purpose for testing should be established. Because the purposes of testing direct how the results are used, qualifications beyond general testing competencies may be needed to interpret and apply data.
- Characteristics of Tests: Understanding of the strengths and limitations of each instrument used is a requirement.
- Settings and Conditions of Test Use: Assessment of the quality and relevance of test user knowledge and skill to the situation is needed before deciding to test or participate in a testing program.
- Roles of Test Selectors, Administrators, Scorers, and Interpreters: The education, training, and experience of test users determine which tests they are qualified to administer and interpret.

Each test user must evaluate his or her qualifications and competence for selecting, administering, scoring, interpreting, reporting, or communicating test results. Test users must develop the skills and knowledge for each test he or she intends to use.

Technical Knowledge

Responsible use of tests requires technical knowledge obtained through training, education, and continuing professional development. Test users should be conversant and competent in aspects of testing including:

- Validity of Test Results: Validity is the accumulation of evidence to support a specific interpretation of the test results. Since validity is a characteristic of test results, a test may have validities of varying degree, for different purposes. The concept of instructional validity relates to how well the test is aligned to state standards and classroom instructional objectives.

- Reliability: Reliability refers to the consistency of test scores. Various methods are used to calculate and estimate reliability depending on the purpose for which the test is used.
- Errors of Measurement: Various ways may be used to calculate the error associated with a test score. Knowing this and knowing the estimate of the size of the error allows the test user to provide a more accurate interpretation of the scores and to support better-informed decisions.
- Scores and Norms: Basic differences between the purposes of norm-referenced and criterion-referenced scores impact score interpretations.

Test Selection

Responsible use of tests requires that the specific purpose for testing be identified. In addition, the test that is selected should align with that purpose, while considering the characteristics of the test and the test taker. Tests should not be administered without a specific purpose or need for information. Typical purposes for testing include:

- Description: Obtaining objective information on the status of certain characteristics such as achievement, ability, personality types, etc. is often an important use of testing.
- Accountability: When judging the progress of an individual or the effectiveness of an educational institution, strong alignment between what is taught and what is tested needs to be present.
- Prediction: Technical information should be reviewed to determine how accurately the test will predict areas such as appropriate course placement; selection for special programs, interventions, and institutions; and other outcomes of interest.
- Program Evaluation: The role that testing plays in program evaluation and how the test information may be used to supplement other information gathered about the program is an important consideration in test use.

Proper test use involves determining if the characteristics of the test are appropriate for the intended audience and are of sufficient technical quality for the purpose at hand. Some areas to consider include:

- The Test Taker: Technical information should be reviewed to determine if the test characteristics are appropriate for the test taker (e.g., age, grade level, language, cultural background).
- Accuracy of Scoring Procedures: Only tests that use accurate scoring procedures should be used.
- Norming and Standardization Procedures: Norming and standardization procedures should be reviewed to determine if the norm group is appropriate for the intended test takers. Specified test administration procedures must be followed.
- Modifications: For individuals with disabilities, alternative measures may need to be found and used and/or accommodations in test taking

procedures may need to be employed. Interpretations need to be made in light of the modifications in the test or testing procedures.

- Fairness: Care should be taken to select tests that are fair to all test takers. When test results are influenced by characteristics or situations unrelated to what is being measured. (e.g., gender, age, ethnic background, existence of cheating, unequal availability of test preparation programs) the use of the resulting information is invalid and potentially harmful. In achievement testing, fairness also relates to whether or not the student has had an opportunity to learn what is tested.

Test Administration

Test administration includes carefully following standard procedures so that the test is used in the manner specified by the test developers. The test administrator should ensure that test takers work within conditions that maximize opportunity for optimum performance. As appropriate, test takers, parents, and organizations should be involved in the various aspects of the testing process including.

Before administration it is important that relevant persons

- are informed about the standard testing procedures, including information about the purposes of the test, the kinds of tasks involved, the method of administration, and the scoring and reporting;
- have sufficient practice experiences prior to the test to include practice, as needed, on how to operate equipment for computer-administered tests and practice in responding to tasks;
- have been sufficiently trained in their responsibilities and the administration procedures for the test;
- have a chance to review test materials and administration sites and procedures prior to the time for testing to ensure standardized conditions and appropriate responses to any irregularities that occur;
- arrange for appropriate modifications of testing materials and procedures in order to accommodate test takers with special needs; and
- have a clear understanding of their rights and responsibilities.

During administration it is important that

- the testing environment (e.g., seating, work surfaces, lighting, room temperature, freedom from distractions) and psychological climate are conducive to the best possible performance of the examinees;
- sufficiently trained personnel establish and maintain uniform conditions and observe the conduct of test takers when large groups of individuals are tested;
- test administrators follow the instructions in the test manual; demonstrate verbal clarity; use verbatim directions; adhere to verbatim directions; follow exact sequence and timing; and use materials that are identical to those specified by the test publisher;

- a systematic and objective procedure is in place for observing and recording environmental, health, emotional factors, or other elements that may invalidate test performance and results; deviations from prescribed test administration procedures, including information on test accommodations for individuals with special needs, are recorded; and
- the security of test materials and computer-administered testing software is protected, ensuring that only individuals with a legitimate need for access to the materials/software are able to obtain such access and that steps to eliminate the possibility of breaches in test security and copyright protection are respected.

After administration it is important to

- collect and inventory all secure test materials and immediately report any breaches in test security; and
- include notes on any problems, irregularities, and accommodations in the test records.

These precepts represent the basic process for all standardized tests and assessments. Some situations may add steps or modify some of these to provide the best testing milieu possible.

Test Scoring

Accurate measurement necessitates adequate procedures for scoring the responses of test takers. Scoring procedures should be audited as necessary to ensure consistency and accuracy of application.

- Carefully implement and/or monitor standard scoring procedures.
- When test scoring involves human judgment, use rubrics that clearly specify the criteria for scoring. Scoring consistency should be constantly monitored.
- Provide a method for checking the accuracy of scores when test takers challenge accuracy.

Interpreting Test Results

Responsible test interpretation requires knowledge about and experience with the test, the scores, and the decisions to be made. Interpretation of scores on any test should not take place without a thorough knowledge of the technical aspects of the test, the test results, and its limitations. Many factors can impact the valid and useful interpretations of test scores. These can be grouped into several categories including psychometric, test taker, and contextual, as well as others.

- Psychometric Factors: Factors such as the reliability, norms, standard error of measurement, and validity of the instrument are important when interpreting test results. Responsible test use considers these basic concepts and how each impacts the scores and hence the interpretation of the test results.

- Test Taker Factors: Factors such as the test taker's group membership and how that membership may impact the results of the test is a critical factor in the interpretation of test results. Specifically, the test user should evaluate how the test taker's gender, age, ethnicity, race, socioeconomic status, marital status, and so forth, impact on the individual's results.
- Contextual Factors: The relationship of the test to the instructional program, opportunity to learn, quality of the educational program, work and home environment, and other factors that would assist in understanding the test results are useful in interpreting test results. For example, if the test does not align to curriculum standards and how those standards are taught in the classroom, the test results may not provide useful information.

Communicating Test Results

Before communication of test results takes place, a solid foundation and preparation is necessary. That foundation includes knowledge of test interpretation and an understanding of the particular test being used, as provided by the test manual.

Conveying test results with language that the test taker, parents, teachers, clients, or general public can understand is one of the key elements in helping others understand the meaning of the test results. When reporting group results, the information needs to be supplemented with background information that can help explain the results with cautions about misinterpretations. The test user should indicate how the test results can be and should not be interpreted.

Closing

Proper test use resides with the test user — the counselor and educator. Qualified test users understand the measurement characteristics necessary to select good standardized tests, administer the tests according to specified procedures, assure accurate scoring, accurately interpret test scores for individuals and groups, and ensure productive applications of the results. This document provides guidelines for using tests responsibly with students and clients.

References and Resource Documents

American Counseling Association. (1997). Code of ethics and standards of practice. Alexandria, VA: Author.

American Counseling Association. (2003). Standards for qualifications of test users. Alexandria, VA: Author.

American Educational Research Association, American Psychological Association, National Council on Measurement in Education. (1999). Standards for educational and psychological testing. Washington, DC: American Educational Research Association.

American School Counselor Association & Association for Assessment in Counseling (1998). Competencies in assessment and evaluation for school counselors. Alexandria, VA: Author.

Joint Committee on Testing Practices. (2000) Rights and responsibilities of test takers: Guidelines and expectations, Washington, DC: Author.

Joint Committee on Testing Practices. (2002). Code of fair testing practices in education. Washington, DC: Author.

RUST Committee. Janet Wall, Chair, James Augustin, Charles Eberly, Brad Erford, David Lundberg, Timothy Vansickle. *Association for Assessment in Counseling, 2003. All rights reserved.*

CODE OF FAIR TESTING PRACTICES
IN EDUCATION
Prepared by
The Joint Committee on Testing Practices

The Code of Fair Testing Practices in Education *(Code)* is a guide for professionals in fulfilling their obligation to provide and use tests that are fair to all test takers regardless of age, gender, disability, race, ethnicity, national origin, religion, sexual orientation, linguistic background, or other personal characteristics. Fairness is a primary consideration in all aspects of testing. Careful standardization of tests and administration conditions helps to ensure that all test takers are given a comparable opportunity to demonstrate what they know and how they can perform in the area being tested. Fairness implies that every test taker has the opportunity to prepare for the test and is informed about the general nature and content of the test, as appropriate to the purpose of the test. Fairness also extends to the accurate reporting of individual and group test results. Fairness is not an isolated concept, but must be considered in all aspects of the testing process.

The *Code* applies broadly to testing in education (admissions, educational assessment, educational diagnosis, and student placement) regardless of the mode of presentation, so it is relevant to conventional paper-and-pencil tests, computer based tests, and performance tests. It is not designed to cover employment testing, licensure or certification testing, or other types of testing outside the field of education. The *Code* is directed primarily at professionally developed tests used in formally administered testing programs. Although the *Code* is not intended to cover tests made by teachers for use in their own classrooms, teachers are encouraged to use the guidelines to help improve their testing practices.

The *Code* addresses the roles of test developers and test users separately. Test developers are people and organizations that construct tests, as well as those that set policies for testing programs. Test users are people and agencies that select tests, administer tests, commission test development services, or make decisions on the basis of test scores. Test developer and test user roles may overlap, for example, when a state or local education agency commissions test development services, sets policies that control the test development process, and makes decisions on the basis of the test scores.

Many of the statements in the *Code* refer to the selection and use of existing tests. When a new test is developed, when an existing test is modified, or when the administration of a test is modified, the *Code* is intended to provide guidance for this process.

The *Code* is not intended to be mandatory, exhaustive, or definitive, and may not be applicable to every situation. Instead, the Code is intended to be aspirational, and is not intended to take precedence over the judgment of those who have competence in the subjects addressed.

The Code provides guidance separately for test developers and test users in four critical areas:

    A. Developing and Selecting Appropriate Tests

    B. Administering and Scoring Tests

    C. Reporting and Interpreting Test Results

    D. Informing Test Takers

The Code is intended to be consistent with the relevant parts of the Standards for Educational and Psychological Testing (American Educational Research Association [AERA], American Psychological Association [APA], and National Council on Measurement in Education [NCME], 1999). The Code is not meant to add new principles over and above those in the Standards or to change their meaning. Rather, the Code is intended to represent the spirit of selected portions of the Standards in a way that is relevant and meaningful to developers and users of tests, as well as to test takers and/or their parents or guardians. States, districts, schools, organizations and individual professionals are encouraged to commit themselves to fairness in testing and safeguarding the rights of test takers. The Code is intended to assist in carrying out such commitments.

The Code has been prepared by the Joint Committee on Testing Practices, a cooperative effort among several professional organizations. The aim of the Joint Committee is to act, in the public interest, to advance the quality of testing practices. Members of the Joint Committee include the American Counseling Association (ACA), the American Educational Research Association (AERA), the American Psychological Association (APA), the American Speech-Language-Hearing Association (ASHA), the National Association of School Psychologists (NASP), the National Association of Test Directors (NATD), and the National Council on Measurement in Education (NCME).

Copyright 2004 by the Joint Committee on Testing Practices. This material may be reproduced in whole or in part without fees or permission, provided that acknowledgment is made to the Joint Committee on Testing Practices. Reproduction and dissemination of this document are encouraged. This edition replaces the first edition of the Code, which was published in 1988. Please cite this document as follows: Code of Fair Testing Practices in Education. (2004). Washington, DC: Joint Committee on Testing Practices. (Mailing Address: Joint Committee on Testing Practices, Science Directorate, American Psychological Association, 750 First Street, NE, Washington, DC 20002-4242; http://www.apa.org/science/jctpweb.html .) Contact APA for additional copies.

A. Developing and Selecting Appropriate Tests

TEST DEVELOPERS	TEST USERS
Test developers should provide the information and supporting evidence that test users need to select appropriate tests.	*Test users should select tests that meet the intended purpose and that are appropriate for the intended test takers.*
A-1. Provide evidence of what the test measures, the recommended uses, the intended test takers, and the strengths and limitations of the test, including the level of precision of the test scores.	A-1. Define the purpose for testing, the content and skills to be tested, and the intended test takers. Select and use the most appropriate test based on a thorough review of available information.
A-2. Describe how the content and skills to be tested were selected and how the tests were developed.	A-2. Review and select tests based on the appropriateness of test content, skills tested, and content coverage for the intended purpose of testing.
A-3. Communicate information about a test's characteristics at a level of detail appropriate to the intended test users.	A-3. Review materials provided by test developers and select tests for which clear, accurate, and complete information is provided.
A-4. Provide guidance on the levels of skills, knowledge, and training necessary for appropriate review, selection, and administration of tests.	A-4. Select tests through a process that includes persons with appropriate knowledge, skills, and training.
A-5. Provide evidence that the technical quality, including reliability and validity, of the test meets its intended purposes.	A-5. Evaluate evidence of the technical quality of the test provided by the test developer and any independent reviewers.
A-6. Provide to qualified test users representative samples of test questions or practice tests, directions, answer sheets, manuals, and score reports.	A-6. Evaluate representative samples of test questions or practice tests, directions, answer sheets, manuals, and score reports before selecting a test.
A-7. Avoid potentially offensive content or language when developing test questions and related materials.	A-7. Evaluate procedures and materials used by test developers, as well as the resulting test, to ensure that potentially offensive content or language is avoided.
A-8. Make appropriately modified forms of tests or administration procedures available for test takers with disabilities who need special accommodations.	A-8. Select tests with appropriately modified forms or administration procedures for test takers with disabilities who need special accommodations.
A-9. Obtain and provide evidence on the performance of test takers of diverse subgroups, making significant efforts to obtain sample sizes that are adequate for subgroup analyses. Evaluate the evidence to ensure that differences in performance are related to the skills being assessed.	A-9. Evaluate the available evidence on the performance of test takers of diverse subgroups. Determine to the extent feasible which performance differences may have been caused by factors unrelated to the skills being assessed.

B. Administering and Scoring Tests

TEST DEVELOPERS	TEST USERS
Test developers should explain how to administer and score tests correctly and fairly.	*Test users should administer and score tests correctly and fairly.*
B-1. Provide clear descriptions of detailed procedures for administering tests in a standardized manner.	B-1. Follow established procedures for administering tests in a standardized manner.
B-2. Provide guidelines on reasonable procedures for assessing persons with disabilities who need special accommodations or those with diverse linguistic backgrounds.	B-2. Provide and document appropriate procedures for test takers with disabilities who need special accommodations or those with diverse linguistic backgrounds. Some accommodations may be required by law or regulation.
B-3. Provide information to test takers or test users on test question formats and procedures for answering test questions, including information on the use of any needed materials and equipment.	B-3. Provide test takers with an opportunity to become familiar with test question formats and any materials or equipment that may be used during testing.
B-4. Establish and implement procedures to ensure the security of testing materials during all phases of test development, administration, scoring, and reporting.	B-4. Protect the security of test materials, including respecting copyrights and eliminating opportunities for test takers to obtain scores by fraudulent means.
B-5. Provide procedures, materials and guidelines for scoring the tests, and for monitoring the accuracy of the scoring process. If scoring the test is the responsibility of the test developer, provide adequate training for scorers.	B-5. If test scoring is the responsibility of the test user, provide adequate training to scorers and ensure and monitor the accuracy of the scoring process.
B-6. Correct errors that affect the interpretation of the scores and communicate the corrected results promptly.	B-6. Correct errors that affect the interpretation of the scores and communicate the corrected results promptly.
B-7. Develop and implement procedures for ensuring the confidentiality of scores.	B-7. Develop and implement procedures for ensuring the confidentiality of scores.

C. Reporting and Interpreting Test Results

TEST DEVELOPERS	TEST USERS
Test developers should report test results accurately and provide information to help test users interpret test results correctly.	*Test users should report and interpret test results accurately and clearly.*
C-1. Provide information to support recommended interpretations of the results, including the nature of the content, norms or comparison groups, and other technical evidence. Advise test users of the benefits and limitations of test results and their interpretation. Warn against assigning greater precision than is warranted.	C-1. Interpret the meaning of the test results, taking into account the nature of the content, norms or comparison groups, other technical evidence, and benefits and limitations of test results.
C-2. Provide guidance regarding the interpretations of results for tests administered with modifications. Inform test users of potential problems in interpreting test results when tests or test administration procedures are modified.	C-2. Interpret test results from modified test or test administration procedures in view of the impact those modifications may have had on test results.
C-3. Specify appropriate uses of test results and warn test users of potential misuses.	C-3. Avoid using tests for purposes other than those recommended by the test developer unless there is evidence to support the intended use or interpretation.
C-4. When test developers set standards, provide the rationale, procedures, and evidence for setting performance standards or passing scores. Avoid using stigmatizing labels.	C-4. Review the procedures for setting performance standards or passing scores. Avoid using stigmatizing labels.
C-5. Encourage test users to base decisions about test takers on multiple sources of appropriate information, not on a single test score.	C-5. Avoid using a single test score as the sole determinant of decisions about test takers. Interpret test scores in conjunction with other information about individuals.
C-6. Provide information to enable test users to accurately interpret and report test results for groups of test takers, including information about who were and who were not included in the different groups being compared, and information about factors that might influence the interpretation of results.	C-6. State the intended interpretation and use of test results for groups of test takers. Avoid grouping test results for purposes not specifically recommended by the test developer unless evidence is obtained to support the intended use. Report procedures that were followed in determining who were and who were not included in the groups being compared and describe factors that might influence the interpretation of results.

C-7. Provide test results in a timely fashion and in a manner that is understood by the test taker.	C-7. Communicate test results in a timely fashion and in a manner that is understood by the test taker.
C-8. Provide guidance to test users about how to monitor the extent to which the test is fulfilling its intended purposes.	C-8. Develop and implement procedures for monitoring test use, including consistency with the intended purposes of the test.

D. Informing Test Takers

Under some circumstances, test developers have direct communication with the test takers and/or control of the tests, testing process, and test results. In other circumstances the test users have these responsibilities.

Test developers or test users should inform test takers about the nature of the test, test taker rights and responsibilities, the appropriate use of scores, and procedures for resolving challenges to scores.
D-1. Inform test takers in advance of the test administration about the coverage of the test, the types of question formats, the directions, and appropriate test-taking strategies. Make such information available to all test takers.
D-2. When a test is optional, provide test takers or their parents/guardians with information to help them judge whether a test should be taken—including indications of any consequences that may result from not taking the test (e.g., not being eligible to compete for a particular scholarship) —and whether there is an available alternative to the test.
D-3. Provide test takers or their parents/guardians with information about rights test takers may have to obtain copies of tests and completed answer sheets, to retake tests, to have tests rescored, or to have scores declared invalid.
D-4. Provide test takers or their parents/guardians with information about responsibilities test takers have, such as being aware of the intended purpose and uses of the test, performing at capacity, following directions, and not disclosing test items or interfering with other test takers.
D-5. Inform test takers or their parents/guardians how long scores will be kept on file and indicate to whom, under what circumstances, and in what manner test scores and related information will or will not be released. Protect test scores from unauthorized release and access.
D-6. Describe procedures for investigating and resolving circumstances that might result in canceling or withholding scores, such as failure to adhere to specified testing procedures.
D-7. Describe procedures that test takers, parents/guardians, and other interested parties may use to obtain more information about the test, register complaints, and have problems resolved.

Note: The membership of the Working Group that developed the Code of Fair Testing Practices in Education and of the Joint Committee on Testing Practices that guided the Working Group is as follows: John J. Fremer, Ph.D., (Co-Chair), Janet E. Wall, Ed.D., (Co-Chair), Peter Behuniak, Ph.D., Lloyd Bond, Ph.D., Gwyneth M. Boodoo, Ph.D., Wayne Camara, Ph.D., Ray Fenton, Ph.D., Sharon M. Goldsmith, Ph.D.,, Bert F. Green, Ph.D.,, William G. Harris, Ph.D., Janet E. Helms, Ph.D., Stephanie

H. McConaughy, Ph.D., Julie P. Noble, Ph.D., Wayne M. Patience, Ph.D., Carole L. Perlman, Ph.D., Douglas K. Smith, Ph.D., (deceased) Pat Nellor Wickwire, Ph.D., Mary Yakimowski, Ph.D., Lara Frumkin, Ph.D., of the APA served as staff liaison.

The Joint Committee intends that the Code be consistent with and supportive of existing codes of conduct and standards of other professional groups who use tests in educational contexts. Of particular note are the Responsibilities of Users of Standardized Tests (Association for Assessment in Counseling and Education, 2003), APA Test User Qualifications (2000), ASHA Code of Ethics (2001), Ethical Principles of Psychologists and Code of Conduct (1992), NASP Professional Conduct Manual (2000), NCME Code of Professional Responsibility (1995), and Rights and Responsibilities of Test Takers: Guidelines and Expectations (Joint Committee on Testing Practices, 2000).

RIGHTS AND RESPONSIBILITIES OF TEST TAKERS: GUIDELINES AND EXPECTATIONS

Preamble

The intent of this statement is to enumerate and clarify the expectations that test takers may reasonably have about the testing process, and the expectations that those who develop, administer, and use tests may have of test takers. Tests are defined broadly here as psychological and educational instruments developed and used by testing professionals in organizations such as schools, industries, clinical practice, counseling settings and human service and other agencies, including those assessment procedures and devices that are used for making inferences about people in the above-named settings. The purpose of the statement is to inform and to help educate not only test takers, but also others involved in the testing enterprise so that measurements may be most validly and appropriately used. This document is intended as an effort to inspire improvements in the testing process and does not have the force of law. Its orientation is to encourage positive and high quality interactions between testing professionals and test takers. The rights and responsibilities listed in this document are neither legally based nor inalienable rights and responsibilities such as those listed in the United States of America's Bill of Rights. Rather, they represent the best judgments of testing professionals about the reasonable expectations that those involved in the testing enterprise (test producers, test users, and test takers) should have of each other. Testing professionals include developers of assessment products and services, those who market and sell them, persons who select them, test administrators and scorers, those who interpret test results, and trained users of the information. Persons who engage in each of these activities have significant responsibilities that are described elsewhere, in documents such as those that follow (American Association for Counseling and Development, 1988; American Speech-Language-Hearing Association, 1994; Joint Committee on Testing Practices, 1988; National Association of School Psychologists, 1992; National Council on Measurement in Education, 1995).

In some circumstances, the test developer and the test user may not be the same person, group of persons, or organization. In such situations, the professionals involved in the testing should clarify, for the test taker as well as for themselves, who is responsible for each aspect of the testing process. For example, when an individual chooses to take a college admissions test, at least three parties are involved in addition to the test taker: the test developer and publisher, the individuals who administer the test to the test taker, and the institutions of higher education who will eventually use the information. In such cases a test taker may need to request clarifications about their rights and responsibilities. When test takers are young children (e.g., those taking standardized tests in the schools) or are persons who spend some or all their time in institutions or are incapacitated, parents or guardians may be granted some of the rights and responsibilities, rather than, or in addition to, the individual. Perhaps the most fundamental right test takers have is to be able to take tests that meet high professional standards, such as those described in Standards for Educational and Psychological Testing (American Educational Research Association, American Psychological Association, & National Council on Measurement in Education, 1999) as well as those of other appropriate professional associations. This statement should be used as an adjunct, or supplement, to those standards. State and federal laws, of course, supersede any rights and responsibilities that are stated here.

References

American Association for Counseling and Development (now American Counseling Association) & Association for Measurement and Evaluation in Counseling and Development (now Association for Assessment in Counseling). (1989). Responsibilities of users of standardized tests: RUST statement revised. Alexandria, VA: Author.

American Educational Research Association, American Psychological Association, & National Council on Measurement in Education. (1999). Standards for educational and psychological testing. Washington, DC.

American Educational Research Association, American Speech-Language-Hearing Association. (1994). Protection of rights of people receiving audiology or speech-language pathology services. ASHA (36), 60-63.

Joint Committee on Testing Practices. (1988). Code of fair testing practices in education. Washington, DC: American Psychological Association.

National Association of School Psychologists. (1992). Standards for the provision of school psychological services. Author: Silver Springs, MD.

National Council on Measurement in Education. (1995). Code of professional responsibilities in educational measurement. Washington, DC: Author.

The Rights and Responsibilities of Test Takers: Guidelines and Expectations

Test Taker Rights and Responsibilities Working Group of the Joint Committee on Testing Practices, August, 1998

As a test taker, you have the right to:

1. Be informed of your rights and responsibilities as a test taker.

2. Be treated with courtesy, respect, and impartiality, regardless of your age, disability, ethnicity, gender, national origin, religion, sexual orientation or other personal characteristics.

3. Be tested with measures that meet professional standards and that are appropriate, given the manner in which the test results will be used.

4. Receive a brief oral or written explanation prior to testing about the purpose(s) for testing, the kind(s) of tests to be used, if the results will be reported to you or to others, and the planned use(s) of the results. If you have a disability, you have the right to inquire and receive information about testing accommodations. If you have difficulty in comprehending the language of the test, you have a right to know in advance of testing whether any accommodations may be available to you.

5. Know in advance of testing when the test will be administered, if and when test

results will be available to you, and if there is a fee for testing services that you are expected to pay.

6. Have your test administered and your test results interpreted by appropriately trained individuals who follow professional codes of ethics.

7. Know if a test is optional and learn of the consequences of taking or not taking the test, fully completing the test, or canceling the scores. You may need to ask questions to learn these consequences.

8. Receive a written or oral explanation of your test results within a reasonable amount of time after testing and in commonly understood terms.

9. Have your test results kept confidential to the extent allowed by law.

10. Present concerns about the testing process or your results and receive information about procedures that will be used to address such concerns.

As a test taker, you have the responsibility to:

1. Read and/or listen to your rights and responsibilities as a test taker.

2. Treat others with courtesy and respect during the testing process.

3. Ask questions prior to testing if you are uncertain about why the test is being given, how it will be given, what you will be asked to do, and what will be done with the results.

4. Read or listen to descriptive information in advance of testing and listen carefully to all test instructions. You should inform an examiner in advance of testing if you wish to receive a testing accommodation or if you have a physical condition or illness that may interfere with your performance on the test. If you have difficulty comprehending the language of the test, it is your responsibility to inform an examiner.

5. Know when and where the test will be given, pay for the test if required, appear on time with any required materials, and be ready to be tested.

6. Follow the test instructions you are given and represent yourself honestly during the testing.

7. Be familiar with and accept the consequences of not taking the test, should you choose not to take the test.

8. Inform appropriate person(s), as specified to you by the organization responsible for testing, if you believe that testing conditions affected your results.

9. Ask about the confidentiality of your test results, if this aspect concerns you.

10. Present concerns about the testing process or results in a timely, respectful way, if you have any.

The Rights of Test Takers: Guidelines for Testing Professionals

Test takers have the rights described below. It is the responsibility of the professionals involved in the testing process to ensure that test takers receive these rights.

1. Because test takers have the right to be informed of their rights and responsibilities as test takers, it is normally the responsibility of the individual who administers a test (or the organization that prepared the test) to inform test takers of these rights and responsibilities.

2. Because test takers have the right to be treated with courtesy, respect, and impartiality, regardless of their age, disability, ethnicity, gender, national origin, race, religion, sexual orientation, or other personal characteristics, testing professionals should:

   a. Make test takers aware of any materials that are available to assist them in test preparation. These materials should be clearly described in test registration and/or test familiarization materials.

   b. See that test takers are provided with reasonable access to testing services.

3. Because test takers have the right to be tested with measures that meet professional standards that are appropriate for the test use and the test taker, given the manner in which the results will be used, testing professionals should:

   a. Take steps to utilize measures that meet professional standards and are reliable, relevant, and useful given the intended purpose and are fair for test takers from varying societal groups.

   b. Advise test takers that they are entitled to request reasonable accommodations in test administration that are likely to increase the validity of their test scores if they have a disability recognized under the Americans with Disabilities Act or other relevant legislation.

4. Because test takers have the right to be informed, prior to testing, about the test's purposes, the nature of the test, whether test results will be reported to the test takers, and the planned use of the results (when not in conflict with the testing purposes), testing professionals should:

   a. Give or provide test takers with access to a brief description about the test purpose (e.g., diagnosis, placement, selection, etc.) and the kind(s) of tests and formats that will be used (e.g., individual/group, multiple-choice/free response/performance, timed/untimed, etc.), unless such information might be detrimental to the objectives of the test.

   b. Tell test takers, prior to testing, about the planned use(s) of the test results. Upon request, the test taker should be given information about how long such test scores are typically kept on file and remain available.

   c. Provide test takers, if requested, with information about any preventative measures that have been instituted to safeguard the accuracy of test scores. Such information would include any quality control procedures that are employed and some of the steps taken to prevent dishonesty in test performance.

   d. Inform test takers, in advance of the testing, about required materials that must be brought to the test site (e.g., pencil, paper) and about any rules that allow or prohibit use of other materials (e.g., calculators).

e. Provide test takers, upon request, with general information about the appropriateness of the test for its intended purpose, to the extent that such information does not involve the release of proprietary information. (For example, the test taker might be told, "Scores on this test are useful in predicting how successful people will be in this kind of work" or "Scores on this test, along with other information, help us to determine if students are likely to benefit from this program.")

f. Provide test takers, upon request, with information about re-testing, including if it is possible to re-take the test or another version of it, and if so, how often, how soon, and under what conditions.

g. Provide test takers, upon request, with information about how the test will be scored and in what detail. On multiple-choice tests, this information might include suggestions for test taking and about the use of a correction for guessing. On tests scored using professional judgment (e.g., essay tests or projective techniques), a general description of the scoring procedures might be provided except when such information is proprietary or would tend to influence test performance inappropriately.

h. Inform test takers about the type of feedback and interpretation that is routinely provided, as well as what is available for a fee. Test takers have the right to request and receive information regarding whether or not they can obtain copies of their test answer sheets or their test materials, if they can have their scores verified, and if they may cancel their test results.

i. Provide test takers, prior to testing, either in the written instructions, in other written documents or orally, with answers to questions that test takers may have about basic test administration procedures.

j. Inform test takers, prior to testing, if questions from test takers will not be permitted during the testing process.

k. Provide test takers with information about the use of computers, calculators, or other equipment, if any, used in the testing and give them an opportunity to practice using such equipment, unless its unpracticed use is part of the test purpose, or practice would compromise the validity of the results, and to provide a testing accommodation for the use of such equipment, if needed.

l. Inform test takers that, if they have a disability, they have the right to request and receive accommodations or modifications in accordance with the provisions of the Americans with Disabilities Act and other relevant legislation.

m. Provide test takers with information that will be of use in making decisions if test takers have options regarding which tests, test forms or test formats to take.

5. Because that test takers have a right to be informed in advance when the test will be administered, if and when test results will be available, and if there is a fee for testing services that the test takers are expected to pay, test professionals should:

a. Notify test takers of the alteration in a timely manner if a previously announced testing schedule changes, provide a reasonable explanation for the change, and inform test takers of the new schedule. If there is a change, reasonable alternatives to the original schedule should be provided.

b. Inform test takers prior to testing about any anticipated fee for the testing process, as well as the fees associated with each component of the process, if the components can be separated.

6. Because test takers have the right to have their tests administered and interpreted by appropriately trained individuals, testing professionals should:

a. Know how to select the appropriate test for the intended purposes.

b. When testing persons with documented disabilities and other special characteristics that require special testing conditions and/or interpretation of results, have the skills and knowledge for such testing and interpretation.

c. Provide reasonable information regarding their qualifications, upon request.

d. Insure that test conditions, especially if unusual, do not unduly interfere with test performance. Test conditions will normally be similar to those used to standardize the test.

e. Provide candidates with a reasonable amount of time to complete the test, unless a test has a time limit.

f. Take reasonable actions to safeguard against fraudulent actions (e.g., cheating) that could place honest test takers at a disadvantage.

7. Because test takers have the right to be informed about why they are being asked to take particular tests, if a test is optional, and what the consequences are should they choose not to complete the test, testing professionals should:

a. Normally only engage in testing activities with test takers after the test takers have provided their informed consent to take a test, except when testing without consent has been mandated by law or governmental regulation, or when consent is implied by an action the test takers have already taken (e.g., such as when applying for employment and a personnel examination is mandated).

b. Explain to test takers why they should consider taking voluntary tests.

c. Explain, if a test taker refuses to take or complete a voluntary test, either orally or in writing, what the negative consequences may be to them for their decision to do so.

d. Promptly inform the test taker if a testing professional decides that there is a need to deviate from the testing services to which the test taker initially agreed (e.g., should the testing professional believe it would be wise to administer an additional test or an alternative test), and provide an explanation for the change.

8. Because test takers have a right to receive a written or oral explanation of their test results within a reasonable amount of time after testing and in commonly understood terms, testing professionals should:

   a. Interpret test results in light of one or more additional considerations (e.g., disability, language proficiency), if those considerations are relevant to the purposes of the test and performance on the test, and are in accordance with current laws.

   b. Provide, upon request, information to test takers about the sources used in interpreting their test results, including technical manuals, technical reports, norms, and a description of the comparison group, or additional information about the test taker(s).

   c. Provide, upon request, recommendations to test takers about how they could improve their performance on the test, should they choose or be required to take the test again.

   d. Provide, upon request, information to test takers about their options for obtaining a second interpretation of their results. Test takers may select an appropriately trained professional to provide this second opinion.

   e. Provide test takers with the criteria used to determine a passing score, when individual test scores are reported and related to a pass-fail standard.

   f. Inform test takers, upon request, how much their scores might change, should they elect to take the test again. Such information would include variation in test performance due to measurement error (e.g., the appropriate standard errors of measurement) and changes in performance over time with or without intervention (e.g., additional training or treatment).

   g. Communicate test results to test takers in an appropriate and sensitive manner, without use of negative labels or comments likely to inflame or stigmatize the test taker.

   h. Provide corrected test scores to test takers as rapidly as possible, should an error occur in the processing or reporting of scores. The length of time is often dictated by individuals responsible for processing or reporting the scores, rather than the individuals responsible for testing, should the two parties indeed differ.

   i. Correct any errors as rapidly as possible if there are errors in the process of developing scores.

9. Because test takers have the right to have the results of tests kept confidential to the extent allowed by law, testing professionals should:

   a. Insure that records of test results (in paper or electronic form) are safeguarded and maintained so that only individuals who have a legitimate right to access them will be able to do so.

b. Should provide test takers, upon request, with information regarding who has a legitimate right to access their test results (when individually identified) and in what form. Testing professionals should respond appropriately to questions regarding the reasons why such individuals may have access to test results and how they may use the results.

c. Advise test takers that they are entitled to limit access to their results (when individually identified) to those persons or institutions, and for those purposes, revealed to them prior to testing. Exceptions may occur when test takers, or their guardians, consent to release the test results to others or when testing professionals are authorized by law to release test results.

d. Keep confidential any requests for testing accommodations and the documentation supporting the request.

10. Because test takers have the right to present concerns about the testing process and to receive information about procedures that will be used to address such concerns, testing professionals should:

a. Inform test takers how they can question the results of the testing if they do not believe that the test was administered properly or scored correctly, or other such concerns.

b. Inform test takers of the procedures for appealing decisions that they believe are based in whole or in part on erroneous test results.

c. Inform test takers, if their test results are under investigation and may be canceled, invalidated, or not released for normal use. In such an event, that investigation should be performed in a timely manner. The investigation should use all available information that addresses the reason(s) for the investigation, and the test taker should also be informed of the information that he/she may need to provide to assist with the investigation.

d. Inform the test taker, if that test taker's test results are canceled or not released for normal use, why that action was taken. The test taker is entitled to request and receive information on the types of evidence and procedures that have been used to make that determination.

The Responsibilities of Test Takers: Guidelines for Testing Professionals

Testing Professionals should take steps to ensure that test takers know that they have specific responsibilities in addition to their rights described above.

1. Testing professionals need to inform test takers that they should listen to and/or read their rights and responsibilities as a test taker and ask questions about issues they do not understand.

2. Testing professionals should take steps, as appropriate, to ensure that test takers know that they:

a. Are responsible for their behavior throughout the entire testing process.

b. Should not interfere with the rights of others involved in the testing process.

   c. Should not compromise the integrity of the test and its interpretation in any manner.

3. Testing professionals should remind test takers that it is their responsibility to ask questions prior to testing if they are uncertain about why the test is being given, how it will be given, what they will be asked to do, and what will be done with the results. Testing professionals should:

   a. Advise test takers that it is their responsibility to review materials supplied by test publishers and others as part of the testing process and to ask questions about areas that they feel they should understand better prior to the start of testing.

   b. Inform test takers that it is their responsibility to request more information if they are not satisfied with what they know about how their test results will be used and what will be done with them.

4. Testing professionals should inform test takers that it is their responsibility to read descriptive material they receive in advance of a test and to listen carefully to test instructions. Testing professionals should inform test takers that it is their responsibility to inform an examiner in advance of testing if they wish to receive a testing accommodation or if they have a physical condition or illness that may interfere with their performance. Testing professionals should inform test takers that it is their responsibility to inform an examiner if they have difficulty comprehending the language in which the test is given. Testing professionals should:

   a. Inform test takers that, if they need special testing arrangements, it is their responsibility to request appropriate accommodations and to provide any requested documentation as far in advance of the testing date as possible. Testing professionals should inform test takers about the documentation needed to receive a requested testing accommodation.

   b. Inform test takers that, if they request but do not receive a testing accommodation, they could request information about why their request was denied.

5. Testing professionals should inform test takers when and where the test will be given, and whether payment for the testing is required. Having been so informed, it is the responsibility of the test taker to appear on time with any required materials, pay for testing services and be ready to be tested. Testing professionals should:

   a. Inform test takers that they are responsible for familiarizing themselves with the appropriate materials needed for testing and for requesting information about these materials, if needed.

   b. Inform the test taker, if the testing situation requires that test takers bring materials (e.g., personal identification, pencils, calculators, etc.) to the testing site, of this responsibility to do so.

6. Testing professionals should advise test takers, prior to testing, that it is their responsibility to:

   a. Listen to and/or read the directions given to them.

   b. Follow instructions given by testing professionals.

   c. Complete the test as directed.

   d. Perform to the best of their ability if they want their score to be a reflection of their best effort.

   e. Behave honestly (e.g., not cheating or assisting others who cheat).

7. Testing professionals should inform test takers about the consequences of not taking a test, should they choose not to take the test. Once so informed, it is the responsibility of the test taker to accept such consequences, and the testing professional should so inform the test takers. If test takers have questions regarding these consequences, it is their responsibility to ask questions of the testing professional, and the testing professional should so inform the test takers.

8. Testing professionals should inform test takers that it is their responsibility to notify appropriate persons, as specified by the testing organization, if they do not understand their results, or if they believe that testing conditions affected the results. Testing professionals should:

   a. Provide information to test takers, upon request, about appropriate procedures for questioning or canceling their test scores or results, if relevant to the purposes of testing.

   b. Provide to test takers, upon request, the procedures for reviewing, retesting, or canceling their scores or test results, if they believe that testing conditions affected their results and if relevant to the purposes of testing.

   c. Provide documentation to the test taker about known testing conditions that might have affected the results of the testing, if relevant to the purposes of testing.

9. Testing professionals should advise test takers that it is their responsibility to ask questions about the confidentiality of their test results, if this aspect concerns them.

10. Testing professionals should advise test takers that it is their responsibility to present concerns about the testing process in a timely, respectful manner.

Members of the JCTP Working Group on Test Taker Rights and Responsibilities: Kurt F. Geisinger, Ph.D. (Co-Chair), William Schafer, Ph.D. (Co-Chair), Gwyneth Boodoo, Ph.D., Ruth Ekstrom, Ed.D., Tom Fitzgibbon, Ph.D., John Fremer, Ph.D., Joanne Lenke, Ph.D., Sharon Goldsmith, Ph.D., Julie Noble, Ph.D., Douglas Smith, Ph.D., Nicholas Vacc, Ed.D., Janet Wall, Ed.D.

STANDARDS FOR MULTICULTURAL ASSESSMENT

Preface

The Association for Assessment in Counseling (AAC) is an organization of counselors, counselor educators, and other professionals that advances the counseling profession by providing leadership, training, and research in the creation, development, production, and use of assessment and diagnostic techniques.

The increasing diversity in our society offers a special challenge to the assessment community, striving always to assure fair and equitable treatment of individuals regardless of race, ethnicity, culture, language, age, gender, sexual orientation, religion or physical ability. This is especially important given the increased emphasis place on assessment spawned by national and state legislation and educational reform initiatives.

This document, *Standards for Multicultural Assessment*, is an attempt to create and maintain an awareness of the various assessment standards that have been produced by various professional organizations. It is a compilation of standards produced by several professional associations.

This publication is based on a study completed by the Committee on Diversity in Assessment under the direction of the AAC Executive Council. The first version of this document was published in 1992, and was also published as an article in *Measurement and Evaluation in Counseling and Development* (Prediger, 1994). The original publication was prompted by a request from Jo-Ida Hansen, Chair of the 1991-1992 Committee on Testing of the American Association for Counseling and Development (now ACA). Dale Prediger prepared the original publication under the direction of the AAC Executive Council.

Because of advances in professional standards in the past decade, it was necessary to update and expand upon the first version. This revised document was created by a committee of members from the AAC, chaired by Dr. Wendy Charkow-Bordeau along with committee members, Drs. Debbie Newsome and Marie Shoffner. This publication was commissioned by the Executive Council of the Association for Assessment in Counseling.

AAC also wishes to thank Drs. Pat Nellor Wickwire and Janet Wall for their care and assistance in finalizing this document and coordinating its production. AAC hopes that all counselors, teachers, and other assessment professionals find this document to be useful in improving their assessment practices.

STANDARDS FOR MULTICULTURAL ASSESSMENT (2nd Ed.)

Purpose

The Association for Assessment in Counseling (AAC), a division of the American Counseling Association (ACA), presents this revised compilation of professional standards. Although AAC believes that tests, inventories, and other assessment instruments can be beneficial for members of all populations, AAC recognizes that the increasing diversity in client backgrounds presents special challenges for test users. The standards assembled here address many of these challenges that are specifically related to the assessment of multicultural populations.

Although a number of standards in this compilation have relevance for the use of assessment instruments in psychological screening, personnel selection, and placement, they were selected because they have special relevance for counseling and for multicultural and diverse populations. Standards that apply in the same way for all populations (e.g., general standards for norming, scaling, reliability, and validity) are not included. Readers may consult the source documents and other publications for universal testing standards.

AAC urges all counselors to subscribe to these standards and urges counselor educators to include this compilation in programs preparing the "culturally competent counselor" (Sue, Arredondo, & McDavis, 1992, p. 447). Finally, AAC supports other professional organizations in advocating the need for a multicultural approach to assessment, practice, training, and research.

Definition of Multicultural and Diverse Populations

A precise definition of multicultural and diverse populations is evolving. The multicultural competencies outlined by Sue et al. (1992), and then revised by Arredondo and Toporek (1996), define the following five major cultural groups in the United States and its territories: African/Black, Asian, Caucasian/European, Hispanic/Latino, and Native American. Arredondo and Toporek differentiated between these cultural groups, which are based on race and ethnicity, and diversity, which applies to individual differences based on age, gender, sexual orientation, religion, and ability or disability.

In revising the Standards for Multicultural Assessment, an inclusive definition of multiculturalism and diversity was used. For the purposes of this document, multicultural and diverse populations include persons who differ by race, ethnicity, culture, language, age, gender, sexual orientation, religion, and ability.

Source Documents

Five documents which include professional standards for assessment in counseling were used as sources for this compilation.

1. Code of Fair Testing Practices in Education (2nd ed) (CODE) (Joint Committee on Testing Practices [JCTP], 2002. Available for download at http://aac.ncat. edu.

2. Responsibilities of Users of Standardized Tests (3nd ed) (RUST). (ACA & AAC, 2003 Available for download at http://aac.ncat.edu.

3. Standards for Educational and Psychological Testing (2nd ed.) (SEPT). (American Educational Research Association, APA, & National Council on measurement in Education, 1999). Ordering information is available from APA, 750 First Street N.E., Washington, D.C. 20002-4242 or on-line at http://www.apa.org/science/standards.html.

4. Multicultural Counseling Competencies and Standards (COMPS). (Association for Multicultural Counseling and Development, 1992). These standards can be viewed in the 1996 article by Arredondo and Toporek. Full reference information is listed below in the reference section.

5. Code of Ethics and Standards of Practice of the American Counseling Association (ETHICS). (ACA, 1996). Ordering information can be obtained from ACA, 5999 Stevenson Avenue, Alexandria, VA, 22304-3300. The ethical code and standards of practice may also be viewed on-line at http://www.counseling.org/resources/ethics.htm.

Classification of Standards

Sixty-eight standards specifically relevant to the assessment of multicultural and diverse populations were identified in a reading of the five source documents. The content and intent of these standards were analyzed and classified. Assessment roles, functions, and tasks cited in these standards were clustered into three major groups.

Selection of Assessment Instruments

Content and Purpose (n=13)

Norming, Reliability, and Validity (n=18)

Administration and Scoring of Assessment Instruments (n=16)

Interpretation and Application of Assessment Results (n=21)

The Standards

The 68 standards are listed below by cluster and source.

Selection of Assessment Instruments: Content and Purpose

1. Evaluate procedures and materials used by test developers, as well as the resulting test, to ensure that potentially offensive content or language is avoided. (CODE, Section A-7)

2. Select tests with appropriately modified forms or administration procedures for test takers with disabilities who need special accommodations. (CODE, Section A-8)

3. For individuals with disabilities, alternative measures may need to be found and used.

4. Care should be taken to select tests that are fair to all test takers. (RUST)

5. Test developers should strive to identify and eliminate language, symbols, words, phrases, and content that are generally regarded as offensive by members of racial, ethnic, gender, or other groups, except when judged to be necessary for adequate representation of the domain. (SEPT 7.4)

6. In testing applications where the level of linguistic or reading ability is not part of the construct of interest, the linguistic or reading demands of the test should

be kept to the minimum necessary for the valid assessment of the intended construct. (SEPT, Standard 7.7)

7. Linguistic modifications recommended by test publishers, as well as the rationale for modifications, should be described in detail in the test manual. (SEPT, Standard 9.4)

8. In employment and credentialing testing, the proficiency language required in the language of the test should not exceed that appropriate to the relevant occupation or profession. (SEPT, Standard 9.8)

9. Inferences about test takers' general language proficiency should be based on tests that measure a range of language features, and not on a single linguistic skill. (SEPT, Standard 9.10)

10. Tests selected for use in individual testing should be suitable for the characteristics and background of the test taker. (SEPT, Standard 12.3)

11. Culturally competent counselors understand how race, culture, and ethnicity may affect personality formation, vocational choices, manifestation of psychological disorders, help-seeking behavior, and the appropriateness or inappropriateness of counseling approaches. (COMPS, 13)

12. Culturally competent counselors have training and expertise in the use of traditional assessment and testing instruments. They not only understand the technical aspects of the instruments but also are aware of the cultural limitations. This allows them to use test instruments for the welfare of clients from diverse cultural, racial, and ethnic groups. (COMPS, 29)

13. Counselors are cautious when selecting tests for culturally diverse populations to avoid inappropriateness of testing that may be outside of socialized behavioral or cognitive patterns. (ETHICS, Section III.C.5)

Selection of Assessment Instruments: Norming, Reliability, and Validity

1. Evaluate the available evidence on the performance of test takers of diverse subgroups. Determine to the extent feasible which performance differences may have been caused by factors unrelated to skills being assessed. (CODE, Section A-9).

2. Technical information should be reviewed to determine if the test characteristics are appropriate for the test taker (e.g., age, grade level, language, cultural background). (RUST)

3. Where there are generally accepted theoretical or empirical reasons for expecting that reliability coefficients, standard errors of measurement, or test information functions will differ substantially for various subpopulations, publishers should provide reliability data as soon as feasible for each major population for which the test is recommended. (SEPT, Standard 2.11)

4. If a test is proposed for use in several grades or over a range of chronological age groups and if separate norms are provided for each grade or age group,

reliability data should be provided for each age or grade population, not solely for all grades or ages combined. (SEPT, Standard 2.12)

5. When significant variations are permitted in test administration procedures, separate reliability analyses should be provided for scores produced under each major variation if adequate sample sizes are available. (SEPT, Standard 2.18)

6. Norms, if used, should refer to clearly described populations. These populations should include individuals or groups to whom test users will ordinarily wish to compare their own examinees. (SEPT, Standard 4.5)

7. When credible research reports that test scores differ in meaning across examinee subgroups for the type of test in question, then to the extent feasible, the same forms of validity evidence collected for the examinee population as a whole should also be collected for each relevant subgroup. Subgroups may be found to differ with respect to appropriateness of test content, internal structure of test responses, the relation of test scores to other variables, or the response processes employed by the individual examinees. Any such findings should receive due consideration in the interpretation and use of scores as well as in subsequent test revisions. (SEPT, Standard 7.1)

8. When credible research reports differences in the effects of construct-irrelevant variance across subgroups of test takers on performance on some part of the test, the test should be used if at all only for the subgroups for which evidence indicates that valid inferences can be drawn from test scores. (SEPT, Standard 7.2)

9. When empirical studies of differential prediction of a criterion for members of different subgroups are conducted, they should include regression equations (or an appropriate equivalent) computed separately for each group or treatment under consideration or an analysis in which group or treatment variables are entered as moderator variable. (SEPT, Standard 7.6)

10. When a construct can be measured in different ways that are approximately equal in their degree of construct representation and freedom from construct-irrelevant variance, evidence of mean score differences across relevant subgroups of examinees should be considered in deciding which test to use. (SEPT, Standard 7.11)

11. When credible research evidence reports that test scores differ in meaning across subgroups of linguistically diverse test takers, then to the extent feasible, test developers should collect for each linguistic group studied the same form of validity evidence collected for the examinee population as a whole. (SEPT, Standard 9.2)

12. When a test is translated from one language to another, the methods used in establishing the adequacy of translation should be described, and empirical and logical evidence should be provided for score reliability and the validity of the translated test's score inferences for the uses intended in the linguistic groups to be tested. (SEPT, Standard 9.7)

13. When multiple language versions of a test are intended to be comparable, test developers should report evidence of test comparability. (SEPT, Standard 9.9)

14. When feasible, tests that have been modified for use with individuals with disabilities should be pilot tested on individuals who have similar disabilities to investigate the appropriateness and feasibility of the modifications. (SEPT, Standard 10.3)

15. When sample sizes permit, the validity of inferences made from test scores and the reliability of scores on tests administered to individuals with various disabilities should be investigated and reported by the agency or publisher that makes the modification. Such investigations should examine the effects of modifications made for people with various disabilities on resulting scores, as well as the effects of administering standard unmodified tests to them. (SEPT, Standard 10.7)

16. When relying on norms as a basis for score interpretation in assisting individuals with disabilities, the norm group used depends upon the purpose of testing. Regular norms are appropriate when the purpose involves the test taker's functioning relative to the general population. If available, normative data from the population of individuals with the same level or degree of disability should be used when the test taker's functioning relative to individuals with similar disabilities is at issue. (SEPT, Standard 10.9)

17. When circumstances require that a test be administered in the same language to all examinees in a linguistically diverse population, the test user should investigate the validity of the score interpretations for test takers believed to have limited proficiency in the language of the test. (SEPT, Standard 11.22)

18. Counselors carefully consider the validity, reliability, psychometric limitations, and appropriateness of instruments when selecting tests for use in a given situation or with a particular client. (ETHICS, Section E.6.a)

Administration and Scoring of Assessment Instruments

1. Provide and document appropriate procedures for test takers with disabilities who need special accommodations or those with diverse linguistic backgrounds. Some accommodation may be required by law or regulation. (CODE, Section B-2)

2. For individuals with disabilities, accommodations in test taking procedures may need to be employed. Appropriate modifications of testing materials and procedures in order to accommodate test takers with special needs are to be arranged. (RUST)

3. Include notes on any problems, irregularities, and accommodations in the test

4. A systematic and objective procedure is in place for observing and recording environmental, health, emotional factors, or other elements that may invalidate test performance and results; deviations from prescribed test administration procedures, including information on test accommodations for individuals

with special needs, are recorded. Carefully observe, record, and attach to the test record any deviation from the prescribed test administration procedures. Include information on test accommodations for individuals with special needs. (RUST)

5. The testing or assessment process should be carried out so that test takers receive comparable and equitable treatment during all phases of the testing or assessment process. (SEPT, Standard 7.12)

6. Testing practice should be designed to reduce threats to the reliability and validity of test score inferences that may arise from language differences. (SEPT, Standard 9.1)

7. When testing an examinee proficient in two or more languages for which the test is available, the examinee's relative language proficiencies should be determined. The test generally should be administered in the test taker's most proficient language, unless proficiency in the less proficient language is part of the assessment. (SEPT, Standard 9.3)

8. When an interpreter is used in testing, the interpreter should be fluent in both the language of the test and the examinee's native language, should have expertise in translating, and should have a basic understanding of the assessment process. (SEPT, Standard 9.11)

9. People who make decisions about accommodations and test modifications for individuals with disabilities should be knowledgeable of existing research on the effects of the disabilities in question on test performance. Those who modify tests should also have access to psychometric expertise for so doing. (SEPT, Standard 10.2)

10. If a test developer recommends specific time limits for people with disabilities, empirical procedures should be used, whenever possible, to establish time limits for modified forms of timed tests rather than simply allowing test takers with disabilities a multiple of the standard time. When possible, fatigue should be investigated as a potentially important factor when time limits are extended. (SEPT, Standard 10.6)

11. Those responsible for decisions about test use with potential test takers who may need or may request specific accommodations should (a) possess the information necessary to make an appropriate selection of measures, (b) have current information regarding the availability of modified forms of the test in question, (c) inform individuals, when appropriate, about the existence of modified forms, and (d) make these forms available to test takers when appropriate and feasible. (SEPT, Standard 10.8)

12. Any test modifications adopted should be considered appropriate for the individual test taker, while maintaining all feasible standardized features. A test professional needs to consider reasonably available information about each test taker's experiences, characteristics, and capabilities that might impact test performance, and document the grounds for the modification. (SEPT, Standard 10.10)

13. If a test is mandated for persons of a given age or all students in a particular grade, users should identify individuals whose disabilities or linguistic background indicates the need for special accommodations in test administration and ensure that those accommodations are employed. (SEPT, Standard 11.23)

14. Counselors provide for equal access to computer applications in counseling services. (ETHICS, Section A.12.c)

15. When computer applications are used in counseling services, counselors ensure that: (1) the client is intellectually, emotionally, and physically capable of using the computer application; (2) the computer application is appropriate for the needs of the client; (3) the client understands the purpose and operation of the computer applications; and (4) a follow-up of client use of a computer application is provided to correct possible misconceptions, discover inappropriate use, and assess subsequent needs. (ETHICS, Section A.12.a)

16. Prior to assessment, counselors explain the nature and purposes of assessment and the specific use of results in language the client (or other legally authorized person on behalf of the client) can understand, unless an explicit exception to this right has been agreed upon in advance. (ETHICS, Section E.3.a)

Interpretation and Application of Assessment Results

1. Interpret the meaning of the test results, taking into account the nature of the content, norms or comparison groups, other technical evidence, and benefits and limitations of test results. (CODE, Section C-1)

2. Review the procedures for setting performance standards or passing scores. Avoid using stigmatizing labels. (CODE, Section C-4)

3. For individuals with disabilities, interpretations need to be made in light of the modifications in the test or testing procedures. (RUST)

4. When test results are influenced by irrelevant test taker characteristics (e.g., gender, age, ethnic background, cheating, availability of test preparation programs) the use of the resulting information is invalid and potentially harmful. (RUST)

5. Factors such as the test taker's group membership and how that membership may impact the results of the test is a critical factor in the interpretation of test results. Specifically, the test user should evaluate how the test taker's gender, age, ethnicity, race, socioeconomic status, marital status, and so forth, impact on the individual's results. (RUST)

6. If local examinees differ materially from the population to which the norms refer, a user who reports derived scores based on the published norms has the responsibility to describe such differences if they bear upon the interpretation of the reported scores. (SEPT, Standard 4.7)

7. In testing applications involving individualized interpretations of test scores other than selection, a test taker's score should not be accepted as a reflection

of standing on a characteristic being assessed without consideration of alternate explanations for the test taker's performance on that test at that time. (SEPT, Standard 7.5)

8. When scores are disaggregated and publicly reported for groups identified by characteristics such as gender, ethnicity, age, language proficiency, or disability, cautionary statements should be included whenever credible research reports that test scores may not have comparable meaning across different groups. (SEPT, Standard 7.8)

9. When tests or assessments are proposed for use as instruments of social, educational, or public policy, the test developers or users proposing the test should fully and accurately inform policymakers of the characteristics of the tests as well as any relevant and credible information that may be available concerning the likely consequences of test use. (SEPT, Standard 7.9)

10. When the use of a test results in outcomes that affect the life chances or educational opportunities of examinees, evidence of mean test score differences between relevant subgroups of examinees should, where feasible, be examined for subgroups for which credible research reports mean differences for similar tests. Where mean differences are found, an investigation should be undertaken to determine that such differences are not attributable to a source of construct under representation or construct-irrelevant variance. While initially the responsibility of the test developer, the test user bears responsibility for users with groups other than those specified by the developer. (SEPT, Standard 7.10).

11. When score reporting includes assigning individuals to categories, the categories should be chosen carefully and described precisely. The least stigmatizing labels, consistent with accurate representation, should always be assigned. (SEPT, Standard 8.8)

12. When there is credible evidence of score comparability across regular and modified administrations, no flag should be attached to a score. When such evidence is lacking, specific information about the nature of the modification should be provided, if permitted by law, to assist test users properly to interpret and act on test scores. (SEPT, Standard 9.5 and 10.11)

13. In testing persons with disabilities, test developers, test administrators, and test users should take steps to ensure that the test score inferences accurately reflect the intended construct rather than any disabilities and their associated characteristics extraneous to the intent of the measurement. (SEPT, Standard 10.1)

14. In testing individuals with disabilities for diagnostic and intervention purposes, the test should not be used as the sole indicator of the test taker's functioning. Instead, multiple sources of information should be used. (SEPT, Standard 10.12)

15. Agencies using tests to conduct program evaluations or policy studies, or to monitor outcomes, should clearly describe the population the program or policy

is intended to serve and should document the extent to which the sample of test takers is representative of that population. (SEPT, Standard 15.5)

16. Reports of group differences in average test scores should be accompanied by relevant contextual information, where possible, to enable meaningful interpretation of these differences. Where appropriate contextual information is not available, users should be cautioned against misinterpretation. (SEPT, Standard 15.12)

17. Culturally competent counselors possess knowledge about their social impact on others. They are knowledgeable about communication style differences, how their style may clash or facilitate the counseling process with minority clients, and how to anticipate the impact it may have on others. (COMPS, 7)

18. Culturally competent counselors have knowledge of the potential bias in assessment instruments and use procedures and interpret findings keeping in mind the cultural and linguistic characteristics of the clients. (COMPS, 22)

19. Counselors recognize that culture affects the manner in which clients' problems are defined. Clients' socioeconomic and cultural experience is considered when diagnosing mental disorders. (ETHICS, Section E.5.b)

20. Counselors are cautious in using assessment techniques, making evaluations, and interpreting the performance of populations not represented in the norm group on which an instrument was standardized. They recognize the effects of age, color, culture, disability, ethnic group, gender, race, religion, sexual orientation, and socioeconomic status on test administration and interpretation and place test results in proper perspective with other relevant factors. (ETHICS, Section E.8)

21. In reporting assessment results, counselors indicate any reservations that exist regarding validity or reliability because of the circumstances of the assessment or the inappropriateness of the norms for the person tested. (ETHICS, Section E.9.a)

References

American Counseling Association. (1996) Code of ethics and standards of practice. Alexandria, VA: Author.

American Counseling Association and Association for Assessment in Counseling (2003). Responsibilities of users of standardized tests. Alexandria, VA: Author.

American Educational Research Association, American Psychological Association, and National Council on Measurement in Education (1999). Standards for educational and psychological testing (2nd ed.). Washington, DC: American Educational Research Association.

Arredondo, P., & Toporek, R. (1996). Operationalization of the multicultural counseling competencies [Electronic version]. Journal of Multicultural Counseling and Development, 24, 42-79.

Association for Multicultural Counseling and Development. (1992) Multicultural counseling competencies and standards. Alexandria, VA: American Counseling Association.

Joint Committee on Testing Practices. (2002). Code of fair testing practices in education. Washington, DC: Author.

Prediger, D. J., (1992) Standards for multicultural assessment. Alexandria, VA: Association for Assessment in Counseling.

Prediger, D. J. (1994). Multicultural assessment standards: A compilation for counselors. Measurement and Evaluation in Counseling and Development, 27, 68-73.

Sue, D. W., Arredondo, P., & McDavis, R. (1992). Multicultural counseling competencies and standards: A call to the profession. Journal of Counseling and Development, 70, 477-486.

A COUNSELOR'S GUIDE USER'S MATRIX: AN ALPHABETICAL LISTING OF CAREER ASSESSMENT INSTRUMENTS BY CATEGORY AND TYPE OF USE[1]

Edwin A. Whitfield
Associate Director (Retired)
Office of Supportive Learning Environments
Office of Assessment
Ohio Department of Education

Sibyl Cato
Doctoral Student
Counselor Education
The Ohio State University

The User's Matrix is an alphabetized listing of all 274 instruments either reviewed or briefly described in the fourth edition of *A Counselor's Guide*. These instruments are identified by *Characteristics* assessed, Level of *Use*, and whether the instruments are particularly appropriate for *Special Populations*. Instruments in boldface type are reviewed and may be located using the Table of Contents. All other instruments are briefly described in the *Additional Career Assessment Instruments* chapter under the appropriate category. The exact page number for either reviewed or briefly described instruments may be obtained from the Index.

The Characteristics used to describe the instruments do not exclusively correspond to those used to group them for either the reviews or brief descriptions, because many instruments fit more than one category. However, they are categorical descriptions of what the instruments are intended to measure. The Values category includes instruments that assess Job Satisfaction and Environments.

The *Use* categories are based on level of schooling or setting for those uses beyond four years of college. The Adult Education/Training category includes instruments used with adults who are receiving counseling for education, training or job change outside the traditional college environment. The Business & Industry/Employment category describes instruments that would be administered by or for employers who typically would use the results to make hiring or advancement decisions.

The *Special Populations* Category is listed separately from those that designate either characteristics assessed or level of use. Instruments identified here may be appropriate for individuals with particular disabilities or academic, economic, or social disadvantages.

The reader may find the matrix useful to provide a quick overview of the instruments, by name, which are available to assess particular characteristics. Furthermore, an initial judgment about an instrument's fit for an intended population also can be made.

---

[1] This Matrix is an update and revision of the work of Jerome T. Kapes and Linda Martinez, Texas A&M University, in the 4th edition of the *Counselor's Guide*.

INSTRUMENT NAME	CHARACTERISTICS						USE						
	Achievement	Aptitude	Interest	Values/Satisfaction/Environments	Career Development/Maturity	Personality	Elementary School	Junior High/Middle School	Senior High School	2-Year or 4-Year College	Adult Education/Training	Business & Industry/Employment	Special Populations
Ability Explorer (AE)		*						*	*	*			
ACCU Vision - Workplace Success Skills System	*				*	*			*	*	*	*	
Activity Vector Analysis (AVA)	*		*		*	*					*	*	
Adaptability Test		*							*		*	*	*
Adult Basic Learning Exam (ABLE)	*								*				*
Adult Career Concerns Inventory (ACCI)					*					*	*	*	
Adult Personality Inventory (API)						*				*	*	*	
Applicant Review				*		*				*		*	
ARC Self-Determination Scale (ARC-SDS)					*	*			*		*		*
Armed Services Vocational Aptitude Battery (ASVAB - CEP)		*	*					*	*	*			
Ashland Interest Assessment (AIA)			*		*			*	*	*	*		*
Barriers to Employment Success Inventory (BESI)					*				*		*		*
Barsch Learning Styles Inventory - Revised						*					*		*
Basic Skills Locater Test	*								*		*		*
Becker Work Adjustment Profile:2 (BWAP:2)					*				*		*	*	*
Bennett Hand Tool Dexterity Test (BHTDT)		*							*		*	*	*

INSTRUMENT NAME	Achievement	Aptitude	Interest	Values/Satisfaction/Environments	Career Development/Maturity	Personality	Elementary School	Junior High/Middle School	Senior High School	2-Year or 4-Year College	Adult Education/Training	Business & Industry/Employment	Special Populations
Bennett Mechanical Comprehension Test (BMCT)	*	*							*	*	*	*	
Brigance Diagnostic Employability Skills Inventory (ESI)					*				*		*		*
Brigance Diagnostic Life Skills Inventory (LSI)	*				*				*		*		*
Business Careers Interest Inventory (BCII)			*						*	*	*	*	
California Life Goals Evaluation Schedules				*							*		
California Psychological Inventory 3rd Edition (CPI 434)						*				*	*	*	
Campbell Interest & Skill Survey (CISS)			*						*	*	*	*	
Campbell Organizational Survey				*							*	*	
Career Ability Placement Survey (CAPS)		*						*	*	*	*		
Career Action Inventory					*						*	*	
Career Anchors: Discovering Your Real Values				*						*	*		
Career and Vocational Form of the SOI-LA Basic Test		*						*	*	*	*	*	
Career Assessment Battery (CAB)			*					*	*	*	*		*
Career Assessment Inventory (CAI)			*						*	*	*	*	
Career Attitudes and Strategies Inventory (CASI)					*			*	*	*	*	*	
Career Beliefs Inventory (CBI)					*			*	*	*	*	*	

INSTRUMENT NAME	CHARACTERISTICS						USE						
	Achievement	Aptitude	Interest	Values/Satisfaction/Environments	Career Development/Maturity	Personality	Elementary School	Junior High/Middle School	Senior High School	2-Year or 4-Year College	Adult Education/Training	Business & Industry/Employment	Special Populations
Career Compass			*					*	*				
Career Decision Scale (CDS)					*				*	*	*		
Career Decision Self-Efficacy Scale (CDSE)					*			*	*	*	*		
Career Development Inventory (CDI)					*				*	*			
Career Directions Inventory (CDI)			*						*	*	*		
Career Exploration Inventory (CEI)			*		*			*	*	*	*		
Career Factors Inventory (CFI)								*	*	*	*		
Career Finder			*				*	*	*	*	*		
Career Interest Inventory (CII)			*					*	*	*	*		
Career Inventories for the Learning Disabled (CILD)		*	*			*			*				*
Career IQ and Interest Test (CIQIT)		*	*						*	*	*		
Career Key			*					*	*	*	*		
Career Leverage Inventory					*						*		
Career Maturity Inventory (CMI)					*			*	*	*			
Career Occupational Preference System Interest Inventory (COPS)			*					*	*	*	*		
Career Orientation Placement and Evaluation Survey (COPES)				*				*	*	*	*		*

INSTRUMENT NAME	CHARACTERISTICS						USE						
	Achievement	Aptitude	Interest	Values/Satisfaction/Environments	Career Development/Maturity	Personality	Elementary School	Junior High/Middle School	Senior High School	2-Year or 4-Year College	Adult Education/Training	Business & Industry/Employment	Special Populations
Career Planning Survey	*	*	*					*	*				
Career Profile Assessment		*	*					*	*				
Career Programs Assessment Test (CPAT)	*	*	*						*	*	*		*
CareerScope		*						*	*	*	*		
Career SnapShot 2001		*							*	*	*		
Career Technical Assistance Program (C-Tap)	*							*	*	*	*		
Career Thoughts Inventory (CTI)					*				*	*	*		
Career Transitions Inventory (CTI)					*						*		
Chronicle Career Quest (CCQ)			*				*	*	*				
Childhood Career Development Scale (CCDS)					*	*	*	*	*				
CITE Learning Styles Inventory								*	*		*		
Clerical Abilities Battery (CAB)	*	*							*	*	*	*	*
Clerical Skills Test Series	*	*							*	*	*	*	
Clifton StrengthsFinder or StrengthsFinder 2.0						*				*	*	*	
COIN Basic Skills and Career Interest Survey		*	*					*	*	*	*		
COIN Career Targets		*	*					*	*				

INSTRUMENT NAME	CHARACTERISTICS						USE						
	Achievement	Aptitude	Interest	Values/Satisfaction/Environments	Career Development/Maturity	Personality	Elementary School	Junior High/Middle School	Senior High School	2-Year or 4-Year College	Adult Education/Training	Business & Industry/Employment	Special Populations
COIN Clue					*			*					
COIN Educational Inventory			*						*				
Comprehensive Ability Battery (CAB)		*							*	*	*	*	
Comp Adult Std Assmnt Sys(CASAS)See Employability Comptncy Sys (ECS)	*								*	*	*	*	
Comprehensive Personality Profile						*				*	*	*	
Computer Operator Aptitude Battery (COAB)		*								*	*	*	
Computer Programmer Aptitude Battery (CPAB)		*								*	*	*	
Crawford Small Parts Dexterity Test (CSPDT)	*	*							*		*	*	*
Customer Service Skills Assessment Program									*	*	*	*	
Deal-Me-In/It's In the Cards			*		*								
Differential Aptitude Tests (DAT)		*						*	*	*	*	*	
Dvorine Color Vision Test		*							*	*	*	*	
Employability Competency System Appraisal Test (ECS Appraisal)	*								*	*	*	*	
Employability Inventory									*		*	*	
Employee Aptitude Survey (EAS)		*								*	*	*	
Employee Reliability Inventory						*					*	*	*

INSTRUMENT NAME	CHARACTERISTICS						USE						
	Achievement	Aptitude	Interest	Values/Satisfaction/Environments	Career Development/Maturity	Personality	Elementary School	Junior High/Middle School	Senior High School	2-Year or 4-Year College	Adult Education/Training	Business & Industry/Employment	Special Populations
Endorele-Severson Transition Rating Scales J-R	*				*				*		*		*
Evaluating the Participant's Employability Skills	*	*	*		*				*	*	*		
Explore													
Explore the World of Work (E-WOW)			*					*			*		*
Flanagan Aptitude Classification Test (FACT)		*							*	*	*	*	*
Flannagan Industrial Tests (FIT)		*							*	*	*	*	*
Fleishman Job Analysis Survey (F-JAS)				*								*	
Functional Assessment Inventory	*				*								*
Fundamental Interpersonal Relations Orientation-Behavior (FIRO-B)						*			*	*	*	*	
Geist Picture Interest Inventory (GPII)			*										
General Clerical Test (GCT)		*							*	*	*	*	*
Gordon Personal Profile-Inventory (GPP-I)						*			*	*	*	*	
Group Test of Musical Ability		*					*	*					
Guide for Occupational Exploration (GOE) Inventory II			*					*	*	*	*		
Guilford-Zimmerman Temperament Survey (GZTS)						*			*	*	*	*	
Hall Occupational Orientation Inventory 4th edition (HALL)			*	*				*	*	*	*		

INSTRUMENT NAME	Achievement	Aptitude	Interest	Values/Satisfaction/Environments	Career Development/Maturity	Personality	Elementary School	Junior High/Middle School	Senior High School	2-Year or 4-Year College	Adult Education/Training	Business & Industry/Employment	Special Populations
Harrington-O'Shea Career Decision-Making System-R (CDM-R)			*					*	*	*	*		
Hay Aptitude Test Battery		*								*	*	*	
Highlands Ability Battery (tHAB)		*						*	*	*	*	*	
High School Career-Course Planner			*					*	*				
Individual Style Survey (ISS)				*						*	*	*	
Industrial Reading Test (IRT)	*								*	*	*	*	
Insight Inventory						*			*	*	*	*	
Interest Explorer			*						*				
Interest, Determination, Exploration & Assessment System (IDEAS)			*					*	*	*	*	*	*
Intuitive Mechanics		*							*	*	*	*	
IPI Aptitude-Intelligence Test Series		*				*			*	*	*	*	
Jackson Personality Inventory Revised (JPI)						*				*	*	*	
Jackson Vocational Interest Inventory (JVIS)			*						*	*	*		
Job Descriptive Index, Revised (JDI Rev)	*			*						*	*	*	
Job Effectiveness Prediction System (JEPS)	*											*	
Job Search Attitude Inventory (JSAI)					*				*	*	*	*	

INSTRUMENT NAME	Achievement	Aptitude	Interest	Values/Satisfaction/Environments	Career Development/Maturity	Personality	Elementary School	Junior High/Middle School	Senior High School	2-Year or 4-Year College	Adult Education/Training	Business & Industry/Employment	Special Populations
		CHARACTERISTICS							USE				
Job Skills	*								*	*	*	*	
Job Skills Tests	*	*							*		*	*	*
Job Style Indicator (JSI)				*							*	*	
Job Survival and Success Scale (JSSS)	*	*									*		
Judgement of Occupational Behavior-Orientation 2000+ (JOB-O 2000)			*		*	*	*	*	*	*	*		*
Keirsey Character Sorter						*		*		*	*		
Keirsey Temperament Sorter II				*		*		*		*	*	*	
Knowdell Career Values Card Sort				*						*	*	*	
Knowdell Leisure and Retirement Activities Card Sort					*						*	*	
Knowdell Motivated Skills Card Sort	*	*		*				*	*	*	*	*	
Knowdell Occupational Interests Card Sort			*		*			*	*	*	*	*	
Kolb Learning Skills Profile (LSP)								*	*	*	*		
Kuder Career Search (KCS)			*					*	*	*			
Kuder Skills Assessment (KSA)	*	*						*	*	*	*		
LCCE Competency Assessments: Knowledge and Performance	*							*	*	*	*		*
Learning Styles Inventory						*	*	*	*		*	*	*

INSTRUMENT NAME	Achievement	Aptitude	Interest	Values/Satisfaction/Environments	Career Development/Maturity	Personality	Elementary School	Junior High/Middle School	Senior High School	2-Year or 4-Year College	Adult Education/Training	Business & Industry/Employment	Special Populations
Learning/Working Styles Inventory		*				*					*		*
Lomaselect: Entry Level		*	*	*		*			*		*		
Making a Terrific Career Happen (MATCH)			*					*	*				
McCarron-Dial System (MDS)		*				*		*	*	*	*		*
Mechanical Aptitudes		*							*	*	*		
Mechanical Movements		*							*		*	*	*
Microcomputer Evaluation of Career Areas (MECA)			*	*						*	*	*	*
Minnesota Clerical Test (MCT)		*							*	*	*	*	
Minnesota Importance Questionnaire (MIQ)				*					*	*	*	*	
Minnesota Job Description Questionnaire (MJDQ)				*								*	
Minnesota Paper Form Board-Revised		*							*	*	*	*	*
Minnesota Rate of Manipulation Test, 1969 Edition (MRMT)		*						*	*	*	*	*	*
Minnesota Satisfaction Questionnaire (MSQ)				*								*	
Minnesota Satisfactoriness Scales (MSS)					*						*	*	
Minnesota Spatial Relations Test, Revised Edition (MSRT)		*							*	*	*	*	*
Missouri Occupational Card Sort (MOCS)			*						*	*	*		

INSTRUMENT NAME	CHARACTERISTICS						USE						
	Achievement	Aptitude	Interest	Values/Satisfaction/Environments	Career Development/Maturity	Personality	Elementary School	Junior High/Middle School	Senior High School	2-Year or 4-Year College	Adult Education/Training	Business & Industry/Employment	Special Populations
Motivational Appraisal of Personal Potential (MAPP)		*	*			*		*	*	*	*	*	
Multidimensional Aptitude Battery (MAB)		*						*	*	*	*	*	*
Musical Aptitude Profile		*					*	*	*				
My Vocational Situation (MVS)					*		*	*	*	*	*		
Myers-Briggs Type Indicator (MBTI)			*		*	*			*	*	*		
NEO Personality Inventory-Revised (NEO PI-R)						*				*	*	*	
NOCTI Occupational Competency Tests	*								*	*	*	*	
O*NET Ability Profiler		*							*	*	*		
O*NET Interest Inventory/Computerized Interest Profiler			*						*	*	*		
O*NET Work Importance Locator/ Computerized WI Profiler				*				*	*	*	*		
Occupational Aptitude Survey & Interest Schedule-3rd ed (OASIS-3)		*	*					*	*	*	*		*
Occupational Interest Profile (OIP)			*								*		
Occupational Personality Assessment						*				*	*	*	
Occupational Personality Questionnaire						*				*	*	*	
Occupational Preference Inventory		*	*						*	*	*	*	
Occupational Stress Inventory Revised (OSI-R)		*				*			*	*	*	*	

INSTRUMENT NAME	Achievement	Aptitude	Interest	Values/Satisfaction/Environments	Career Development/Maturity	Personality	Elementary School	Junior High/Middle School	Senior High School	2-Year or 4-Year College	Adult Education/Training	Business & Industry/Employment	Special Populations
					CHARACTERISTICS					USE			
O'Conner Finger Dexterity Test		*							*		*	*	*
O'Conner Tweezer Dexterity Test		*							*		*	*	*
Office Skills Test		*							*	*	*	*	
Pennsylvania Bi-Manual Worksample		*						*	*		*	*	*
Perceptual Speed		*							*	*	*	*	*
Personal Style Indicator (PSI)				*		*		*	*		*	*	
Personality Research Form (PRF)				*		*			*	*	*	*	
Personnel Tests for Industry - Oral Directions Test (PTI-ODT)		*						*	*		*	*	*
Pictorial Inventory of Careers (PIC)			*					*	*	*	*	*	*
Pictorial Reasoning Test (PRT)		*						*	*		*		
Plan													
Position Analysis Questionnaire (PAQ)	*											*	
Position Classification Inventory (PCI)				*								*	
Practical Assessment Exploration System (PAES)	*		*		*			*	*				*
Prevocational Assessment Screen (PAS)		*						*	*				*
Professional Employment Test		*										*	

INSTRUMENT NAME	Achievement	Aptitude	Interest	Values/Satisfaction/Environments	Career Development/Maturity	Personality	Elementary School	Junior High/Middle School	Senior High School	2-Year or 4-Year College	Adult Education/Training	Business & Industry/Employment	Special Populations
				CHARACTERISTICS						USE			
PSI Basic Skills Test	*	*										*	*
Purdue Pegboard		*			*				*		*	*	*
Quality of Life Inventory (QOLI)				*						*	*	*	
Reading-Free Vocational Interest Inventory: 2 (RFVII: 2)			*					*	*		*		*
Responsibility and Independence Scale for Adolescents	*				*								*
Retirement Activities Card Sort			*								*		*
Revised Beta Examination-Third Edition (BETA-III)		*						*	*	*	*	*	
Rokeach Value Survey				*				*	*	*	*	*	*
Sales Attitude Checklist						*						*	
Salience Inventory (SI)				*					*	*	*	*	
Scholastic Level Exam (SLE)		*						*	*	*	*	*	*
School to Work Career Survey			*						*		*	*	
Schubert General Ability Battery (GAB)		*						*	*	*	*	*	
Self Directed Search (SDS)			*					*	*	*	*	*	*
Short Employment Tests (SET)		*							*	*	*	*	*
Short Tests of Clerical Ability (STCA)		*						*	*	*	*	*	*

INSTRUMENT NAME	CHARACTERISTICS						USE						
	Achievement	Aptitude	Interest	Values/Satisfaction/Environments	Career Development/Maturity	Personality	Elementary School	Junior High/Middle School	Senior High School	2-Year or 4-Year College	Adult Education/Training	Business & Industry/Employment	Special Populations
Singer-Loomis Inventory of Personality (SLIP)						*			*	*	*	*	
Sixteen Personality Factors (16PF)						*			*	*	*	*	
Skills Assessment Module (SAM)		*			*				*		*	*	*
Skills Confidence Inventory (SCI)		*							*	*	*	*	
Space Relations (Paper Puzzles)		*							*	*	*	*	*
Space Thinking (Flags)		*							*	*	*	*	*
SRA Mechanical Aptitudes		*						*	*	*	*	*	
SRA Pictorial Reasoning Test (PRT)		*						*	*	*	*	*	*
SRA Test of Mechanical Concepts		*							*	*	*	*	*
Strategic Assessment of Readiness for Training (START)	*					*					*		
Street Survival Skills Questionnaire (SSSQ)					*	*	*	*	*	*	*		*
Strength Deployment Inventory								*	*		*	*	*
Stromberg Dexterity Test (SDT)		*							*	*	*	*	
Strong Interest Inventory Assessment Tool (SII)			*					*	*	*	*	*	*
Student Styles Questionnaire (SSQ)						*	*	*	*		*		

INSTRUMENT NAME	Achievement	Aptitude	Interest	Values/Satisfaction/Environments	Career Development/Maturity	Personality	Elementary School	Junior High/Middle School	Senior High School	2-Year or 4-Year College	Adult Education/Training	Business & Industry/Employment	Special Populations
Styles of Teamwork Inventory	*					*						*	
Success Skills 2000		*				*			*	*	*	*	
Super's Work Values Inventory-revised (SWVI-r)				*				*	*	*	*	*	
SureHire		*				*					*	*	
Survey of Interpersonal Values (SIV)				*					*	*	*	*	
Survey of Personal Values (SPV)				*					*	*	*	*	
Survey of Work Styles (SWS)						*				*	*	*	
Survey of Work Values				*					*	*	*	*	
System for Assessment and Group Evaluation (SAGE 2001)	*	*	*			*			*	*	*	*	*
Talent Assessment Program (TAP)		*						*	*	*	*	*	*
Technical Test Battery		*								*	*	*	
Technology and Internet Assessment	*							*	*	*	*	*	
Temperament Comparator (TC)						*					*	*	
Tests of Adult Basic Education (TABE) Forms 9 and 10	*								*	*	*	*	*
Test of Mechanical Concepts		*						*	*	*	*		
Thurstone Temperament Schedule						*		*	*	*	*	*	

INSTRUMENT NAME	Special Populations	Business & Industry/Employment	Adult Education/Training	2-Year or 4-Year College	Senior High School	Junior High/Middle School	Elementary School	Personality	Career Development/Maturity	Values/Satisfaction/Environments	Interest	Aptitude	Achievement
	USE							CHARACTERISTICS					
Training House Assessment Kit	*	*						*				*	*
Transition Behavior Scale–2nd edition (TBS-2)	*				*			*	*				
Transition Planning Inventory (TPI)	*		*		*	*			*				
Transition-to-Work Inventory			*		*	*					*		
UNIACT IV				*	*	*					*		
USES Basic Occupational Literacy Test (BOLT)	*	*	*		*								*
Valpar 300 Series Dexterity Modules	*	*	*	*								*	*
Valpar Aviator	*		*		*						*	*	
Valpar Component Work Sample Series	*		*									*	*
Valpar Pro 3000	*		*	*	*				*		*		*
Valpar Test of Essential Skills (VTES)	*		*		*	*							*
Values Preference Indicator		*	*							*			
Values Scale (VS)		*	*	*	*					*			
Viewpoint		*						*					*
Vocational Adaptation Rating Scales (VARS)	*	*	*		*	*			*				
Vocational Decision-Making Interview	*		*			*			*				

INSTRUMENT NAME	Achievement	Aptitude	Interest	Values/Satisfaction/Environments	Career Development/Maturity	Personality	Elementary School	Junior High/Middle School	Senior High School	2-Year or 4-Year College	Adult Education/Training	Business & Industry/Employment	Special Populations
Vocational Evaluation Systems (Singer)		*	*					*	*				*
Vocational Implications of Personality (VIP)						*		*	*	*	*	*	*
Vocational Interest Assessment System (VIAS)			*					*	*	*	*		*
Vocational Interest Exploration (VIE) System			*					*	*	*	*		*
Vocational Interest Inventory & Exploration Survey (VOC-TIES)			*					*	*		*		*
Vocational Interest Temperament and Aptitude System (VITAS)		*									*		*
Vocational Preference Inventory			*			*				*	*	*	
Vocational Training Inventory and Exploration Survey (VOC-TIES)			*						*	*	*	*	*
VOC-TECH Quick Screener (VTQS)		*	*					*	*				*
V-TECS Assessments	*								*	*	*	*	
Watson-Glaser Critical Thinking Appraisal		*							*	*	*	*	
Wesman Personnel Classification Test (PCT)		*								*	*	*	
Wide Range Achievement Test-3 (WRAT-3)	*		*					*	*	*	*		*
Wide Range Interest and Occupation Test-2nd Edition (WRIOT-2)							*	*	*	*	*		*
Wiesen Test of Mechanical Aptitude		*						*	*	*	*	*	
Wonderlic Basic Skills Test (WBST)		*									*	*	*

INSTRUMENT NAME	CHARACTERISTICS						USE						
	Achievement	Aptitude	Interest	Values/Satisfaction/Environments	Career Development/Maturity	Personality	Elementary School	Junior High/Middle School	Senior High School	2-Year or 4-Year College	Adult Education/Training	Business & Industry/Employment	Special Populations
Wonderlic Personnel Test	*	*										*	*
Work Adjustment Inventory					*	*			*		*		
Work Environment Scale				*					*			*	
Work Exploration Checklist			*					*					
WorkKeys Assessments (WorkKeys)	*								*	*	*	*	
Work Motivation Inventory (WMI)				*				*			*	*	
Work Performance Assessment					*	*			*		*		*
Work Personality Profile					*	*					*		*
Work Preference Questionnaire			*									*	
Work Readiness Cognitive Screen (WCS)	*	*							*		*		*
Work Skills Development Package (WSD)	*	*									*		*
Work Temperament Inventory					*	*		*	*		*	*	*
Workmate				*					*	*	*		
Workplace Skills Survey	*	*						*	*	*			
World of Work Inventory (WOWI)	*	*	*	*				*	*	*	*		*

574

INDEX